AMERICAN GOVERNMENT

D.C. HEATH AND COMPANY

Lexington, Massachusetts   Toronto

James Q. Wilson

HARVARD UNIVERSITY

AMERICAN GOVERNMENT

Institutions and Policies

Charts and graphs by B. J. & F. W. Taylor
Illustrations by Terry Presnall and Irene Roman/
  Rep. Gwen Goldstein
Cartography by Norman C. Adams
Cover illustration and title page: The Image Bank
Photo credits appear on the following page.

PHOTOGRAPH CREDITS

American Antiquarian Society 23 (right), 32 (left)

Alan Band Associates 304

The Bettmann Archive, Inc. 10 (left), 23 (left), 82, 142, 146 (left, center), 267, 309, 374 (right), 384, 398 (both), 404 (left), 484, 535 (top), 558, 604

Black Star 548 (right); Michael Abramson 79, 219; John Blair 520 (left); Dennis Brack 9 (right), 199, 227, 255, 320, 325 (right), 395, 411, 425, 545, 574, 601; Geoffrey Clifford 589; Ted Cowell 176, 242, 520 (right); Tom Ebenhoh 595; Shelly Katz 112; Jean-Claude Lejeune 158 (right); Martin A. Levick 46 (bottom), 108 (left), 206 (right), 207, 211, 529; Andy Levin 607 (right); Claus Meyer 158 (left); Bert Miller 543 (left); Owen D. B. 544; David Rubinger 565; Christopher Springmann 7; Steve Schapiro 325 (left), 518; Andrew Schneider 134, 417; St. Louis Post Dispatch 358, 413 (left); Michael D. Sullivan 563 (right); Paul Thomas 371; Karin Vismara 454 (bottom); George L. Walker III 115; Fred Ward 113

Jean Boughton 444 (left), 593

Brown Brothers xiii (left), xiv (bottom, left), 16, 38 (left), 78, 116 (left), 230, 261 (center), 404 (right), 433, 466, 578

Ken Buck 68

Camera 5 Terry Arthur 356; Steve Northup xiii (top, right), 3

Chicago Tribune–New York Times, Syndicate, Inc. MacNelly 362; Shoe 364

Jim Collison 422

Condé Nast Publications © 1935 xvi (bottom, left), © 1963 410

Paul S. Conklin xiv (center), xvi (center), 55 (right), 62, 126, 193, 205, 226 (right), 257, 268, 280 (both), 281, 296, 365 (top), 430 (right), 443, 561 (right), 579, 597, 607 (left)

Culver Pictures xiii (bottom, right), 42, 374 (left), 540

Eastern Airlines Public Relations Office 224 (left)

Editorial Photocolor Archives (EPA) Daniel S. Brody 373

Dwight D. Eisenhower Library 127

Benedict J. Fernandez from *In Opposition* © 1968 500

The Free Library of Philadelphia 27

German Information Center 10 (right)

Steve Hansen 178

Grant Heilman Photography 438; John Colwell 427

Harvard College Library 21, 24, 36, 148, 233 (both), 288; Theodore Roosevelt Collection 315, 560

Harvard Theatre Collection 513

Historical Pictures Service, Inc. 18, 209

Karl Hubenthal 332 (left)

Jeroboam, Inc. Emilio Mercado 444 (right), 531 (left); Barbara Paup 55 (left), Rose Skytta 610

Lyndon Baines Johnson Library Yoichi R. Okamoto xvi (top, left), 239, 326 (right), 416, 467, 474, 509, 528, 547 (left), 591 (right)

Brent Jones 537

Jean-Claude Lejeune 91 (left), 536 (right)

Library of Congress xv (left), xvii (bottom, right), xviii (top), 26 (left), 29, 32 (far right—top, bottom), 44, 50, 140, 156 (left), 164, 170 (left), 180 (both), 188 (left), 204, 254, 261 (left), 266, 321 (right), 314 (bottom), 380 (both), 381, 382 (left), 508, 511, 534 (right), 588

Lincoln University Library 382 (center)

Louis Mercier Fred J. Maroon 335, 377

Magnum Photos, Inc. Bob Adelman 523; Bruno Barbey 153; Cornell Capa 249, 569; Henri Dauman 463, 563 (left), 587; Elliott Erwitt 341; Leonard Freed 4, 102, 501; Charles Gatewood 91 (right); Burt Glinn 231, 415, 561 (left); Mark Godfrey 337; Charles Harbutt 9 (left), 81 (left) 448, 495; Hiroji Kubota 154, 453; Roger Malloch 576; Alex Webb 430 (left)

David Muench 409

Cliché des Musées Nationaux-Paris 80

NASA 224 (right)

For Roberta, Matthew, Annie . . . again.
And Annabelle.

James Q. Wilson has taught government at Harvard since 1961, where he is now the Henry Lee Shattuck Professor of Government. Raised in California, Wilson attended the University of Redlands and received his Ph.D. from the University of Chicago. He is the author of seven books: *Negro Politics*, *The Amateur Democrat*, *City Politics* (with Edward C. Banfield), *Varieties of Police Behavior*, *Political Organizations*, *Thinking About Crime*, and *The Investigators*. While at Harvard, he has been chairman of the Department of Government, director of the Joint Center for Urban Studies of MIT and Harvard, chairman of the Standing Committee on Athletic Sports, and chairman of a task force whose report led to the creation of a Core Curriculum.

Wilson has served in a number of advisory posts in the federal government: chairman of the White House Task Force on Crime in the Lyndon Johnson administration, chairman of the Task Force on Order and Justice for Vice-President Hubert Humphrey, and chairman of the National Advisory Commission for Drug Abuse Prevention in 1972–1973. In 1977 the American Political Science Association conferred on him the Charles E. Merriam Award for advancing the art of government through the application of social science knowledge.

He is a Fellow of the American Academy of Arts and Sciences and a member of the National Association of Underwater Instructors.

PREFACE

I wrote this text with the conviction that students want to know not only who governs but also what difference it makes who governs. These questions can be answered, I believe, only by linking the analysis of governmental institutions and political processes to an explanation of how and why major policy decisions are made as they are.

It has been my experience in teaching an introductory course in American government that one must try both to describe and explain—to make clear how people and institutions behave in political matters and as well to show that this behavior importantly affects the kinds of policies we do (or do not) get.

These two goals cannot be met by writing a descriptive account of government that appends, almost as an afterthought, a chapter on "policy" at the end. A one-chapter discussion of policy is probably worse than no discussion at all, since about all that can be said in so little space is too general to be useful or too opinionated to be credible. Conclusions about an "imperial presidency" or an "imperial judiciary," about the "power" of the media or the "role" of the parties, strike me as little more than conjecture if they are not based on a careful examination of how presidents, judges, reporters, and party leaders actually affect, or fail to affect, a range of policy questions. Nor will a "policy analysis" book be satisfactory if there is no reference to the structure of governing supplied by the Constitution, by laws and institutions, and by political values and opinions.

The first three parts of this book should serve as a comprehensive introduction to the institu-tions and processes of American government. But the very first chapter raises questions about who rules, and to what ends, and promises that the answers will not be found until one has at least sampled the analysis of specific policies. Part IV is devoted to the politics of policy-mak-ing, organized around a simple—but I think useful—conceptual scheme that can help students understand why the politics of certain policies are different from those of others, and to see why certain actors and institutions have more in-fluence in some matters than in others.

I also believe that American politics must be seen as an evolutionary process growing out of political beliefs and institutional arrangements different from those found in other democratic nations. Each chapter about a governmental institution or a major political process begins by placing the American system in a larger con-text. I try, in a brief space, to show how historical forces have shaped our present-day arrangements and how they differ in interesting ways from similar arrangements in Britain and Europe.

Some topics are treated in greater detail in this book than in many others. There is an entire chapter on the media—their structure, historical evolution, and political role. The chapter on public opinion deals at length with elite as well as mass opinion. To show how the less obvious, more fundamental features of the American mind may affect politics, I supply a chapter on Ameri-can political culture that emphasizes its dis-tinctive features. The Supreme Court obviously is important, but the greatest impact of the judiciary comes from the decisions of lower federal courts that never receive a systematic review by the highest court. Therefore, I devote considerable space in the chapter on the judiciary to how and at what cost people get access to lower courts and the resulting influence on public policy.

This book can be used in a variety of ways. A teacher can assign it to be read in sequence. I do this, and it works well. Or one can skip about. For example, one can assign the chapter on the presidency and then follow it with policy chapters (such as those on foreign affairs and military spending) in which the president plays an especially important role. Then one can assign the chapters on Congress and the media, followed by policy chapters (such as those on business regulation and social welfare) in which these actors are particularly influential. And the chapter on the judiciary can be followed by chapters on civil liberties and civil rights wherein the courts have obviously played a major part.

It is not necessary to read all the policy chapters to understand the conclusions I draw from them since the highlights of these chapters are summarized in Chapter 22. It is important, however, to read Chapter 14, because the conceptual tools introduced there are repeatedly referred to in the rest of the policy chapters.

In any book, but especially in a textbook, an author must consider carefully how to handle personal beliefs. The study of politics is not a value-free science, but admitting that ought not to confer a license for the author to pontificate at will. To me, the crucial question is the attitude one takes to problems of evidence and inference. I believe an author ought to write a text in which major controversies are clearly labeled as such, competing arguments are summarized, and the problems of evidence and inference are taken seriously. I have tried to avoid describing politics as a struggle between the good guys and the bad guys, to shun snap judgments and loaded language, and to postpone reaching conclusions about who wins and who loses until after a review of several policy areas.

This is not the same as claiming that I have been "objective" or "detached"—I doubt any text writer ever has or ever can be—but it does represent a genuine effort (no doubt inadequate) to avoid sloganeering and indoctrination. I think there ought to be more "discipline" in our academic discipline than is sometimes apparent.

I have tried to select illustrative material that will catch the students' attention *and* direct that attention to political matters. In the chapter on civil liberties students are challenged to choose how they would decide actual Supreme Court cases. At the back of the book there is a complete listing of presidents and Congresses showing the partisan composition of each. I also decided to put in lists of "political trivia" and some of the popular "laws" of politics, because the student mind tends to be fascinated with these and to find them memorable. Since I believe politics is fascinating and ought to be memorable, I hope these and other illustrative materials will help convey to the student the excitement of studying—and practicing—politics.

Others will decide whether this text has any merit, but I am confident that the supplementary materials available are of remarkably high quality. Richard Pious of Barnard College has prepared an imaginative Student Handbook. By using some self-administered tests, simple data-analysis projects, and some larger student exercises, he shows students how they can expand their own knowledge of politics while remembering (or criticizing) the key concepts supplied by the text. John McAdams of Marquette University has produced an extraordinary Instructor's Guide that offers, not only interesting references and discussion topics, but classroom projects (such as polls of student opinion) that focus attention on the relationship—if any—between popular beliefs and public policy. There is also a Test Item File with text page references.

Since I have drawn on the work of so many other scholars in writing this book, I hope they—and any reader—will feel free to write me with suggestions on how it can be improved.

ACKNOWLEDGMENTS

Every author depends on others in writing any book, but writing a textbook requires the services of so many persons that one almost feels as though he were the recording secretary for an academic conference. The words in this book are all mine, but my debts for ideas, facts, and illustrations are so diverse as to defy enumeration. I am delighted, however, to mention those who have been of special value.

Several students at Harvard University served ably as research assistants: Leslie Cornfeld, Michael Cornfield, Robert Katzmann, William Kristol, John McAdams, Joan Meier, Patricia Rachal, Victoria Radd, Beth Rubinstein, and George White.

As it was being written, the entire manuscript was read with great care and effect by Gottlieb J. Baer of American River College, John McAdams of Marquette University, Richard Pious of Barnard College, James Sheffield of Wichita State University, and Manfred Stevens of Lamar University. Several chapters were reviewed by my old friend and former collaborator Peter B. Clark. On completion, the manuscript was reviewed by Murray C. Havens of Texas Tech University, James Perkins of San Antonio College, and Robert Weissberg of the University of Illinois, Urbana-Champaign.

Individual chapters were reviewed by experts in these subjects. To avoid imputing to them responsibility for the chapters they saw, I list them here, with my deep gratitude, in alphabetical order:

Henry J. Abraham, *University of Virginia*
Robert J. Art, *Brandeis University*
Joseph Cooper, *Rice University*
Martha Derthick, *Brookings Institution*
Daniel J. Elazar, *Temple University*
Richard F. Fenno, Jr., *University of Rochester*
Paul J. Halpern, *Environmental Protection Agency*
Charles V. Hamilton, *Columbia University*
Harry N. Hirsch, *Harvard University*
Herbert Kaufman, *Brookings Institution*
Xandra Kayden
Louis W. Koenig, *New York University*
Lawrence J. Korb, *Naval War College*
Everett Carll Ladd, Jr., *University of Connecticut*
David Lawrence, *Fordham University*
Seymour Martin Lipset, *Stanford University*
Norman R. Luttbeg, *Texas A & M University*
Thomas K. McCraw, *Harvard Business School*
Forrest McDonald, *University of Alabama*
Ernest R. May, *Harvard University*
John E. Mueller, *University of Rochester*
Mark V. Nadel
Pietro Nivola, *University of Vermont*
Gary Orfield, *University of Illinois*
Joseph Pechman, *Brookings Institution*
Gerald M. Pomper, *Rutgers University*
Henry J. Pratt, *Wayne State University*
C. Herman Pritchett, *University of California, Santa Barbara*
Austin Ranney, *American Enterprise Institute*
Michael J. Robinson, *Catholic University*
Stanley Rothman, *Smith College*
Francis E. Rourke, *Johns Hopkins University*
Robert H. Salisbury, *Washington University*
Martin Shefter, *Cornell University*
James L. Sundquist, *Brookings Institution*
Edward R. Tufte, *Yale University*
Christopher Wolfe, *Marquette University*
Gordon Wood, *Brown University*

Various typists, but principally Sally Cox, Wendy Gelberg, Jennifer Hitchcock, and Mary Marvin, performed splendidly. D.C. Heath and Company supplied me with the services of an exceptionally able staff of editors and designers, notably Betty Ann Tyson, Sharon Mallar Donahue, and Esther Agonis. John Harney talked me into this; I didn't think it was possible.

Given all this assistance, all that remained for me was to make the mistakes. That I no doubt have done.

J.Q.W.

CONTENTS

PART II Opinions, Interests, and Organizations   *97*

PART III   Institutions of Government   253

PART IV   The Politics of Public Policy   *409*

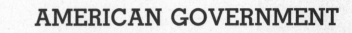

AMERICAN GOVERNMENT

PART I

The American System

66 In framing a government which is to be administered by men over men, the great difficulty lies in this: You must first enable the government to control the governed; and in the next place oblige it to control itself. 99

FEDERALIST NO. 51

1 The Study of American Government

Who holds political power · Formal authority ·
Legitimacy of government · Forms of democ-
racy · Democratic centralism · Participatory
democracy · Representative democracy ·
Popular rule · Theories as to who rules ·
Influence

There are two great questions about politics:
Who governs? To what ends?

We want to know the answer to the first question because we believe that the nature of those
who rule—their personalities and beliefs, their
virtues and vices—will affect what they do to and
for us. Many people already think they know the
answer to the question, and they are prepared
to talk and vote on that basis. That is their right
and the opinions they express may be correct;
but they may also be wrong. Indeed, many of
these opinions *must* be wrong because they are in
conflict. When asked, "Who governs?", some
persons will say "the unions" and some will say
"big business"; others will say "the politicians"
or "the people" or "the Communists." Still
others will say "Wall Street," "the military,"
"crackpot liberals," "the media," "bureaucrats,"
or "pointy-headed intellectuals." Not all these
answers can be correct—at least, not all of the
time.

Senator Huey P. Long of Louisiana, a spellbinding
orator, in 1932 (left). Senator John Tower of Texas
shakes hands with constituents (right).

The answer to the second question is important because it tells us how government affects our lives. We want to know not only who governs, but what difference it makes who governs. In our day-to-day lives, we may not think government makes much difference at all. In one sense that is right because our most pressing personal concerns—work, play, love, family, health—are essentially private matters on which government touches but slightly. But in a larger and longer perspective, government makes a substantial difference. Consider: forty-five years ago 96 percent of all American families paid no federal income tax, and for the 4 percent or so who did pay, the average rate was only about 4 percent of their incomes. Today almost all families pay federal income taxes, and the average rate is 20 percent of their incomes. Through laws that have been enacted in the past forty-five years, the federal government has taken charge of an enormous amount of the nation's income, with results that are still being debated. Or consider: twenty years ago in many parts of the country blacks could ride only in the backs of buses, had to use washrooms and drinking fountains that were labeled "colored," and could not be served in most public restaurants. Such restrictions have been almost eliminated, in large part because of decisions by the federal government.

It is important to bear in mind that we wish to answer two different questions, and not two versions of the same question. You cannot always predict what goals government will establish knowing only who governs, nor can you always tell who governs by knowing what activities government undertakes. Most people holding national political office are middle-class, middle-aged, white Protestant males, but we cannot then conclude that the government will only adopt policies that are to the narrow advantage of the middle class, or the middle-aged, or to whites, or to Protestants, or to men. If we thought that, we would be at a loss to explain why the rich are taxed more heavily than the poor, why a War on Poverty was declared, why constitutional amendments giving rights to blacks and women passed Congress by large majorities, or why Catholics and Jews have been appointed to so many important governmental posts.

This book is chiefly devoted to answering the question, "Who governs?" It is written in the belief that this question cannot be answered without looking at how government makes—or fails to make—decisions about a large variety of concrete issues. Thus, especially in Part IV, we shall inspect government policies to see what individuals, groups, and institutions seem to exert the greatest power in the continuous struggle to define the purposes of government. Power and purpose are inextricably intertwined.

WHAT IS POLITICAL POWER?

By "power" we mean the ability of one person to get another person to act in accordance with the first person's intentions. Sometimes an exercise of power is obvious, as when the president tells the air force that it cannot build the B-1 bomber. More often, power is exercised in subtle ways that may not be evident even to the participants, as when the president's economic advisers persuade him to impose wage and price controls. The advisers may not think they are using power—after all, they are the president's

subordinates—but if the president acts in accord with their intentions as a result of their arguments, they have used power.

Power is found in all human relationships, but we shall be concerned here only with power as it is used to affect who will hold government office and how government will behave. This leaves many important things out of account. If a corporation closes a factory in a small town where it was the major employer, it is using power in ways that affect deeply the lives of people. When a university refuses to admit a student or a medical society refuses to license a would-be physician, it is also using power. But to explain how all these things happen would be tantamount to explaining how society as a whole, and in all its particulars, operates. We limit our view to government, and chiefly to the American federal government. However, we shall repeatedly pay special attention to how things once thought to be "private" matters become "public"—that is, how they manage to become objects of governmental action. In Chapter 14, where we begin the discussion of policy-making, we will look closely at how issues get onto the governmental agenda. Indeed, one of the most striking transformations of American politics has been the extent to which, in recent decades, almost every aspect of human

“Much of American political history has been a struggle over what constitutes legitimate authority.”

life has found its way onto the governmental agenda. Twenty years ago the federal government would have displayed no interest in a factory closing its doors, a university refusing an applicant, or a profession not accrediting a member. Now governmental actions can and do affect all these things.

Persons who exercise political power may or may not have the authority to do so. By "authority" we mean the right to use power. The exercise of rightful power—that is, of authority—is ordinarily easier than the exercise of power that is not supported by any persuasive claim of right. We accept decisions, often without question, if they are made by persons who we believe have the right to make them; we may bow to naked power because we cannot resist it, but by our recalcitrance or our resentment we put the users of naked power to greater trouble than the wielders of authority. We will on occasion speak of "formal authority." By this we mean that the right to exercise power is vested in a governmental office. A president, a senator, and a federal judge have formal authority to do certain things.

Dramatic changes have occurred in popular beliefs in the legitimacy of government intervention in what were once regarded as private matters. Not long ago the government—and public opinion—tolerated overt segregation in private business. Today such segregation is illegal. People now also support the right of the government to search passengers boarding aircraft, unthinkable before aircraft hijackings made it seem necessary.

What makes power rightful varies from time to time and from country to country. In the United States we usually say that a person has political authority if his or her right to act in a certain way is conferred by a law or a state or national constitution. But what makes a law or constitution a source of right? That is the question of legitimacy. In the United States the Constitution today is widely, if not unanimously, accepted as a source of legitimate authority, but that was not always the case.

Much of American political history has been a struggle over what constitutes legitimate authority. The Constitutional Convention in 1787 was an effort to see whether a new, more powerful federal government could be made legitimate; the succeeding administrations of George Washington, John Adams, and Thomas Jefferson were in large measure preoccupied with disputes over the kinds of decisions that were legitimate for the federal government to make. The Civil War was a bloody struggle over the legitimacy of the federal union; the New Deal of Franklin Roosevelt was hotly debated by those who disagreed over whether it was legitimate for the federal government to intervene deeply in the economy.

In the United States today no government at any level would be considered legitimate if it were not in some sense democratic. That was not always the prevailing view, however; at one time, people disagreed over whether democracy itself was a good idea. In 1787 Alexander Hamilton worried that the new government he helped create might be too democratic while George Mason, who refused to sign the Constitution, worried that it was not democratic enough. Today virtually everyone believes that "democratic government" is the only proper kind. Most people probably believe that our existing government is democratic; and a few believe that other institutions of public life—schools, universities, corporations, trade unions, churches—should be run on democratic principles if they are to be legitimate. We shall not discuss the question of whether democracy is the best way of governing all institutions.

Rather we shall consider the different meanings that have been attached to the word "democratic" and which, if any, best describes the government of the United States.

WHAT IS DEMOCRACY?

Democracy is a word used to describe at least three different political systems. In one system the government is said to be democratic if its decisions will serve the "true interests" of the people whether or not those people directly affect the making of those decisions. It is by using this definition of democracy that various authoritarian regimes—the Soviet Union, China, Cuba, and certain European, Asian, and Latin American dictatorships—have been able to claim that they were "democratic." The Soviet Union, for example, has claimed that it operates on the principle of "democratic centralism" whereby the true interests of the masses are discovered through discussion within the Communist party and then decisions are made under central leadership to serve those interests. Whether or not the "true interests" are in fact discovered and served is obviously a matter of dispute.

The second way in which the term democracy is used is to describe those regimes that come as close as possible to the Aristotelian ideal of the "rule of the many."[1] A government is democratic if all, or most, of its citizens participate directly in either holding office or making policy. In Aristotle's time—Greece in the fifth century B.C.—such a government was possible. The Greek city-state, or *polis,* was quite small and within it citizenship was extended to all free adult male property-holders. (Slaves, women, minors, and those without property were excluded from participation in government.) In more recent times, the New England town meeting approximates the Aristotelian ideal. In such a meeting the adult citizens of a community gather once or twice a year to vote directly on all major issues and expenditures of the town. As towns have become larger and issues more compli- cated, many town governments have abandoned the pure town meeting in favor of either the representative town meeting (in which a large number, perhaps two or three hundred, of elected representatives meet to vote on town affairs) or representative government (in which a small number of elected city councillors make decisions).

Some people have argued that the virtues of direct or participatory democracy can and should be reclaimed even in a modern, complex society. This can be done either by allowing individual neighborhoods in big cities to govern themselves (community control) or by requiring those affected by some government program to participate in its formulation (citizen partici- pation). In many states a measure of direct democracy exists when voters can decide on referendum issues—that is, policy choices that appear on the ballot. The proponents of direct democracy defend it as the only way to ensure that the "will of the people" prevails.

The third definition of democracy is an alternative to the former and is the principle of governance of most nations that are called democratic. It was most concisely stated by the economist Joseph Schumpeter: "The democratic method is that institutional arrangement for arriving at political decisions in which individuals [i.e., leaders] acquire the power to decide by means of a competitive struggle for the people's vote."[2] Sometimes this method is called ap- provingly "representative democracy"; at other times it is referred to, disapprovingly, as the "elitist" theory of democracy. It is justified by one or both of two arguments: First, it is impractical, owing to limits of time, information, energy, interest, and expertise, for the people to decide on public policy, but it is not impractical to expect them to make reasonable choices among competing leadership groups. Second, some persons (including, as we shall see in the next chapter, many of the Framers of the Constitution) believe that direct democracy is likely to lead to bad decisions because people often decide large

❝This fear of direct democracy persists today, as can be seen from the statements of persons who do not like what the voters have decided.**❞**

Direct democracy exists in some states in the form of referenda elections. Voters in California passed Proposition 13, which forced a cut in property taxes, over the opposition of many elected officials.

issues on the basis of fleeting passions and in response to popular demagogues. This fear of direct democracy persists today, as can be seen from the statements of persons who do not like what the voters have decided. For example, politicians who favored Proposition 13, the referendum measure that in 1978 sharply cut property taxes in California, spoke approvingly of the "will of the people." Politicians who disliked Proposition 13 spoke disdainfully of "mass hysteria."

For representative government to work, there must, of course, be an opportunity for genuine leadership competition. This requires in turn that individuals and parties be able to run for office, that communication (through speeches, the press, and in meetings) be free, and that the voters perceive that a meaningful choice exists. Many questions still remain to be answered. For instance: How many offices should be elective and how many appointive? How many candidates or parties can exist before the choices become hopelessly confused? Where will the money come from to finance electoral campaigns? There is more than one answer to such questions. In some European democracies, for example, very few offices—often, just those in the national or local legislature—are elective, and much of the money for campaigning for these offices comes from the government. In the United States many offices—executive and judicial as well as legislative—are elective, and most of the money the candidates use for campaigning comes from industry, labor unions, and private individuals.

Whenever the word "democracy" is used alone in this book, it will have the meaning Schumpeter gave it. As we shall see in the next chapter, the men who wrote the Constitution did not use the word "democracy" in that document. They wrote instead of a "republican form of government," but by that they meant what we call "representative democracy." Whenever we refer to that form of democracy involving the direct participation of all or most citizens, we shall use the term "direct" or "participatory" democracy.

HOW IS POWER DISTRIBUTED IN A DEMOCRACY?

Representative democracy is any system of government in which leaders are authorized to make decisions by winning a competitive struggle for the popular vote. It is obvious, then, that very different sets of hands can control political power depending on what kinds of persons can become leaders, how the struggle for votes is carried on, how much freedom to act is given to those who win the struggle, and what other sorts of influence (besides the desire for popular approval) affect the leaders' actions.

In some cases what the leaders do will be so sharply constrained by what most people want that the actions of officeholders will follow the preferences of citizens very closely. We shall call such cases examples of "majoritarian" politics. In this case elected officials are the delegates of the people, acting as the people (or a majority of them) would act were the matter put to a popular vote. The issues handled in a majoritarian fashion can only be those that are sufficiently important to command the attention of most citizens, sufficiently clear to elicit an informed opinion from citizens, and sufficiently feasible so that what citizens want done can, in fact, be done. In Chapter 14 we shall discuss what features of an issue create the circumstances that facilitate majoritarian decision-making, and in other chapters in Part IV give examples of them.

When circumstances do not permit majoritarian decision-making, then some group of officials will have to act without knowing (and perhaps not caring) exactly what people want. Indeed, even on issues that do evoke a clear opinion from a majority of citizens, the shaping of the details of a policy will reflect the views of those persons who are sufficiently motivated to go to the trouble of becoming active participants in policy-making. These active participants usually will be a small, and probably an unrepresentative, minority. Thus, the actual distribution of political power even in a democracy will depend importantly on the composition of the political elites who are actually involved in the struggles over policy. By "elite," we mean an identifiable group of persons who possess a disproportionate share of some valued resource—in this case, political power.

> **❝**Even on issues that do evoke a clear opinion from a majority of citizens, the shaping of the details of a policy will reflect the views of those persons who are sufficiently motivated to go to the trouble of becoming active participants in policy-making.**❞**

Political activists differ from most citizens: they take politics more seriously, they feel more strongly attached to a candidate or an issue, and they may even earn a living from politics. Increasingly, activists are young people.

There are at least four theories that purport to describe and explain the actions of political elites. One theory is associated with the writings of Karl Marx. To Marxists—or at least to some of them, since not all Marxists agree—government, whatever its outward form, is merely a reflection of underlying economic forces, primarily the pattern of ownership of the means of production. All societies, they claim, are divided into classes on the basis of the relations of people to the economy—capitalists (the bourgeoisie), workers, farmers, intellectuals. In modern society two major classes contend for power, capitalists and workers. Whichever class dominates the economy also controls the government,

which is nothing more than a piece of machinery designed to express and give legal effect to underlying class interests. In the United States the government "is but a committee for managing the common affairs of the whole bourgeoisie."[3] To a traditional Marxist, it would be pointless to study the government as if it had any independent power in society, since it is controlled by the dominant social class. There are many variations, some quite subtle, on this fundamental argument, and some newer Marxists find it more interesting to study how the government actually operates than did Marx himself, for whom government was a mere "epiphenomenon." But even neo-Marxists believe that the

Max Weber (1864–1920), a German scholar, was a founder of sociology. Trained in law and history, he produced a major analysis of the evolution of modern society, which stressed the role of bureaucracy.

Karl Marx (1818–1883), a German philosopher and radical political leader, was the founder of modern socialist thought. A brilliant, complex, and vituperative writer, Marx was best known for his "Communist Manifesto." His major work was *Das Kapital*, a four-volume analysis of nineteenth-century capitalism.

answer to the questions of who really governs, and to what ends, is to be found in the pattern of economic interests, especially those represented by the large corporation.

A second theory, closely related to the first, argues that a nongovernmental elite makes most of the major decisions but that this elite is not composed exclusively, or even primarily, of corporate leaders. C. Wright Mills, an American sociologist, expresses this view in his book *The Power Elite*.[4] To him, the most important policies are set by a loose coalition of three groups—corporate leaders, top military officers, and a handful of key political leaders. Different persons have different versions of the "power elite" theory. Some would add to the triumvirate listed by Mills the leaders of the major communications media, and others would add major labor leaders. The essential argument is the same, however: government is dominated by a few top leaders, most of whom are outside the government and enjoy great advantages in wealth, status, or organizational position. They act in concert, and the policies they make serve the interests of the elite. Some people have such leaders in mind when they use the term "The

Establishment," though when that expression was first coined it referred to the influence exercised by Wall Street lawyers who alternated between governmental and private employment.[5]

A third theory directs attention to the appointed officials—the bureaucrats—who operate government agencies and large corporations from day to day. Max Weber, a German historian and sociologist who wrote in the early years of this century, criticized the Marxist position because it assigned exclusive significance to economic power. Weber thought Marx had neglected the dominant social and political fact of modern times—that all institutions, governmental and nongovernmental, have fallen under the control of large bureaucracies whose expertise and specialized competence are essential to the management of contemporary affairs. Capitalists or workers may come to power, but the government agencies they create will be dominated by those who operate them on a daily basis. This dominance would have advantages, Weber thought, because decisions would be made more rationally; but it would also have disadvantages because the political power of the bureaucrats would become "over-towering."[6]

A fourth answer has no single intellectual parent but can be described, loosely, as the pluralist view. Political resources, such as money, prestige, expertise, organizational position, and access to the mass media, are so widely scattered in our society and in the hands of such a variety of persons that no single elite has anything like a monopoly on them. Furthermore, there are so many governmental institutions in which power may be exercised—city, state, and federal governments and, within these, the offices of mayors, managers, legislators, governors, presidents, judges, bureaucrats—that no single group, even if it had many political resources, could dominate most, or even much, of the political process. Policies are the outcome of a complex pattern of political haggling, innumerable compromises, and shifting alliances.[7] Pluralists do not argue that political resources are distributed equally—that would be tantamount to saying that all decisions are made on a majoritarian basis. They believe that political resources are sufficiently divided among such different kinds of elites (businessmen, politicians, union leaders, journalists, bureaucrats, professors, environmentalists, lawyers, and whatever) that all, or almost all, relevant interests have a chance to affect the outcome of decisions. Not only are the elites divided, they are responsive to their followers' interests, and thus they provide representation to almost all citizens affected by a policy.

Contemplating these contending theories may lead some persons to the cynical conclusion that, whichever theory is correct, politics is a self-seeking enterprise in which everybody is out for personal gain. Though there is surely plenty of self-interest among political elites (at least as much as there is among college students!), it does not necessarily follow that the resulting policies will be wholly self-serving. For one thing, a policy may be good or bad independently of the motives of the person who decided it, just as a product sold on the market may be useful or useless regardless of the profit-seeking or wage-seeking motives of those who produced it. For another thing, the self-interest of persons is often an incomplete guide to their actions. People must frequently choose between two courses of action, neither of which has an obvious "payoff" to them. We caution against the cynical explanation of politics which Americans seem especially prone to adopt. Alexis de Tocqueville, the French author of a perceptive account of American life and politics in the early nineteenth century, noticed this trait among us:

Americans . . . are fond of explaining almost all the actions of their lives by the principle of self-interest rightly understood. . . . In this respect I think they frequently fail to do themselves justice; for in the United States as well as elsewhere people are sometimes seen to give way to those disinterested and spontaneous impulses that are natural to man; but the Americans seldom admit that they yield to emotions of this kind; they are more anxious to do honor to their philosophy than to themselves.[8]

The belief that people will usually act on the basis of their self-interest, narrowly defined, is a theory to be tested, not an assumption to be made. One example of how such an assumption can prove misleading will suffice for now. In the 1960s leaders of the AFL-CIO in Washington were among the most influential forces lobbying Congress for the passage of certain civil rights bills. Yet at the time they did this, the leaders did not stand to benefit either personally (they were almost all white) or organizationally (rank-and-file labor union members were not enthusiastic about such measures).[9] To understand why they took these positions, it is not enough to know their incomes or their jobs, one must also know something about their attitudes, their allies, and the temper of the times. In short, political preferences cannot invariably be predicted simply by knowing economic or organizational position.

POLITICAL CHANGE

The question of who governs will be answered differently at different times. Circumstances change as does our knowledge about politics. As we shall see in Part III, the presidency and Congress in the second half of the nineteenth century were organized rather differently from how they are today. Throughout this book we shall make frequent reference to the historical evolution of institutions and policies. We shall do this partly because what government does today is powerfully influenced by what it did yesterday, and partly because the evolution of our institutions and policies has not stopped but is continuous. If we get some sense of how the past has shaped the government, we may better understand what we see today and are likely to see tomorrow.

We tend to judge government and its policies by contemporary standards, even though the way government operates and the policies it may now apply are the products of the very different circumstances of an earlier era. The federal government today administers a social security system based in part on the concept of "insurance" and operated in large part by the states. To understand why that is so, we must understand the economic realities, constitutional interpretations, and political beliefs that existed in 1935, when the present law was passed.

Nor can we explain why the federal government played so small a role in the shaping of the national economy and the national industrial structure in the late nineteenth and early twentieth centuries merely by assuming that it was captured by the industrialists, corrupted by the politicians, or enfeebled by popular beliefs in laissez-faire economics. Throughout this period *state* governments were quite active in subsidizing, shaping, and regulating economic enterprise; indeed, there is scarcely a present-day federal policy toward business that does not have a precedent in state policies of fifty or a hundred years earlier. What has changed are

beliefs about what it was proper for the federal government to do, beliefs (and supporting institutions) that were originally shaped by events that occurred over two hundred years ago.

At certain times in our history we have taken an active interest in foreign affairs—at the time the nation was founded, when France and England seemed to have it in their power to determine whether or not America would survive as a nation; in the 1840s, when we sought to expand the nation into areas where Mexico and Canada had claims; in the late 1890s, when many leaders believed we had an obligation to acquire an overseas empire in the Caribbean and the Pacific; and in the period from the 1940s to the 1960s, when we openly accepted the role of the world's policeman. At other times the nation has looked inward, spurning opportunities for expansion and virtually ignoring events that in other periods would have been a cause for war, or at least mobilization.

The existence of deep-seated beliefs, major economic developments, and widely shared (or competing) perspectives as to what constitutes the dominant political problem of the time shapes the nature of day-to-day political conflict. What this means is that, in any broad historical or comparative perspective, politics is *not just* about "who gets what," though that is part of the story. It is about how people, or elites claiming to speak for people, define the public interest. Lest one think that such definitions are mere window dressing, signifying nothing of importance, bear in mind that on occasion men and women have been prepared to fight and die for one definition or another. Suppose you, the reader, had been alive in 1861. Do you think you would have viewed slavery as a matter of gains and losses, costs and benefits, winners and losers? Some people did. Or do you think you would have been willing to fight to abolish or preserve it? Many others did just that. The differences in the two ways of thinking about such an issue are at least as important as how institutions are organized or elections conducted.

FINDING OUT WHO GOVERNS

Ideally, political scientists ought to be able to give clear answers, amply supported by evidence, to the questions, How is political power distributed? and To what purposes will it be used under various circumstances? In reality, they can (at best) give partial, contingent, and controversial answers. The reason is to be found in the nature of our subject. Unlike economists, who assume that people have more or less stable preferences and can compare ways of satisfying those preferences by looking at the relative prices of various goods and services, political scientists are interested in how preferences are formed, especially for those kinds of services, such as national defense or pollution control, that cannot be evaluated chiefly in terms of monetary costs.

Understanding preferences is vital to understanding power. Who did what in government is not hard to find out, but who wielded power—that is, who made a difference in the outcome and for what reason—is much harder to discover. "Power" is a word that conjures up images of deals, bribes, power-plays, and arm-twisting. In fact, most power exists because of shared understandings, common friendships, communal or organizational loyalties, and differing degrees of prestige. These are hard to identify and almost impossible to quantify.

Nor can the distribution of political power be inferred simply by knowing what laws are on the books or what administrative actions have been taken. The enactment of a consumer protection law does not mean that consumers are powerful any more than the absence of such a law means that corporations are powerful. The passage of such a law could reflect an aroused public opinion, the lobbying of a small group claiming to speak for consumers, the ambitions of a senator, or the intrigues of one business firm seeking to gain a competitive advantage over another. A close analysis of what the law entails and how it was passed and administered is necessary before much of anything can be said.

The public speaks in many ways. Popular influence on government can be orderly, as in this New England town meeting, or disorderly, as in this Boston rally against the court-ordered busing of schoolchildren.

"Judgments about institutions and interests can only be made after one has seen how they behave on a variety of important issues or potential issues.**"**

This book will avoid sweeping claims that we have an "imperialistic" presidency (or an impotent one), an "obstructionist" Congress (or an innovative one), or "captured" regulatory agencies. Such labels simply do an injustice to the different roles that presidents, congressmen, and administrators play in different kinds of issues and in different historical periods.

The view taken in this book is that judgments about institutions and interests can only be made after one has seen how they behave on a variety of important issues or potential issues. Thus, Part IV of this book on policy-making is an essential part of the analysis, not an appendage. The issues discussed there—economic policy, the regulation of business, social welfare, civil rights and liberties, foreign and military affairs—are the daily business of government. The policies adopted or blocked, the groups heeded or ignored, the values embraced or rejected—these constitute the raw material out of which one can fashion an answer to the central questions we have asked: Who rules, and to what ends?

The way in which our institutions of government handle social welfare, for example, differs from the way other democratic nations handle it, and differs as well from the way our own institutions once treated it. Thus, the description of our institutions to be found in Part III will include not only an account of how they work today but also a brief historical background on their workings and a comparison of them with similar institutions in other countries. There is a tendency to assume that how we do things today is the only way they could possibly be done. In fact, there are other ways to operate a government based on some measure of popular rule. History, tradition, and belief weigh heavily on all that we do.

In any event, the place to begin a search for how power is distributed in national politics and what purposes that power serves is with the founding of the federal government in 1787: the Constitutional Convention and the events leading up to it. Though the decisions made then were not made by philosophers or professors, the practical men who made them had a philosophic and professorial cast of mind, and thus they left behind a fairly explicit account of what values they sought to protect and what arrangements they thought ought to be made for the allocation of political power.

SUMMARY

There are two major questions about politics: Who governs? To what ends? This book will focus mainly on answering the first.

There are four answers that have traditionally been given to the question of who governs.

- The *Marxist*—those who control the economic system will control the political one.
- The *elitist*—a few top leaders, not all of them drawn from business, make the key decisions without reference to popular desires.
- The *bureaucratic*—appointed civil servants run things.
- The *pluralist*—competition among affected interests shapes public policy.

To choose among these theories or to devise new ones requires more than describing governmental institutions and processes. In addition, one must examine the kinds of issues that do (or do not) get taken up by the political system and how that system resolves them.

"Democracy" can mean many things. In this book it will mean a system of governing in which persons acquire the power to make decisions by means of a free and competitive struggle for the people's vote.

Suggested Readings

Banfield, Edward C. *Political Influence.* New York: The Free Press, 1961. A method of analyzing politics—in this case, in the city of Chicago—comparable to the approach adopted in this book.

Crick, Bernard. *The American Science of Politics.* London: Routledge & Kegan Paul, 1959. A critical review of the methods of studying government and politics.

Dahl, Robert A. *A Preface to Democratic Theory.* Chicago: University of Chicago Press, 1956. A theoretical analysis of the meaning of democracy.

Marx, Karl, and Friedrich Engels. "The Manifesto of the Communist Party," in Robert C. Tucker, ed., *The Marx-Engels Reader,* 2nd ed. New York: W. W. Norton, 1978, pp. 469–500. The classic statement of the Marxist view of history and politics. Should be read in conjunction with Engels,

"Socialism: Utopian and Scientific," in the same collection, pp. 683–717.

Mills, C. Wright. *The Power Elite.* New York: Oxford University Press, 1956. An argument that self-serving elites dominate American politics.

Schumpeter, Joseph A. *Capitalism, Socialism, and Democracy,* 3rd ed. New York: Harper Torchbooks, 1950, Chs. 20–23. A lucid statement of the theory of representative democracy and how it differs from participatory democracy.

Truman, David B. *The Governmental Process,* 2nd ed. New York: Alfred A. Knopf, 1971. A pluralist interpretation of American politics.

Weber, Max. *From Max Weber: Essays in Sociology,* trans. and ed. by H. H. Gerth and C. Wright Mills. London: Routledge & Kegan Paul, 1948, Ch. 8. A theory of bureaucracy and of its power.

2 The Constitution

Revolution fought for liberty • Colonists' views on government • Problems with the Confederation • Innovative state constitutions • Shays's Rebellion • Framing the Constitution • *Federalist Papers* • Checks on popular rule • Protecting liberty • Need for Bill of Rights • Position on slavery • Motives of the Framers • Factional competition

The goal of the American Revolution was liberty. It was not the first revolution with that object, it may not have been the last, but it was perhaps the clearest case of a people altering the political order, violently, simply in order to protect their liberties. Subsequent revolutions had more complicated, or utterly different, objectives. The French Revolution in 1789 sought, not only liberty, but "equality and fraternity." The Russian Revolution (1917) and the Chinese Revolution (culminating in 1948) chiefly sought equality and were little concerned with liberty as we understand it.

THE PROBLEM OF LIBERTY

What the American colonists sought to protect when they signed the Declaration of Independence in 1776 were the traditional liberties to

This parade celebrated New York's ratification of the Constitution in 1788 (left). President Gerald Ford speaks at Independence Hall, Philadelphia, on July 4, 1976 (right).

protected while they remained a part of the British Empire.

Slowly but inevitably opinion shifted. By the time war broke out in 1775, a large number of colonists (though perhaps not a majority) had come to the conclusion that the colonies would have to become independent of Great Britain if their liberties were to be assured. The colonists had many reasons for regarding independence as the only solution, but one is especially important: they no longer had confidence in the English constitution. This constitution was not a single written document, but rather a collection of laws, charters, and traditional understandings that proclaimed the liberties of British subjects. Yet these liberties, in the eyes of the colonists, were regularly violated despite their constitutional protection. Clearly, then, the English con-

were, they thought, widely understood. They were based, not on the generosity of the king or the language of statutes, but on a "higher law" embodying "natural rights" that were ordained by God, discoverable in nature and history, and essential to human progress. These rights, John Dickinson wrote, "are born with us; exist with us; and cannot be taken away from us by any human power."[3] There was general agreement that the essential rights included life, liberty, and property long before Thomas Jefferson wrote them into the Declaration of Independence. (Jefferson changed "property" to "the pursuit of happiness," but almost everybody else went on talking about property.)

This emphasis on property did not mean that the American Revolution was thought up by the rich and wellborn to protect their interests or that there was a struggle between property-owners and the propertyless. In late-eighteenth-century America, most people (except the black slaves) had property of some kind. The overwhelming majority of citizens was self-employed —as farmers or artisans—and rather few persons benefited financially by gaining independence from England. Taxes were higher during and after the war than before, trade was disrupted by the conflict, and debts mounted perilously as various expedients were invented to pay for the struggle. There were, of course, war profiteers and those who tried to manipulate the currency to their own advantage, but most Americans at the time of the war saw the conflict clearly in terms of political rather than economic issues. It was a war of ideology.

Everyone recognizes the glowing language with which Jefferson set out the case for independence in the second paragraph of the Declaration:

We hold these truths to be self-evident, that all men are created equal, that they are endowed by their Creator with certain unalienable Rights, that among these are Life, Liberty and the pursuit of Happiness.—That to secure these rights, Governments are instituted among Men, de-

❝The Revolution was more than the War of Independence. It began before the war, continued after it, and involved more than driving out the British army by force of arms.❞

riving their just powers from the consent of the governed—that whenever any Form of Government becomes destructive of these ends, it is the Right of the People to alter or to abolish it, and to institute new Government, laying its foundation on such principles, and organizing its powers in such form, as to them shall seem most likely to effect their Safety and Happiness.

What almost no one recalls, but what is an essential part of the Declaration, are the next twenty-seven paragraphs in which, item by item, Jefferson listed the specific complaints the colonists had against George III and his ministers. None of these items spoke of social or economic conditions in the colonies; all spoke, instead, of specific violations of political liberties. The Declaration was, in essence, a lawyer's brief prefaced by a stirring philosophical claim that the rights being violated were "unalienable"—that is, based on nature and Providence, and not on the whims or preferences of men. Jefferson, in his original draft, added a twenty-eighth complaint—that the king had allowed the slave trade to continue *and* was inciting slaves to revolt against their masters. Congress, faced with so contradictory a charge, decided to include a muted reference to slave insurrections and omit all reference to the slave trade.

The Real Revolution
The Revolution was more than the War of Independence. It began before the war, continued after it, and involved more than driving out the British army by force of arms. The *real* Revolution, as John Adams afterward explained in a letter to a friend, was the *"radical change in the principles, opinions, sentiments, and affections of the people."* [4] This radical change had to do with a

new vision of what could make political authority legitimate and personal liberties secure. Government by royal prerogative was rejected; instead, legitimate government would require the consent of the governed. Political power could not be exercised on the basis of tradition but only as a result of a direct grant of power contained in a written constitution. Human liberty existed before government was organized, and government must respect that liberty. The legislative branch of government, in which the people were directly represented, should be superior to the executive branch.

These were, indeed, revolutionary ideas. No government at the time had been organized on the basis of these principles. And to the colonists, such notions were not empty words but rules to be put into immediate practice. In 1776 eight states adopted written constitutions. Within a few years every former colony but Connecticut and Rhode Island had adopted one. Most had detailed bills of rights defining personal liberties, and most placed the highest political power in the hands of elected representatives.

Written constitutions, representatives, and bills of rights are so familiar to us now that we forget how bold and unprecedented those innovations were in 1776. Indeed, many Americans did not think they would succeed: either they would be so strong that they would threaten liberty or so weak they they would permit chaos.

The eleven years that elapsed between the Declaration of Independence and the signing of the Constitution in 1787 were years of turmoil, uncertainty, and fear. George Washington had to wage a bitter, protracted war without anything resembling a strong national government to support him. The supply and financing of his army were based on a series of hasty improvisations, most badly administered and few adequately supported by the fiercely independent states. When peace came, many parts of the nation were a shambles. At least a quarter of New York City was in ruins, and many other communities were nearly devastated. Though the British lost the war, they still were a powerful factor on the North American continent with an army available in Canada and a large navy at sea. Spain claimed the Mississippi River Valley and occupied what are now Florida and California. Men who had left their farms to fight came back to discover themselves in debt with no money and heavy taxes. The paper money that had been printed to finance the war was now virtually worthless.

Weaknesses of the Confederation

The thirteen states had only a faint semblance of a national government with which to bring order to the nation. The Articles of Confederation, which went into effect in 1781, created little more than a "league of friendship" that could not levy taxes or regulate commerce. Each state retained its sovereignty and independence, each state (regardless of size) had one vote in Congress, nine (of thirteen) votes were required to pass any measure, and the delegates who cast these votes were picked and paid for by the state legislatures. Congress did have the power to make peace, and thus it was able to ratify the treaty with England in 1783. It could coin money, but there was precious little to coin; it could appoint the key army officers, but the army was small and dependent for support on independent state militias. It was allowed to deal with the Indians and run the post office—then, as now, thankless tasks that nobody else wanted. John Hancock, who in 1785 was elected to the meaningless office of "president" under the Articles, never showed up to take the job. Several states claimed the unsettled lands in the West, and occasionally pressed those claims with guns. Pennsylvania and Virginia went to war near Pittsburgh, and Vermont threatened to become part of Canada. There was no national judicial system to settle these or other claims among the states. To amend the Articles of Confederation, all thirteen states had to agree.

Many of the leaders of the Revolution, such as George Washington and Alexander Hamilton, believed that a stronger national government was essential. They lamented the disruption of commerce and travel caused by the quarrelsome states and deeply feared the possibility of foreign military intervention, with England or France playing one state off against another. A small group of men, conferring at Washington's home at Mount Vernon in 1785, decided to call a meeting to discuss trade regulation. That meeting, held at Annapolis, Maryland, in September 1786, was not well attended (no delegates arrived from New England), and so another meeting, this one in Philadelphia, was called for the following spring—in May 1787—to consider ways of remedying the defects of the Confederation.

THE CONSTITUTIONAL CONVENTION

The delegates assembled at Philadelphia for what was advertised (and authorized by Congress) as a meeting to revise the Articles; they adjourned four months later having written a wholly new constitution. When they met, they were keenly aware of the problems of the confederacy but far from agreeing as to what should be done about those problems. The protection of life, liberty, and property were their objectives in 1787 as they had been in 1776, but they had no accepted political theory that would tell them what kind of national government, if any, would serve that goal.

The Constitutional Convention met in 1787 in the Philadelphia State House where the Declaration of Independence had been signed eleven years before.

" Confederacies were too weak to govern and tended to collapse from internal dissension, while all stronger forms of government were so powerful as to trample the liberties of the citizens. "

The Lessons of Experience

They had read ancient and modern political history only to learn that nothing seemed to work. James Madison spent a good part of 1786 studying books sent to him by Thomas Jefferson, then in Paris, in hopes of finding some model for a workable American republic. He took careful notes on various confederacies in ancient Greece and on the more modern confederacy of the United Netherlands. He reviewed the history of Switzerland and Poland and the ups and downs of the Roman Republic. He concluded that there was no model; as he later put it in one of the *Federalist* papers, history consists only of beacon lights "which give warning of the course to be shunned, without pointing out that which ought to be pursued."[5] The problem seemed to be that confederacies were too weak to govern and tended to collapse from internal dissension, while all stronger forms of government were so powerful as to trample the liberties of the citizens.

State Constitutions.   Madison and the others did not need to consult history, or even the plight of the Articles of Confederation, for illustrations of the problem. These could be found in the government of the American states at the time. Pennsylvania and Massachusetts exemplified two aspects of the problem. The Pennsylvania constitution, adopted in 1776, created the most radically democratic of the new state regimes. All power was given to a one-house (unicameral) legislature, the Assembly, the members of which were elected annually for one-year terms. No legislator could serve more than four years. There was no governor or president, only an Executive Council that had few powers. Thomas Paine, whose pamphlets had helped precipitate

the break with England, thought the Pennsylvania constitution was the best in America, and in France philosophers hailed it as the very embodiment of the principle of rule by the people. Though popular in France, it was a good deal less popular in Philadelphia. The Assembly disfranchised the Quakers, persecuted conscientious objectors to the war, ignored the requirement of trial by juries, and manipulated the judiciary.[6] To Madison and his friends, the Pennsylvania constitution demonstrated how a government, though democratic, could be tyrannical as a result of concentrating all powers into one set of hands.

The Massachusetts constitution, adopted in 1780, was a good deal less democratic. There was a clear separation of powers among the various branches of government, the directly elected governor could veto acts of the legislature, and judges served for life. Both voters and elected officials had to be property-owners; the governor, in fact, had to own at least £1,000 worth of property. The principal officeholders had to swear they were Christians.

Shays's Rebellion.   But if the government of Pennsylvania was thought to be too strong, that of Massachusetts seemed too weak, despite its "conservative" features. In January 1787 a group of ex–Revolutionary War soldiers and officers, plagued by debts and high taxes and fearful of losing their property to creditors and tax collectors, forcibly prevented the courts in western Massachusetts from sitting. This became known as "Shays's Rebellion" after one of the officers, Daniel Shays. The governor of Massachusetts asked the Continental Congress to send troops to suppress the rebellion, but it could not raise the money or the manpower. Then he turned to his own state militia, but discovered he did not have one. In desperation, private funds were collected to hire a volunteer army that marched on Springfield and, with the firing of a few shots, dispersed the rebels who fled into neighboring states.

Shays's Rebellion in western Massachusetts in 1786–1787 stirred deep fears of anarchy in America. The ruckus was put down by a hastily assembled militia, and the rebels were eventually pardoned.

Commonwealth of MASSACHUSETTS,

By BENJAMIN LINCOLN, Esquire,

Commanding General of the Troops now in the Field, by Order of
GOVERNMENT.

WHEREAS there are some of the Citizens of this Commonwealth, who have acted in Arms as Non-Commissioned Officers and Privates against the Government of this State, who have caused it to be represented, that they would willingly return to their Allegiance and Duty, could they hope for a Pardon.

To all such I declare, That if they will come in, surrender their Arms, and take and subscribe the Oath of Allegiance to this Commonwealth, that they will be recommended to a Pardon.

B. LINCOLN.

Dated at Head-Quarters, Pittsfield, *February* 19, 1787.

Shays's Rebellion, occurring between the aborted Annapolis convention and the coming Philadelphia convention, had a powerful effect on opinion. Delegates who might have been reluctant to attend the Philadelphia meeting, especially those from New England, were galvanized by the fear that state governments were about to collapse from internal dissension. George Washington wrote a friend despairingly: "For God's sake . . . , if they [the rebels] have *real* grievances, redress them; if they have not, employ the force of government against them at once."[7] Thomas Jefferson, living in Paris, took a more detached view: "A little rebellion now and then is a good thing," he wrote. "The tree of liberty must be refreshed from time to time with the blood of patriots and tyrants."[8] Though Jefferson's detachment might be explained by the fact that he was in Paris and not

in Springfield, there were others, like Governor George Clinton of New York, who shared the view that no strong central government was required. (Whether Clinton would have agreed about the virtues of spilled blood, especially his, is another matter.)

The Framers

The Philadelphia convention attracted fifty-five delegates, only about thirty of whom participated regularly in the proceedings. One state, Rhode Island, refused to send anyone. The convention met during a miserably hot Philadelphia summer with the delegates pledged to keep their deliberations secret. (The talkative and party-loving Benjamin Franklin was often accompanied by other delegates to make sure that neither wine nor his delight in telling stories would lead him to divulge delicate secrets.)

John Locke (1632–1704), an English philosopher, believed government should be based on the consent of the governed. His *Two Treatises on Civil Government* (1690) influenced those who wrote the Declaration of Independence and the Constitution.

Those who attended were for the most part young (Hamilton was 32; Madison, 36) and experienced. Eight delegates had signed the Declaration of Independence, seven had been governors, thirty-four were lawyers and reasonably well-to-do, a few were wealthy. They were not "intellectuals," but men of practical affairs. Thirty-nine had served in the ineffectual Congress of the Confederation; a third were veterans of the Continental army.

Some names made famous by the Revolution were conspicuously absent. Thomas Jefferson and John Adams were serving as ministers abroad; Samuel Adams was ill; Patrick Henry was chosen to attend but refused, commenting that he "smelled a rat in Philadelphia, tending toward monarchy."

The convention produced, not a revision of the Articles of Confederation as it had been authorized to do, but instead a wholly new written constitution creating a true national government unlike any that had existed before. That document is today the world's oldest written constitution. The delegates who wrote it were neither saints nor schemers, and the deliberations were not always lofty or philosophical—much hard bargaining, not a little confusion, and the accidents of personality and time helped shape the final product. The delegates were split on many issues—whether there should be a strong central government, how the states should be represented, what was to be done about slavery, the role of the people—each of which was resolved by a compromise. The speeches of the delegates (known to us from the detailed notes kept by Madison) did not explicitly draw on political philosophy or quote from the writings of John Locke. Everybody present was quite familiar with the traditional arguments and, on the whole, well-read in history. But though the leading political philosophers were only rarely mentioned, the debate was profoundly influenced by philosophical beliefs, some formed by the revolutionary experience and others by the eleven-year attempt at self-government.

From the debates leading up to the Revolution, the delegates had drawn a commitment to liberty, which, despite the abuses sometimes committed in its name, they continued to share. Their defense of liberty as a natural right was drawn from the writings of Locke and based on his view that such rights are discoverable by reason. In a "state of nature," Locke argued, all men cherish and seek to protect their life, liberty, and property. But in a state of nature—that is, a society without a government—the strong can use their liberty to deprive the weak of theirs. The instinct for self-preservation leads men to want a government that will prevent this exploitation. But if the government is not itself to deprive men of their liberty, it must be limited. The chief limitation on it, he said, should derive from the fact that it is created, and governs, by the consent of the governed and by means of institutions wielding separate powers. People will not agree to be ruled by a government that threatens their liberty; therefore, the government to which they freely choose to submit themselves will be a limited government designed to protect liberty.

The Pennsylvania experience as well as the history of British government led the Framers to doubt that popular consent would be a sufficient guarantor of liberty. A popular government may prove too weak (as in Massachusetts) to prevent one faction from abusing another, or a popular majority can be tyrannical (as in Pennsylvania). In fact, the tyranny of the majority can be an even graver threat than the rule by the few. In the former case there may be no defenses for the individual—one lone person cannot count on the succor of public opinion or the possibility of popular revolt.

The problem, then, was a delicate one: how to devise a government strong enough to preserve order but not so strong that it would threaten liberty. The answer, the delegates believed, was not "democracy" as it was then understood. To many conservatives in the late eighteenth century democracy meant mob rule—it meant, in short, Shays's Rebellion (or, if they had been candid about it, the Boston Tea Party). On the other hand, aristocracy—the rule of the few—was no solution, since the few were likely to be self-seeking. Madison, writing later in the *Federalist* papers, put the problem this way:

If men were angels, no government would be necessary. If angels were to govern men, neither external nor internal controls on government would be necessary. In framing a government which is to be administered by men over men, the great difficulty lies in this: you must first enable the government to control the governed; and in the next place oblige it to control itself.[9]

Striking this balance could not be done, Madison believed, simply by writing a constitution that set limits on what government could do. The example of British rule over the colonies proved that laws and customs were inadequate checks on political power. As he expressed it, "A mere

> **"The problem, then, was a delicate one: how to devise a government strong enough to preserve order but not so strong that it would threaten liberty."**

demarcation on parchment of the constitutional limits [of government] is not a sufficient guard against those encroachments which lead to a tyrannical concentration of all the powers of government in the same hands."[10]

THE CHALLENGE

The resolution of political issues, great and small, often depends crucially on how the central question is phrased. The delegates came to Philadelphia in general agreement that there were defects in the Articles of Confederation that ought to be remedied. Had they, after convening, decided to make their business that of listing these defects and debating alternative remedies for them, the document that emerged would in all likelihood have been very different from what in fact was adopted. But immediately after the convention had organized itself and chosen Washington to be its presiding officer, the Virginia delegation, led by Governor Edmund Randolph but relying heavily on the draftsmanship of James Madison, presented to the convention a comprehensive plan for a wholly new national government. The plan quickly became the major item of business of the meeting; it, and little else, was debated for the next two weeks.

The Virginia Plan
When the convention decided to make the Virginia Plan its agenda, it had, whether it realized it or not, fundamentally altered the nature of its task. The business at hand was not to be the Articles and their defects, but rather how one should go about designing a true national government. The Plan called for

William Paterson (1745–1806) was attorney general of New Jersey when he was chosen to be a delegate to the Constitutional Convention. He opposed a strong national union, and offered a plan that would have given more power to the states. He later became a U.S. senator and a member of the Supreme Court.

Edmund Randolph (1753–1813), a delegate to the Constitutional Convention, was governor of Virginia. His Virginia Plan, in large part the work of James Madison, called for a strong central government. Though the Constitution followed his plan in many respects, he opposed its adoption at first, but then with a change of heart supported its ratification at the Virginia convention. He later became attorney general and secretary of state of the United States.

a "strong *consolidated* union" organized into three governmental branches—the legislative, executive, and judicial. The legislature was to be composed of two houses, the first elected directly by the people and the second chosen by the first house from among persons nominated by state legislatures. An executive was to be chosen by the national legislature, as were members of a national judiciary. The executive and some members of the judiciary were to constitute a "council of revision" that could veto acts of the legislature; that veto, in turn, could be overridden by the legislature. There were other interesting details, but the key features of the Virginia Plan were two: (1) a national legislature would have supreme powers on all matters on which the separate states were not competent to act, as well as the power to veto any and all state laws, and (2) at least one house of the legislature would be elected directly by the people.

The New Jersey Plan

As the debate went on, the opponents of a strong national government became increasingly worried that the convention was not going to con-

sider any alternative to the Virginia Plan. Accordingly, a group of delegates, chiefly from New Jersey but including representatives from other states as well, offered a substitute plan. Led by William Paterson of New Jersey, these delegates produced a set of resolutions that were designed to amend, not replace, the Articles of Confederation. The powers of Congress to raise revenue were increased and an executive chosen by Congress was authorized, but Congress would remain the creature of the states, its members chosen by them. In essence, whereas the Virginia Plan was based on the notion of popular sovereignty and a national government with broad powers, the New Jersey Plan was based on the concept of state sovereignty and a national government with limited powers.

If the New Jersey resolutions had been presented first and become the major item of business, it is quite possible that they would have become the framework for the document that finally emerged. But they were not. Offered after the convention had been discussing the Virginia Plan for two weeks, they encountered a reception very different from what they would have received if introduced earlier. The debate had got the delegates thinking in terms of a national government and thus had accustomed them to proposals that, under other circumstances, might have seemed quite radical. On June 19 the first decisive vote of the convention was taken: seven states preferred the Virginia Plan, three states the New Jersy Plan, and one state was split.

With the tide running in favor of a strong national government, the supporters of states' rights had to shift their strategy. Many of the critics of the Virginia Plan were from small states, and they now began to focus their efforts on ensuring that they could not be outvoted by the larger ones in Congress. One way was to have the members of the lower house elected by the state legislatures rather than the people, with each state getting the same number of seats rather than seats proportional to its population.

The debate was long and feelings ran high, so much so that Benjamin Franklin, at eighty-one the oldest delegate present, suggested that each day's meeting begin with a prayer. It turned out that the convention could not even agree on this: Hamilton is supposed to have objected, sarcastically, that the convention did not need "foreign aid," and others pointed out that the group had no funds with which to hire a minister. And so the argument continued.

The Compromise

Finally, a committee was appointed to meet during the Fourth of July holidays to work out a compromise, and the convention adjourned to await its report. Little is known of what went on in that committee's session, though some were later to say that Franklin played a key role in hammering out the plan that finally emerged. That compromise, the most important reached at the convention, and later called the Great Compromise, was submitted to the full convention on July 5 and debated for another week and a half. The debate might have gone even longer, but suddenly the hot weather moderated and Monday, July 16, dawned cool and

The presiding officer at the Constitutional Convention was George Washington (1732–1799). He rarely participated in the debates, but the effect of his presence was great. He was a national military hero, and it was generally expected that he would be the nation's first president.

fresh after a month of misery. On that day the plan was adopted: five states in favor, four opposed, and two not voting.* Thus, by the narrowest of margins, the structure of the national legislature was set, as follows:

- A House of Representatives consisting initially of 65 members apportioned among the states roughly on the basis of population and elected by the people.
- A Senate consisting of two senators from each state to be chosen by the state legislatures.

---

*The states in favor were Connecticut, Delaware, Maryland, New Jersey, and North Carolina. Those opposed were Georgia, Pennsylvania, South Carolina, and Virginia. Massachusetts was split down the middle; the New York delegates had left the convention. New Hampshire and Rhode Island were absent.

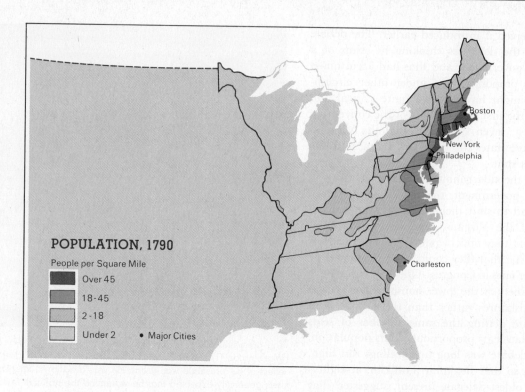

POPULATION, 1790

People per Square Mile

- Over 45
- 18 - 45
- 2 - 18
- Under 2   • Major Cities

Boston
New York
Philadelphia
Charleston

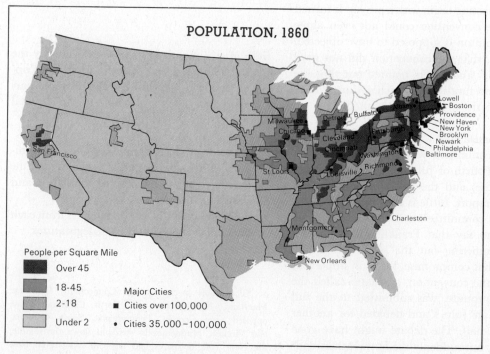

POPULATION, 1860

Lowell
Albany
Boston
Providence
New Haven
New York
Brooklyn
Newark
Philadelphia
Baltimore
Buffalo
Detroit
Milwaukee
Chicago
Cleveland
Pittsburgh
Cincinnati
Washington
St. Louis
Louisville
Richmond
San Francisco
Montgomery
New Orleans
Charleston

People per Square Mile

- Over 45
- 18 - 45
- 2 - 18
- Under 2

Major Cities
■ Cities over 100,000
• Cities 35,000 – 100,000

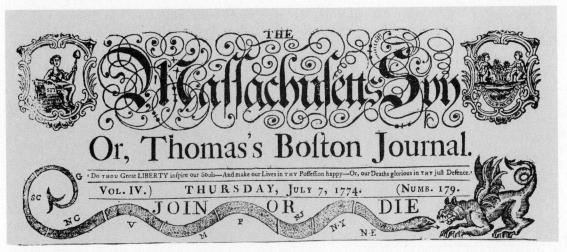

Even before the Revolutionary War, many felt that some form of union would be necessary if the rebellious colonies were to survive. In 1774 the *Massachusetts Spy* portrayed the colonies as segments of a snake that must "Join or Die."

The Great Compromise reconciled the interests of small and large states by allowing the former to predominate in the Senate and the latter in the House. This reconciliation was necessary to ensure that there would be support for a strong national government from both small as well as large states. It represented major concessions on the part of several groups. Madison, for one, was deeply opposed to the idea of having the states equally represented in the Senate. He saw in that a way for the states to hamstring the national government and much preferred some measure of proportional representation in both houses. Delegates from other states worried that representation on the basis of population in the House of Representatives would enable the large states to dominate legislative affairs. The margin by which the compromise was accepted was razor-thin (five states in favor, four opposed), but it held firm. In time, most of the delegates from the dissenting states accepted it.

After the Great Compromise many more issues had to be resolved, but by now a spirit of accommodation had developed. When one delegate proposed having the Congress choose the president, another, James Wilson, proposed that he be elected directly by the people. When neither side of that argument could prevail, a committee invented a plan for an "Electoral College" that would choose a president. When some delegates wanted a president chosen for life terms, others proposed seven-year terms, and still others wanted the term limited to three years without eligibility for reelection. The convention settled on a four-year term with no bar to reelection. Some states wanted the Supreme Court picked by the Senate; others wanted it chosen by the president. They finally agreed to let the president nominate the justices who would then have to be confirmed by the Senate.

Finally, on July 26, the proposals that were already accepted, together with a bundle of unresolved issues, were handed over to a "Committee of Detail" of five delegates. This committee included Madison and Gouverneur Morris, who was to be (so far as we know) the chief draftsman of the document that finally emerged.

The committee hardly contented itself with mere "details," however. It inserted some new proposals and made changes in old ones, drawing for inspiration on existing state constitutions and the members' beliefs as to what the other delegates might accept. On August 6 the report—the first complete draft of the Constitution—was submitted to the convention. There it was debated, item by item, revised, amended, and finally, on September 17, approved by all twelve states in attendance. (Not all *delegates* approved, however; three, including Randolph, refused to sign.)

THE CONSTITUTION AND DEMOCRACY

A debate continues to rage over whether the Constitution created, or was even intended to create, a democratic government. The answer is complex. The Framers did not intend to create a "pure democracy"—one in which the people rule directly. For one thing, the size of the country and the distances between settlements would have made that physically impossible. But for another, the Framers worried that a government in which all citizens directly participate, as in the New England town meeting, would be a government excessively subject to temporary popular passions and one in which minority rights would be insecure. They intended instead to create a republic, by which they meant a government in which a system of representation operates. In designing that system, the Framers chose, not without argument, to have the members of the House of Representatives elected directly by the people. Some delegates did not want to go even that far. Elbridge Gerry of Massachusetts, who refused to sign the Constitution, argued that though "the people do not want [i.e., lack] virtue" they are often the "dupes of pretended patriots." Roger Sherman of Connecticut agreed. But George Mason of Virginia and James Wilson of Pennsylvania carried the day when they argued that "no government could long subsist

without the confidence of the people," and this required "drawing the most numerous branch of the legislature directly from the people." Popular elections were approved: six states in favor, two opposed.

But though popular rule was to be one element of the new government, it was not to be the only one. State legislatures, not the people, would choose the senators; electors, not the people directly, would choose the president. As we have seen, without these arrangements, there would have been no Constitution at all, for the small states adamantly opposed any proposal that would have given power to the large ones. And direct popular election of the president would clearly have made the populous states the dominant ones. In short, the Framers wished to observe the principle of majority rule, but they felt that, on the most important questions, two kinds of majorities were essential—a majority of the voters and a majority of the states.

The power of the Supreme Court to declare an act of Congress unconstitutional—"judicial review"—is also a way of limiting the power of popular majorities. It is not clear whether the Framers intended that there be judicial review, but there is little doubt that in the Framers' minds the fundamental law, the Constitution, had to be safeguarded against popular passions. They made the process for amending the Constitution easier than it had been under the Articles but still relatively difficult.

An amendment can be proposed by either a two-thirds vote of both houses of Congress *or* by a national convention called by Congress at the request of two-thirds of the states.* Once

*There have been many attempts to get a new constitutional convention. In the 1960s thirty-three states, one short of the required number, requested a convention to consider the reapportionment of state legislatures. At present (1979), efforts are under way to call a convention to consider amendments to ban abortions and to require a balanced federal budget.

proposed, an amendment must be ratified by three-fourths of the states, either through their legislatures or through special ratifying conventions in each state. Twenty-six amendments have survived this process, all of them proposed by Congress and all but one (the Twenty-First) ratified by state legislatures rather than state conventions.

In short, the answer to the question of whether the Constitution brought into being a democratic government is "yes," if by "democracy" is meant a system of representative government based on popular consent. The degree of that consent has changed since 1787, and the institutions embodying that consent can take different forms. One form, rejected in 1787, gives all political authority to one set of representatives directly elected by the people. (That is the case, for example, in most parliamentary regimes, such as Great Britain, and in some city governments in the United States.) The other form of democracy is one in which different sets of officials, chosen directly or indirectly by different groups of people, share political power. (That is the case with the United States and a few other nations where the separation of powers is intended to operate.)

Key Principles

The American version of representative democracy was based on two major principles, the separation of powers and federalism. In America political power was to be shared by three separate branches of government; in parliamentary democracies that power was concentrated in a single, supreme legislature. In America political authority was divided between a national government and several state governments—federalism—whereas in most European systems authority was centralized in the national government. Neither of these principles was especially controversial at Philadelphia. The delegates began their work in broad agreement that separated powers and some measure of federalism were necessary, and both the Virginia and New Jersey

"The American version of representative democracy was based on two major principles, the separation of powers and federalism."

plans contained a version of each. How much federalism should be written into the Constitution was quite controversial, however.*

Government and Human Nature

Though the concepts of separated powers and federalism were widely shared at the convention, they were distinctively American ideas that grew out of the Framers' experience with colonial and Confederation governments and were linked, in their minds, with certain principles of human nature. As Madison was later to explain, the self-interest of men that could lead to disunity and tyranny might, if channeled by appropriate governmental institutions, provide a source of unity and a guarantee of liberty.

Persons sought their own advantage, in and out of politics; unchecked, this pursuit would lead some persons or factions to exploit others. But if the pursuit of self-interest were harnessed to political office, and if these offices were in competition with one another, then self-interest could prevent one set of officeholders from gathering all political power into its hands. "Ambition must be made to counteract ambition" so that "the private interest of every individual may be a sentinel over the public rights."[11] If men were angels, or if government were able to turn imperfect men into angels, all this would

---

*To the delegates a truly "federal" system was one, like the New Jersey Plan, that allowed for very strong states and only a weak national government. When the New Jersy Plan lost, the delegates who defeated it began using the word "federal" to describe their plan even though it called for a stronger national government. Thus, men who began as "federalists" at the convention ultimately became known as "antifederalists" during the struggle over ratification.

be unnecessary. But Madison and the other delegates were resigned to taking human nature pretty much as it was, and therefore they adopted "this policy of supplying, by opposite and rival interests, the defect of better motives."[12] The separation of powers would work, not in spite of the imperfections of human nature, but because of them.

So also with federalism. By dividing power between the states and the national government, one level of government can serve as a check on the other. This should provide a "double security" to the rights of the people: "The different governments will control each other, at the same time that each will be controlled by itself."[13] This was especially likely to happen in America, Madison thought, because it was a large country filled with diverse interests—rich and poor, Protestant and Catholic, Northerner and Southerner, farmer and merchant, creditor and debtor. Each

James Madison

John Jay

Alexander Hamilton

of these interests would constitute a faction that would seek its own advantage. One faction may come to dominate government, or a part of government, in one place, and another and rival faction may dominate it in another. The pulling and hauling among these factions would prevent any single government—say, that of New York—from dominating all of government. The division of powers among several governments would give to virtually every faction an opportunity to gain some—but not full—power.

THE CONSTITUTION AND LIBERTY

A more difficult question to answer is whether the Constitution created a system of government that would respect personal liberties. And that, in fact, is the question that was debated in the states when the document was presented for ratification. The proponents of the Constitution called themselves the Federalists (though they might more accurately be called "nationalists"). The opponents came to be known as the Antifederalists (though they might more accurately be called "states'-righters"). To be put into effect, the Constitution had to be approved by ratifying conventions in at least nine states. This was perhaps the most democratic feature of the Constitution: it had to be accepted, not by the existing Congress (still limping along under the Articles of Confederation), not by the state legislatures, but by special conventions elected by the people.

Though democratic, the ratification process was technically illegal. The Articles of Confederation, which still governed, could only be amended with the approval of all thirteen state legislatures. The Framers wanted to bypass these legislatures because they feared that, for reason of ideology or out of a desire to retain their powers, the legislators would oppose the Constitution. The Framers wanted ratification with less than the consent of all thirteen states because they knew such unanimity could not

Most Americans at the time of the convention were small farmers, who wanted as little government as possible.

be attained. (And, indeed, the conventions in North Carolina and Rhode Island did initially reject the Constitution.)

Reactions to the Constitution

The great issue that was before the state conventions was liberty, not democracy. Opponents of the new government did not argue that the federal government had so many checks and balances operating in it that the popular will would be defeated, but rather that it had too few such checks. The Antifederalists had no agreed-upon alternative to the Constitution, and that, of course, hurt their cause—it is hard to beat something with nothing. But they did have some shared objections: the House of Representatives was too small and too infrequently elected; there was an insufficient separation of the powers of the president and Senate; Congress had too many powers, and—most important—there was no bill of rights.

Historians have long argued over why the Framers, preoccupied with liberty, should have

❝It quickly became clear that without at least the promise of a bill of rights, the Constitution would not be ratified.**❞**

put no bill of rights in the Constitution. Some have suggested that this omission was evidence that liberty was not their chief concern. In fact, when one delegate suggested that a bill of rights be drawn up, the state delegations at the convention voted unanimously against the idea. There were several reasons for this action.

First, the Constitution, as written, *did* contain a number of specific guarantees of individual liberty, including the right of trial by jury in criminal cases and the privilege of the writ of habeas corpus. These rights are shown below.

Liberties Guaranteed in the Constitution
(before the Bill of Rights was added)

- Writ of habeas corpus* may not be suspended (except during invasion or rebellion).
- No bill of attainder may be passed by Congress or the states.
- No ex post facto law may be passed by Congress or the states.
- Right of trial by jury in criminal cases.
- Citizens of each state are entitled to the privileges and immunities of the citizens of every other state.
- No religious test or qualification for holding federal office.
- No law impairing the obligation of contracts.

---

*The meaning of words used to define certain rights:
Writ of habeas corpus: An order issued by a judge to a police officer or sheriff ordering that the person being held in custody be brought before the judge; designed to prevent illegal arrests.
Bill of attainder: A law that declares a person, without a trial, to be guilty of a crime.
Ex post facto law: A law that makes criminal an act that was legal when it was committed, or that increases the penalty for a crime after it has been committed; a retroactive criminal law.

Second, most states in 1787 had bills of rights. When Elbridge Gerry proposed to the convention that a federal bill of rights be drafted, Roger Sherman rose to observe that it was unnecessary because the state bills of rights were sufficient.[14]

But third, and perhaps most important, the Framers thought they were creating a government with specific, limited powers. It could do, they thought, only what the Constitution explicitly permitted it to do, and nowhere in that document was there permission to infringe freedom of speech or of the press or to impose cruel and unusual punishments. Some delegates probably feared that if any serious effort were made to list the rights that were guaranteed, later officials might assume that they had the power to do anything not explicitly forbidden.

Need for a Bill of Rights

Whatever their reasons, the Framers made at least a tactical and perhaps a fundamental mistake. It quickly became clear that without at least the promise of a bill of rights, the Constitution would not be ratified. Though the small states, pleased by their equal representation in the Senate, quickly ratified (in Delaware, New Jersey, and Georgia, the vote in the conventions was unanimous), the battle in the large states was intense and the outcome uncertain. In Pennsylvania, Federalist supporters dragged boycotting Antifederalists to the legislature in order to ensure that a quorum was present so that a convention could be called.

There were rumors of other rough tactics. In Massachusetts, the Constitution was approved by a narrow majority, but only after key leaders promised to obtain a bill of rights. In Virginia, James Madison fought against the fiery Patrick Henry, whose climactic speech against ratification was dramatically punctuated by a noisy thunderstorm outside. The Federalists won, by ten votes. In New York, Alexander Hamilton argued the case for six long weeks against the determined opposition of most of the state's key political leaders; he carried the day, but only by three votes, and then only after New York City threatened to secede from the state if it did not ratify. By June 21, 1788, the ninth state—New Hampshire—had ratified and the Constitution was law.

Despite the bitterness of the ratification struggle, the new government that took office in 1789–1790, headed by President Washington, was greeted enthusiastically. By the spring of 1790, all thirteen states had ratified. There remained, however, the task of fulfilling the promise of a bill of rights. To that end, James Madison introduced into the first session of the First Congress a set of proposals, many based on the existing Virginia bill of rights. Twelve were approved by Congress; ten of these were ratified by the states and went into effect in 1791. These amendments did not limit the power of state governments over citizens, only the power of the federal government. (Later, the Fourteenth Amendment, as interpreted by the Supreme Court, extended many of the guarantees of the Bill of Rights to cover state governmental action.)

THE CONSTITUTION AND SLAVERY

Nowhere in the Constitution can one find the words "slave" or "slavery." Yet at the time the document was written, one-third of the population of five southern states was made up of black slaves. Everyone at the Philadelphia convention was fully aware of this fact, but there was little debate on the morality of slaveholding. The only major argument was over the implications of slavery for the apportioning of seats in the House of Representatives, on the power of the government to restrict the slave trade, and on some related issues.

To some, the failure of the Constitution to address the question of slavery was a great betrayal of the promise of the Declaration of Independence that "all men are created equal."[15] For the Constitution to be silent on the subject

The
Bill of Rights

The First Ten Amendments to the Constitution, Grouped by Topic and Purpose

PROTECTIONS AFFORDED CITIZENS TO PARTICIPATE IN THE POLITICAL PROCESS

Amendment 1: Freedom of religion, speech, press, assembly, and of the right to petition the government.

PROTECTIONS AGAINST ARBITRARY POLICE AND COURT ACTION

Amendment 4: No unreasonable searches or seizures.

Amendment 5: Grand jury indictment required to prosecute a person for a serious crime.

No "double jeopardy"—being tried twice for the same offense.

Cannot be forced to testify against oneself.

No loss of life, liberty, or property without due process.

Amendment 6: Right to speedy, public, impartial trial with defense counsel and right to cross-examine witnesses.

Amendment 7: Jury trials in civil suits where value exceeds $20.

Amendment 8: No excessive bail or fines, no cruel and unusual punishment.

PROTECTIONS OF STATES' RIGHTS AND UNNAMED RIGHTS OF PEOPLE

Amendment 9: Unlisted rights are not necessarily denied.

Amendment 10: Powers not delegated to the United States or denied to states are reserved to the states.

OTHER AMENDMENTS

Amendment 2: Right to bear arms.

Amendment 3: Troops may not be quartered in homes in peacetime.

"The blunt fact, however, was that any effort to use the Constitution to end slavery would have meant the end of the Constitution."

The Constitutional Convention did not face the slavery issue head on. Although slave auctions, such as this one in Richmond, Virginia, were commonplace, some leaders wanted to rid the country of this "national sin." But to attempt this would have prevented the formation of a national government.

of slavery, and thereby to allow that odious practice to continue, was to convert, by implication, the Declaration into reading, "all *white* men are created equal."

It is easy to accuse the signers of the Declaration and the Constitution of hypocrisy. They knew of slavery, many of them owned slaves, and yet they were silent. Indeed, British opponents of the independence movement took special delight in taunting the colonists about their complaints of being "enslaved" to the British Empire while ignoring the slavery in their very midst.[16] Increasingly, revolutionary leaders during this period spoke to this issue. Thomas Jefferson had tried to get a clause opposing the slave trade put into the Declaration of Independence. James Otis of Boston had attacked slavery and argued that black as well as white men should be free. As revolutionary fervor mounted, so did northern criticisms of slavery. The Massachusetts legislature and then the Continental Congress voted to end the slave trade; Delaware prohibited the importation of slaves; Pennsylvania voted to tax it out of existence; and Connecticut and Rhode Island decided that all slaves brought into their states would automatically become free.

Slavery continued unabated in the South, defended by some whites because they thought it right, by others because they found it useful. But even in the South there were opponents, though rarely conspicuous ones. George Mason, a large Virginia slaveholder and a delegate to the convention, warned prophetically that "by an inevitable chain of causes and effects, providence punishes national sins [slavery] by national calamities."[17] The blunt fact, however, was that any effort to use the Constitution to end slavery would have meant the end of the Constitution. The southern states would never have signed a document that seriously interfered with slavery. Without the southern states there would have been a continuation of the Articles of Confederation, which would have left each state entirely sovereign and thus entirely free of any prospective challenge to slavery.

Thus, the Framers compromised with slavery; Theodore Lowi calls this their Greatest Compromise.[18] Slavery is dealt with in three places in the Constitution, though never by name. In determining the representation each state was to have in the House, "three-fifths of all other persons" (i.e., of slaves) are to be added to "the whole number of free persons."[19] The South originally wanted slaves to count fully even though, of course, none would be elected to the House; they settled for counting 60 percent of them. The convention also agreed not to allow the new government by law or even constitutional amendment to prohibit the importation of slaves until the year 1808.[20] The South, thus, had twenty years in which it could acquire more slaves from abroad; after that, Congress was free (but not required) to end the importation. Finally, the Constitution guaranteed that if a slave were to escape his or her master and flee to a nonslave state, the slave would be returned by that state to "the party to whom . . . service or labour may be due."[21]

The unresolved issue of slavery was to prove the most explosive question of all and, in the end, led to a great Civil War. Nor did the problem end with the war's end, for the legacy of slavery continues to the present. The enslavement of the blacks in the United States proved to be a social and political catastrophe of the first magnitude. The Framers managed to postpone that catastrophe in order to create a union that would eventually be strong enough to deal with the problem when it could no longer be postponed.

THE MOTIVES OF THE FRAMERS

Some persons prefer to judge political phenomena, not by what was said or done, but by the motives of those who spoke and acted. To these persons, what is most interesting about the Constitutional Convention was not the document that emerged but the motives of those who attended. More accurately, the true meaning of the provisions of the Constitution can only be understood by knowing what the Framers intended to achieve. In this view, to understand those intentions, one must look to the personal circumstances of the Framers.

There is nothing wrong with attempting to understand a difficult and complex document by examining intentions. Earlier in this chapter, certain arguments were made about what the Framers intended based on an examination of what they said about the problems of disunity, the fear of foreign intervention, the disruption of commerce, and the threats to liberty posed by oppressive rule and unchecked factionalism. Some scholars, however, find the words of the Framers an unpersuasive guide to their true intentions. To these critics, intentions are better revealed by the economic interests of the Framers and of those who attended the state ratifying conventions.

Since one of the main issues with which this book will deal is the relative importance of economic interests and political opinion in explaining how American government operates, it is premature to offer any general conclusions now. We can, however, ask whether the Constitutional Convention was made up of opposed factions that spoke and voted in ways consistent with clear economic interests. That such was the case was first and most powerfully argued by the historian Charles A. Beard in his book, *An Economic Interpretation of the Constitution*.[22] Beard attempted to show that there were two major economic interests in conflict at the time and that one dominated the convention and the state ratification process to the disadvantage of the other. The dominant group were those holding *personal* property—money, public securities (the IOUs issued by the states and the Continental Congress to pay for the war), and capital invested in manufacturing, shipping, and land speculation. He called this group, largely urban and commercial in orientation, the "personalty interest." Its opponent was the "realty interest"—persons who owned *real* property, including farmers (small and large) and southern slaveholders. In the state conventions, Beard said,

James Wilson (1742–1798) of Pennsylvania, a brilliant lawyer and terrible businessman, was the principal champion of the popular election of the House. He wanted to be chief justice of the United States but had to settle for being a member. Near the end of his life he was jailed repeatedly for debts incurred by his business speculations.

Elbridge Gerry (1744–1814) was a wealthy Massachusetts merchant and politician who participated in the convention but refused to sign the new Constitution.

the same group of well-off urban and commercial leaders secured the ratification of the Constitution to the disadvantage of small farmers, debtors, and a propertyless mass.

Beard claimed, in short, that the Constitution was devised, adopted, and ratified by persons whose economic interests were primarily in capital other than land, and that, to protect those interests, they produced a document that gave special protection to the kind of property represented by money, capital, and the ownership of public securities.[23]

This argument has been subjected to searching analysis by many historians and by and large disproved. The economic interests of the Federalists and the Antifederalists were so complex and diverse as largely to offset each other. Forrest McDonald painstakingly analyzed the economic position of the Framers and of the members of the state ratifying conventions and found almost no support for the Beard thesis. The delegates at Philadelphia did not have a common economic interest, nor did they divide, on the major issues, along obvious lines. Some of the richest men there—Elbridge Gerry of Massachusetts and George Mason of Virginia—refused to sign the Constitution and worked to block

its ratification, while many of the key proponents of the document—Madison, Wilson, and Hamilton—were men of modest means and heavy debts. Even George Washington, a huge landowner, was in arrears on his taxes at the time and had little or no cash.

At the ratifying conventions matters were equally complex. Small farmers were in the majority in states where the vote for ratification was unanimous and more or less equally represented on both sides in states where the vote was divided. Only in two states—Massachusetts and Connecticut—were the commercial, securities-owning groups disproportionately represented among the supporters of ratification.[24] Nor were the "propertyless masses" excluded from the process. In most states the great majority of adult white males owned property and could vote.[25]

In fact, economic interests in 1787 were so complex that it is almost impossible to make any general statements about who won and who lost from the adoption of the Constitution. Small farmers benefited in some places and not in others; merchants who imported goods were affected differently from those who exported; some large landholders stood to lose power and some to gain; some economic groups were probably not affected at all. Though in states such as Massachusetts economic issues were explicitly raised in the debate over ratification, in most states the debate centered on political questions—chiefly, on whether liberty could prosper under national as well as under local government.

LIBERTY, EQUALITY, AND SELF-INTEREST

The Constitution reflected a set of compromises made by men struggling to balance the competing demands of liberty and order. To the Antifederalists, the government they created was too strong, too centralized. To some Federalists, especially Alexander Hamilton, it was barely strong enough. Those who carried the day in Philadelphia were united less by their economic interest than by their view of human nature. They had a common view of how that nature might be harnessed to operate the machinery of a republic so that liberty of person and property might be secure from internal and external threats. The problems which they did not squarely face and which were to reappear again and again in American political history involved the consequences of relying on self-interest as the motive for politics and of making liberty its chief object.

There were many at the time who believed that good government requires good people. Thus, the cure for the problems of the day was to be found not in constitutional machinery but in improving the spirit of the people. Samuel Adams, a leader of the Boston Tea Party, thought the nation would have to become a "Christian Sparta."[26] Benjamin Austin of Massachusetts wrote that "no government under heaven" can prevent "ruin" so long as the people engage in "folly and dissipation."[27] What was needed were "frugality, industry, temperance, and simplicity."[28] To achieve these virtues, perhaps less liberty rather than more was necessary.

A Pragmatic Solution

Madison, on the other hand, felt that self-interest, freely pursued, was a more practical and durable solution to the problem of government than any effort to educate the citizenry or heighten their sense of virute. He wanted, he said, to make republican government possible "even in the absence of political virtue." But he did not believe that the policies of the government would or should reflect only self-interest. The citizens had to have a reasonable degree of virtue and disinterestedness for popular government to function at all. Furthermore, he believed that in so large a nation, with so many factions contending, no policy would be adopted unless many different factions were willing to support it, and he assumed that any policy that obtained such broad support would be a good one. "In the extended republic of the United States," he wrote, "a coalition of a majority of the whole society could seldom take place on any other principles than those of justice and the general good."[29] We shall want to look closely at this belief, and see to what extent factional competition has in fact led to policies that are of general value rather than of narrow advantage.

Finally, neither the Federalists nor the Antifederalists could have anticipated the way in which equality would become a concern of citizens, or the degree to which the national government would be led to intervene in society and the economy in order to deal with inequalities. The perceptions people have of the sources and remedies of inequality have changed profoundly since the eighteenth century. To Jefferson and Madison, citizens naturally differed in their talents and qualities. What was to be guarded against was the use of governmental power to create *un*natural and undesirable inequalities. This would happen if the government allowed political power to be concentrated in a few hands or conferred special privileges on the few by granting them exclusive charters and monopolies. To prevent such artificial inequalities from developing, government, especially a na-

66This changing view of the meaning of equality and its relationship to personal liberty has animated much of the debate over public policy in this country.99

tional government that was remote from the daily lives of citizens, should be strictly confined to the exercise of limited powers.

The Modern View

Today many people think of inequality quite differently. To them, it is the natural social order, or the acquisitive talents of people operating in society, that produces undesirable inequalities. It is the task of government to restrain these natural tendencies and to produce, by political and legal action, a greater degree of equality than society fosters when left alone. Thus, the government, especially the national government because of its superior powers and wider scope, should play a large and active role in human affairs.

To Jefferson and Madison, there was no obvious contradiction between liberty and equality. By "equality" they meant *political* equality, or equal rights before the law. In the Declaration, Jefferson wrote of the necessity for the Americans to assume their "separate and equal station" among the powers (i.e., nations) on earth. Americans were henceforth to be considered equal to Englishmen.[30] Liberty was the necessary protector of equality—to be free of unjust laws or patterns of political subordination was to retain one's natural political equality.

To the modern mind, on the other hand, liberty and equality appear to be inconsistent principles. If the task of government is to overcome social and economic inequalities that arise from the workings of society, then law will have to be used to restrict personal liberty so that greater equality can be produced.

This changing view of the meaning of equality and its relationship to personal liberty has animated much of the debate over public policy in this country. That debate, indeed, broke out almost immediately after the new government

was formed in 1789. One group of Framers, led by Alexander Hamilton, was eager to see the national government encourage the development of a vigorous commercial economy and, above all, a powerful national union. Jefferson and Madison were initially ready to accept this, for the alternative seemed to be the chaos and disunity of the old Confederation. But in time, they began to oppose the enlargement of the national government. They opposed this growth of government partly because they had greater faith in a localistic and agrarian society than in a nationalistic and commercial one, but partly also because they saw the Hamiltonian program as fostering inequality and weakening the natural virtues of the citizens. It was not a clash between those with and without property—in 1789, most adult white males owned property—but rather a clash between beliefs about the meaning of liberty and equality and the relationship between the two.

SUMMARY

The Framers of the Constitution sought to create a government capable of protecting both liberty and order. The solution they chose—one without precedent at that time—was a government based on a written constitution that combined the principles of popular consent, the separation of powers, and federalism.

Popular consent was embodied in the procedure for choosing the House of Representatives but limited by the indirect election of senators and the Electoral College system for selecting a president. Political authority was to be shared by three branches of government in a manner deliberately intended to produce conflict among these branches. This conflict, motivated by the self-interest of the persons occupying each branch, would, it was hoped, prevent tyranny, even by a popular majority.

Federalism came to mean a system in which both the national and state governments had independent authority. Allocating powers between the two levels of government and devising means to ensure that neither large nor small states would dominate the national government required the most delicate compromises at the Philadelphia convention. The decision to do nothing about slavery was another such compromise.

In the drafting of the Constitution and the struggle over its ratification in the states, the positions people took were not chiefly determined by their economic interests but by a variety of factors. Among these were profound differences of opinion over whether state governments or a national government would be the best protector of personal liberty.

Suggested Readings

Bailyn, Bernard. *The Ideological Origins of the American Revolution.* Cambridge, Mass.: Harvard University Press, 1967. A brilliant account of how the American colonists formed and justified the idea of independence.

Beard, Charles A. *An Economic Interpretation of the Constitution.* New York: Macmillan, 1913. The controversial thesis that the Framers were chiefly motivated by economic interests.

Becker, Carl L. *The Declaration of Independence.* New York: Vintage Books, 1942. The classic account of the meaning of the Declaration.

Corwin, Edward S. *The Constitution and What It Means Today,* 14th ed. Rev. by Harold W. Chase and Craig R. Ducat. Princeton, N.J.: Princeton University Press, 1978. A section-by-section analysis of the Constitution in light of Supreme Court interpretations.

Farrand, Max. *The Framing of the Constitution of the United States.* New Haven, Conn.: Yale University Press, 1913. A good, brief account of the Philadelphia convention, by the editor of Madison's notes on the convention.

Federalist Papers. By Alexander Hamilton, James Madison, and John Jay. A convenient edition was edited by Clinton Rossiter. New York: New American Library, 1961.

McDonald, Forrest. *We the People.* Chicago: University of Chicago Press, 1958. A refutation of the Beard thesis on the economic motives of the Framers.

Rossiter, Clinton. *1787: The Grand Convention.* New York: Macmillan, 1966. A well-written account of the Philadelphia convention and the ratification struggle.

Wills, Garry. *Inventing America.* Garden City, N.Y.: Doubleday, 1978. A fascinating but flawed effort to disprove Becker's interpretation of the Declaration.

Wood, Gordon S. *The Creation of the American Republic.* Chapel Hill, N.C.: University of North Carolina Press, 1969. A detailed study of American political thought before the Philadelphia convention.

3 Federalism and the States

Contrast of federal and unitary systems ·
Intent of Founders to disperse power · Necessary
and proper clause · *McCulloch* v. *Maryland* ·
Dual federalism · National supremacy · Politics
of financial aid programs · Intergovernmental
lobbies · Federal aid and federal control ·
Judicial power · Power in state and local governments · Governors and power of parties ·
Types of city government

Since the adoption of the Constitution in
1787, the single most persistent source of
political conflict has been the relations between
the national and the state governments. The
political conflict over slavery, for example, was
intensified because some state governments con-
doned or supported slavery, while others took
action to discourage it. The proponents and opponents of slavery were thus given territorial
power centers from which to carry on the dispute. Other issues, such as the regulation of business and the provision of social welfare programs,
were in large part fought out, for well over a
century, in terms of "national interests" versus
"states' rights." While other nations, such as
Great Britain, were debating the question of
whether the national government *ought* to provide old-age pensions or regulate the railroads,

An adamant defender of states' rights, John C.
Calhoun (1782–1850), senator from South Carolina
(left). The growing dependence of cities and states on
Washington is exemplified by President Jimmy Carter
signing a federal loan guarantee to New York City
(right).

the United States debated a different question—whether the national government *had the right* to do these things. Even after these debates had ended—almost invariably with a decision favorable to the national government—the administration and financing of the programs that resulted have usually involved a large role for the states. In short, federalism has long been a central feature of American politics. It continues to be even today when most Americans think of the government in Washington as vastly powerful and state governments as weak or unimportant.

GOVERNMENTAL STRUCTURE

"Federalism" refers to a political system in which there are local (territorial, regional, provincial, state, or municipal) units of government, as well as a national government, that can make final decisions with respect to at least some governmental activities and whose existence is specially protected.[1] Almost every nation in the world has local units of government of some kind, if for no other reason than to decentralize the administrative burdens of governing. But these governments are not federal unless the local units exist independently of the preferences of the national government and can make decisions on at least some matters without regard to those preferences.

The United States, Canada, Australia, India, West Germany, and Switzerland are federal systems, as are a few other nations. France, Great Britain, Italy, and Sweden are not: they are unitary systems, because such local governments as they possess can be altered or even abolished by the national government and cannot plausibly claim to have final authority over any significant governmental activities.

The special protection that subnational governments enjoy in a federal system derives in part from the constitution of the country but also from the habits, preferences, and dispo-

"Though the national government has come to have vast powers, it exercises many of those powers through state governments.**"**

Persons obtaining welfare benefits or using the interstate highway system are benefiting from federal programs that are largely run by the states.

sitions of the citizens and the actual distribution of political power in society. The constitution of the Soviet Union has in theory created a federal system, as claimed by that country's full name— the Union of Soviet Socialist Republics—but in fact none of these "socialist republics" is in the slightest degree independent of the central government in Moscow. Were the American Constitution the only guarantee of the independence of the American states, they would have long since become mere administrative subunits of the government in Washington. Their independence depends in large measure on the commitment of Americans to the idea of local self-government and on the fact that Congress consists of persons who are selected by and responsive to local constituencies.

"The basic political fact of federalism," writes David B. Truman, "is that it creates separate,

self-sustaining centers of power, prestige, and profit."[2] Political power is locally acquired by persons whose careers depend for the most part on satisfying local interests. As a result, though the national government has come to have vast powers, it exercises many of those powers through state governments. What many of us forget when we think about "the government in Washington" is that it spends much of its money and enforces most of its rules, not on citizens directly, but on other, local units of government. A large part of the welfare system, all of the interstate highway system, virtually every aspect of programs to improve cities, the largest part of the effort to supply jobs to the unemployed, the entire program to clean up our water, and even much of our military manpower (in the form of the National Guard) are enterprises in which the national government does not govern so

Federalism has provided opportunities for experimentation and protest. Women were able to vote in the Wyoming Territory in 1888, long before they could do so in most states. Attempts to block the landing of the supersonic Concorde in New York were made easier by local rather than federal control over airports.

much as it seeks, by regulation, grant, plan, argument, and cajolery, to get the states to govern in accordance with nationally defined (though often vaguely defined) goals.

In France, welfare, highways, education, the police, and the use of land are all matters that are directed nationally. In the United States, highways and some welfare programs are largely state functions (though they make use of federal money), while education, policing, and land-use controls are primarily local (city, county, or special-district) functions.

Federalism: Good or Bad?

A measure of the importance of federalism is the controversy that surrounds it. To some, federalism means allowing states to block action, prevent progress, upset national plans, protect powerful local interests, and cater to the self-interest of hack politicians. Harold Laski, a British observer, described American states as "parasitic and poisonous,"[3] and William H. Riker, an American political scientist, argues that "the main effect of federalism since the Civil War has been to perpetuate racism."[4] By contrast, another political scientist, Daniel J. Elazar, believes that the "virtue of the federal system lies in its ability to develop and maintain mechanisms vital to the perpetuation of the unique combination of governmental strength, political flexibility, and individual liberty, which has been the central concern of American politics."[5]

So diametrically opposed are the Riker and the Elazar views that one wonders if they are talking about the same subject. They are, of course, but they are stressing different aspects of the same phenomenon. Whenever the opportunity to exercise political power is widely available (as among the fifty states, three thousand counties, and many thousands of municipalities), it is obvious that in different places different persons will be able to make use of that power for different purposes. There is no question that allowing states and cities to make autonomous, binding political decisions will allow some people in some places to make those decisions in ways that maintain racial segregation, protect vested interests, and facilitate corruption. It is equally true, however, that this arrangement also enables other persons in other places to pass laws that attack segregation, regulate harmful economic practices, and purify politics, often long before these ideas gain national support or become national policy.

For example: in a unitary political system, such as that of Great Britain, a small but intensely motivated group could not have blocked civil rights legislation for as long as some southern senators blocked it in this country. But by the same token, it would have been equally difficult for another small but intensely motivated group to block plans to build a highway through an attractive residential neighborhood, as citizens frequently do in this country but rarely are able to do in Britain. An even more dramatic illustration involved the efforts of citizens in England, France, and the United States to prevent the Concorde supersonic transport from landing at airports near certain populated areas. Such groups had no success in England or France, where the national government alone makes these decisions. But they enjoyed considerable (albeit temporary) success in the United States where they were able to persuade the Port of New York Authority to deny landing rights to the Concorde. British and French officials were incredulous that such matters could be decided by local authorities. (Eventually, the courts ruled that these restrictions had to be lifted.)

The plain fact is that the existence of independent state and local governments means that different political groups pursuing different political purposes will come to power in different places. (While groups opposed to the Concorde had the most influence in New York, those welcoming it were most influential in Dallas.)

❝A federal system, by virtue of the decentralization of authority, lowers the cost of organized political activity.❞

The smaller the political unit, the more likely it is to be dominated by a single political faction. James Madison understood this fact perfectly and used it to argue (in *Federalist* No. 10) that it would be in a large (or "extended") republic, such as that of the United States as a whole, that one would find the greatest opportunity for all relevant interests to be heard. When William Riker condemns federalism, he is thinking of the fact that in some places, the ruling factions in cities and states have been groups opposed to granting equal rights to blacks. When Daniel Elazar praises federalism, he is thinking of the fact that in other states and cities, the ruling factions have been ones that have taken the lead (long in advance of the federal government) in developing measures to protect the environment, extend civil rights, and improve social conditions. If you live in California, whether you like federalism depends in part on whether you like the fact that California has, independently of the federal government, cut property taxes, strictly controlled coastal land use, heavily regulated electric utilities, and increased (at one time) and decreased (at another time) its welfare rolls.

Increased Political Activity
Federalism has many effects, but its most obvious effect has been to facilitate the mobilization of political activity. (At the end of this chapter, some evidence will be presented as to what other effects have been.) Unlike Don Quixote, the average citizen does not tilt at windmills. He or she is more likely to become involved in organized political activity if he or she feels there is a reasonable chance of having a practical effect. The chances of having such an effect are greater where there are many elected officials

and independent governmental bodies, each with a relatively small constituency, than where there are few elected officials, most of whom have the nation as a whole for a constituency. In short, a federal system, by virtue of the decentralization of authority, lowers the cost of organized political activity; a unitary system, because of the centralization of authority, raises the cost. We may disagree about the purposes of organized political activity, but the fact of widespread organized activity can scarcely be doubted—or if it can be doubted, it is only because you have not yet read Chapters 5 and 8 of this book.

It is impossible to say whether the Founders, when they wrote the Constitution, planned to produce such widespread opportunities for political participation. Unfortunately, they were not very clear (at least in writing) about how the federal system was supposed to work, and thus most of the interesting questions about the jurisdiction and powers of federal governments had to be settled by a century and a half of protracted, often bitter, conflict.

THE FOUNDING

The intention of the Founders seems clear: federalism was one device whereby personal liberty was to be protected. (The separation of powers was another.) They feared that placing final political authority in any set of hands, even in the hands of persons popularly elected, would so concentrate power as to risk tyranny. On the other hand, they had seen what happened when independent states tried to form a compact, as under the Articles of Confederation; what the states put together, they could also take apart. The alliance among the states that existed from 1776 to 1787 was a confederation: that is, a system of government in which the people create state governments which, in turn, create and operate a national government. Since the national government in a confederation de-

rives its powers from the states, it is dependent on their continued cooperation for its survival. By 1786, that cooperation was barely forthcoming.

A Bold, New Plan

A federation—or a "federal republic," as the Founders called it—derives its powers directly from the people, as do the state governments. As the Founders envisioned it, both levels of government, the national and the state, would have certain powers but neither would have supreme authority over the other. Madison, writing in *Federalist* No. 46, said that both the state and the federal governments "are in fact but different agents and trustees of the people, constituted with different powers." In *Federalist* No. 28, Hamilton explained how he thought the system would work: the people could shift their support between state and federal levels of government as needed to keep the two in balance. "If their rights are invaded by either, they can make use of the other as the instrument of redress."

It was an entirely new plan, for which no historical precedent existed. Nobody came to the Philadelphia convention with a clear idea of what a federal (as opposed to a unitary or a confederal) system would look like, and there was not much discussion at Philadelphia of how the system would work in practice. Few delegates then used the word "federalism" in the sense we now employ it (it was originally used as a synonym for "confederation" and only later came to stand for something different).[6] The Constitution does not spell out the powers states are to have and, until the Tenth Amendment was added at the insistence of various states, there was not even a clause in it saying (as did the amendment) that "the powers not delegated to the United States by the Constitution, nor prohibited by it to the states, are reserved to the states respectively, or to the people." The Founders assumed from the outset that the federal government would only have those powers given to it by the Constitution;

the Tenth Amendment was an afterthought, added to make that assumption explicit and to allay fears that something else was intended.[7]

Elastic Language

The need to reconcile competing interests of large and small states and of northern and southern states, especially as they affected the organization of Congress, was sufficiently difficult without trying to spell out exactly what relationship ought to exist between the national and the state systems. For example: Congress was given the power to regulate commerce "among the several states." The Philadelphia convention would have gone on for four years rather than four months if the Founders had decided that it was necessary to describe, in clear language, how one was to tell where commerce *among* the states ended and commerce wholly *within* a single state began. The Supreme Court, as we shall see, devoted over a century to that task before giving up.

Though some clauses bearing on federal-state relations were reasonably clear (see the boxed insert), other clauses were quite vague. The Founders knew, correctly, that they could not make an exact and exhaustive list of everything the federal government was empowered to do—circumstances would change, new exigencies would arise. Thus, they added the following elastic language to Article I: Congress shall have the power to "make all laws which shall be necessary and proper for carrying into execution the foregoing powers."[8]

The Founders carried away from Philadelphia different views of what federalism meant. One view was championed by Hamilton. Since the people had created the national government, since the laws and treaties made pursuant to the Constitution were "the supreme law of the land" (Article VI), and since the most pressing needs were the development of a national economy and the conduct of foreign affairs, Hamilton thought the national government was the superior and leading force in political affairs and its

The States and the Constitution

The Framers made some attempt to define the relations between the states and the federal government and how states were to relate to one another. The following points were made in the original Constitution—before the Bill of Rights was added.

Restrictions on powers of the states

States may not make treaties with foreign nations, coin money, issue paper currency, grant titles of nobility, pass a "bill of attainder" or an "ex post facto law,"* or, without the consent of Congress, levy any taxes on imports or exports, keep troops and ships in time of peace, or enter into an agreement with another state or with a foreign power.   *Article I, Section 10*

Guarantees by the federal government to the states

The national government guarantees to every state a "republican form of government" and protection against foreign invasion and (provided the states request it) protection against domestic insurrection.   *Article IV, Section 4*

An existing state will not be broken up into two or more states or merged with all or part of another state without that state's consent.   *Article IV, Section 3*

Congress may admit new states into the Union.
    Article IV, Section 3

Taxes levied by Congress must be uniform throughout the United States—they may not be on some states but not others.
    Article I, Section 8

The Constitution may not be amended to give states unequal representation in the Senate.   *Article V*

Rules governing how states deal with each other

"Full faith and credit" shall be given by each state to the laws, records, and court decisions of other states. (For example, a civil case settled in the courts of one state cannot be retried in the courts of another.)   *Article IV, Section 1*

The citizens of each state shall have the "privileges and immunities" of the citizens of every other state. (No one is quite sure what this is supposed to mean.)   *Article IV, Section 2*

If a person charged with a crime by one state flees to another, he is subject to extradition—that is, the governor who finds him is supposed to return him to the governor who wants him.
    Article IV, Section 2

* For definitions of "bill of attainder" and "ex post facto law" see Chapter 2.

Thomas Jefferson (1743–1826) was not at the Constitutional Convention. His doubts about the new national government eventually led him to oppose the Federalist administration of John Adams and to argue for states' rights.

powers ought to be broadly defined and liberally construed. The other view, championed by Jefferson, was that the federal government, though important, was the product of an agreement among the states and though "the people" were the ultimate sovereigns, the principal threat to their liberties was likely to come from the national government. (Madison, a strong supporter of national supremacy at the convention, later became a champion of states' rights.) Thus, the powers of the federal government should be narrowly construed and strictly limited. As Madison put it in *Federalist* No. 45, in language that probably made Hamilton wince, "The powers delegated by the proposed Constitution to the federal government are few and defined. Those which are to remain in the State governments are numerous and indefinite."

Hamilton argued for national supremacy; Jefferson for states' rights. Though their differences were greater in theory than in practice (as we shall see in Chapter 11, Jefferson while president sometimes acted in a positively Hamiltonian manner), the differing interpretations they offered of the Constitution were to shape political debate in this country until well into the 1960s.

THE CHANGING MEANING OF FEDERALISM

The Civil War was fought, in part, over the issue of national supremacy versus states' rights, but it only settled one part of that argument—namely, that the national government was supreme, its sovereignty derived directly from the people, and thus the states could not lawfully secede from the Union. Virtually every other aspect of the national supremacy issue continued to animate political and legal debate for another century.

The Court Speaks

As arbiter of what the Constitution means, the Supreme Court became the focal point of that debate. In Chapter 13 we shall see in some detail how the Court made its decisions. For now it is enough to know that during the formative years of the new Republic, the Supreme Court was led by a staunch and brilliant advocate of the Hamiltonian position, Chief Justice John Marshall. In a series of decisions, he and the Court powerfully defended the national supremacy view of the newly formed federal government.

The most important decision was in a case, seemingly trivial in its origins, that arose when James McCulloch, the cashier of the Baltimore branch of the Bank of the United States, which had been created by Congress, refused to pay a tax levied on that bank by the state of Maryland. He was hauled into state court and convicted of failing to pay a tax. In 1819 McCulloch appealed all the way to the Supreme Court in a case known as *McCulloch* v. *Maryland*. The Court, in a unanimous opinion, answered two questions in ways that expanded the powers of Congress and confirmed the supremacy of the federal government in the exercise of those powers.

The first question was whether Congress had the right to set up a bank, or any other corporation, since such a right is nowhere explicitly mentioned in the Constitution. Marshall said that, though the federal government possessed only those powers enumerated in the Constitution, the "extent"—that is, the meaning—of those powers required interpretation. Though the word "bank" is not in that document, there is to be found there the power to manage money: to lay and collect taxes, issue a currency, and borrow funds. To carry out these powers, Congress may reasonably decide that chartering a national bank is "necessary and proper." Marshall's words were carefully chosen to endow the "necessary and proper" clause with the widest possible sweep:

Let the end be legitimate, let it be within the scope of the Constitution, and all means which are appropriate, which are plainly adapted to that end, which are not prohibited, but consistent with the letter and spirit of the Constitution, are constitutional.[9]

The second question was whether a federal bank could lawfully be taxed by a state. To answer it, Marshall went back to first principles. The government of the United States was not established by the states, but by the people, and thus it was supreme in the exercise of those powers conferred upon it. Having already concluded that chartering a bank was within the powers of Congress, Marshall then argued that the only way for such powers to be supreme was for their use to be immune from state challenge and for the products of their use to be protected against state destruction. Since "the power to tax involves the power to destroy," and since the power to destroy a federal agency would confer upon the states using it supremacy over the federal government, the states may not tax any federal instrument. Hence, the Maryland law was unconstitutional.

McCulloch won, and so did the federal government. Half a century later, the Court decided that what was sauce for the goose was sauce for the gander. It held that, just as state govern-

ments could not tax federal instrumentalities, so the federal government could not tax state ones.[10] Matters have become much more complex since then, but it is still the case that if you earn interest from a municipal bond, you do not have to pay federal income tax on it, just as you do not have to pay state income tax on interest from a United States bond.[11]

Though the Supreme Court may decide a case, it does not always settle an issue. The battle over states' rights versus national supremacy continued to rage in Congress, in presidential elections, and ultimately on the battlefield. John C. Calhoun of South Carolina expounded the doctrine of "nullification," based on the view, rejected by Marshall, that the Constitution was a compact among states which any state was free to nullify by refusing to enforce within its boundaries any federal law that in the state's opinion exceeded federal authority. This view, first advanced in opposition to a tariff opposed by the South, ultimately led to crises that no court could resolve. The Civil War, ironically, had an effect opposite to what the southern states had hoped for: the necessities of war led to an expansion of the powers of the Union leaders and thus, with their victory, to an enlargement of the powers of the federal government.

Dual Federalism
After the war the debate about the meaning of federalism focused on the interpretation of the commerce clause of the Constitution. Out of this debate there emerged the doctrine of "dual federalism," which held that though the national government was supreme in its sphere, the states were equally supreme in theirs, and that these two spheres of action should and could be kept separate. Applied to commerce, the concept of dual federalism implied that there was such a thing as *inter*state commerce, which Congress could regulate, and *intra*state commerce, which only the states could regulate, and that the Court could tell which was which.

❝The principle of national supremacy has triumphed over that of states' rights.❞

For a while the Court tried to decide what was interstate commerce by the kind of business that was being conducted. Transporting things between states was obviously interstate commerce, and so subject to federal regulation. Thus, federal laws affecting the interstate shipment of lottery tickets,[12] prostitutes,[13] liquor,[14] and harmful foods and drugs[15] were upheld. On the other hand, manufacturing,[16] insurance,[17] and farming[18] were *intra*state commerce, and so only the state governments were allowed to regulate them.

Such product-based distinctions turned out to be hard to sustain. For example, if you ship a case of whiskey from Kentucky to Kansas, how long is it in interstate commerce (and thus subject to federal law), and when does it enter intrastate commerce and become subject only to state law? For a while the Court's answer was that the whiskey was in interstate commerce so long as it was in its "original package,"[19] but that only precipitated long quarrels as to what was the original package, and how one is to treat things, like gas and grain, that may not be shipped in packages at all. And how could one distinguish between manufacturing and transportation when one company did both or when a single manufacturing corporation owned factories in different states? And if an insurance company sold policies to customers both inside and outside a given state, were there to be different laws regulating identical policies that happened to be purchased from the same company by persons in different states?

In time, the effort to find some clear principles that distinguished interstate from intrastate commerce was pretty much abandoned. Commerce was like a stream flowing through the country, drawing to itself contributions from thousands of scattered enterprises and depositing its products in millions of individual homes. The Court began to permit the federal government to regulate almost anything that affected this stream, so that by the 1940s, not only had farming and manufacturing been redefined as part of interstate commerce,[20] but even the janitors and window washers in buildings that housed companies engaged in interstate commerce were now said to be part of that stream.[21]

The current Court interpretation of various laws pertaining to commerce is immensely complex, difficult to summarize, and impossible to explain. (For example: lawyers are said to engage in interstate commerce but professional baseball players are not, so that federal antitrust laws affect the former but not the latter.)[22] It would be only a mild overstatement, however, to say that the doctrine of dual federalism is virtually extinct and that, provided it has a good reason for wanting to do so, Congress can pass a law that will regulate, constitutionally, almost any kind of economic activity located anywhere in the country. In short, the principle of national supremacy has triumphed over that of states' rights.

FEDERAL-STATE RELATIONS

Though constitutionally the federal government may be supreme, politically it must take into account the fact that the laws it passes must be approved by congressmen and senators selected from, and responsive to, state and local constituencies. Thus, what Washington lawfully may do is not the same thing as what politically it may wish to do. For example, in 1947 the Supreme Court decided that the federal government and not the states had supreme authority over oil under the ocean off the nation's coasts.[23] Six years later, after an intense debate, Congress passed and the president signed a law transferring title to these tidelands oil reserves back to the states.

Grants-in-Aid

The best illustration of how political realities modify legal authority can be found in federal grants-in-aid. The first of these programs began even before the Constitution was adopted, in the form of land grants made by the federal government to the states in order to finance education. (State universities all over the country were built with the proceeds from the sale of these land grants; hence the name, "land-grant colleges.") Land grants were also made to support the building of wagon roads, canals, railroads, and flood-control projects. These measures were hotly debated in Congress (President Madison thought some were unconstitutional) even though the use to which the grants were put was left almost entirely to the states.

Cash grants-in-aid began almost as early. In 1808 Congress gave $200,000 to the states to pay for their militia, with the states in charge of the size, deployment, and command of these troops. However, grant-in-aid programs remained few in number and small in price until the twentieth century, when scores of new ones came into being. In 1915, less than $6 million was spent per year in grants-in-aid; by 1925, over $114 million was spent; by 1937, nearly $300 million.[24] The purposes to which the money was put reveal, as clearly as anything, the changing priorities of American politics. In 1915, federal grants-in-aid went primarily for agricultural training and experimentation; in 1920, with the advent of the automobile, the bulk of the funds went for highway construction; in 1937, with the onset of the Depression, most of the money went for assistance to the elderly and other persons in need.

The grant-in-aid system, once under way, grew rapidly because it helped state and local officials resolve a dilemma. On the one hand, they wanted access to the superior taxing power of the federal government. On the other hand, prevailing constitutional interpretation, at least until the late 1930s, held that the federal government could not spend money for purposes not

Among the earliest examples of federal grants-in-aid were the land-grant colleges. Pictured here are students at the University of Missouri in the early 1900s. The school was founded to teach—among other things—agricultural science.

authorized by the Constitution. The solution was, obviously, to have federal money put into state hands—Washington would pay the bill, the state would run the programs.

There were four reasons why federal money seemed, to state officials, so attractive. For one thing, during most of the nineteenth century and the early decades of the twentieth, the federal government was taking in more money than it was spending. The high-tariff policies of the Republicans produced a healthy budget surplus; in the 1880s Washington literally had more money than it knew what to do with. Some went to pay off a large part of the national debt, some was given to Civil War veterans as a pension, and some went to the states or was otherwise used for internal improvements.[25] By the mid-twentieth century, when budget surpluses had pretty much become a thing of the past, a second reason for turning to Washington became evident: the income tax. Inaugurated in the

1920s, it proved to be a marvelously flexible tool of public finance, for it automatically brought in more money as economic activity (and thus personal income) grew. Third, the federal government, unlike the states, managed the currency, and thus could print more money whenever it needed it. (Technically, it borrowed this money, and of course it paid interest on what it had borrowed, but it was under no obligation to pay it all back because, as a practical matter, it had borrowed from itself.) The size of the federal public debt stayed more or less constant, or even declined, in the second half of the nineteenth century. By the mid-twentieth century, for reasons to be explained in a later chapter, people no longer worried about the national debt so much, or at least worried about it for reasons other than the fear of being in debt. Thus the federal government came to accept, as a matter of policy, the proposition that when it needed money, it would print it. States could not do this: if they borrowed (and many could not), they had to pay it all back, in full.

These three economic reasons for the attractiveness of federal grants were probably not as important as a fourth reason, politics. Federal money seemed to a state official to be "free money." If Nebraska could get Washington to put up the money for improving navigation on the Platte River, the citizens of the entire nation, and not just of Nebraska, would pay for it. Of course, if Nebraska gets money for that purpose, every state will want it (and will get it). Even so, it was still an attractive political proposition: the governor of Nebraska did not have to propose, collect, or take responsibility for federal taxes. Indeed, he could denounce the federal government for being profligate in its use of the people's money. Meanwhile, he would cut the ribbon opening the new dam on the Platte.

Meeting National Needs

Until the 1960s most federal grants-in-aid were conceived by, or in cooperation with, the states and designed to serve essentially state purposes. Large blocs of voters and a variety of organized interests would press for grants to help farmers, build highways, or support vocational education. During the 1960s, however, an important change occurred: the federal government began devising grant programs based less on what states were demanding and more on what federal officials perceived to be important *national* needs. Federal officials, not state and local ones, were the principal proponents of grant programs to aid the urban poor, combat crime, reduce pollution, and deal with drug abuse. Some of these programs even attempted to bypass the states, providing money directly to cities or even to local citizen groups. These were worrisome developments for governors who were accustomed to

TABLE 3.1   Historical Trend of Federal Grant-in-Aid Outlays
(fiscal years; dollar amounts in millions)

	Total grants	Composition of grants-in-aid		Federal grants as a percent of state and local expenditures
		Grants for payments to individuals	Other	
1950	$ 2,253	$ 1,421	$ 832	10.4%
1955	3,207	1,770	1,437	10.1
1960	7,020	2,735	4,285	14.7
1965	10,904	3,954	6,950	15.3
1970	24,018	8,867	15,151	19.4
1971	28,109	10,789	17,320	19.9
1972	34,372	13,421	20,951	22.0
1973	41,832	13,104	28,728	24.3
1974	43,308	14,030	29,278	22.7
1975	49,723	16,106	33,618	23.2
1976	59,037	19,511	39,526	24.7
1977	68,396	23,002	45,394	26.4
1978 est.	80,288	25,151	55,137	27.5
1979 est.	85,020	27,190	57,830	26.2

Source: Budget of the U.S. Government, Fiscal Year 1979: Special Analyses, p. 184.

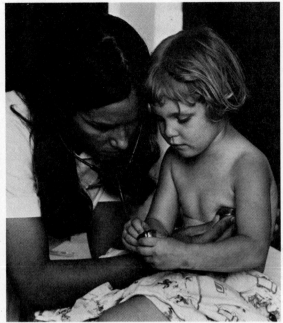

Federal aid now supports in part almost every local governmental service, including public health and elementary and secondary education.

being the conduit for money on its way from Washington to local communities.

The rise in federal activism in setting goals and the efforts on occasion to bypass state officials occurred at a time when the total amount of federal aid to states and localities had become so vast that many jurisdictions were completely dependent on it for the support of vital services. Whereas federal aid amounted to less than 2 percent of state and local spending in 1927, by 1970 it amounted to 19 percent and by 1978 to 28 percent (see Table 3.1). Some of the older, larger cities had become what one writer called "federal aid junkies," so dependent were they on these grants. In 1978 in Detroit, 77 percent of the revenue the city raised came from Washington.[26]

The Intergovernmental Lobby

State and local officials, both elected and appointed, began to form an important new lobby— the "intergovernmental lobby," made up of mayors, governors, superintendents of schools, state directors of public health, county highway commissioners, local police chiefs, and others who had come to count on federal funds.[27] The five largest of these lobbies employed, in 1976, a total of thirty-four lobbyists and spent around $6 million (see Table 3.2). But there are many other, more specialized ones as well. It is important to understand that these interest groups did not, by and large, create the programs they now seek to influence; rather, the programs tended to create the interest groups. Police chiefs, for example, did not demand in 1967 the creation of the Law Enforcement Assistance Administration, which today spends over $1 billion a year on local criminal justice agencies. But once the LEAA was created, organized police chiefs developed a strong interest in its continuation.

TABLE 3.2   A Look at the State-Local Lobbies

Membership	Number of lobbyists	Resources from dues
National Governors' Conference 54 state and territorial governors	6	$684,950
National Conference of State Legislatures 7,600 state legislators plus staff	6	$1.3 million
National League of Cities 14,700 cities	6	$1.8 million
U.S. Conference of Mayors 500 cities with 30,000 population or more	4	$708,000
National Association of Counties 1,500 counties	12	$1.4 million

Source: *National Journal*, August 14, 1976, p. 1137.

The purpose of the intergovernmental lobby is the same as the purpose of a private lobby: to obtain more money with fewer strings. In general, it has succeeded. Federal spending on grants-in-aid has continued to rise (see Figure 3.1) and, even more important, the restrictions on the use of these monies have been loosened.

This loosening took the form of shifting much federal aid from *categorical* grants to *block* grants or to *revenue sharing*. A categorical grant is one for a specific purpose defined by federal law: to build an airport or a college dormitory, for example, or to make welfare payments to low-income mothers. Such grants usually require that the state or locality put up money to "match" some part of the federal grant, though the amount of matching funds can be quite small. (In the federal highway program, Washington pays about 90 percent of the construction costs and the states only about 10 percent.) Governors and mayors complained about these categorical grants because their purposes were often so narrow that it was impossible for a state to adapt federal grants to local needs. A mayor may have wanted federal money to build parks but discovered that the city could only get money if

it launched an urban renewal program that entailed bulldozing several blocks of housing or small businesses.

One response to this problem was to consolidate several categorical grant-in-aid programs into a single "block" grant devoted to a general purpose and with a minimum of specific restrictions on its use. Block grants (sometimes called "special revenue sharing" or "broad-based aid") were begun during the Nixon administration and are now made in such areas as community development, help for the unemployed, and assistance to criminal justice agencies. The Housing and Community Development Act of 1974 consolidated seven separate categorical grant programs aimed at cities; the Comprehensive Employment and Training Act of 1973 brought together several formerly separate categorical programs intended for the unemployed. In 1978 block grants accounted for about 14 percent of all federal aid programs.

Revenue sharing (sometimes called "general revenue sharing") is even more permissive. Adopted in 1972 with the passage of the State and Local Fiscal Assistance Act, it provides for the distribution of about $6 billion a year in

President Carter meets with
a delegation of governors
to discuss his energy bill.

FIGURE 3.1   Federal Grants to State and Local Governments

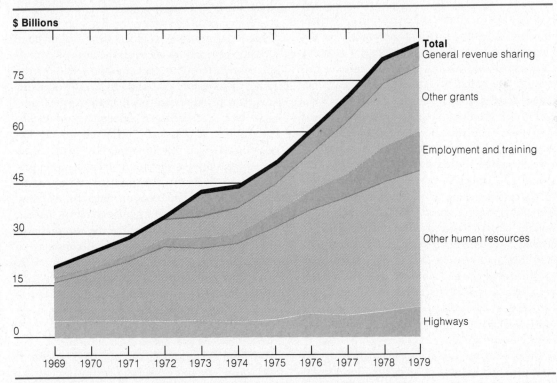

Source: Budget of the U.S. Government, Fiscal Year 1979: Special Analyses, p. 175.

federal funds to the states and localities. Distribution is determined by a statistical formula that takes into account population, local tax effort, and the wealth of the local populace in a way that is supposed to ensure that poorer, heavily taxed communities get more of the money than better-off, lightly taxed ones. One-third of the money goes to the states and two-thirds to localities (cities, counties, and townships). There are only a few restrictions on how the money is used (it must be spent in ways that do not discriminate on the basis of race, color, sex, or ethnicity, and do not violate federal wage and hour laws) and practically no restrictions on what it may be used for (almost anything except education or welfare). Moreover, the cities and states need not put up matching funds. In 1978 revenue sharing accounted for about 12 percent of all federal aid.

Politics of Aid Programs

The politics of these different aid programs illustrate the ways in which federalism works. The categorical grants were preferred by many congressmen and almost all federal bureaucrats because the specificity of these programs enhanced federal control over how the money was used. These groups opposed revenue sharing and were joined in this by some liberal interest groups, such as organized labor, that did not trust the states and cities to make wise use of no-strings-attached money. Some conservative interest groups, such as the Chamber of Commerce, feared the possibility of a tax increase to pay for revenue sharing. Supporting revenue sharing were governors and mayors (but only after they had worked out an agreement as to how the money would be divided between states and cities) and public opinion (which liked the the idea of having spending decisions made locally, where presumably citizens would have more influence).[28]

Once block grants and revenue sharing became law, they did not grow in size as rapidly as the old categorical grant programs. Though block grants (like revenue sharing) are popular with governors and mayors, they cover such a broad range of activities that no single interest group has a vital stake in pressing for their enlargement. Revenue sharing, for example, provides a little money to lots of city agencies, but rarely does it provide all or even most of the money for any single agency. Thus, no single agency acts as if the expansion of revenue sharing is a life-and-death matter. Categorical grants, on the other hand, are often a matter of life and death for many agencies—state departments of welfare, highways, and health, for example, are utterly dependent on federal aid. Accordingly, the administrators in charge of these programs will press strenuously for their expansion. Moreover, categorical programs are supervised by specialized committees of Congress and, as we shall see in Chapter 10, many of these committees have an interest in seeing their programs grow.

As a result of the political differences between categorical grants and block grants or revenue sharing, the amount spent on the former tends to increase faster than the amount spent on the latter. Between 1975 and 1978, the amount spent on revenue sharing increased by 11 percent, but that spent on categorical grants increased by 56 percent.[29] The reason was explained this way by one observer: "You dilute the constituency when you make aid more general. Say you had a program [to control a disease]. You'd get everyone in the country interested in that disease to focus on that one subject, and a congressman to become the champion of [it]. . . . There just is not that much sympathy to increase revenue sharing."[30] As we shall see in Part IV, this pattern is not unique to federal grants but is a general feature of the politics of almost all government spending programs.

Rivalry Among the States

The more important federal money becomes to the states, the more likely they are to compete among themselves for the largest share of it.

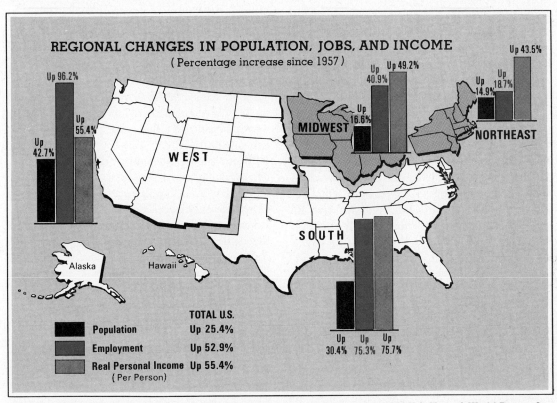

REGIONAL CHANGES IN POPULATION, JOBS, AND INCOME
(Percentage increase since 1957)

Up 96.2%
Up 55.4%
Up 42.7%
WEST

Up 40.9% Up 49.2%
Up 16.6%
MIDWEST

Up 43.5%
Up 14.9% Up 18.7%
NORTHEAST

SOUTH

Alaska Hawaii

Up 30.4% Up 75.3% Up 75.7%

	TOTAL U.S.
Population	Up 25.4%
Employment	Up 52.9%
Real Personal Income (Per Person)	Up 55.4%

For a century or better, the growth of the United States—in population, business, income—was concentrated in the industrial Northeast. In recent decades, however, that growth—at least in population and employment, if not in income —has shifted to the South, Southwest, and Far West.[31] This change has precipitated an intense debate over whether the federal government, by the way it distributes its funds and awards its contracts, is unfairly helping some regions and states at the expense of others. Journalists and politicians dubbed the struggle as one between "Snowbelt" (or "Frostbelt") and "Sunbelt" states.

Whether in fact there is anything worth arguing about is far from clear: the federal government has had great difficulty in figuring out where it ultimately spends what funds for what purposes. For example: a $1 billion defense contract may go to a company with headquarters in California, but much of the money may actually be spent in Connecticut or New York, as the prime contractor in California buys from subcontractors located in the other states. It is even less clear whether federal funds actually affect the growth rate of the regions. The uncertainty about the facts has not prevented a debate about the issue. That debate focuses on the formulas written into federal laws by which block grants and revenue sharing funds are allocated. These formulas take into account such things as a county or city's population, personal income in the area, and housing quality. A slight change in a formula can shift millions of dollars in grants in ways that either favor the older declining cities of the Northeast or the newer and still growing cities of the Southwest.

No better revelation of the importance of local considerations in national decisions can be found than by watching the extent to which senators and representatives calculate the effects on their states and districts of any proposed aid distribution formula. They are assisted in this by computers that can tell them instantly how much money will be available to their constituents under various formulas. As one staff member of the House of Representatives put it, "Members now vote by printout. It is a tool of the trade."[32]

FEDERAL AID AND FEDERAL CONTROL

So pervasive has federal aid to states and localities become that many persons fear (or hope) that the federal government is well on its way toward controlling state and local governments, to their detriment (or benefit). Indeed, one argument made on behalf of revenue sharing and block grants was that they would arrest this trend by reducing the extent to which federal controls would accompany federal aid.

On the surface, such a view seems quite plausible—"he who pays the piper calls the tune." In the case of federal aid, calling the tune presumably occurs in this way: A city or state must apply for a grant, sometimes in competition with other cities or states. It must file a voluminous plan, acceptable to federal officials. If it obtains the grant, it must accept as conditions scores of federal rules as to how that money should be spent; moreover, it must put up matching funds of its own, whether it can afford them or not. Though some of the strings are quite reasonable (for example, the ban on racial discrimination), others are more debatable (for example, the requirement that "citizen advisory boards" be created or that metropolitan

or regional planning agencies be formed). And if a city or state starts a program on the basis of a grant, it must worry that next year or the year after the grant may be reduced or terminated. This would leave the city or state with the unpleasant choice of either raising taxes to make up the difference or explaining to irate citizens why a benefit they had once received was now being withdrawn.

There is a good deal of truth in the view that federal dollars mean federal control. Every local official has his or her favorite story of unreasonable federal controls. The Department of Health, Education, and Welfare attached as a condition to federal aid to education that local high schools could not hold father-son banquets or send boys to "Boys' State," and ruled that, in an Iowa case, all-girl basketball teams were illegal. (The first two rulings were overturned by Congress; the third, as of early 1979, seems to be a dead letter.)

What Really Happens

The theory that federal aid means rigid federal control is not the whole story, however. Though Washington requires a staggering amount of paper work in order to obtain a grant, much of it is simply wasted motion because the grant usually is awarded in any case. The reason is simple: no federal official wants to explain to the senator from Kentucky why his state did not get an equivalent grant to the one that neighboring Tennessee got. In the American federal system, when Washington wants to send money to one state or congressional district, it must usually send money to every state and district. In 1966, for example, President Lyndon Johnson proposed a "Model Cities" plan under which federal funds would be spent on experimental programs in a small number of large cities with especially acute urban problems. When the bill went to Congress, however, it quickly became clear that no such plan would be passed unless the number of cities was increased so that there would be federal money available for cities of virtually any size located in every state. Senator Edmund Muskie of Maine, whose support was crucial, would not vote for a bill that did not make Augusta, Bangor, and Portland eligible for a plan originally conceived to help New York, Chicago, and Philadelphia.[33]

There is a plethora of federal rules about how money is to be spent, but the penalty for evading the rules—namely, having the money withdrawn—is rarely invoked. Again, Congress is the reason. It takes a brave federal official to tell some representatives and senators that the flow of money to their constituents is being turned off. For example, the federal government currently spends over $3 billion a year to assist elementary and secondary schools in every state in the Union, all pursuant to a law passed in 1965. The bulk of the money was supposed to go to school districts with large concentrations of children from poor families. The funds were to add to local expenditures on schools rather than substitute for them. Futhermore, the effects of efforts to help educate poor children were to be evaluated. A few years later, studies showed that the money was going to all districts and not primarily poor ones, that many things were being purchased that had little to do with basic education, and that scarcely any effort at evaluation was being made. When a federal official tried to withhold money from the Chicago school system on grounds that it was segregated, the mayor of Chicago went to Washington and got the decision reversed. When federal audits disclosed that some of the funds were being spent improperly, little happened. Finally, because of intense public criticism by civil rights groups, some of the problems were corrected. But the fundamental lesson was clear. The federal government cannot easily impose its will by means of money grants on states that are willing to use their leverage in Congress to resist such controls.[34]

Even when decisions are made in Washington, circumstances can force federal officials to be accountable to local concerns. Here an official of the Nuclear Regulatory Commission answers questions about an accident at a nuclear power plant at Three Mile Island, Pennsylvania, while Governor Richard Thornburgh looks on.

Similarly, the Medicare law of 1965 authorized the payment of billions of dollars in federal funds to hospitals to reimburse them for the care they provided to elderly and needy persons. The Department of Health, Education, and Welfare (HEW) was directed to draw up rules to ensure that no substandard hospital would be eligible for this reimbursement. The political reality, however, led HEW to draft flexible criteria that would allow all but the most defective hospitals to participate; to have done otherwise would have been to risk having persons who were denied care in their local hospitals write angry letters to their congressmen about "meddling federal bureaucrats."[35]

Political Bargaining

Federal rules are more likely to achieve certain goals than others. Washington provides much

66 The grant-in-aid system works, not by having the 'supreme' federal government 'dictate' to 'powerless' states and cities, but rather by placing federal and state agencies in a kind of bargaining relationship in which each side has resources the other wants. 99

Though Washington pays for the CETA (Comprehensive Education and Training Act) program to train unemployed workers, it has left the design and management of these programs to the states and cities.

of the money that the states spend on Aid to Families with Dependent Children (AFDC, popularly known as "welfare"). Because it pays the piper, Washington can and does insist that each state spend its public assistance money without favoritism or discrimination, with strict regard for financial accountability, and in a way that will make it easier rather than harder for people to become eligible for these funds. Explicit federal rules are in part responsible for this. Equally important has been the encouragement federal administrators give to

their state counterparts and allies—that is, the heads of state welfare agencies—to develop and enforce their own rules that reduce or eliminate differences in how cities and counties handle welfare. On the other hand, the federal government has not been able—indeed, has not seriously tried—to get the states to have the same eligibility rules or to pay the same amounts to welfare recipients. The reason is simple: Congress, sensitive to state interests, has not enacted any uniform federal standards in this regard (efforts to do so are described in Chapter 17), and federal administrators are not eager to antagonize either Congress or state officials whose cooperation is essential if there is to be a welfare program at all.[36] As a result, the size of the average monthly welfare payment received by an AFDC family varies enormously among the states. In 1974, for example, an AFDC family in Mississippi received $50 per month while one living in New York received $346.

In these and other cases, the grant-in-aid system works, not by having the "supreme" federal government "dictate" to "powerless" states and cities, but rather by placing federal and state agencies in a kind of bargaining relationship in which each side has resources the other wants. The federal agency can provide money, but the state agency has influence with congressmen who determine how much money the federal agency gets in the first place.[37]

In this relationship, the power of the federal agency is greatest when it is enforcing some clear, widely accepted rule, such as honesty in handling and accounting for money. Its power is least when it is attempting to get the state agency to achieve a complex, vaguely defined goal (such as "improving the education of poor children" or "improving the quality of hospitals"). Since the 1960s the federal government increasingly has sought just such hard-to-define and hard-to-achieve objectives, with the result that the implementation of many federal programs has become increasingly difficult. For example, in 1966 the Economic Development Administration (EDA), a part of the United States Department of Commerce, sought to reduce unemployment and ease racial tensions in Oakland, California, by giving agencies in that city over $23 million to build an aircraft maintenance hangar, a ship terminal, and some smaller projects. Many jobs on these projects were earmarked for unemployed persons, especially blacks and other minorities. Four years later, in 1970, the terminal was only partially built, the plans for the hangar were not yet complete, and only a small number of jobs for minorities had been created.[38] The reason for this rather poor showing was not the incompetence or indifference of the persons involved, but rather that several different and complex goals had to be achieved by coordinating the efforts of many private parties and several different agencies at every level of government. Each of these groups and agencies had to concur if plans were to be implemented, and here, as in most human affairs, it was hard to produce that concurrence by simply "issuing orders."

Judicial Direction

Federal restrictions on state and local government have increased dramatically in the last decade or two, but only partly because "Washington bureaucrats" are "giving orders" to local officials. Though these things are hard to measure, it is likely that the principal source of the increased constraints on the freedom of action of localities has been the federal courts. As the range of federal activities has enlarged, as the number of programs funded by federal dollars has grown, as the courts have become (in ways to be described in Chapter 13) more open to the complaints of citizen groups, *legal*, not political, action has become the chief means by which local officials are made to act in accordance with somebody's version of federal standards.

The Complex Web of Federal, State, and Local Agencies

The Case of Oakland, California

To get an aircraft hangar and a ship terminal built in a way that would help reduce minority unemployment in Oakland, California, the following groups and agencies had to cooperate:

Federal
- Economic Development Administration, U.S. Department of Commerce
- Seattle Regional Office of the EDA
- Oakland Office of the EDA
- U.S. General Accounting Office
- U.S. Department of Health, Education, and Welfare
- U.S. Department of Labor
- U.S. Navy

Local
- Mayor of Oakland
- Oakland City Council
- Port of Oakland

Private
- World Airways Company
- Oakland business leaders
- Oakland black leaders
- Conservation and environmental groups in Oakland

There were at least seventy important decisions to which some or all of these groups had to agree.

Source: Jeffrey L. Pressman and Aaron B. Wildavsky, *Implementation* (Berkeley: University of California Press, 1973), pp. 95–96, 102–107.

Rules governing local police conduct are often set by federal courts. These courts have increasingly provided a forum for citizens to challenge local governmental decisions.

Judges, usually but not always in federal court, have ordered Massachusetts to change the way in which it hires firefighters; Philadelphia, the manner in which it handles police brutality complaints; and Chicago, the location in which it builds public housing projects. (Such suits are not always decided against a city's freedom of action. Federal courts have generally allowed cities to decide for themselves what constitutes obscene matter and how their land is to be zoned.) In all of the cases in which a federal standard is applied to a local situation, what happens is not that some remote "federal" authority gets its way, but that some *local* group (public housing tenants, police officers, parents, blacks, or whatever) uses the courts as a way of challenging the decisions of other local groups. Federal aid, and especially the enlarged role of federal courts, provides more opportunities for such local struggles to be waged.

POWER IN STATE AND LOCAL GOVERNMENTS

Given the importance of state and local governments in the American federal system, one must know something of how politics is carried on in these places if one is to have a complete understanding of government in the United States. To supply that understanding is beyond the scope of this book, but a few key facts can be described that will help the reader put the matter in perspective.

Overview

The most important of these facts is the great diversity of state and local political systems. State government in Georgia is very different—in structure, procedures, and popular attitudes—from state government in New York, and the politics of Los Angeles could not be more different from that of Chicago. The preservation of this diversity has always been to some people one of federalism's advantages and to others one of its defects.

In recent years that diversity has become less as politics, like the economy and the arts, has become more national—which is to say, more uniform. Modern communications and transportation have led to the development of a national market for goods, services, and entertainment. (Today we buy nationally advertised beer, whereas in the 1920s much of the beer we drank was locally brewed and sold.) They have also led to the migration of persons from one region to another (a large fraction of the persons living in Miami or Atlanta were born in the North, just as a large fraction of those living in Detroit and Chicago were born in the South). Politically, the nationalizing forces can be seen in the decline of the Democratic monopoly on elected offices in the South and the Republican monopoly on such offices in New England. As we shall see in Chapter 7, regions that were once dominated by one party are becoming less so.

But political institutions are slower to change than tastes for beer, and thus the nationalization of politics has taken place more gradually than the nationalization of consumer preferences. Though state and local governments differ in many ways, perhaps the most important is between those that are "executive-centered" and those that are "legislature-centered."

Initially, almost all state and local governments were legislature-centered: that is, state legislatures and city councils (not governors or mayors) had most of the power. This pattern reflected the early distrust most Americans had of executive authority, based on their unhappy experiences with royal governors during the colonial period. Indeed, in 1787 the new federal constitution gave more power to the president than most states were yet willing to give to their governors. And most cities and villages did not even have mayors—they were governed by the people directly (in town meetings) or by boards of selectmen or city councils. Throughout most of the nineteenth century, governors (and, as the posts were created, mayors) had relatively little authority in most places.

Around the turn of the century—from the 1880s to the 1920s—there appeared an effort to strengthen the executive at the expense of the legislature, especially in cities where mayors gained more authority and where appointed city managers began to take over many of the administrative powers formerly held by independent elected officials. The changes begun in this period, and which continue to be pressed

For a long time popular opinion was suspicious of strong governors and tried to keep them dependent on state legislatures. The Progressive movement in the early twentieth century sought to give governors more formal authority. The movement was especially strong in states such as California and Wisconsin, where today governors have become important presidential candidates. Shown here are California's governor, Edmund G. ("Jerry") Brown, and the Wisconsin state legislature.

in many places today, were described as an effort at "reform." And there was, in truth, a genuine desire to reform in the sense of purify: it was thought that legislatures and the local political parties that dominated them were often corrupt and wasteful and that transferring more authority to a single executive would improve the honesty and efficiency of government. The theory was that a single, prominent official was more easily held accountable and less easily corrupted than many obscure politicians.

But purity was not the only objective. Giving more authority to executives was a way of changing the kinds of policies that might be adopted and the kinds of groups and interests that might be specially favored in the policy-making process. An executive who is elected statewide or citywide will presumably take a statewide or citywide view of public policy. That executive will probably be particularly attentive to interests that can organize on a statewide or citywide basis (business firms, labor unions, professional groups) or that control political resources that have a statewide or citywide reach (newspapers, television stations). Executives, more than legislatures, are likely to favor "planning," worry about the state of the economy "as a whole," and rely on "experts" in making decisions. (The quotation marks are to remind the reader that, despite their attractive connotations, these terms are both ambiguous and controversial—what is a plan or an expert to one person is a scheme or a manipulator to another.)[39]

There are ideological implications of reform as well. Whatever may have been the motives of the original proponents of executive-centered political systems, today it is generally the case that liberals tend to support strong executives and the policies they propose, and conservatives tend to support legislatures and the policies they favor. There are many exceptions to this generalization. During the Vietnam War, for example, liberals came to distrust the American presidents who were leading the war effort and to call for greater congressional control over, and

limitations on, that effort. And when Ronald Reagan was governor of California, liberals in that state looked to the legislature, not the executive, for leadership. Nevertheless, over the long run, liberals—persons who want government to do many things—favor executive power because executives tend to be proponents of change and an enlarged role for government. On the other hand, conservatives—persons who want government to play a small role in society—look to the legislature because it has the ability and often the inclination to block executive proposals.

The struggle between reformers and anti-reformers produced a mixture of state and local political systems that can be classified as "executive-centered" or "legislature-centered" only at the cost of a good deal of oversimplification. Though the classification conceals many important distinctions, it at least directs the reader's attention to some central differences.

State Politics

The formal authority of a governor depends on the incumbent's tenure of office, the right to appoint other important administrative officials, the right to make up a budget for the executive branch, and the ability to veto bills the legislature had passed. A strong governor is something of a rarity:

- In 40 states, the governor serves a four-year term and can be reelected at least once, but in 6 states, no consecutive reelection is allowed after one four-year term and in 4 states the governor's term is but two years.[40]
- In most states, the governor must share formal authority with an independently elected attorney general, treasurer, and secretary of state (as well as with a lieutenant governor). But in some states a host of other officials are also elected—superintendent of education, auditor, insurance commissioner, mining commissioner, tax commissioner, printer, and even fish and game commissioner.[41]

- Most governors prepare the budget for their states, but in 7 states the governor's authority in this matter is shared with other, independent officials.[42]
- In about half the states, the governor has a strong veto power over the legislation. The governor can veto particular items in a bill as well as the whole bill; a two-thirds vote of the legislature is required to override the veto. In other states the governor's veto power is quite weak or easily overridden, and in one state (North Carolina) the governor has no veto at all.[43]

These four dimensions of a governor's formal authority can be combined into a single index of gubernatorial power for each of the fifty states. The governors with the most formal authority are found in New York, Illinois, and Hawaii; those with the least in Texas, West Virginia, and South Carolina (at least as of 1971).[44] In some cases a governor with little *formal authority* may be able to exercise a great deal of *actual power* because he or she has access to other political resources. He or she may, for example, command a strong party organization or have the ability to distribute political jobs and contracts to reward friends and punish enemies. We have no good measure of how these informal sources of power are distributed among the states, but the reader should be aware that in states such as Indiana the existence of strong, well-organized political parties and a large amount of political patronage may more than make up for the formal weakness of the governor.

Where the Strong Governors Are. In general, the strongest governors, at least as measured by their formal authority, are found in the larger, more urbanized and industrialized states of the North, whereas the weakest governors are found in the South and Southwest. (In many of these executive-centered state political systems, the governor has a substantial amount of informal power as well as formal authority—for example,

❝Political authority in most American states remains highly fragmented, more so than in the national government.❞

the governors of Illinois and Pennsylvania control thousands of political jobs.) Some observers have suggested that strong governors are found in the industrialized states because these places have the most complex problems and the largest state bureaucracies. It is just as likely that the strong governors exist in such places, not because of the problems these states confront (after all, what is a "problem" is a matter of political judgment), but rather because of the kinds of people who live in the big northern cities. Reformers who believe in strong executives are more likely to be found in large cosmopolitan areas and to have influence there.

A movement has developed of late to strengthen the power of governors at the expense of other state elected officials. Since 1965 at least nineteen states have reorganized their executive branches, generally in the direction of enlarging the authority of the governor. In Oklahoma, for example, the voters in 1975 approved amendments to the state constitution to abolish five of thirteen elective executive offices. No longer will Oklahomans vote for a commissioner of charities and corrections, a labor commissioner, a chief mine inspector, or a secretary of state; these jobs are now either appointive or nonexistent. The object of such changes is to make it easier for the governor to take control over—and thus be accountable for—the executive branch and to reduce the chances that little-known officials in low-visibility posts will make policy without being effectively supervised.

Even with all these changes, political authority in most American states remains highly fragmented, more so than in the national government. Not only are there many independently elected executive offices (such as state treasurer, attorney general, and secretary of state), but

These campaign signs on a street corner in Providence, Rhode Island, graphically illustrate the number of different elective offices in American cities and states.

in about half the states even the lieutenant governor is elected, not jointly with the governor, but separately. This means that the person who will take over upon the governor's death and who often presides over the state senate may well be from a different political party (or from a different faction within the same party) than the governor. In Illinois in 1971, for example, the governor was a Republican but the lieutenant governor was a Democrat; moreover, because the lieutenant governor had a vote in an evenly divided state senate, he was able to tip the party balance in that body in favor of the Democrats. In 1979 governors in twenty-five states were of a different party from that which controlled one or both houses of the state legislature.

Scholars disagree about the effect these institutional and political arrangements have on the kinds of policies adopted by the states. To some, the policies a state has depends on the way it is organized to make decisions; to others, the decisive factors are the economic conditions of the state or its distinctive political culture.

Party Strength. There is no disagreement, however, about one consequence of our pattern of state government—its fragmentation and diversity greatly affect the organization and behavior of American political parties and the relations between federal and state governments. Since most political conflicts are over local offices and local issues, most people active in politics have a local perspective. Since political power is divided among so many offices and persons at the state level, it is inconceivable that the political parties would be able to display much unity or leadership at the national level. If we see people working at cross-purposes at the peak of the political pyramid, it is in large part because they are working at cross-purposes at the bottom of that pyramid. Indeed, as we shall see in Chapter 6, the fragmentation of political parties that results from their being organized around fragmented state and local governmental institutions means that it is a mistake to speak of them as if they were "pyramids" at all.

There are exceptions. In some states, parties,

as they operate in state legislatures, are quite strong. In New York, Massachusetts, Rhode Island, and Pennsylvania, the great majority—usually well over three-fourths—of the votes on controversial pieces of legislation follow party lines fairly closely (that is, a majority of the Democrats vote against a majority of the Republicans).[45] This tends to be the result of the unusual powers given party leaders in these state legislatures: they are able to control their colleagues by deciding who gets to be chairman of what committee and by influencing the distribution of other favors. In most states, however, rarely more than half the legislative votes follow party lines, and in some states, such as Utah, Idaho, and Oregon, party-line voting is quite rare.

The implications of this for federal-state relations are clear. Political power in the states is highly fragmented and only rarely can one person speak "for" the state in its entirety. A Democratic governor may go to Washington to ask for federal aid for one program, only to have a Republican attorney general or superintendent of education go there and ask for something quite different. Even where one political party is dominant, that party (for reasons to be explained in Chapter 6) is likely to be made up of many warring factions, rarely able to speak with one voice. Thus, the congressmen and senators from a state often represent different local interests even when they are members of the same party.

Local Politics

Just as the existence of the states tends to give a local orientation to much of national politics, so also the existence of cities, towns, and counties gives a local cast to much of state politics. But unlike the states, whose existence and boundaries are guaranteed by the federal Constitution, cities enjoy no constitutional protection: legally, they are entirely the creatures of the state which could, in theory, reorganize their governments, redraw their boundaries, or even abolish them altogether.[46]

But what is possible in theory is rarely tried in practice, because cities and towns have political power—the votes of their residents, of course, but even more important the political organizations and elected representatives whose roots are deep in the local soil. In most states the county is the unit around which the political party is organized; in some states the cities, especially the larger ones, provide an additional unit of party organization.

The localistic nature of political parties is explained largely by the existence at the city and county levels of those resources—elective offices, appointive jobs—which politicians seek and which form the basis of any party system. Chicago, and Cook County of which it is a part, had, in the 1960s, 341 positions to be filled by election: 50 aldermen, a mayor, and two other citywide officers; 21 county officials; 95 judges

Local political machines are powerful—until they are beaten. Jane Byrne was elected mayor of Chicago in 1979, having first defeated the organization's candidate in the primary election.

of county and municipal courts; 160 party officials (ward and township committeemen, all elected); and 12 officials of various special district governments, such as the Metropolitan Sanitary District.[47] This total does not include the dozens of representatives chosen from Chicago–Cook County to the state legislature and the Congress. The Republican or Democratic party in Cook County will naturally care who is elected president or senator, but they will care even more who is elected to the numerous local offices. Even in localities where the parties, unlike those of Chicago, are weak and disorganized, most political conflicts will be over, not who rules in Washington, but who rules, and to what ends, in Lubbock, Columbus, Allentown, or Springfield.

Types of City Government.   City governments, like state ones, differ primarily in the extent to which the executive has much or little power. Unlike the states, however, there is a greater variety in the identity of that executive. There are three kinds of municipal executives: a mayor, a city manager, and a commission. The mayor may be elected either directly by the voters (as are the mayors of Boston, New York, and Los Angeles) or by the other members of the city council (as in Cambridge, Massachusetts). A city manager is a full-time administrator, supposedly (and often actually) professional in skills and nonpartisan in attitudes, who is appointed by a city council to take charge of the executive departments of the government. City managers are found in about one-fourth of all cities; the larger ones include Cincinnati, Dallas, Kansas City, and San Diego. A commission is a many-headed executive: a board, elected by the voters, that exercises both executive and legislative functions. It is relatively uncommon, but still can be found in St. Paul and Salt Lake City.

There are two ways by which political power can become centralized in the hands of the city executive. First, the mayor may have, by law

or city charter, much formal authority. The mayor of Boston is a "strong mayor" in this sense: directly elected by the people, he generally can dominate the city council. The council may cut but may not increase the mayor's budget and has little say over whom he appoints to many of the top administrative positons. There are only a few independent boards and commissions, and those that exist, such as the Boston Redevelopment Authority, are often dominated by the mayor's appointees.

Second, executive power may be great, not because of the formal authority of the mayor, but because of the informal powers he or she can muster. There are at least three sources of such informal power: a strong political party or machine, well-organized business or labor support, and the mayor's personal following. Chicago is the classic case of a party machine providing a mayor who has little formal authority with enough power to dominate city politics almost completely. The machine, which is described in greater detail in Chapter 6, is a tightly organized, strongly hierarchical party organization that relies on jobs, favors, and contracts to maintain discipline. At one time many cities had machines; today only a few do. In addition to Chicago, Philadelphia is an example, albeit one weaker than once was the case, and Albany is another. The impact of political reformers and changes in voter attitudes have made such organizations increasingly difficult to sustain.

Informal power may also be supplied by nonpolitical groups, such as business leaders and labor unions, provided they can control such things as campaign funds and publicity needed by politicians and provided they face no serious challenge from a party organization. For many years business leaders were highly influential in the politics of Atlanta and Dallas, helping elect councilmen and mayors who were in sympathy with such business objectives as economic development and low taxes. Labor unions have been an important source of power in St. Paul and Detroit. (Interestingly, the United Auto Workers union, though a powerful force in Michigan state politics, has had much less influence in the politics of Detroit even though many of its members live in that city.)[48] Unions made up of municipal employees have become an especially important source of power in many cities.

Finally, a mayor with a strong personality may develop a personal following among the voters so great that, though they are not organized into a machine, they make him politically unassailable. James Michael Curley had such a following in Boston, as did Fiorello La Guardia in New York. Neither was a strong party leader; neither had, by law, a great deal of authority; neither had the organized backing of powerful business leaders; but each was able to get his way on many matters because few other politicians dared challenge him for the public's support.

Shifts in Power. Over the last few decades, the trend of local politics has been in the direction of weakening the sources of informal power (party machines, business or labor organizations) and increasing the formal authority of city executives. Unfortunately for most mayors and city managers, the informal sources of their power have declined faster than their formal authority has grown. Though Atlanta, Boston, and New York, among other cities, have adopted charters that give more authority to the mayor, these cities have witnessed the decline in the importance of organized business (Atlanta), the power of party machines (New York), and the availability of politicians able to attract strong personal followings (Boston). Thus, the ability of the mayors of these cities to dominate the political process has not increased as fast as they would like or as the reformers who were responsible for these new charters had hoped. In other cities, such as Los Angeles, the mayor has scarcely gained any formal authority at all.

Moreover, events since the 1960s have sharply

" A mayor with a strong personality may develop a personal following among the voters so great that, though they are not organized into a machine, they make him politically unassailable. **"**

No one was more skillful at developing a personal following than Fiorello La Guardia, mayor of New York from 1934–1945. Here he coaches the cast of a play, written and directed by His Honor, intended to show his constituents how an early food stamp plan would work.

increased the variety of political forces with which a mayor must deal. Municipal employee unions have grown rapidly in size and power as they have won the right to bargain collectively. As a result, mayors have been forced to negotiate labor contracts with police officers, firefighters, schoolteachers, and others who constitute a significant force in city elections. A city employee may work for the mayor, but the mayor may hold office at the pleasure of city employees. Federal programs, such as the War on Poverty

An important new force in local politics is the public employee union movement. Here San Francisco police officers walk a picket line in 1975.

and Model Cities, have stimulated the formation of neighborhood organizations to deal with employment, housing, and other problems. These groups often receive all or part of their funds from the federal government. They are run by persons elected by citizens or appointed by self-perpetuating boards, giving them substantial independence from city hall. Such organizations have created new opportunities to mobilize neighborhood residents and to represent interests that once may have been neglected. They have also proliferated the number and diversity of power centers with which mayors are confronted. Some mayors, of course, will try to incorporate these groups into a political apparatus supportive of their efforts at reelection, but usually the mayor needs the neighborhood groups more than they need the mayor.

Effects of Fragmentation. These political forces affect federalism in several ways. The weak and fragmented nature of local political parties means that most congressmen and senators, while quite sensitive to local interests and opinions, are not part of any strong organization that can shape their careers or determine their votes. As will be explained in Chapter 10, most congressmen and senators have an *individual* rather than an organizational relationship with their constituents.

Very few mayors ever rise to important national office. The difficult problems that cities face, the absence of sufficient authority and power to govern without challenge, and the deep social divisions (between races, neighborhoods, and social classes) in cities tend to make mayors controversial persons, more likely to receive blame than credit. The former mayor of Indianapolis, Richard Lugar, was an exception—he became senator from Indiana; another was Hubert Humphrey, who became senator from Minnesota and later vice-president after having been the mayor of Minneapolis. But Mayors Kevin White of Boston and Fiorello La Guardia and John Lindsay of New York had no chance of being nominated for national office even though all wanted it. Perhaps the best-known big-city mayor, Richard Daley of Chicago, never aspired to national office. Governors do better: at times, as many as one-fourth of all United States senators are former governors.[49]

Strong executives are often more effective in getting federal aid for their cities than are weak ones. When Washington began, in 1964, to distribute money to the cities to reduce poverty, those big cities with strong executives, such as Chicago and Philadelphia, got a larger share (in proportion to their population) of this money than did those big cities, such as New York and Los Angeles, with weak executives. This result occurred, not simply because the executives were strong, but because of *why* they were strong. The mayors of Chicago and Philadelphia headed powerful political machines and thus were able to control their city's representatives in Congress, directing them, as a united block, to back moves in Washington designed to bring money to their cities. The mayors of Los Angeles and New York, by contrast, could not control their city's congressional delegations or otherwise display their power to federal officials. While the mayors of Chicago and Philadelphia were skilled at getting money, they were loathe to share power: poor persons in these cities participated much less in setting policies aimed at poverty than did the representatives of the poor in New York and Los Angeles.[50]

Public policy is affected by the political independence of the cities and states. Their partial autonomy means that decisions over many important matters will reflect local political values and tastes. Federal systems such as the United States (and also Canada, Switzerland, and West Germany) allow the amount of money spent on such services as education to vary much more among regions than do unitary political systems (such as England and Sweden).[51] Similarly with welfare expenditures: the South spends much less per capita on welfare programs than do the larger northern states, even allowing for local differences in the standard of living.[52]

SUMMARY

States participate actively both in determining national policy and in administering national programs. Moreover, they reserve to themselves or the localities within them important powers over public services, such as schooling and law enforcement, and important public decisions, such as land-use control, that in unitary systems are dominated by the national government.

How one evaluates federalism depends in large part on the value one attaches to the competing criteria of equality and participation. Federalism means that citizens living in different

parts of the country will be treated differently, not only in spending programs, such as welfare, but in legal systems that assign in different places different penalties to similar offenses or that differentially enforce civil rights laws. But federalism also means that there are more opportunities for participation in making decisions: in influencing what is taught in the schools and in deciding where highways and government projects are to be built. Indeed, differences in public policy—that is, unequal treatment—are in large part the result of participation in decision-making. It is difficult, perhaps impossible, to have more of one of these values without having less of the other.

Politics, and public policy, have become somewhat more nationalized of late, with the federal government, and especially the federal courts, imposing increasingly uniform standards on the states. But there are limits as to how far and how fast this will proceed, for the states and localities continue to play a powerful, independent role in managing federal programs. The more complex or difficult the objective of these programs, the more state and local cooperation must be obtained by persuasion rather than by directive.

Suggested Readings

Banfield, Edward C., and James Q. Wilson. *City Politics.* Cambridge, Mass.: Harvard University Press, 1963. How politics is organized and carried out in American cities.

Derthick, Martha. *Between State and Nation: Regional Organizations of the United States.* Washington, D.C.: Brookings Institution, 1974. Analyzes governmental structures that involve more than one state, including the Appalachian Regional Commission, the Delaware River Basin Commission, and the Tennessee Valley Authority.

Derthick, Martha. *The Influence of Federal Grants.* Cambridge, Mass.: Harvard University Press, 1970. Considers the extent to which federal aid leads to federal control in the area of welfare.

Diamond, Martin. "The Federalist's View of Federalism," in George C. S. Benson, ed., *Essays in Federalism.* Claremont, Calif.: Institute for Studies in Federalism of Claremont Men's College, 1961, pp. 21–64. A profound analysis of what the Founders meant by "federalism."

Elazar, Daniel J. *American Federalism: A View from the States,* 2nd ed. New York: Thomas Y. Crowell, 1972. A sympathetic analysis of the historical development and present nature of American federalism.

Grodzins, Morton. *The American System.* Chicago: Rand McNally, 1966. Argues that American federalism has always involved extensive sharing of functions between national and state governments.

Haider, Donald H. *When Governments Come to Washington.* New York: The Free Press, 1974. A description of the intergovernmental lobby—state and local officials who attempt to influence federal policy.

Jacob, Herbert, and Kenneth N. Vines, eds. *Politics in the American States: A Comparative Analysis,* 3rd ed. Boston: Little, Brown, 1976. The best survey of state politics, governments, and policy-making, with chapters (by various authors) on governors, legislatures, parties, courts, federal-state relations, and other matters.

Pressman, Jeffrey L., and Aaron B. Wildavsky. *Implementation.* Berkeley: University of California Press, 1973. An excellent case study of how federalism affected the implementation of a single economic development project in Oakland, California.

Riker, William H. *Federalism: Origin, Operation, Significance.* Boston: Little, Brown, 1964. An explanation and critical analysis of federalism here and abroad.

Diversity and Union

From the beginning, American politics has had to cope with social diversity. Though the total white population of the United States in 1790 was not much more than that of Connecticut today, and though most people shared a common background (Protestant Britons), Americans at the time of the Founding exhibited a remarkable range of manners and interests, differences that quickly became deeper as cities grew and the westward movement began.

Many critics of the Constitution believed that the nation was already so diverse as to make a national government either unworkable or oppressive. James Madison advanced the novel idea that this diversity was a strength: it would help to ensure against a tyrannical majority. "The larger the society" —and the more various its interests—"the more duly capable it will be of self-government." In the mid-nineteenth century, faced with the prospect of civil war, it took a brave or far-sighted person to cling to that belief.

By Andrew Jackson's time, social diversity had combined with popular participation to make local politics a rowdy, festive affair, where both whiskey and money flowed freely. George Bingham, a politician himself, painted *The County Election* in 1852.

"The County Election," *by George Caleb Bingham. Collection of The Boatmen's National Bank of St. Louis*

There were large differences in wealth in the new nation. Thousands of persons, many resplendent in the most elegant finery, came to the splendid Oakland House in Louisville, Kentucky, to watch the horse races. But the principal cleavage in the early nineteenth century was not between rich and poor, but between slave and non-slave regions. By 1860 prime black field hands would bring $1,200 in slave auctions like this one in Richmond, Virginia; women, unless "fancy," sold for 25 percent less.

The challenge to slavery arose in large measure out of evangelical Christianity. Portrayed here are Anabaptists in Philadelphia, who watch as one of their number is baptized. This and other sects were part of the Great Revival that swept the country in the 1830s and provided the impetus for the anti-slavery movement. Young preachers such as

(Left), "Oakland House and Race Course, Louisville, 1840." *Collection of the S. B. Speed Art Museum, Louisville, Kentucky*

"The Slave Auction." *Kennedy Galleries, Inc., New York*

Theodore Weld from Lane Seminary would give abolitionist speeches in churches, sometimes in the face of a hostile crowd.

Many persons, however, wanted nothing to do with the turmoil of the East and went west. In *The Robe Traders,* Charles M. Russell portrayed the confluence of three cultures outside a trading post in the West: an Easterner in the dress of a boat captain, a trapper in a Hudson's Bay coat, and a Blackfoot Indian on horseback, signaling that he wishes to trade.

After the Civil War industrialization produced sharper cleavages among economic classes. But owing to the enormous increase in immigration, ethnicity rather than class became the major source of social diversity. Between 1851 and 1924, when legal quotas restricted immigration, over 33 million persons entered the United States. By 1900 one

(Right), "A Philadelphia Anabaptist Immersion During a Storm," *by Pavel Petrovich Svinin. The Metropolitan Museum of Art, Rogers Fund, 1942*

"The Robe Traders," *by C. M. Russell. The Thomas Gilcrease Institute of American History and Art, Tulsa, Oklahoma*

out of every eight Americans had been born abroad. Ben Shahn's mural depicts the variety of persons arriving: amidst an anonymous crowd of refugees is Albert Einstein clutching a violin case.

Politics increasingly had to reconcile class and ethnic interests. No better example of the conflict can be found than the election of 1896, when people divided both along lines of class (in their attitudes toward "hard" versus "soft" money) and along lines of culture (in their beliefs about liquor and religion).

In the twentieth century these complicated struggles centered in the cities. By 1920, for the first time, more Americans lived in urban than in rural places. The growing cities brought together rich and poor, ethnic neighborhoods and racial or religious ghettos, commercial and cultural activities. Cities offered both opportunity and loneliness, freedom and squalor. Edward Hopper's *Night-*

Scala/Editorial Photocolor Archives © Estate of Ben Shahn

"Nighthawks," by Edward Hopper. The Art Institute of Chicago

hawks, painted in 1942, vividly conveyed one aspect of the urban mood. Urban political machines—the distinctly American form of political party—had to find ways of organizing voters divided along so many lines.

In a nation fractured by a civil war and rent by many issues, the political system has done remarkably well in forging a semblance of national unity out of America's social diversity. For more than a century political parties—though never mentioned by the Founders, save in disapproving tones—were one of the major devices for managing diversity. Today the parties are in retreat, their influence giving way to that of the mass media, higher education, and interest groups. But the diversity of the nation persists and even deepens. Ways must still be found to reconcile the beliefs and interests of middle-class blacks at a church service in Montgomery, Alabama, with those of poor blacks in rural Alabama,

Owen Franken, Stock, Boston

Owen Franken, Stock, Boston

Ilka Hartmann, Jeroboam, Inc.

Sepp Seitz, Woodfin Camp & Associates

Donald Dietz, Stock, Boston

to bring into a governing coalition groups as different as these Jews at a bar mitzvah ceremony, American Indians stepping from a camper, and Cuban-Americans living in Miami's "Little Havana."

Even among persons similar in wealth and education there are profound differences in political opinion. This was true at the Founding; it is no less true today. It is hard to imagine that a family enjoying a hot tub in Marin County, California, and a couple picnicking at the Rolling Rock Steeple Chase in Pennsylvania have the same political beliefs, even if they have roughly the same incomes.

William Strode, Woodfin Camp & Associates

Cary Wolinsky, Stock, Boston

Donald Dietz, Stock, Boston

In Jackson's time and for many decades thereafter, politics was the great American sport. Today sports are the great American sport. People always enjoy spectacles and develop loyalties. Once, politics supplied both; now, it often supplies neither. Government affects our lives more than formerly, but a diverse nation is less confident that it can affect government. Political parties once brought different kinds of people together for a common purpose. Today what draws us together is more likely to be a baseball game on a warm Sunday afternoon at Fenway Park.

*　*　*

4 American Political Culture

Tocqueville's observations • Attitudes and values • Phenomenon of Americanism • Almond and Verba's comparative study • Experience of a libertarian revolution • Legitimization of an opposition party • Influence of religious heritage • Family life • Trust in government • Increase in cynicism • Political efficacy • Support for civil liberties

If the Republic, created in 1787, had depended for its survival entirely on the constitutional machinery designed by the Founders, it probably would not have endured. That machinery was copied by many other nations, notably those of Latin America, but in virtually no other country did such devices as federalism, the elected president, the bicameral legislature, and the separation of powers produce a political system capable of both effective government and the protection of liberty. In many nations (such as Argentina, Brazil, and the Philippines) that adopted the American model, there have been, at best, brief periods of democratic rule interrupted by military takeovers, the rise to power of unscrupulous demagogues, or the spread of wholesale corruption. The Constitution of the United States, like an old wine, has rarely survived an ocean crossing.

Alexis de Tocqueville, the perceptive French observer of American politics, noticed this as

The political culture of a nation is revealed by its symbolic acts, such as this Fourth of July parade around 1910. Within that culture, great diversity can exist, as exemplified by a Puerto Rican parade in New York City (right).

❝Neither the Constitution nor the physical advantages of the country can alone explain the persistence of democratic institutions.❞

Alexis de Tocqueville (1805–1859) was a young French aristocrat who came to the United States to study the American prison system. He remained to write the brilliant *Democracy in America* (1835), a profound analysis of our political culture.

early as the 1830s. The maintenance of a democratic republic, he wrote, depends, not only on the laws and constitution of a nation, but on the physical circumstances in which a people find themselves and on their manners and customs.[1] The vast territory of the United States created innumerable opportunities for the average person to acquire land, grow crops, and engage in trade. The frontier seemed to expand endlessly (or at least as fast as the native Indians could be driven from their ancestral homes), conferring on persons with pluck and luck a chance to become economically and socially independent. No feudal aristocracy monopolized the land, and no powerful central government imposed more than minimal taxes or restraints on its use. These small, independent farmers and tradesmen, unlike a nation of landless peasants or indentured servants, could make democratic government work.

Other nations have been similarly favored, but without the same result. As Tocqueville noted, much of South America contains fertile lands and rich resources, but democracy did

not take firm root there.[2] Had he returned to the United States fifty years later, when the frontier was no longer expanding and large, crowded cities were becoming commonplace, Tocqueville would have observed that, despite the lessened availability of abundant land, democratic government was more or less intact.

Neither the Constitution nor the physical advantages of the country can alone explain the persistence of democratic institutions. Though both are important, even more important are what Tocqueville called the customs of the American people, by which he meant their "moral and intellectual characteristics."[3]

From Tocqueville's time to the present, writers have argued about what these characteristics are, whether they are unique to Americans, and how—if at all—they actually shape the operation of government.

POLITICAL CULTURE

There have been over two dozen attempts to describe systematically the distinctive political customs—or in the modern parlance, the "political culture"—of the American people.[4] Though there were differences in emphasis and language, there was also a surprisingly large measure of agreement among them. Almost all of these attempts drew attention to certain values their authors believed are widely shared:

Liberty   Freedom from restraint, especially from that imposed by law.

Individualism   Personal effort or achievement and the award of recognition based on it (rather than recognition based on family, class, or privilege).

Equality   Equality of opportunity (rather than equality of condition or outcome).

Rule of law   As opposed to arbitrary power.

Civic duty   The obligation to vote and otherwise take seriously communal and civic affairs.

A Look at the Evidence

At least three questions about such a political culture immediately come to mind. First, how do we know that people share these beliefs? For most of our history, there have been no public opinion polls, and even after they became commonplace they were rather crude tools for measuring the existence and meaning of complex, abstract ideas. There is, in fact, no way to prove that such values as those listed above are important to Americans. But neither is there good reason for dismissing the list out of hand. One can infer, as have many scholars, the existence of certain values by a close study of the kinds of books Americans read, the speeches they hear, the slogans to which they respond, and the political choices they make, as well as by noting the observations of insightful foreign visitors. Personality tests as well as opinion polls, particularly those asking similar questions in different countries, also supply useful evidence, some of which will be reviewed below.

Second, if these values are important to Americans, how can we explain behavior that is so obviously inconsistent with them? For example, if white Americans say they believe in equality of opportunity, why did so many of them for so long deny that equality to black

America has both a shared political culture and some distinctive subcultures associated with various ethnic and religious groups.

The Meaning of Political Culture

A political culture is a patterned set of ways of thinking about how politics and governing ought to be carried out. A nation, if it is made up of persons who are quite similar to one another, may have a single political culture, part of what is sometimes referred to as a "national character." Most nations are not homogeneous, however, being made up instead of distinctive regions, religions, and ethnic groups. Each of these parts may have a distinctive political subculture. The American South, for example, has a political culture that differs in important ways from that of the Northeast.

Because a political culture consists of our fundamental assumptions about how the political process should operate, we often take it for granted or are completely unaware of how important these assumptions are. For instance, we assume that a person who loses an election should not try to prevent the winner from taking office, that it is wrong to use public office to enrich oneself or one's family, and that nobody should have a greater claim to political authority simply because he or she comes from a rich or wellborn family. In many other societies these are not widely shared assumptions, and in some societies the opposite is often believed.

A political culture is not the same as a political ideology. The concept of ideology will be explained in Chapter 5. As used there, it will refer to more or less consistent sets of views as to the policies government ought to pursue. A doctrinaire conservative, liberal, or radical has an ideology. Up to a point, people can disagree on ideology (what government should do) but share a common political culture (how government ought to be operated). Some ideologies, however, are so critical of the existing state of affairs that they require a fundamental change in the way politics is carried on, and thus they embody a different political culture as well.

At the height of immigration to this country there was a striking emphasis on creating a shared political culture. Schoolchildren, whatever their national origin, were taught to salute this country's flag.

Americans? That people act contrary to their professed beliefs is an everyday fact of life: we believe in honesty, yet we steal from our employer and sometimes underreport our taxable income. Self-interest and social circumstances, as well as values, shape behavior. Gunnar Myrdal, a Swedish observer of American society, described race relations in this country as "an American dilemma" resulting from the conflict between the "American creed" (a belief in equality of opportunity) and American behavior (denying blacks full citizenship).[5] But the creed remains important because it is a source of change: as more and more persons become aware of the inconsistency between their values and their behavior, that behavior slowly changes.[6] Race relations in this country would take a very different course if, instead of the abstract but widespread belief in equality, there were an equally widespread belief that one race is in-

herently inferior to another. (No doubt some white Americans believe that, but most do not.)

Third, if there is agreement on certain political values, why has there been so much political conflict in our history? How can Americans who agree on fundamentals fight a bloody civil war, engage in violent labor-management disputes, take to the streets in riots and demonstrations, and sue each other in countless court battles? Conflict, even violent struggle, can occur over specific policies even among persons who share, at some level of abstraction, common beliefs. Many political values may be irrelevant to specific controversies: there is no abstract value, for example, that would settle the question of whether steelworkers ought to organize unions. More important, much of our conflict has occurred precisely because we have strong beliefs that happen, as each of us interpret them, to be in conflict. Equality of opportunity seems an attractive idea, but sometimes it can be pursued only by curtailing personal liberty, another attractive idea. The states went to war in 1861 over one aspect of that conflict—the rights of slaves versus the liberties of slave-owners.

Indeed, the Civil War is a remarkable illustration of the extent to which certain fundamental beliefs about how a democratic regime ought to be organized have persisted despite bitter conflict over the policies that regime adopted. When the southern states seceded from the Union, they formed, not a wholly different government, but one modeled, despite some important differences, on the United States Constitution. Even some of the language of the Constitution was duplicated, suggesting that the southern states believed, not that a new form of government or a different political culture ought to be created, but that the South was the true repository of the existing constitutional and cultural order.[7]

Perhaps the most frequently encountered evidence that Americans believed themselves bound by common values and common hopes has been the persistence of the word "Americanism" in our political vocabulary. Throughout the nineteenth and most of the twentieth centuries, "Americanism" and "American way of life" were familiar terms, not only in Fourth of July speeches, but in everyday discourse. For many years a committee of the House of Representatives existed, called the House UnAmerican Activities Committee. There is hardly any example to be found abroad of such a way of thinking: there is no "Britishism" or "Frenchism," and when Britons and French people become worried about subversion, they call it a problem of internal security, not a manifestation of "UnBritish" or "UnFrench" activities.

A Comparative Study
There have been a number of efforts to describe more precisely and measure more accurately the kinds of political values Americans may

share. One of the most ambitious of these was a study of citizens in five nations in 1959–1960 by Gabriel Almond and Sidney Verba.[8] Almond and Verba were interested in discovering the extent to which people in these countries had the attitudes that they, the authors, believed were essential to a democratic government. Among these attitudes were a sense of civic duty (a belief that one has an obligation to participate in political or civic affairs) and a sense of civic competence or political efficacy (a belief that one can affect government policies). They found that Americans, and to a lesser degree citizens of Great Britain, had a stronger sense of both civic duty and civic competence than did citizens of Germany, Italy, or Mexico. In Table 4.1 we see that over half the Americans and over a third of the Britons believed the ordinary person ought to "be active in his community," compared to only a tenth in Italy and a fifth in Germany.

TABLE 4.1 Beliefs About the Obligations of Citizenship

Percent who say the ordinary man should:	United States	Great Britain	Germany	Italy	Mexico
Be active in his community	51%	39%	22%	10%	26%
Only participate in more passive ways (be interested, etc.)	27	31	38	22	33
Only participate in church affairs	5	2	1	0	0
Total who mention some outgoing activity	83%	72%	61%	32%	59%
Only be upright in personal life	1%	1%	11%	15%	2%
Do nothing in local community	3	6	7	11	2
Don't know	11	17	27	35	30
Other	2	5	1	7	7
Total percent	100%	100%	100%	100%	100%
Total number of cases	970	963	955	995	1,007

Source: Gabriel A. Almond and Sidney Verba, *The Civic Culture: Political Attitudes and Democracy in Five Nations,* p. 169. Copyright © 1963 by Princeton University Press. Reprinted by permission of Princeton University Press.

Popular confidence in American political leaders has declined since the early 1960s. The man here is protesting President Carter's farm policies. Other people protest against different "broken promises."

TABLE 4.2   Percent Who Say They Can Do Something About an Unjust Local or National Regulation, by Nation

Nation	Can do something about local regulation	Can do something about national regulation
United States	77%	75%
Great Britain	78	62
Germany	62	38
Italy	51	28
Mexico	52	38

Source: Gabriel A. Almond and Sidney Verba, *The Civic Culture: Political Attitudes and Democracy in Five Nations*, p. 185. Copyright © 1963 by Princeton University Press. Reprinted by permission of Princeton University Press.

In Table 4.2 many more Americans and Britons than Germans, Italians, or Mexicans believed that they could "do something" about a national law or a local regulation that they considered unjust.

Obviously, people may not act in accordance with their professed sense of duty, and they may exaggerate how effective such action is likely to be, but what is important is that they have these beliefs. They think their political system is and should be participant, and those beliefs are a form of professed support for the political system that is not found in all nations, including some we think of as democratic.

In the course of their inquiry, Almond and Verba learned of other political attitudes held by Americans that may in fact be even more important than a (perhaps unrealistic) sense of duty or competence. When asked what aspect of their country they were most proud of, Americans overwhelmingly mentioned their governmental and political institutions; Britons were only half as likely to do so, and Germans and Italians scarcely mentioned government at all. (Germans were more likely to mention the characteristics of the people; Italians more likely to mention the physical attributes of the country or "nothing.") (See Table 4.3.) One should recall that this question was asked in 1959–1960; as we shall see, popular pride in our political institutions has declined in recent years.

Moreover, for all our contentiousness and despite all the claims that Americans are "materialistic," citizens of this country, together with those of Great Britain, are much more likely than persons in Germany, Italy, or Mexico to describe human nature as fundamentally cooperative, to believe that people can be trusted, and to think that people are often willing to help others. (See Table 4.4.) A democratic system will almost certainly find it difficult to survive if its citizens do not trust each other (they have to be willing, for example, to allow their opponents to take office when the latter win an election.)

TABLE 4.3   Aspects of Nation in which Respondents Report Pride, by Nation

Percent who say they are proud of:	United States	Great Britain	Germany	Italy	Mexico
Governmental, political institutions	85%	46%	7%	3%	30%
Social legislation	13	18	6	1	2
Position in international affairs	5	11	5	2	3
Economic system	23	10	33	3	24
Characteristics of people	7	18	36	11	15
Spiritual virtues and religion	3	1	3	6	8
Contributions to the arts	1	6	11	16	9
Contributions to science	3	7	12	3	1
Physical attributes of country	5	10	17	25	22
Nothing or don't know	4	10	15	27	16
Other	9	11	3	21	14
Total % of responses*	158%	148%	148%	118%	144%
Total % of respondents	100%	100%	100%	100%	100%
Total number of cases	970	963	955	995	1,007

Source: Gabriel A. Almond and Sidney Verba, *The Civic Culture: Political Attitudes and Democracy in Five Nations*, p. 102. Copyright © 1963 by Princeton University Press. Reprinted by permission of Princeton University Press.

*Percentages exceed 100 because of multiple responses.

TABLE 4.4   Social Trust and Distrust, by Nation

Percent who agree that:	United States	Great Britain	Germany	Italy	Mexico
Statements of *Distrust*					
"No one is going to care much what happens to you, when you get right down to it."	38%	45%	72%	61%	78%
"If you don't watch yourself, people will take advantage of you."	68	75	81	73	94
Statements of *Trust*					
"Most people can be trusted."	55	49	19	7	30
"Most people are more inclined to help others than to think of themselves first."	31	28	15	5	15
"Human nature is fundamentally cooperative."	80	84	58	55	82
Total number of respondents	970	963	955	995	1,007

Source: Gabriel A. Almond and Sidney Verba, *The Civic Culture: Political Attitudes and Democracy in Five Nations*, p. 267. Copyright © 1963 by Princeton University Press. Reprinted by permission of Princeton University Press.

As we shall see in Part III, there are different ways of organizing democratic governmental systems; so also there are different political cultures, and not just the American one, that are supportive of democratic government. Sweden, for example, has a well-developed democratic government, with a constitution, an elective legislature, competing political parties, free speech, and a reasonably honest and nonpartisan bureaucracy. The Swedes take great pride in their political institutions and in many of the policies that result. But their political culture is significantly different from ours: it is more deferential than participatory. Though almost all adult Swedes vote in national elections, few participate in politics in any other way. They defer to the decisions of experts and specialists who work for the government, rarely challenge governmental decisions in court, believe leaders and legislators ought to decide issues on the basis of "what is best" more than on "what the people want," and value equality as much as (or more than) liberty.[9] Where Americans are contentious, Swedes value harmony; where Americans tend to assert their rights, Swedes tend to observe their obligations.

The contrast in political cultures is even greater when one looks at a nation, such as Japan, with a wholly different history and set of traditions. One study compared the values expressed by a small number of upper status Japanese with those of some similarly situated Americans. Where the Americans emphasized the virtues of individualism, competition, and equality in their political, economic, and social relations, the Japanese attached greater value to maintaining good relations with colleagues, having decisions made by groups, preserving social harmony, and displaying respect for hierarchy. Americans were more concerned than the Japanese with rules and with treating others fairly but impersonally, with due regard for their rights. The Japanese, on the other hand, stressed the importance of being sensitive to the personal needs of others, avoiding conflict, and reaching decisions through discussion rather than the application of rules.[10] These cultural differences affect in profound but hard-to-measure ways the workings of the political and economic systems of the two countries, making them function quite differently despite the fact both are industrialized, capitalist nations.

It is easy to become carried away by the more obvious differences among national cultures and to overgeneralize from them. Thinking in stereotypes about the "typical" American, the "typical" Swede, or the "typical" Japanese is as risky as thinking of the "typical" white or the "typical" black American. This can be especially misleading in nations, such as the United States and Canada, that have been settled by a variety of ethnic and religious groups (English-speaking versus French-speaking Canadians, for example, or Jewish, Protestant, and Catholic Americans).[11] But it is equally misleading to suppose that the operation of a political system can be understood entirely from the objective features—its laws, economy, or physical circumstances.

THE SOURCES OF POLITICAL CULTURE

That Americans bring a distinctive way of thinking to their political life is easier to demonstrate than to explain. But even a brief, and necessarily superficial, effort to understand the sources of our political culture can help make its significance clearer.

The American Revolution, as we saw in Chapter 2, was essentially over liberty: an assertion by colonists of what they took to be their rights. Though the Constitution produced eleven years after the Revolution had to deal with other issues as well, its animating spirit reflected the effort to reconcile personal liberty with the needs of social control. These founding experiences, and the political disputes that followed, have given to American political thought and culture a preoccupation with the assertion and maintenance of *rights*. This tradition of a concern for rights has imbued the daily conduct of politics with a kind of adversary spirit quite foreign to the political life of countries that did not undergo a libertarian revolution or that were formed out of an interest in other goals, such as social equality, national independence, or ethnic supremacy.

The contentiousness of a people animated by a suspicion of government and devotion to individualism could easily have made democratic politics so tumultuous as to be impossible. After all, one must be willing to trust others with power if there is to be a democratic government at all. And sometimes those others will be people not of one's own choosing. The first great test case took place around 1800 in a battle between the Federalists, led by John Adams and Alexander Hamilton, and the Democratic-Republicans, led by Thomas Jefferson and James Madison. The two factions deeply distrusted each other: the Federalists had passed laws (see Chapter 18) designed to suppress Jeffersonian journalists; Jefferson suspected the Federalists were out to subvert the Constitution; the Federalists believed he intended to sell out the country to France. But as we shall see in Chapter 6, the threat of civil war never materialized, and the Jeffersonians came to power peacefully. Within a few years the role of an opposition party had become legitimate, and serious efforts to suppress one's opponents had been abandoned. By happy circumstance, people were reconciled to the view that liberty and orderly political change could coexist.[12]

The Constitution, by creating a federal system and dividing political authority among competing institutions, provided ample opportunity for widespread—though hardly universal—participation in politics. The election of Jefferson in 1800 produced no political catastrophe, and those who had predicted one were, to a degree, discredited. But other, more fundamental

❝This tradition of a concern for rights has imbued the daily conduct of politics with a kind of adversary spirit quite foreign to the political life of countries that did not undergo a libertarian revolution.❞

features of American life contributed to the same end. One of the most important of these was the religious diversity.

The absence of an established or official religion for the nation as a whole, reinforced by a constitutional prohibition of such an establishment and the migration to this country of persons with different religious backgrounds, meant that religious diversity was inevitable. Since there could be no orthodox or official religion, it became difficult for a corresponding political orthodoxy to emerge. Moreover, the conflict between the Puritan tradition, with its emphasis on faith and good works, and the Catholic church, with its devotion to the sacraments and priestly authority, provided a recurrent source of cleavage in American public life. The differences in values between these two groups showed up, not only in their religious practices, but in areas involving the regulation of manners and morals and even in the choice of a political party. For more than a century candidates for state and even national office were deeply divided over whether the sale of liquor should be prohibited, a question that arose ultimately out of competing religious doctrines.

Even though there was no established church, there was certainly a dominant religious tradition, and that was Protestantism and especially Puritanism. The Protestant churches provided both a set of beliefs and an organizational experience that had profound effects on American political culture. Those beliefs were consistent with, and even required, a life of personal achievement as well as religious conviction: a believer had an obligation to work, save money, obey the secular law, and do good. Max Weber explained the rise of capitalism in part by what he called the "Protestant ethic" and what we now sometimes call the "work ethic."[13] Such values had political consequences as well; persons holding them were motivated to civic and communal action.

Churches offered a ready opportunity for developing and practicing civic and political skills. Since most Protestant churches were organized along congregational lines—that is, the church was controlled by its members, who put up the building, hired the preacher, and supervised the finances—they were, in effect, miniature political systems, with leaders and committees, conflict and consensus. Developing a participant political culture was undoubtedly made easier by the existence of a participant religious culture.

None of this should be taken as implying that a democratic political culture cannot exist in a Catholic country; obviously, France, Belgium, Costa Rica, and Puerto Rico, among other societies with large Catholic populations, have been governed by democratic institutions, and American Catholics have fully shared in this nation's political culture. But the Protestant organizational experience, and to some extent its religious doctrines as well, facilitated the development of *one kind* of democratic political tradition, an especially participant kind.

All aspects of culture, including the political, are preserved and transmitted to new generations primarily by the family. Though some believe that the weakening of the family unit has eroded the extent to which it transmits any-

The family is the most important source of political values. It is not hard to imagine that this family, which was photographed in Black River Falls, Wisconsin, around 1900, held somewhat different values than would a modern family.

thing, particularly culture, and has enlarged the power of other sources of values—the mass media and the world of friends and fashion, leisure and entertainment—there is still little doubt that the ways we think about the world are largely acquired within the family. In Chapter 5 we shall see that the family is the primary source of one kind of political attitude—identification with one or another political party. Even more important, the family shapes in subtle ways how we think and act on political matters. Erik Erikson, the psychologist, noted certain traits that are more characteristic of American than of European families—the greater freedom enjoyed by children, for example, and the larger measure of equality among family members. These familial characteristics promote a belief, carried through life, that every person has rights deserving protection, and that a variety of interests have a legitimate claim to consideration when decisions are made.[14]

Though a political culture has an enduring and powerful effect, it, like other aspects of culture, is not immune to change. We cannot here consider in detail whether, in the last few generations, there has been an important change in American political culture, but the possibility should be borne in mind. The writings of Horatio Alger are no longer popular, perhaps because we are less willing today to believe that personal effort and virtue are alone sufficient to achieve worldly success. (The continued popularity of "self-improvement" books and programs suggests, however, that the belief persists in only a slightly changed form.) No longer do we so readily refer to the "American way of life" or to "Americanism," possibly because we are less comfortable than we once were with public declarations of our collective self-esteem (though we may still make such declarations privately, to ourselves, where they cannot be overheard by persons who think such views are naive). We may worry that "other-directed" or conformist Americans have replaced "inner-direc-

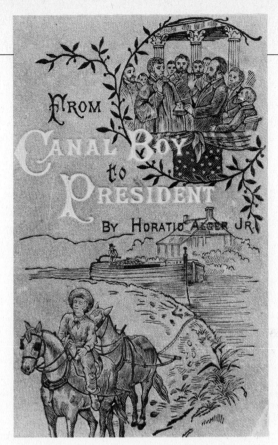

The books of Horatio Alger—such as this one entitled *From Canal Boy to President*, published in 1881—conveyed to millions of Americans a belief in individual effort and success as rewards for right living.

ted" or individualistic Americans, though in fact our love of both achievement and equality probably means that we were always both conformists and individualists at one and the same time.[15]

TRUST IN GOVERNMENT

That the American political culture may have changed is suggested by the fact that, however measured, popular trust in American government and confidence in the responsiveness of government to citizen concerns have declined sharply since the early 1960s.

In Figure 4.1 we see that various measures of our distrust of government increased slowly between 1958 and 1970 and then sharply from 1972 through 1976. By 1976, nearly twice as many Americans as in 1958 thought that there were "quite a few" crooks in government, that government was run for the benefit of a "few big interests" (rather than for the benefit of all), that "a lot" of tax money was wasted, and that only "some of the time" can we expect the government in Washington to "do what is right." There was a smaller increase in the proportion believing that the people running the government "don't seem to know what they are doing."[16] The largest single increase in these measures occurred between 1972 and 1974 at the time of the Watergate scandal, when close

aides to the president were shown to have interfered illegally in the electoral system, and the president himself was shown to have participated in the cover-up of those bungled efforts. Were the change only related to Watergate it would scarcely be worthy of comment, for that sorry episode is now over and presumably no longer blighting public confidence in government. But as one can see, much of the increased distrust occurred during the 1960s, well before Watergate.

Four Kinds of Dissatisfaction

These findings, worrisome as they are, do not prove that Americans are turning against their system of government. One must be careful to differentiate among at least four kinds of

---

FIGURE 4.1   The Growth of Mistrust of Government

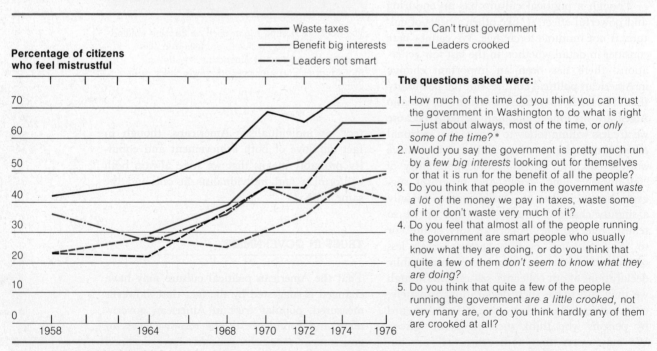

The questions asked were:

1. How much of the time do you think you can trust the government in Washington to do what is right —just about always, most of the time, or *only some of the time?* *
2. Would you say the government is pretty much run by a *few big interests* looking out for themselves or that it is run for the benefit of all the people?
3. Do you think that people in the government *waste a lot* of the money we pay in taxes, waste some of it or don't waste very much of it?
4. Do you feel that almost all of the people running the government are smart people who usually know what they are doing, or do you think that quite a few of them *don't seem to know what they are doing?*
5. Do you think that quite a few of the people running the government *are a little crooked,* not very many are, or do you think hardly any of them are crooked at all?

Source: Tabulated by John McAdams from data supplied by the Survey Research Center, University of Michigan.

* Mistrustful answers are italicized.

By and large, the increase in cynicism has been directed at officials and policies, and possibly also at outcomes, and not at the system itself.

The impassioned conflict over American involvement in Vietnam brought out protesters on both sides, each side seeking to associate important symbols ("peace," "patriotism") with its cause.

popular dissatisfactions—rejection of the *system* of government, dislike for the *leaders* of that government, disapproval of the *policies* of that government, and dissatisfaction over the *outcomes* of those policies.[17] By and large, the increase in cynicism has been directed at officials and policies, and possibly also at outcomes, and not at the system itself. Some persons who are on the left politically (liberals) are upset because government has been unwilling or unable to produce more social change and solve more problems. Some persons who are on the right (conservatives) are disappointed because government has been unable to ensure law and order and has engaged in what they regard as unwise social experiments. For example, a black voter may have become disenchanted with government because it has failed to integrate society and eliminate urban poverty, while a white voter may have become equally disenchanted because the government has tried to integrate schools by forced busing and has spent too much money on welfare.[18]

From the evidence we have, it is hard to tell the difference between popular attitudes toward government officials and policies, on the one hand, and attitudes toward the system of government on the other. Indeed, the citizenry may not always be able to make that distinction itself. When we become disgusted with a president, with Congress, or with a set of policies, for example, we do not often stop and ask ourselves whether this also means that we are fed up with our constitutional system and prefer an alternative way of doing things. There is some evidence, however, that support for the constitutional system remains strong despite the increased distrust of those who hold power

TABLE 4.5   Percentage of Americans Saying They Had a "Great Deal of Confidence" in People Running Various Institutions

	February 1966	February 1979
Congress	42%	18%
Executive branch of federal government	41	17
Supreme Court	50	28
Military	61	29
Organized religion	41	20
Major companies	55	18
Organized labor	22	10
The press	29	28
Higher education	61	33

Source: ABC News–Harris Surveys. Reprinted by permission of the Chicago Tribune–New York News Syndicate, Inc.

Schoolchildren in the 1970s seemed to have less favorable attitudes toward public officials than they did in the early 1960s. It remains unclear whether love of country, of the sort displayed by this young Cub Scout, has been affected.

in that system. In 1972, when distrust in government was quite high, 86 percent of the persons interviewed in a national survey agreed with the following statement: "I am proud of many things about our form of government." Even among those who expressed a low level of trust in officials, three-fourths agreed with this expression of pride. As we shall see in the next section, people have become in recent years increasingly supportive of some of the important "rules of the game" by which our system is supposed to be conducted.[19]

Moreover, the dissatisfaction with governmental policies and their results extends to the other institutions and occupations of society. In Table 4.5 we see that the percentage of Americans saying they had a "great deal of confidence" in the people running organized religion fell by nearly half between 1966 and 1979. The leaders of the military, major companies, and organized labor suffered equally great or even larger declines in confidence. Only the press held its own. (One wonders why.)

The 1960s and early 1970s, when these declines occurred, were periods of great turmoil—the civil rights movement, the war in Vietnam, the rapid rise in crime, the assassination of various leaders, urban riots and campus demonstrations, and economic inflation. People thought, not unreasonably, that things were getting out of hand and leaders ought to take some of the blame. In addition, this was a period of rapid political change. The government was expanding dramatically the range of problems it tackled, and some of these problems—crime, racism, poverty, disorder, drug abuse—proved extraordinarily difficult to solve. The more government—or any institution—attempts to achieve, the greater the risk it runs of failure, real or apparent.

Though the growth in popular dissatisfaction with government policies and officials is not equivalent to a withdrawal of popular support from government, and though the reasons for its growth can be explained, its long-term effects are unknown but perhaps damaging. Adults who once admired government leaders may in time, with an easing of tensions, recover that admiration. But young persons who grew up in this tumultuous period and whose first, and perhaps most important, exposure to politics was one that elicited feelings of cynicism and dissatisfaction may carry those feelings with them throughout their lives. One study found that the attitudes of schoolchildren toward the president in 1973 were significantly less favorable than had been true of similar schoolchildren in 1962. (By 1975, they had improved somewhat, but not to anything like the levels of support revealed in 1962.)[20] How the adult political behavior of this generation will be affected by their formative political experiences, if it will be affected at all, will not be known for many years.

Political Efficacy

Another measure of the change, if any, in political culture is the decline in the extent to which people have a sense of political competence or efficacy. In Figure 4.2 we see that three ways of asking about this all reveal an increase between 1960 and 1976 in the proportion of Americans who think that "people like me don't have any say about what the government does," that politics and government are "too complicated" to understand, and that public officials "don't care much what people like me think." In 1976 many more persons than in 1960 felt powerless or ineffective as citizens.[21]

Unlike the increased distrust of government, the change in the sense of political efficacy was unaffected by Watergate—there was no particular difference in the responses given in 1974

FIGURE 4.2   The Growth of a Sense of Political Ineffectiveness

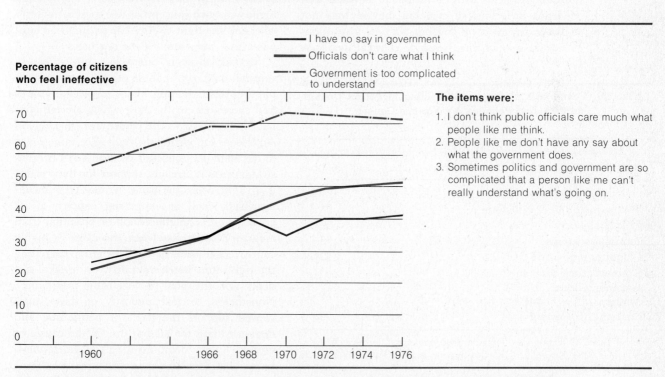

Percentage of citizens who feel ineffective

——— I have no say in government
——— Officials don't care what I think
—·—· Government is too complicated to understand

The items were:

1. I don't think public officials care much what people like me think.
2. People like me don't have any say about what the government does.
3. Sometimes politics and government are so complicated that a person like me can't really understand what's going on.

Source: Tabulated by John McAdams from data supplied by the Survey Research Center, University of Michigan.

(after Watergate) from those offered in 1972 (before Watergate). Government, apparently, has simply become too big and pervasive for citizens to think any longer that they can affect it. (In 1976 half of all Americans thought the federal government was too powerful; in 1964 less than a third did.)[22]

There is evidence that many of these changes in mood and perception have occurred in other countries as well, so that, compared to citizens of other nations, Americans may still feel relatively satisfied and efficacious. In any case, it would be astonishing and perhaps troubling if most persons were to believe that popular opinion always determines what the government does, since that opinion is deeply divided on many questions and nonexistent on others.

POLITICAL TOLERANCE

Disagreement with government policies that leads to feelings of cynicism may or may not have any effect on how our political institutions work; a heightened sense of political inefficacy may reveal nothing more than that citizens now have a sharper sense of reality. But if the American political culture does not include a widely shared respect for the essential rules by which politics is carried on, then democratic government may not be possible at all. It is this concern that has led many scholars to investigate whether people accept and support the essential political rights of others—to speak, publish, and peacefully demonstrate. If unpopular speakers are always shouted down, if government efforts to censor newspapers meet with ready public approval, if orderly protest marches are regularly broken up by mobs, then the political liberties on which democratic government depends would be so deeply in jeopardy and so difficult to protect as to make that democracy a sham.

Public opinion surveys provide a complicated picture of popular attitudes toward essential political freedoms and the extent of popular tolerance for controversial activities. First, an overwhelming majority of people interviewed agree with such concepts as free speech, majority rule, and the right to circulate petitions, at least when they are stated in the abstract.[23]

Second, there is much less—but still substantial—support for these principles when people are asked to apply them to specific groups and causes, especially those which are unpopular. Table 4.6 gives the percentage (in 1971) of Americans supporting the right of certain groups to circulate petitions and hold peaceful demonstrations. As is obvious, support for these rights is greatest when the cause is relatively uncontroversial (such as expressing concern about crime in one's neighborhood or pollution from a factory) and least when the cause is highly controversial (such as when the group exercising the rights are "black militants" or "radical students" or the goal is legalizing marijuana). Nonetheless, a clear majority of those interviewed support the right of petitioning and demonstrating for all but one of the causes or groups. (Only "demonstrating to legalize marijuana" had less than majority support.)

TABLE 4.6   Percentage of Americans Willing to Permit Demonstrations and Petitions, by Various Causes

Cause	Percentage Tolerant of	
	Demonstrations	Petitions
About crime in community	81%	95%
About pollution from a factory	80	93
By black militants	61	69
By radical students	60	72
To legalize marijuana	41	52
To protect blacks buying or renting homes in white neighborhoods (asked of whites only)	55	70

Source: David G. Lawrence, "Procedural Norms and Tolerance: A Reassessment," *American Political Science Review*, Vol. 70 (March 1976), p. 88. Reprinted by permission.

Third, popular support for civil liberties, even when exercised by unpopular groups, appears to have increased significantly in the last twenty years or so. In the 1950s at least three studies showed much less support for these political freedoms than that revealed by the 1971 study.[24] For example, in the late 1950s only 44 percent of those responding to one survey were willing to allow a Communist to speak; in 1971, 60 percent were willing to allow "radical students" to hold public demonstrations. In the mid-1950s, 37 percent of the public were willing to tolerate a speech against religion; in 1971, 41 percent were willing to tolerate a demonstration in favor of legalizing marijuana.[25]

Fourth, tolerance of political dissent and support for civil liberties increase as education increases. Table 4.7 shows that, especially on controversial matters, college graduates are much more likely than persons who have only been through grade school to tolerate demonstrations and petitions by black militants and

> **"Popular support for civil liberties, even when exercised by unpopular groups, appears to have increased significantly in the last twenty years or so."**

radical students on behalf of unpopular causes such as integrated housing and legalized marijuana use. This holds true even among those college graduates who happen to dislike militants and radicals or who disapprove of the causes being advocated.[26] Because higher education tends to increase one's level of political tolerance (it also, as we shall see in Chapter 5, increases one's tendency to support "liberal" causes), some of the increase in the public's general level of tolerance during the last twenty years or so is probably due to the increased educational level of that public.

In short, the political culture of Americans supports but does not guarantee the exercise of essential freedoms; thus, those freedoms cannot be safely entrusted to the care of public

TABLE 4.7 Percentage of Americans Tolerating Certain Acts, by Level of Education

Acts	Percentage Tolerant			
	Grade School	Some High School	High School	College
Demonstrations				
By black militants	48%	51%	63%	76%
By radical students	45	48	65	76
For legalized marijuana	24	31	40	64
For integrated housing	33	47	58	76
Petitions				
By black militants	55	60	71	85
By radical students	53	65	76	88
For legalized marijuana	33	45	53	73
For integrated housing	51	47	58	88

Source: David G. Lawrence, "Procedural Norms and Tolerance: A Reassessment," *American Political Science Review*, Vol. 70 (March 1976), p. 88. Reprinted by permission.

Note: When the respondents are divided into those favoring and those opposing a group or policy, the same relationship between education and tolerance tends to occur.

opinion alone. Constitutional protections of minority rights—an important limitation on popular rule—are necessary to ensure that, where the cause is controversial, the divided state of public opinion will not lead to an unjustified denial of freedom.

SUMMARY

The American constitutional system is supported by a democratic political culture that fosters a sense of civic duty, takes pride in the nation's constitutional arrangements, and provides support (though not always overwhelmingly) for the exercise of essential civil liberties. In recent years satisfaction with the behavior of government and confidence in the efficacy of the citizenry have declined, but tolerance for the employment of political liberties on behalf of unpopular causes has increased. The former has occurred despite the increase in educational levels, the latter because of it.

Political culture contributes to both *consensus* (the acceptance of electoral decisions, the absence of mass-based revolutionary parties, and strong support for the constitutional system) and *conflict* (the emphasis on individual rights, the tension between the principles of liberty and equality, the lack of deference to government officials, and the willingness to resist—sometimes violently—government policies).

The political culture gives to American politics a flavor different from that found in many other democratic nations: a preoccupation with rights and an adversary style, revealed by the greater inclination to precipitate conflict—in the courts, in administrative agencies, and in the media.

Suggested Readings

Almond, Gabriel, and Sidney Verba. *The Civic Culture.* Princeton, N.J.: Princeton University Press, 1963. A public opinion survey of the political cultures of five nations—the United States, Germany, Great Britain, Italy, and Mexico—as they were in 1959.

Almond, Gabriel, and Sidney Verba, eds. *The Civic Culture Revisited.* Boston: Little, Brown, forthcoming. A criticism and updating of some of the findings of the original study.

Devine, Donald J. *The Political Culture of the United States.* Boston: Little, Brown, 1972. A summary of several studies about American political values.

Hartz, Louis. *The Liberal Tradition in America.* New York: Harcourt Brace Jovanovich, 1955. A stimulating interpretation of American political thought since the Founding, emphasizing the notion of consensus.

Lipset, Seymour Martin. *The First New Nation.* New York: Basic Books, 1963. How the origins of American society gave rise to the partially competing values of equality and achievement and the way in which these values animate American political institutions.

Potter, David. *People of Plenty.* Chicago: University of Chicago Press, 1954. The consequences for American politics of economic abundance.

Tocqueville, Alexis de. *Democracy in America,* ed. by Phillips Bradley. New York: Alfred A. Knopf, 1951, 2 vols. First published in 1835, this was and remains the single greatest interpretation of the distinctive features of American political culture.

PART II
Opinions, Interests, and Organizations

❝ The latent causes of faction are thus sown in the nature of man; and we see them everywhere brought into different degrees of activity, according to the different circumstances of civil society. ❞

FEDERALIST NO. 10

5 Public Opinion and Political Participation

Democracy and public opinion · Acquiring party identification from parents · Effect of religion, peers, and college · Conducting polls · Cleavages in public opinion · Activists and ideology · Elite opinion · Emergence of a "New Class" · Forms of participation · Why people vote as they do · Effect of opinion on policy

Government in the United States is supposed to be influenced by the opinions and activities of individual citizens, but what that influence is and what it should be are much in dispute. If you believe that the major or sole objective of government is to do "what the people want," then American government falls far short of the ideal, and always will. There is simply no way for a government that each year enacts hundreds of laws, issues thousands of executive and judicial orders, and makes tens of thousands of administrative decisions to discover, much less act upon, some clear idea of the public's opinion.

Indeed, it is impossible for the public as a whole to even have an opinion on more than a small fraction of the matters on which government acts. There are more elections and more elected officials in the United States than in any other country, and this allows those citizens who vote (usually a minority of those eligible to vote) to pass judgment on officials who

Public opinion polls, and even newspapers that were printed too early on election night, guessed wrong in the 1948 presidential contest (left). Since then, opinion polling has improved in quality and grown in importance (right).

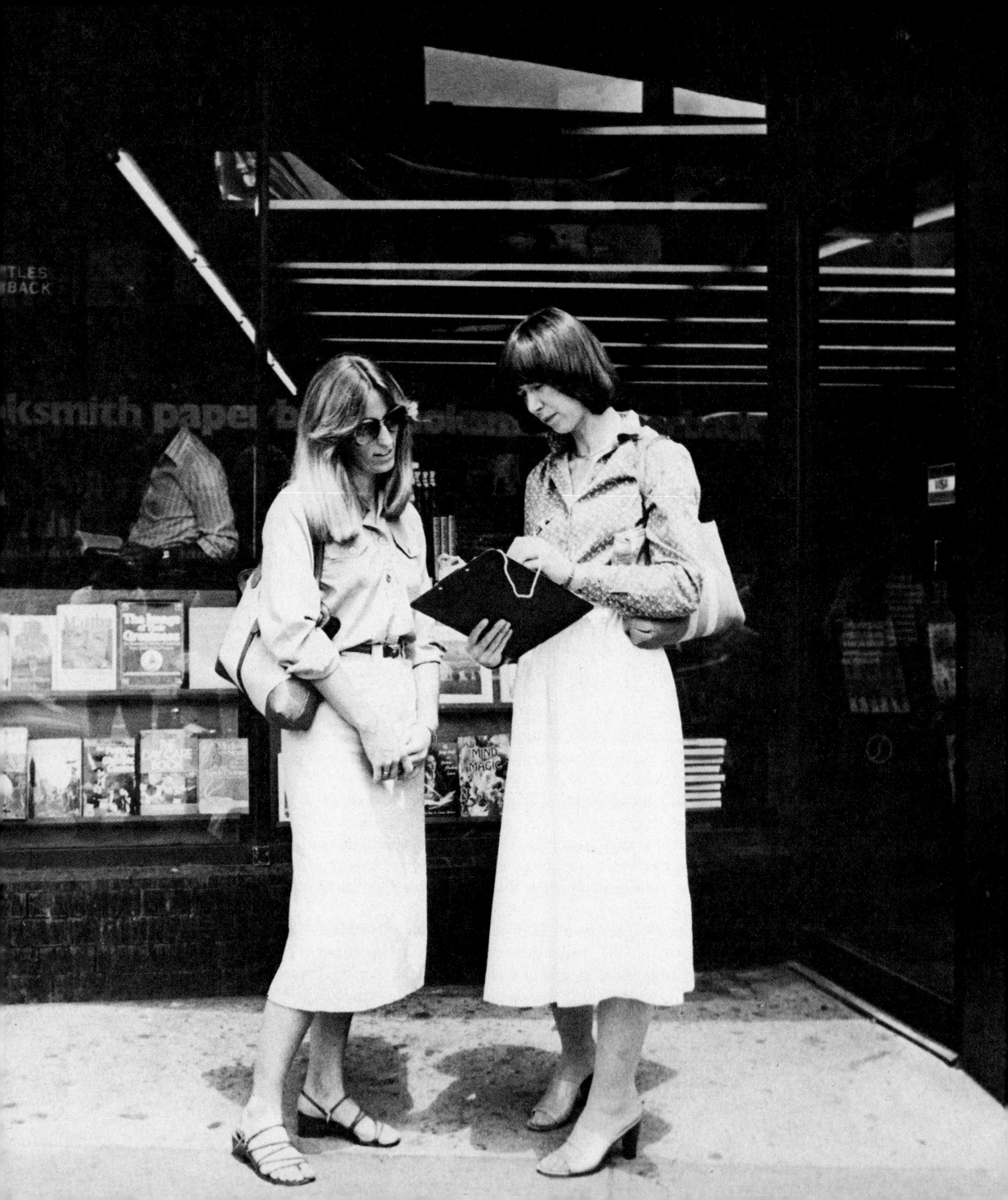
TLES
BACK
ksmith paper
THE DAY CARE BOOK
MIND MAGIC

will make decisions. But important as this popular check on government rule may be, at best it can only be a judgment about the broad outlines of the policies elected officials support or enact.

To the Framers of the Constitution, however, government was not created to do from day to day what the people want; it was created to achieve certain substantive goals that most people share when they think disinterestedly about government. The preamble to the Constitution listed six such goals: union, justice, domestic tranquility, the common defense, the general welfare, and liberty. One means to achieve these goals was popular rule, as provided for by the opportunity to vote for members of the House of Representatives (and, later, for members of the Senate and for presidential electors). But there were other means as well: federalism, the separation of powers, a Bill of Rights, and an independent judiciary. Moreover, the Framers clearly understood that factions and interest groups, rather than the public "as a whole," would be the chief source of opinion on most matters. They hoped, however, that in a nation as large and diverse as the United States there would be so many factions and so complex an array of interests that every relevant opinion would get a hearing, and that for a proposal to succeed it would have to command the support of a broad coalition of groups. Whether their hopes in this regard were realized is a question to which we shall frequently return.

This chapter is concerned, not with the extent to which American politics approaches the unobtainable ideal of direct popular rule, but with the following: (1) the nature and origin of political opinions; (2) the major differences in the opinions of important groups in our society; and (3) the ways in which the opinions of those persons most active in politics (and presumably most influential in policy-making) compare with the opinions of rank-and-file citizens or square with widely shared values.

THE ORIGINS OF POLITICAL ATTITUDES

How we learn our political attitudes is not a question of only academic importance. For a government to be truly responsive to popular opinion, that opinion must, to an important extent, be formed independently of the preferences of persons in power. This can be made clearer by considering an economic analogy: the market for automobiles will only operate efficiently if people can decide for themselves whether they prefer Chevrolets or Fords or Plymouths. If what we think of these cars depends entirely on what the advertising agencies employed by car manufacturers tell us, then how many cars of what kind we buy will depend largely on the money and skill devoted to the advertising campaigns. We would be happy, not because we own a good car, but because Madison Avenue tells us we own a good car.

If political opinion can be largely manipulated by government—by buying up votes, promoting its services, controlling the schools, conducting slick election campaigns—then citizens are no longer in a position to make meaningful choices even in those few cases where the opportunity for a choice is presented. Public opinion is no longer autonomous, but dependent.

Now, just as automobile advertising affects to some degree what cars we buy (though rarely what we think of them after we buy), government action affects to some degree our preferences among public policies. But there are limits to the impact of any kind of advertising, economic or political, at least in a free society.

The Role of the Family
The best-studied (though not necessarily the most important) case of opinion formation is that of party identification. The majority of young persons identify with their parents' political party. A study of high school seniors showed that, of these young men and women, almost all (91 percent) knew accurately the presidential

preference of their parents, the great majority (71 percent) knew accurately their parents' party identification, and most shared that identification (only 7 percent identified with the party opposite to that of their parents).[1] (See Table 5.1.) This process begins fairly early in life: by the time they are in the fifth grade (age eleven), over half of all schoolchildren identify with one party or the other and another fifth claim to be independents.[2]

Naturally, as people grow older they become more independent of their parents in many ways, including politically, but there nonetheless remains a great deal of continuity between youthful partisanship, learned from one's parents, and adult partisanship. One study of adults found that around 60 percent still had the party identification—Democrat, Republican, or independent—of their parents. Of those who differ with at least one parent, the overwhelming majority do so, not by identifying with the opposite party, but by describing themselves as "independents."[3]

The ability of the family to inculcate a strong sense of party identification has declined in recent years. The proportion of citizens who say they consider themselves to be Democrats or Republicans has become steadily smaller since the early 1950s. This drop has been greatest among persons who strongly identify with one party or another. In 1952, 22 percent of the voters said they were strong Democrats and 13 percent said they were strong Republicans; by 1976, only 15 percent claimed to be strong Democrats and 9 percent to be strong Republicans. Accompanying this decline in partisanship has been a sharp rise in the proportion of citizens describing themselves as independents.

Part of this change results from the fact that young voters have always had a weaker sense of partisanship than older ones, and today there are, proportionally, a larger number of young voters than twenty or thirty years ago. But the youthfulness of the population cannot explain

❝So far, the evidence suggests that children are more independent of their parents in policy preferences than in party identification.❞

Young children in Trenton, New Jersey, display the party affiliation learned from their parents.

TABLE 5.1 Parent and Child Agreement in Party Identification

| | Child | | |
Parents	Democrat	Independent	Republican
Democrat	33%	13%	4%
Independent	7	13	4
Republican	3	10	14

Source: M. Kent Jennings and Richard G. Niemi, "The Transmission of Political Values from Parent to Child," *American Political Science Review,* Vol. 62 (March 1968), p. 173. Reprinted by permission.

all of the changes, for the decline in partisanship has occurred at all age levels. Moreover, persons who reached voting age in the 1960s were less likely than those who came of age in the 1950s to acquire or maintain the party identification of their parents.[4]

Religion shapes political attitudes. Chances are that this young Jewish boy, shown at his bar mitzvah party, will grow up to have more liberal attitudes than will a young Protestant boy.

TABLE 5.2 Religion and Political Opinions: Percent "Liberal" Among Northern Whites, by Religion

Issue	Protestant	Catholic	Jewish
Economic and welfare issues			
Tax reform	46%	52%	48%
Domestic spending	73	82	94
Medical care	40	60	77
Guaranteed standard of living	28	35	47
Military spending	17	19	43
Civil rights and civil liberties issues			
Aid to minorities	40	38	56
School busing	9	6	13
Rights of accused	44	37	50
Legalize marijuana	28	34	74
Women's rights	66	71	86
Mean percent liberal, all issues	39%	43%	59%

Source: Center for Political Studies, University of Michigan, 1976 survey, as reported in Robert S. Erikson and Norman G. Luttbeg, *American Public Opinion: Its Origins, Content, and Impact,* 2nd ed. (New York: John Wiley, 1979). Reprinted by permission of John Wiley & Sons, Inc.

Though we still tend to acquire some measure of partisanship from our parents, the meaning of that identification is far from clear. There are, after all, liberal and conservative Democrats, as well as liberal and conservative Republicans. So far, the evidence suggests that children are more independent of their parents in policy preferences than in party identification. The correlation of children's attitudes with parental attitudes on issues involving civil liberties and racial questions is much lower than the correlation of party identification.[5] This may be because issues change from one generation to the next, because children are more idealistic than their parents, or because most parents do not communicate to their children clear, consistent positions on a range of political issues. The family dinner table is not a seminar in political philosophy, but a place where people discuss jobs, school, dates, and chores.

In some families, however, the dinner table *is* a political classroom. Fairly clear political ideologies (a term we shall define in a later section) seem to be communicated to that small proportion of children raised in families where politics is a dominant topic of conversation and political views are strongly held. Studies of the participants in various student radical movements in the 1960s suggested that college radicals were often the sons and daughters of persons who had themselves been young radicals; some commentators dubbed them the "red-diaper babies." Presumably, deeply conservative young persons come disproportionately from families that were also deeply conservative (perhaps they should be called "black-diaper babies"). This transfer of political beliefs from one generation to the next does not appear in large national studies because so small a proportion is at either the far left or the far right of the political spectrum.

Effect of Religion

How the family forms and transmits political attitudes is not well understood, but one important factor seems to be its religious traditions.

In general, Catholic families are somewhat more liberal, especially on economic issues, than white Protestant ones, while Jewish families are decidedly more liberal on both economic and noneconomic issues than either.[6] (See Table 5.2.) Among northern whites, Protestants are likely to be Republican, Catholics are likely to be Democratic, and Jews are overwhelmingly Democratic.[7] This may strike some readers as strange, since in most elections and political debates no explicitly religious questions are at stake. But religion in the United States, and probably elsewhere, conveys to its adherents not simply a set of beliefs about God and morality but also a way of looking at human nature and human affairs. A religious tradition that emphasizes salvation through faith alone, the wickedness of human nature, and the need to avoid personal dissipation and worldly sin is likely to imbue a different way of looking at politics than one that has an optimistic view of human nature, stresses the obligation to do good works, and is concerned as much about social justice as personal rectitude. Moreover, immigrants often had distinctive experiences (Irish and Italian Catholics, for example, came here under different circumstances than Polish and Russian Jews), and the memory of these experiences may well become part of an ethnic and religious tradition that is handed down from one generation to the next.

One might suppose that the public schools would rival the family as a source of political attitudes, and perhaps, because public schools are instruments of government, they would be a more manipulative source. While it is true that how a child thinks in general terms of government tends, during the elementary grades, to become more like the views of his or her teacher, there is as yet not much hard evidence that schools implant any distinctive political orientation, or at least one that is sharply different from what is learned in the home.[8]

Peer Influence

Friendship groups formed in the neighborhood, the schoolyard, or the workplace also influence political attitudes. They can have the effect of modifying or weakening family influence, though not as greatly as one might suppose. In Table 5.3 we see the extent to which high school students agree or disagree with parents and friends on a

---

TABLE 5.3 Agreement Between High School Students and Their Friends and Parents

	Party identification	1964 presidential vote	Political trust	Political efficacy	18-year-old vote
Overall agreement with					
Friends	52%	78%	62%	72%	66%
Parents	72	83	66	57	55
When friends and parents disagree, agreement with					
Friends	12[a]	42	46	65	62
Parents	64	58	54	35	38

Source: Suzanne Koprince Sebert, M. Kent Jennings, and Richard G. Niemi, "The Political Texture of Peer Groups," from M. Kent Jennings and Richard G. Niemi, *The Political Character of Adolescence* (Princeton, N.J.: Princeton University Press, 1974), p. 246. Copyright © 1974 by Princeton University Press. Reprinted by permission of Princeton University Press.

[a]This pair of figures will, unlike the others in these two rows, equal less than 100 percent. This is because party identification was not treated as a dichotomous variable, whereas the others were.

number of issues. The crucial test is what happens when a student must deal with disagreements between the political views of parents and friends. When the disagreement is over party identification or presidential preference, the student tends to side with the parents over the friends. When the issue is whether eighteen-year-olds should vote or whether one has a strong sense of political "efficacy" (i.e., feels able to cope with political affairs and to have an impact on decisions), the student, not surprisingly, is more likely to agree with friends than with parents.

At one time disagreements between the old and the young were described as a "generation gap." Youths were portrayed as more liberal and even radical, more opposed to existing institutions, more hostile to conventional values, and more opposed to the war in Vietnam than their elders. In fact, most of these conclusions were journalistic exaggerations. Young people naturally are a bit less concerned with economic security and a bit more concerned with personal friendships than are adults, but no great "gap" in political attitudes exists.[9] Indeed, as we shall see in Chapter 20, young persons were *less* likely to be opposed to the war in Vietnam than were older persons.

Effect of Education

There is one institutional experience, however, that does have a marked effect on political attitudes, and that is college. Studies going back over half a century seem to show that attending college makes a difference, usually in a liberal direction. College students are more liberal than the population generally, and students at the most prestigious or selective colleges are the most liberal of all.[10] Students studying the social sciences tend to be more liberal—and to become even more liberal as time goes on—than those studying engineering or the physical sciences.[11] Students become more liberal the longer they remain in college, with seniors more liberal than freshmen and graduate students more liberal than seniors.[12]

These changes in political attitudes tend to persist beyond the end of college. One study found that former college students still described themselves as more liberal than their parents seven years after graduation.[13] Another study found that students who changed from being conservative to being liberal tended to maintain that liberalism for at least twenty years after graduation.[14] Since college graduates tend, as adults, to be better-off financially than those who did not attend college, and since better-off persons are more likely to be Republicans, the persistence of the liberalizing effect of college

---

TABLE 5.4 Automobiles and Ideology: Kinds of Automobiles Owned by College Faculty Members Who Have Differing Political Ideologies (in percent)

Brand of Automobile	Most Liberal 1	2	3	4	Most Conservative 5
GM	12%	18%	18%	23%	29%
Ford	15	19	20	22	24
Chrysler	19	22	18	21	20
AMC	21	17	12	23	26
Japanese	22	22	17	20	18
Volkswagen	26	26	16	17	15
Fiat	27	18	30	11	13
Leyland	27	31	15	15	12
Mercedes-Benz	32	19	21	17	11
Volvo	32	19	18	18	14
No car	31	28	23	11	7

Source: Data from survey of faculty opinion by Everett Carll Ladd, Jr., and Seymour Martin Lipset, 1975. B. Bruce-Briggs, *The War Against the Automobile* (New York: E. P. Dutton, 1977), p. 184. Reprinted by permission.

Note: The more liberal the faculty member, the more likely he is to own no car or an imported car, especially a Volvo or a Mercedes-Benz. The more conservative the faculty member, the more likely he is to own an American car, especially a General Motors product.

seems puzzling or even contradictory. Later in this chapter we shall offer an explanation of this apparent paradox.

No one is entirely certain why college has the effect it does, but the attitudes and role of the faculty are surely an important part of the explanation. Professors are more liberal than members of other occupations, professors at the most prestigious schools are more liberal than those at the less-celebrated ones, professors in the social sciences more liberal than those in engineering or business, and younger faculty members are more liberal than older ones.[15] (College faculty members often develop a life-style that reveals their political convictions. As shown in Table 5.4, a professor who drives a Volvo or Mercedes tends to be politically more liberal than one who drives a Chevrolet or Ford.)

The political disposition of professors is in part the result of the kinds of persons who become college teachers, but it is also the result of the nature of intellectual work. Intellectuals require freedom to explore new or unpopular ideas and thus tend to be strong supporters of civil liberties. Intellectuals work with words and numbers to develop general or abstract ideas; frequently they do not take personal responsibility for practical matters. Thus, they are often critical of persons who do take such responsibility and who, in the management of complex human affairs, inevitably make compromises. Intellectuals are by training and profession skeptical of common opinions, and thus they are often critical of accepted values and existing institutions. They are interested in ideas and the ideal and thus are sometimes disdainful of the interests and institutions of society.

At one time the liberalizing effect of college had only a small impact on national politics because so few persons were college graduates. In 1900 only 6 percent of Americans seventeen years of age had even graduated from high school, and less than 1 percent of twenty-three-year-olds were college graduates. By 1970, 76

"College has become, along with the family, an important source of political opinion for the American electorate."

The importance of college as a source of political ideas has grown with the rapid increase in college enrollments.

percent of all Americans of age seventeen were high school graduates, and 22 percent of those of age twenty-three were college graduates.[16] College has become, along with the family, an important source of political opinion for the American electorate.

CLEAVAGES IN PUBLIC OPINION

The way in which political opinions are formed helps explain the cleavages that exist among these opinions and why these cleavages do not follow any single political principle, but instead overlap and cross-cut in bewildering complexity.

If, for example, the United States were composed almost entirely of white Protestants, the
great majority of whom did not attend college,
and all of whom lived in the North, there would
still be plenty of political conflict—the rich would
have different views from the poor, the workers
different views from the farmers—but that conflict would be much simpler to describe and
explain. It might even lead to political parties
that were more clearly aligned with competing
political philosophies than those we now have.
In fact, of course, some democratic nations in
the world today do have a population very much
like the one I have asked you to imagine, and
the United States itself, during the first half of
the nineteenth century, was overwhelmingly
white, Protestant, and without much formal
schooling.

Today, however, there can be found cross-
cutting cleavages based on race, ethnicity, religion, region, and education, in addition to those
created by income and occupation. To the extent
politics is sensitive to public opinion, it is sensitive to a variety of different and even competing
publics. Not all these publics have influence
proportionate to their numbers or even to their
numbers adjusted for the intensity of their feelings. As will be described later, a filtering process
occurs that makes the opinions of some publics
more influential than those of others.

Whatever this state of affairs may mean for
democracy, it creates a messy situation for political scientists. It would be so much easier if everyone's opinion on political affairs reflected some
single feature of one's life—one's income, occupation, age, race, or sex. Of course, some writers have argued that political opinion *is* a reflection of one such feature, social class, usually
defined in terms of income or occupation, but
that view, though containing some truth, is be-
set with inconsistencies—poor blacks and poor
whites disagree sharply on many issues involving
race, well-to-do Jews and well-to-do Protestants
often have opposing opinions on social welfare
policy, and low-income elderly people are much

pretend we know things that in fact we don't, or to be helpful to interviewers by inventing opinions on the spur of the moment.

Third, *the questions must be asked fairly*—in clear language, without the use of "loaded" or "emotional" words. They must give no indication of what the "right" answer is, but offer a reasonable explanation, where necessary, of the consequences of each possible answer. For example, in 1971 the Gallup Poll asked people whether they favored a proposal "to bring home all U.S. troops [from Vietnam] before the end of the year." Two-thirds of the public agreed with that. Then the question was asked in a different way: Do you agree or disagree with a proposal to withdraw all U.S. troops by the end of the year "regardless of what happens there [in Vietnam] after U.S. troops leave"? In this form, substantially less than half the public agreed.

Fourth, *the answer categories offered to a person must be carefully considered.* This is no problem when there are only two candidates for office—say, Jimmy Carter and Gerald Ford—and you want only to know which one the voters prefer. But it can be a big problem when you want more complex information. For example, if you ask people (as does George Gallup) whether they "approve" or "disapprove" of how the president is handling his job, you will get one kind of answer—let us say that 55 percent approve and 45 percent disapprove. On the other hand, if you ask them (as does Louis Harris) how they rate the job the president is doing, "excellent, pretty good, only fair, or poor," you will get very different results. It is quite possible that only 46 percent will pick such positive answers as "excellent" or "pretty good," and the rest will pick the negative answers, "only fair" and "poor." If you

are president, you can choose to believe Mr. Gallup (and feel pleased) or Mr. Harris (and be worried). The differences in the two polls do not arise from the competence of the two pollsters, but entirely from the choice of answers that they include with their questions.

Finally, it is important to remember that not every difference in answers is a significant difference. A survey is based on a sample of people. Select another sample, by equally randomized methods, and you might get slightly different results. This difference is called a *sampling error*, and its likely size can be computed mathematically. In general, the bigger the sample and the bigger the differences between the percentage of people giving one answer and the percentage giving another, the smaller the sampling error. In a poll of 1,500 persons in which 51 percent said they favored Jimmy Carter and 49 percent said they favored Gerald Ford, the *true* division of opinion among *all* voters might vary by as much as 3 percentage points, so that in fact somewhere between 48 and 54 percent actually favor Carter. The size of that sampling error can be reduced with bigger samples, but the cost of getting a sample big enough to make the error much smaller is huge.

As a result of sampling error and for other reasons, it is very hard for pollsters to predict the winner in a close election. Since 1952 every major national poll has in fact picked the winner of the presidential election, but there may have been some luck involved in such close races as the 1960 Kennedy-Nixon and the 1976 Carter-Ford contests. The best use of polls is not to predict elections but to find out what people think about those candidates and issues on which they are reasonably well informed.

Two views of the Equal Rights Amendment.

more worried about crime than are low-income graduate students. Plumbers and professors may have similar incomes, but they rarely have similar views, and businessmen in New York City often take a very different view of government from businessmen in Houston or Birmingham.

In some other democracies, a single factor such as class may explain more of the differences in political attitudes than it does in the more socially heterogeneous United States. Manual workers in England prefer the Labour party by a margin of three to one, whereas white-collar and professional workers prefer the Conservative party by a similar margin.[17] In the United States manual workers prefer the Democratic party, but not by so large a margin, and nonmanual workers such as managers and executives are shifting away from the Republican party.[18]

Occupations

Indeed, there is some evidence that occupation is becoming less important as an explanation of political opinions in this country. In the 1950s V. O. Key, Jr., found differences in opinion on current political issues to be closely associated with occupation: persons holding managerial or professional jobs had distinctly more conservative views on social welfare policy and more internationalist views on foreign policy than did persons having jobs as manual workers.[19] For example, professional and business persons in 1952 were much more likely than manual workers to say that the government was doing "too much" in trying to deal with problems such as unemployment, education, and housing; much less likely to favor government provision of low-cost health care; and somewhat more likely to support American involvement with problems in other parts of the world.[20]

During the next decade this pattern changed greatly. Opinion surveys taken in the late 1960s showed that business and professional persons had views quite similar to those of most manual workers on such matters as the poverty program, health insurance, American policy in Vietnam, and government efforts to create jobs.[21] There remained some differences, naturally—unskilled workers had more liberal views on economic issues than did any other occupational category, and business persons differed sharply from others on the merits of price controls and in their support for foreign aid. But over a long period of time—the data go back to the 1930s—the correlation between occupation and policy preferences (and between income and policy preferences) has become steadily weaker. No one is quite certain why this has happened, but it is probably due in part to the changing effects of education on all levels of society but especially on persons entering higher status occupations.

Race

If occupation has become less important in explaining political attitudes, race has become more important. It is hardly surprising that blacks and whites differ on a number of matters. Over the last thirty or forty years the extent of those differences has narrowed on some issues and widened on others. What may be surprising is that the differences are not limited to issues involving race. Table 5.5 shows the opinion of whites and blacks on several issues as of 1968. There was substantial disagreement not only over desegregation and the speed with which civil rights leaders were pressing for change but also over government job guarantees, trade with Communist nations, policy in Vietnam, and protest activity.[22]

One study compared attitudes of blacks in five issue areas during the 1970s with their attitudes during the 1950s. Whereas blacks had expressed quite liberal views on these matters

in the earlier period, they had become even more liberal by the later period. No other definable social group had become as consistently liberal during these two decades and no other group had become as strongly supportive of the Democratic party.[23]

As we shall see in Chapter 19, white opposition to extending equal opportunity to blacks in such areas as housing, employment, and schooling has declined significantly since the

---

TABLE 5.5 Opinions of Blacks and Whites on Public Issues, 1968

Issue and Position	*Percent Support Among Opinion Holders*	
	Whites	Blacks
The government should see to it that every person has a job and a good standard of living	34%	88%
Our farmers and businessmen should be allowed to do business with Communist countries	43	65
Do not disapprove of all protest meetings or marches that are permitted by local authorities	43	73
Oppose stronger Vietnam stand that might mean invading North Vietnam	60	81
On relations between the races: there should be—		
desegregation	33	78
strict segregation	17	4
something in between	50	18
On whether civil rights leaders are pushing too fast:		
not fast enough	5	63
too fast	71	8
about right	24	29

Source: Robert S. Erikson and Norman G. Luttbeg, *American Public Opinion* (New York: John Wiley, 1973), pp. 186–187. Reprinted by permission of John Wiley & Sons, Inc.

1940s. A large majority of whites today give at least verbal support to integrationist beliefs and values that many of them would have opposed two or three decades ago. Despite this change, there remains a wide gulf between black and white opinions on many issues of national politics. There is a much smaller gulf, or no gulf at all, between the races on some matters of local concern, however. For example, in 1972 large and virtually identical majorities of blacks and whites favored stricter police measures and stiffer court sentences to deal with crime.[24] Blacks and whites also have similar views on abortion.

Region

It is widely believed that geographic region affects political attitudes and in particular that Southerners and Northerners disagree importantly on many policy questions. As we will see,

southern congressmen tend to vote differently—and more conservatively—than northern ones,[25] and it should stand to reason that this is because their constituents, southern voters, expect them to vote differently. The available evidence suggests this difference among regions is greatest for noneconomic issues. In Table 5.6 we can compare the proportion of white Protestants in each of four regions of the country who gave liberal answers to questions regarding economic/welfare issues and civil liberties/civil rights issues in 1976. (The table is limited to white Protestants to eliminate the effect of the very different proportions of blacks, Catholics, and Jews living in the various regions.) Southerners were conspicuously less liberal than Easterners, Midwesterners, or Westerners, chiefly on such questions as aid to minorities, legalizing marijuana, school busing, and enlarging the rights of persons accused of crimes.

This helps to explain why the South was for so long a part of the Democratic party coalition: on national economic and social welfare policies (and on foreign policy), Southerners express views not very different from Northerners. That coalition is threatened, however, by the divisiveness produced by issues of race and liberty.

The southern life-style is different from that of the Northeast, as is readily apparent to anyone who has lived in both regions. The South has, on the whole, been more accommodating to business enterprise and less accommodating to organized labor than the Northeast; it has given greater support to the third-party candidacy of George Wallace, which was a form of protest against big government and the growth of national political power as well as against civil rights; and it was in the South that the greatest opposition arose to income redistribution plans, such as the Family Assistance Plan of 1969 (to be discussed in Chapter 17). Moreover, there is some evidence that white Southerners became by the 1970s more conservative than they had been in the 1950s, at least when compared to

TABLE 5.6   Regional Differences in Political Opinions: Percent Giving "Liberal" Response Among White Protestants, 1976

Issue	East	Midwest	South	West
Economic and welfare issues				
Tax reform	45%	47%	44%	44%
Domestic spending	75	72	73	74
Medical care	49	34	39	43
Guaranteed standard of living	35	28	33	24
Military spending	41	37	34	41
Civil rights and civil liberties issues				
Aid to minorities	50	35	27	40
School busing	10	7	2	11
Rights of accused	40	41	32	51
Legalize marijuana	27	26	17	32
Women's rights	64	64	58	72
Mean percent liberal, all issues	41%	37%	34%	41%

Source: Center for Political Studies, University of Michigan, 1976 survey, as reported in Robert S. Erikson and Norman G. Luttbeg, *American Public Opinion: Its Origins, Content, and Impact,* 2nd ed. (New York: John Wiley, 1979). Reprinted by permission of John Wiley & Sons, Inc.

white Northerners.[26] Finally, white Southerners have become less attached to the Democratic party: whereas over three-fourths described themselves as Democrats in 1952, less than half did by 1972.[27]

These changes in the South can have great significance, as we shall see in the next two chapters when we consider how elections are fought out. It is enough for now to remember that, without the votes of the southern states, no Democrat except Lyndon Johnson in 1964 would have been elected president from 1940 through 1976. (Without the South, Roosevelt would have lost in 1944, Truman in 1948, Kennedy in 1960, and Carter in 1976. And even though Carter carried the South, he did not win a majority of white southern votes.)[28]

POLITICAL IDEOLOGY

To now, the words "liberal" and "conservative" have been used as if everyone agreed what they meant and as if they accurately described general sets of political beliefs held by large segments of the population. Neither of these assumptions is correct. Like many useful words—love, peace, happiness—they are as vague as they are indispensable.

When we refer to persons as liberals, conservatives, socialists, or radicals, we are implying that they have a patterned set of beliefs about how government and other important institutions in fact operate and how they ought to operate, and in particular about what kinds of policies government ought to pursue. They are said to display to some degree a political *ideology*—that is, a coherent and consistent set of beliefs about who ought to rule, what principles rulers ought to obey, and what policies rulers ought to pursue. (There are other definitions of ideology; to Marx, for example, "ideology" meant a set of ideas that constituted a rationalization of the economic interest of a person or class.) Political scientists measure the extent to which people

have a political ideology in two ways: first, by seeing how frequently people use broad political categories (such as "liberal," "conservative," "radical") to describe their own views or to justify their preferences for various candidates and policies and, second, by seeing to what extent the policy preferences of a citizen are consistent over time or based at any one time on certain consistent principles. This second method involves a simple mathematical procedure: measuring how accurately one can predict a person's view on a subject at one time from having known his or her view on that subject at an earlier time or measuring how accurately one can predict a person's view on one issue from knowing his or her view on a different issue. The higher the accuracy of such predictions (or correlations), the more we say a person's political opinions display "constraint" or ideology.

Most studies of public opinion suggest that the great majority of citizens display relatively little ideology in their thinking, however that term is defined or measured. According to a leading study, people do not usually employ words like "liberal" or "conservative" in explaining or justifying their preferences for candidates or policies, not many more than half can give plausible meanings for these terms, and there are relatively low correlations among the answers to similar questions given by people at different points in time and to comparable questions asked at one point in time. From this, many scholars have concluded that the great majority of Americans do not think about politics in an ideological or even a very coherent manner and make little use of such concepts, so dear to political commentators and professors, as "liberal" or "conservative."[29]

Consistent Attitudes

This does not settle the question entirely, however. Critics of the view that Americans are nonideological have argued that people can have general, and strongly felt, political predispositions even though they are not able to use

Busing children in order to integrate public schools is a deeply controversial issue, but it divides people along different lines than would an economic issue such as employment.

say what constitutes a "consistent" set of positions? A voter might well believe that he or she was being quite consistent if, for example, he or she favored both strong government efforts on behalf of various social programs and a tough government stance toward Communist nations.

Finally, some scholars argue that the dramatic events of the 1960s—the civil rights revolution, the war in Vietnam, the riots and protest demonstrations—increased the extent to which voters followed coherent ideological lines. They point to surveys taken in the 1960s and early 1970s that seem to show that Americans were more likely, compared to the 1950s, to give "consistent" answers to policy questions. The big increase in ideological thinking apparently occurred in 1964, when the election for president offered about as clear a choice as one could imagine between a defender of a large, activist federal government (Lyndon Johnson) and a staunch critic of such a government (Barry Goldwater).[31] Other scholars disagree with this interpretation, arguing that changes in the way the questions were worded on opinion polls taken during the 1950s and 1960s makes any comparison invalid. People did not give more "consistent" or ideological answers to questions in 1964 than they did in 1956; rather, they simply gave answers to different questions.[32] It is hard to judge this argument, but a fair summary might be this: there is evidence of some increase in the extent to which citizens are self-consciously "liberal" or "conservative," but the extent of that change and the meaning of those terms to the citizens are still very much in dispute.

Our understanding of how the American public views political issues remains incomplete. No doubt a large fraction of the public is poorly informed on policies, parties, and candidates. There is also little evidence that more than a minority use the ideological categories employed by intellectuals and political activists to describe their own political views or those of others. (The proportion who do so, however, seems to have increased during the 1960s.) Nor do most people

such terms as "liberal" correctly. Moreover, public opinion polls must, of necessity, ask rather simple questions, and the apparent "inconsistency" in the answers people give in different time periods may show that the nature of the problem and the wording of the question have changed in ways not obvious to persons analyzing the surveys.[30]

What constitutes "consistency" is very much in the mind of the observer. For example, citizens are regarded as having "consistent" or "ideological" views if they want the government to have larger social welfare programs, help blacks, enforce school integration, and avoid taking a tough line against Communist nations. These are all considered to be "liberal" views. (Persons would also be described as having "consistent" or "ideological" opinions if they took the opposite position on each of these questions; they would then be called "conservatives.") But all this is a bit arbitrary—who is to

Senator Barry Goldwater in 1964 ran as an ideologically conservative candidate for president and lost badly.

take positions on issues that intellectuals define as "consistent," though, again, the proportion who are consistent in this way increased in the 1960s.

Activists

Political activists, on the other hand, are much more likely than the average citizen to think in ideological terms and to take "consistent" positions on various issues. One scholar found that candidates for Congress in 1958 took "consistent" positions on domestic and foreign policy issues much more frequently than the public at large.[33] (Unfortunately, we have no attitude studies of such candidates since 1958, but there is little reason to suppose that their views have become less structured or constrained.) In part, this may be the result simply of better information—activists spend all or most of their time on political affairs and they may see relationships among issues that others do not. In part, it may also reflect the kinds of persons with whom activists associate: politics, contrary to popular lore, does not ordinarily make strange bedfellows, rather it brings like-minded people together. People who have a similar political outlook on some matters will tend, as a consequence of frequent association with each other and a desire to eliminate sources of friction, to develop outlooks that are similar on most or all matters. And activists have more structured opinions because, in part, the motives that lead them to engage in politics arise in many cases out of strong convictions about how the country ought to be run—that is to say, out of having a political ideology to begin with.

THE CATEGORIES OF OPINION: "LIBERALS" AND "CONSERVATIVES"

The words most frequently used to describe people who have a patterned set of beliefs about politics are "liberal" and "conservative." Unfortunately, these terms have a long and complicated history, and their casual usage today often creates more confusion than clarity. In the early nineteenth century, when these words first came into circulation in Europe, a "liberal" was a person who favored personal and economic liberty—that is, freedom from the controls and powers of the state. An economic liberal, for example, supported the free market and opposed government regulations of trade. A "conservative" was originally a person who opposed the excesses of the French Revolution and its emphasis on personal freedom, and favored instead a restoration of the power of the state, the church, and the aristocracy.

Beginning around the time of Franklin Roosevelt and the New Deal, the meaning of these terms began to change. Roosevelt used the term "liberal" to refer to his political program—one that called for an active national government that would intervene in the economy, create social welfare programs, and assist certain groups (such as organized labor) to acquire greater bargaining power. In time, the opponents of an activist national government began using the term "conservative" to describe themselves. (Barry Goldwater, in 1964, was the first major politician to proclaim himself a conservative.) In general, a conservative favored a free market rather than a regulated one, states' rights over national supremacy, and greater reliance on individual choice in economic affairs.

Though the meaning of these terms changed, they did not in the process become more precise. Two persons may describe themselves as liberals even though the first favors both the welfare state and a strong national defense and the second favors the welfare state but wants a sharp reduction in military spending. Similarly, one conservative may favor enforcement of laws against drug abuse and another may believe that the government should let people decide for themselves what drugs to take. Once, liberals favored laws guaranteeing equality of opportunity among the races; now, some liberals favor "affirmative action" plans involving racial quotas or goals. Once, conservatives opposed American intervention abroad; today, many conservatives believe the United States should play an active role in foreign affairs.

In view of this confusion, one is tempted to throw up one's hands in disgust and consign words like "liberal" and "conservative" to the garbage can. While understandable, such a reaction would be a mistake because, in spite of their ambiguities, these words remain in general use, convey some significant meaning, and point to real differences between, for example, the liberal and conservative wings of the Democratic and Republican parties. Our task is to clarify these differences by showing the particular meanings these words have.

Various Categories

We can imagine certain broad categories of opinion to which different persons subscribe. These categories are found by analyzing the answers people give to dozens of questions about political issues. Different analysts come up with slightly different categories, but on the whole there is a substantial amount of agreement. Three categories in particular have proved useful.

The first involves questions about government policy toward the economy. We will describe as "liberal" those persons who favor government efforts to ensure that everyone has a job, to spend more money on medical and educational programs, and to increase rates of taxation for well-to-do persons.

The second involves questions about civil rights and race relations. We will describe as "liberal" those persons who favor strong federal action to desegregate schools, to increase hiring opportunities for minorities, to provide compensatory programs for minorities, and to enforce strictly civil rights laws.

The third involves questions about public and political conduct. We will describe as "liberal" those persons who are tolerant of protest demonstrations, who favor legalizing marijuana and in other ways wish to "decriminalize" so-called "victimless crimes," who emphasize protecting the rights of the accused over punishing criminals, and who see the solution to crime in eliminating its causes rather than in getting tough with offenders.

Analyzing Consistency

Now, it is obvious that a person can take a liberal position on one of these issues and, without feeling in the slightest degree "inconsistent," take a conservative position on the others. Several studies, such as those by Seymour Martin Lipset and Earl Rabb and James A. Stimson,[34] suggest that this is exactly what most citizens do. Lipset and Rabb, for example, analyzed the characteristics of persons who embraced each of the four possible combinations of belief on economic and cultural tolerance issues. They found that certain groups were more likely than others to embrace a particular combination of views, though no single group expressed one combination to the exclusion of all others. For example, persons who are liberal on economic issues but conservative on cultural tolerance ones are more likely to be manual workers, to have a high school education or less, and to be female. Persons who are conservative on economic issues but liberal on cultural tolerance ones, on the other hand, are more likely to be in business, to have a college education, and to be male. Persons who are liberal on both economic and cultural questions are more likely to be college-educated persons in professional occupations, while those who are conservative on both economic and cultural issues are more likely to be Southerners who were raised on a farm and who belong to fundamentalist Protestant churches.

There are, it must be stressed, many exceptions to these patterns, and many persons do not fit into any of these categories. Moreover, the classification scheme would become even more complicated if additional issues were added—for example, foreign policy. Nevertheless, the notion that there are several categories of opinions and that these categories are packaged together in different ways by different people can help us understand the diversity of political opinion in the United States and the difficulty in putting together a coalition of groups that can obtain passage of a new law or secure the victory of a candidate for election.

For example: the Democratic party consists of an enormously diverse array of persons who, to oversimplify, can be described in terms of the following "policy packages":

Liberal on economic policy and civil rights, conservative on law and order
  Example: Many members of organized labor; most blacks

Liberal on economic policy, conservative on civil rights and law-and-order issues
  Example: Followers of George Wallace; small-town Southerners

Liberal on economic policy, civil rights, and law-and-order issues
  Example: Intellectuals

" Though the average citizen cannot be described as being purely "liberal" or purely "conservative," it is important to bear in mind that political activists often *do* display a great deal of attitude consistency. **"**

This young McGovern worker displays a concern for issues ("peace") that is stronger than that shown by most rank-and-file voters.

A comparable variety of policy packages can be found in the Republican party. Obviously, trying to keep these groups united behind a single presidential candidate or a single legislative program can be excruciatingly difficult. Just as obviously, it would be absurd to describe the resulting coalition as being "liberal" or "conservative" *as a whole.*

Though the average citizen cannot be described as being purely "liberal" or purely "conservative," it is important to bear in mind that political activists often *do* display a great deal of attitude consistency. In other words, if they are liberal on one set of issues, they are likely

66 At one time . . . persons who ranked high in education and income held more conservative views than those who lacked these advantages. . . . By the mid-1960s this had begun to change dramatically. 99

These businessmen of the 1930s were probably conservative Republicans. Those who comprise the elite groups of today—such as research scientists, college instructors, government officials, journalists—are more likely to be liberal and Democratic.

to be liberal on all others, and if they are conservative on one set of issues, they are likely to be conservative on all others. We have already seen this to be the case with congressional candidates. This tendency toward ideological thinking is also characteristic of voters who have the highest levels of education and the most information about politics and government.[35]

The informed, educated voter is more likely to see all issues in a left-right perspective and to vote on that basis. Since such persons are more likely to vote and otherwise participate in politics than uninformed, uneducated persons, the former's ideology is more important than their numbers might indicate. Candidates, activists, and knowledgeable followers of politics may, thus, impart to political decision-making a greater degree of ideological consistency than

the average voter wishes. This may be one reason (though surely not the only one) why some policies preferred by voters get filtered out by the process of political representation.

POLITICAL ELITES AND THE "NEW CLASS"

If the persons who were elected or appointed to office or who occupied positions of influence in the political parties were exact replicas of the average voter (or the average Democratic or Republican voter), our analysis of public opinion would be nearly at an end. Those in power would think and act as would the average voter, were he or she in their place.

But obviously those in power are different from the average voter—we have already seen that congressmen, bureaucrats, and judges are more likely than the average voter to be males, college graduates, and reasonably well paid. Later in this chapter we shall review evidence that those who participate the most in politics are different in other important ways from the average citizen. No study of opinion is complete, therefore, without a study of elite opinion as well as mass opinion.

By "elite" we do not mean people who are "better" than other people. "Elite" is a technical term used by social scientists to describe persons who have a disproportionate amount of some valued social resource—money, schooling, prestige, political power, or whatever. Every society, capitalist or Communist, has an elite because in every society government officials will have more power than ordinary citizens, some persons will earn more money than others, and some persons will have more prestige (because of popularity, beauty, wealth, athletic prowess, artistic talents, or political power) than others.

At one time American elites were overwhelmingly conservative and Republican. Persons who ranked high in education and income held more conservative views than those who lacked these advantages. Even more important, college education and high incomes tended to produce similar effects. (For example, a clear majority of Harvard college students—and probably of most college students—preferred Republican candidates for president during most elections right up to the early 1960s.)[36] Those who went to college, especially private colleges, tended to come from well-to-do families, and college had only a moderate liberalizing effect on these persons.

Shift to Liberalism

By the mid-1960s this had begun to change dramatically. Certain elite groups were becoming much more liberal, so much so that one could no longer take for granted that anybody with a high income or a professional occupation

A Tale of Two Counties

If you thought that people vote on the basis of their incomes and occupations, you would expect the citizens of Marin County (in Northern California) and Orange County (in Southern California) to behave pretty much alike. In 1970 both counties had family incomes that were distinctly above the average ($12,238 in Orange, $13,931 in Marin). In each county, about one-third of the work force had professional or managerial jobs. Both are overwhelmingly white.

But politically, they are poles apart. Barry Goldwater carried Orange County but lost Marin County in 1964. George McGovern in 1972 received 46 percent of the Marin County vote but only 27 percent of the Orange County vote. In the 1972 Democratic primary election, McGovern swept Marin County while his rival, Hubert Humphrey, easily carried Orange County.

Marin County is heavily populated with members of the liberal New Class; Orange County is filled with persons who are much more conservative. Some of the difference may be accounted for by education—whereas 27 percent of Marin County adults are college graduates, only 16 percent of Orange County adults are. But much of the difference is rooted in the very different life-style and family experiences of the two communities.

Marin County is liberal, upper-middle-class, and with family and educational ties to the East Coast and to prestige universities. Orange County is conservative, upwardly mobile, and with family ties to the Midwest and South. Marin County residents are more likely to drive foreign cars, Orange County residents to drive American ones.

These two counties—and similar communities elsewhere—reveal the kinds of cultural cleavages that divide the American middle class.

Source: Adapted from William Schneider, "The New Moralism," Politics Today, November–December 1978, pp. 12–13.

was a conservative. Figure 5.1, developed by Everett Carll Ladd, Jr., shows the change over three decades in the degree of identification with the Democratic party and the likelihood of voting for Democratic congressional candidates for three groups of voters: persons with a college education, business executives, and whites under age thirty with higher-than-average incomes. Throughout the 1940s and 1950s, each of these three groups was less Democratic in its prefer-

FIGURE 5.1   The Upper Middle Class Abandons the G.O.P.

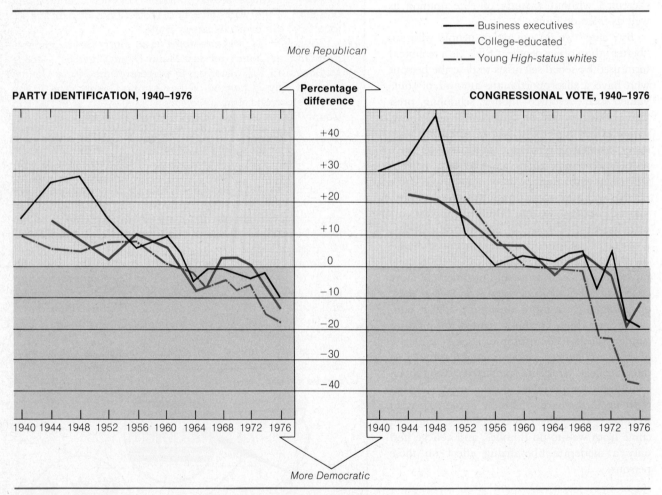

Note: As those descending lines make clear, the American upper middle class, once strongly Republican, has defected to the Democratic party in terms both of partisan self-identification (the chart on the left) and of congressional voting (right). The lines represent the percentage difference between Republican support and Democratic support in three upper-middle-class groups—business executives, the college-educated, and young whites with high socioeconomic status. Republican leads are shown above the zero line, Democratic leads below it.

ences than the average citizen. Beginning around 1964, they became more Democratic than the average person and, with some temporary reversals around 1968–1970, that trend has continued. Ladd calls this change a "class inversion," by which he means that certain measures—such as education and occupation—of a higher social class are no longer a reliable indication of Republican or conservative political views.[37]

This change should not be overstated. Well-off business leaders continue to have more conservative views on many economic issues than manual workers or lower income blacks. In 1976, for example, there was a difference of 12 or 13 percentage points in the rate at which high-status whites and low-status whites supported Democratic presidential and congressional candidates, with the former giving less support than the latter.[38] But in 1948 that gap had been on the order of 30 percentage points.

The change in attitude on some specific issues helps illustrate the point. In 1940 people were asked in a poll whether the federal government should regulate business more or less than it was doing; in 1961 a similar question was asked. As can be seen from Table 5.7, persons holding professional or managerial jobs were strongly opposed in 1940 to more government regulation and disagreed sharply with manual workers on the question. But by 1961 twice as many professional and managerial persons thought there should be *more* such regulation than thought there should be less, and the differences from manual workers on the issue had virtually disappeared. Another study produced similar findings. It looked at the proportion of higher status, northern white Protestants who had "liberal" or "conservative" views on a range of policy questions in the 1950s and again in the 1970s. In the 1950s this group was the most conservative of any identifiable part of the American population—over 60 percent could be found at the most conservative end of the scale. By the 1970s, however, a profound change

had occurred. Some members of this group had become even more conservative, but other members had become much more liberal, with the result that this segment of society (which includes many persons who are in some sense "elite") was deeply split or polarized—some very liberal and some very conservative, with not many persons in between.[39]

That there could be so many upper status persons with liberal views will seem strange only if you think that people with good jobs, high incomes, and a lot of education are—as they once were—bankers, doctors, corporation presidents, and Wall Street lawyers. In fact, a larger and larger fraction of persons with prestige jobs, good incomes, and much education are not in business at all, but rather are government officials, research scientists, professors,

---

TABLE 5.7   Opinions on Government Regulation of Business, Selected Occupation Groups, 1940 and 1961

1940 Question: "During the next four years, do you think there should be more regulation or less regulation of business by the Federal Government, than at present?"

	More	About same	Less
Professional/managerial	14%	16%	70%
Manual	40	26	35

1961 Question: "Do you think the laws regulating business corporations are too strict, or not strict enough?"

	Not strict enough	About right	Too strict
Professional/managerial	37%	47%	16%
Manual	38	49	13

Source: Gallup Poll data as tabulated in Everett Carll Ladd, Jr., *Transformations of the American Party System*, 2nd ed. (New York: W. W. Norton, 1978), p. 109. Reprinted by permission.

TABLE 5.8 Attitudes of "New Class" and "Old Class" Democrats on Social and Cultural Issues

Policy Preference	Percent Agreeing Among	
	"New Class" Democrats	"Old Class" Democrats
Should divorce be easier or more difficult to obtain than it is now? *Percentage answering "easier"*	59%	21%
Should a pregnant woman be able to obtain a legal abortion if she is married and does not want any more children? *Percentage answering "yes"*	73	32
What is your opinion of someone having sexual relations with someone other than the marriage partner? *Percentage thinking extramarital sex is always wrong*	38	80
What is your opinion of sexual relations between two adults of the same sex? *Percentage feeling homosexuality is always wrong*	27	89
Do you think we are spending the right amount of money to protect the environment? *Percentage thinking we are spending too little*	85	49
Do you think there should be laws against marriages between blacks and whites? *Percentage favoring laws against miscegenation*	5	67
Which statement comes closest to your feelings about pornography laws? *Percentage thinking "there should be laws against the distribution of pornography whatever the age"*	13	55
In a community-wide vote on the housing issue, which law would you favor? *Percentage choosing law allowing homeowner to decide, even if he prefers not to sell to blacks*	33	78

Source: Everett Carll Ladd, Jr., "The Democrats Have Their Own Two-Party System," *Fortune*, October 1977, p. 217. Reprinted by permission of Social Science Data Center, University of Connecticut and Fortune Art Department/ Joe Argenziano © 1977 Time, Inc.

Note: "New Class" Democrats are respondents under 40 years of age, college-educated, in professional and managerial jobs. "Old Class" Democrats are those over age 50, without college training, in blue-collar occupations. The data are from the combined 1972–1977 NORC surveys.

executives of voluntary associations and foundations, and members of the mass media of communication or of advertising firms. Between 1950 and 1970 the number of persons in nonbusiness occupations that involve writing and speaking (teachers, writers, researchers, bureaucrats, lawyers, the clergy) more than doubled, to at least 5 million.[40]

Education and Expertise

Some writers have described what has happened as the arrival on the scene of a "New Class." Old class distinctions were based purely on wealth or income. (To Marx, for example, the major classes were the proletariat—the workers—and the bourgeoisie—the businessmen.) The "New Class" consists, in the opinion of those who offer this theory, of persons whose elite positions are the result, not of their wealth or business position, but of their education and technical skills. Expertise rather than wealth defines this group, the members of which can be found concentrated in such places as the high-technology industries along Route 128 near Boston, the research enterprises near Stanford and Berkeley in California and in the Raleigh-Durham area of North Carolina, and in the offices of the federal bureaucracy and of the publishing companies of New York City.

The opinions and political significance of such a New Class are a matter of dispute. Some believe that its members not only disagree with business leaders and other members of the Old Upper Class on matters of public policy but are in fact hostile to the very concept of business enterprise. Others find it to be either closely allied with business on important questions or, if hostile, lacking in great influence.[41]

Whatever one makes of the long-term significance of the rising importance of advanced education as a source of both political views and social power, there can be little doubt that it has created great strains within the political parties. As we shall see in Chapter 10, both parties, but especially the Democratic, have been deeply split by the conflict between their ideological and nonideological wings. In Table 5.8, one dimension of that split within the Democratic party is vividly portrayed. The views of two factions within that party on various social and cultural issues are shown. In the first column are the views of those Democrats who are under the age of forty, college-educated, and hold professional or managerial jobs (what Ladd, who devised this table, calls New Class Democrats); in the second column are the opinions of Democrats who are over fifty, without college training, and hold blue-collar jobs (Old Class Democrats). The differences could not be greater—on divorce, abortion, homosexuality, environmental protection, civil rights laws, and pornography, New Class and Old Class Democrats disagree profoundly. (If the table had included some economic issues, the differences would have been less.) Given these differences in opinion, especially on "social" issues, between New Class and Old Class Democrats, agreeing on a Democratic presidential candidate is likely to be difficult.

POLITICAL PARTICIPATION

Persons of different social and especially educational backgrounds not only have different political opinions, they also participate in politics at different rates. Ordinarily, we think of such participation in terms of voting, but there are many other—and probably more important—ways to participate: by working in political campaigns, joining politically active organizations, contributing money to candidates, writing letters to congressmen, and even by talking politics with one's friends and neighbors.

Forms of Participation

Table 5.9 shows the results of asking Americans about their involvement in various kinds of political activities. As can be seen, voting is by far the most common form of political participation, while giving money to a candidate and being a member of a political organization

TABLE 5.9 Political Involvement

Type of Political Participation	Percentage
1. Report regularly voting in presidential elections[a]	72%
2. Report always voting in local elections	47
3. Active in at least one organization involved in community problems	32
4. Have worked with others in trying to solve some community problems	30
5. Have attempted to persuade others to vote as they were	28
6. Have ever actively worked for a party or candidates during an election	26
7. Have ever contacted a local government official about some issue or problem	20
8. Have attended at least one political meeting or rally in last three years	19
9. Have ever contacted a state or national government official about some issue or problem	18
10. Have ever formed a group or organization to attempt to solve some local community problem	14
11. Have ever given money to a party or candidate during an election campaign	13
12. Presently a member of a political club or organization	8

Source: Sidney Verba and Norman H. Nie, *Participation in America* (New York: Harper & Row, 1972), p. 31. Copyright © 1972 by Sidney Verba and Norman H. Nie. Reprinted by permission of Harper & Row, Publishers, Inc.

[a] Composite variable created from reports of voting in 1960 and 1964 presidential elections. Percentage is equal to those who report they have voted in both elections.

are the least common. And even these figures overstate matters since most persons tend to exaggerate how frequently they vote or how active they are in politics.

Sidney Verba and Norman H. Nie did an elaborate statistical analysis of the ways in which people participate in politics and came up with six forms of participation that are characteristic of six different kinds of citizens (Table 5.10). About one-fifth (22 percent) of the population is completely inactive—they rarely vote, they do not get involved in organization, and they probably do not even talk about politics very much. These *inactives* typically have little education and low incomes, are relatively young, and many of them are black. At the opposite extreme are the *complete activists,* constituting about one-tenth of the population (11 percent), who are highly educated, have high incomes, and tend to be middle-aged rather than young

or old. They tend to participate in all forms of politics.

Between these extremes are four categories of limited forms of participation. The *voting specialists* are persons who vote but do little else; they tend not to have much schooling or income, and to be substantially older than the average person. *Campaigners* not only vote but like to get involved in campaign activities as well. They are better educated than the average voter, but what seems to distinguish them most is their interest in the conflicts, passions, and struggle of politics, their clear identification with a political party, and their willingness to take strong positions. *Communalists* are much like campaigners in social background but have a very different temperament: they do not like the conflict and tension of partisan campaigns. They tend to reserve their energies for community activities of a more nonpartisan nature—forming and

TABLE 5.10 Political and Community Participation: A Summary

Type of Participant	Pattern of Activity	Leading Orientations	Main Social Characteristics
The inactives (22%)	No activity.	Totally uninvolved, no interest, skill, sense of competence, or concern with conflict.	Lower socioeconomic levels and blacks are over-represented, as are older and younger citizens (but not middle-aged ones) and women.
The voting specialists (21%)	They vote regularly, but do nothing else.	Strong partisan identity but otherwise relatively uninvolved and with low skills and competence.	Lower socioeconomic levels are overrepresented. Older citizens are over-represented, as are those in big cities. Underrepresented in rural areas.
The parochial participants (4%)	They contact officials on particularized problems and are otherwise inactive.	Some political skill (information) but otherwise no political involvement.	Lower socioeconomic groups are overrepresented, but blacks are underrepresented. Catholic rather than Protestant. Big cities rather than small towns.
The communalists (20%)	They contact officials on broad social issues and engage in co-operative activity. Vote fairly regularly, but avoid election campaigns.	High sense of community contribution, involvement in politics, skill and competence. Nonpartisan and avoid conflict.	Upper socioeconomic levels very overrepresented, blacks underrepresented. Protestant rather than Catholic. Overrepresented in rural areas and small towns; underrepresented in big cities.
The campaigners (15%)	Heavily active in campaigns and vote regularly.	Politically involved, relatively skilled and competent, partisan and involved in conflict, but little sense of community contribution.	Overrepresentation of upper-status groups. Blacks and particularly Catholics overrepresented. Big-city and suburbs rather than small towns and rural areas.
The complete activists (11%)	Active in all ways.	Involved in politics in all ways, highly skilled and competent.	Heavy overrepresentation of upper-status groups. Old and young underrepresented.

Source: Sidney Verba and Norman H. Nie, *Participation in America* (New York: Harper & Row, 1972), pp. 118–119. Copyright © 1972 by Sidney Verba and Norman H. Nie. Reprinted by permission of Harper & Row, Publishers, Inc.

Note: 7% of sample unclassified.

joining organizations to deal with local problems and contacting local officials about these problems. Finally, there are some *parochial participants* who do not vote and stay out of election campaigns and civic associations, but who are willing to contact local officials about specific, often personal, problems.

It is striking that over 40 percent of Amer-

icans either do not participate in politics at all or limit that participation strictly to voting. There are a number of reasons why people do not get involved in politics, but one deserves special mention: for most persons, politics offers few rewards. Even voting imposes a number of burdens (registering to vote, waiting in line, missing work, making sense of a long ballot),

TABLE 5.11   How Citizens Participate in Seven Countries

	Austria	India	Japan	Netherlands	Nigeria	United States	Yugoslavia
Voting							
Regular voters[b]	85%	48%	93%	77%	56%	63%	82%
Campaign activity							
Members of a party or political organization	28	5	4	13	[a]	8	15
Worked for a party	10	6	25	10	[a]	25	45
Attended a political rally	27	14	50	9	[a]	19	45
Communal activity							
Active members in a community action organization	9	7	11	15	34	32	39
Worked with a local group on a community problem	3	18	15	16	35	30	22
Helped form a local group on a community problem	6	5	5	[a]	26	14	[a]
Contacted an official in the community on some social problem	5	4	11	6	2	13	11
Contacted an official outside the community on a social problem	3	2	5	7	3	11	[a]
Particularized contacting							
Contacted a local official on a personal problem	15	12	7	38	2	6	20
Contacted an official outside the community on a personal problem	10	6	3	10	1	6	[a]
Number of cases	1,769	2,637	2,657	1,746	1,799	2,544	2,995

Source: Norman H. Nie and Sidney Verba, "Political Participation," in Fred I. Greenstein and Nelson W. Polsby, eds., *Handbook of Political Science* (Reading, Mass.: Addison-Wesley, 1975), Vol. 4, pp. 24–25.

[a] Not asked.   [b] Vote regularly in both local and national elections.

and offers the hope of few tangible results (hardly anybody ever casts a vote that affects the outcome of an election). The wonder is not that only 60 percent or so of the populace votes, but that the proportion is not smaller.

Why People Participate

One of the reasons the percentage of participants is as high as it is is that most Americans have a strong sense of civic duty. They believe they have an obligation to vote, even when their vote will not make a difference, and they feel good about having voted after it is over. As we have seen in Chapter 4, a sense of civic obligation is stronger in the United States than in many other democratic nations. Twice as many Americans as Britons said, in answer to a question about the role the ordinary person ought to play in his or her community, that the citizen should vote and take part in local organizations.[42] But if more Americans than Britons say they *should* vote, why do fewer *actually* vote? Are Americans hypocrites? Not really. Americans face greater difficulties in registering to vote than do citizens of almost any other country. American political parties do not do as well at luring people to the polls as the parties of most European nations. And most important, Americans find being active in the community a more rewarding form of participation than merely voting.

Compared to citizens of other countries, many Americans find communal activity to be more enjoyable and more important than simply voting. In Table 5.11 we see how persons in seven nations described their political activities. Americans did not vote as often as citizens of Austria, the Netherlands, or Japan, but they were much more likely to be active members of a community organization and to work with others on community problems. Many people do not think of these activities as "politics," but that is a mistake: anything that influences the policies government follows is politics in the broad sense.

"The wonder is not that only 60 percent or so of the populace votes, but that the proportion is not smaller."

The low turnout in American elections has led to many advertising campaigns to increase the vote, with little success.

Who Participates

Whatever the form of participation, those who are the most active tend to be those with more education (and, to a lesser degree, with higher incomes) than those who are the least active. Indeed, educational differences explain more of the variation in political participation in the United States than they do in any other country in which comparable studies have been done.[43] Older persons are more active than younger ones, and men more active than women.[44]

Overall, blacks participate in politics less frequently than whites, but among persons of the same socioeconomic status—that is, having roughly the same income and level of education—blacks tend to participate *more* than whites.[45] This is particularly true for blacks who are financially better off or who are especially sensitive to racial issues. But the forms of participation among blacks are somewhat different from those of whites. Blacks, compared to whites, are less likely to contact public officials about problems and slightly less likely to vote, but much more likely to join civic organizations or become active in political campaigns.[46]

There is evidence that the rate at which peo-

The flood of mail that arrives daily in a congressional office is an important form of political participation.

ple have been participating in politics in ways other than by voting has increased in recent years. One survey found that the proportion of citizens who had written a letter to a public official increased from about 17 percent in 1964 to over 27 percent by 1976. Citizens also participate in politics (though they do not think of it in that way) whenever they make a demand on a government official, such as a welfare administrator or a highway planner. And public demonstrations, protest marches, and sit-ins have become a much more common form of political participation. By one count, there were only 6 demonstrations per year between 1950 and 1959 but 140 per year between 1960 and 1967. Such forms of political participation may have begun among blacks, civil rights workers, and antiwar protesters, but they have spread to include truck drivers upset with national speed limits, farmers complaining of low prices for their products, parents objecting to busing to achieve racial balance in schools, and conservationists seeking to block the construction of nuclear power plants. Though the rate at which Americans vote in elections has been declining (see Chapter 7), the rate at which they have been taking up other forms of political participation has been increasing.[47]

The effect of the differences among people in the rate of political participation has not been exhaustively studied. The evidence, however, suggests that government officials tend to be better informed about and more in agreement with the opinions of persons most active in politics than they are with the views of the rank-and-file citizenry.[48] There is nothing particularly sinister about this: people who try to have influence are going to have more of it than people who do not try. This means that we should be especially interested in the political opinions of the political activists. To recapitulate what we have already said, activists tend to have more extreme views than the citizens for whom they supposedly speak: Republican activists are often more consistently conservative than the average Republican, Democratic activists often more consistently liberal than the average Democrat.

OPINION AND VOTING

For most citizens, casting a vote is their only significant form of political participation. Political scientists have lavished enormous effort on the task of explaining how people cast their votes. Perhaps because so many studies have been done by so many scholars, there is more conflict than consensus about what is going through a voter's mind when he or she steps into the polling place.

There are two major explanations of voting. The first is based on party identification. Most voters are poorly informed on many issues and on the positions that the rival political parties have on these issues. Opinion surveys done in 1956, for example, found that no more than one-third of the voters were familiar with a list of current issues and with the positions on these issues taken by the parties. Since more than a third voted, the votes of this majority would have to be based on something other than issue preference. To the authors of this study, all associated with the University of Michigan, that something was party identification.[49]

Party Votes

To these scholars, the sense of being a Republican or a Democrat, largely inherited from one's parents, is the chief determinant of how a person votes in a national election. Naturally, party identification is not the *sole* source of the voter's choice—if it were, the Democrats would have won every presidential election since the 1930s. The other factor, according to these scholars, is the voter's response to the personality of the candidate. A popular Republican, such as Dwight Eisenhower, or an unpopular Demo-

Republicans must have a popular candidate, such as Dwight D. Eisenhower, or the Democrats must nominate an especially unpopular one, for the Republicans to overcome the Democrats' advantage among voters.

crat, such as George McGovern, can swing the election to the Republicans. Issues are not irrelevant, but they are of minor importance in any given election. Over a long period of time, however, issues might play a role in changing party identification, as happened during the Great Depression of the 1930s.

Policy Votes

The rival theory is based on the belief that the voters are not fools or helplessly in the grip of party loyalties acquired at their parents' dinner table. V. O. Key, Jr., examined voters who changed their minds between presidential elections—those that switched from one party to another—and found that most of these switchers acted rationally on the basis of their assessment of the policies of the two parties.[50] David RePass noted that the University of Michigan studies had judged voter knowledge of issues on the basis of answers to questions on things the *pollsters* thought important. When people were asked about what they, the voters, thought important, the citizens mentioned issues, recognized that in many cases the parties differed in what they promised to do about them, and made their voting decision in many cases on the basis of this difference.[51]

It is possible that both theories are correct, at least in part. The Michigan studies were done in the 1950s, when major domestic issues were conspicuous by their absence and political parties seemed to be in agreement. As we have seen, issues became more important to voters in the 1960s; many analysts of these later elections contend that such issues as civil rights, campus protests, crime, and the war in Vietnam dominated public attention sufficiently to cause a much larger fraction of the electorate to vote on the basis of issues rather than party identification or candidate personality.[52] In short, times had changed, and voters with them.

The debate continues to rage, with ever more complex and sophisticated statistical techniques being used to assess the rival theories. Though the newest analyses are so complicated as to defy summary, at least in an introductory book, they probably have moved our understanding of voters closer to the truth. After all, the voters are complicated human beings not easily or fairly described by any simple push-pull theory of elections. Consider the possibilities: voters may (1) select their party identification because of how they see the issues; (2) reinterpret the issues in light of a prior party loyalty; or (3) select a preferred candidate on the basis or his or her real as well as imagined stand on issues. Small wonder that opinion analysts often feel like the man who turns a corner only to meet himself coming in the opposite direction.

OPINION AND POLICY

We began this chapter asking what influence popular opinion has on government in the United States, and we end with the same question. In Part IV evidence will be assembled that will permit at least a partial answer. Here, we can sketch the outlines of that answer. Mass opinion may be a *source* of policy, a *reflection* of policy, a *constraint* on policy, or *irrelevant* to policy.

Mass opinion is a *source* of policy whenever a law is enacted or a decision is made in order to do what policy-makers perceive that a majority of the citizens want. For this to occur, people must know enough and care enough about a matter to have a clear opinion about it, and the political process must make that opinion apparent to officials and provide them with an incentive to act on it. These conditions are often met when a problem arises that touches the lives of ordinary citizens with enough force (or "salience," as political scientists term it) to lead people to organize and vote on the basis of this mass opinion. As we shall see in Part IV, inflation, mass unemployment, and high medical costs (especially for the elderly) have been issues of this sort.[53] Social security, unemployment compensation, and Medicare were enacted in response to the public concerns these problems stimulated. We shall also see that, at least initially, it was not enough that people wanted these programs. Often political circumstances had to occur—a crisis, intensive lobbying, a lopsided election victory by one party—to overcome the resistance to such programs offered by their opponents. There are also some issues that people care about greatly on which the federal government, for various reasons, does little—perhaps because it does not know what to do. Street crime has been one such problem.

Public opinion may also be created by government actions taken for other reasons. As we shall see in Part IV, there was little or no

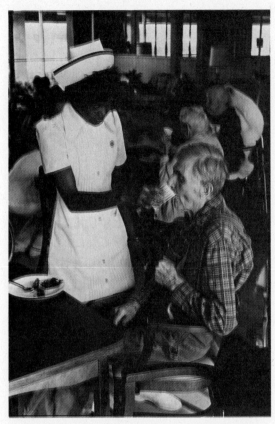

The Medicare law, passed in 1965, brought federally supported medical assistance to the elderly. It was a clear case of public policy being molded by public opinion.

public demand for federal laws concerning automobile safety or environmental protection in advance of the legislation passed on these matters. A few persons cared passionately about such issues, but the majority of citizens were indifferent. Once the government debated and acted, however, public opinion was stimulated. Then many consumer and environmental programs attracted broad support (though, as we shall see, some of that support waned when environmental policies appeared to conflict with economic growth). Here, public opinion has been a *reflection* of public policy.

Opinion may affect government powerfully without directing its actions. Widely held beliefs, of the sort described in Chapter 4, about how government ought to be conducted *constrain* the actions of officials. In many policy areas, especially those remote from the daily concerns of citizens, officials are free to act without concern for mass opinion, provided that they do not publicly violate important procedural norms—fairness, honesty, and due regard for the apparent interests of the many. If much or most of the government's business could be conducted in secret, these norms might exercise only a weak constraint on official decision. But the checks and balances created by rival executive and legislative branches, a decentralized and individualistic Congress, and an aggressive mass media ensure a reasonably high probability that virtually any government action will become public knowledge. (A man experienced in government service once defined an important secret as something you couldn't wait to tell your wife.) More public careers are ruined by scandals and allegations of misconduct than by stupid or unwise decisions, and hence many officials worry more about making a decision the right way than about making the right decision.

Finally, majority opinion can sometimes be *ignored*. A substantial majority of American citizens have repeatedly expressed to public opinion polls their opposition to forced busing to promote racial integration in the schools, quotas for the hiring of minority persons on the job, choosing presidents through the Electoral College, and spending more money on economic aid to foreign countries.[54] Yet all these policies have been in effect—some because they are required by courts that are not directly responsible to public opinion, some because they represent constitutional traditions that are hard to change, and some because elected officials believe that public opinion is wrong and should, up to a point, be ignored.

In later chapters, and especially in Part IV,

we shall try to explain why opinion dictates government action in some areas, merely constrains it in others, and is irrelevant in still others. It is important to remember, however, that "public opinion" is not usually a clear, fixed, easily interpreted political fact. Though citizens are usually alert to matters that touch their lives directly and quite rational in deciding, among things they know well, what is best for them, many government programs are so complex or remote that there may either be no serious public opinion about them at all or (to say the same thing in other words) "opinion" may vary depending on how the question is put, the alternatives that are offered, and which elected officials are known to support a particular position. For example, most citizens have little interest in foreign affairs most of the time and are skeptical of policies that might get this country more deeply involved in the problems of other nations. But should the president take action that produces that involvement, the initial public response is to support him strongly (see Chapter 20). By and large, most people do not think much about government or politics, and for perfectly good reasons—they have enough to worry about in holding a job, paying off a mortgage, managing their children, and keeping their health.

SUMMARY

Political opinions are shaped by family, religious, and ethnic traditions, by occupational and peer-group experiences, and by higher education. Though still important, economic and occupational sources of opinion have become less significant with the increase in the number of persons attending college and holding high-paying but nonbusiness jobs (the New Class).

Most Americans do not have highly ideological (i.e., systematic and "consistent") political views, but a substantial proportion of those persons active in political life can be described as "liberals" or "conservatives." Among the citizenry at large, many persons are likely to have mixed ideologies—for example, to be liberal on economic issues but conservative on social ones or vice versa.

Party identification has been far more important than political ideology in explaining how people cast their votes, and this sense of identification remains important even though it has been getting weaker among many voters. Though parental influence is strong in shaping one's party identification, it is not decisive, nor do persons vote on the basis of their identification in blind disregard of the particular issues (if any) in a campaign.

There are many ways of participating in politics, of which voting may be among the least important. Though Americans vote at a lower rate than do citizens of other countries, they are more likely to participate in communal and civic affairs and to contact public officials. Persons active in politics in whatever ways tend to have different characteristics than persons who are not active.

Suggested Readings

Erikson, Robert S., and Norman G. Luttbeg. *American Public Opinion: Its Origins, Content, and Impact,* 2nd ed. New York: John Wiley, 1979. A good summary of studies of public opinion and its relation to politics.

Jennings, M. Kent, and Richard G. Niemi. *The Political Character of Adolescence: The Influence of Families and Schools.* Princeton, N.J.: Princeton University Press, 1974. A study of political attitudes among high school students.

Key, V. O., Jr. *The Responsible Electorate.* Cambridge, Mass.: Harvard University Press, 1966. An argument, with evidence, that American voters are not fools.

Ladd, Everett Carll, Jr. *Where Have All the Voters Gone?* New York: W. W. Norton, 1978. A stimulating essay on recent changes in public opinion and its connection with political parties.

Lane, Robert E. *Political Ideology*. New York: The Free Press, 1962. A sensitive account of the average American voter based on in-depth interviews that explore the beliefs of a small number of citizens.

Lipset, Seymour Martin. *Political Man: The Social Bases of Politics*. Garden City, N.Y.: Doubleday, 1959. An exploration of the relationship between society, opinion, and democracy in America and abroad.

Milbrath, Lester W., and M. L. Goel. *Political Participation*, 2nd ed. Chicago: Rand McNally, 1977. A summary of studies of how people participate in politics.

Nie, Norman H., Sidney Verba, and John R. Petrocik. *The Changing American Voter*. Cambridge, Mass.: Harvard University Press, 1976. Traces shifts in American voter attitudes since 1960.

Verba, Sidney, and Norman H. Nie. *Participation in America*. New York: Harper & Row, 1972. Analyzes the relationship between social class and political participation.

6 Political Parties

The political parties of the United States are
the oldest in the world; among democratic
nations, they may also be the weakest. It is not
their age that has enfeebled them, however;
when they were a hundred years old, they were
still vigorous and played a dominant role in national politics. Rather, they have declined in
significance as a result of changes in the legal
rules under which they operate and in the attitudes of the citizens whom they seek to organize.
All of this has occurred—and is still occurring—in
a constitutional system that has caused the parties, even in their heyday, to be decentralized
and fragmented.

PARTIES—HERE AND ABROAD

A political party is a group that seeks to elect
candidates to public office by supplying them
with labels—a "party identification"—by which

Tammany Hall, decked out in flags for the 1924
Democratic convention (left). Two young delegates to a
party convention typify the contemporary party
activists (right).

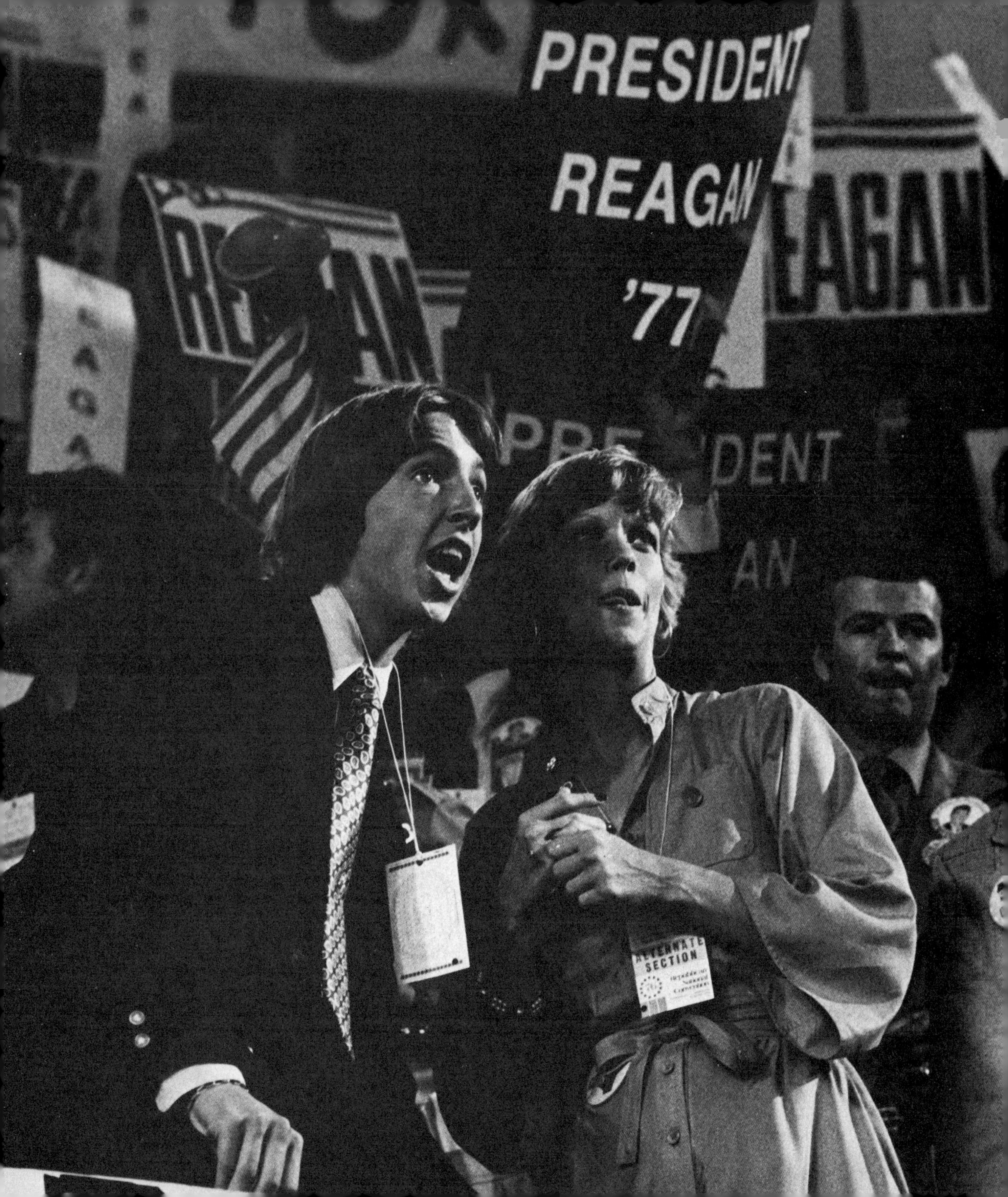
PRESIDENT
REAGAN
'77
EAGAN
ALTERNATE
SECTION

The decline of party: Campaign buttons show the names of the candidates but rarely the names of the parties to which they belong.

they are known to the electorate.[1] This definition is purposefully broad so that it will include both familiar parties (Democratic, Republican) and unfamiliar ones (Whig, Libertarian, Socialist Worker) and will cover periods in which a party is very strong (having an elaborate and well-disciplined organization that provides money and workers to its candidates) as well as periods in which it is quite weak (supplying nothing but the label to candidates). The label by which a candidate is known may or may not actually be printed on the ballot opposite a candidate's name—in the United States it does appear on the ballot in all national elections but in only a minority of municipal ones; in Australia and Israel (and in Great Britain before 1969) it never appears on the ballot at all.

This definition suggests the three political arenas within which parties may be found. A party exists as a label in the minds of the voters, as an organization that recruits and campaigns for candidates, and as a set of leaders who try to organize and control the legislative and executive branches of government. A powerful party is one whose label has a strong appeal for the voters, whose organization can decide who will be candidates and how their campaigns will be managed, and whose leaders can dominate one or all branches of government.

In the United States the labels of the two major parties have always had a relatively strong appeal for the voters, so much so that third parties and independent candidates have rarely had much success at the national or even state level. As we shall see, however, even the party label has of late begun to lose its hold on the voters' minds. There has rarely—perhaps never—been a strong *national* party organization in this country, though there have been long periods in which certain state, city, or county components of the Democratic or Republican parties have been organizationally powerful. (The Cook County—that is, Chicago—Democratic "machine" is one example of this.) And only occasionally have the political parties been able to dominate the Congress, though parties have always been able to influence the choice of congressional leaders and the votes of many congressmen on at least certain matters.

In Europe matters are very different. Virtually the only way a person can become a candidate for an elective office is to be nominated by party leaders. Campaigns are run by the party, using party funds and workers, not by the candidate. Once in office, the elected officials are expected to vote and act together with other members of their party. The principal criterion by which voters choose among candidates is their party identification or label. (This has been changing somewhat of late—European parties, like American ones, have not been able to count as heavily as in the past on party loyalty among the voters.)

Decentralization

Several factors explain the striking differences between American and European political parties. First, the federal system of government in the United States decentralizes political authority and thus decentralizes political party organizations. For nearly two centuries most of the important governmental decisions were made at the state and local level—decisions regarding education, criminal justice, land use, business regulation, and public welfare—and thus it was at the state and local level that the important struggles over power and policy occurred. Moreover, most persons with political jobs—either elective or appointive—worked for state and local government, and thus a party's interest in obtaining these jobs for its followers meant that it had to focus attention on who controlled city hall, the county courthouse, and the state capitol. Federalism, in short, meant that political parties would acquire jobs and money from local sources and fight local contests. This, in turn, meant that the national political parties would be coalitions of local parties, and though these coalitions would have a keen interest in capturing the presidency (with it, after all, went control of large numbers of federal jobs), the national party leaders rarely had as much power as the local ones. The Republican leader of Cuyahoga County, Ohio, for example, could often ignore the decisions of the Republican national chairman and even of the Ohio state chairman.

Political authority in the United States has of late come to be far more centralized: the federal government now makes decisions affecting almost all aspects of our lives, including those—such as schooling and welfare—once left entirely in local hands. Yet the political parties have not become more centralized as a result. If anything, they have become even weaker and more decentralized. One reason for this apparent paradox is that in the United States, unlike in most other democratic nations, political parties are closely regulated by state and federal laws, and these regulations have had the effect of weakening

> **"Federalism, in short, meant that political parties would acquire jobs and money from local sources and fight local contests."**

the power of parties substantially. Perhaps the most important of these regulations are those that prescribe how a party's candidates are to be selected.

In the great majority of American states the party leaders do not select persons to run for office; by law, those persons are chosen by the voters in primary elections. Though sometimes the party can influence who will win a primary contest, in general persons running for state or national office in this country owe little to party leaders. In Europe, by contrast, there is no such thing as a primary election—the only way to become a candidate for office is to persuade party leaders to put your name on the ballot. In a later section of this chapter, the impact of the direct primary will be discussed in more detail; for now, it is enough to note that its use removes from the hands of the party leadership its most important source of power over officeholders.

Furthermore, if an American political party wins control of Congress, it does not—as in most European nations with a parliamentary system of government—also win the right to select the chief executive of the government. The American president, as we have seen, is independently elected, and this means that he will choose his principal subordinates, not from among congressmen, but from among persons out of Congress. Should he pick a representative or senator for his cabinet, that person would have to resign from Congress in order to accept the job. Thus, an opportunity to be a cabinet secretary is not an important reward for congressmen, and so the president cannot use the prospect of that reward as a way of controlling congressional action. All this weakens the significance and power of party as a means of organizing the government and conducting its business.

Parties play a larger role in the lives of Europeans than in the lives of Americans. Citizens in this Italian village during a 1978 campaign are probably affected in many ways by political parties—through their unions, the church, their clubs.

Political Culture

The attitudes and traditions of American voters reinforce the institutional and legal factors that make American parties relatively weak. Political parties in this country have rarely played an important part in the life of the average citizen; indeed, one does not (usually) "join" a party here except by voting for its candidates. In many European nations, on the other hand, many citizens will join a party, pay dues, and attend regular meetings. Furthermore, in countries such as France, Austria, and Italy, the political parties supply a wide range of activities and dominate a variety of associations to which a person may belong—labor unions, youth groups, educational programs, even chess clubs.

In the United States we tend to keep parties separate from other aspects of our lives. As Democrats or Republicans, we may become ex-

cited by a presidential campaign and a few of us may even participate in helping elect a congressman or state senator. Our social, business, working, and cultural lives, however, are almost entirely nonpartisan. Indeed, most Americans, unlike many Europeans, would resent partisanship becoming a conspicuous feature of other organizations to which we belong. All this is a way of saying that American parties play a segmental, rather than comprehensive, role in our lives and that even this role is diminishing as more and more of us proclaim ourselves to be "independents."

THE RISE AND DECLINE OF THE POLITICAL PARTY

Our nation began without parties; today parties, though far from extinct, are about as weak as at any time in our history. In between the Founding and the present, however, parties arose and became powerful. We can see this process in four broad periods of party history: when political parties were created (roughly from the Founding to the 1820s); when the more or less stable two-party system developed (roughly from the time of President Jackson to the Civil War); when parties developed a comprehensive organizational form and appeal (from roughly the Civil War to the 1930s); and finally when party "reform" began to alter the party system (beginning in the early 1900s but taking effect chiefly from the New Deal to the present).[2]

The Founding

The Founders disliked parties, thinking of them as "factions" motivated by ambition and self-interest. George Washington, dismayed by the quarreling between Hamilton and Jefferson in his cabinet, devoted much of his Farewell Address to condemning parties. This hostility to party was understandable: the legitimacy and success of the newly created federal government were still very much in doubt. When Jefferson organized his followers to oppose Hamilton's policies, it seemed to Hamilton and *his* followers that Jefferson was opposing, not just a policy or a leader, but the very concept of a national government. Jefferson for his part thought Hamilton was not simply pursuing bad policies, but was subverting the Constitution itself. Before political parties could become legitimate, it was necessary for people to be able to separate in their minds quarrels over policies and elections from disputes over the legitimacy of government itself. The ability to make that distinction was slow in coming, and thus parties were objects of profound suspicion and defended, at first, only as temporary expedients.

The first organized political party in American history was made up of the followers of Jefferson who, beginning in the 1790s, called themselves "Republicans" (hoping to suggest thereby that their opponents were secret monarchists). The followers of Hamilton kept the label "Federalist" that once had been used to refer to all supporters of the new Constitution (hoping to imply that *their* opponents were "antifederalists" or enemies of the Constitution). These parties were loose caucuses of political notables in various localities, with New England being strongly Federalist and much of the South passionately Republican. Jefferson and his ally James Madison thought their Republican party was a temporary arrangement designed to defeat John Adams, a Federalist, in his bid to succeed Washington in 1796. (Adams narrowly defeated Jefferson who, under the system then in effect, became vice-president because he had the second most electoral votes.) In 1800 Adams's bid to succeed himself intensified party activity even more, but this time Jefferson won and the Republicans assumed office. The Federalists feared that Jefferson would dismantle the Constitution, but Jefferson adopted a conciliatory posture, saying in his Inaugural Address that "we are all Republicans, we are all Federalists."[3] It was not true, of course—the Federalists detested Jefferson and some were planning to have New England secede from the Union—but it was good politics, expressive of the need every president

"Before political parties could become legitimate, it was necessary for people to be able to separate in their minds quarrels over policies . . . from disputes over the legitimacy of government itself.**"**

has to persuade the public that, despite partisan politics, the presidency exists to serve all the people.

So successful were the Republicans that the Federalists virtually ceased to exist as a party. Jefferson was reelected in 1804 with almost no opposition; Madison easily won two terms; James Monroe carried sixteen out of nineteen states in 1816 and was reelected without opposition in 1820. Political parties had seemingly disappeared, just as Jefferson had hoped. The weakness of this "first party system" can be explained by the fact that it *was* the first—nobody had been born a Federalist or a Republican, there was no ancestral party loyalty to defend, the earliest political leaders did not think of themselves as professional politicians, and the Federalist party had such a limited sectional and class base that it could not compete effectively in national elections. The parties that existed in

---

TWO VIEWS OF PARTIES

President George Washington, in his 1796 Farewell Address:

"Let me warn you in the most solemn manner against the baneful effects of the spirit of party generally. This spirit . . . exists under different shapes in all government, more or less stifled, controlled, or repressed; but in those of the popular form it is seen in its greatest rankness and is truly their worst enemy."

Political scientist E. E. Schattschneider, in a 1942 book:

"Political parties created democracy and . . . modern democracy is unthinkable save in terms of the parties."

these early years were essentially small groups of local notables. Political participation was limited, and nominations for most local offices were arranged rather casually.

Even in this early period, the parties, though they had very different views on economic policy and somewhat different class bases, did not represent clear, homogeneous economic interests. Farmers in Virginia were Republicans, but farmers in Delaware were Federalists; the commercial interests of Boston were firmly Federalist, but commercial leaders in urban Connecticut were likely to be Republican. From the beginning to the present, elections have created heterogeneous coalitions.

The Jacksonians

What is often called the "second party system" emerged around 1824 with Andrew Jackson's first run for the presidency and lasted until the Civil War became inevitable. Its distinctive feature was that political participation became a mass phenomenon. For one thing, the number of voters to be reached had become quite large. Only about 365,000 popular votes were cast in 1824. But as a result of laws that enlarged the number of persons eligible to vote and of an increase in the population, by 1828 well over a million votes were tallied and by 1840 well over two million. (In England at this time there were only 650,000 eligible voters.) For another, by 1832 presidential electors were selected by popular vote in virtually every state. (As late as 1816, electors were chosen by the state legislatures, rather than by the people, in about half the states.) Presidential politics had become a truly national, genuinely popular activity; indeed, in many communities election campaigns had become the principal public spectacle.

The party system of the Jacksonian era was built from the bottom up rather than, as during the period of the Founding, from the top down. No change better illustrates this transformation than the abandonment of the system of having caucuses composed of members of Congress

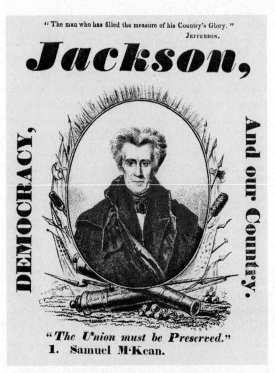

"The man who has filled the measure of his Country's Glory."
JEFFERSON.

Jackson,

DEMOCRACY,   And our Country.

"The Union must be Preserved."
1. Samuel M'Kean.

When Andrew Jackson ran for president in 1828, over a million votes were cast for the first time in American history. This poster, from the 1832 election, was part of the emergence of truly mass political participation.

nominate presidential candidates. The caucus system was an effort to unite the legislative and executive branches by giving the former some degree of control over who would have a chance to capture the latter. The caucus system became unpopular when the caucus candidate for president in 1824 ran third in a field of four in the general election and was completely discredited when Congress denied the presidency to Jackson, the candidate with the most popular votes.

To replace the caucus, the party convention was invented. The first convention in American history was that of the Anti-Masonic party in 1831; the first convention of a major party was that of the anti-Jackson Republicans later that year (it nominated Henry Clay for president).

The Democrats held a convention in 1832 that ratified Jackson's nomination for reelection and picked Martin Van Buren as his running mate. The first convention to select a man who would be elected president and who was not already the incumbent president was held by the Democrats in 1836; it chose Van Buren.

Considering the many efforts made in recent years to curtail or even abolish the national nominating convention, it is worth remembering that the convention system was first developed in part as a reform—a way of allowing for some measure of local control over the nominating process. Virtually no other nation adopted this method, just as no other nation was later to adopt the direct primary after the convention system became the object of criticism. It is interesting, but perhaps futile, to speculate on how American government would have evolved if the legislative caucus had remained as the method for nominating presidents.

The Civil War and Sectionalism

Though the party system created in the Jacksonian period was the first truly national system, with Democrats (followers of Jackson) and Whigs (opponents of Jackson) fairly evenly balanced in most regions, it could not withstand the deep split in opinion created by the agitation over slavery. Both parties tried, naturally, to straddle the issue since neither wanted to divide its followers and thus lose the election to its rival. But slavery and sectionalism were issues that could not be straddled. The parties divided and new parties emerged. The modern Republican party (not the old Democratic-Republican party of Thomas Jefferson) began as a third party. As a result of the Civil War, it came to be a major-party (the only third party ever to gain major party status) and to dominate national politics with only occasional interruptions for three-quarters of a century.

Republican control of the White House, and to a lesser extent of Congress, was in large measure the result to two events that gave to Repub-

❝Slavery and sectionalism were issues that could not be straddled. The parties divided and new parties emerged.❞

licans a marked advantage in the competition for the loyalties of voters. The first of these was the Civil War. This bitter, searing crisis deeply polarized popular attitudes. Those who supported the Union side became, for generations, Republicans; those who supported the Confederacy, or who had opposed the war, became Democrats. As it turned out, this partisan division was, for a while, nearly even—though the Republicans usually won the presidency and the Senate, they often lost control of the House. There were many northern Democrats. In 1896, however, another event—the presidential candidacy of William Jennings Bryan—further strengthened the Republican party. Bryan, a Democrat, alienated many voters in the populous northeastern states while attracting voters in the South and Midwest. The result was to confirm and deepen the split in the country, especially North versus South, begun by the Civil War. From 1896 to the 1930s, with only rare exceptions, the northern states were solidly Republican, the southern ones solidly Democratic.

This had a profound effect on the organization of political parties, for it meant that most states were now one-party states. As a result, competition for office at the state level had to go on *within* a single dominant party (the Republican party in Massachusetts, New York, Pennsylvania, Wisconsin, and elsewhere; the Democratic party in Georgia, Mississippi, South Carolina, and elsewhere). There emerged, as a result, two major factions within each party, but especially within the Republican. One was composed of the party regulars, the professional politicians, the "stalwarts," or the Old Guard. They were preoccupied with building up the party machinery, developing party loyalty, and acquiring and dispensing patronage—jobs and other favors—for themselves and their faithful followers. Their great skills were those of organization, negotiation, bargaining, compromise; their great interest was in winning.

The other faction, variously called "Mugwumps" or "Progressives" or "reformers," was opposed to the heavy emphasis on patronage, disliked the party machinery because it only permitted bland candidates to rise to the top, was fearful of the heavy influx of immigrants into American cities and of the ability of the party regulars to organize them into "machines," and wanted to see the party take unpopular positions on certain issues (such as free trade). Their great skills were those of advocacy and articulation; their great interest was in principle.

At first the Mugwumps tried to play a balance-of-power role, sometimes siding with the Republican party of which they were members, at other times defecting to the Democrats (as when they bolted the Republican party to support Grover Cleveland, the Democratic nominee, in 1884). But later, as the Republican strength in the nation grew, Progressives within that party became less and less able to play a balance-of-power role, especially at the state level. Wisconsin, Michigan, Ohio, and Iowa were solidly Republican; Georgia, the Carolinas, and the rest of the Old South by 1880 had become so heavily Democratic that the Republican party in many areas had virtually ceased to exist. If the Progressives were to have any power, it would require, they came to believe, an attack on the very concept of partisanship itself.

The Era of Reform

Progressives began to espouse measures to curtail or even abolish political parties. They favored primary elections to replace nominating conventions because the latter were viewed as manipulated by party bosses; they favored nonpartisan elections at the city level and in some cases at the state level as well; they argued against corrupt alliances between parties and businesses. They wanted strict voter registration requirements that would reduce vote frauds but would

CLEAVAGES AND CONTINUITY IN THE TWO-PARTY SYSTEM

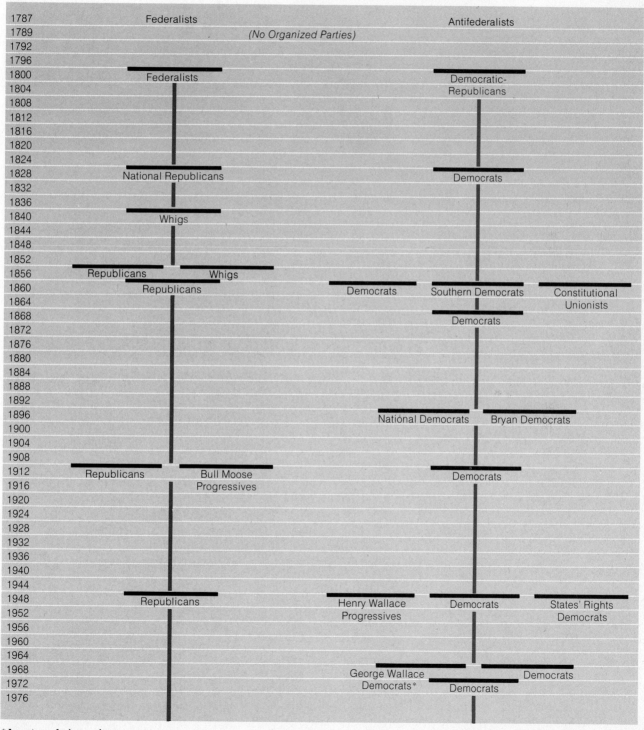

1787	Federalists	Antifederalists
1789	*(No Organized Parties)*	
1792		
1796		
1800	Federalists	Democratic-Republicans
1804		
1808		
1812		
1816		
1820		
1824		
1828	National Republicans	Democrats
1832		
1836		
1840	Whigs	
1844		
1848		
1852		
1856	Republicans · Whigs	
1860	Republicans	Democrats · Southern Democrats · Constitutional Unionists
1864		
1868		Democrats
1872		
1876		
1880		
1884		
1888		
1892		
1896		National Democrats · Bryan Democrats
1900		
1904		
1908		
1912	Republicans · Bull Moose Progressives	Democrats
1916		
1920		
1924		
1928		
1932		
1936		
1940		
1944		
1948	Republicans	Henry Wallace Progressives · Democrats · States' Rights Democrats
1952		
1956		
1960		
1964		
1968		George Wallace Democrats* · Democrats
1972		Democrats
1976		

*American Independent party.

Senator Robert M. La Follette of Wisconsin, here speaking to supporters from his front steps, was a leader of the Progressive movement in the early twentieth century. He ran as a third-party candidate for president in 1924.

also, as it turned out, keep ordinary citizens who found the requirements cumbersome from voting; they pressed for civil service reform to eliminate patronage; and they made heavy use of the mass media as a way of attacking the abuses of partisanship and of promoting their own ideas and candidacies.

The Progressives were more successful in some places than in others. In California, for example, Progressives led by Governor Hiram Johnson in 1910–1911 were able to institute the direct primary and to adopt procedures—called the "initiative" and the "referendum"—so that citizens could vote directly on proposed legislation, thereby bypassing the state legislature. Governor Robert La Follette brought about similar changes in Wisconsin.

The effect of these changes was to reduce substantially the worst forms of political corruption and ultimately to make boss rule in politics difficult if not impossible. But they also had the effect of making political parties, whether led by bosses or statesmen, weaker, less able to hold officeholders accountable, and less able to assemble the power necessary for governing the fragmented political institutions created by the Constitution. Party votes in Congress, as we shall see in Chapter 10, began to decline, as did the power of congressional leadership. Above all, the Progressives did not have an answer to the problem first faced by Jefferson: if there is not a strong political party, by what other means will candidates for office be found, recruited, and supported? Political candidacies, like people, are not the products of a virgin birth. Some group or organization must arrange a candidacy, and if that group is not a party, then it can only be another kind of interest group, the mass media, or the personal supporters and family of the candidate. These alternatives are best seen by looking at the forms of party structure now operating.

PARTY STRUCTURE TODAY

At the national level the formal structure of American political parties is relatively simple; much of it is unimportant. The ultimate source of rules and authority in the Democratic and Republican parties is the national convention, held every four years to nominate a presidential candidate. (In 1974 and again in 1978 the Democrats held an interim or midterm convention—that is, one meeting two years after the regular nominating convention—to discuss issues and modify party rules.) The convention not only selects the presidential and vice-presidential candidates, it also decides on the party's rules, adopts a platform, and chooses the national committee members.

National Committees and Chairmen
The national committee of each party consists of varying numbers of persons, men and women, from each state and from Puerto Rico, the District of Columbia, and certain territories, chosen

by the state parties in a variety of ways. The exact composition of these national committees is of little consequence since they rarely have much to do. Perhaps their most important duty is to choose the party's national chairman, but if the party controls the White House, the president actually makes the choice which the committee merely ratifies. If the committee's party is out of power, there may be some intense bargaining among potential presidential candidates over who is to be chairman in order to ensure that the major duty of this person—to plan the next national nominating convention—is done in a way that does not give an unfair advantage to one candidate. The chairman employs a staff to run the national office. Staff members spend much of their time worrying about how to raise money to pay their own salaries and to settle any debts the party may have accrued.

In addition to the national committees, each party has two committees—a National Congressional Committee and a Senatorial Campaign Committee—with the task of raising and distributing money to help congressional candidates of that party. These committees are made up entirely of representatives and senators and are independent of the Democratic and Republican National Committees.

In the Republican party the National Committee, the Congressional Committee, and the Senatorial Campaign Committee play a somewhat larger role in the affairs of the party than do their Democratic counterparts. The three Republican committees raise a large amount of money from many small contributors by direct-mail advertising. In 1978, for example, the Republicans had nearly half a million donors, the great majority of whom gave $25 or less. With this money the party rents computers and hires staff workers and political and legal advisers. It also gives contributions to Republican candidates, up to the limits imposed by the campaign finance laws described in Chapter 7. The Democratic committees have contributed less to their candidates, allowing local party organizations and candidates to support them-

selves. Given the Democrats' great numerical superiority in Congress, it is not hard to understand why the national party should feel that no elaborate national campaign organization is necessary.

National Conventions

The national committee selects the time and place of the national convention and issues a "call" for the convention that sets forth the number of delegates each state and territory is to have and indicates the rules under which delegates must be chosen. The number of delegates, and their manner of selection, can significantly influence the chances of various presidential candidates, and considerable attention is thus devoted to these matters. In the

The hoopla and hijinks of the national party conventions have been restrained of late by the need to appear dignified on television, but there is still plenty of noise and confusion, as shown here at the 1976 Democratic National Convention.

Democratic party, for example, there was a long struggle between those who wished to see southern states receive a large share of the delegates to the convention in recognition of their firm support of Democratic candidates in presidential elections and those who preferred to see a larger share of delegates allotted to northern and western states that, though less solidly Democratic, were larger or more liberal. A similar conflict within the Republican party has pitted conservative Republican leaders in the Midwest against liberal ones in the East. Though a compromise formula is usually chosen, the drift of these formulas over the years has been gradually to shift voting strength in the Democratic convention away from the South and toward the North and West and in the Republican convention away from the East and toward the South and Southwest. These delegate allocation formulas are but one sign—others will be mentioned later in this chapter—of the tendency of the two parties' conventions to move in opposite ideological directions—the Democrats more to the left, the Republicans more to the right.

The exact formula for apportioning delegates is extremely complex. For the Democrats it takes into account the vote each state cast for Democratic candidates in past elections and the number of electoral votes of each state; for the Republicans, it takes into account the number of representatives in Congress and whether the state in past elections cast its electoral votes for the Republican presidential candidate and elected Republicans to the Senate, the House, and the governorship. Thus, the Democrats give extra delegates to large states while the Republicans give extra ones to loyal states.

The way in which delegates are chosen can be even more important than their allocation. The Democrats, beginning in 1972, have developed an elaborate set of rules designed to weaken the control over delegates by local party leaders and to increase the proportion of women, young persons, blacks, and native Americans attending the convention. These rules were first drafted by a party commission chaired by Senator George

McGovern (who was later to make skillful use of these new procedures in his successful bid for the Democratic presidential nomination). They were revised in 1974 by another commission chaired by Barbara Mikulski, whose decisions were ratified by the 1974 midterm convention. After the 1976 election, yet a third commission, chaired by Morley Winograd, produced still another revision of the rules, approved in June 1978.

Though the details differ in important ways, the general thrust of each Democratic commission that has considered delegate selection has been to broaden or at least maintain the antiparty changes begun by the Progressives at the beginning of this century. Whereas the earlier reformers tried to minimize the role of parties in the election process, those of the 1970s sought to weaken the influence of party leaders and enlarge the role of the rank and file—to create, in short, *intra*party democracy as well as *inter*party democracy. Within the Democratic party, this goal was sought by rules that, for the 1980 convention, require:

- The equal division of delegates between men and women.
- The establishment of "goals" for the representation of "constituency groups" (such as blacks, Hispanics, or native Americans) in proportion to their presence in a state's Democratic electorate.
- Open delegate-selection procedures, with advance publicity and written rules.
- The selection of 75 percent of the delegates at the level of congressional districts or lower.
- The allocation of delegates among presidential candidates in proportion to the votes they get in a primary election or nominating convention, *except* that no delegates are to be given to any candidate who receives less than a minimum percentage of such votes. (The "minimum percentage," apparently designed to make it difficult for marginal candidates to challenge President Carter for the nomination, is set by a complex formula but in general is between 15 and 20 percent.)

> **❝**The general thrust of each Democratic commission that has considered delegate selection has been to broaden or at least maintain the antiparty changes begun by the Progressives at the beginning of this century.**❞**

- No "unit rule"—that is, no delegate may be required to vote as the majority of the delegation votes.
- Restrictions on the number of party leaders and elected officials who can be voting members of the delegation.

The general effect of these and other rules has been to convert the national convention from a place where established party leaders—many of them holding elective office—meet to bargain over who the party's presidential candidate shall be into a meeting that by and large ratifies the decisions made at the state level by voters participating in primary elections or local caucuses. Once, national conventions were portrayed as public circuses whose members were manipulated by party bosses meeting in smoke-filled rooms in nearby hotels. Though much hoopla and not a little smoke remain, the degree of manipulation has been dramatically reduced.

For example, the ability of one state's party leader to bargain with another by offering to swing his bloc of delegates to one candidate if the other leader does the same is sharply limited by Democratic party regulations. These regulations make it hard to "deliver" a state because they prohibit the unit rule, require that a state's delegation proportionately represent each candidate's popularity in that state, and encourage the delegates to be chosen by primary elections or public meetings rather than by the leadership. The delegate-selection rules of the Republican party do not go as far in this direction, but they have increasingly tended to make delegate selection more "open."

Most Americans dislike "manipulation," "bosses," and "deals" and approve of "democracy," "reform," and "openness." These are

First national political convention	*Anti-Masonic party, 1831, in Baltimore*
First time incumbent governors were nominated for president	*Rutherford B. Hayes of Ohio (by Republicans, in 1876) Samuel J. Tilden of New York (by Democrats, in 1876)*
First black to receive a vote at a national party convention	*Frederick Douglass (at Republican convention in 1888)*
First year in which women attended conventions as delegates	*1900 (one woman at both Democratic and Republican conventions)*
Most ballots needed to choose a presidential nominee	*103, by Democrats in 1924 to select John W. Davis*
Closest vote in convention history	*543 3/20 to 542 7/20, defeating a motion to condemn the Ku Klux Klan at 1924 Democratic convention*
First Catholic nominated for president by major party	*Al Smith, by Democrats in 1928*
Only person nominated for president four times by major political party	*Franklin D. Roosevelt (by Democrats in 1932, 1936, 1940, and 1944)*
Only persons nominated for president three times by major political party	*Grover Cleveland (by Democrats in 1884, 1888, and 1892) William Jennings Bryan (by Democrats in 1896, 1900, and 1908) Richard M. Nixon (by Republicans in 1960, 1968, and 1972)*

commendable instincts. But such instincts, if not carefully tested against practical results, may mislead us into supposing that anything described as a "reform" is a good idea. Rules affect the distribution of power: under any rules, some groups win and others lose. Whether we like certain rules depends in part on whether we think them fair and in part on whether we like the outcomes they produce. Later in this chapter we shall consider what outcomes result from the new delegate-selection rules by looking at the effect, if any, they have on who gets to attend a convention and what kinds of presidential candidates are helped or hurt as a result.

STATE AND LOCAL PARTIES

To the extent there is anything like regular, ongoing party organizations, they are found at the city, county, and state levels. Though affiliated with the national Democratic or Republican parties, they are not under the direction or control of the national committee or the national chairman, except insofar as they select delegates to the national conventions. In their day-to-day affairs, they are autonomous, independent units.

Formally, these party units are organized under state law. In a typical state there will be a state committee that nominally is the highest party authority. Below it, there will usually be county committees and sometimes city or town committees. In some places even precincts have a formal party organization. The members of these party committees are selected in a variety of ways—sometimes in primary elections, some-

POLITICAL
PARTY
trivia

Frederick Douglass

Al Smith

Franklin D. Roosevelt

times by conventions, sometimes by a building-block process whereby persons elected to serve on precinct or town committees in turn choose the members of county committees who then choose state committee members.

Occasionally the power in the local party follows the formal structure. But more often, the party can only be understood in terms of the informal processes whereby workers are recruited and leaders selected. Rather than describe a "typical" local party organization—there is no such thing—we shall look at five kinds of party organization and give examples of each. The reader should understand, of course, that each of these types operates within a party structure described by law: legally, they are all precinct, city, or county committees. The names they are given here are not the names by which they are officially known.

The Machine

A political machine is a party organization that recruits its members by the use of tangible incentives—money, political jobs, an opportunity to get favors from government—and that is characterized by a high degree of leadership control over member activity. At one time, many local party organizations were machines, and the struggle over political jobs—patronage—was the chief concern of their members. Though Tammany Hall in New York City began as a caucus of well-to-do notables in the local Democratic party, by the latter part of the nineteenth century it had become a machine organized on the basis of political "clubs" in each assembly district. These clubs were composed of party workers whose job it was to get out the straight party vote in their election districts and who hoped for a tangible reward if they were successful.

And there were abundant rewards for which to hope. During the 1870s, it was estimated that one out of every eight voters in New York City had a federal, state, or city job.[4] The federal bureaucracy was one important source of those jobs. The New York Custom House alone em-

ployed thousands of persons, virtually all of whom were replaced if their party lost the presidential election. The postal system was another source, and it was frankly recognized as such. When James N. Tyner became postmaster general in 1876, he was "appointed not to see that the mails were carried, but to see that Indiana was carried."[5] Elections and conventions were so frequent and the intensity of party competition so great that being a party worker was for many a paid full-time occupation.

Well before the arrival of vast numbers of poor immigrants from Ireland, Italy, and elsewhere, old-stock Americans had perfected the machine, run up the cost of government, and systematized vote frauds. Kickbacks on contracts, payments extracted from officeholders, and funds raised from businessmen made some politicians rich but also paid the huge bills of the elaborate party organization. When the immigrants began flooding the eastern cities, the party machines were there to provide them with all manner of services in exchange for their support at the polls: the machines were a vast welfare organization operating before the creation of the welfare state.

The abuses of the machine were well known and gradually curtailed. Stricter voter registration laws reduced fraud, civil service reforms cut back on the number of patronage jobs, and competitive bidding laws made it harder to award overpriced contracts to favored businesses. The Hatch Act (passed by Congress in 1939) made it illegal for federal civil service employees to take an active part in political management or political campaigns by serving as a party officer, soliciting campaign funds, running for partisan office, working in a partisan campaign, endorsing partisan candidates, taking voters to the polls, counting ballots, circulating nominating petitions, or being a delegate to a party convention. (They may still vote and make campaign contributions.)

These restrictions gradually took federal employees out of machine politics, but they did not end the machines. In many cities, such as

❝It is easy either to scorn the machine as a venal and self-serving organization or to romanticize it as an informal welfare system. In truth, it was a little of both.❞

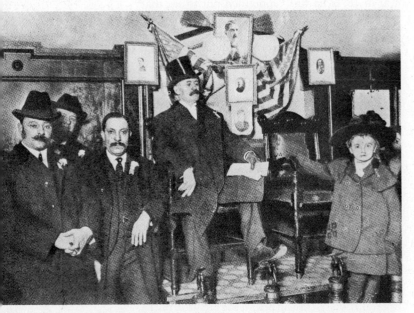

Ex-Senator George Washington Plunkitt of Tammany Hall explains machine politics from atop the bootblack stand in front of the New York County Court House, around 1905.

Chicago, Philadelphia, and Albany, ways were found to maintain the machine even though city employees were technically under civil service. Far more important than the various Progressive reforms that weakened machines were changes among voters. As voters grew in education, income, and sophistication, they depended less and less on the advice and leadership of local party officials. And as the federal government created a bureaucratic welfare system, the party's welfare system declined in value.

It is easy either to scorn the machine as a venal and self-serving organization or to romanticize it as an informal welfare system. In truth, it was a little of both. Above all, it was a frank recognition of the fact that politics requires organization; the machine was the supreme expression of

the value of organization. Even allowing for vote frauds, in elections where machines were active, voter turnout was huge: more people participated in politics when mobilized by a machine than when appealed to by television or good government associations.[6] Moreover, because machines are interested in winning, they will subordinate any other consideration to that end. This has meant that machines were usually willing to support the presidential candidate with the best chance of winning, regardless of his policy views (provided, of course, that he was not determined to wreck the machine once in office). Republican machines helped elect Abraham Lincoln as well as Warren G. Harding; Democratic machines were of crucial importance in electing Franklin D. Roosevelt and John F. Kennedy. As we shall see, some other kinds of party organization may be more interested in supporting a principle than in winning an election.

Ideological Parties

At the opposite extreme from the machine is the ideological party. Where the machine values winning above all else, the ideological party values principle above all else. Where the former depends on money incentives, the latter spurns them. And whereas the former is strongly hierarchical and disciplined, the latter is usually contentious and factionalized.

Most ideological parties have never been part of the Democratic or Republican parties because to be such would require that the former compromise their principles in order to accommodate the electoral needs of the latter. The typical ideological party is a "third party," such as the Socialist, Socialist Workers, Prohibition, and Libertarian parties. But within both the Democratic and Republican parties there can be found local units that are, if not rigidly ideological, then certainly more devoted to issues and principles than to party loyalty.

Important examples of this are the "reform" or "amateur" clubs that sprang up in the late

1950s and early 1960s in such cities as New York, Los Angeles, and San Francisco and in many parts of states such as Wisconsin and Minnesota. These clubs had two traits in common: the members became active in politics because of their interest in issues, and they expected that decisions within the party would be as participatory and democratic as possible.

Sometimes, as with the reform clubs in New York during the 1960s, they arose initially to challenge the machine bosses, such as Carmine de Sapio of Tammany Hall. Loosely allied as the Committee for Democratic Voters, they became a dominant force in Manhattan. In California, on the other hand, where there was no machine to attack, the clubs moved to fill the vacuum created by the absence of any other kind of organization. These clubs, collectively known as the California Democratic Council, have been from time to time the major locus of political power in the state, far more important than the Democratic state committee which is, by law, the formal head of the party.[7]

Because persons who join these clubs are interested in issues, the conflict within and among the clubs over the proper position to take on issues is often intense. By the same token, the leaders of these clubs, unlike those of machines, have much less room for maneuvering or bargaining: if, in negotiations with other politicians, they demand too little or give up too much, they will be accused by their followers of a "sell-out" and, in all likelihood, replaced. Since politics, especially in a two-party system, requires that coalitions be built among groups and persons who do not always agree on everything, this constraint on the ability of a club leader to make useful alliances can be a weakness.

Not all issue-oriented clubs are Democratic. Many are Republican, as in California where the Republican Assembly—a collection of such clubs—was for a long time far more important than the formal party machinery in promoting candidates. The policies in which Republican volunteers are interested differ, of course, from those of their Democratic counterparts, but the organizational consequences are very much the same. Where Democratic club members tend to be much more left-liberal than the average Democratic voter, Republican club members tend to be much more right-conservative than the typical Republican voter.[8] As we shall see later in this chapter, the increased importance of such issue-oriented activists in national nominating conventions has affected the kinds of decisions made there.

Solidary Groups

Machines, ideological groups, and issue-oriented clubs may be the most visible or dramatic forms of party organization, but they are not the most common. Most people who participate in politics derive neither money benefits nor an enlarged sense of purpose from their activity; rather, they simply find it fun. Sometimes they get into politics because they enjoy the game, sometimes because it is a way of meeting and being with people. When people get together on a regular, organized basis to participate in politics out of gregarious or game-loving instincts, we call the group that results a "sociability" or "solidary" association.

Some of these associations were once machines. When a machine loses its patronage, some of its members—especially the older ones—may continue to serve in the organization out of a desire for camaraderie. In other cases, precinct, ward, and district committees are built up from the first on the basis of friendship networks. One study of political activists in Detroit found that most of them mentioned friendships and a liking for politics, rather than an interest in issues, as their reason for joining the party organization.[9] Members of ward and town organizations in St. Louis County gave the same answer when asked why they joined.[10] Since patronage has declined in value and since the appeals of ideology are limited to a minority of citizens, the motivations for participating in politics have increasingly become very much like those for joining a bowling league or a bridge club.

The advantage of such groups is that they are neither corrupt nor inflexible; the disadvantage is that they often do not work very hard. Knocking on doors on a rainy November evening to try to talk people into voting for your candidate is a chore under the best of circumstances; it is especially unappealing if you joined the party primarily because you like to attend meetings or drink coffee with your friends.[11]

Sponsored Parties

Sometimes a relatively strong party organization can be created among volunteers without heavy reliance on money or ideology and without depending entirely on persons finding the work fun. This occurs when another organization exists in the community that can create, or at least sponsor, a local party structure. The clearest example of this is the Democratic party in and around Detroit, which has been developed, led, and to a degree financed by the political action arm of the United Auto Workers union. The UAW has had a long tradition of rank-and-file activism, stemming from its formative struggles in the 1930s, and since the city is virtually a one-industry town, it was not hard to transfer some of this activism from union organizing to voter organizing.

By the mid-1950s, union members and leaders made up over three-fourths of all the Democratic party district leaders within the city.[12] On election day, union funds were available for paying persons to canvass voters; between elections, political work on an unpaid basis was expected of union leaders. Though the UAW–Democratic party alliance in Detroit has not always been successful in city elections (the city is nonpartisan), it has been quite successful in carrying the city for the Democratic party in state and national elections. This electoral power enhanced the influence of the UAW in deciding what candidates would get the party's nomination.

Not many areas have organizations as effective or as dominant as the UAW that can bolster, sponsor, or even take over the weak formal party structure. Thus, sponsored local parties are not common in the United States.

Personal Followings

Because candidates can no longer count (in most areas) on the backing of a machine, because issue-oriented clubs are limited to upper-middle-class areas and sponsored parties to a few unionized areas, and because solidary groups are not always very productive, a person wanting to win an election will usually try to form a personal following who will work for him, without pay, during a specific election campaign and then disband until the next election rolls around.

For this to succeed, the candidate must have an appealing personality, a lot of friends, or a big bank account. The Kennedy family has had all three, and the electoral success of the personal followings of John F. and Edward M. Kennedy in Massachusetts and of Robert Kennedy in New York became legendary. James Michael Curley was sometimes described as the "boss" of Boston when he was mayor, but he was nothing of the kind—he relied, not on a political machine, but on his ability to build a personal following. Southern politicians, perhaps because so many operate in one-party states that lack machines, have been the grand masters at building followings, such as those of Eugene Talmadge and his son, Herman, in Georgia, or those of Huey, Earl, and Russell Long in Louisiana.

Before radio and television, many politicians wishing to build a personal following had to content themselves with running for office in small constituencies where they could easily become known. In building a state or national "name" for themselves, newspapers were sometimes useful, but since editors decide what shall and shall not be printed, not every aspiring candidate could be certain that his message would get printed to his liking. Radio and television, as

Two generations of political followings: Senator Herman Talmadge of Georgia sits at a desk beneath a picture of his father, Eugene Talmadge, who was governor of Georgia for three terms.

we shall see, changed all this, permitting a candidate to speak directly to large numbers of voters, without editing, and thus to build statewide and even national followings completely outside the party structure.

Some readers may take it for granted that a personal following is a good thing, since it makes it easier to vote for the person rather than the party and to keep party "bosses" from interfering with the popular will. That may often be the case, but there is another side to the story. A politics of personal followings is a politics of personality; with so many offices to be filled and so many personalities offering to fill them, the average voter will be lucky if he or she can form a

reasonable judgment about even two or three candidates in the course of a year or two. Personality politics can lead to individualistic, uninformed politics, as V. O. Key, Jr., found when he studied the way "nonparty" politics operated in the South.[13] In those places where the South was free of machines, it often had demagogues instead. It is not easy to decide whether one prefers strong party politics, with a risk of bossism and corruption but with the advantage of the ability to get things done and the opportunity to hold the party collectively responsible for its leaders' actions, or nonparty politics, with a freedom from party controls but little opportunity to build cohesive governing coalitions.

THE TWO-PARTY SYSTEM

With so many different varieties of local party organizations (or nonorganizations) and with such a great range of opinion found within each party, it is remarkable that we have had only two major political parties for most of our history. In the world at large, a two-party system is a rarity; by one estimate, only 15 out of 131 nations have it.[14] Most European democracies are multiparty systems. Not only do we have but two parties with any chance of winning nationally, these parties have been, over time, rather evenly balanced—between 1888 and 1976, the Republicans won twelve presidential elections and the Democrats eleven. Furthermore, whenever one party has achieved a temporary ascendancy and its rival has been pronounced dead (as were the Democrats during the Republican dominance in the first third of this century and as were the Republicans during the 1930s and again in the 1960s), the "dead" party has displayed remarkable powers of recuperation, coming back to win important victories.

At the state or congressional district level, however, the parties are not evenly balanced. For a long time the South was so heavily Democratic at all levels of government as to be a one-party area while upper New England and the Dakotas were strongly Republican. All regions are more competitive today than once was the case, but even now one party or the other tends to enjoy a substantial advantage in at least half the states and in perhaps two-thirds of the congressional districts. Nevertheless, though the parties are not as competitive in state elections as they are in presidential ones, there have rarely been in the states, at least for any extended period of time, political parties other than the Democrats and the Republicans. (See Table 6.1.)

Scholars are not entirely in agreement as to why the two-party system should be so permanent a feature of American political life, but two kinds of explanations are of major importance. The first has to do with the system of elections, the second with the distribution of public opinion.

Elections at every level of government are based on the plurality, winner-take-all method. The plurality system means that in all elections for representative, senator, governor, and president, and in almost all elections for state legislator, mayor, and city councillor, the winner is that person who gets the most votes, even if they do not constitute a majority. We are so familiar with this system we sometimes forget there are other ways of running an election. For example, one could require that the winner get a majority of the votes, thus producing runoff elections if

TABLE 6.1   The Rise of Republican Politics in the South, 1950–1978

Year	Number of congressmen		Number of senators		Number of governors		Number of states voting for presidential nominee	
	D	R	D	R	D	R	D	R
1950	103	2	22	0	11	0		
1952	100	6	22	0	11	0	7	4
1954	99	7	22	0	11	0		
1956	99	7	22	0	11	0	6	5
1958	99	7	22	0	11	0		
1960	99	7	22	0	11	0	8[a]	2
1962	95	11	21	1	11	0		
1964	89	17	21	1	11	0	6	5
1966	83	23	19	3	9	2		
1968	80	26	18	4	9	2	1	5[b]
1970	79	27	16 (1)[c]	5	9	2		
1972	74	34	14 (1)[c]	7	8	3	0	11
1974	81	27	15 (1)[c]	6	8	3		
1976	82	26	16 (1)[c]	5	9	2	10	1
1978	77	31	15 (1)[c]	6	8	3		

[a] Eight Mississippi electors voted for Harry Byrd.
[b] George Wallace won five states on the American Independent ticket.
[c] Harry Byrd, Jr., was elected in Virginia in 1970 and 1976 as an Independent.

nobody got a majority on the first try. France does this in choosing its national legislature. In the first election, candidates for parliament who win an absolute majority of the votes cast are declared elected. A week later, the remaining candidates who received at least one-eighth but less than one-half the vote go into a runoff election; those who then win an absolute majority are also elected.

The French method encourages many political parties to form, each hoping to win at least one-eighth of the vote in the first election and then to enter into an alliance with its ideologically nearest rival in order to win the runoff. In the United States the plurality system means that a party must make all of the alliances it can before the first election—there is no second chance. Hence, every party must be as broadly based as possible; a narrow, minor party has no hope of winning.

The winner-take-all feature of American elections has the same effect. Only one congressman is elected from each district. In many European countries, the elections are based on proportional representation. Each party submits a list of candidates for parliament, ranked in order of preference by the party leaders. The nation votes. A party winning 37 percent of the vote gets 37 percent of the seats in parliament; a party winning 2 percent of the vote gets 2 percent of the seats. Since even the smallest parties have a chance of winning something, minor parties have an incentive to organize.

The most dramatic example of the winner-take-all principle is the American Electoral College. Whichever candidate for president wins the most popular votes in a state wins *all* of that state's electoral votes. In 1968, for example, Richard Nixon only won 45 percent of the popular vote in Missouri, but he got all of Missouri's twelve electoral votes because his two rivals (Hubert Humphrey and George Wallace) each got fewer popular votes. Minor parties cannot compete under this system. Voters know this and

In France, as in many European countries, parties are both more numerous and more influential than in the United States. In this French election, the voter can choose one of six lists of candidates offered by six different parties.

are often reluctant to "waste" their vote on a minor-party candidate who cannot win.

The United States has experimented with other electoral systems. Proportional representation was used for municipal elections in New York City at one time and is still in use for that purpose in Cambridge, Massachusetts. Many states have elected more than one state legislator from each district. In Illinois, for example, three legislators have been elected from each district with each voter allowed to cast two votes, thus virtually guaranteeing that the minority party will be able to win one of the three seats. But none of these experiments has altered the national two-party system, probably because of the existence of a directly elected president chosen by a winner-take-all Electoral College.

❝The presidency is the great prize of American politics; to win it, you must form a party with as broad an appeal as possible.❞

George Wallace in 1968 received nearly 14 percent of the popular presidential vote. But many persons who liked him probably were reluctant to "waste" their votes on a minor-party candidate with no chance of winning.

The presidency is the great prize of American politics; to win it, you must form a party with as broad an appeal as possible. As a practical matter, that means there will be, in most cases, only two serious parties—one made up of those who support the party already in power and the other made up of everybody else. Only one third party ever won the presidency—the Republicans in 1860—and it went on to become a major party.

The second kind of explanation for the persistence of two parties is to be found in the opinions of the voters. Though there have been periods of bitter dissent, most of the time most citizens have agreed enough to permit them to come together into two broad coalitions. There has not been a massive and persistent body of opinion that has rejected the prevailing economic system (and thus we have not had, except occasionally, a Marxist party with mass appeal); there has not been in our history an aristocracy or monarchy (and thus there has been no party that has sought to restore aristocrats or monarchs to power). Churches and religion have almost always been regarded as matters of private choice that lie outside politics (and thus there has not been a party seeking to create or abolish special governmental privileges for one church or another). In some European nations, the organization of the economy, the prerogatives of the monarchy, and the role of the church have been major issues with long and bloody histories. So divisive have these issues been that they have helped prevent the formation of broad coalition parties.

But Americans have had other deep divisions—between white and black, for example, or between North and South—and yet the two-party system has endured. This suggests that electoral procedures are of great importance—the winner-take-all, plurality election rules have made it useless for anyone to attempt to create an all-white or an all-black national party except as an act of momentary defiance or in the hope of taking enough votes away from the two major parties to force the presidential election into the House of Representatives. (That may have been George Wallace's strategy in 1968.)

For many years there was an additional reason for the two-party system: the laws of many states made it difficult, if not impossible, for third parties to get on the ballot. In 1968, for example, the American Independent party of George Wallace found that it would have to collect 433,000 signatures (15 percent of the votes cast in the last statewide election) in order to get on the presidential ballot in Ohio. Wallace took the issue to the Supreme Court which ruled, six to three, that such a restriction was an unconstitutional violation of the equal protection clause of the Fourteenth Amendment.[15] Wallace got on the ballot, and other states in the future will no doubt find it difficult to use burdensome restrictions for the purpose of maintaining the two-party system. But for the reasons already indicated, that system will probably persist even without the aid of these legal protections.

MINOR PARTIES

The electoral system may prevent minor parties from winning, but it does not prevent them from forming. Minor parties—usually called, erroneously, "third parties"—have been a permanent feature of American political life. Four major kinds of minor parties, with examples of each, are described on this page.

The minor parties that have endured have been the ideological ones. Their members feel themselves to be outside the mainstream of American political life and sometimes, as in the case of various Marxist parties, look forward to a time when a revolution or some other dramatic change in the political system will vindicate them. They are usually not interested in immediate electoral success and thus persist despite their poor showing at the polls. One such party, however, the Socialist party of Eugene Debs, won nearly 6 percent of the popular vote in the 1912 presidential election and during its heyday elected 1,200 candidates to local offices, including 79 mayors. Part of the Socialist appeal arose from its opposition to municipal corruption, part from its opposition to American entry into World War I, and part from its critique of American society. No ideological party has ever carried a state in a presidential election.

Apart from the Republicans, who quickly became a major party, the only minor parties to carry states and thus win electoral votes were one party of economic protest (the Populists, who

Types of Minor Parties

1. **Ideological parties**
   Parties professing a comprehensive view of American society and government that is radically different from that of the established parties. Most of these have been Marxist in outlook, but some are quite the opposite, such as the Libertarian party.

   Examples:
   Socialist party (1901 to 1960s)
   Socialist Labor party (1888 to present)
   Socialist Workers party (1938 to present)
   Communist party (1920s to present)
   Libertarian party (1972 to present)

2. **One-issue parties**
   Parties seeking a single policy, usually revealed by their names, and avoiding other issues.

   Examples:
   Free Soil party (to prevent spread of slavery) 1848–1852
   American or "Know-Nothing" party (to oppose immigration and Catholics) 1856
   Prohibition party (to ban the sale of liquor) 1869 to present

3. **Economic protest parties**
   Parties, usually based in a particular region, especially involving farmers, that protest against depressed economic conditions. These tend to disappear as conditions improve.

   Examples:
   Greenback party (1876–1884)
   Populist party (1892–1908)

4. **Factional parties**
   Parties that are created by a split in a major party, usually over the identity and philosophy of the major party's presidential candidate.

   Examples:
   Split off from the Republican party—
      "Bull Moose" Progressive party (1912)
      La Follette Progressive party (1924)

   Split off from the Democratic party—
      States' Rights ("Dixiecrat") party (1948)
      Henry Wallace Progressive party (1948)
      American Independent (George Wallace) party (1968)

The Socialist party and the Progressive party were both minor parties, but their origins were different. The Socialist party was an ideological party; the "Bull Moose" Progressive party split off from the Republican party.

carried five states in 1892) and several factional parties (most recently, the States' Rights Democrats in 1948 and the American Independent party of George Wallace in 1968). Though factional parties may hope to cause the defeat of the party from which they split, they have not always been able to achieve this. Harry Truman was elected in 1948 despite the defections of both the leftist Progressives, led by Henry Wallace, and the right-wing Dixiecrats, led by J. Strom Thurmond. In 1968 Hubert Humphrey would probably have lost even if George Wallace had not been in the race (Wallace voters would probably have switched to Nixon rather than to Humphrey, though of course one cannot be certain). It is quite possible, on the other hand, that a Republican might have beaten Woodrow Wilson in 1912 if the Republican party had not split in two (the regulars supporting William Howard Taft, the Progressives supporting Theodore Roosevelt).

What is striking is not that we have had so many minor parties, but that we have not had more. There have been several major political movements that did not produce a significant third party: the civil rights movement of the 1960s, the antiwar movement of the same 1960s, the antiwar movement of the same

decade, and most important the labor movement in this century. Blacks were part of the Republican party after the Civil War and part of the Democratic party after the New Deal (even though the southern wing of that party for a long time kept them from voting). The antiwar movement found candidates with whom it could identify within the Democratic party (Eugene McCarthy, Robert F. Kennedy, George McGovern) even though it was a Democratic president, Lyndon B. Johnson, who was chiefly responsible for our commitment in Vietnam. After Johnson only narrowly won the 1968 New Hampshire primary, he withdrew from the race. Unions in this century have not tried to create a labor party—indeed, they were for a long time opposed to almost any kind of national political activity. Since labor became a major political force in the 1930s, the largest industrial unions have been content to operate as a part (and a very large part) of the Democratic party.

One reason why some potential sources of minor parties never formed such parties, in addition to the dim chance of success, is that the direct primary and the national convention have made it possible for dissident elements of a major party, unless they become completely disaffected, to remain in the party and affect the choice of candidates and policies. The antiwar movement had a profound effect on the Democratic conventions of 1968 and 1972; blacks have played a growing role in the Democratic party; only in 1972 did the unions feel that the Democrats nominated a presidential candidate (McGovern) unacceptable to them.

The impact of minor parties on American politics is hard to judge. One bit of conventional wisdom holds that minor parties develop ideas that the major parties later come to adopt. The Socialist party, for example, is supposed to have called for major social and economic policies that the Democrats under Roosevelt later embraced and termed the New Deal. It is possible that the Democrats did "steal the thunder" of the Socialists, but it hardly seems likely that they did it because the Socialists had proposed these things or proved them popular. (In 1932 the Socialists got only 2 percent of the vote and in 1936 less than one-half of 1 percent.) Roosevelt probably adopted the policies he did in part because he thought them correct and in part because dissident elements within his *own* party—leaders such as Huey Long of Louisiana— were threatening to bolt the Democratic party if it did not move to the left. Even Prohibition was adopted more as a result of the efforts of interest groups such as the Anti-Saloon League than as the consequence of its endorsement by the Prohibition party.

The minor parties that have probably had the greatest influence on public policy have been the factional parties. Mugwumps and Liberal Republicans, by bolting the regular party, may have made that party more sensitive to the issue of civil service reform; the Bull Moose and La Follette Progressive parties probably helped encourage the major parties to pay more attention to issues of business regulation and party reform; the power of the Dixiecrat and Wallace movements probably strengthened the hands of those who wished to go slow on desegregation. The threat of a factional split is a risk both major parties must face, and it is in the efforts each makes to avoid such splits that one finds the greatest impact, at least in this century, of minor parties.

NOMINATING A PRESIDENT

The major parties face, as we have seen, two contrary forces: one, generated by the desire to win the presidency, pushes them in the direction of nominating a candidate who can appeal to the majority of voters and who will thus have essentially middle-of-the-road views. The other, produced by the need to keep dissident elements in the party from bolting and forming a third party, leads them to compromise with dissidents or extremists in ways that may damage the party's standing with the voters.

The Democrats and Republicans have always faced these conflicting pressures, but of late they have become especially acute. When the presidential nomination was made by a party convention that was heavily influenced, if not controlled, by party leaders and elected officials, it was relatively easy to ignore dissident factions and pick candidates on the basis of who could win. The *electoral* objectives of the party were predominant. The price that was paid for this was that often a faction left the party and ran a separate ticket—as happened in 1912, 1924, 1948, and 1968. Today the power of party leaders and elected officials within the parties is greatly diminished, with most delegates now selected by primary elections. A larger proportion of the delegates is likely to be more interested in issues and to be less amenable to compromise over those issues than was once the case. In these circumstances the *policy* interests of the party activists are likely to be important.

Are the Delegates Representative of the Voters?
There would be no conflict between the electoral and policy interests of a political party if the delegates to its nominating convention had the

Party activists often have opinions quite different from those of rank-and-file party supporters. The women pictured here supporting legalized abortions would have much support at a Democratic national convention; the woman with the sign opposing abortion would have little.

same policy views as most voters, or at least as most party supporters. In fact, this is not the case—in parties as in many organizations, the activists and leaders tend to have views different from those of the rank and file.[16] In American political parties in recent years, this difference has become very great.

At both the 1972 and 1976 Democratic national conventions, the delegates had views on a variety of important issues that were vastly different from those of rank-and-file Democrats. On welfare, military policy, school desegregation, crime, and abortion, Democratic delegates expressed opinions that were almost diametrically opposed to those of most Democrats (see Table 6.2). The Republican national convention in 1972, on the other hand, was composed of

delegates whose views were quite similar to those of rank-and-file Republicans. Indeed, so divergent were the Democratic delegate opinions that the attitudes of most *Republican* delegates were closer to the views of rank-and-file Democrats.[17]

In 1964 the Republican party nominated Barry Goldwater for president. We have no opinion data for delegates to that convention as detailed and comprehensive as those available for the 1972 and 1976 conventions, but it seems clear that the Republican delegates then, like the Democratic delegates in 1972, selected as their nominee a person who was not the most popular candidate among voters at large and thus was not the candidate most likely to win.

What accounts for the sharp disparity between delegate opinion (and often delegate candidate preference) and voter attitudes? Some have blamed the discrepancy on the rules, described earlier in this chapter, under which delegates are chosen, especially those rules that require increased representation for women, minorities, and the young. Close examination suggests that this is not a plausible explanation. For one thing, it will not explain why the Republicans nominated Goldwater in 1964 (and almost nominated Ronald Reagan, another non-mainstream candidate, in 1976). For another, women, minorities, and youth have among them all shades of opinions—there are plenty of middle-of-the road women and young persons as well as very liberal or very conservative ones. (There are not many very conservative blacks, at least on race issues, but there are certainly plenty who are moderate on race and conservative on other issues.) The question to be answered is why only *certain* elements of these groups were heavily represented at the 1972 convention.

Who Votes in Primaries?

A second explanation is the increased importance of primaries. In 1968, seventeen states held primaries and thereby picked about 38 percent of the Democratic delegates; in 1972, twenty-three states held primaries and thereby chose 61 percent of the delegates. By 1976, thirty states were picking delegates by primaries, accounting for 73 percent of the votes at the Democratic convention (and 68 percent of those at the Republican).[18] Now, if voters were to turn out in large numbers in primary elections, we might assume that delegates picked by that process would have attitudes very much like those of the voters themselves. But in fact far fewer voters participate in primaries than in general elections. In 1976, for example, only about 28 percent of the voting-age population participated in the presidential primaries (by contrast, 54 percent voted in the general election).[19]

If only half as many people turn out in primary as in general elections, then there is a good chance that those who turn out in the former are different in important ways from those who vote in the latter. They would obviously be more strongly motivated, and they may have different policy views as well. Unfortunately, we have little evidence that measures with any accuracy the extent to which primary voters are alike or unlike voters generally.

Who Are the New Delegates?

A third explanation is that, however delegates are chosen, they are a different breed today than they once were. Whether picked by caucuses or primaries, and of whatever sex or race, a far larger proportion of convention delegates, both Republican and Democratic, are issue-oriented activists—persons with an "amateur" or "purist" view of politics. Far fewer delegates are in it for the money (there is no longer much patronage to pass around) or simply for the fun of the game. And there has been a sharp rise in the proportion

---

TABLE 6.2   How Democratic Voters and Democratic Delegates Differ:
A Comparison of the Views of Voters Identifying Themselves as Democrats with the Views of the Delegates to the 1976 Democratic National Convention

Policy Preference	Democratic Voters	Democratic Delegates
Favor busing for school integration	24%	50%
Believe we are spending too much on defense	30	60
Favor right to abortion	42	83
Favor death penalty for serious crimes	76	54
Believe too much attention is paid to minorities	42	14
Describe self as "conservative"	36	8

Source: Everett Carll Ladd, Jr., *Where Have All the Voters Gone? The Fracturing of America's Political Parties* (New York: W. W. Norton, 1978), p. 65. Reprinted by permission.

of delegates with college degrees (three times as many Democratic delegates in 1972 had post-graduate degrees as did Democratic delegates in 1948).[20] Many of the Democratic delegates in 1972 and 1976 were part of what was called in Chapter 5 the "New Class."

Party activists, especially those who do the work without pay and who are in politics out of an interest in issues, are not likely to resemble the average citizen, for whom politics is merely an object of observation, discussion, and occasional voting. In 1972 such activists at the Democratic convention were most likely to be supportive of one of the two candidates with the strongest ideological appeal—McGovern or Wallace—and least likely to be supportive of those candidates that represented party regularity (Edmund Muskie, Hubert Humphrey).[21] It seems likely that the same thing was true at the Republican conventions of 1964 and 1976: the activists favored the more ideological candidates.

In sum, the changing incentives for participation in party work, in addition to such effect as the primary system may have, have contributed to the development of a national presidential nominating system different from that which once existed. The advantage of the new system is that it increases the opportunity for persons with strong policy preferences to play a role in the party and thus reduces the chance that they will bolt the party and form a factional minor party. The disadvantage of the system is that it increases the chances that one or both parties may nominate presidential candidates who are not appealing to the average voter or even to a party's rank and file.

DO THE PARTIES DIFFER?

Though the presidential nomination process may sometimes produce candidates whose opinions are at odds with those of the voters, in general the words "Democrat" or "Republican" on the ballot cover candidates who espouse a great variety of views. So large is the umbrella of the party label that many citizens wonder whether the parties differ at all. Might they not be, as some have suggested, no different than Tweedledum and Tweedledee?

Appearances would certainly suggest that, as George Wallace liked to say, there is not a "dime's worth of difference" between the Democrats and Republicans. The Democrats include senators as liberal as George McGovern and Edward Kennedy and as conservative as Herman Talmadge and John Stennis; among the Republicans are such liberals as Charles Mathias and Jacob Javits and such conservatives as Jesse Helms and Strom Thurmond.

These differences within the parties are enough to convince some persons that the parties are utterly lacking in principle or philosophy. It should be clear by now why, in a two-party, winner-take-all system, the parties have good reason to avoid organizing around a clear principle or philosophy. When they have tried to do so, they have often discovered that enunciating any clear, specific party philosophy costs them more votes than they gain, especially since the party activists who are the likely source of these principles will probably have views very different from those of the average voter.

Though the need to win elections pulls each party toward the center as the party tries to attract the uncommitted voter, there is still a significant difference in the general policy attitudes of the two parties, especially among leaders and activists. Even among rank-and-file voters who identify with one party or the other, some differences in preferences are evident. In 1972, for example, voters who identified with the Democratic party were slightly more liberal on a number of policy questions than were voters who identified with the Republican party. Democratic identifiers were somewhat more likely than Republican ones to favor busing for school integration, to believe that abolishing poverty by government action is more important than emphasizing the obligation to work, and to favor

TABLE 6.3   Policy Preferences of Voters Who Identify with Democratic and Republican Parties, 1972

Issue and Position	Preferences of Democratic Voters	Republican Voters
Welfare:		
"No one should live in poverty whether or not they work"	22%	13%
"Persons able to work should be required to work"	69	79
Busing to integrate schools:		
Favor busing	15	5
Oppose busing	82	93
Crime:		
More important to protect rights of accused	36	28
More important to stop crime	50	56
Attitude toward military:		
Favorable	67	71
Unfavorable	16	12
Neutral	16	18

Source: Jeane Kirkpatrick, *The New Presidential Elite* (New York: Russell Sage Foundation, 1976), Tables 10-1, 10-2, 10-3, 10-7.

protecting the rights of the accused as opposed to reducing crime (see Table 6.3). If these were the only differences between the parties, one might be justified in concluding that they are but two slightly different versions of the same political creed.

Among party activists, leaders, and officeholders, however, the differences between the two parties are very large. The delegates to the 1972 Democratic and Republican presidential nominating conventions had almost totally opposed views on such questions as welfare, busing, crime, and the military. For example, whereas 66 percent of the Democratic delegates favored school busing to achieve racial balance, only 8 percent of the Republican delegates sup-

66 Most voters cluster toward the middle of the political spectrum; to win an election, the parties must appeal to such middle-of-the-road voters. **99**

ported busing (see Table 6.4). Another study of 1972 attitudes found that Republican party activists were significantly more conservative than Republican identifiers and Democratic party activists were substantially more liberal than Democratic identifiers.[22] A study done at the time of the 1976 elections showed the same thing.[23]

Among persons elected to office, the same partisan differences are apparent. As we shall see in Chapter 10, the Democratic members of the House of Representatives and of the Senate are much more liberal in their voting behavior than are the Republican members of the two houses of Congress.

It is possible the two parties became more different in the 1960s and 1970s than they had been earlier. As we saw in Chapter 5, there is some evidence, though not yet clear proof, that more persons consider themselves liberals or conservatives now than formerly. This change has especially affected activists in the Democratic party. In 1968 and again 1972, the proportion of Democratic activists who had distinctly liberal views was more than twice that in 1956 or 1960.[24]

These facts suggest the central problem faced by a political party today. Most voters cluster toward the middle of the political spectrum; to win an election, the parties must appeal to such middle-of-the-road voters. But the activists, leaders, convention delegates, and officeholders within each party have views that tend to be closer to the political extremes than to the middle. Thus, a person seeking to obtain power in a party, become a convention delegate, or win a party's nomination for office must often move closer to the extremes than to the center. This creates a potential dilemma: the stance one takes to obtain the support of party activists must often be quite different from the stance one must take to win a general election. In the next chapter, we shall look closely at how politicians try to cope with that dilemma.

SUMMARY

A political party exists in three arenas: among the voters who psychologically identify with it, as a grass-roots organization staffed and led by activists, and as a group of elected officials who follow its lead in law-making. In this chapter we have looked at the party primarily as an organization and seen the various forms it takes at the local level—the machine, the ideological party, the solidary group, the sponsored party, and the personal following.

TABLE 6.4   Policy Preferences of Delegates to Democratic and Republican Presidential Nominating Conventions, 1972

Issue and Position	Preferences of Democratic Delegates	Republican Delegates
Welfare:		
"No one should live in poverty whether or not they work"	57%	10%
"Persons able to work should be required to work"	28	75
Busing to integrate schools:		
Favor busing	66	8
Oppose busing	25	84
Crime:		
More important to protect rights of accused	78	21
More important to stop crime	13	56
Attitude toward military:		
Favorable	42	84
Unfavorable	43	4
Neutral	14	12

Source: Jeane Kirkpatrick, *The New Presidential Elite* (New York: Russell Sage Foundation, 1976), Tables 10-1, 10-2, 10-3, 10-7.

Nationally, the parties are weak, decentralized coalitions of these local forms. As organizations that influence the political systems, parties are getting weaker. Voters no longer strongly identify with one of the major parties as they once did. The spread of the direct primary has made it harder for parties to control who is nominated for elective office, thus making it harder for the parties to influence the behavior of these people once elected. Delegate-selection rules, especially in the Democratic party, have helped shift the center of power in the national nominating convention. Because of the changes in rules, power has moved away from officeholders and party "regulars" and toward the more ideological wings of the parties.

Minor parties have arisen from time to time, but the only ones that have affected the outcome of presidential elections have been those that represented a splinter group within one of the major parties (such as the Bull Moose Progressives). The two-party system is maintained, and minor parties are discouraged, by an election system (winner-take-all, plurality elections) that makes voters reluctant to "waste" a vote on a minor party and by the ability of potential minor parties to wield influence within a major party by means of the primary system.

In the next chapter we shall look at the role of parties in shaping voter attitudes and in Chapter 10 at the role of parties in Congress. In each of these other areas we will find more evidence of party decay.

Suggested Readings

Chambers, William Nisbet, and Walter Dean Burnham, eds. *The American Party Systems: Stages of Political Development,* 2nd ed. New York: Oxford University Press, 1975. Essays tracing the rise of the party system since the Founding.

Epstein, Leon D. *Political Parties in Western Democracies.* New York: Praeger, 1967. Compares party organization and functions in the United States, Great Britain, and Europe.

Goldwin, Robert A., ed. *Political Parties, U. S. A.* Chicago: Rand McNally, 1964. Essays evaluating the performance of the American parties.

Keech, William R., and Donald R. Matthews. *The Party's Choice.* Washington, D. C.: Brookings Institution, 1977. Analyzes how presidential candidates were nominated from 1940 through 1976.

Key, V. O., Jr., *Southern Politics.* New York: Alfred A. Knopf, 1949. A classic account of how politics operated in the one-party South.

Kirkpatrick, Jeane. *The New Presidential Elite.* New York: Russell Sage Foundation, 1976. Detailed analysis of the delegates to the 1972 Democratic and Republican conventions.

Ranney, Austin. *Curing the Mischiefs of Faction: Party Reform in America.* Berkeley: University of California Press, 1975. History and analysis of party "reforms" with special attention to the 1972 changes in the Democratic party rules.

Riordan, William L. *Plunkitt of Tammany Hall.* New York: Alfred A. Knopf, 1948 (first published in 1905). Amusing and insightful account of how an old-style party boss operated in New York City.

Schattschneider, E. E. *Party Government.* New York: Holt, Rinehart and Winston, 1942. An argument for a more disciplined and centralized two-party system.

Sorauf, Frank J. *Political Parties in the American System,* 3rd ed. Boston: Little, Brown, 1976. Good basic text on how American political parties are organized and behave.

Sundquist, James L. *Dynamics of the Party System.* Washington, D.C.: Brookings Institution, 1973. History of the party system, emphasizing the impact of issues on voting.

Wilson, James Q. *The Amateur Democrat.* Chicago: University of Chicago Press, 1962. Analysis and evaluation of the issue-oriented political clubs that arose in the Democratic party in the 1950s and 1960s.

7 Elections and Campaigns

Early control of elections by states · Expansion of the electorate · Voting turnout · Kinds of elections · Who runs campaigns · Campaign strategy · Use of the media · Use of polls · Effects of campaigns · Analyzing election results · Party realignments · Changes in balloting · Elections and policy change · Costs and benefits of voting · Financing the campaigns · Controlling the finances

Socialist presidential candidate Eugene Debs in 1912 (left); and Jimmy Carter, campaigning in 1976 (right).

There are more elections to fill more offices in the United States than in perhaps any other major democracy; public participation in American elections, however, is lower than in elections elsewhere. Moreover, political parties, as both organizations and labels, play a smaller role in American elections and campaigns than they do in other countries.

These three facts—the large number of offices to be filled by election, the low participation in those elections, and the weak condition of political parties—have important implications for a theory of democracy. That many offices are filled by election would presumably make many officials accountable to the voters. But if the turnout for those elections is low and no political party exists that can be held responsible for the behavior of these officeholders, then many offices will be filled with persons unknown to most voters and with no higher loyalty than their own ambition. If democracy means majority rule,

66 The multitude of elective offices in the United States reflects two facts: the desire for a system of checks and balances . . . and a long-standing distrust of governmental power. **99**

then the low turnout of voters in many elections allows something less than a majority to rule. If, on the other hand, we were to get rid of many lesser elective offices in order to focus public attention—and public participation—on a single elective office, then we might get large turnouts and majority rule, but that majority would control only a small segment of the governmental structure.

FIGURE 7.1   Voting Turnout in Western Nations Since 1960

Country	Number of elections	Average turnout
Australia	8	95.0%
Italy	4	93.0
Belgium	6	91.8
Germany	5	88.6
Sweden	7	88.3
Netherlands	5	88.1
Norway	5	82.3
France	4	77.7
Canada	6	76.7
Britain	5	75.4
Ireland	5	75.1
Switzerland	4	59.4
UNITED STATES	5	59.1

0   10   20   30   40   50   60   70   80   90   100

Source: T. T. Mackie and Richard Rose, *The International Almanac of Electoral History* (New York: The Free Press, 1974).

In a parliamentary system such as that of Great Britain, there may be no more than two offices for which a citizen can vote—the member of Parliament from his or her district and the member of his or her local city council. A citizen of Massachusetts, by contrast, can vote during a four-year period for president, senator, congressman, governor, state representative, state senator, attorney general, state auditor, state treasurer, secretary of state, county commissioner, sheriff, and clerks of various courts, as well as (in cities) mayor, city councillors, and school committee members, and (in towns) selectmen, town meeting members, moderator, library trustees, health board members, tax assessors, water commissioners, town clerk, housing authority members, tree warden, and commissioner of the public burial grounds. There are an estimated 521,000 elective offices in the United States, and almost every week of the year there will be an election going on somewhere in this country.[1]

The multitude of elective offices in the United States reflects two facts: the desire for a system of checks and balances based on the separate election of the executive and legislative branches and a long-standing distrust of governmental power that can only be controlled (it is thought) by directly electing most officials. (To these original reasons a third can be added: once an office is elective, the person holding that office will bitterly resist any effort to make his or her office appointive, or worse, to abolish it altogether.)

Perhaps because there are only one or—possibly—two elective offices in most European countries, voter participation in elections to fill those offices is very high (see Figure 7.1). Some of these countries, such as Australia and Italy, make voting compulsory. As a result, their turnout is often well over 90 percent. But even in nations such as France and Great Britain, where voting is voluntary, turnout regularly exceeds 70 or 80 percent of the eligible population. In the 1976 presidential election in the United States, voter turnout was only 54 percent. As we shall see, however, there are other factors besides the multitude of elections that account for the low level of American voter participation.

Political parties in this country are increasingly unable to get out the vote, present an organized slate of candidates for the many offices to be filled, or hold the occupants of these offices accountable to any single set of leaders. Evidence of this can be seen, for example, in the rise in "split-ticket" voting whereby a citizen votes for the candidate of one party for president and the candidate of a different party for governor or senator. A split-ticket is a meaningless concept in most of Europe where the voter, in a given election, can only fill one office.

THE RISE OF THE AMERICAN ELECTORATE

It is ironic that relatively few persons vote in American elections since it was in this country that the mass of people first became eligible to vote. At the time the Constitution was ratified, the vote was limited to property-owners or taxpayers, but by the administration of Andrew Jackson it had been broadened to include virtually all white male adults. Only in the South did property restrictions persist—they were not abolished in Louisiana until the 1840s or in Virginia until 1852. And of course in many parts of the North as well as in the South, black males could not vote in many states, even if they were not slaves. Women could not vote in most states until the twentieth century; Chinese-Americans were widely denied the vote; and being in prison is grounds for losing the franchise even today. Aliens, on the other hand, were often allowed to vote if they had at least begun the process of becoming a citizen. By 1880 only an estimated 14 percent of all adult males in the United States could not vote; in England in the same period, about 40 percent of adult males were disfranchised.[2]

From State to Federal Control
Initially, it was left entirely to the states to decide who could vote and for what offices. The Con-

stitution gave to Congress only the right to pick the day on which presidential electors would gather and to alter state regulations regarding congressional elections. The only provision of the Constitution requiring a popular election was the clause in Article I that members of the House of Representatives be chosen by the "people of the several states."

Because of this permissiveness, early federal elections varied greatly. Several states picked their members of the House at large (i.e., statewide) rather than by district, others used districts but elected more than one representative from each. Still others had their elections in odd-numbered years, and some even required that a congressional candidate win a majority, rather than simply a plurality, of votes to be elected (when that requirement was in effect, runoff elections—in one case as many as twelve—were necessary). Furthermore, presidential electors were at first picked by state legislatures rather than by the voters directly.

Congress, by law and constitutional amendment, has steadily reduced state prerogatives in these matters. In 1842 a federal law required that all members of the House be elected by districts; other laws over the years required that all federal elections be held in even-numbered years on the Tuesday following the first Monday in November.

The most important changes in elections have been those that extended the suffrage to women, blacks, and eighteen-year-olds and made mandatory the direct popular election of United States senators. The Fifteenth Amendment, adopted in 1870, said that the "right of citizens of the United States to vote shall not be denied or abridged by the United States or by any state on account of race, color, or previous condition of servitude." Reading those words today, one would assume that they gave blacks the right to vote. That is not what the Supreme Court during the 1870s thought they meant. By a series of decisions, it held that the Fifteenth Amendment did not necessarily confer the right to vote on anybody, it merely asserted that if someone was denied that right, the denial could not be explicitly on the grounds of race. And the burden of proving that it was race that led to the denial fell on the black who was turned away at the polls.[3]

This interpretation opened the door to all manner of state stratagems to keep blacks from voting. One was a literacy test (a large proportion of former slaves were illiterate), another was a requirement that a poll tax be paid (most former slaves were poor), a third was the practice of keeping blacks from voting in primary elections (in the one-party South the only meaningful election was the Democratic primary). To allow whites to vote who were illiterate or poor, a "grandfather clause" was added to the law saying that you could vote, even though you did not meet the legal requirements, if you or your ancestors voted before 1867 (blacks, of course, could not vote before 1867). When all else failed, blacks were intimidated, threatened, or harassed if they showed up at the polls.

There began a long, slow legal process of challenging in court each of these restrictions in turn. One by one, the Supreme Court set most of them aside. The grandfather clause was declared unconstitutional in 1915,[4] the "white primary" finally fell in 1944.[5] Some of the more blatantly discriminatory literacy tests were also overturned.[6] The practical result of these rulings was slight: only a small proportion of voting-age blacks were able to register and vote in the South, and they were found mostly in the larger cities. A dramatic change did not begin until 1965,

Immediately after the Civil War blacks voted in large numbers throughout the South. With the end of Reconstruction, restrictive state laws and practices steadily reduced the number of enfranchised blacks. By the 1890s white supremacy had been reestablished and was publicly defended.

WHITE SUPREMACY!

Attention, White Men!

Grand Torch-Light Procession

At JACKSON,

On the Night of the

Fourth of January, 1890.

The Final Settlement of Democratic Rule and White Supremacy in Mississippi.

GRAND PYROTECHNIC DISPLAY!
Transparencies and Torches Free for all.

All in Sympathy with the Grand Cause are Cordially and Earnestly Invited to be on hand, to aid in the Final Overthrow of Radical Rule in our State.

Come on foot or on horse-back; come any way, but be sure to get there.
Brass Bands, Cannon, Flambeau Torches, Transparencies, Sky-rockets, Etc.

A GRAND DISPLAY FOR A GRAND CAUSE.

with the passage of the Voting Rights Act. This act suspended the use of literacy tests and authorized the appointment of federal examiners who could order the registration of blacks in states and counties (mostly in the South) where fewer than 50 percent of the voting-age population were registered or had voted in the last presidential election. It also provided criminal penalties for interfering with the right to vote.

Though implementation was slow, during the 1960s the number of blacks voting rose sharply. In 1940, only 5 percent of voting-age blacks in the South were registered; by 1966, 45 percent were registered; by 1970, 62 percent (see Table 7.1). In just ten years—from 1960 to 1970—the number of blacks registered in Mississippi rose from 5 percent to over 70 percent. Since blacks make up a large fraction of the southern population, this change began to have a dramatic effect on political behavior. Some southern politicians who had previously supported segregation and campaigned against blacks began to court the black vote and to modify rather strikingly their opinions on racial issues. However, there were still incidents of harassment and intimidation as late as the mid-1970s.

Women were kept from the polls by law more than by intimidation, and when the laws changed women began almost immediately to vote in large numbers. By 1915 several states, mostly in the West, had begun to permit women to vote. But it was not until the Nineteenth Amendment to the Constitution was ratified in 1920, after a struggle lasting many decades, that women generally were allowed to vote. At one stroke, the size of the eligible voting population almost doubled. Contrary to the hopes of some and the fears of others, however, no dramatic changes occurred in the conduct of elections, the identity of the winners, or the substance of public policy. Initially, at least, women voted more or less in the same manner as men, though not quite as frequently.

The political impact of the youth vote was also less than expected. The Voting Rights Act of 1970 gave the right to vote in federal elections to eighteen-year-olds, beginning January 1, 1971. It also contained a provision lowering the voting age to eighteen in state elections, but the Supreme Court declared this unconstitutional. As a result, a constitutional amendment, the Twenty-Sixth, was proposed by Congress and ratified by the states in 1971. The 1972 elections became the first in which all persons between

TABLE 7.1   Voter Registration in the South
Percentage of Voting-Age Population

		Ala.	Ark.	Fla.	Ga.	La.	Miss.	N.C.	S.C.	Tenn.	Tex.	Va.	Total
1960	White	63.6	60.9	69.3	56.8	76.9	63.9	92.1	57.1	73.0	42.5	46.1	61.1
	Black*	13.7	38.0	39.4	29.3	31.1	5.2	39.1	13.7	59.1	35.5	23.1	29.1
1970	White	85.0	74.1	65.5	71.7	77.0	82.1	68.1	62.3	78.5	62.0	64.5	69.2
	Black	66.0	82.3	55.3	57.2	57.4	71.0	51.3	56.1	71.6	72.6	57.0	62.0
1976	White	79.3	62.6	61.3	65.9	78.4	80.0	69.2	58.4	73.7	69.1	61.6	67.9
	Black	58.4	94.0	61.1	74.8	63.0	60.7	54.8	56.5	66.4	65.0	54.7	63.1

Source: Voter Education Project, Inc., Atlanta, Ga., *Voter Registration in the South.*
*Includes other minority races.

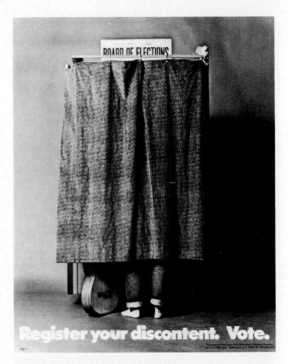

The campaign to win the vote for women nationwide succeeded with the adoption of the Nineteenth Amendment in 1920. Eighteen-year-olds won the right to vote in 1971.

the ages of eighteen and twenty-one could cast ballots (before then, four states had allowed persons under twenty-one to vote). About 25 million persons had suddenly become eligible to participate in elections, but their turnout was lower than for the population as a whole, and they did not flock to any particular party or candidate. George McGovern, the Democratic candidate for president in 1972, counted heavily on attracting the youth vote, but did not. Most young voters supported Nixon (though college students favored McGovern).[7]

National standards now govern almost every aspect of voter eligibility. All persons eighteen years of age and older may vote; there may be no literacy test or poll tax; states may not require residency of more than thirty days in that state before a person may vote; areas with significant numbers of citizens not speaking English must give those persons ballots written in their own language; and federal voter registrars and poll watchers may be sent into areas where less than 50 percent of the voting-age population participates in a presidential election. Before 1961 residents of the District of Columbia could not vote for the president; the Twenty-Third Amendment to the Constitution, ratified in that year, gave them this right.

Voting Turnout
Given all these legal safeguards, one might expect that participation in elections would have risen sharply. In fact, the proportion of the voting-age population that has gone to the polls in presidential elections has remained about the same—between 55 and 60 percent of those eligible—for the last twenty years or so and appears today to be much smaller than it was in the latter part of the nineteenth century (see Figure 7.2). In every presidential election between 1840

and 1900, at least 70 percent of the eligible population apparently went to the polls, and in some years (1840 and 1876) over 80 percent seem to have voted. After 1900 there was not a single presidential election in which turnout reached 70 percent, and there have been two occasions (1920 and 1924) when it did not even reach 50 percent.[8] Even outside the South, where efforts to disfranchise blacks make data on voting turnout especially hard to interpret, turnout seems to have declined: over 84 percent of the voting-age population participated in presidential elections in nonsouthern states between 1884 and 1900, but only 68 percent between 1936 and 1960 and even fewer since 1960.[9]

Scholars have vigorously debated the meaning of these figures. One view is that this decline in turnout, even allowing for the shaky data on

which the estimates are based, has been real and the result of a decline of popular interest in elections and a weakening of the extent to which the two major parties are closely competitive. During the nineteenth century, according to this theory, the parties fought hard, worked strenuously to get as many voters as possible to the polls, afforded the mass of voters a chance to participate in party politics through caucuses and conventions, kept the legal barriers to participation (such as complex registration procedures) low, and looked forward to close, exciting elections. After 1896, by which time the South had become a one-party Democratic region and the North heavily Republican, both parties became more conservative, national elections usually resulted in lopsided victories for the Republicans, and citizens began to lose interest

FIGURE 7.2   Voter Participation in Presidential Elections, 1860–1976

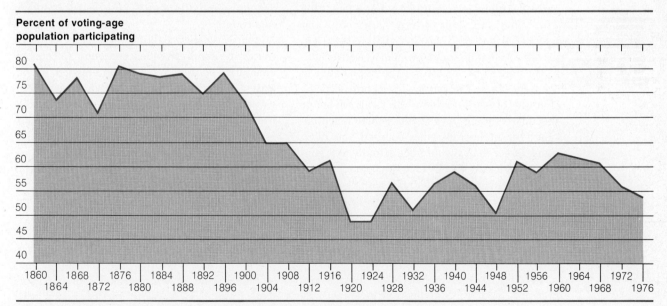

Source: For years 1860–1928, Bureau of the Census, *Historical Statistics of the United States, Colonial Times to 1970,* Pt. 2, p. 1071; and for years 1932–1976, *Statistical Abstract of the United States, 1978,* p. 520.

Note: Several southern states did not participate in the 1864 and 1868 elections.

in politics because it no longer seemed relevant to their needs. The parties ceased functioning as organizations to mobilize the mass of voters, and fell under the control of leaders, mostly conservative, who resisted mass participation.[10]

There is another view, however. It argues that the decline in voter turnout has been more apparent than real and that though elections were certainly more of a popular sport in the nineteenth century than they are today, the parties were no more democratic then than now, and voters then may have been more easily manipulated. Until around the beginning of the twentieth century, vote frauds were commonplace because they were easy. The political parties, not the government, printed the ballots; they were often cast in public, not in private voting booths; there were few serious efforts to decide who was eligible to vote, and the rules that did operate were easily evaded. Under these circumstances, it was easy for a person to vote more than once, and the party machines made heavy use of these "floaters" or repeaters. "Vote early and often" was not a joke, but a fact. "Big Tim" Sullivan, a boss in New York's old Tammany Hall, once had his party's ballots soaked in perfume so that he could use scent as well as sight to ensure that his voters put the right ballot in the right box.[11] The parties often controlled the counting of votes, padding the totals whenever they feared losing. As a result of these machinations, the number of votes counted was often much larger than the number actually cast, and the number cast was in turn often much larger than the number of individuals eligible to vote. For example, in 1888 West Virginia officially claimed there were 147,408 persons in the state eligible to vote, but mysteriously 159,440 votes were cast in the presidential election, for a "voter turnout" of 108 percent![12]

In short, if votes had been legally cast and honestly counted in the nineteenth century, the statistics on turnout in elections might well be much lower than the inflated figures we now have.[13] To the extent this is true, we may not have had a decline in voter participation as great

as some have suggested. Nevertheless, most scholars believe that, even accurately measured, turnout probably did decline somewhat since the 1890s. One reason was that voter registration regulations became more burdensome. There were longer residency requirements, aliens who had announced their intention of becoming citizens could no longer vote in most states, it became harder for blacks to vote, educational qualifications for voting were adopted by several states, and voters had to register long in advance of the elections. These changes, designed to purify the electoral process, were aspects of the Progressive reform impulse described in Chapter 6, and served to cut back on the number of persons who could participate in elections.

Furthermore, state after state began adopting the "Australian ballot" around 1890. This was a government-printed ballot of uniform size and shape that was cast in secret to replace the old party-printed ballot that was cast in public. By 1910 only three states were without the Australian ballot. Its use cut back on (but certainly did not eliminate) vote-buying and fraudulent vote counts.

The Australian ballot and strict voter registration procedures tended, like most reforms in American politics, to have unintended (or at least less obvious) as well as intended consequences. These changes not only reduced fraudulent voting, they reduced voting generally, because they made it more difficult for certain groups of perfectly honest voters—those with little education, for example, or those who had recently moved—to register and vote. As we shall see when we examine later in this chapter more recent changes in election laws, the "reforms" adopted by one generation are often designed to correct the unintended consequences of the "reforms" of an earlier generation.

Finally, the growing weakness of party organizations, coupled with the frequency with which one party won a lopsided election victory in the twentieth century, probably reduced voter participation. As we shall see, the persons least likely to vote are usually those with little education and the least experience in politics. Intense organized efforts are necessary to get these people to the polls, but such efforts are hard to mount when party organization no longer exists.

RUNNING A CAMPAIGN

Political campaigns, once mounted by party organizations, are today largely run by the personal followers of the candidate. If the election is contested, and especially if it is likely to be close, the candidate will create an organization to work for him, but it will be a temporary one that goes out of existence the day after the election. Furthermore, campaigns for national offices are usually organized on behalf of an individual candidate, not a slate of candidates of the same party.

Several features of our political system have contributed to the rise of personalistic campaigns. Primary elections, as we have seen, have weakened or eliminated a major source of party power in many states—the ability to select the party's nominee. Often a nominee will win a

Mobilization Politics in the Nineteenth Century

Politics was a national sport during much of the nineteenth century. Torchlight parades, massive rallies, colorful banners, and public orations were commonplace then; today, they have been replaced with television interviews and sedate meetings in auditoriums.

Morton Keller notes that in 1888 twenty-five possible presidential candidates were pictured on cards placed in packages of Honest Long Cut Tobacco. The cards were collected and traded as if they were pictures of baseball players.[1]

The very language of politics emphasized the warlike nature of the effort to mobilize voters, as suggested by this pastiche of typical phrases:

◆ ◆ ◆

From the *opening gun* of the *campaign* the *standard bearer,* along with other *war-horses fielded* by the party, *rallied* the *rank and file* around the party *standard,* the *bloody shirt,* and other *slogans.* Precinct *captains* aligned their *phalanxes* shoulder-to-shoulder to *mobilize* votes for the *Old Guard.* . . . Finally the *well-drilled fugelmen* in the *last ditch* closed *ranks,* overwhelmed the enemy *camp,* and divided the *spoils* of victory.[2]

◆ ◆ ◆

[1] Morton Keller, *Affairs of State* (Cambridge, Mass: Harvard University Press, 1977), p. 535.
[2] Richard Jensen, *The Winning of the Midwest* (Chicago: University of Chicago Press, 1971), p. 11.

PRESIDENTIAL POSSIBILITIES
MELVILLE W. FULLER,
OF ILLINOIS.

PRESIDENTIAL POSSIBILITIES
JOHN M. PALMER,
OF ILLINOIS.

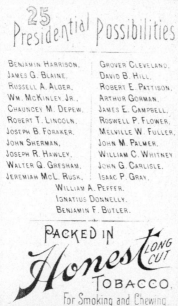

25 Presidential Possibilities

BENJAMIN HARRISON,	GROVER CLEVELAND,
JAMES G. BLAINE,	DAVID B. HILL,
RUSSELL A. ALGER,	ROBERT E. PATTISON,
WM. McKINLEY JR.,	ARTHUR GORMAN,
CHAUNCEY M. DEPEW,	JAMES E. CAMPBELL,
ROBERT T. LINCOLN,	ROSWELL P. FLOWER,
JOSEPH B. FORAKER,	MELVILLE W. FULLER,
JOHN SHERMAN,	JOHN M. PALMER,
JOSEPH R. HAWLEY,	WILLIAM C. WHITNEY,
WALTER Q. GRESHAM,	JOHN G. CARLISLE,
JEREMIAH McL. RUSK,	ISAAC P. GRAY,
WILLIAM A. PEFFER,	
IGNATIUS DONNELLY,	
BENJAMIN F. BUTLER.	

PACKED IN
Honest LONG CUT
TOBACCO,
For Smoking and Chewing.

primary over the opposition of the party leadership; in such cases, it is hardly surprising that the party may feel little obligation to work hard for that person's victory in the general election.

Political funds and political jobs are increasingly under the control of candidates and officeholders, not party leaders. The public finance of presidential campaigns means, as we shall see, that most of the money used to help elect a candidate goes to the candidate, or his personal organization, and is not funneled through the party. The ability to reward followers with patronage jobs is in many places in the hands of an elected official rather than a party boss.

The increased reliance on the mass media for campaigning—especially the reliance on radio and television—means that candidates purchase advertising and give interviews largely to bolster their own chances of victory. Given the cost of radio and television advertising, it hardly makes sense for one candidate to give any other a "free ride" by including him on a slate. Moreover, electronic advertising is usually devoted to building a candidate's "image"—that is, to emphasizing the candidate's *personal* qualities—and that cannot easily be done for a slate or a party ticket.

Finally, the decline in party identification that we observed in Chapter 5 has made any appeal to party loyalty a weaker basis for building a winning coalition than once was the case. In heavily Democratic or heavily Republican areas, the candidate of the dominant party will continue, naturally, to mention his party affiliation; his opponent, just as naturally, will avoid mentioning his own affiliation. And in closely competitive states or districts, both candidates may omit references to their party identification lest they inadvertently alienate voters who might like them as individuals.

The Support Staff

The temporary, personal organizations of candidates tend to be composed of certain distinct groups of workers. At the core there is usually a small number of paid professionals, either hired for the occasion or drawn from an incumbent's office staff. A senator or representative will use his congressional staff (at the public's expense, of course) to organize his reelection campaign. A president will have most of the White House staff and many of the cabinet and subcabinet officials at his disposal. A challenger must hire his own staff. With the decline of party, there has come into being a sizable group of professional campaign managers available for hire by a variety of candidates. (Some of these professionals, though, prefer to work only for candidates who share their views.) A few, such as Spencer-Roberts, Inc., of California, are well-paid, full-time campaign consultants; others are part-timers who, between campaigns, find jobs in government, or with public relations or advertising firms, or as lawyers.

The paid staff usually has charge of the most important work of the campaign—scheduling the candidate, raising money (though sometimes this is done by wealthy supporters who volunteer for the task), issuing press releases, and dealing with the media. The 1976 presidential campaign of Jimmy Carter was directed by a closely knit group of young supporters from Atlanta, including Hamilton Jordan, Jody Powell, and Stuart Eizenstat. They were supplemented by various paid specialists, such as Patrick Caddell, a polltaker, and Jerry Rafshoon, an advertising executive. Gerald Ford's campaign was run by hired specialists from Spencer-Roberts, supplemented by White House aides.

The second group of campaign workers is made up of the unpaid senior advisers—usually old and trusted acquaintances of the candidate, some of whom may never have held political office—to whom the candidate turns for counsel on major strategic and tactical issues. Charles Kirbo, an Atlanta lawyer, and Bert Lance, a Georgia banker, played such roles for Carter.

The third group consists of citizen volunteers who type letters, stuff envelopes, make telephone

Kinds of Elections

There are two kinds of elections in the United States: **general** and **primary.** A general election is used to fill an elective office. A primary election is one intended to select a party's candidates for an elective office, though in fact those who vote in a primary election may or may not consider themselves party members. Some primaries are **closed**—you must declare in advance, sometimes several weeks, that you are a registered member of the political party in whose primary you wish to vote. About forty states have closed primaries. Other primaries are **open**—that is, you can decide when you enter the voting booth on election day in which party's primary you wish to participate. You are given every party's primary ballot; you may vote on one. Michigan, Minnesota, Montana, North Dakota, Utah, Vermont, and Wisconsin have open primaries. A variant on the open primary is the **blanket** or "free love" primary—in the voting booth you mark a ballot that contains the candidates for nomination of all the parties, and thus you can help select the Democratic candidate for one office and the Republican candidate for another. Alaska and Washington have blanket primaries. The differences among these kinds of primaries should not be exaggerated, for even the closed primary does not create any great barrier for a voter who wishes to vote in the Democratic primary in one election and the Republican in another. All he or she has to do is (in the extreme case) change his or her registration or (in the typical case) simply pick on election day the preferred party's ballot. Some states also have a **runoff primary**—if no candidate gets a majority of the votes, there is a runoff between the two candidates with the most votes. Runoff primaries are common in the South. A special kind of primary is that used to pick delegates to the presidential nominating conventions of the major parties—these are **presidential** primaries, and they come in a bewildering variety. A simplified list of the kinds of presidential primaries would look like this:

1. *Delegate selection only*
   Only the names of prospective delegates to the convention appear on the ballot. They may or may not indicate their presidential preference.

2. *Delegate selection with advisory presidential preference*
   Voters pick delegates and indicate their preferences among presidential candidates. The delegates are not legally bound to observe these preferences.

3. *Binding presidential preference*
   Voters indicate their preferred presidential candidate. Delegates must observe these preferences, at least for a certain number of convention ballots. The delegates may be chosen in the primary or by a party convention. The presidential candidate who carries a binding preference primary may receive:
   a. all the delegates ("winner take all," allowed only in the Republican party), or
   b. the number of delegates that corresponds to his proportion of the preference vote.

The ballot from a state with a "blanket" primary election.

STATE OF ALASKA
Primary Election August 22, 1978

GOVERNOR
Vote For One (1)

CROFT, CHANCY	Democrat	+
FINK, TOM	Republican	+
HAMMOND, JAY	Republican	+
HICKEL, WALTER J.	Republican	+
KERTTULA, JALMAR M. (JAY)	Democrat	+
LOCKHART, JIMMIE DREW (JDL)	Republican	+
MERDES, ED	Democrat	+

LIEUTENANT GOVERNOR
Vote For One (1)

ALEXANDER, JOHN L.	Democrat	+
BEIRNE, M. F. (MIKE)	Republican	+
BRADLEY, BOB	Democrat	+
BRADLEY, W. E. (BRAD)	Republican	+
DALTON, KATHLEEN (MIKE)	Republican	+
HOHMAN, GEORGE H., JR.	Democrat	+
HURLEY, KATHERINE T. (KATIE)	Democrat	+
KONIGSBERG, CHARLES	Democrat	+
MILLER, TERRY	Republican	+
SWANSON, LESLIE E. (RED)	Democrat	+
THOMPSON, D. E. (DUX)	Democrat	+
WARD, ROBERT W. (BOB)	Republican	+
WARREN, CLIFF	Democrat	+

UNITED STATES SENATOR
Vote For One (1)

HOBBS, DON	Democrat	+
SONNEMAN, JOE	Democrat	+
STEVENS, TED	Republican	+

UNITED STATES REPRESENTATIVE
Vote For One (1)

"To win the primary, one must mobilize a relatively small number of enthusiasts; to win the general election, one must attract a much larger and perhaps much different group of supporters."

George McGovern had a great appeal for liberal Democrats in 1972 but could not attract the middle-of-the-road voters.

calls, drive cars, crank mimeograph machines, canvass door-to-door, and pass out leaflets. They include young persons looking for excitement, older persons who are friends of the candidate, job-seekers hoping for patronage appointments, and individuals attracted by issues. Volunteers do routine jobs which they often find boring. Many would like to help define the issues, but, as we shall see, defining issues in any detail is rarely an important part of a campaign. Some volunteers resent the power and privileges of the inner circle and especially of the paid staff; members of the inner circle, on the other hand, frequently grumble about the inefficiency or meddlesomeness of the volunteers.

A fourth group represents a new development in campaigns—the issue consultants. Candidates often believe they must have positions on the

issues of the day, and many like to formalize this by producing "position papers." Lawyers, professors, college students, and lobbyists are recruited to help write these papers, most of which play little role in the campaign and no role in the subsequent term of office. As we shall see, campaigns are rarely organized around a detailed or extensive discussion of issues. Ordinarily, candidates can afford to take only general and equivocal positions on most matters and explicit positions—and then not in much detail—on but a few matters. Why, then, have issue consultants? Probably for three reasons: the media expect it, such tasks provide work for eager volunteers, and the candidate wishes to become better informed on matters with which he or she may have to deal.

A campaign, except one for a safe seat in Congress, is an exercise in uncertainty. No one knows in advance what will win or lose the election; no one can be certain what tactics will make a difference. Given the many divisions in public opinion, a winning majority is a coalition of many diverse parts; the problem for the campaigner is to decide which parts can be taken for granted and which can be attracted. A strategy must be devised to attract wavering voters away from the opposition without irritating or alienating one's own dedicated supporters.

Reliance on the primary to win the nomination makes this problem all the greater. To win the primary, one must mobilize a relatively small number of enthusiasts; to win the general election, one must attract a much larger and perhaps much different group of supporters. There will be little conflict if one's primary supporters are attracted by one's personality—that does not entail making commitments on issues. There will be a large conflict if the primary was won by attracting voters through strong issue positions. Table 7.2 shows how George McGovern was hurt by this dilemma. Those who voted for him in the presidential primaries of 1972 had positions to the left of all Democratic voters—and especially of Democratic voters who supported Nixon—on a variety of issues—amnesty for Vietnam draft resisters, decriminalizing marijuana, policies toward minorities, and policies toward Vietnam.

This conflict may not seem important—after all, who else can the enthusiasts support if their candidate backs away from their position on the issues? What, in short, is to prevent the candidate, once he has the nomination, from moving immediately to the center of the political spectrum?

Two things prevent it. First, his opponent will not let him forget the positions he took while winning the primary. The opposition will use these more extreme positions to hurt his standing with the voters. Second, even though the enthusiasts find it impossible to vote for the opposition, they will find it quite easy to stop contributing time, effort, and money to their candidate if he starts waffling on the issues of importance to them. In 1972 McGovern found himself trapped by just this predicament. He had run in the primaries as a leftist candidate. As his campaign manager later explained:

Our strategy [in the primaries] was always to co-opt the left, become the candidate of the liberal wing of the party. . . . We always knew it would be a two-man race between a liberal and a conservative. There was, in fact, no center.[14]

TABLE 7.2　Policy Preferences of Voters Supporting George McGovern and Richard Nixon in 1972 Election

Policy Preference	Voters Supporting McGovern in Primaries	All Voters Who Were Democrats	Democrats Who Voted for Nixon
U.S. policy in Vietnam			
Liberal	79%	52%	30%
Conservative	5	24	39
Amnesty for draft resisters			
Liberal	52	34	18
Conservative	48	66	82
Decriminalizing marijuana			
Liberal	41	20	10
Conservative	41	72	83
Help for minorities			
Liberal	49	39	25
Conservative	26	39	51
Busing to integrate schools			
Liberal	19	14	0.2
Conservative	70	81	96

Source: Adapted from Arthur H. Miller *et al.*, "A Majority Party in Disarray: Policy Polarization in the 1972 Election," *American Political Science Review*, Vol. 70 (September 1976), p. 757. Reprinted by permission.

Note: Persons with "center" or middle-of-the-road positions omitted from table.

❝For most voters an election is a retrospective judgment on the performance of whoever has been in office.**❞**

Senator Edward Brooke of Massachusetts won his first two elections by large margins. But in 1978 he lost after a campaign in which his marital and financial difficulties received a great deal of press attention.

During the general election, McGovern did move toward the center, but he could not move very far because Nixon kept mentioning the positions he had taken (or was alleged to have taken) in the primaries and because the campaign contributions on which he depended came from thousands of small donors who were solicited for money by mail. To keep the money coming in— and thus to keep the campaign alive—McGovern would from time to time have to make a dramatic appeal, by mail or on television, to those donors. The appeals that would arouse them were often appeals that only irritated the average voter on whom the outcome of the election depended.[15] In 1976, by contrast, Jimmy Carter won the nomination by emphasizing his personality and general themes such as "trust"; in

the general election, he was not encumbered by a need to defend particular policy positions taken in the primaries. Furthermore, public finance of the presidential campaign reduced his dependence on mobilizing many small donors by emotional or issue-laden appeals.

Picking a Course

To cope with the uncertainty of campaigns, every candidate develops a strategy. Events will often upset the best-laid plans, but at the beginning, at least, the candidate and his staff try to make the following kinds of choices:

- Should we run a "positive" (build me up) or a "negative" (attack the opponent) campaign?
- What "theme" can we develop? A theme is a simple idea of (one hopes) broad appeal that can be repeated over and over again. For Jimmy Carter in 1976, it was "trust"; for John F. Kennedy in 1960, it was "get the country moving again"; for Dwight Eisenhower in 1952, it was "Korea, communism, and corruption."
- What should be the timing of the campaign— a major effort early, or start slowly and build to a peak?
- What kinds of voters can be swayed by a campaign—workers? farmers? suburbanites?
- Where shall we spend most of our money—on television? direct mail? campaign trips?

Sometimes one has little choice in these matters. For example, an incumbent, whether he likes it or not, will have to run on his record. For most voters an election is a retrospective judgment on the performance of whoever has been in office. Incumbents, as we have seen, enjoy great advantages in a campaign and are usually hard to unseat, but an incumbent who has taken some controversial positions, or been the subject of a scandal, or who has been in office when the economy has taken a turn for the worse, can be in trouble. Whatever such an incumbent may prefer, his campaign is likely to involve defending his record in office. On the other hand, an incumbent who has escaped serious trouble while in office is in an enviable position—he can take a lofty position, speak in a statesmanlike way about his knowledge and experience, and refuse to debate (or even to mention) his opponent. President Eisenhower in 1956 and President Nixon in 1972 were in exactly these positions.

If no incumbent is running, then the choice of strategies is wider, with one exception. A person running for president who is of the same party as the outgoing president will be saddled, for better or worse, with the record of the incumbent. Hubert Humphrey in 1968 had to defend the administration of Lyndon Johnson; Richard Nixon in 1960 had to defend the record of Dwight Eisenhower; and Gerald Ford in 1976 had to cope with the legacy of the Nixon administration.

All of these strategic considerations can go out the window if one or the other candidate commits an apparent blunder. In a closely watched race, such as that for president, the media record every word and, in their need to have a daily headline, leap on every mistake. In 1976 President Ford erroneously implied in a television debate against Carter that certain Eastern European nations were independent of the Soviet Union. It was obviously a slip of the tongue—Ford knew it was a mistake—but for days the press and the opposition dwelt on this lapse. Similarly, Carter was quoted in a famous interview with *Playboy* magazine as saying that he sometimes had lust in his heart. It is hard to imagine anyone who has not experienced lust, but presidents, even those with children, are supposed to be above that sort of thing. Giving the interview was probably a mistake—indeed, Carter later admitted it was a mistake—but the damage was done. Every candidate, every campaign organization, lives in mortal fear of the unexpected blunder.

At one time almost all campaigning was aimed at making personal contact with as many voters as possible through rallies, parades,

> **"**Every candidate, every campaign organization, lives in mortal fear of the unexpected blunder.**"**

"whistle-stop" train tours, and shaking hands outside factory gates or in shopping-center parking lots. All of this still goes on, but more and more candidates for statewide and national office devote their energies to getting on television. Television reaches more people than all other campaign methods put together, and voters say in polls that they get more of their political information from television than from any other single source, including newspapers.

Using Television

There are two ways to use television—by running paid advertisements and by getting on the nightly news broadcasts. In the language of campaigners, short television ads are called "spots," and a campaign activity that appears on a news broadcast is called a "visual." Much has been written about the preparation of spots, usually under titles such as "the selling of the president" or "packaging the candidate." Most of it has been written by advertising executives, persons not known for a tendency to underestimate their abilities. No doubt spots can have an important effect in some cases. A little-known candidate can increase his or her visibility by frequent use of spots (and this is what Carter did in the 1976 presidential primaries). Sometimes a complete unknown can win a primary by clever use of television, as allegedly happened when Mike Gravel became the Democratic nominee for senator from Alaska in 1968 and Milton Shapp became the Democratic nominee for governor of Pennsylvania in 1966. Nelson Rockefeller was helped in his difficult campaign to be reelected governor of New York in 1966 by television spots that did *not* show Rockefeller—his advertising agency decided he did not come across well on TV—but showed instead clever commercials describing his policies and programs.

CAMPAIGN HOOPLA

In the 1888 presidential campaign, supporters of Benjamin Harrison rolled a huge ball covered with campaign slogans across the country. The gimmick, first used in 1840, gave rise to the phrase, "keep the ball rolling."

Candidates first made phonographic recordings of their speeches in 1908. Warren G. Harding is shown here recording a speech during the 1920 campaign.

The effect of television advertising on general elections is probably a good deal less than in primaries; indeed, as we shall see in Chapter 9, most scientific studies of television influence on voting decisions show that either it has no effect or the effect is subtle and hard to detect. Nor is it surprising that this should be the case. In a general election, after all, especially one for high-visibility offices (such as president or governor), the average voter has many sources of information—his own party or ideological preference, various kinds of advertising, the opinions of friends and family, and newspaper and magazine stories. Furthermore, both sides will use TV spots; if well done, they are likely to cancel each other out. In short, it is not yet clear that a "gullible" public is being sold a bill of goods by slick Madison Avenue advertisers, whether the goods are automobiles or politicians.

Visuals are a vital part of any major campaign effort because, unlike spots, they cost the campaign little and, being "news," they may have greater credibility with the viewer. A visual is a brief filmed episode showing the candidate doing something that a reporter thinks is newsworthy. Simply making a speech, unless the speech contains important new facts or charges, is often thought by TV editors to be uninteresting—television viewers are not attracted by pictures of "talking heads," and in the highly competitive world of TV, audience reactions are all-important determinants of what gets on the air. Knowing this, campaign managers will strive to have their candidates do something visually interesting every day, no later than 3 P.M. (if the visual is to be on the 6 P.M. news)—talk to elderly folks in a nursing home, shake hands with people waiting in an unemployment line,

"Whistle-stopping" from the back of a railroad car was for long a popular tactic. Here Franklin and Eleanor Roosevelt shake hands with supporters in Fremont, Nebraska.

Urbanization and the movement of people to big cities made railroad tours of small towns an increasingly inefficient way to meet voters. Thus the motorcade through city streets began to take its place, such as this one in 1968 where the public greeted Robert F. Kennedy.

commiserate about inflation with shoppers in a supermarket, or sniff the waters of a polluted lake. Obviously, all these efforts are for nought if a TV camera crew is not around; great pains are taken, therefore, to schedule these visuals at times and in places that make it easy for the photographers to be present.

Ironically, the visuals—and television newscasts generally—may give the viewer less information than commercial spots. This, of course, is the exact opposite of what many people believe. It is commonplace to deplore political advertising, especially the short spots, on the grounds that it is either devoid of information or manipulative in effect, and to praise television news programs, especially longer debates and interviews, because they are informative and balanced. In fact, the best research we have so far suggests the reverse is true—news programs

The first televised presidential campaign debate occurred in 1960 between John F. Kennedy and Richard M. Nixon.

"In the general election, most citizens—probably two-thirds—will vote on the basis of their traditional party loyalties."

covering elections tend to convey very little information (they often show scenes of crowds cheering or candidates shouting slogans) and to make little or no impression on viewers, if indeed they are watched at all. Paid commercials, on the other hand, especially the shorter spots, often contain a good deal of information that is seen, remembered, and evaluated by a public that is quite capable of distinguishing between fact and humbug.[16]

A special kind of television campaigning is the campaign debate. Incumbents or well-known candidates rarely have an incentive to debate their opponents; by so doing, they only give more publicity to lesser-known rivals. Despite the general rule among politicians to never help an opponent, Vice-President Nixon debated the less-well-known John Kennedy in 1960, and President Gerald Ford debated the less-well-known Jimmy Carter in 1976. Nixon and Ford lost. Lyndon Johnson would not debate Barry Goldwater in 1964, nor would Nixon debate Humphrey in 1968 or McGovern in 1972. Johnson and Nixon won. What effect TV debates have on election outcomes is unclear, though Kennedy's performance in 1960 and Carter's in 1976 probably helped them.

Television is the most visible example of modern technology affecting a campaign; less visible, but perhaps just as important, is the computer. The computer makes possible sophisticated direct-mail campaigning, and this in turn makes it possible for a candidate easily to address specific appeals to particular voters and rapidly to solicit persons for campaign contributions. Representative David Stockman, Republican of Michigan, keeps a computer in his Washington office in which hundreds of paragraphs on various issues are stored together with the names and addresses of thousands of voters in his dis-

trict. It can answer letters from constituents and address letters to voters on almost any conceivable subject.[17] George McGovern and George Wallace both made heavy use of computerized mailing lists in their presidential bids.

Whereas television is heard by everybody, and thus leads the candidate using it to speak in generalities to avoid offending anyone, direct mail is aimed at particular groups (college students, American Indians, bankers, auto workers) to whom specific views can be expressed with much less risk of offending someone. So important are the lists of names of potential fund-givers to whom the computer sends appeals that a prize resource of any candidate, guarded as if it were a military secret, is "The List." Novices in politics must slowly develop their own lists or beg sympathetic incumbents for a peek at theirs.

THE EFFECTS OF CAMPAIGNS

The great source of uncertainty for candidates, and the great source of frustration for their managers, is that no one knows whether campaigns make a difference, and if so, which parts make what difference for which voters. In the general election, most citizens—probably two-thirds—will vote on the basis of their traditional party loyalties. In most House and Senate races, that fact is enough to ensure that the candidate of the dominant party will win. Presidential races, however, are usually much closer.

Why this should be so is not immediately clear. Nationally, far more persons identify with the Democratic than with the Republican party; why, then, do the Democrats not always win? One reason is that persons who consider themselves Democrats are less firmly wedded to their party than are Republicans wedded to theirs. Table 7.3 shows the percentage of persons who identify themselves as Democrats or Republicans who voted for various presidential candidates since 1952. At least 80 percent of the Republican voters supported the Republican candidate; indeed, if we omit the unusual 1964 election when Goldwater was the candidate, at least 86 percent of the Republican identifiers regularly voted Republican. By contrast, there have been more defections among the Democratic voters—in 1968, 26 percent supported someone other than Humphrey, and in 1972, 33 percent supported Nixon.

The other reason, also clear in Table 7.3, is that the Republicans do much better than the Democrats among the self-described "independent" voters. In every election since 1952 but one (1964) the Republican candidate has won a larger percentage of the independent vote than has the Democratic nominee; in fact, the Republicans usually got a majority of the independents.

Most voters make up their minds whom they will support for president by the time the nominating conventions are over. In every election since 1948, no more than about one-third of the voters told pollsters that they waited until during the campaign to make up their minds. The people who wait are not greatly different from those who decide early—over the course of several elections, they are about as likely to be Democrats as Republicans, to be well informed as to be poorly informed.[18]

Just who these poeple are and what they want is the concern of the growing number of professional polling organizations hired by candidates. Scarcely any serious politician running for major office would dream of proceeding without commissioning a poll—and sometimes several. The purpose of these private polls, unlike the pub-

TABLE 7.3   Percentage of Popular Vote by Groups in Presidential Elections, 1952–1976

		National	Republicans	Democrats	Independents
1952	Stevenson	44.6%	8%	77%	35%
	Eisenhower	55.4	92	23	65
1956	Stevenson	42.2	4	85	30
	Eisenhower	57.8	96	15	70
1960	Kennedy	50.1	5	84	43
	Nixon	49.9	95	16	57
1964	Johnson	61.3	20	87	56
	Goldwater	38.7	80	13	44
1968	Humphrey	43.0	9	74	31
	Nixon	43.4	86	12	44
	Wallace	13.6	5	14	25
1972	McGovern	38	5	67	31
	Nixon	62	95	33	69
1976	Carter	51	11	80	48
	Ford	49	89	20	52

Source: Gallup Poll data compiled by Robert D. Cantor, *Voting Behavior and Presidential Elections* (Itasca, Ill.: F. E. Peacock, 1975), p. 35, and Gerald M. Pomper, *The Election of 1976* (New York: David McKay, 1977), p. 61. Reprinted by permission of the American Institute of Public Opinion.

lished ones by George Gallup, Lou Harris, and others, is not to predict who will win but to find out how the voters perceive the candidates and what appeals will reach what kinds of undecided voters.

These polls can sometimes be quite helpful to the candidate. In 1952 Americans wanted some honorable way to end the Korean War. Discovering this, Eisenhower went on television to announce that, if elected, he would go to Korea to end the war. Now traveling to Korea had little to do with ending the war; obtaining a truce there required military and diplomatic efforts, not presidential journeys. But the promise captured the mood and bolstered the hopes of the public, and helped elect Eisenhower. In 1966 Edward Brooke, running for the Senate from Massachusetts, learned from polls that some voters were critical of him for not having spoken out on the black riots then occurring in many cities. Brooke went on television with a statement that criticized extremists of both races; shortly thereafter, his standing in the polls rose.[19]

But just as often the polls tell the candidate things he already knows or can do nothing about. During the 1972 presidential race, the polls showed that even among persons planning to vote for them, neither Nixon nor McGovern had a broad appeal. (In October 1972 the polls asked Americans who had the most attractive personality—McGovern, Nixon, or neither. "Neither" won handily.)[20] What did distinguish Nixon and McGovern in the voters' minds was that those who supported Nixon thought of McGovern as an "extremist" and a person who had a "permissive" attitude on such "social issues" as marijuana, abortion, and amnesty. McGovern supporters, by contrast, did not trust Nixon and found him too conservative on foreign policy and too slow in getting us out of Vietnam.[21] The voters, in short, found Nixon and McGovern to be quite different persons, as indeed they were, and likely to carry out very different policies if put in office. It is hard to see

what either candidate, especially McGovern, who lost, could have done about all this.

No one is sure what effect campaigns have on general elections, especially for president. Because the voter receives stimuli from so many sources, perhaps we shall never know which, if any, are of decisive importance. Probably a good rule of thumb is this: a campaign makes more difference, the fewer the other sources of voter information. Campaigns are likely to be more important, thus, for low-visibility offices (library trustee in Belmont, Massachusetts), in primary elections (the voter is confronted with many candidates who all have the same party identification), and in elections not extensively covered by the media. The less the voter can learn from other sources and the more confusing the choices he or she faces, the more helpful may be campaign literature, door-to-door canvassing, coffee parties, and speeches.

Studies in Gary, Indiana, and Detroit, Michigan, of the effect of door-to-door canvassing by precinct workers suggest that, in these highly organized cities, campaign activity of this sort may have a small but significant effect on elections and that the effect is largest in primaries and local elections.[22] Few cities are so well organized or so heavily canvassed, however. National studies show that during a presidential election, about one-fifth of the voters are contacted or visited by a campaign worker.[23] No one knows what difference it makes.

Campaigns do have one indisputable effect: they provide for the passage of time between the nomination and the election. During that time— in a national election, from roughly the beginning of September to the first week in November—several things happen. Traditional party loyalties start to reassert themselves. (Right after a presidential convention, the person just nominated tends to have a big lead in the polls. This usually dwindles as time goes on.) The candidates have a chance to make mistakes. Generalized perceptions of the candidates' personalities begin to take hold in the voters' minds as they become more familiar with the candidates' voices, faces, and behavior. Finally, events happen during campaigns—strikes, riots, disasters, economic changes—and voters can watch how the candidates respond to these challenges.[24]

ELECTION OUTCOMES

To the candidates and perhaps to the voter, the only interesting outcome of an election is who won. To a political scientist, the interesting outcomes are the broad trends in winning and losing and what they imply about the attitudes of voters, the operation of the electoral system, and the fate of political parties.

Figure 7.3 shows the trend in the popular vote for president since the Civil War. From 1876 to 1896 the Democrats and Republicans were hotly competitive. The Republicans won three times, the Democrats twice in close contests. Beginning in 1896, the Republicans became the dominant party and, except for 1912 and 1916 when Woodrow Wilson, a Democrat, was able to win owing to a split in the Republican party, the Republicans carried every presidential election until 1932. Then, Franklin Roosevelt put together what has since become known as the "New Deal coalition," and the Democrats became the dominant party. They won every election until 1952, when Eisenhower, a Republican and a popular military hero, was elected for two terms.

FIGURE 7.3   Partisan Division of the Presidential Vote in the Nation, 1824–1976

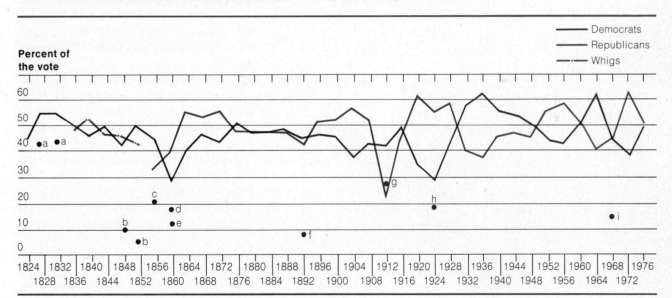

Source: Historical Data Archive, Inter-university Consortium for Political Research, as reported in William H. Flanigan and Nancy H. Zingale, *Political Behavior of the American Electorate,* 3rd ed., p. 32. Copyright © 1975 by Allyn and Bacon, Inc., Boston. Reprinted with permission.

Other parties gaining at least 5% of the vote: [a]National Republican; [b]Free Soil; [c]American; [d]Southern Democratic; [e]Constitutional Union; [f]People's; [g]Bull Moose; [h]Progressive; [i]American Independent.

Party Realignments

There have clearly been important turning points in the strength of the major parties, especially in the twentieth century when for long periods we have had not so much close competi-

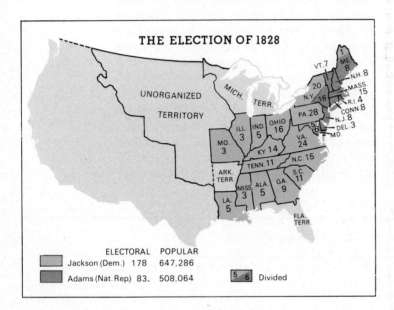

THE ELECTION OF 1828

ELECTORAL	POPULAR
Jackson (Dem.) 178	647,286
Adams (Nat. Rep) 83.	508,064

5 6 Divided

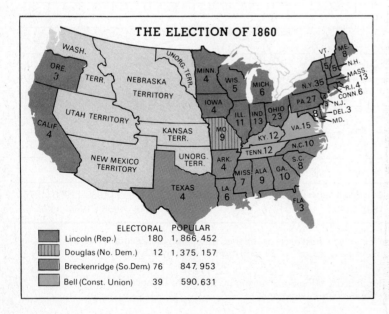

THE ELECTION OF 1860

	ELECTORAL	POPULAR
Lincoln (Rep.)	180	1,866,452
Douglas (No. Dem.)	12	1,375,157
Breckenridge (So.Dem)	76	847,953
Bell (Const. Union)	39	590,631

tion between two parties as an alternation of dominance by one party and then another. To help explain these major shifts in the tides of politics, scholars have developed the notion of "critical" or "realigning" elections. Such an election is one in which there occurs—perhaps not all at once, but within a short period of time—a reorganization of the coalitions that make up the two major parties so that one party gains lasting dominance over the other.[25] By some accounts, there have been five realigning elections in American history—1800 (when the Jeffersonian Republicans defeated the Federalists), 1828 (when the Jacksonian Democrats came to power), 1860 (when the Whig party collapsed and the Republicans under Lincoln came to power), 1896 (when the Republicans defeated William Jennings Bryan), and 1932 (when the Democrats under Roosevelt came into office). Some observers are struck by the fact that these realignments have occurred with marked regularity every twenty-eight to thirty-six years and have speculated on whether they are the result of inevitable cycles in American political life.

Such speculations need not concern us, for what is more important is to understand why a realignment occurs at all. That is not entirely clear. For one thing, there are at least two kinds of realignments—one in which a major party is so badly defeated that it disappears and a new party emerges to take its place (this happened to the Federalists in 1800 and to the Whigs in 1856–1860), another in which the two existing parties continue but voters shift their support from one to the other (this happened in 1896 and 1932). Furthermore, not all critical elections have been carefully studied.

The three clearest cases seem to be 1860, 1896, and 1932. By 1860 the existing parties could no longer straddle the fence on the slavery issue. The Republican party was formed in 1856 on the basis of clear-cut opposition to slavery; the Democratic party split in half in 1860, with one part (led by Stephen A. Douglas and based in the North) trying to waffle on the issue, and the other (led by John C. Breckinridge and drawing its support from the South) categorically denying that any government had any right to outlaw slavery. The remnants of the Whig party, renamed the Constitutional Union party, tried to unite the nation by writing no platform at all, thus remaining silent on slavery. Lincoln and the anti-slavery Republicans won in 1860; Breckinridge and the pro-slavery southern Democrats came in second. From that moment on the two major political parties had acquired different sources of support and stood (at least for a decade) for different principles. The parties that had tried to straddle the fence were eliminated. The Civil War fixed these new party loyalties deeply into the popular mind, and the structure of party competition was set for nearly forty years.

In 1896 a different kind of realignment occurred. Economics rather than slavery was at issue. There was a series of depressions during the 1880s and 1890s that fell especially hard on farmers in the Midwest and parts of the South. The prices paid farmers for their commodities had been falling more or less steadily since the Civil War, making it increasingly difficult for them to pay their bills. A bitter reaction against the two major parties, which were straddling this issue as they had straddled slavery, spread like a prairie fire, leading to the formation of parties of economic protest—the Greenbackers and the Populists. Reinforcing the economic cleavages were cultural ones: Populists tended to be fundamentalist Protestants; urban voters were increasingly Catholic. Matters came to a head in 1896 when William Jennings Bryan captured the Democratic nomination for president and saw to it that the party adopted a Populist platform. The existing Populist party endorsed the Bryan candidacy. In the election, anti-Bryan Democrats deserted the party in droves to support the Republican candidate, William McKinley.

Once again, a real issue divided the two parties: the Republicans stood for industry, business, hard money, protective tariffs, and urban interests; the Democrats, for farmers, small towns, low tariffs, and rural interests. The Republicans

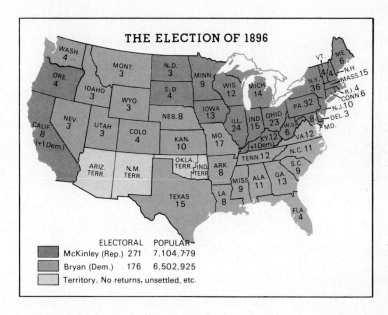

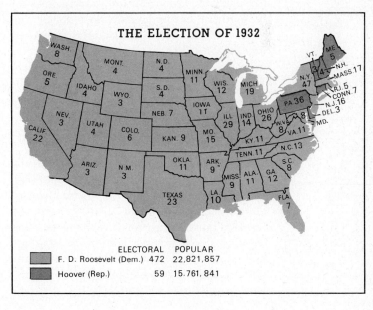

The 1896 election was a watershed in American politics—a "realigning election" that brought together new party coalitions. It pitted William Jennings Bryan, a fiery midwestern champion of strict religion and easy money (left), against William McKinley, the Republican defender of the gold standard (right). McKinley campaigned from his front porch in Canton, Ohio.

won, carrying the cities, workers and businessmen alike; the Democrats lost, carrying most of the southern and midwestern farm states. The old split between North and South that resulted from the Civil War was now replaced in part by an East versus West, city versus farm split.[26] It was not, however, only an economic cleavage—the Republicans had been able to appeal to Catholics and Lutherans who disliked fundamentalism and its hostility to liquor and immigrants.

This alignment persisted until 1932. Again, change was triggered by an economic depression; again, more than economic issues were involved. The "New Deal coalition" that emerged was based on bringing together into the Democratic party urban workers, northern blacks, southern whites, and Jewish voters. Unlike 1860 and 1896, it was not preceded by any third-party movement; it occurred suddenly (though some

groups had begun to shift their alliance in 1928) and gathered momentum throughout the 1930s. The Democrats, isolated as a sectional party based in the South since 1896, had now become the majority party by finding a candidate and a cause that could lure urban workers, blacks, and Jews away from the Republican party where they had been for decades. It was obviously a delicate coalition—blacks and southern whites disagreed on practically everything except their liking for Roosevelt; Jews and the Irish bosses of the big-city machines also had little in common. But the federal government under Roosevelt was able to supply enough benefits to each of these disparate groups to keep them loyal members of the coalition and to supply a new basis for party identification.

To some degree, these critical elections involved, not simply converting existing voters to new party loyalties, but recruiting into the dominant party the new voters—young persons just coming of voting age, immigrants just receiving their citizenship papers, and blacks just receiving, in some places, the right to vote. But there were also genuine conversions—northern blacks, for example, had been heavily Republican before Roosevelt but became heavily Democratic after his election.

In short, an electoral realignment occurs when a new issue of utmost importance to the voters (slavery, the economy) arises that cuts across existing party divisions and replaces old issues that had formerly been the basis of party identification. Some observers have speculated that we are due for a new party realignment as the tensions within the New Deal coalition become more evident. As the memory of Roosevelt and the Great Depression fades, as new voters come of age, the ability of the Democrats to keep within their party both persons who are liberal

❝Though the old coalitions are becoming frayed at the edges, as yet no convulsive new issue has arisen that would split the existing parties into enduring new alignments.**❞**

and those who are conservative on "social" issues may decline. (See Chapter 5.) One Republican strategist predicted, in fact, that a new Republican majority could be fashioned by bringing together Republicans and dissatisfied elements of the Democratic coalition, such as blue-collar workers, but nothing of the sort has yet happened.[27] Though the old coalitions are becoming frayed at the edges, as yet no convulsive new issue has arisen that would split the existing parties into enduring new alignments.

Party Decline

What seems to be happening instead is that political parties are decaying, not realigning. This can be seen in several ways. We have already noted (Chapter 5) that the proportion of persons identifying with one or the other party has been declining since the 1960s. There has also been an increase in the proportion of persons voting a split ticket. Figure 7.4, for example, shows the steep increase in the percentage of congressional districts carried by one party for the presidency and by the other for Congress. Whereas in the 1940s one party would carry a given district for both its presidential and congressional candidates, today nearly half the districts split their votes between one party's presidential candidate and the other's congressional candidate.

Public opinion shows the same thing. In 1948 about a third of the voters interviewed said they had split their tickets; by 1968 nearly one-half had; in 1972 over 60 percent did. The increase was greatest in the South and Northeast. So far, this ticket-splitting has helped the Democrats keep control of Congress even when they have lost the presidency and enabled the Republicans

Franklin Roosevelt greets Dr. George Washington Carver at Tuskegee Institute in Alabama. Blacks had long voted Republican; during the New Deal they shifted to the Democratic party. This change was part of the political realignment that occurrred in the elections of 1932 and 1936.

FIGURE 7.4   Trends in Split-Ticket Voting for President and Congressmen, 1920–1976

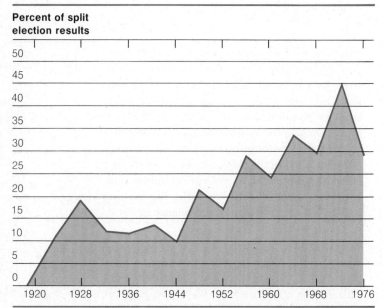

Percent of split election results

Note: The figure is the percentage of congressional districts carried by presidential and congressional candidates of different parties in each election year.

to capture the White House when unable to win in Congress.

Ticket-splitting was almost unheard of in the nineteenth century, and for a very good reason. In those days the voter was either given a ballot by the party of his choice and he dropped it, intact, into the ballot box (thereby voting for everybody listed on the ballot), or he was given a government-printed ballot that listed in columns all the candidates of each party. All the voter had to do was make a mark at the top of one column in order to vote for every candidate in that column. (When voting machines came along, they provided a single lever that, when pulled, cast votes for all the candidates of a particular party.) Progressives around the turn of the century began to persuade states to adopt the "office-bloc" (or "Massachusetts") ballot in place of the "party-column" (or "Indiana") bal-

lot. This office-bloc ballot lists all candidates by office; there is no way to vote a straight party ticket by making one mark. Not surprisingly, states using the office-bloc ballot show much more ticket-splitting than those without it.[28]

A Winning Coalition

If the strength of each party's hold on the loyalty of its voters is declining, then we would expect the composition of each party's voting coalition to vary from election to election. This happens, though the persistence of party loyalty and policy preferences among various groups provides some continuity in the votes that each party receives.

There are two ways to look at it. One is to ask what percentage of various identifiable groups in the population supported the Democratic or Republican candidate for president. The other is to ask what proportion of a party's total vote came from each of these groups. The answer to the first question tells us how *loyal* blacks, farmers, union members, and others are to the Democratic or Republican party or candidate; the answer to the second question tells us how *important* each group is to a candidate or party. These figures describe both the continuity and the changes within the coalitions supporting each party.

For the Democrats, the two most loyal groups have been black and Jewish voters. Blacks and Jews have always given at least two-thirds of their votes to Democrats. The only presidential elections in which their preferences differed significantly were 1960 and 1972; Jewish voters liked John F. Kennedy more than did blacks, but blacks liked George McGovern more than did Jews. Union members and Catholics, long thought to be a major part of the New Deal coalition, have showed a great deal of variation in their partisan loyalties. Catholics voted overwhelmingly for John Kennedy (a Catholic), but supported Nixon in 1972 and Eisenhower in 1956, and divided almost evenly between the two parties in 1952 and 1968. Union members did not give a majority of their votes to Humphrey in

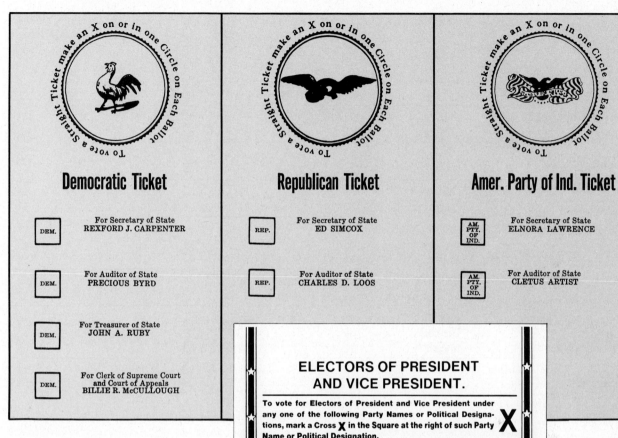

SAMPLE BALLOTS

The party-column or "Indiana" ballot lists all candidates of one party under the party name or emblem, thereby making it easy to vote a straight party ticket by putting an X in the emblem (or, if a voting machine is used, by pulling the party lever). The office-bloc or "Massachusetts" ballot, on which candidates of all parties are grouped by office, makes it harder for the voter to cast a straight party vote.

TABLE 7.4   Who Likes the Democrats?
Percentage of Various Groups Saying They Voted for the Democratic Presidential Candidate

Group		1952	1956	1960	1964	1968[a]	1972	1976
Sex	Men	47%	45%	52%	60%	41%	37%	53%
	Women	42	39	49	62	45	38	48
Race	White	43	41	49	59	38	32	46
	Nonwhite	79	61	68	94	85	87	85
Education	College	34	31	39	52	37	37	42
	Grade school	52	50	55	66	52	49	58
Occupation	Professional and business	36	32	42	54	34	31	42
	Blue-collar	55	50	60	71	50	43	58
Age	Under 30	51	43	54	64	47	48	53
	50 and over	39	39	46	59	41	36	52
Religion	Protestant	37	37	38	55	35	30	46
	Catholic	56	51	78	76	59	48	57
	Jewish[b]	71	77	89	89	85	66	68
Southerners		51	49	51	52	31	29	54

Source: Gallup Poll data as tabulated in Jeane J. Kirkpatrick, "Changing Patterns of Electoral Competition," in Anthony King, ed., *The New American Political System* (Washington, D.C.: American Enterprise Institute, 1978), pp. 264–265. Copyright © 1978 by the American Enterprise Institute. Reprinted by permission.

[a] 1968 election had three major candidates (Humphrey, Nixon, and Wallace).

[b] Jewish vote estimated from various sources; since the number of Jewish persons interviewed is often less than 100, the error in this figure, as well as that for nonwhites, may be large.

TABLE 7.5   The Contribution Made to Democratic Vote Totals by Various Groups, 1952–1976[a]

	1952	1956	1960	1964	1968	1972	1976
Poor (income under $3,000)	28%	19%	16%	15%	12%	10%	7%
Black (and other nonwhite)	7	5	7	12	19	22	16
Union member (or union member in family)	38	36	31	32	28	32	33
Catholic (and other non-Protestant)	41	38	47	36	40	34	35
South (including border states)	20	23	27	21	24	25	36
Central cities (or 12 largest metropolitan areas)	21	19	19	15	14	14	11

Source: Extracted from figures presented by Robert Axelrod, "Communications," *American Political Science Review*, Vol. 68 (June 1974), pp. 718–719; and *ibid.* (June 1978).

[a] The figures presented represent the percentage of the party's vote in any specific election due to the group in question.

1968 (they supported Nixon or Wallace) and split about evenly between Democrats and Republicans in 1952 and 1956. Once a firm part of the Democratic coalition, Southerners deserted that party in 1968 and 1972 (only to return in 1976). (See Table 7.4.)

The Republican coalition is often described as the party of business and professional persons. The loyalty of these groups to Republicans in fact is strong—only in 1964 did they desert the Republican candidate to support Lyndon Johnson. Farmers have usually been Republican, but they are a volatile group, highly sensitive to the level of farm prices, and thus quick to change parties. They abandoned the Republicans in 1948 and 1964. Contrary to popular wisdom, the Republican party usually wins a majority of the votes of poor persons (defined as those earning under $3,000 a year). Only in 1964 did most poor persons support the Democratic candidate. This can be explained by the fact that the poor include quite different elements—low-income blacks (who are Democratic) and many elderly, retired persons (who usually vote Republican).

In sum, the loyalty of most identifiable groups of voters to either party is not overwhelming. Only blacks, business persons, and Jews regularly give two-thirds or more of their votes to one party or the other; other groups display tendencies, but none that cannot be changed.

The contribution each of these groups makes to the party coalitions is a different matter. Though blacks are overwhelmingly and persistently Democratic, they make up so small a portion of the total electorate that only in recent years have they accounted for as much as one-fifth of the total Democratic vote (see Table 7.5). The groups that make up the largest part of the Democratic vote—Catholics, union members, Southerners—are also the least dependable parts of that coalition.[29]

This means that, when representatives of various segments of society make demands on party leaders and presidential candidates, they usually stress either their numbers or their loyalty, but

❝Thus, for any president and for either party, putting together a winning coalition is something that must be done anew in every election.**❞**

Union leaders usually support the Democratic party, but their ability to deliver the votes of the workers is limited. Many of the rank and file will vote Republican.

rarely both. Black leaders, for example, sometimes describe the black vote as of decisive importance to Democrats and thus deserving of special consideration from a Democratic president. But blacks are so loyal that a Democratic candidate can almost take their votes for granted and, in any event, they are not as numerous as other groups. Union leaders, by contrast, will emphasize how many union voters there are, but a president will know that union leaders cannot "deliver" the union vote and that this vote may well go to the president's opponent whatever the leaders say. Thus, for any president and for either party, putting together a winning coalition is something that must be done anew in every election. There are few voters who can either be taken for granted or written off as a lost cause.

❝The constitutional system within which our elections take place was designed to moderate the pace of change—to make it neither easy nor impossible to adopt radical proposals.❞

The difficulty in getting federal, state, and local governments to cooperate effectively is one barrier to efforts to rebuild slums. President Carter, HUD Secretary Patricia Harris, and Mayor Abe Beame of New York City inspect a burned out area of the South Bronx in 1977.

THE EFFECTS OF ELECTIONS ON POLICY

Cynics complain that elections are meaningless—no matter who wins, crooks, incompetents, or self-serving politicians still hold office. Persons of a more charitable disposition may concede that elected officials are decent enough persons but argue that public policy remains more or less the same no matter which official or which party is in office.

There is no brief and simple response to this view. Much depends on which office or policy we examine, something we shall do in greater detail in Part IV. One reason it is so hard to

generalize about the policy effects of elections is that the offices to be filled by the voters are so numerous and the ability of the political parties to unite these officeholders behind a common policy is so weak that any policy proposal must run a gauntlet of potential opponents. Though we have but two major parties, and though only one party can win the presidency, each party is a weak coalition of diverse elements that reflect the many divisions in public opinion. Proponents of a new law must put together a majority coalition almost from scratch, and a winning coalition on one issue tends to be somewhat different—often, dramatically different—from a winning coalition on another issue.

In a parliamentary system with strong parties such as that in Great Britain, an election can often have a major effect on public policy. When the Labour party won office in 1945, it put several major industries under public ownership and launched a comprehensive set of social services, including a nationalized health care plan. Its ambitious and controversial campaign platform was converted, almost item by item, into law. When the Conservative party returned to power in 1951, it accepted some of these changes but rejected others (for example, it denationalized the steel industry).

American elections, unless accompanied by a national crisis such as war or a depression, rarely produce changes of the magnitude of those that occurred in Britain in 1945. The constitutional system within which our elections take place was designed to moderate the pace of change—to make it neither easy nor impossible to adopt radical proposals. But the fact that the system is intended to moderate the rate of change does not mean it will always work that way. The election of 1860 brought to national power a party committed to opposing the extension of slavery and southern secession; it took a bloody war to vindicate that policy. The election of 1896 led to the dominance of a party committed to high tariffs, a strong currency, urban growth, and business prosperity—a commitment that was not significantly altered until 1932. The election of that year led to the New Deal, which produced the greatest single enlargement of federal authority since 1860. The election of 1964 gave the Democrats such a large majority in Congress (as well as control of the presidency) that there began to issue forth an extraordinary number of new policies of sweeping significance—Medicare and Medicaid, federal aid to education and to local law enforcement, two dozen environmental and consumer protection laws, the Voting Rights Act of 1965, a revision of the immigration laws, and a new cabinet-level Department of Housing and Urban Development.

In view of all this, it is hard to argue that the pace of change in our government is always slow or that elections never make a difference. Studies by scholars confirm that elections are often significant, despite the difficulty of getting laws passed. One analysis of about fourteen hundred promises made between 1944 and 1964 in the platforms of the two major parties revealed that 72 percent were carried into effect.[30]

Another study examined the party platforms of the Democrats and Republicans from 1844 to 1968 and all the laws passed by Congress between 1789 and 1968. By a complex statistical method, the author of the study was able to show that during certain periods the differences between the platforms of the two parties were especially large (1856, 1880, 1896, 1932) and that there was at about the same time a high rate of change in the kinds of laws being passed.[31] This study supports the general impression conveyed by history that elections can often be central to important policy changes.

Why, then, do we so often think that elections make little difference? It is because public opinion and the political parties enter a phase of consolidation and continuity between periods of rapid change. During this phase the changes are, so to speak, digested and party leaders adjust to the new popular consensus that may (or may not) evolve around the merits of these changes. During the 1870s and 1880s, Democratic politicians had to come to terms with the failure of the southern secessionist movement and the

abolition of slavery; during the 1900s, the Democrats had again to adjust to the fact that national economic policy was going to support industrialization and urbanization, not farming; during the 1940s and 1950s, the Republicans had to learn to accept the popularity of the New Deal.

Elections in ordinary times are not "critical," do not produce any major party realignment, are not fought out over a dominant issue, and provide the winners with no clear mandate. In most cases an election is little more than a retrospective judgment on the record of the incumbent president and the existing congressional majority. If times are good, incumbents win easily; if times are bad, incumbents may lose even though their opponents may have no clear plans for change. As we shall see in Chapter 16, even such retrospective judgments about the economy and government can affect policy greatly.

ELECTORAL PROBLEMS: TURNOUT

Earlier we saw that participation in American elections is low. Many people worry about this and various plans have been devised to correct it. These include efforts to educate voters so they will not be "apathetic."

Voter "apathy" may not be a good explanation of why turnout is so low, however. Indeed, given the obstacles placed before the voter, and the slight chance that any individual's vote will make any difference in the outcome, what is surprising (and pleasing) is that so many people vote anyway. Consider the costs and benefits of voting:

Costs
- Register in advance, often several weeks in advance, of the election by going to a registration place several blocks or miles from your home.
- Learn enough about the candidates so that you feel competent to vote. (Remember, there may be dozens of names on the ballot.)

- Take time off from work or other duties. (Remember, elections in this country, unlike in France, are always on weekdays.)
- Get to the polls on your own. (Once, party organizations would take you there, but now only a few civic or political groups will do this.)
- Wait in line at the polls. (Remember, federal elections are in November, when it is often cold and rainy.)

Benefits
- One chance in a million that your vote will make a difference in the results.
- The sense of satisfaction that comes from having done your duty.

The costs of voting are quite large compared to the benefits. Indeed, if we sold breakfast food the way we promote voting, the cereal companies would go bankrupt. Studies have shown, for example, that registration requirements cut down drastically on the number of persons voting—by one estimate, there may be as many as 10 million persons who on election day would like to vote

but cannot because they forgot to register.[32] Others may remember to register, but because they have moved recently (and nearly half the population moves in any five-year period) and cannot meet the residency requirements, they cannot vote.

Steps have been taken to reduce the burdens of registration, but not with much effect so far. Since 1970 federal law has prohibited residency requirements of more than thirty days for presidential elections; a Supreme Court decision in 1972 declared that requirements much in excess of this for state and local elections would also be improper.[33] By 1976 seventeen states and the District of Columbia, containing about 47 percent of the nation's population, had adopted laws permitting voters to register by mail. Voter turnout in these states, however, actually *declined* (it was 2 percent lower in 1976 than in 1972, when the register-by-mail plans did not exist).[34] One state (North Dakota) does not require voter registration at all, and two states (Minnesota and Wisconsin) allowed persons wishing to vote in 1976 to register at the time they voted (thus in effect eliminating preregistration requirements). These states experienced an increase in turnout of about one or two percentage points.[35] A nationwide register-by-mail plan has been proposed but has not been enacted, partly because of uncertainty as to its effectiveness, partly because of objections to its cost or administration, and partly because Republicans feel it might give an advantage to Democrats.

In short, the physical and administrative barriers to voting may not be the principal cause of low voter turnouts. Some states that have unusually high participation rates (Utah, Idaho, South Dakota, New Hampshire, Connecticut) do not have registration systems that are appreciably simpler than those places with low turnouts (South Carolina, the District of Columbia, Texas). Much of the difference in turnout must be explained by the political traditions of the states, the composition of the population, the closeness of the elections, and the attitudes of local officials (see Table 7.6).

TABLE 7.6   States with Highest and Lowest Rates of Participation in Presidential Elections

Highest States		Lowest States	
South Dakota	68.7%	District of Columbia	30.8%
Utah	68.4	Georgia	37.9
Minnesota	68.0	South Carolina	38.6
North Dakota	68.0	North Carolina	43.4
Montana	67.8	Alabama	43.5
Connecticut	66.3	Tennessee	43.6
New Hampshire	64.2	Louisiana	44.3
Washington	63.8	Mississippi	45.0
Wyoming	63.8	Texas	45.3
Iowa	63.3	Virginia	45.5
Idaho	63.1	Arkansas	47.9

Source: U.S. Bureau of the Census as reported in *Statistical Abstract of the United States, 1975,* p. 451.

Note: Percentage of voting-age population voting in 1972 presidential election.

For certain persons, the material and psychic costs of voting are lower than for the general population and the benefits are higher. Business and professional persons find it easier to arrange their working schedules than persons punching a time clock or tending five children at home. Persons with more schooling tend to have a stronger sense of civic duty and more political information than those with less schooling, and consequently are more likely to vote. Older persons are more likely to vote than younger ones (except for those with a college education), perhaps because young people have yet to acquire much interest in politics. Areas where elections are competitive are more likely to have a high turnout than those where they are one-sided. Therefore, one-party areas of the South have lower participation rates than two-party states of the North and West. Blacks are less likely to participate than whites, especially in the South but even in the North, in part, perhaps, because a large proportion of blacks have low incomes or otherwise find the costs of voting high (see Table 7.7).

Finally, voting in all social groups is less among those with little interest in politics or a weak sense of party identification. The more strongly you identify with the Democratic or Republican party, the more likely you are to vote. This means that any program that succeeds in getting the nonvoter to the polls will bring into the electorate many persons who are not interested in or confident about politics. Both parties like to believe that this group might help them if they could be brought to the polls. The Democrats believe that, since many are low-income, they would vote Democratic; the Republicans sometimes feel that the nonvoters are uninterested in politics because they have been "turned off" by decades of Democratic programs and await only a clear alternative ("a choice, not an echo") to energize them. In fact, how nonvoters would vote is unknown and probably would depend very much on the nature of the appeals that were made (if there *are* any appeals that would be successful).

TABLE 7.7 Participation in National Elections, by Population Characteristics, 1968–1976

Characteristics		*Percent Reporting They Voted*		
		1968	1972	1976
Male		69.8%	64.1%	59.6%
Female		66.0	62.0	58.8
White		69.1	64.5	60.9
Black		57.6	52.1	48.7
Age[a]	18–20 years	33.3	48.3	38.0
	21–24 years	51.1	50.7	45.6
	25–34 years	62.5	59.7	55.4
	35–44 years	70.8	66.3	63.3
	45–64 years	74.9	70.8	68.7
	65 and over	65.8	63.5	62.2
Residence	Metropolitan	68.0	64.3	59.2
	Nonmetropolitan	67.3	59.4	59.1
	North and West	71.0	66.4	61.2
	South	60.1	55.4	54.9
Education	8 years or less	54.5	47.4	44.1
	9–11 years	61.3	52.0	47.2
	12 years	72.5	65.4	59.4
	More than 12 years	81.2	78.8	73.5
Employment	Employed	71.1	66.0	62.0
	Unemployed	52.1	49.0	43.7
	Not in labor force	63.2	59.3	56.5

Source: Statistical Abstract of the United States, 1978, p. 520.

Note: These are the percentages of people who say to an interviewer that they voted. People tend to overreport their participation, and thus these percentages are higher than the percentage actually voting.

[a] Covers civilian noninstitutional population 18 years old and over in Georgia and Kentucky, 19 and over in Alaska, 20 and over in Hawaii, and 21 years and older elsewhere in 1968.

The parties, especially the Democrats, spend a lot of money on drives to register voters and get out the vote. Presidential elections are often so close that the shift of a few thousand votes in a few states could make the difference between victory and defeat. As with all other aspects of campaigning, however, there is great uncertainty as to the effectiveness of such drives.

ELECTORAL PROBLEMS: MONEY

"Money is the mother's milk of politics," a powerful California politician once observed, and few candidates who have struggled to raise a campaign chest would disagree. Indeed, money has become more important to the candidate as party organization has declined. If no machine can supply battalions of precinct workers paid for with patronage jobs, then such workers must either be dispensed with, hired on a temporary basis, or recruited from among the not always dependable ranks of volunteers. Even more important, increased reliance on radio and television advertising and on direct-mail campaigning has dramatically raised the cost of running for office. A one-minute commercial on national television in prime time can cost $150,000; sixty-second "drive-time" radio spots in a city such as Detroit cost roughly $100 each; mailing a letter to 100,000 voters will cost around $25,000. As Will Rogers said, "You have to be loaded just to get beat."

In 1952, perhaps the first presidential election to make extensive use of television, the two parties spent on that medium about $3.5 million. By 1968, in the hard-fought Nixon-Humphrey contest, radio-TV expenses in just the general election had risen to $18.7 million; another $7.8 million had been spent in the primaries. Expenditures on the broadcast media accounted for about half of the campaign budget of a presidential candidate. In 1972 the pattern shifted somewhat—Nixon, way ahead in the polls and having the advantage of being an incumbent president whose activities were regularly covered by the media, spent on radio and TV less than one-third of what he had spent four years earlier. McGovern, on the other hand, was behind in the polls and thus spent more on radio and TV than Humphrey had four years before and in addition mounted an expensive direct-mail campaign.[36] In the 1974 senate races, $24.5 million was spent, about a fifth of it on broadcasting.[37]

Sources of Campaign Funds

Our knowledge of how campaign money is raised or spent has, until recently, been rather spotty. Federal law did not effectively require public disclosure of political contributions until 1972, when the name, address, and occupation of every contributor of $100 or more to a congressional or presidential candidate had to be publicly listed. The law also required a complete reporting of campaign expenditures and set limits on the amounts individuals and campaign organizations could contribute to an election (to be discussed below).

The first source of money is the candidate. In 1970, for example, there were forty-five candidates for office who spent out of their own or their families' resources between $500,000 and $1,000,000. This group included:

- Nelson Rockefeller, a Republican, whose family spent $4.5 million on his campaign for governor of New York.
- Richard Ottinger, a Democrat, who spent $3.9 million of his family's money in an unsuccessful effort to become a senator from New York.
- Norton Simon, a Democrat, who spent $1.8 million of his own money in trying to become a senator from California.
- Howard Metzenbaum, a Democrat, who used $500,000 of his family's money trying to become a senator from Ohio.

In 1974 Congress passed a law that would have set a limit on how much a person or his family could spend on his own campaign, but the Supreme Court overturned this restriction on the grounds that it abridged the right of free speech guaranteed by the First Amendment.[38]

The second source is other well-to-do persons. On April 7, 1972, the rules requiring disclosure of the names of persons making federal campaign contributions went into effect. The Committee to Re-elect the President, President Nixon's campaign organization, managed to raise nearly $20 million before the disclosure laws took effect, most of it from very wealthy contributors who preferred to remain anonymous. Later investigations revealed that about 100 persons contributed $40,000 or more each; about 40 of these contributed $100,000 or more each; and a few contributed in excess of $1,000,000 each. After the disclosure rules became law, the scale of giving dropped somewhat, but there were still 37 persons who gave $50,000 or more apiece between April and December, including 18 who gave in excess of $100,000 each. George McGovern, the Democratic nominee, collected $50,000 or more from at least 18 individuals, 9 of whom gave over $100,000 and one of whom gave $724,430.[39]

Wealthy persons give for many reasons—a liking for a candidate, strong ideological attraction to a candidate's position, or ambition for prestige and power. Most large donors get little of personal value in return, though for decades it has been customary for presidents of both parties to give a certain number of high federal appointments, especially ambassadorships, to large donors. In 1972 President Nixon appointed thirteen noncareer ambassadors to Western European countries; eight of them had contributed at least $50,000 to his reelection campaign.

When men hired by the Nixon reelection organization broke into the headquarters of the Democratic National Committee in the Watergate office building in 1972, they were caught by an alert security guard. The investigation of this break-in, which gathered momentum only after the election was over, led to the disclosure of dubious or illegal campaign finance practices and stimulated public demands for reform. The 1974 campaign finance reform law was a response to this. Among other things, it set a limit of $1,000 on the amount any individual could contribute to any single candidate in any given federal election (primary or general), outlawed cash contributions in excess of $100 (to ensure that checks would be written so that the source of funds could more easily be traced), and prohib-

A computerized mailing center, such as this one in Virginia run by Richard Viguerie, can help a political candidate raise millions of dollars by direct-mail solicitation of small donors.

ited foreign contributions. The Supreme Court upheld these restrictions in a test case.[40]

Third, campaign funds come from organizations and interest groups. Until recently, it was illegal for corporations or labor unions to contribute money directly to political campaigns, but the law was easy to circumvent—corporation executives could give money as individuals (and be covertly reimbursed by their companies), corporate money could be "laundered" by first sending it abroad, and labor unions could set up "political action committees" to raise money from members for campaign purposes. And other interest groups—whether those with a tangible or an ideological interest in policy—could make unlimited contributions. The investigations following the 1972 campaign led to the indictment of twenty-one individuals and fourteen corporations for making illegal campaign contributions, mostly to the Nixon campaign but some also to the campaigns of Democratic candidates such as Hubert Humphrey, Edmund Muskie, and

Henry M. Jackson. Most of those indicted were found guilty.

The interest groups that supply money to campaigns include those affected materially by public policy (labor unions, milk producers, schoolteachers, doctors, business organizations) and those interested in promoting candidates with a liberal or a conservative ideology. The National Committee for an Effective Congress has, for nearly three decades, raised money for liberals running for Congress. In 1972 it gave nearly $400,000 to eighty-eight candidates. Conservative groups, such as Americans for Constitutional Action, also make donations.[41]

The 1974 law put effective restrictions for the first time on such organizations. As modified by certain amendments in 1976, it allowed corporations, labor unions, and special-interest groups to set up political action committees (PACs) which, provided they raised money from at least fifty volunteer donors and gave funds to at least five candidates in a federal election, could contribute up to $5,000 to each candidate in each election. Strict accounting rules were introduced, and each corporation or union was limited to one PAC. The corporate PACs solicit their funds primarily from the executives in their firms (though they are allowed to solicit from workers and stockholders as well); the unions solicit their members. In 1978 there were 778 PACs sponsored by corporations, 550 by trade associations, and 263 by labor unions.

Though the campaign finance laws have restricted the amount of money that a PAC or individual may contribute to any given candidate, the legal authorization of PACs has probably increased the total amount of business (and labor) expenditure on politics. Business-oriented PACs contribute more money to campaigns than do union members, but this does not give Republicans, traditionally thought to be favored by business, any substantial advantage. The reason is simple—as we shall see in Chapters 8 and 10, interest groups have strong incentives to support incumbent politicians. As a result, in the 1978 congressional elections in which the great majority of incumbents running for reelection were Democrats, business-oriented PACs gave almost half their funds to Democratic candidates. Almost all the labor contributions also went to Democrats.

Fourth, campaign money is contributed by small individual donors. Before 1964 no serious effort was made to reach such givers on the assumption that it would not be worthwhile. Then, Barry Goldwater, in a televised campaign speech during 1964, asked persons who supported him to send in checks. To everyone's amazement, 300,000 persons followed his advice. In 1968 George Wallace based his entire third-party campaign for the presidency on small contributors and got money from 750,000 of them—a record that still stands. In 1972 George McGovern followed the same path; though his campaign was launched with the aid of a few wealthy donors who made large contributions, he raised most of his money by direct-mail and television appeals that stimulated 640,000 donors to send in checks averaging about $25 each.[42]

The recent campaign finance laws have given a strong impetus to candidates to solicit the small donor, not only by limiting each contribution to a candidate to $1,000, but by creating a fifth source of funds—a system of publicly financed presidential elections. If you seek your party's presidential nomination, the federal government will pay to your campaign committee an amount equal to the sum you raise from individuals who contribute $250 or less, up to a limit of $5 million. (You also must show you are a serious contender by raising at least $5,000 —in individual contributions of $250 or less—in each of twenty states.) Thus, the opportunity to get a federal subsidy encourages the primary candidate to solicit many small donations. In 1976 the various Democratic and Republican primary candidates received a total of $24 million in federal matching dollars.

Once you win the presidential nomination, you are then entitled to full federal support for your general election campaign (provided you are the nominee of a "major party," defined as one that received at least 5 percent of the popular vote in the preceding presidential election). This support is for the actual expenditures you make. If you elect to accept public financing as a presidential candidate, you and your family may not personally contribute more than $50,000 to the campaign. Furthermore, if you take public money, you may not accept private donations to pay for the general election. In 1976 the Carter and Ford campaigns each received a $21.8 million federal grant for their general election campaigns. If you choose not to accept federal funding, there is no limit on what you can spend.

There still remain ways to spend money on politics outside these limits. A person can spend unlimited amounts on "independent" efforts on behalf of candidates, provided he or she shows that the effort is truly independent and is not done in concert with the candidate or his campaign staff. The Supreme Court has made it clear that the right to buy political advertisements, print leaflets, and otherwise work for candidates is a form of speech protected by the First Amendment; that such efforts cost money does not make it permissible for Congress to restrict them.[43] Individuals and organizations can also contribute substantial sums to political parties, though not to individual candidates. (See box for summary of contribution limits.)

The Effect of Campaign Finance Reform

The effects of these new laws are not entirely clear, but some trends seem likely. First, those candidates for federal office (Congress or the presidency) who are either personally wealthy or who can appeal successfully to many small donors by the use of television or direct-mail solicitation will have an advantage. A candidate of modest means and little television appeal, however substantial his other qualifications and experience, is likely to be at a disadvantage.

Second, any congressional candidate who is not rich will have to devote more, not less, time to

Major Federal Campaign Finance Rules

General

- All federal election contributions and expenditures are reported to a six-person Federal Election Commission with power to investigate and prosecute violators.
- All contributions over $100 must be disclosed, with name, address, and occupation of contributor.
- No *cash* contributions over $100; no foreign contributions.
- No ceiling on amount a candidate or campaign may spend (unless a presidential candidate accepts federal funding).

Individual Contributions

- May not exceed $1,000 to any candidate in any election per year.
- May not exceed $20,000 per year to a national party committee or $5,000 to a political action committee.
- No limit on individual expenditures for "independent advertising."

Political Action Committees

- A corporation, union, or other association may each establish one PAC.
- A PAC must register 6 months in advance, have at least 50 contributors, and give to at least 5 candidates.
- PAC contributions to a candidate may not exceed $5,000 per election.

Presidential Primaries

- Federal matching funds, dollar for dollar, are available for all money raised by candidates from donors giving $250 or less, up to a limit of $5 million.
- To be eligible, a candidate must raise $5,000 in each of 20 states in contributions of $250 or less.

Presidential Election

- Federal government will pay all campaign costs of major party candidates.

fund-raising than before. The days when a few dinners with wealthy supporters could produce a campaign war chest are practically over. Now, either a candidate will have to find a powerful issue with which he or she can be identified (as did George Wallace and George McGovern) or spend much of his or her campaign time speaking to many groups of potential small donors. Proposals have been made for federal funding of congressional campaigns, but none has been passed.

Third, incumbents will continue to enjoy a substantial advantage in fund-raising. Before the reform laws, congressional incumbents got more money than challengers; after the laws, the same pattern held. In 1972, for example, incumbent members of the House, Democratic or Republican, were able to spend about twice as much money as challengers.[44] Where there was no incumbent, the rival candidates each spent about the same amount. An incumbent has the advantage, in raising money, of being a known quantity, having a good chance of winning (he may come from a safe district), and perhaps holding the power to act adversely to the interests of those who might support his opponent. (Remember, campaign contributions can no longer be secret.) The appeal of incumbents explains why even corporate PACs, generally led by conservative businessmen, gave about 40 percent of their 1976 congressional contributions to Democrats—they were generally the incumbents. Yet if challengers are to have a reasonable chance, they must often spend more than incumbents to overcome the greater name recognition that the latter enjoy among the voters.

Fourth, "late-starters" are likely to be discouraged. If money must be raised in small amounts and by expensive campaigns, then a candidate for office is well advised to start long in advance of the election in order to raise a campaign chest. Someone who decides at the last minute to run will not be able to get started with a few large contributions from well-heeled supporters.

Fifth, the laws further weaken the political parties. The federal funding of presidential campaigns goes to the candidate and to his campaign committee, not to the party organization. Furthermore, federal matching funds for presidential primaries will make it possible for several candidates to stay in the primary races longer, thus making the primaries even more important as mechanisms for selecting a presidential candidate.

Sixth, the role of celebrities in politics will increase. An efficient and perfectly legal fund-raising device is to have a benefit show or rock music concert. Thousands of persons will come; though each will pay a modest admission fee, the total sum raised may be huge, with all of it (less expenses) going to the candidate. Obviously, to attract such a crowd, a popular figure must appear. Each party has its stable of celebrities—Republicans have used John Wayne, Bob Hope, and Frank Sinatra; Democrats have used Robert Redford, Paul Newman, and Shirley MacLaine; both parties have used various rock groups.

These changes are the consequence of efforts to purify the electoral process. The object in every case has been to minimize the extent to which large contributors can unduly influence or even control the process of nomination and election. The 1976 elections suggest that there was no undue or improper solicitation of large givers. It has become extremely difficult to "sell" ambassadorships and harder for interest groups wanting special favors to conceal the money incentives they offer politicians under the guise of campaign contributions.

At the same time it should be recognized that the campaign finance laws were not based on evidence that elected officials or policy decisions in the past had been for sale on a wholesale basis. There is some strong evidence that milk price support levels may have been altered in recognition of large donations from dairymen and that a Securities and Exchange Commission investigation into a certain financial manipulator may have been terminated in reward for that person's large contributions. And some ambassadorships may have been given chiefly on the basis of money (though one must bear in mind that no person of ordinary means could afford the expense of being an ambassador to a major foreign capital). Overall, however, there was little evidence of systematic corruption of the political process.

The new laws governing campaign finance are based, at root, on the conviction that elections must not only be fair, they must appear to be fair. Whether or not special-interest groups used campaign funds to buy and sell favors, the public is not likely to feel comfortable about a process in which millions of dollars are raised from a handful of people, funds are "laundered" in Mexico, or unaccounted-for cash is kept in safes and used to hire burglars.

SUMMARY

The United States has more elective offices and more elections than any other major nation in the world. The decision as to who can vote in those elections—originally made almost entirely by the states—is now largely under federal control. Though the franchise has gradually been extended to include all persons eighteen years of age and over, there has been an accompanying decline in voter participation in elections. This change is not so great as it appears because miscounting and vote frauds artificially inflated the turnout in the nineteenth century. But some decline has indisputably occurred, perhaps because politics is less interesting to citizens today than half a century ago, perhaps also because the political parties have become weaker and less able to mobilize voters.

Political campaigns have increasingly become personalized with little or no connection to formal party organizations as a result of the decay of parties, the rise of the direct primary and the electronic media, and campaign finance laws.

Candidates face the problem of creating a temporary organization that can raise money from large numbers of small donors, mobilize enthusiastic supporters, and win a nomination in a way that will not harm their ability to appeal to a broader, more diverse constituency in the general election. Campaigning has an uncertain effect on election outcomes, but election outcomes can have important effects on public policy, especially at those times—during "critical" or "realigning" elections—when new voters are coming into the electorate in large numbers, old party loyalties are weakening, or a major issue is splitting the majority party.

Suggested Readings

Alexander, Herbert. *Financing Politics: Money, Elections, and Political Reform.* Washington, D. C.: Congressional Quarterly, 1976. A summary of campaign financing and of the new laws designed to regulate it.

Asher, Herbert. *Presidential Elections and American Politics.* Homewood, Ill.: The Dorsey Press, 1976. A useful, brief analysis of how Americans have voted.

Burnham, Walter Dean. *Critical Elections and the Mainsprings of American Politics.* New York: W. W. Norton, 1970. An argument about the decline in voting participation and the significance of the realigning election of 1896.

Kayden, Xandra. *Campaign Organization.* Lexington, Mass.: D. C. Heath, 1978. A close look at how political campaigns are organized, staffed, and led at the state level.

Page, Benjamin I. *Choices and Echoes in Presidential Elections.* Chicago: University of Chicago Press, 1978. Analyzes the interaction between the behavior of candidates and of voters in American elections.

Patterson, Thomas E., and Robert D. McClure. *The Unseeing Eye: The Myth of Television Power in National Politics.* New York: G. P. Putnam's Sons, 1976. Analyzes the impact, usually small, of television newscasts and advertising during the 1972 presidential election.

8 Interest Groups

Reasons for proliferation of interest groups ▪
Wave theory of interest group formation ▪ Who
joins organizations ▪ Americans' participation
in civic and political associations ▪ Operation
of interest groups ▪ Comparison of views of
leaders and of rank and file ▪ Enlisting
support ▪ Nader's organizations ▪
Intergovernmental lobbies ▪ Sources of
information ▪ Fund-raising and spending ▪
Tactics ▪ Governmental regulations

Though no exact count exists, it is likely that a greater number and variety of interest groups are active in the politics of the United States than in the politics of any other country. (An "interest group" is any organization that seeks to influence public policy.) Such organizations are found in every political system—democratic or authoritarian, capitalist or socialist—but certain features of American society and politics contribute to their proliferation here.

In general, the more cleavages there are in society, the greater the variety of interests and thus (usually) the greater the number of political organizations. Many European nations, such as Sweden, are populated by persons of essentially one race and one national background and often of one religion. The United States is a nation of immigrants, made up of whites, blacks, Chicanos, Europeans, Chinese-Americans, and countless others; there are at least eighty-five

Interest groups representing farmers have existed for over a century. The Grangers gathered in Illinois in 1873 (left), and farmers marched in Washington, D.C., in 1979 (right).

❝The more places at which policy can be influenced, the more organizations will arise seeking to exercise that influence.**❞**

religions claiming fifty thousand or more believers each in this country; Americans live in a vast land made up of distinct regions with differing traditions and cultures. And on top of all these sources of diversity there are the inevitable differences, found in every society, between those with more wealth and those with less, between those in manufacturing and those in farming, between those of one opinion and those of another. As James Madison said in *Federalist* No. 10, "The latent causes of faction are thus sown in the nature of man."

The American constitutional system also

contributes to the multiplicity of interest groups. In a nation where all, or most, political authority is lodged in a single national government and where that national government is under the direction of a single leader (such as a prime minister), there will be only a few places where important political decisions can be made and thus only a few opportunities for political influence to be exerted. Great Britain is such a country. While it has interest groups in abundance, they are fewer in number and larger in scale than those found in a decentralized political system such as that of the United States. The more places at which policy can be influenced, the more organizations will arise seeking to exercise that influence.

Thus, one finds in Great Britain a single organization of farmers, a single organization of

Interest groups, such as these pro- and anti-nuclear power marchers, have become more important as political parties have declined.

veterans, a single major business organization, and a single medical society. Since all the important governmental decisions about agriculture, industry, veterans' affairs, and medicine are made nationally by a particular ministry, the farmers, businessmen, veterans, and doctors who wish to influence those policies each find it advantageous, if not essential, to band together into a single organization to deal effectively with that ministry. In the United States, by contrast, there are at least three major farm organizations (the American Farm Bureau Federation, the National Farmers' Union, and the Grange), and each of these is made up of state and county branches, many of which act quite independently of national headquarters. There is one major labor organization, the AFL-CIO, but it is in fact a loose coalition of independent national unions (such as the steelworkers, the coal miners, and the plumbers); in addition, some large unions, such as the Teamsters, are not part of the AFL-CIO at all. There are countless business organizations, several veterans' associations, many different civil rights groups, and so on.

Where political power is not consolidated, interest groups have little incentive to coalesce. For example, a plumbers' union in the United States will deal with city governments over modifications to local building codes, with state governments concerning the requirements for becoming a licensed plumber, and with the federal government over regulations governing the hiring of minority workers and the pay rates of persons employed by federal contractors. Since each component of the union—the city, state, and national offices—has something it can do for its members, it has an independent basis for existence. The local union need not obey the orders of its national office, and the national office of a union need not obey the orders of the AFL-CIO. As we saw in Chapter 3, one of the chief consequences of federalism has been to stimulate a variety of organized political activity.

There may also be a third reason, in addition

Labor unions, such as the American Federation of State, County, and Municipal Employees (AFSCME), are among the interest groups that have begun to play a larger role in politics as parties have declined.

to social diversity and governmental fragmentation, for the proliferation of interest groups in this country. There are essentially two kinds of organizations that can assemble and use political power—parties and interest groups. Where political parties are strong, interest groups are likely to be weak. As parties decline in strength, interest groups are likely to become more powerful. The evidence gathered by scholars does not permit us to say confidently that this relationship always works this way, but it seems plausible. For example, the powerful Cook County Democratic machine has long controlled the government of Chicago; interest groups—labor unions, civic associations—have been, as a consequence, less powerful. When such groups want to get something done, they must usually do it in coopera-

❝As parties decline in strength, interest groups are likely to become more powerful.**❞**

tion with the party or not at all. In New York City or Boston, by contrast, political parties are quite weak and various interest groups can play a large and independent role in policy-making.[1] As American political parties have been declining, interest groups have been becoming more numerous and more active; it is possible that the former change has helped cause the latter.[2]

In Austria, France, Italy, and some other nations where parties are strong, many if not most of the major interest groups are closely linked to one or another political party. In Italy, for example, each party—Socialist, Communist, centrist, and conservative—will have a cluster of interest groups (labor unions, professional societies, social clubs) closely allied with it.[3] Though some American interest groups regularly support the candidates and policies of a particular party (the AFL-CIO, for instance, almost always backs Democrats), the relationship is not as close as in Europe: interest groups feel free to act independently of the parties or to ignore them altogether.

THE RISE OF INTEREST GROUPS

"The formation of associations," David B. Truman has observed, "tends to occur in waves."[4] During the 1770s many groups arose to agitate for American independence; during the 1830s and 1840s the number of religious associations increased sharply and the anti-slavery movement began. In the 1860s trade unions based on crafts emerged in significant numbers, farmers formed the Grange, and various fraternal organizations were born. In the 1880s and 1890s business associations proliferated. The great era of organization-building, however, was in the first two decades of the twentieth century. Within this twenty-year period, many of the

best-known and largest associations with an interest in national politics were formed: the Chamber of Commerce, the National Association of Manufacturers, the American Medical Association, the NAACP, the Urban League, the American Farm Bureau, the Farmers' Union, the National Catholic Welfare Conference, the American Jewish Committee, and the Anti-Defamation League. The most recent wave of interest group formation occurred in the 1960s, and led to the emergence of environmental, consumer, and political reform organizations such as those sponsored by Ralph Nader.

The fact that associations in general, and political interest groups in particular, are created more rapidly in some periods than in others suggests that these groups do not arise inevitably out of natural social processes. There have always been farmers in this country, but there were no national farm organizations until the latter part of the nineteenth century. Blacks had been victimized by various white supremacy policies from the end of the Civil War on, but the NAACP did not emerge until 1910. Men and women worked in factories for decades before industrial unions were formed.

There are at least four factors that help explain the rise of interest groups. The first consists of broad economic developments that create new interests and redefine old ones. Farmers had little reason to become organized for political activity so long as most of them consumed what they produced. The importance of regular political activity only became evident after most farmers began to produce cash crops for sale in markets that were unstable or affected by forces (the weather, the railroads, foreign competition) that farmers could not control. Similarly, for many decades most workers were craftsmen working alone or in small groups. Such unions as existed were little more than craft guilds interested in protecting their jobs and in training apprentices. The reason for large, mass-membership unions did not exist until there arose mass-production industry operated by large corporations.

Second, government policy itself helped create interest groups. Wars create veterans who in turn demand pensions and other benefits. The first large veterans' organization, the Grand Army of the Republic, was made up of Union veterans of the Civil War. By the 1920s these men were receiving about a quarter of a billion dollars a year from the government and naturally had created organizations to watch over the distribution of this money. The federal government encouraged the formation of the American Farm Bureau Federation (AFBF) by paying for county agents who would serve the needs of farmers under the supervision of local farm organizations; these county bureaus eventually came together as the AFBF. The Chamber of Commerce was launched at a conference attended by President William Howard Taft. Professional societies, such as those made up of lawyers and doctors, became important in part because state governments gave to such groups quasi-governmental authority to decide who was and who was not qualified to become a lawyer or a doctor. Workers had a difficult time organizing so long as the government, by the use of injunctions enforced by the police and the army, prevented strikes. Unions, especially those in mass-production industries, began to flourish after Congress passed laws in the 1930s that prohibited the use of injunctions in private labor disputes, that required employers to bargain with unions, and that allowed a union representing a majority of the workers in a plant to require all workers to join it.[5]

Third, political organizations do not emerge automatically even when government policy permits them and social circumstances seem to require them. Somebody must exercise leadership, often at substantial personal cost. These organizational entrepreneurs are found in greater numbers at certain times than at others. They are often young, caught up in a social movement, drawn to the need for change, and inspired by some political or religious doctrine. Anti-slavery organizations were created in the

W. E. B. Du Bois was one of the founders of the NAACP in 1910 and the editor of its magazine, *The Crisis.*

1830s and 1840s by enthusiastic young persons influenced by a religious revival that was then sweeping the country. The period from 1890 to 1920 when so many national organizations were created was a time when the college-educated middle class was growing rapidly. (The number of men and women who received college degrees each year tripled between 1890 and 1920.)[6] During this era, natural science and fundamentalist Christianity were locked in a bitter contest as the competing ideas of personal salvation and social progress, the Gospels and Darwinism, became the watchwords of rival social movements. The 1960s, when many new organizations were born, was a decade in which young persons were powerfully influenced by the civil rights and antiwar movements and when college enrollments more than doubled.

Finally, organization begets counterorganization. When unions began to form, employers began to organize trade associations to resist them. As employers organized to deal with workers, workers felt a greater need to join unions.

MEMBERSHIP IN ORGANIZATIONS

It is often said that America is a nation of joiners, but that is only partially true. A study by Gabriel Almond and Sidney Verba of citizens of five nations found that Americans are less frequently members of labor unions than are the British or Germans and no more likely than the British, Germans, and Italians to be members of business, professional, or charitable organizations[7] (see Table 8.1). A smaller proportion of the work force in the United States are members of labor unions than in any of the other major industrial democracies. About two-thirds of all workers belong to unions in Austria and Sweden, around one-half belong in Belgium and Italy, and over a third belong in England, the Netherlands, and Germany; less than 27 percent belong in the United States.[8] This difference in union membership is all the more striking when one realizes that in most European countries there is no legal or contractual obligation to join a union in order to hold a job, whereas such an obligation (called the "union shop") does exist in many American industries.

There are, however, two kinds of organizations that Americans are much more likely to join than citizens of other countries—religious and political associations. About 11 percent of American adults report that they belong to a civic or political organization, more than three times the percentage who say they are members of such groups in Britain or Germany. And religious associations (not churches, but church-related organizations) have as participants nearly one-fifth of all American adults, but no more than one-twentieth of the adults in the other countries studied by Almond and Verba.

The reason for the higher participation by Americans in civic and political associations is, we think, the greater sense of political efficacy and the stronger sense of civic duty among Americans. When Almond and Verba asked citizens of various countries what they would do to protest an unjust local regulation, 56 percent of the Americans—but only 34 percent of the British and 13 percent of the Germans—said they would try to organize their neighbors to write letters, sign petitions, or otherwise act in concert.[9] Americans are also more likely than the citizens of other nations to try to form or use an organization when they wish to influence the national government, remote as that institution may seem.[10] The inclination of Americans to think that organized activity is an effective way to influence government is not the result of the greater education of Americans compared to Italians or Germans: at every level of schooling

TABLE 8.1   Membership in Various Types of Organizations, by Nation

Organization	United States	Great Britain	Germany	Italy	Mexico
Trade unions	14%	22%	15%	6%	11%
Business	4	4	2	5	2
Professional	4	3	6	3	5
Farm	3	0	4	2	0
Social	13	14	10	3	4
Charitable	3	3	2	9	6
Religious[a]	19	4	3	6	5
Civic-political	11	3	3	8	3
Cooperative	6	3	2	2	0
Veterans'	6	5	1	4	0
Fraternal[b]	13				
Other	6	3	9	6	0
Percentage who are members of any organization	57%	47%	44%	30%	24%

Source: Gabriel A. Almond and Sidney Verba, *The Civic Culture: Political Attitudes and Democracy in Five Nations,* p. 302. Copyright © 1963 by Princeton University Press. Reprinted by permission of Princeton University Press.

[a] This refers to church-related organizations, not to church affiliation itself.
[b] U.S. only.

Americans are more likely than others to attempt to form groups.[11]

Not all citizens are equally likely to join organizations, and thus organizational activity will not represent a faithful cross section of American opinion. Joiners are much more likely than nonjoiners to be upper status persons: those with higher-than-average incomes, more educational experience, and better-than-average occupations.[12] This is, of course, about what one would expect: higher income persons can afford more organizational memberships than lower income ones, persons in professional and business occupations often find it easier to attend meetings during business hours than do blue-collar workers, and persons with college degrees often have a wider range of interests than those without.

Some observers find in these facts evidence that interest group activity will be tilted in favor of the rich, the wellborn, and the privileged. As one political scientist put it, "The pressure system has an upper-class bias."[13] That conclusion, however, is meaningful only if there is such a thing as an "upper-class bias." The striking feature of interest groups is that, even among those composed entirely of better-off persons, the amount of conflict and disagreement is so great. A business association will be opposed by an environmentalist organization; an association favoring a strong military posture will be opposed by one favoring cuts in the defense budget; groups of women favoring the Equal Rights Amendment will be faced by groups of women opposing it. In each case, the members of both sets of organizations will be better-off than the average American, but they disagree nonetheless.

That there is conflict among interest groups with upper status members does not prove either that all interests in society have adequate organizational representation or that all political issues will mobilize comparably strong opponents and proponents. Some groups may have great

❝The reason for the higher participation by Americans in civic and political associations is, we think, the greater sense of political efficacy and the stronger sense of civic duty among Americans.❞

Signing petitions is a form of political participation that is more common in America than in most other democracies.

difficulty in forming organizations at all; others may form organizations that are too weak to handle their adversaries. For decades blacks found it almost impossible to form effective interest groups; indeed, the two leading civil rights organizations today—the NAACP and the Urban League—were originally begun by whites who had the time, money, and opportunities that blacks lacked. Today blacks belong to more organizations than do whites of comparable income,[14] blacks control the NAACP and the Urban League, and changes in laws and judicial attitudes have made it easier for black organizations to affect public policy than once was the case. At one time consumer organizations had scarcely any effect on public policy; today their effect is considerable. On the other hand, neighborhood groups seeking to influence the quality of public services in their area, taxpayer associations seeking to reduce taxes, or organizations seeking to place tighter government controls on guns are still, in many areas, relatively ineffective even though they may be composed, in each case, of persons of relatively high incomes.

In short, one cannot judge the power of an interest group simply by knowing the social and economic characteristics of its members. That power will also be affected by the nature of the issue, the tactics the organization is prepared to use, the resources it commands, and the attitudes of the public officials with which the organization must deal.

Each citizen has many interests, and sometimes they compete. This whale-lover urges the boycott of Japanese goods with a bumper sticker on his or her Japanese car.

THE POLITICAL ACTIVITY OF INTEREST GROUPS

Whose Interests

We often make the mistake of assuming that what an interest group does in the political arena is simply to give expression to the interests of its members; know those interests and you know what the organization will do. Though this may be the case for some interest groups, especially small ones representing a narrow segment of society with a direct stake in some policy, it is not always the case. Every political organization must do two things—attract and hold members, and devise and carry out a political strategy. The organization faces in two directions: internally, toward its members, and externally, toward the political system. Sometimes its internal, member-attracting posture is different from or even in conflict with its external, policy-influencing posture.

Recall the example given in Chapter 1. In the mid-1960s a survey of the white members (the majority) of a large industrial union showed that 32 percent thought that the desegregation of schools, housing, and job opportunities for blacks had gone too fast, while only 21 percent thought it had gone too slowly. Among the national staff and officers of the union, however, none thought desegregation had gone too fast and 69 percent thought it had been too slow.[15] Furthermore, this union had aggressively lobbied in Congress for the passage of civil rights laws even though its (white) members were opposed or skeptical. Obviously, the politics of this interest group were not based simply on the expressed interests of most of its members.

The National Council of the Churches of Christ, an organization of various Protestant denominations claiming more than 40 million members, has spoken out frequently on matters of political interest. It has supported civil rights legislation, opposed American involvement in Vietnam, and favored the diplomatic recognition of the People's Republic of China at a time (1966) when that was a deeply controversial policy. No careful survey of the opinion of rank-and-file Protestants on these matters was done, but, given the fact that other studies have shown white Protestants to be fairly conservative[16] and that a large proportion of the NCC's members lived in the South, it seems quite likely that the leadership of the NCC was taking positions, as its critics charged, considerably at variance with the beliefs of its grass-roots members.[17]

There are business organizations in which the same pattern can be observed. A group called the Foreign Oil Policy Committee lobbied long and hard in the mid-1950s for legislation that would restrict the amount of foreign oil imported into this country. The moving force behind the Committee was coal mine owners who wanted to reduce the competition their product had to face on the market. But a number of railroad companies whose interests were quite divided were also members of it. On the one hand, the railroads transported coal, and so would be happy if more coal were sold. On the other hand, they also transported oil and used oil to power their diesel locomotives, and thus would be hurt by the price increases resulting from the exclusion of foreign oil. Nevertheless, they went along with the organization and admitted later to an interviewer that they had not given the matter much thought.[18]

Analyzing What Happens

To understand how interest groups formulate and carry out their political objectives, it is clearly not enough to know the interests and opinions of rank-and-file members: though these are important, they are often not decisive. There are at least four other factors that should be taken into account.

First, the homogeneity of the group being represented will affect the organization's position: the more homogeneous the interest, the more likely an organization will represent that interest accurately. The American Cotton Manufacturers Institute represents southern textile mills. They are few enough in number and similar enough in outlook to be able to formulate and carry out clear policies squarely based on their money interests: to try to get laws passed and government decisions made that will keep foreign-made textiles from competing with American-made goods. Sometimes they are successful, sometimes not, but it is not hard to explain what they do or why. By contrast, the United States Chamber of Commerce represents thousands of different kinds of businesses in hundreds of different communities. Its membership is so large and diverse that the Chamber in Washington can only speak out clearly and forcefully on relatively few matters. All businesses would like lower taxes, and so the Chamber will certainly support that view. On the other hand, some businesses would like higher tariffs and some lower ones, and so the Chamber says little or nothing about tariffs.

Second, the reasons people have for joining an organization are often unrelated to many of the policies the organization takes. When businessmen, farmers, or workers join an organization that promises to protect and advance their direct money interests, they usually expect the organization to deliver on those matters. If the trade association persuades the government to change the tax laws, if the union gets a big wage increase for its workers, if the farm organization helps farmers buy and sell their products, the members are satisfied. If these organizations then want to take positions on other issues—reforming the Electoral College, for example, or sending foreign aid to Israel—most of the members will tolerate this (or ignore it), whatever their personal views may be. Thus, the AFL-CIO in Washington can take positions on a number of issues without worrying about rank-and-file opinion so long as the rank and file is satisfied with union performance on the important bread-and-butter questions. So also with Protestant churchgoers:

so long as they receive in their local congregations the spiritual or social satisfaction that comes from church attendance, they will not pay much attention to the national pronouncements of the National Council of Churches. If they disagree, they will have little incentive to change things.

Third, organizations with large staffs are, other things being equal, likely to take political positions more in accordance with staff beliefs than with membership opinion. Bureaucrats in the private sector, like those in the public one, have their own views, and though these are never entirely at odds with those of rank-and-file members, neither are they always the same. The National Council of Churches has a large national staff; so also does the Chamber of Commerce, the AFL-CIO, and the American Farm Bureau Federation. Members of these staffs will usually have backgrounds, educational experiences, personal attitudes, and daily routines that are considerably at variance with those of rank-and-file members.

Finally, the views of the militant and active members are more likely to influence organizational behavior than the opinions of the less militant, less active members. Many persons participate in the Sierra Club, the Friends of the Earth, the John Birch Society, the Communist party, the National Organization for Women, and the American Civil Liberties Union out of a passionate conviction in the rightness of the organization's stated purposes. The leaders of the more ideological groups cannot count on all members being indifferent or easily satisfied; they must instead worry about members who vigorously debate every issue, resist leadership control, and insist that strong (and sometimes impolitic) stands be taken. These activists are not always representative of the membership as a whole. Moreover, to raise funds for such organizations, dramatic stands must be taken that will appeal to those members who have money to give, even if what is dramatic may not (in the

eyes of the leaders) be the most important issue. For example, an officer of an environmentalist association in Washington told an interviewer that he wanted to press the government to design and implement national standards for air and water pollution, but had to spend some of his time waging campaigns to save whales and porpoises from fishermen. The members of the organization would give little attention or money to the dull business of measuring air quality but would devote much passion and many dollars to the plight of whales and porpoises.

THE SPECIAL PROBLEM OF MASS ORGANIZATIONS

Many interest groups have the advantage of representing small groups of individuals or organizations that have a direct and substantial stake in the success of the group's lobbying activities. It is an advantage because it is relatively easy to persuade persons or organizations in these circumstances to become members and contribute time, energy, and money. This fact helps explain why most lobbying organizations in Washington are small associations composed of specialized business firms or occupations.

Organizing large constituencies—consumers, for example, or blacks, or women, or taxpayers—is a different and much more difficult matter. No organization exists that can claim to have, as members, more than a tiny fraction of these groups. (The NAACP, for example, enrolls only a tiny percentage of all blacks.) These low participation rates do not necessarily mean that consumers, blacks, women, or taxpayers are "selfish" or "apathetic," but only that they are numerous. A single consumer, for example, knows full well that whether he or she joins a consumer organization will not make an appreciable difference in the power or resources of that organization. It will succeed or fail regardless of whether he or she joins; furthermore, if the organization is successful, he or she will get the benefits of its success whether or not he or she is a member. Therefore, the average consumer has very little incentive to join such a group. This has been called by Mancur Olson the "free rider" problem.[19]

Enlisting Support

Organizations desirous of speaking on behalf of, or of obtaining support from, a mass constituency clearly have their work cut out for them. There are essentially two ways of overcoming the free rider problem: finding incentives in addition to the appeal of the organization's purposes with which to attract members or locating a sponsor who will support the organization even though it has no mass base.

Farm organizations have recruited many members, not only by promising to make their voices heard in Washington (very few farmers, one suspects, think that their voices are heard no matter what organization they join), but also by offering a wide range of services. The Illinois Farm Bureau, for example, offers to its members—and *only* to its members—an opportunity to buy farm supplies at discount prices, to market their products through efficient cooperative organizations, and to purchase low-cost insurance. These monetary advantages to membership help explain why the Illinois Farm Bureau has been able to enroll as members almost every farmer in the state as well as many nonfarmers who value its services.[20] Farm Bureaus in other states have followed the Illinois example. Similarly, the American Association of Retired Persons has been able to recruit nearly 10 million older citizens, in large part by supplying its members with health insurance, travel benefits, tax advice, and discounts on prescription drugs. As a result of these incentives, both the Farm Bureau and the Association of Retired Persons have the money to afford—and the broad membership base to make legitimate—the policy papers issued on matters of national interest.

> **❝** There are essentially two ways of overcoming the free rider problem: finding incentives in addition to the appeal of the organization's purposes with which to attract members or locating a sponsor who will support the organization even though it has no mass base. **❞**

The other method for sustaining an organization seeking to speak on behalf of a mass constituency is to find a sponsor who can recruit the members or pay the bills. The National Council of Senior Citizens, which claims several million members, was started by the AFL-CIO. Many of its members come from the ranks of organized labor, and the unions still pay a part of the Council's bills.[21] Consumers Union (CU) maintains a staff in Washington that lobbies on behalf of consumers before government committees and agencies and brings suit in federal court on consumer issues. This staff is paid for by the earnings of *Consumer Reports*, a magazine published by CU that provides readers with tests on various consumer products. Various foundations have given grants to political organizations to support their efforts on behalf of a wide range of causes.

Such organizations proliferated in the 1960s and 1970s. One study of eighty-three so-called "public interest" organizations found that many of them relied heavily on foundations or direct-mail campaigns for money. One-third of these groups received at least half their funds from foundations and a tenth received over 90 percent from such sources. The Ford Foundation was the most important of these (between 1970 and 1974 it contributed over $10 million to political or legal-action groups, though of late it has cut back on such giving). This means that many "public interest" groups have either no members or no means for members to shape policy. Over half the groups in this study did not give rank-and-file members a voice in decision-making and over two-thirds were dominated by their paid staffs. As a result, the goals of a consumer or environmental protection group will often reflect the

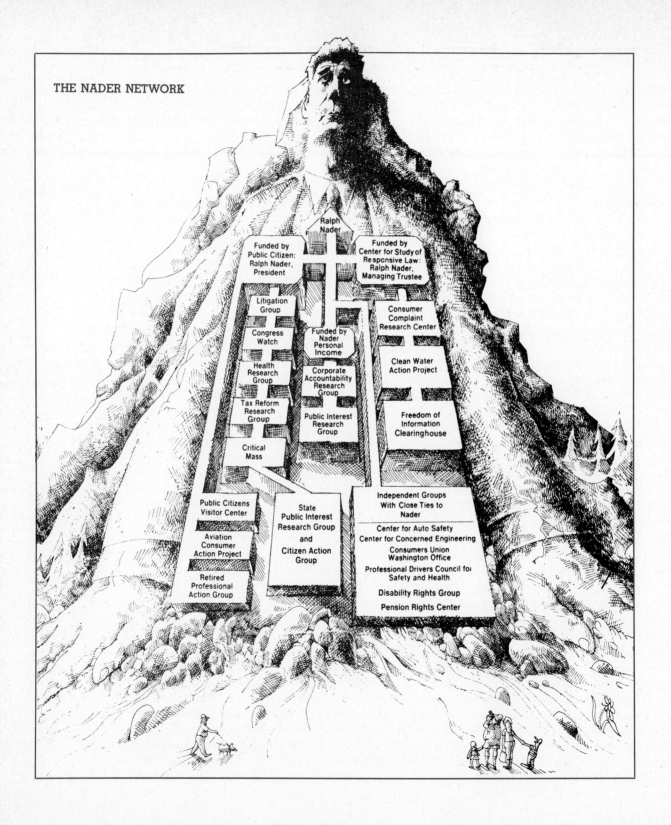

THE NADER NETWORK

Ralph Nader

Funded by Public Citizen: Ralph Nader, President

Funded by Center for Study of Responsive Law: Ralph Nader, Managing Trustee

Litigation Group

Congress Watch

Health Research Group

Tax Reform Research Group

Critical Mass

Funded by Nader Personal Income

Corporate Accountability Research Group

Public Interest Research Group

Consumer Complaint Research Center

Clean Water Action Project

Freedom of Information Clearinghouse

Public Citizens Visitor Center

Aviation Consumer Action Project

Retired Professional Action Group

State Public Interest Research Group and Citizen Action Group

Independent Groups With Close Ties to Nader

Center for Auto Safety
Center for Concerned Engineering
Consumers Union Washington Office
Professional Drivers Council for Safety and Health
Disability Rights Group
Pension Rights Center

views of those elites that dominate it just as the goals of a business organization will reflect the views of the individuals who control it.[22] The difference, obviously, is that the "public interest" elites are drawn from the ranks of what was called, in Chapter 5, the liberal "New Class" whereas the business elites represent more conservative opinions.

The best-known examples of sponsored organizations claiming to represent mass constituencies are, of course, the various groups associated with Ralph Nader. Nader became a popular national figure in the mid-1960s after General Motors made a clumsy attempt to investigate and discredit his background when Nader was testifying in favor of an auto safety bill (see Chapter 15). Nader won a large out-of-court settlement against GM, his books began to earn royalties, and he was able to command substantial lecture fees; most of this money was turned over to various organizations he created to investigate matters of interest to consumers. In addition, he founded a group called Public Citizen that raised money by direct-mail solicitation from thousands of small contributors. With his own money and that raised by Public Citizen, he was able to support, or at least get under way, various "Naderite" associations. These include, as of early 1978:[23]

- Congress Watch, with a staff of eleven, that lobbies in Congress and reports on its activities.
- Critical Mass, with a staff of four, that takes positions critical of nuclear energy.
- Public Citizen Litigation Group, with a staff of ten, that brings lawsuits on behalf of various groups.
- Tax Reform Research Group, with a staff of eight, that lobbies for changes in the tax laws.
- Health Research Group, with a staff of eight, that criticizes the health care system.

In addition, there are in most states local Public Interest Research Groups (PIRGs) run and financed by local college students, often by persuading campus officials to set aside for the local PIRG a percentage of the mandatory activities fee that each student pays. Nader plays a large role in helping PIRGs get started, though he does not direct their activities once they are under way.

The use of material incentives (as with the Farm Bureau) and financial sponsors (as with Consumers Union and Nader groups) has advantages and disadvantages. It permits organizations to exist and even flourish without having to persuade large numbers of persons to accept the organizations' goals or contribute voluntarily to their attainment. This means that certain interests that might otherwise go unrepresented acquire a political voice. By the same token, the farmers, senior citizens, or consumers on whose behalf the organizations claim to speak may not, in fact, have their true interests represented by these groups and may have no way of expressing their disagreement with the people who supply them with this vicarious representation.

Not all diffuse interests need go unrepresented unless they find a sponsor or an organization with the resources to make membership attractive. Some groups have perfected the art of direct-mail fund-raising. Common Cause, an organization founded in 1970 with an interest in altering the procedures of American politics (such as campaign finance rules), has been remarkably successful in recruiting a large (over two hundred thousand) group of people willing to pay dues ($15 a year) without getting any personal benefit in return. Nader's Public Citizen has emulated the Common Cause approach, as have a growing number of liberal and conservative organizations.

Vicarious Representation

In addition, unorganized interests often get represented by existing organizations that have a money stake in obtaining a policy that would confer benefits on nonorganization members as well. For example, the users of first-class mail are not organized, nor could they be—they number in the tens of millions. But the interest of these users in preventing the price of first-class mail from going up is staunchly defended by the National Association of Greeting Card Publishers, a group that, for obvious reasons, would like to see the cost of sending greeting cards (and thus of all first-class mail) kept as low as possible. Similarly, individual citizens could not be organized in large numbers to insist on having air pollution reduced or automobile bumpers made stronger, but there are many business firms that make and sell smokestack scrubbers, the ingredients for catalytic converters, and automobile bumpers that will lobby strenuously on behalf of any laws that require more of their products to be purchased. The existence of this form of vicarious representation does not mean that all worthy interests will be represented, or represented accurately, but it does mean that the difficulty in organizing mass constituencies does not automatically result in the neglect of the preferences of such constituencies.

THE INFLUENCE OF INTEREST GROUPS

We can only know the power of an interest group, or of interest groups in general, by watching it in action and evaluating the results. In Part IV of this book, we shall look at these groups, as well as other institutions, as they attempt to determine what issues get placed on the public agenda and what policies get accepted or rejected. Here we shall simply sketch out the methods such groups use in trying to wield influence and make general remarks about the value of each.

Public officials want certain resources that interest groups can help supply: information, political support (not only votes, but public expressions of approval), money (not only campaign finances, but budgets for agencies and, on occasion, opportunities for nongovernmental employment), and the absence of "trouble." The organizations that can produce information, votes, money, and trouble are not limited to the conventional private interest groups or "lobbies" with which we are all familiar. Government agencies are themselves interest groups, especially in a governmental system as fragmented and decentralized as ours. For example, not only will drug companies lobby Congress over the kinds of laws that ought to regulate the manufacture of drugs, so also will the Food and Drug Administration and the Drug Enforcement Administration. Just because these two agencies are part of the same government, do not suppose that they will always see eye-to-eye or will refrain from using interest group tactics, such as letter-writing campaigns and leaks to the newspapers. The armed services will provide junkets for congressmen just as will private businesses. By law, a government agency is not supposed to lobby Congress; in fact, a good deal of discreet lobbying must be undertaken by any agency that hopes to prosper.

Information

Congressmen, bureau chiefs, and other public officials confront an enormous variety of bewildering problems; legislators in particular must take positions on a staggering number of issues on which they cannot possibly become experts. Once every two or six years they need money with which to run a reelection campaign, but every day of the week they need information.

Though there are nonpartisan, nonpolitical sources of information—the world almanac or an encyclopedia, for example—the kind of detailed, specific, up-to-the-minute information that legislators need is hard to get and expensive to collect. Thus, in most cases only groups with a strong interest in some issue are likely to produce the information. Most lobbyists (or "legislative representatives") are not flamboyant, party-giving arm-twisters; they are specialists who gather information (favorable to their client, naturally) and present it in as organized, persuasive, and factual a manner as possible. All lobbyists no doubt exaggerate, but few can afford to misrepresent the facts or mislead a legislator, and for a very simple reason: almost every lobbyist must develop and maintain the confidence of a legislator over the long term, with an eye on tomorrow's issues as well as today's. Misrepresentation or bad advice can embarrass a legislator who accepts it or repel one who detects it, leading him to reduce his reliance on the lobbyist. Maintaining contacts and channels of communication is vital; to that end, maintaining trust is essential.

To anticipate what will be said in Part IV, the value of the information provided by a lobbyist is often greatest when the issue is fairly narrow, involving only a few interest groups or a complex economic or technical problem. The value of information, and thus the power of the lobbyist, is likely to be least when the issue is one of broad and highly visible national policy.

Sometimes the nature of an issue or the governmental process by which an issue is resolved gives a great advantage to the suppliers of certain information and imposes a great burden on would-be suppliers of contrary information. In Part IV we shall see in more detail how this happens with what will be called "client politics." For example, the Civil Aeronautics Board (CAB) has set airline fares and decided what airlines would fly to what cities. Historically, the only organizations with any incentive to appear before the CAB and supply the necessary information were, naturally, the airlines. Until the CAB began to deregulate civil aviation, CAB decisions often tended to favor the established airlines. For a long time, only radio and television broadcasters had any incentive (or could afford) to appear before the Federal Communications Commission (FCC), which decides what broadcasters shall be licensed and on what terms. Owing to changes in the industry (such as the rise

❝Public officials want certain resources that interest groups can help supply: information, political support, money, and the absence of 'trouble'.❞

Chinese supporters of President Carter parade in New York City in 1976.

of cable television) and to the growth of sponsor-funded consumer groups, FCC hearings are now often hotly contested. When the Federal Energy Administration (FEA) was trying to allocate scarce oil and gasoline supplies among competing users, it discovered that the information it needed was possessed only by the oil companies. (It later took steps to develop its own sources of data.)

❝Most legislators tend to hear what they want to hear and to deal with interest groups that agree with them.

. . . Members of an interest group will also tend to work primarily with legislators with whom they agree.**❞**

Public officials not only want technical information; they also want political cues. A cue is a signal telling the official what values are at stake in an issue—who is for, who against a proposal— and how that issue fits into his or her own set of political beliefs. Some legislators feel comfortable when they are on the "liberal" side of an issue, and others feel comfortable when they are on the "conservative" side, especially when they are not familiar with the details of the issue. A liberal legislator will look to see if the AFL-CIO, the NAACP, the Americans for Democratic Action, the Farmers' Union, and various Naderite organizations favor a proposal; if they do, that is often all he or she has to know. If these groups are split, then the legislator will worry about the matter and try to look into it more closely. Similarly, a conservative legislator will feel comfortable if the Chamber of Commerce, the Farm Bureau Federation, the American Medical Association, various business associations, and Americans for Constitutional Action are in agreement; he or she will feel less comfortable if they are divided. As a result of this process, lobbyists often work together in informal coalitions based on general political ideology.

One important way in which these cues are made known is by "ratings" that interest groups make of legislators. These are regularly compiled by the AFL-CIO (on who is "pro-labor"), by the Americans for Democratic Action (on who is "liberal"), by the Americans for Constitutional Action (on who is "conservative"), by the Consumer Federation of America (on who is "pro-consumer"), and by the League of Conservation Voters (on who is "pro-environment"). These ratings are designed to generate public support

for (or opposition to) various legislators. They can be helpful sources of information, but they are sometimes biased by the arbitrary selection of what constitutes a "liberal" or a "pro-consumer" or a "conservative" vote.

Public Support

Considering that conflict is the essence of politics, it may seem strange that politicians dislike controversy. But they do, and for perfectly human reasons: no one enjoys dealing with persons who are upset or who find you objectionable or unworthy. One consequence of this fact is that most legislators tend to hear what they want to hear and to deal with interest groups that agree with them.[24] Two senators from the same state may choose to listen to very different constituencies in that state and to take very different policy positions. Neither senator may feel he has been "pressured" or "lobbied" because each has heard mostly from groups or persons who share his views. (Politicians define "pressure" as arguments and inducements supplied by somebody with whom they disagree.)

Members of an interest group will also tend to work primarily with legislators with whom they agree; a lobbyist does not find it pleasant to argue with somebody who is suspicious of him and not likely to change his mind whatever he says. For the lobbyist, the key target is the undecided or wavering legislator or bureaucrat. Sometimes the lobbyist will make a major effort to persuade the undecided legislator that public opinion is strongly inclined in one direction. He will do this by commissioning public opinion polls, by stimulating local citizens to write letters or send telegrams, by arranging for constituents to pay personal visits to the legislator, or by getting newspapers to run editorials supporting the lobbyist's position.

Though most lobbying organizations cultivate the goodwill of government officials, there are important exceptions. Some groups, especially those that use an ideological appeal to attract supporters or that depend for their maintenance and influence on media publicity, will deliberately attack actual or potential allies in government in order to embarrass them. Ralph Nader is as likely to denounce as to praise those officials who tend to agree with him if their agreement is not sufficiently close or public. He did this with Senator Edmund Muskie, the author of the Clean Air Act, and with William Haddon, Jr., an early administrator of the National Highway Traffic Safety Administration. The head of the Fund for Animals is not reluctant to attack those officials in the Forest Service and the Interior Department on whose cooperation the Fund must rely if it is to achieve its goals.[25] Sometimes, as we shall see in a later section, the use of threats instead of rewards extends to physical confrontations.

It is not clear how often public pressure works. Congressmen are skilled at recognizing and discounting organized mail campaigns and are usually satisfied that they can afford to go against even legitimate expressions of hostile public opinion on a few occasions. Only a few issues, of great symbolic significance and high visibility, are so important that a congressman would think that to ignore public opinion would mean the difference between winning and losing the next election. In 1978 being for or against the Panama Canal treaties or for or against abortion created serious electoral problems for several congressmen.

Some observers believe that the decay of the political parties and the growing involvement of the government in issues with powerful emotional significance (such as abortion, nuclear power, and school busing) have contributed to the rise of "single-issue politics" and "grass-roots lobbying." As the ability of political parties to form stable governing coalitions declines and as citizens find certain governmental decisions deeply troubling, interest groups increasingly seek to obtain their goals by mobilizing citizens to bombard their congressmen with mail and

Ralph Nader acquired substantial political power by his skill at attacking public officials whom he felt did not serve consumer interests.

visits and to vote for or against them on the basis of some single issue.

The largest interest groups have always worked to defeat legislators opposed to them. The Committee on Political Education (COPE) of the AFL-CIO supports friends of labor (mostly Democrats); the Business Industry Political Action Committee (BIPAC) supports friends of business. This support consists chiefly of campaign contributions; both sides usually claim success, but since both often endorse candidates (especially incumbents) who would win anyway, it is hard to know how much of this credit is deserved.

One particularly aggressive interest group that intervenes actively in elections (with publicity and organizing rather than campaign contributions) is Environmental Action, Inc. Since 1970 it has designated a "Dirty Dozen" members of the House of Representatives who it claims are "anti-environment." Of the thirty-one congressmen so listed since 1970, only seven still serve in the House. Many congressmen believe that the "Dirty Dozen" label hurts them in their districts, and though they are angry over what they feel is the unfair use of the label, they will often strive to avoid it if at all possible.[26]

Money

Interest groups can legally supply money to public officials running for office under limitations described in Chapter 7 and summarized later in this chapter. They can also lobby Congress to increase or reduce the appropriations for government agencies (and thus these agencies have an incentive to cultivate the goodwill of interest groups). Some interest groups can provide opportunities for employment to former government officials (and thus members of Congress and of agencies sometimes have an incentive to impress potential future employers). On occasion—obviously, no one knows how often—an interest group or an individual will offer a cash bribe to a public official.

The largest interest group contributors in the 1978 congressional elections were professional, labor, and business associations. As these organizations have gained experience with creating and operating political action committees (PACs), the amounts raised and spent have increased; the 1978 contributions to congressional candidates were much larger than those in 1976 or 1974 (see Table 8.2).

Two of the most important committees in Congress are the House Ways and Means Committee and the Senate Finance Committee; these groups write the major tax laws. In 1976 forty-nine men and women on these committees ran for reelection. They received on the average

TABLE 8.2   Political Action Committees

During the 1977–1978 election season, the ten political action committees making the largest contributions to candidates were:

Committee	Contribution*
1. American Medical Political Action Committee	$1,563,000
2. Realtors Political Action Committee	1,170,000
3. Automobile and Truck Dealers Election Action Committee	970,000
4. United Auto Workers Voluntary Community Action Program	898,000
5. AFL-CIO Political Contributions Committee	830,000
6. United Steelworkers of America Political Action Fund	558,000
7. Transportation Political Education League	541,000
8. American Dental Political Action Committee	493,000
9. Communications Workers of America Political Contributions Committee	459,000
10. Machinists Non-Partisan Political League	453,000

* Figures are rounded because reports, as of March 1979, were not completely tabulated.

about $42,000 each from special-interest-group PACs. This sum, however, was only about one-fifth the total expenditures of the candidates; the remainder came from individuals (who can give a maximum of $1,000 to a candidate), various fund-raising dinners, and the candidate's own resources.[27]

Labor groups in 1978 gave almost all their contributions (95 percent) to the Democrats among these candidates, while business groups split their donations (60 percent to Republicans, 40 percent to Democrats). Most won handily. The extent to which candidates rely on special-interest contributions varies greatly, depending on the closeness of the race, the views of the candidate, and the committee assignment held. For example, Senators Russell B. Long of Louisiana and John C. Stennis of Mississippi were unopposed in the 1976 general election. They only received a small proportion of their cam-

paign funds from interest groups and, of course, did not even need that.[28] On the other hand, Senator Harrison A. Williams, Jr., of New Jersey had an opponent. In addition he was chairman of the Senate Human Resources Committee (and thus handled legislation of interest to labor) and of the Securities Subcommittee of the Senate Banking, Housing, and Urban Affairs Committee (and thus handled bills of interest to business). He received over 40 percent of his campaign funds from interest groups, with about equal amounts from business and labor.[29]

Many top government officials come to Washington from business jobs, law firms, or labor unions. When some officials leave government they often accept positions with organizations that had previously been doing business with the government. This "revolving door" is obviously a matter of concern since it raises the possibility of conflicts of interest. On the other hand, it would

During the 1977–1978 election season, 1,360 political action committees spent money on federal candidates. Here is where the money came from and went:

PAC Sponsor	Contributions (in millions)				
	By Party		By Incumbency		
	Dem	Rep	Incumbent	Challenger	Open
Corporations	$3.5	$5.4	$5.4	$1.8	$1.6
Trade & professional associations	4.7	6.0	6.6	1.9	2.2
Labor unions	8.8	0.5	5.7	2.0	1.7
Citizen organizations	0.6	1.6	0.7	0.9	0.6
Other	0.6	0.2	0.6	0.1	0.1
Totals	$18.2	$13.7	$19.1	$6.7	$6.2

Source: Federal Election Commission, "Interim Summary" of Non-Party Political Action Committee financial activity, 1977–1978 (dated January 24, 1979).

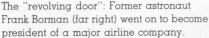

The "revolving door": Former astronaut Frank Borman (far right) went on to become president of a major airline company.

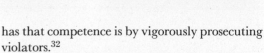

be foolish to disqualify from public service persons who have acquired in private life expert knowledge about a policy or to disqualify from private employment public officials who retire from government or who are forced to resign when a different party comes to power.[30]

An example of a serious conflict of interest: A retired naval officer was indicted for trying, while in the Navy Department, to award a government contract to a private firm for which he later went to work, three weeks after his retirement.[31]

An example of no conflict of interest: A lawyer in the Justice Department prosecuted antitrust cases for the government. While still young, he left the department to take a job with a large law firm that specializes in defending corporations accused of antitrust violations. There was no conflict there because the law firm wanted to hire a competent expert in antitrust law and the only way a Justice Department attorney can prove he

has that competence is by vigorously prosecuting violators.[32]

The in-between cases: Between 1969 and 1973, 1,406 Pentagon officials left government to take jobs in the defense industry.[33] These persons might use their contacts in government unfairly to help their companies get defense contracts, or they might simply apply their expert knowledge of government rules and requirements to assist their companies in making perfectly proper bids.

Several laws and presidential orders govern the way in which the revolving door is used. Their application presents a problem, however. If regulations are applied too stringently, the government will lose the ability to hire the best-qualified persons and will punish former government officials with entirely proper ambitions. If they are applied too loosely, some persons will use their government positions to arrange "sweetheart" deals with private interests.

Trouble

Public displays and disruptive tactics—protest marches, sit-ins, picketing, and violence—have always been a part of American politics. Indeed, they were among the favorite tactics of the American colonists seeking independence in 1776.

Both ends of the political spectrum have used display, disruption, and violence. On the left, feminists, anti-slavery agitators, coal miners, auto workers, welfare mothers, blacks, anti-nuclear-power groups, public housing tenants, the American Indian Movement, the Students for a Democratic Society, and the Weather Underground have created "trouble" ranging from peaceful sit-ins at segregated lunch counters to bombings and shootings. On the right, the Ku Klux Klan has used terror, intimidation, and murder; parents opposed to forced busing of schoolchildren have demonstrated; business firms have used strong-arm squads against workers; and an endless array of "anti-" groups (anti-Catholics, anti-Masons, anti-Jews, anti-immigrants, anti-saloons, anti-blacks, anti-protesters, and probably even anti-antis) have taken their disruptive turns on stage. These activities are not morally the same—a sit-in demonstration is quite different from a lynching—but politically they constitute a similar problem for a government official.

An explanation of why and under what circumstances disruption occurs is beyond the scope of this book. To understand interest group politics, however, it is important to remember that "making trouble" has of late become a quite conventional political resource and is no longer simply the last resort of extremist groups. Making trouble is now an accepted political tactic of ordinary middle-class citizens as well as of disadvantaged or disreputable persons.

There is, of course, a long history of "proper" persons using disruptive methods. In a movement that began in England at the turn of the century and which then spread here, feminists

Conflict of Interest

In 1978 a new federal law codified and broadened the rules governing possible conflicts of interest among senior members of the executive branch. (The law also covered congressmen, as described in Chapter 10.) The key provisions were these:

Financial disclosure: The president, vice-president, and top-ranking (GS-16 and above) executive branch employees must each year file a public financial disclosure report that lists:

- The source and amount of all earned income as well as income from stocks, bonds, and property, the worth of any investments or large debts, and the source of a spouse's income, if any.

- Any position held in business, labor, or certain nonprofit organizations.

Employment after government service: Former executive branch employees may *not:*

- Represent anyone before their former agencies in connection with any matter that the former employees had been involved in before leaving the government.

- Appear before an agency, for two years after leaving government service, on matters that were under the former employees' official responsibility even if they were not personally involved in the matter.

- Represent anyone on any matter before their former agency, for one year after leaving it, even if the former employees had no connection with the matter while in the government.

In addition, another law prohibits **bribery:** it is illegal to ask, solicit, or receive anything of value in return for being influenced in the performance of one's duties.

Finally, an executive order forbids **outside employment:** an official may not hold a job or take a fee, even for lecturing or writing, if such employment or income might create a conflict, or an apparent conflict, of interest.

Sources: National Journal, November 19, 1977, pp. 1796–1803; and *Congressional Quarterly Weekly Report,* October 28, 1978, pp. 3121–3127.

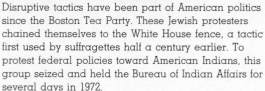

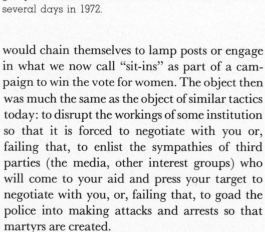

Disruptive tactics have been part of American politics since the Boston Tea Party. These Jewish protesters chained themselves to the White House fence, a tactic first used by suffragettes half a century earlier. To protest federal policies toward American Indians, this group seized and held the Bureau of Indian Affairs for several days in 1972.

would chain themselves to lamp posts or engage in what we now call "sit-ins" as part of a campaign to win the vote for women. The object then was much the same as the object of similar tactics today: to disrupt the workings of some institution so that it is forced to negotiate with you or, failing that, to enlist the sympathies of third parties (the media, other interest groups) who will come to your aid and press your target to negotiate with you, or, failing that, to goad the police into making attacks and arrests so that martyrs are created.

The civil rights and antiwar movements of the 1960s gave experience in these methods to thousands of young persons and persuaded others of the effectiveness of such methods under certain conditions. Though these movements have abated or disappeared, their veterans and emulators have put such tactics to new uses—trying to block the construction of the Seabrook, New Hampshire, nuclear power plant, for example, or occupying the office of the secretary of Health, Education, and Welfare to obtain concessions for handicapped persons.

Government officials dread this kind of trouble. They usually find themselves in a "no-win" situation. If they ignore the disruption, they are accused of being "insensitive," "unresponsive," or "arrogant." If they give in to the demonstrators, they encourage more demonstrations by proving that this is a useful tactic. If they call the police, they run the risk of violence and injuries, followed by not only bad publicity but lawsuits. (When mass arrests were made during an antiwar demonstration in Washington, D.C., subsequent lawsuits were filed that were decided in favor of the protesters, and millions of dollars in damages had to be paid.)

REGULATING INTEREST GROUPS

Interest group activity is a form of political speech protected by the First Amendment to the Constitution: it cannot lawfully be abolished or even much curtailed. In 1946 Congress passed the Federal Regulation of Lobbying Act which requires groups and individuals seeking to influence legislation to register with the secretary of the Senate and the clerk of the House and file quarterly financial reports. The Supreme Court upheld the law but restricted its application to lobbying efforts involving direct contacts with members of Congress.[34] More general, "grassroots" interest group activity may not be restricted by the government. The 1946 act has had little practical effect. Not all lobbyists take the trouble to register and there is no guarantee that the financial statements filed are accurate or complete. There is no staff in the Senate or House in charge of enforcing the law or of investigating violations of it.[35]

Several suggestions have been made for stricter or better-enforced laws. The issues involved are complex, and some important principles are at stake. One proposal, for example, would require that contributors to an interest group be disclosed, much as contributors to an election campaign must now be disclosed. This could well discourage people from giving money for fear of reprisals. Suppose you are an executive of the Ford Motor Company who happens to believe in tougher government controls on auto pollution. If you give money to the Environmental Defense Fund, and this becomes known, your career prospects at Ford might suddenly become a good deal dimmer. Matters get even tougher if you are a covert homosexual who gives money to a gay liberation group, only to have your name disclosed.

Even without disclosure rules, complex reporting requirements can place substantial burdens on smaller, less affluent interest groups that might well find the cost and bother of filling out endless forms so great as to make it difficult or impossible for them to function. For example, one proposal would require any interest group that sends a letter to five hundred or more people or to twelve branches of the group to send a copy of the letter to the comptroller general.[36] Such a rule would produce a blizzard of paper work and give Congress access to essentially private correspondence. Needless to say, most lobbying groups, including the Naderites, oppose the requirements in this proposal (they are favored, however, by Common Cause). A comparable law in California has produced little beneficial effect.[37]

The significant legal constraints on interest groups come, not from the current federal lobbying law (though that may change), but from the tax code and the campaign finance laws. A nonprofit organization—which includes not only charitable groups but almost all voluntary associations that have an interest in politics—need

Lobbying in action: Common Cause representative Michael Cole (right) talks in the House with Representative Tom Railsback of Illinois.

not pay income taxes, and financial contributions to it can be deducted on the donor's income-tax return, provided the organization does not devote a "substantial part" of its activities to "attempting to influence legislation."[38] Many tax-exempt organizations do take public positions on political questions and testify before congressional committees. If the organization does any serious lobbying, however, it will lose its tax-exempt status (and thus find it harder to solicit donations and more expensive to operate). Exactly this happened to the Sierra Club in 1968 when the Internal Revenue Service revoked its tax-exempt status because of its extensive lobbying activities. Some voluntary associations try to deal with this problem by setting up separate organizations to collect tax-exempt money—for example, the NAACP, which lobbies, must pay taxes, but the NAACP Legal Defense and Educational Fund, which does not lobby, is tax exempt.[39]

Finally, the campaign finance laws, described in detail in Chapter 7, limit to $5,000 the amount any political action committee can spend on a given candidate in a given election. These laws have sharply curtailed the extent to which any single group can give money, though they may well have increased the total amount different groups in the same sector of society (labor, business, dairy farmers, lawyers) are providing.

Beyond making bribery or other manifestly corrupt forms of behavior illegal and restricting the sums that campaign contributors can donate, there is probably no system for controlling interest groups that would both make a useful difference and leave important constitutional and political rights unimpaired. Ultimately, the only remedy for imbalances or inadequacies in interest group representation is to devise and sustain a political system that gives all affected parties a reasonable chance to be heard on matters of public policy. That, of course, is exactly what the Founders thought they were doing.

Whether they succeeded or not is a question to which we shall return at the end of this book.

SUMMARY

Interest groups in the United States are more numerous and more fragmented than those in nations, such as Great Britain, where the political system is more centralized. The goals and tactics of interest groups reflect not only the interests of their members but also the size of the groups, the incentives with which they attract supporters, and the role of the professional staffs. Because of the difficulty of organizing large numbers of persons, a group purporting to speak for mass constituencies will often have to provide material benefits to members or acquire an affluent sponsor (such as a foundation). The chief source of interest group influence is information; public support, money, and the ability to create "trouble" are also important. The right to lobby is protected by the Constitution, but the tax and campaign finance laws impose significant restrictions on how money may be used.

Suggested Readings

Bauer, Raymond A., Ithiel de Sola Pool, and Lewis A. Dexter. *American Business and Public Policy.* New York: Atherton, 1963. A study of how business organizations attempted to shape foreign trade policy, set in a broad analysis of how pressure groups and Congress operate.

Berry, Jeffrey M. *Lobbying for the People.* Princeton, N. J.: Princeton University Press, 1977. Discusses the general characteristics of more than eighty "public interest" lobbies, with a detailed discussion of two.

Lowi, Theodore J. *The End of Liberalism.* New York: W. W. Norton, 1969. A critique of the role of interest groups in American government.

Milbrath, Lester W. *The Washington Lobbyists.* Chicago: Rand McNally, 1963. A description of lobbyists and their work.

Olson, Mancur. *The Logic of Collective Action*. Cambridge, Mass.: Harvard University Press, 1965. A theory of interest group formation from an economic perspective.

Truman, David B. *The Governmental Process*, 2nd ed. New York: Alfred A. Knopf, 1971. An interpretation of American politics, first published in 1951, emphasizing the importance of groups and group conflict.

Wilson, James Q. *Political Organizations*. New York: Basic Books, 1973. A theory of interest groups and political parties that emphasizes the incentives they use to attract members.

Zisk, Betty H., ed. *American Political Interest Groups: Readings in Theory and Research*. Belmont, Calif.: Wadsworth, 1969. A useful collection of some of the major writings on interest groups.

9 The Media

Politicians' dependency on the media • Early partisan sponsorship of the press • Emergence of mass newspapers • National magazines of opinion • Electronic journalism • Local vs. national orientation of the media • Regulation of radio and TV and nonregulation of newspapers • Effects of the media on politics • Attempts by government to shape public opinion • Interpreting political news

All public officials have a love-hate relationship with newspapers, television, and the other media of mass communication. They depend on the media for the advancement of their careers and policies but fear the media's power to criticize, expose, and destroy. As political parties—and especially strong local party organizations—have declined, politicians have become increasingly dependent on the media. Their efforts to woo the press have become ever greater and their expressions of rage and dismay when that courtship is spurned, ever stronger. At the same time, the media have been changing, especially in the kinds of persons who have been attracted into leading positions in journalism and in the attitudes such persons have brought with them. There has always been an adversary relationship between those who govern and those who write, but events of recent decades have, as we shall see, made that conflict especially keen.

Journalists were once anonymous and poorly paid, as these covering President Theodore Roosevelt (left). Today a journalist such as Walter Cronkite is a household name and a wealthy person (right).

The relationships between government and the media in this country are shaped by laws and understandings that accord the media a degree of freedom greater than that to be found in almost any other nation. Though many public officials secretly might like to control the media, and though no medium of communication in the United States or elsewhere is totally free of government influence, the press in this country is among the freest in the world. A study of ninety-four countries found only sixteen in which the press enjoyed a high degree of freedom; the United States was one of these.[1] Some democratic nations, such as France and Great Britain, place more restrictions on the communications media than are found here. The laws governing libel in England are so strict that public figures frequently sue newspapers for printing statements that tend to defame or ridicule them—and they collect. In the United States, as will be explained, the law of libel is loose enough to permit intense and even inaccurate criticism of anybody who is in the public eye. England also has an Official Secrets Act that can be used to punish any present or past public official who divulges to the press private government business.[2] In this country, by contrast, the Freedom of Information Act, together with a long tradition of leaking inside stories and writing memoirs of one's public service, virtually guarantees that very little can be kept very secret for very long.

Almost all American radio and television stations are privately owned, though they require government licenses (issued for three-year terms) to operate. In France, broadcasting is operated by a government agency (Radiodiffusion-Télévision Française) under the control of the minister of information, who is not averse to using that control to protect the government's image. Until recently, the French government had the power to ban the showing of any motion picture that was thought likely to "disturb the public order" or for other "reasons of state."[3] A French newspaper editor was heavily fined by a court

for having written an article critical of the president of France.[4] While the federal government does impose rules on American broadcasters, it does not have the power routinely to censor or dictate the contents of particular stories. As we shall see though, its power to license broadcasters has been used, on occasion, to harass station owners who were out of favor with the White House.

The freedom from government control that comes with the private ownership of the mass media of communication has a price, of course—newspapers, magazines, and broadcast stations are businesses that must earn a profit. Some critics believe that the need for profit leads publishers and station owners to distort the news coverage of politics to satisfy the desires of advertisers, the pecuniary interests of stockholders, or the private ideology of the managers. This is much too simple a view, however. Every owner of a communications medium must satisfy the often competing interests of a number of distinct constituencies—advertisers, readers or viewers, editors and reporters, and organized external pressure groups. How each newspaper or broadcaster balances the preferences of these groups varies from case to case. Moreover, the relative strength of these groups has changed over time. In general, the history of American journalism, at least among newspapers, has been the history of the growing power and autonomy of editors and reporters.

JOURNALISM IN AMERICAN POLITICAL HISTORY

Important changes in the nature of American politics have gone hand in hand with major changes in the organization and technology of the press. This is not to say that the nature of journalism dictates the nature of politics, but only that politics, being essentially a form of communication, will respond to changes in how communications are carried on. This can be seen by considering four important periods in journalistic history.

The Party Press

In the early years of the Republic, politicians of various factions and parties created, sponsored, and controlled newspapers to further their interests. This was possible because newspapers were of necessity small (they could not easily be distributed to large audiences owing to poor transportation) and expensive (the type was set by hand and the presses printed copies slowly). Moreover, there were few large advertisers to pay the bills. These newspapers circulated chiefly among the political and commercial elites who could afford the high subscription prices. Even with high prices, the newspapers, to exist, often required subsidy. That money frequently came from the government or from a political party.

During the Washington administration, the Federalists, led by Alexander Hamilton, created the *Gazette of the United States*. The Republicans, led by Thomas Jefferson, retaliated by creating the *National Gazette* and made its editor, Philip

> **"Important changes in the nature of American politics have gone hand in hand with major clanges in the organization and technology of the press;"**

Freneau, the "clerk for foreign languages" in the State Department at $250 a year to help support him. After Jefferson became president, he induced another publisher, Samuel Harrison Smith, to start the *National Intelligencer*, subsidizing him by giving him a contract to print government documents. Andrew Jackson, when he became president, aided in the creation of the *Washington Globe*. By some estimates, there were over fifty journalists on the government payroll during this era.[5] Naturally, these newspapers were relentlessly partisan in their views. Citizens could choose among different party papers but only rarely could they find a paper that tried to present both sides of an issue.

The *National Gazette*, edited by Philip Jefferson faction in national politics. Jefferson, as secretary of state, helped Freneau by giving him a job in the State Department. The *Gazette of the United States*, published by John Fenno, supported Jefferson's rival, Alexander Hamilton.

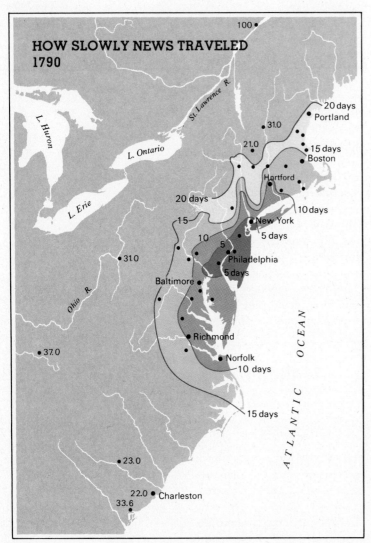

HOW SLOWLY NEWS TRAVELED 1790

100

20 days
Portland

31.0

21.0

15 days
Boston

Hartford

20 days

10 days

15

New York

10

5 days

5

Philadelphia

31.0

5 days

Baltimore

Richmond

Norfolk
10 days

37.0

15 days

ATLANTIC OCEAN

23.0

22.0 Charleston
33.6

L. Huron

L. Ontario

L. Erie

St. Lawrence R.

Ohio R.

Source: *Atlas of Early American History*, 1976, p. 69. Adapted from map in Allan R. Pred, *Urban Growth and the Circulation of Information: The United States System of Cities, 1790–1840*, p. 37. By permission of Princeton University Press and Harvard University Press, © 1973 by the President and Fellows of Harvard College.

The numbers on this map mark the average lag, in days, between the occurrence of an event in an outlying place and the published report of that event in the Philadelphia newspapers. The lines connect places with similar lag times. For example, it took over ten days in 1790 for news of an event in Boston to be published in Philadelphia.

The Popular Press

Changes in society and technology made possible the rise of a self-supporting, mass-readership daily newspaper. The development of the high-speed rotary press enabled publishers to print thousands of copies of a newspaper cheaply and quickly. The invention of the telegraph meant that news from Washington could be flashed almost immediately to New York, Boston, Philadelphia, and Charleston, thus providing local papers with access to information that once only the Washington papers enjoyed. The creation in 1848 of the Associated Press put the telegraphic dissemination of information to newspaper editors on a systematic basis. Since the AP provided stories to newspapers of every political hue and in every geographic region, it could not afford to be partisan or biased; out of an interest in attracting as many subscribers as possible, it had to present the facts objectively. Meanwhile, the nation was becoming more urbanized, bringing together large numbers of people in densely settled areas. These people could support a daily newspaper by paying only a penny per copy and by patronizing merchants who advertised in its pages. Newspapers no longer needed political patronage to prosper, and soon such subsidies began to dry up. In 1860 the Government Printing Office was established, thereby putting an end to most of the printing contracts that Washington newspapers had once enjoyed.

The mass-based newspaper was scarcely nonpartisan, but the partisanship it displayed arose from the convictions of its publishers and editors rather than from the influence of its party sponsors. And these convictions were of a certain kind, ones that blended political beliefs with economic interest. The way to attract a large readership was with sensationalism: violence, romance, and patriotism, coupled with exposés of government, politics, business, and society. As practiced by Joseph Pulitzer and William Randolph Hearst, founders of large newpaper empires, this editorial policy had great appeal for

Two journalistic styles: William Randolph Hearst's *New York Journal* gave sensational coverage to the sinking of the *USS Maine* in 1898. The stately *New York Times* of Adolph Ochs produced a more restrained story on the event. Then, the *Journal* had the larger circulation of the two, but as the nation became more middle class, it was the *Times* that survived and prospered.

the average citizen and especially for the immigrants flooding into the large cities.

Strong-willed publishers could often become powerful political forces. Hearst used his papers to agitate for war against Spain when the Cubans rebelled against Spanish rule. Conservative Republican political leaders were opposed to the war, but a steady diet of newspaper stories about real and imagined Spanish brutalities whipped up public opinion in favor of intervention. At one point, Hearst sent the noted artist Frederic Remington to Cuba to supply paintings of the conflict. Remington cabled back: "Everything is quiet. . . .There will be no war." Hearst supposedly replied: "Please remain. You furnish the pictures and I'll furnish the war."[6] When the battleship *USS Maine* blew up in Havana harbor, President William McKinley

felt helpless to resist popular pressure, and war was declared in 1898.

For all their excesses, the mass newspapers began to create a common national culture, to establish the feasibility of a press that was free of government control or subsidy, and to demonstrate how exciting (and profitable) could be the criticism of public policy and the revelation of public scandal.

Magazines of Opinion

The growing middle class was often repelled by what it called "yellow journalism" and was developing, around the turn of the century, a taste for political reform and a belief in the doctrines of the Progressive movement. To meet this market, there arose a variety of national magazines that, unlike those devoted to manners and literature that already existed, discussed issues of public policy. Among the first of these were the *Nation, Atlantic,* and *Harper's,* founded in the 1850s and 1860s; later there came the more broadly based mass-circulation magazines such as *McClure's, Scribner's,* and *Cosmopolitan.* They provided the means for developing a national constituency on behalf of certain issues, such as regulating business (or, in the language of the times, "trust-busting"), purifying municipal

politics, and reforming the civil service system. Lincoln Steffens and other so-called "muckrakers" were frequent contributors to the magazines, setting a pattern for what we now call "investigative reporting."

The national magazines of opinion provided an opportunity for individual writers to gain a national following. The popular press, though initially under the heavy influence of their founder-publishers, made the names of certain reporters and columnists household words. In time, the great circulation wars between the big-city daily newspapers started to wane as the more successful papers bought up or otherwise eliminated their competition. This reduced the need for the more extreme forms of sensationalism, a change that was reinforced by the growing sophistication and education of the readers. And the founding publishers were gradually replaced by less flamboyant managers. All of these changes—in circulation needs, in audience interests, in managerial style, in the emergence of nationally known writers—helped increase the power of editors and reporters and make them a force to be reckoned with along with advertisers, readers, and other interest groups.

McClure's Magazine featured such muckraking journalists as Lincoln Steffens, who in this issue wrote about corruption in Minneapolis in 1903. The illustration is an actual page from an accounts book showing bribes paid to the mayor.

Electronic Journalism

Radio came on the national scene in the 1920s, television in the late 1940s. They represented a major change in the way news was gathered and disseminated, though few politicians at first understood the importance of this change. A broadcast permits public officials to speak directly to audiences without their remarks being filtered through editors and reporters. This was obviously an advantage to politicians, provided they were skilled enough to use it—they could, in theory, reach the voters directly, on a national scale, without the services of political parties, interest groups, or friendly editors.

But there was an offsetting disadvantage—people could easily ignore a speech broadcast on a radio or television station by either not listening at all or by tuning in to a different station. By contrast, the views of at least some public figures would receive prominent and often unavoidable display in newspapers, and in a growing number of cities there was only one daily paper. Moreover, space in a newspaper is cheap compared to time on a television broadcast. Adding one more story, or one more name to an existing story, costs the newspaper little; much less news can be carried on radio or television, and each news segment must be quite brief if the audience is not to become bored. As a result, the number of political personalities that can be covered by radio and television news is much smaller than is the case with newspapers, and the cost (to the station) of making a news item or broadcast longer is often prohibitively large.

Thus, to obtain the advantages of electronic media coverage, public officials must do something sufficiently bold, or in a manner sufficiently colorful, that they gain free access to radio and television news broadcasts, or they must find the money to purchase radio and television time. The president of the United States, of course, is routinely covered by radio and television and can, ordinarily, get free time to speak to the nation on matters of importance. All other officials must struggle for access to the electronic media by making controversial statements, acquiring a national name, or purchasing expensive time.

The efforts, described in Chapter 7, made by political candidates to get "visuals"—filmed stories—on the evening television news continue after they are elected. Since the president always is news, a politician wishing to make news is well advised to attack the president. Even better, attack him with the aid of a photogenic prop: when Senator John Heinz III of Pennsylvania wanted to criticize President Carter's bridge repair program, Heinz had himself filmed making the attack, not in his office, but standing on a bridge.

In sum, the transformations in the nature of

❝ To obtain the advantages of electronic media coverage, public officials must do something sufficiently bold, or in a manner sufficiently colorful, that they gain free access to radio and television news broadcasts. **❞**

journalism have altered significantly the way public officials and candidates can use communications. In the era of the party press, only a small number of better-off citizens regularly read newspapers and those they read were typically highly partisan. This was an era when politics consisted of competition among relatively small groups of notables and in which presidential candidates were nominated by legislators. The era of the mass newspaper made easier the emergence of mass politics: national conventions, the mobilization of voters at election time by broad appeals, mass rallies, and the development of strong party loyalties. The emergence of national magazines of opinion facilitated the development (discussed in Chapter 8) of national interest groups organized around policy questions and gave voice to the middle-class "reform" movement that agitated for a reduction in the role and power of political parties. Electronic journalism made it possible for politicians to develop personal followings independent of party structure, perhaps contributing to the decline of party loyalties and organization.

THE STRUCTURE OF THE MEDIA

The relationship between journalism and politics is not a one-way street: though politicians take advantage, as best they can, of the media of communication available to them, these media, in turn, attempt to use politics and politicians as a way of both entertaining and informing their audiences. The mass media, whatever they may say to the contrary, are not simply a mirror held up to reality or a "messenger" that carries the news. There is, inevitably, a process of selection,

❝The national press plays the role of gatekeeper, scorekeeper, and watchdog for the federal government.**❞**

of editing, and of emphasis, and this process reflects, to some degree, the way in which the media are organized, the kinds of audiences they seek to serve, and the preferences and opinions of the members of the media.

Degree of Competition

Contrary to popular belief, there has not been any significant decline in the number of daily newspapers in this country: there were 1,763 in 1946, there were 1,756 in 1978. And such decline as has occurred has been with respect to the small-town papers; there are more newspapers today (252) in cities of over fifty thousand population than there were in 1946 (199).

There has been a decline, however, in the number of cities in which there are competing daily papers. There were competing newspapers in 60 percent of American cities in 1900, but in only 4 percent by 1972. The largest cities—New York, Chicago, Detroit, Philadelphia, Los Angeles, Washington, Atlanta, Boston—have at least two central-city newspapers, but most other cities have but one. This is partially offset by the fact that in many metropolitan areas, two or more neighboring cities will each have a newspaper whose readership overlaps. Residents of Manchester, New Hampshire, for example, can easily obtain the *Manchester Union Leader*, the *Boston Globe*, and the *Boston Herald American*.

Radio and television, by contrast, are intensely competitive and becoming more so. Almost every American home has a radio and a television set. Though there are only three national television networks, local television stations have their own news programs as well as the ones supplied by the networks and can run their own political advertisements as well as those carried nationally. Local affiliates can refuse to accept network offerings. Moreover, in most metropolitan areas there are many tele-

vision stations not affiliated with a network at all and a dozen or more radio stations that are independent, especially FM stations that often develop a distinctive individual appeal. The number of news sources, not counting magazines, available to the citizens of some American cities is quite large.

To a degree that would astonish most foreigners, the American press—radio, television, and newspapers—is made up of locally owned and managed enterprises. In Britain, France, West Germany, Japan, Sweden, and elsewhere, the media are owned and operated with a national audience in mind. The *Times* of London may be published in that city, but it is read throughout Great Britain, as are the *Guardian*, the *Daily Telegraph*, and the *Daily Mirror*. Radio and television broadcasts are centrally planned and nationally aired. The American newspaper, however, is primarily oriented to its local market and local audience, and there will typically be more local than national news in it. Radio and television stations accept network programming, but the early and late evening news programs provide a heavy diet of local political, social, and sports news. Government regulations developed by the Federal Communications Commission are in part responsible for this. No one, including the networks, may own and operate more than one AM radio, one FM radio, and one television station in a given market; nationally, no one may own more than seven television stations and seven AM and seven FM radio stations; and the networks may not compel a local affiliate to accept any particular broadcast. (In fact, almost all network news programs are carried by the affiliates.) The result has been the development of a decentralized broadcast industry.

The National Media

The local orientation of much of the American communications media is partially offset, however, by the emergence of certain publications and broadcast services that constitute a kind of national press. The wire services—the Associated Press and United Press International—supply most of the national news that local papers publish. Certain news magazines—*Time, Newsweek, U. S. News & World Report*—have a national readership. The network evening news broadcasts produced by ABC, CBS, and NBC are carried by most television stations with a network affiliation. Certain newspapers, such as the *New York Times*, the *Washington Post*, and the *Wall Street Journal*, have acquired national influence even without a national readership because they are read daily by virtually every important public official in the federal government (and thus have become an important channel by which these officials keep track of each other) and because the television networks and many local newspapers use the stories that the *Times* and the *Post* print. In fact, one study found that the front page of the morning *Times* importantly shapes the contents of each network's evening news broadcasts.[7]

The existence of a national press is important for two reasons: First, government officials in Washington pay great attention to what these media say about them and their programs. They pay much less attention to what local papers and broadcasters say (if, indeed, they even know about it). Second, the kinds of persons who are reporters and editors for the national press tend to be different from those who work for the local press. They are usually better paid than most journalists, they have often graduated from the more prestigious colleges and universities, and they tend to have more liberal political views.[8] Above all, they seek—and frequently obtain—the opportunity to write stories that are not merely accounts of a particular news event, but that are "background," "investigative," or interpretive stories about issues and policies.[9]

The national press plays the role of gatekeeper, scorekeeper, and watchdog for the federal government. As gatekeeper, it can influence what subjects become national political issues, and for how long. Automobile safety, water pol-

The national press wields great influence because it is read by presidents and virtually every other top government official. President Lyndon Johnson surveys his daily collection of newspapers in the Oval Office.

lution, and the quality of prescription drugs were not major political issues before the national press began giving substantial attention to these matters and thus helped place them on the political agenda in ways to be described more fully in Chapters 14 and 15. When crime rates and drug abuse were rapidly increasing during the early 1960s, they were given little political attention, in part because the media did not cover them extensively. During the late 1960s and early 1970s, media and political attention to these matters heightened. In the mid- and latter-1970s, attention again slackened. *Reality* had not changed during this time, but the focus of media and political attention had shifted. As we shall see in Chapter 20, elite opinion about the war in Vietnam changed significantly as the attitude toward that war expressed by the national media changed.

As scorekeeper, the national media keep track of, and help make, political reputations, note who is being "mentioned" as a presidential candidate, and help decide who is winning and who losing in Washington politics. When Jimmy Carter, then a virtually unknown former governor of Georgia, was planning his campaign to get the Democratic nomination for president, he understood clearly the importance of being "mentioned." So successful was he in cultivating members of the national press that, in the period between November 1975 and February 1976 before the first primary election was held, he was the subject of more stories in the *New York Times*, the *Washington Post*, and the *Columbus Dispatch* than any other potential Democratic presidential candidate, even though most of the others (such as Henry Jackson, Hubert Humphrey, and George Wallace) were much better known. (He did almost as well in getting mentioned on the three television networks.) The scorekeeper function continues during the campaign. Because the New Hampshire presidential primary is always the first one held, it gets heavy national press attention even though that state casts less than 1 percent of the delegate votes in the Democratic and Republican presidential conventions. In 1976 there were more television news stories about the New Hampshire primary than about the New York, Illinois, and North Carolina primaries combined. Whoever wins in New Hampshire gains a great media advantage. Indeed, one can even lose in that state and still "win." Eugene McCarthy's clear defeat by Lyndon Johnson was interpreted by parts of the national press as a moral victory, as was George McGovern's loss in 1972 to Edmund Muskie. In 1976 Ronald Reagan's narrow loss to Gerald Ford was interpreted as a "setback." These interpretations probably affected how these candidacies were later perceived by voters.[10]

As a watchdog, the media—and especially the national media—have both a natural instinct and a strong incentive to expose scandals and intrigues. To some degree, all reporters probably share the belief of H. L. Mencken that the role of the press is to "comfort the afflicted and afflict the comfortable." Older, more established writers may sometimes develop such close relations with powerful personages as to inhibit their search for wrongdoing, but the younger, less well-connected ones often find investigative reporting to be both fascinating and rewarding. Bob Woodward and Carl Bernstein, who wrote most of the Watergate stories for the *Washington Post*, simultaneously served an important public purpose, received the accolades of their colleagues, and (through their subsequent books) earned a substantial amount of money.

The national press may give its reporters more freedom than the local press, though all reporters and editors probably have more independence today than they did fifty years ago. Television gives its newscasters less freedom than newspapers give to their journalists. This restriction is imposed, not for political reasons, but because television news is essentially entertainment that is judged by its ability to attract and hold an audience that has many other channels to which it can turn. Newspapers are, of course, edited to attract an audience, but since newspapers face less competition than television and since readers are free to skim through the paper to find whatever may interest them, no given story is likely to be shaped by political or commercial interests. The result is that a $20,000-a-year reporter for a big-city newspaper will have more freedom to develop stories than will a $200,000-a-year network news anchorman or anchorwoman who will be expected, first and foremost, to draw an audience.

RULES GOVERNING THE MEDIA

Ironically, the least competitive part of the media—the big-city newspapers—is almost entirely free from government regulation while the most competitive part—radio and television broadcasting—must have a government license to operate and must conform to a variety of governmental regulations.

Newspapers and magazines need no license to publish, their freedom to publish what they wish may not be restrained in advance, and they are liable for punishment for what they do publish only under certain highly restricted circumstances. The First Amendment to the Constitution has been interpreted as meaning that no government, federal or state, can place "prior restraints" (i.e., censorship) on the press except under very narrowly defined circumstances.[11] When the federal government sought to prevent the *New York Times* from publishing the Pentagon Papers, a set of secret government documents that had been stolen by an antiwar activist, the Court held that the paper was free to publish them.[12]

Once something is published, a newspaper or magazine may be liable for prosecution if the material is deemed libelous or obscene or if it directly incites someone to commit an illegal act. But the definitions of libel, obscenity, and "fighting words" have been more or less steadily narrowed. For a paper to be guilty of libeling a public official or other prominent person, that person must show not only that what was printed was inaccurate, but also that it was printed maliciously—that is, with "reckless disregard" for its truth or falsity.[13] There is, in short, a wide latitude given the American press in commenting, even erroneously, on public figures.

Though publications can and do get in trouble with the law over obscenity, this restriction has had no effect on newspapers and magazines primarily interested in reporting political news (and some would say little effect on any magazine at all). It is illegal to use the printed word to advocate the violent overthrow of the government if, by your advocacy, you incite persons to immediate action,[14] but this law has rarely been applied to newspapers, and in recent years almost never. There are also laws intended to protect the privacy of citizens, but they do not significantly affect the ability of papers to cover the news: in general, your name and picture can be used without your consent if they appear in a true news story of some conceivable public interest.[15]

When the federal government tried to prevent the *New York Times* from publishing a stolen copy of the Pentagon Papers, the Supreme Court upheld the newspaper.

❝The Supreme Court has upheld the right of the government, in a properly conducted criminal investigation, to compel reporters to divulge information if it bears on the commission of a crime.**❞**

Myron Farber, a *New York Times* reporter, leaves jail where he had been sent in 1978 for refusing to supply his notes to a defense attorney in a trial.

Confidentiality of Sources

Reporters believe they should have the right to keep confidential the sources of their stories. Some states agree, and have passed laws to that effect. Most states, and the federal government, do not agree, and there the courts must decide, in each case, whether the need of a journalist to protect confidential sources of information does or does not outweigh the interest of the government in gathering evidence in a criminal inves-

tigation. In general, the Supreme Court has upheld the right of the government, in a properly conducted criminal investigation, to compel reporters to divulge information if it bears on the commission of a crime.[16]

The conflict is not only between a reporter and law enforcement agencies, but often between a reporter and a person accused of a crime. Myron Farber, a reporter for the *New York Times*, wrote a series of stories that led to the indictment and trial of a physician on charges that he had murdered five patients. Lawyers for the doctor demanded to see Farber's notes in hopes of finding material useful in the defense of their client. The judge ordered Farber to show him the notes so that the judge could determine if they were relevant to the case. Farber refused, arguing that revealing his notes would infringe the confidentiality promised to his sources; the *Times* supported Farber, claiming that "to betray one source would be to jeopardize all." The judge fined the *Times* and sent Farber to jail for contempt of court. On appeal, the New Jersey Supreme Court, supported by the United States Supreme Court, decided against Farber, holding that the accused's right to a fair trial includes the right to compel the production of evidence, even from reporters. (Farber was released from jail when the doctor was acquitted.)

Broadcasting operates under more government regulations than do newspapers. No one may operate a radio or television station without getting a license, renewable every three years, from the Federal Communications Commission (FCC). An application for renewal is rarely refused, but the possibility of its being refused, or of being renewed for only one year, together with the opportunity afforded by renewal hearings for interested people to criticize the broadcaster, means that station owners are often quite sensitive to FCC opinions and suggestions.

For example, few if any broadcasters have lost their licenses because they showed programs that contained violence or made various ethnic groups unhappy, and probably no station has been denied a license renewal for failing to produce enough news and public affairs programs. But every broadcaster knows that violating current FCC expectations (and they change frequently) regarding violence, the portrayal of ethnic groups, or the presentation of public affairs programming will cause difficulties and lead to challenges at renewal time. To avoid this, each station goes out of its way to show that it is complying with FCC guidelines and is meeting the "informational needs" (whatever that may mean) of the community. A determined president, or a White House aide, may sometimes try to use this power of the FCC to make life difficult for critics in the broadcast media.

Though the law under which the FCC operates specifically forbids that agency from engaging in censorship or the control of the content of broadcasts, it does permit the FCC to impose a variety of requirements. For example, it can limit a local TV broadcaster to no more than three hours of network shows during evening "prime time." More important for politics, however, is the "fairness doctrine," an FCC ruling that obliges broadcasters to present contrasting sides of controversial public issues, to give a person who is attacked free time in which to reply (newscasts are exempt from this obligation), and to seek out the views of those who disagree with the opinions of the station.

The fairness doctrine may seem "fair," but its effects are quite uncertain. Some stations, unwilling to make expensive air time available at no charge to certain groups, may simply broadcast no editorials and run no controversial programs. Other stations that do present controversy may discover that the FCC's opinion as to who is eligible to reply may differ greatly from theirs. (In 1964, for example, the FCC published a compilation of its "fairness" policies that said that stations are not obliged to give time to "Communists or to the Communist viewpoint.")[17]

Campaigning

When political candidates wish to campaign on radio or television, more rules apply. A broadcaster is required to provide "reasonable access"

to candidates for public office, to provide equal opportunity for candidates in a particular contest, and to charge the candidates rates no higher than the cheapest rate applicable to commercial advertisers for comparable time. The most troublesome part of these rules is the so-called "equal-time" provision. Under this, if the Democratic and Republican candidates for federal office wish to debate, the broadcasters must also invite the candidates for that office of all minor parties to appear as well. Since this is hardly what the public has in mind when it thinks of watching a debate, special provisions have had to be made for presidential debates. In 1960 Congress suspended the equal-opportunity rule so that the four debates held in that campaign could be limited to John F. Kennedy and Richard M. Nixon. In 1976 the FCC allowed Jimmy Carter and Gerald M. Ford to debate on television, provided it was not sponsored by the networks (the League of Women Voters sponsored it instead) and not held in a TV studio.

Though laws guarantee that candidates can buy time at favorable rates on television, not all candidates take advantage of this. The reason is that television is not always an efficient means of reaching voters. A television message is literally "broad cast"—spread out to a mass audience without regard to the boundaries of the district in which a candidate is running. Presidential candidates, of course, always use television because their constituency is the nation as a whole. Candidates for senator or representative, however, may or may not use television depending on whether the boundaries of their state or district conform well to the boundaries of a television "market."

A market is an area easily reached by a television signal; there are about two hundred such markets in the country. Congressman John Brademas comes from a district in Indiana centered on the city of South Bend, which is also the hub of a distinct TV market. Brademas can use television relatively cheaply (dollars per viewer reached). By contrast, a congressman from New York City is in a market in which a local television signal will reach viewers in at least forty different congressional districts. Since television advertising rates are based on the total size of the market, it would be ridiculously expensive for a New York congressional candidate to buy TV time and pointless besides: most of the people who saw the ad would not be able to vote for the candidate. In 1972, 85 percent of the candidates for senator, but only 53 percent of those for representative, bought television time.[18]

THE EFFECTS OF THE MEDIA ON POLITICS

Everyone believes the media have a profound effect, for better or for worse, on politics. Unfortunately, there is very little scholarly evidence that would prove or measure that effect. The reason for this discouraging gap between what "everyone knows" and no one can prove is probably to be found in the fact that scholars have chiefly tried to measure the effect of the media on election outcomes. But as we have already seen (Chapter 7), elections—especially those for important, highly visible offices—are occasions when the voter is bombarded with all manner of cues from friends, family, interest groups, candidates, radio, television, newspapers, memories, and loyalties. It would be surprising if the effect of the media would be very strong, or at least very apparent, under these circumstances.

Efforts to see whether voters who watch a lot of television, or see candidates on television frequently, vote differently from those who do not watch television at all, or who watch only nonpolitical messages, have generally proved unavailing.[19] This is quite consistent with studies of political propaganda generally. At least in the short run, television and radio suffer from processes called "selective attention" (the citizen sees and hears only what he or she wants) and "mental tune-out" (the citizen simply ignores, or gets irritated by, messages that do not accord

with existing beliefs). Radio and television may tend to reinforce existing beliefs, but it is not clear they change them.[20]

But if this is true, why do companies spend millions of dollars advertising deodorants and frozen pizza? And if advertising can sell these products, why cannot it also sell candidates? The answer is quite simple: citizens are not idiots. They can tell the difference between a deodorant and a Democrat, between a pizza and a Republican. If an ad persuades them to try a deodorant or a pizza, they will do so, knowing that not much is at stake, the costs are small, and if they do not like it they can change brands in an instant. But they know that government is a more serious business, that one is stuck with the winning candidate for two, four, or even six years, and that as citizens they have a lot of information about the past behavior of the two major parties and their principal figures.

Local newspapers have generally endorsed Republican candidates for president throughout this century. Indeed, only in 1964 did more newspapers endorse the Democrat (Johnson) than the Republican (Goldwater). Since the Democrats won eight of the twelve presidential elections between 1932 and 1976, you might think that newspaper endorsements are worthless assets. They may have some value, however, under some circumstances. A careful study of the effect of such endorsements on the 1964 presidential election found that, at least in the North, a newspaper endorsement may have added about five percentage points to what the Democratic candidate would otherwise have obtained.[21]

The major effects of the media, however, probably have much less to do with how people vote in an election and much more to do with how politics is conducted, policies are formulated, and candidates selected. National nominating conventions have been changed to fit the needs of television broadcasters. Some candidates have found it possible to win their party's nomination for senator or governor with expensive advertising campaigns that bypass the parties and ultimately weaken them. Unknown politicians can overnight acquire a national reputation by being shrewd enough—or lucky enough—to be at the center of an event heavily covered by the press.

In 1950 Estes Kefauver was a little-known senator from Tennessee. Then he chaired a special senate investigating committee that brought before it various figures in organized crime. When these dramatic hearings were televised to audiences numbering in the millions, Kefauver became a household word and, in 1952, a leading contender for the Democratic nomination for president. He was a strong vote-getter in the primaries and actually led on the first ballot at the Chicago convention, only to lose to Adlai Stevenson.

The lesson was not lost on other politicians. From that time on, developing through the media a recognized name and a national constituency became important to many senators. It also became, as we shall see in Part IV, a strategy whereby a variety of issues could be placed on the national agenda and pressed on Congress. Envi-

> **❝The media help set the political agenda on matters with which citizens have little personal experience but have much less influence on how people react to things that touch their lives directly.❞**

ronmental and consumer issues benefited especially from the attention given them by the national press. A survey of public opinion in North Carolina found that the issues which citizens believed to be important politically were very similar to the issues that newspapers and television newscasts had featured.[22] On the other hand, people are much less likely to take their cues from the media on matters that affect them personally. Everybody who is unemployed, the victim of crime, or worried about high food prices will identify these matters as issues whether or not the media emphasize them.[23] In short, the media help set the political agenda on matters with which citizens have little personal experience but have much less influence on how people react to things that touch their lives directly.

Senator Estes Kefauver pioneered the televised Senate investigation with hearings into organized crime and (pictured here) teenage drug addiction.

THE MAXIMS OF MEDIA RELATIONS

The importance of the national media to politicians has given rise to some shared understandings among office-holders about how one deals with the media. Some of these are caught in the following maxims:

All secrets become public knowledge. The more important the secret, the sooner it becomes known.

■

All stories written about me are inaccurate; all stories written about you are entirely accurate.

■

The rosier the news, the higher-ranking the official who announces it.

■

Always release bad news on Saturday night. Fewer people notice it.

■

Never argue with a person who buys ink by the barrel.

Press Secretary Jody Powell meets the press at a typical White House news conference during the Carter administration.

GOVERNMENT AND THE NEWS

Every government agency, every public official, spends a great deal of time trying to shape public opinion. From time to time, somebody publishes an "exposé" of the efforts of the Pentagon, the White House, or some bureau to "sell" itself to the people, but in a government of separated powers, weak parties, and a decentralized legislature, any government agency that fails to cultivate public opinion will sooner or later find itself weak, without allies, and in trouble.

Prominence of the President

Though Herbert Hoover was probably the first president to have a press secretary, Franklin D. Roosevelt was undoubtedly the first to make his press secretary, Stephen Early, a major instrument for cultivating, informing, managing, and arguing with the reporters assigned to the White House.[24] Today the press secretary heads a large staff that not only gives reporters answers (or non-answers) to questions, but also supplies the president with digests of what the press is saying about him, attempts to control the information that press officers in various cabinet departments give out, and arranges briefings for out-of-town newspaper editors (in order to bypass the special interests of the national press that covers the White House daily). Most presidents play an active part in all this. Before a press conference a president will be carefully briefed about questions that are likely to be asked, and even subjected to a mock question period to sharpen his answers. When the president is especially upset by what the media are saying about him, he is not averse to calling publishers, editors, and network executives personally to complain.

The White House press corps—the men and women assigned full time to cover the president—have a lounge in the White House where they spend their days, waiting for a story to break or for the press secretary to hold a daily (sometimes twice daily) press briefing. Probably no other nation in the world has brought the press into such close physical proximity to the center of government. The result, of course, is that whatever the president does—make a speech, take a walk, greet an ambassador, or come down with a cold—is at the center of press attention. The enlargement of the role of the president in our system of government has come not only from the force of circumstance and the efforts of presidents, but as well from a national press that devotes great resources to the daily coverage of the unimportant as well as the important details of presidential life.

Coverage of Congress

Congress has watched all this with irritation and envy. It resents the attention given the president, but it is not certain how it can compete. The 435 members of the House are so numerous, and play such specialized roles, that there is little chance they will get much individualized press attention. Traditionally, the House has been quite restrictive about television or radio coverage of its proceedings. Until 1978 it prohibited television cameras on the floor, except on purely ceremonial occasions (such as the annual State of the Union message delivered by the president). From 1952 to 1970 the House would not even allow electronic coverage of its committee hearings (except for a few occasions during those periods when the Republicans were in the majority). Beginning in 1970 certain committee hearings could be covered by cameras, but live coverage did not occur to any significant degree until 1974 when the deliberations of the House Judiciary Committee on the possible impeachment of President Nixon were broadcast.[25]

The Senate has used television much more fully, a fact that has heightened the already substantial advantage senators have over representatives in getting in the public eye. Radio and television coverage of the Senate floor was not allowed until 1978, when the debates on the Panama Canal treaties were broadcast live,

❝Probably no other nation in the world has brought the press into such close physical proximity to the center of government.**❞**

Even a presidential swim, such as this by Gerald Ford, attracts media attention.

but Senate committee hearings have been frequently televised, to produce either news films or live broadcasts, ever since Estes Kefauver demonstrated the power of this medium in 1950–1951.

Senatorial use of television has helped turn the Senate into the incubator for presidential candidates. If you are a governor, you are located, in most states, far from network television news cameras; the best you can hope for is that some disaster—a flood or a blizzard—will bring the cameras to you and focus them on your leadership. But senators all work in Washington, a city filled with cameras. No disaster is necessary to get on the air; only an investigation, a scandal, a major political conflict, or an articulate and telegenic personality.

INTERPRETING POLITICAL NEWS

Because of the importance of the news media in politics, it is important for a citizen to know how to interpret what he or she reads or hears. Political advertisements, of course, are always taken with a grain of salt, but news stories are often accepted without question. Because television is a visual medium, enabling us to judge the personality as well as the words of those who appear on it, Americans arc cspecially inclined to find television news believable and to rely on it (more than newspapers) for their political news (see Table 9.1). At the same time, some people harbor the suspicion that the media are biased in their handling of political news.

This suspicion deepens when one realizes that most members of the national media have views quite different from those of the average citizen. One study of the opinions of editors, executives, commentators, and columnists working for the largest papers, the news magazines, and the broadcast networks found them to be significantly more liberal on all foreign policy questions and most economic ones than were the opinions of business leaders, federal civil servants, or Democratic politicians.[26] Another survey of reporters, most of whom worked in Washington, D.C., disclosed that, in 1972, 61 percent had voted for George McGovern and only 22 percent for Richard Nixon. Among the public at large, the proportions were almost exactly reversed—61 percent voted for Nixon, 38 percent for McGovern.[27]

Kinds of Stories

One should not assume, however, that the political opinions of journalists automatically lead them to slant their stories in a predictable direction. Other factors influence how these stories are written, including most reporters' belief that they have an obligation to be fair and many reporters' need to develop good relations with persons holding different views who might prove to be useful sources. On the other hand, it would be astonishing if strongly held beliefs had no effect at all. To understand the circumstances under which a reporter's or editor's opinion is more or less likely to affect journalism, and thus to be able to interpret intelligently the kinds of stories we as citizens read and hear, we must first distinguish among *kinds* of stories. There are at least three:

1. *Routine Stories:* These are public events, regularly covered by reporters, involving relatively simple, easily described acts or statements. For example: the president takes a trip, a bill passes Congress, the Supreme Court rules on an important case.

2. *Selected Stories:* These are public events knowable to any reporter who cares to inquire, but involving acts and statements not routinely covered by a group of reporters. Thus, a reporter must take the initiative and select a particular event as newsworthy, decide to write about it,

TABLE 9.1 The Sources and Credibility of News

Source of Most News*	1959	1978
Television	51%	67%
Newspapers	57	49
Radio	34	20
Magazines	8	5
Other	4	5

Most Believable Source of News	1959	1978
Television	29%	47%
Newspapers	32	23
Radio	12	9
Magazines	10	9

Source: The Roper Organization, Inc. Reprinted by permission.

* Percentages add to more than 100 because people mentioned more than one source.

and persuade an editor to run it. Examples: an obscure agency issues a controversial ruling, an unknown congressman conducts an investigation, an interest group works for the passage of a bill.

3. *Insider Stories*: Things not usually made public become public because someone with knowledge of these things tells a reporter. The reporter may have worked hard to learn these facts, in which case we say it is "investigative reporting," or he may have had the story dumped in his lap, in which case we call it a "leak."

Routine stories are covered in almost exactly the same way by almost all the media, differing only in their length, the kinds of headlines written, and the position the story occupies on the pages or in the evening news broadcast. The wire services—AP and UPI—will supply routine stories immediately to practically every daily newspaper in America. (The headlines and placement, however, can make a big difference in how the same story is perceived.) The political opinions of journalists have the least effect on these stories, especially if several competing journalists are covering the same story over a protracted period of time. Even a routine or "hard" news story can be incorrectly reported, however, if it is a sudden, unique, and especially complex event. In 1968, for example, toward the end of the Vietnam War, the North Vietnamese and the National Liberation Front gambled on a massive, all-out attack on the cities held by the South Vietnamese and their American allies. The attack failed—the North Vietnamese were repulsed with heavy casualties, the local populace did not rally to their cause, and the cities were held. The journalistic account, on the other hand, was exactly the opposite—the North Vietnamese could move and fight at will, and the Americans were helpless to defend the cities or even their own fortified positions. Peter Braestrup, who later analyzed the Tet Offensive and its journalistic coverage, painstakingly described

Washington-based reporters personally favored George McGovern as the presidential candidate in 1972. The electorate, however, preferred Richard Nixon.

the errors and omissions that led to the misleading versions published. He did not conclude that the political views of reporters explained the mistakes, and surely it would be difficult for any reporters however fair to grasp quickly and accurately an event as complex, dramatic, and violent as a major military struggle. But it is also probably the case that the antiwar attitudes of most reporters reinforced the interpretation of Tet that they wrote.[28]

Nonroutine stories must be selected, and thus someone must do the selecting. The grounds on which the selections are made include not only the intrinsic interest of a story but also the reporter's or editor's beliefs about what *ought* to be interesting. Among these beliefs are the political ideologies of the journalists. A "liberal" paper may well select for coverage stories about white-collar crime, consumerism, the problems of minorities, environmentalism, and the "arms race"; a "conservative" paper might instead select for coverage stories about street crime, the decline of the central business district, the threat of Soviet military strength, and the problems of school busing. Nor are selected stories rare: as I write this, I have before me the April 17, 1978, edition of the *Boston Globe*. In its first fourteen pages, there are seventeen news stories of any length—four are "routine" or "hard" news, thirteen are "selected" (or "background" or "feature") news. Each reader should examine selected or nonroutine stories with the following question in mind: What beliefs or ideas led the editors to decide that this story, rather than some other story on a quite different subject, was important enough to print? Sometimes the answer is simple: human interest or the desire to attract a particular segment of the market. At other times the answer is more complicated: a belief in the goodness or badness of corporations, civil rights groups, generals, conservationists, or labor unions.

News Leaks

Insider stories raise the most difficult questions of all, those of motive. When somebody inside government with private or confidential information gives a story to a reporter, that somebody must have a reason for doing so. But the motives of those who leak information are almost never reported. Sometimes the reporter does not know the motives. More often, one suspects, the reporter is dependent on his or her "highly placed source" and is reluctant to compromise it.

The reliance on the insider leak is as old as the Republic. At one time reporters were grateful for "background briefings" at which top government officials tried to put themselves in the best possible light while explaining the inner meaning of American policy. In the aftermath of Vietnam and Watergate, which weakened the credibility of "the Establishment," many reporters became more interested in the leaks from insiders critical of top officials. In neither

case were the motives of the sources discussed, leaving the reader or viewer to accept at face value whatever remarks are attributed to unnamed "highly placed sources" or "well-informed observers."

Whatever problems exist in selection, editing, access, and motive in the coverage of political events arise, not from any defects in the nature of journalists or politicians, but from the fact that, in a reasonably free society, journalists and public officials will both depend on each other and mistrust one another. The strain is intensified by a system of government, such as ours, in which political authority is so fragmented that every group seeking to advance a policy or a person must make extensive and skillful use of communications in order to acquire, by persuasion, the influence that institutional authority alone is unable to confer.

SUMMARY

Changes in the nature of American politics have been accompanied by—and influenced by—changes in the nature of the mass media of communication. The rise of mass-based political parties was facilitated by the emergence of mass-circulation daily newspapers. Political reform movements depended in part on the development of national magazines catering to middle-class opinion. The weakening of political parties was accelerated by the ability of candidates to speak directly to constituents by radio and television.

The role of journalists in a democratic society poses an inevitable dilemma: if they are to serve well their functions as information-gatherer, gatekeeper, scorekeeper, and watchdog, they must be free of governmental control. But to the extent they are free of such controls, they are also free to act in their own interests, whether political or economic. In the United States a competitive press largely free of governmental controls (except in the area of broadcast licenses) has produced a substantial diversity of opinion and a general (though not unanimous) commitment to the goal of fairness in news reporting. The "national media" are in general more liberal than the local media, but the extent to which any opinion affects reporting varies greatly with the kind of story—routine, selective, or insider.

Suggested Readings

Braestrup, Peter. *Big Story: How the American Press and Television Reported and Interpreted the Crises of Tet 1968 in Vietnam and Washington.* Boulder, Col.: Westview Press, 1977, 2 volumes. A massive, detailed account of how the press reported one critical event; the factual accuracy or inaccuracy of each story is carefully checked.

Clor, Harry M., ed. *The Mass Media and American Democracy.* Chicago: Rand McNally, 1974. Essays from competing points of view about the political influence of the press.

Crouse, Timothy. *The Boys on the Bus.* New York: Random House, 1973. A lively, irreverent account by a participant of how reporters cover a presidential campaign.

Epstein, Edward J. *Between Fact and Fiction: The Problem of Journalism.* New York: Random House, 1975. Essays by a perceptive student of the press on media coverage of Watergate, the Pentagon Papers, the deaths of Black Panthers, and other major stories.

———. *News from Nowhere.* New York: Random House, 1973. Analysis of how television network news programs are produced and shaped.

Patterson, Thomas E., and Robert D. McClure. *The Unseeing Eye: The Myth of Television Power in National Elections.* New York: G. P. Putnam, 1976. Study of 1972 presidential election suggesting that television had little effect on the outcome.

Pool, Ithiel de Sola, Wilbur Schramm, *et al. Handbook of Communication.* Chicago: Rand McNally, 1973. Survey of what is known about the effects of all forms of communication, including the mass media.

Robinson, Michael J. "Television and American Politics, 1956–1976," *The Public Interest* (Summer 1977), pp. 3–39. Essay on the effect of both television entertainment and news stories on perceptions of American politics.

Weaver, Paul. "The New Journalism and the Old," *The Public Interest* (Spring 1974), pp. 67–88. Discusses the rise of newer, more issue-oriented "advocacy journalists" in the national press.

PART III

Institutions of Government

❝But the great security against a gradual concentration of the several powers in the same department consists in giving to those who administer each department the necessary constitutional means and personal motives to resist encroachments of the others.❞

FEDERALIST NO. 51

10 Congress

There are essentially two kinds of national legislative (i.e., law-making) bodies: congresses and parliaments. The United States, along with most Latin American nations, has a congress; Great Britain, along with most Western European nations, has a parliament. A hint as to the difference between the two kinds of legislatures can be found in the original meanings of the words: "Congress" derives from a Latin term that means "a coming together," a meeting, as of representatives from various places. "Parliament" comes from a French word, *parler*, that means "to talk."

There is, of course, plenty of talking—some critics say there is nothing *but* talking—in the United States Congress, and certainly members of a parliament represent to a degree their local districts. But the differences implied by the names of the law-making groups are real ones, with profound significance for how laws are made and how the government is run. These

Henry Clay addressing the United States Senate around 1850 (left), and House Speaker Tip O'Neill (right).

differences affect two important aspects of law-making bodies: how one becomes a member and what one does as a member.

Ordinarily, a person becomes a member of a parliament (such as the British House of Commons) by persuading a political party to put his or her name on the ballot. Though usually a local party committee selects a person to be its candidate, that committee often takes suggestions from national party headquarters. In any case, the local group selects as its candidate someone willing to support the national party program and leadership. In the election voters in the district choose, not between two or three personalities running for office, but between two or three national parties. By contrast, a person becomes a candidate for representative or senator in the United States Congress by running in a primary election. Except in a very few places, political parties exercise little control in the choice of who is nominated to run for congressional office. (This is the case even though the person who won the primary will describe himself or herself in the general election as a "Democrat" or a "Republican.") Voters select candidates in the primaries because of their personalities, positions on issues, or general reputation; even in the general election, where the party label affects who votes for whom, many citizens vote "for the man" (or for the woman), not for the party. As a result of these different systems, a parliament tends to be made up of persons loyal to the national party leadership who meet to debate and vote on party issues. A congress, on the other hand, tends to be made up of persons who think of themselves as independent representatives of their districts or states and who, while willing to support their party on many matters, expect to vote as their (or their constituents') beliefs and interests require.

Once they are in the legislature, members of a parliament discover that they can make only one important decision—whether or not to support the government. The government in a parliamentary system such as Britain's consists of a prime minister and various cabinet officers selected from the party that has the most seats in parliament. As long as the members of that party vote together, that government will remain in power (until the next election). Should members of a party in power in parliament decide to vote against their leaders, the leaders lose office and a new government must be formed. With so much at stake, the leaders of a party in parliament have a powerful incentive to keep their followers in line. They insist that all members of the party vote together on almost all issues; if someone refuses, the penalty is often drastic—the party does not renominate the offending member in the next election.

Members of the United States Congress do not select the head of the executive branch of government—that is done by the voters when they choose a president. Far from making members of Congress less powerful, this makes them more powerful. Representatives and senators can vote on proposed laws without worrying that their votes will cause the government to collapse and without fearing that a failure to support their party will lead to their removal from the ballot in the next election. Congress has independent powers, defined by the Constitution, that it can and does exercise without regard to presidential preferences. Political parties do not control nominations for office, and thus they cannot discipline members of Congress who fail to support the party leadership. Because Congress is constitutionally independent of the president and because its members are not tightly disciplined by a party leadership, individual members of Congress are free to express their views and vote as they wish. They are also free to become involved in the most minute details of law-making, budget-making, and supervision of the administration of laws. They do this through an elaborate and growing set of committees and subcommittees.

In short, a parliament, such as that in Britain, is an assembly of party representatives who choose a government and who discuss major national issues. The principal daily work of a parliament is debate. A congress, such as that in the

United States, is a meeting place of the representatives of local constituencies—districts and states. Members of Congress can initiate, modify, approve, or reject laws, and they share with a president the supervision of the administrative agencies of the government. The principal work of a congress is representation and action, most of which takes place in committee.

What this means in practical terms to the typical legislator is easy to see. Since members of the British House of Commons have little independent power, they get rather little in return. They are poorly paid, may have no offices of their own and virtually no staff, are allowed only small sums to buy stationery, and can make a few free local telephone calls. Each is given a desk, a filing cabinet, and telephone, but not always in the same place. A member of the United States House of Representatives, even the most junior one, has power and is rewarded accordingly. A representative earns a substantial salary ($57,500 a year as of 1978), receives generous retirement benefits, has at least a three-room suite of offices, is supplied with at least eighteen staff persons, can make thirty-three free trips to the home district each year, receives several thousand dollars for stationery and postage, and can mail newsletters and certain other documents to constituents free under the "franking privilege." Representatives with more seniority and senators receive even larger benefits—a senator from New York, for example, is allowed about $1 million a year to hire staff assistants. This example is not given to suggest that members of Congress are overrewarded but only that their importance, as individuals, in our political system can be inferred from the resources they command.

THE EVOLUTION OF CONGRESS

The Framers chose to place legislative powers in the hands of a congress rather than a parliament for philosophical and practical reasons. They did not want to have all powers concentrated in a single governmental institution, even one that

❝The principal work of a congress is representation and action, most of which takes place in committee.❞

The Senate Agriculture Committee hears then-Secretary of Agriculture Earl Butz.

was popularly elected, because they feared that such a concentration could lead to rule by an oppressive or impassioned majority. At the same time, they knew that the states were jealous of their independence and would never consent to a national constitution if it did not protect their interests and strike a reasonable balance between large and small states. Hence, they created a bicameral (two-chamber) legislature—with a House of Representatives to be elected directly by the people and a Senate, consisting of two members from each state, to be chosen by the legislatures of each state. Though "all legislative powers" were to be vested in the Congress, those powers would be shared with a president (who could veto acts of Congress), limited to those explicitly conferred on the federal government and, as it turned out, subject to the power of the

The Powers of Congress

The powers of Congress are found in Article I, Section 8, of the Constitution:

- To lay and collect taxes, duties, imposts, and excises.

- To borrow money.

- To regulate commerce with foreign nations and among the states.

- To establish rules for naturalization (i.e., becoming a citizen) and bankruptcy.

- To coin money, set its value, and punish counterfeiting.

- To fix the standard of weights and measures.

- To establish a post office and post roads.

- To issue patents and copyrights to inventors and authors.

- To create courts inferior to (i.e., below) the Supreme Court.

- To define and punish piracies, felonies on the high seas, and crimes against the law of nations.

- To declare war.

- To raise and support an army and navy and make rules for their governance.

- To provide for a militia (reserving to the states the right to appoint militia officers and to train the militia under congressional rules).

- To exercise exclusive legislative powers over the seat of government (i.e., the District of Columbia) and over places purchased to be federal facilities (forts, arsenals, dockyards, and "other needful buildings").

- To "make all laws which shall be necessary and proper for carrying into execution the foregoing powers, and all other powers vested by this Constitution in the government of the United States." (*Note:* This "necessary and proper" or "elastic" clause has been generously interpreted by the Supreme Court in a manner explained in Chapter 13.)

Supreme Court to declare acts of Congress unconstitutional.

Although they designed these checks and balances to prevent legislative tyranny, the Framers nonetheless expected that Congress would be the dominant institution in the national government. And for a century and a half at least, it was, except for a few brief periods when activist presidents (such as Andrew Jackson, Abraham Lincoln, Theodore Roosevelt, and Woodrow Wilson) were able to challenge congressional supremacy. Until the twentieth century, and during some periods since, the major struggles for national political power have been struggles *within* Congress, over the rules and leadership of that body, rather than between Congress and the president.

The struggles within Congress were generally over issues of great national significance—slavery, the admission of new states, the development of internal improvements, tariffs against foreign goods, and the regulation of business—but cutting across most of these substantive issues was a conflict over the distribution of power within the Congress itself. Two competing values were at stake: centralization versus decentralization. If Congress were to act as a body, quickly and decisively, there must be strong central leadership, restrictions on debate, few opportunities for stalling tactics, and minimal committee interference. If, on the other hand, the interests of individual members, and the beliefs and constituencies they represent, were to be protected or enhanced, then leadership should be weak, the rules must allow for delay and extended discussion, and many opportunities must exist for committee or subcommittee activity.

Though there have been periods of strong central leadership in Congress, the general trend, especially in this century, has been toward decentralizing decision-making and enhancing the power of the individual member at the expense of congressional leadership. This may not have been inevitable. Most American states have constitutional systems quite similar to the federal one, yet in many state legislatures, such as those in New York, Massachusetts, and Indiana, the leadership is quite powerful. In part, the position of these state legislative leaders may be the result of the greater strength of political parties in some states than in the nation as a whole. In large measure, however, it is a consequence of permitting state legislative leaders to decide who shall be chairman of what committee and who shall receive what favors. Congress has left such matters to the workings of time (the seniority system), the decisions of large caucuses, or the rights of individual legislators.

The Period of the Founding

During the first three administrations—of George Washington, John Adams, and Thomas Jefferson—leadership in Congress was often supplied by the president or his cabinet officers. Alexander Hamilton, as secretary of the treasury, acted as Washington's leader in Congress, even though he was not a member of that body. Albert Gallatin, Jefferson's secretary of the treasury, performed essentially the same function, working through intermediaries.

Rather quickly, however, Congress began to assert its independence and to develop its own leadership. The House of Representatives was the preeminent institution, overshadowing the tiny Senate. It originated most legislation. Henry Clay as Speaker of the House was a powerful leader who appointed the members and chairmen of the committees and kept his party, the Democratic-Republicans, under reasonable control. The party caucus,* dominated by Clay, was often influential in shaping policy questions before they were debated on the floor of the House. Indeed, during these early years, the caucus selected its party's candidate for president. The Democratic-Republican caucus, for

---

*Caucus: a meeting of the members of a political party—in this case, the Democratic-Republican members of the House—to decide questions of policy.

> **Until the twentieth century, and during some periods since, the major struggles for national political power have been struggles *within* Congress . . . rather than between Congress and the president.**

example, nominated Jefferson in 1804, James Madison in 1808 and again in 1812, and James Monroe in 1816. The caucus system of nomination enhanced the power of the House, for it meant that the president of the United States, though not elected by Congress, was nominated for that office by important members of Congress. This political fact of life helped make the presidents quite sensitive to congressional desires.

Decline of the House

In the late 1820s the preeminence of the House began to wane. Andrew Jackson asserted the power of the presidency by vetoing legislation he did not like. The caucus system of nominations had fallen into disrepute and was replaced (as we saw in Chapter 6) with a system of national nominating conventions. Most important, the party unity necessary for a Speaker, or any other leader, to control the House was shattered by the issue of slavery. So divided were the parties over this question that the choice of a Speaker became a protracted struggle; one contest in 1856 took 133 ballots before the outcome was decided. A Speaker chosen under these circumstances could hardly wield much power.

During and after the Civil War, the House reclaimed some of its lost stature, in part because the war eliminated the cleavage between the parties that had been caused by the slavery issue. Most of the representatives from the pro-slavery states were absent—the South had seceded from the Union—and their seats remained vacant for several years after the end of the war. Opinion in the House was strongly anti-slavery and anti-South, and this view tended to unify the House. It was led by "Radical Republicans"—men from the North, such as Thaddeus Stevens of Pennsylvania, determined to punish the South for its secession—and their fierce ideology made them influential figures even when they did not always occupy formal positions of leadership. Perhaps the high watermark of their power came in 1868, when the House voted to impeach President Andrew Johnson who was regarded as too "soft" on the South. (The Senate, by a margin of one vote, acquitted Johnson of the impeachment.)

During this period when the House either had weak leadership or leadership based on ideology rather than institutional power, the Senate was growing in stature. (The decision by Henry Clay in 1831 to move from the House to the Senate was symbolic of this shift.) One reason for the greater role of the Senate was the increasing importance of issues that the Senate was constitutionally required to deal with. (Foreign affairs was one such issue: the Senate must approve all treaties.) Equally important, however, were various political circumstances that enhanced the Senate's role. One was the slavery issue. The Senate had two senators from each state, and the admission of new states to the Union was carefully arranged to ensure that there would be equal numbers of senators from slave and free states. This meant that this great issue would be debated in a Senate where the two sides were equally matched. The Senate, unlike the House, had no rule limiting debate; hence, slavery could not only be debated equally, but at great length. As a result, the great orators and statesmen of the time—Clay, Daniel Webster, John Calhoun—sought seats in the Senate. Finally, senators were picked by state legislatures, not by the voters, and the Senate confirmed all major presidential appointments. This gave the Senate a crucial role in the development of local political parties. Often the most powerful party leaders in the various states became senators—men such as Roscoe Conkling, for example, an important party boss from New York. Many senators used their power to funnel jobs—political patronage—to their local party organizations.

Powerful as the Senate was, it was not tightly organized. Its individual members were too independent, too securely based in their own local party organizations to tolerate strong central leadership. The small size of the Senate meant that relatively few rules were necessary to keep business moving in an orderly manner.

The Rise of Party Control in the House

During the period 1889 to 1910, strong, partisan, central leadership emerged for the last time in the House of Representatives. This era was the high point of efforts to produce party government and a centrally controlled House. It began shortly after Thomas B. Reed of Maine was chosen by the Republicans to be Speaker. Reed used his power as Speaker and as leader of the Republican party caucus effectively. He selected all committee members and all committee chairmen, rewarding his supporters and punishing his opponents. He would not allow members to engage in dilatory tactics. He chaired the Rules Committee that decided what business would come up for a vote and what limitations on debate should be. During his heyday an extraordinary amount of party unity was obtained—Republicans voted together as a bloc against the Democrats.

Not long after Reed resigned in 1899, another powerful man became Speaker, Joseph G. Cannon of Illinois. He sought to maintain the Reed tradition, but by now circumstances had changed. Whereas Reed had political views quite similar to those of most Republicans, Cannon was distinctly more conservative than many Republicans around the turn of the century. Moreover, the desire of individual members to act independently was becoming more pronounced. Within a few years the revolt came.

The Decentralization of the House and the "Democratization" of the Senate

In 1910–1911 the House revolted against Cannon, voting to strip the Speaker of his right to appoint committee members or committee chair-

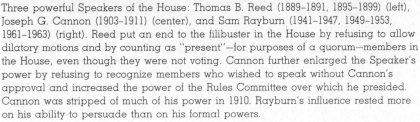

Three powerful Speakers of the House: Thomas B. Reed (1889–1891, 1895–1899) (left), Joseph G. Cannon (1903–1911) (center), and Sam Rayburn (1941–1947, 1949–1953, 1961–1963) (right). Reed put an end to the filibuster in the House by refusing to allow dilatory motions and by counting as "present"—for purposes of a quorum—members in the House, even though they were not voting. Cannon further enlarged the Speaker's power by refusing to recognize members who wished to speak without Cannon's approval and increased the power of the Rules Committee over which he presided. Cannon was stripped of much of his power in 1910. Rayburn's influence rested more on his ability to persuade than on his formal powers.

men and to remove him from membership on the powerful Rules Committee. What power Cannon lost did not flow immediately into the hands of individual members, however. Three other sources of power emerged.

One was the party caucus. For a time, the members of each political party in the House, meeting in their caucuses, would take positions on issues coming before the House and induce each member to support them. On occasion, the leader of the caucus was an especially influential or respected figure, and the caucus was strong. But the caucus lacked any real sanctions and soon its influence waned. Individual members increasingly discovered they could defy it without penalty.

A second was the Rules Committee. Though the Speaker was no longer a member, the committee still decided what bills would come up for

a vote, in what order, and under what restrictions on the length of debate and the right to offer amendments. From the time of Reed down to the present, the Rules Committee has used that power to boost certain bills and block others. A favored bill, for example, could be brought to the floor under a rule that said that debate would be limited to one hour, that no member could speak more than five minutes, and that no amendments could be offered without the support of the committee in charge of the bill. To those who favored these bills, it was an excellent device for ensuring that action was taken; to the opponents of the bills, it was a "gag rule."

Third, the power of the chairmen of the standing committees rose as the power of the Speaker fell. Until the 1970s these chairmen had substantial ability to decide what business the committees they chaired would take up, what

"The House has committed itself . . . to the view that the autonomy and power of the individual member are to be protected at the expense of opportunities for leadership.**"**

bills would be sent out of the committees to the full House, and even what some of these bills would contain. In the days when these chairmen were chosen by the Speaker they often used their power to follow his leadership or that of the party as a whole. But once the Speaker no longer appointed them, they acquired office strictly on the basis of seniority. The seniority principle, though later criticized, was at first seen as a "reform." It meant that representatives could become committee chairmen automatically, subject neither to party control nor to leadership manipulation, simply by having served in Congress longer than anyone else of their party on the committee. When it later became apparent that the seniority system gave power to congressmen whose political views were not shared by other congressmen on the same committees, the system was attacked.

Recent Changes. The decentralization of the House begun in 1910 was made complete by further changes in the 1960s and 1970s. The power of individual members against committee chairmen was strengthened, the number of subcommittees was increased, the staffs of congressmen were enlarged, and three persons who had become committee chairmen by virtue of seniority were removed from those posts to establish that, at least in principle, the seniority system was not sacrosanct.

In sum, during nearly two centuries of growth and experimentation, the House has committed itself, by a series of changes, to the view that the autonomy and power of the individual member are to be protected at the expense of opportunities for leadership. After brief flirtations with party rule in the early nineteenth century under Clay and at the end of that century under Reed and Cannon, the House has rejected the notion that it will play the deliberative, general-policy

role of a parliament. It has chosen instead to emphasize the importance of work in committees, subcommittees, and individual congressional offices. Naturally, laws are passed, many of them of the greatest importance, but legislative action is achieved, not by leadership direction, but only by an elaborate and necessarily slow process of building consent among individual members.

Popular Election of Senators. The Senate never created a position equivalent to that of the Speaker of the House, and it did not give to anyone else the power of a Reed or Cannon. There was a Rules Committee but not one that could control the Senate's business, which was always carried on under a tradition that allowed for unlimited debate. The major change in the Senate came, not from a struggle over its internal control, but from an attack on its membership. For more than a century after the founding of the nation, members of the Senate were chosen by state legislatures. Though often these legislatures picked popular local figures to be senators, just as often there was intense political maneuvering among the leaders of various factions, each struggling to win (and sometimes buy) the votes necessary to become senator. By the end of the nineteenth century, the Senate was known as the "Millionaires' Club," because of the number of wealthy party leaders and businessmen in it. There arose a demand for the direct, popular election of senators.

Naturally, the Senate resisted, and without its approval the necessary constitutional amendment could not pass Congress. When some states threatened to demand a new constitutional convention, the Senate feared that such a convention would change more than just the way in which senators were chosen. A protracted struggle ensued, during which many state legislatures devised ways to ensure that senators they picked would already have won a popular election. The Senate finally agreed to a constitutional amendment that required the popular election of its members, and in 1913 the Seventeenth Amend-

THE WAY WE BECOME SENATOR NOWADAYS.

A cartoon from *Puck* in 1890 expressed popular resentment over the "Millionaires' Club," as the Senate had become known.

ment was approved by the necessary three-fourths of the states. Ironically, given the intensity of the struggle over this question, no great change in the composition of the Senate resulted; most of those members who had been first chosen by state legislatures managed to win reelection by popular vote.

The other major issue in the development of the Senate was the filibuster. A filibuster is a prolonged speech, or series of speeches, made to delay action in a legislative assembly. It had become a common—and unpopular—feature of Senate life by the end of the nineteenth century. It was used by liberals and conservatives alike and for lofty as well as self-serving purposes. The first serious effort to restrict the filibuster came in 1917 after an important foreign policy measure submitted by President Wilson had been talked

to death by, as he put it, "eleven willful men." Rule 22 (to be explained later) was adopted by a Senate fearful of tying a president's hands during a wartime crisis. It provided that debate could be cut off if two-thirds of the senators present and voting agreed to a "cloture" motion. Two years later it was first invoked successfully when the Senate voted cloture to end, after fifty-five days, the debate over the Treaty of Versailles. Cloture is rarely used, and the tradition of unlimited debate remains strong in the Senate.

WHO IS IN CONGRESS?

The fact that power is so decentralized in Congress means that the kind of person elected to it is especially important: since each member exercises some influence, the beliefs and interests of each affect policy. Viewed simplistically, most members of Congress seem the same: the average representative or senator is a middle-aged white Protestant male lawyer. If all such persons usually thought and voted alike, that would be an interesting fact, but they do not, and so it is not.

By Sex and Race

Even these obvious characteristics are changing, though slowly. The number of women has increased—though not much of late—from eight who served in the 80th Congress (1947–1948) to seventeen who served in the 96th (1979–1980). The number of blacks has been increasing as well. During the period immediately after the Civil War, when blacks could vote in the South, more than twenty were elected to Congress. Then, as southern states began to restrict black suffrage, no more blacks were chosen until 1929, when Oscar DePriest was elected from Chicago. Since then, several dozen blacks have entered Congress, including one (Edward W. Brooke of Massachusetts, defeated for reelection in 1978) in the Senate. In the 96th Congress there were sixteen blacks in the House, none in the Senate (see Table 10.1).

TABLE 10.1   Blacks and Women in Congress, 1947–1980

Congress	Senate		House	
	Blacks	Women	Blacks	Women
96th (1979–1980)	0	1	16	16
95th	1	2	16	18
94th	1	0	15	19
93rd	1	0	15	14
92nd	1	2	12	13
91st	1	1	9	10
90th	1	1	5	11
89th	0	2	6	10
88th	0	2	5	11
87th	0	2	4	17
86th	0	1	4	16
85th	0	1	4	15
84th	0	1	3	16
83rd	0	3	2	12
82nd	0	1	2	10
81st	0	1	2	9
80th (1947–1948)	0	1	2	7

Source: Data from *Congressional Quarterly Almanac,* various years.

By Years of Service

The most important change that has occurred in the composition of Congress, however, has been so gradual that most people have not noticed it. In the nineteenth century, a large fraction—often a majority—of congressmen served only one term. In 1869, for example, more than half the members of the House were serving their first term in Congress. Being a congressman in those days was not regarded as a career. This was in part because the federal government was not very important (most of the interesting political decisions were made by states), in part because travel to Washington, D.C., was difficult and the city was not a pleasant place to live, and in part because being a congressman did not pay well. Furthermore, many congressional districts were highly competitive, with the two political parties fairly evenly balanced in each.

Today Congress has become a career, and congressmen are full-time professional politicians. Figure 10.1 shows the decline in the proportion of first-term members of the House. Whereas in 1869 the average representative had served only one term in Congress, by the 1970s the typical representative had served four or five.[1]

Related to this change is a fact of the greatest significance regarding our concept of democracy: most congressmen face no serious challenge for reelection. The length of time the average member has been in Congress has increased because the chances of being defeated have decreased. In the period 1952–1974, only 16 percent of the incumbent senators and only about 6 percent of the incumbent representatives seeking reelection were defeated.[2] To be sure, some congressmen may have decided to retire rather than risk losing an election to a strong opponent, but even allowing for this the odds favoring a congressman's reelection are very high.

Furthermore, the number of instances in which an incumbent congressman wins a hotly contested election has been getting smaller. In 1948 most races where an incumbent representative was running were quite close—that is, the winner got less than 55 percent of the vote. By 1972, however, the winner in the great majority of these contests won 60 percent or more of the vote.[3] Political scientists call districts that have close elections (in which the winner gets less than 55 percent) "marginal" districts. Of late, marginal districts have been getting fewer and fewer. Senators are a bit less secure: their races are much more likely to be close than those involving representatives.

Why congressional seats should have become less marginal—that is, safer—is a matter on which scholars are not entirely in agreement. Some feel it is the result of television and other ways of reaching the voters through the media. But challengers can go on television too—why should this benefit incumbents? Another possibility is that voters are becoming less and less likely to support whatever candidate wins the nomination of the voters' party. They are more likely, in short, to vote for the person rather than the party. And they are more likely to have heard of a person who is an incumbent—he or she can, after all, deluge the voter with free mailings, travel frequently (and at public expense) to meet constituents, and get his or her name in the newspaper by sponsoring bills or conducting investigations. Simply having a familiar name is important in getting elected, and incumbents find it easier than challengers do to make their names known.

Finally, it is possible that incumbents can use their powers to get programs passed or funds spent in ways that benefit their districts. They can help keep an army base open, support the building of a new highway (or block the building of an unpopular one), take credit for federal grants that go to local schools and hospitals, make certain that a particular industry or labor union is protected by tariffs against foreign competition, and so on.[4]

By Party

Probably all of these factors make some difference. Whatever the explanation, the tendency of voters to return incumbents to office means that in ordinary times, no one should expect any dramatic changes in the composition of Congress. Because the advantages of incumbency began to take effect after the Democrats were in control of Congress, these advantages help explain why the Democrats have so thoroughly dominated Congress for the last four decades. Since 1933 the Democrats have had a majority in the House of Representatives and in the Senate in every Congress but two (the 80th, in 1947–1948, and the 83rd, in 1953–1954). Other factors also explain this dominance; more

FIGURE 10.1   Decline in Percentage of First-Term Members of the House of Representatives

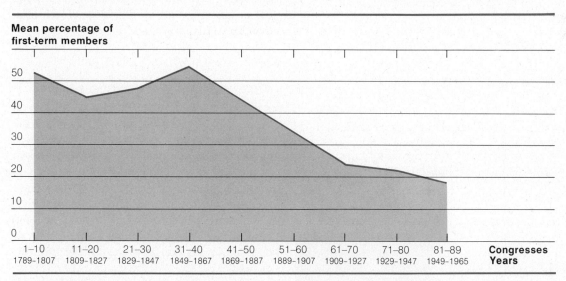

Source: Nelson W. Polsby, "The Institutionalization of the U.S. House of Representatives," *American Political Science Review*, March 1968, p. 147. Reprinted by permission.

• First woman in Congress	*Jeannette Rankin (Mont., 1916)*
• First black in Congress	*Joseph H. Rainey (S.C., 1870)*
• Longest session of Congress	*366 days (75th Congress, meeting from Jan. 3, 1940, to Jan. 3, 1941)*
• Shortest length of time for states to ratify a constitutional amendment	*7 months, 6 days—12th Amendment*
• Longest period of time to ratify an amendment	*3 years, 11 months—22nd Amendment*
• Longest service in Congress by one member	*56 years, Carl Hayden of Arizona (15 years in House, 41 years in Senate), 1912–1968*
• First member of the House to be elected president	*James Madison*
• First member of the Senate to be elected president	*James Monroe*
• First Catholic priest to serve in Congress	*Robert Drinan of Massachusetts*
• States with only one representative in Congress	*Alaska, Delaware, Nevada, North Dakota, Vermont, Wyoming*
• Longest speech ever made in the Senate	*24 hours, 18 minutes, made on August 28–29, 1957, by Senator J. Strom Thurmond (D, S.C.) seeking to block a civil rights bill*
• First woman elected to Senate for full term who was not preceded in office by her husband	*Nancy Landon Kassebaum, elected in 1978 from Kansas*

CONGRESSIONAL
trivia

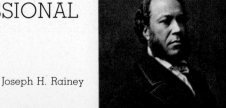

Joseph H. Rainey

voters consider themselves Democrats than consider themselves Republicans, and many parts of the South still afford Republicans little chance of victory. Increasingly, a majority of representatives and senators come from one-party, or at least one-candidate, areas. (Some of these districts are much more competitive in presidential elections than they are in congressional ones.)

From time to time there are major electoral convulsions that alter the membership of Congress, if not its party control. For example, in the election of 1938 the Democrats lost seventy seats in the House, in 1942 they lost fifty, in 1950 they lost twenty-nine, and in 1966 they lost forty-eight. Despite these losses, the Democrats retained a majority in the House elected in each of these years. Because representatives do not always vote along strict party lines, the size of that majority is important. The kinds of bills that get passed will be affected by how many conservative Democrats are prepared to join with Republicans (the so-called "conservative coalition") or how many liberal Republicans are willing to vote with liberal Democrats. When the number of seats is rather evenly divided in Congress, one party may "control" Congress and still not be able to get all, or even most, of its legislative program approved.

GETTING ELECTED TO CONGRESS

Who serves in Congress, and what interests are represented there, is affected by the mechanisms by which congressmen are elected. Each state is entitled to two senators who serve six-year terms and at least one representative who serves a two-year term. How many more representatives a state has will depend on its population; what groups these representatives will speak for depends in part on how the district lines are drawn.

The Constitution says very little about how representatives will be selected except to require that they be inhabitants of the states from which they are chosen. It says nothing about districts and originally left it up to the states to decide who would be eligible to vote for congressmen. The size of the first House was set by the Constitution at sixty-five members, and the apportionment of the seats among the states was spelled out in Article I, Section 2. From that point on, it has been up to Congress to decide how many representatives each state would have (provided each had at least one).

Determining Fair Representation

Initially, some states did not create congressional districts; all their representatives were elected at large. Others elected them from multimember as well as single-member districts. In time, all states with more than one representative elected each from a single-member district. How those district boundaries were drawn, however, could profoundly affect the outcomes of elections. There were two problems. One was malapportionment, which results from having districts of very unequal sizes. If one district is twice as populous as another, twice as many votes are needed in the larger district to elect a congressman. Thus, a citizen's vote in the smaller district is worth twice as much as a vote in the larger. The other problem was gerrymandering, which means drawing a district boundary in some bizarre or unusual shape to make it easy for the candidate of one party to win election in that district. In a state entitled to ten representatives, where half the voters are Democrats and half are Republicans, district lines could be drawn so that eight districts would have a slight majority of citizens from one party and two districts would have lopsided majorities from the other. Thus it can be made easy for one party to win eight of the ten seats.

Malapportionment and gerrymandering have been conspicuous features of American congressional politics. In 1962, for example, one district in Texas had nearly a million residents while

66 The states did little about malapportionment and gerrymandering until ordered to do so by the Supreme Court. **99**

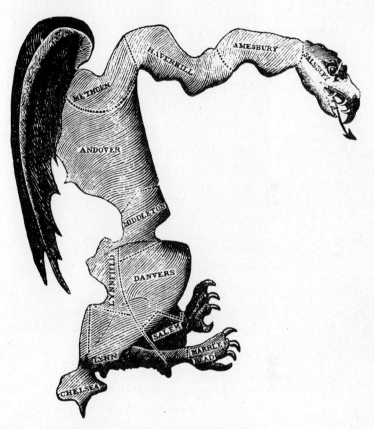

The original Gerrymander: Elbridge Gerry had this Massachusetts district drawn to ensure the election of a Republican. Cartoonist Elkanah Tinsdale in 1812 compared the district to a salamander and termed it a "Gerry-Mander."

another had less than a quarter million. In California, Democrats in control of the state legislature drew district lines in the early 1960s so that two pockets of Republican strength in Los Angeles separated by many miles were connected by a thin strip of coastline. In this way most Republican voters were thrown into one district while Democratic voters were spread more evenly over several.

Senator Nancy Kassebaum of Kansas talks with one of her staff members.

There are thus four problems to solve in deciding who gets represented in the House:

1. establishing the total size of the House;
2. allocating seats in the House among the states;
3. determining the size of congressional districts within states; and
4. determining the shape of those districts.

By and large, Congress has decided the first two questions, and the states have decided the last two—but under some rather strict Supreme Court rules.

In 1911 Congress decided that the House had become large enough and voted to fix its size at 435 members. There it has remained ever since (except for a brief period when it had 437

members owing to the admission of Alaska and Hawaii to the Union in 1959). Once the size was decided upon, it was necessary to find some formula for performing the painful task of apportioning seats among the states as they gained and lost population. The Constitution requires such reapportionment every ten years. A more or less automatic method was selected in 1929 based on a complex statistical system that has withstood decades of political and scientific testing. Under this system, many states—such as New York, Indiana, Pennsylvania, Georgia, Illinois, and Massachusetts—lost representation in the House as other states grew more rapidly in population. The largest gainers have been California and Texas. The average congressional district in 1979 had just under a half million residents.

The states did little about malapportionment and gerrymandering until ordered to do so by the Supreme Court. In 1964 the Court ruled in a case that began in Georgia that the Constitution requires that districts be drawn so that, as nearly as possible, one man's vote would be worth as much as another's.[5] The Court rule, "one man, one vote," seems clear, but in fact leaves a host of questions unanswered. How much deviation from equal size is allowable? Should other factors be taken into account besides population? (For example, a state legislature might want to draw district lines to make it easier for blacks—or Italian-Americans or farmers or some other group with a distinct interest—to elect a representative; the requirement of exactly equal districts might make this impossible.) And the gerrymandering problem remains: districts of the same size can be drawn to favor one party or another. The courts have struggled to find answers to these questions, but they remain far from settled.

Winning the Primary

Once the district lines are set, the other major procedural arrangement that affects the election of a candidate has to do with the system for getting one's name on the ballot. At one time the political parties nominated candidates and even printed ballots with the party slates listed on them. All the voter had to do was take the ballot of the preferred party and put it in the ballot box. Today, with rare exceptions, a candidate gets on the ballot by winning a primary election, the outcome of which is often beyond the ability of political parties to influence. Candidates tend to form organizations of personal followings and win "their party's" nomination simply by getting more primary votes than the next candidate. It is quite unusual for an incumbent congressman to lose a primary—from 1952 to 1974, only 5 percent of the incumbent senators and fewer than 2 percent of the incumbent representatives failed to win renomination in primaries. These factors suggest how little opportunity parties have to control or punish their congressional members.

Congressional campaigns have become "personalized" in the ways described in Chapter 7. This means that candidates not only run without much regard to party structure, they run in ways designed to develop among their constituents a good opinion of *the candidates* and not of the party, their party in Congress, or even of Congress itself. They work to build trust in themselves. To the extent they succeed, they enjoy great freedom in how they vote on particular issues and have less need to explain away votes that their constituents might not like. (If, however, any single-issue groups are actively working in their districts for or against abortion, gun control, nuclear energy, or tax cuts, muting the candidates' voting record may not be possible.) Moreover, as Richard Fenno has found, many congressmen cater to their constituents' heightened distrust of Congress and the federal government and portray themselves as "different," "better," and deserving of being sent to Congress to help "clean things up." This helps explain a paradoxical fact: though opinion polls show many people have a low opinion of Congress, they have a high opinion of their own congressman. Congressmen run *for* Congress by running *against* it.[6]

Qualifications for Entering Congress and Privileges of Being in Congress

Qualifications

Representative

- Must be 25 years of age (when seated, not when elected).
- Must have been a citizen of the United States for seven years.
- Must be an inhabitant of the state from which elected. (*Note:* Custom, but *not* the Constitution, requires that a representative live in the district he or she represents.)

Senator

- Must be 30 years of age (when seated, not when elected).
- Must have been a citizen of the United States for nine years.
- Must be an inhabitant of the state from which elected.

Judging Qualifications

Each house is the judge of the "elections, returns, and qualifications" of its members. Congress alone thus decides disputed congressional elections. On occasion, it has excluded a person from taking a seat on grounds that the election was improper. Either house can punish a member—by reprimand, for example—or, by a two-thirds vote, expel a member.

Privileges

Members of Congress have certain privileges, the most important of which, conferred by the Constitution, is that "for any speech or debate in either house they shall not be questioned in any other place." This doctrine of "privileged speech" has been broadly interpreted by the Supreme Court to mean that congressmen cannot be sued, charged, or enjoined for anything they (or their staff assistants) say or write in connection with their legislative duties. When Senator Mike Gravel of Alaska read the Pentagon Papers—a collection of then-secret government documents about the Vietnam War—into the *Congressional Record* in defiance of a court order restraining publication of the Papers, the Court held that this was "privileged speech" and beyond challenge. [*Gravel* v. *United States*, 408 U.S. 606 (1972).]

THE UNITED STATES CONGRESS

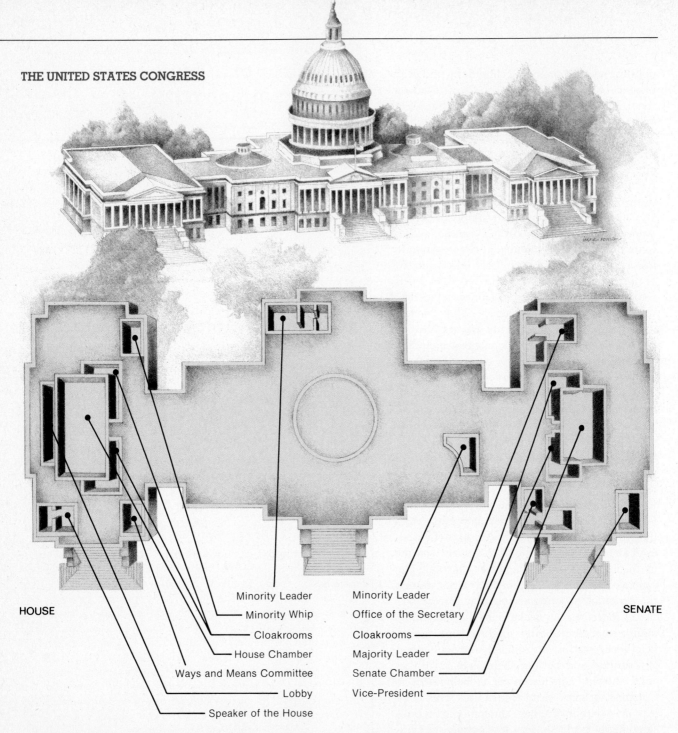

HOUSE

SENATE

Minority Leader
Minority Whip
Cloakrooms
House Chamber
Ways and Means Committee
Lobby
Speaker of the House

Minority Leader
Office of the Secretary
Cloakrooms
Majority Leader
Senate Chamber
Vice-President

The House and Senate meet at opposite ends of the Capitol building. When there is a joint session of Congress—for example, to hear the president's State of the Union address—the senators sit with the representatives in the House chamber. Though the most important work of Congress goes on in committee meetings, which are held in office buildings behind the Capitol, some important political negotiations occur in the offices surrounding the chambers—especially in the cloakrooms (actually, lounges), the offices of the majority and minority leaders, of the Speaker and the vice-president, and of the secretary of the Senate.

THE ORGANIZATION OF CONGRESS: PARTIES AND INTERESTS

Congress is not a single organization; it is a vast and complex collection of organizations by which the business of Congress is carried on and through which congressmen form alliances. If we were to look inside the British House of Commons, we would find only one kind of organization of any importance—the political parties. Though party organization is important in the United States Congress, it is only one of many important units. In fact, other organizations have grown in number as the influence of party has declined.

Party Organization

The Democrats and Republicans in the House of Representatives and the Senate are organized by party leaders. The key leaders, in turn, are elected by the full party membership within the House and Senate. The description that follows is confined to the essential positions.

The Senate. The majority party (of late, the Democrats) chooses one of its members—usually the person with the greatest seniority—to be pres-

ident pro tempore of the Senate. It is largely an honorific position, required by the Constitution so that the Senate will have a presiding officer in the absence of the vice-president of the United States, who is also, according to the Constitution, the president of the Senate. In fact, presiding over the Senate is a tedious chore that neither the vice-president nor the president pro tem relishes, and so it is usually assigned to some junior senator.

The real leadership is in the hands of the majority leader (chosen by the senators of the majority party) and the minority leader (chosen by the senators in the other party). In addition, the senators of each party elect a whip. The principal task of the majority leader is to schedule the business of the Senate, usually in consultation with the minority leader. The majority leader has the right to be recognized first in any floor debate. A majority leader with a strong personality who is skilled at political bargaining may do much more. Lyndon B. Johnson, who was Senate majority leader for the Democrats during much of the 1950s, used his prodigious ability to serve the needs of fellow senators. He helped them with everything from obtaining extra office space to getting choice

---

PARTY LEADERSHIP IN THE SENATE, 1979–1980

Democrats	Republicans
President Pro Tempore	
Warren G. Magnuson (Wash.)	
Majority Leader	Minority Leader
Robert C. Byrd (W. Va.)	*Howard H. Baker, Jr. (Tenn.)*
Whip	Whip
Alan Cranston (Calif.)	*Ted Stevens (Alaska)*
Chairman of the Policy Committee	Chairman of the Policy Committee
Robert C. Byrd (W. Va.)	*John G. Tower (Tex.)*
Chairman of the Steering Committee	Chairman of the Committee on Committees
Robert C. Byrd (W. Va.)	*Jake Garn (Utah)*

66 The key—and delicate—aspect of selecting party leaders, making up the important party committees, and assigning freshman senators to Senate committees is achieving ideological and regional balance. **99**

committee assignments, and in this way acquired substantial influence over the substance as well as the schedule of Senate business. Johnson's successor, Mike Mansfield, was a less assertive majority leader and had less influence.

The whip is a senator who helps the majority leader stay informed about what party members are thinking, rounds up members when important votes are to be taken, and attempts to keep a nose count of how the voting on a controversial issue is likely to go. The whip has several senators who assist him in this task.

Each party in the Senate also chooses a Policy Committee composed of a dozen or so senators who help the party leader schedule Senate business, choosing what bills are to be given major attention and in what order.

From the point of view of individual senators, however, the key party organization is the group that assigns senators to the standing committees of the Senate. The Democrats have a twenty-four member Steering Committee that does this; the Republicans have a fourteen member Committee on Committees. These assignments are especially important for newly elected senators—their political careers, their opportunities for favorable publicity, and their chances for helping their states and their supporters depend in great part on the committees to which they are assigned. For example, when Daniel Patrick Moynihan was elected to the Senate from New York in 1976, he waged an intensive and successful effort to get appointed to the Finance Committee. That body handles bills providing aid to cities and welfare to citizens—two areas of great importance to the big urban areas in Moynihan's state. During the 1960s many new senators fought to get on the Foreign Relations Committee because of the controversy surrounding the war in Vietnam and the highly visible role of members of that committee in criticizing or defending American policy.

The key—and delicate—aspect of selecting party leaders, making up the important party committees, and assigning freshman senators to Senate committees is achieving ideological and regional balance. Liberals and conservatives in each party will fight over the choice of majority and minority leader. When Robert Byrd was elected majority leader, his opponent was Hubert Humphrey. Most moderates and conservatives backed Byrd, and many liberals backed Humphrey. Byrd had made so many friends and seemed so skillful (and Humphrey's health seemed so precarious) that many liberal senators voted for Byrd despite his being a moderate.

The House of Representatives.   The party structure is essentially the same in the House as in the Senate, though the titles of various posts are different. But leadership carries more power in the House than in the Senate because of the House rules. Being so large (435 members), the House must restrict debate and schedule its business with great care; thus, leaders who do the scheduling and who determine how the rules shall be applied usually have substantial influence.

The Speaker is the most important person in the House. He is elected by whichever party has a majority, and he presides over the meetings of that body. Unlike the president pro tem of the Senate, however, his position is anything but honorific. He is the principal leader of the majority party as well as the presiding officer of the entire House. Though Speakers-as-presiders are expected to be fair, Speakers-as-party-leaders are expected to use their powers to help pass legislation favored by their party. In helping his party, the Speaker has some important formal powers at his disposal: he decides who shall be recognized to speak on the floor of the House; he rules whether a motion is relevant and germane to the business at hand; he decides (subject to certain rules) the committees to which new bills shall be assigned. He influences what bills are brought up for a vote; and he appoints the members of special and select committees (to be explained later). Since 1975 he has been able to nominate the majority party members of the Rules Committee. He also has some informal powers: he controls some patronage jobs in the Capitol building and the assignment of extra office space. Even though the Speaker is far less powerful than in the days of Clay, Reed, and Cannon, he is still an important person to have on one's side. Sam Rayburn of Texas exercised great influence as Speaker, and Tip O'Neill, the current Speaker, is doing the same.

In the House, as in the Senate, the majority party elects a floor leader, called the majority leader. The other party also chooses a leader—the minority leader. Traditionally, the majority leader becomes Speaker when the person in that position dies or retires—provided, of course, that their party is still in the majority. Each party also has a whip, with several assistant whips in charge of rounding up votes from various state delegations. Committee assignments are made and the scheduling of legislation is discussed, by the Democrats, in a Steering and Policy Committee, chaired by the Speaker. The Republicans have divided committee assignments and policy discussions, with the former task assigned to a Committee on Committees and the latter to a Policy Committee. Each party also has a congressional campaign committee to provide funds and other assistance to party members running for election or reelection to the House.

Party Voting. The effect of this elaborate party machinery can be crudely measured by the extent to which members of a party vote together in the House and the Senate. A "party vote" can be defined in various ways; naturally, the more

---

PARTY LEADERSHIP IN THE HOUSE, 1979–1980

Democrats	**Republicans**
Speaker *Thomas P. O'Neill, Jr. (Mass.)*	
Majority Leader *Jim Wright (Tex.)*	Minority Leader *John J. Rhodes (Ariz.)*
Whip *John Brademas (Ind.)*	Whip *Robert H. Michel (Ill.)*
Chairman of the Steering and Policy Committee *Thomas P. O'Neill, Jr. (Mass.)*	Chairman of the Committee on Committees *John J. Rhodes (Ariz.)*
	Chairman of the Republican Policy Committee *Bud Shuster (Pa.)*
Chairman of the Democratic Caucus *Thomas S. Foley (Wash.)*	Chairman of the Republican Conference *John B. Anderson (Ill.)*

❝Party *does make a difference in Congress . . . party affiliation is still the single most important thing to know about a congressman.***❞**

stringent the definition, the less party voting we will observe. Figure 10.2 shows two measures of party voting in the House of Representatives during this century. By the strictest measure, a party vote occurs when 90 percent or more of the Democrats vote together against 90 percent or more of the Republicans. A looser measure counts as a party vote any case where at least 50 percent of the Democrats vote together against at least 50 percent of the Republicans. As is plain, by either measure the extent of party voting is low and has declined since the turn of the century. Today, using the 90 percent test, scarcely 3 percent of the votes in the House are party votes; using the 50 percent test, less than two-fifths are.

Given the fact that political parties as organizations do not tightly control a congressman's ability to get elected, what is surprising is not that party votes are relatively rare, but that they occur at all. Why do congressional members of one party ever vote together against a majority of the other party? There are several reasons. First, congressmen do not randomly decide to be Democrats or Republicans; these choices reflect some broad policy agreements, at least for most members. Several interest groups tabulate the votes of congressmen on important issues to see

FIGURE 10.2   The Decline of Party Votes in the House of Representatives, 1897–1969

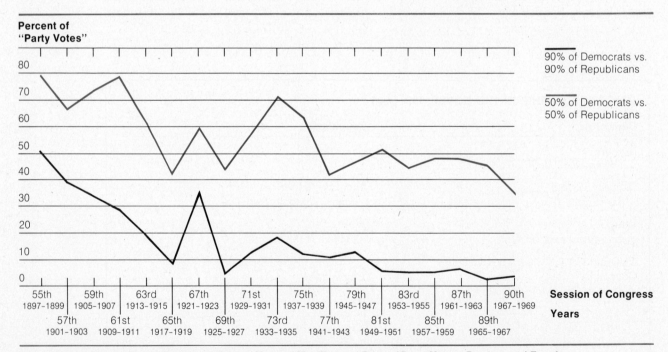

Source: Joseph Cooper, David Brady, and Patricia Hurley, "The Electoral Basis of Party Voting: Patterns and Trends in the U.S. House of Representatives, 1887–1969," in Louis Maisel and Joseph Cooper, eds., *The Impact of the Electoral Process* (Beverly Hills, Calif.: Sage Publications, 1977), p. 139.

who is most and least favorable to their positions. Two such groups are the liberal Americans for Democratic Action (ADA) and the conservative Americans for Constitutional Action (ACA). If we combine the ratings given to each congressman by these two organizations, we can get a rough idea of who is a liberal and who a conservative and how many of each are in the two political parties (see Table 10.2). These ratings for the period 1975 to 1978 show clearly that Democrats and Republicans in Congress differed in their ideological orientation. Two-thirds of the Democratic senators and nearly three-fourths of the Democratic representatives were liberals; only about one-fourth of the Senate Republicans and less than one-tenth of the House Republicans were liberals. There continues to be, of course, a significant minority of conservative Democrats, mostly southern, who on occasion vote together with many Republicans to form a "conservative coalition."

In addition to their personal views, congressmen have other reasons for supporting their party's position at least some of the time. On many matters that come to a vote, a congressman has little information and no opinion. He has no chance of becoming personally familiar with more than a small fraction of the hundreds of items with which Congress must deal each session. He must get advice on how to vote, and it is only natural that Democrats look to Democratic leaders and fellow partisans for that advice, and Republicans look to Republicans. Furthermore, supporting the party position can work to the long-term advantage of a member interested in rising in status and influence in Congress. Though the party leaders are weaker today than in the past, they are hardly powerless. If you are a congressman who wants to get a good committee assignment, obtain a favorable hearing for a bill you submit, become chairman of an important subcommittee, or be taken seriously by other members in the party caucus, it pays not to go out of your way to insult, ignore, or challenge

TABLE 10.2   Policy Views of Congressmen, 1975–1978

| | Number of Congressmen | | | |
| | House | | Senate | |
	Dem	Rep	Dem	Rep
Strongly liberal	71	1	15	1
Liberal	68	4	14	3
Moderately liberal	63	9	11	6
Moderately conservative	43	29	12	5
Conservative	31	40	7	10
Strongly conservative	12	59	3	13

Source: Calculated from data in *Politics Today*, March/April 1979, p. 52.
Note: Scores based on combined ADA–ACA rankings of congressmen.

party leaders. Sam Rayburn, who served as Speaker for seventeen years (in the 1940s and 1950s), reputedly told freshmen congressmen that "if you want to get along, go along." That is less true today, but still good advice.

In short, party *does* make a difference in Congress—not as much as it once did, and not nearly as much as it does today in a parliamentary system, but party affiliation is still the single most important thing to know about a congressman. Knowing whether a member is a Democrat or a Republican will not tell you everything about the member, but it will tell you more than any other one fact.

Opinion and Interest Groupings

In addition to the formal party structure, there are in Congress many informal organizations that reflect the political opinions and interests of the members. Indeed, as party influence has weakened, the importance of these other caucuses and coalitions has increased. Some of the more important are:

Democratic Study Group (DSG). Organized in 1959 to facilitate communication and encourage unity among liberal Democrats, it chose the

President Carter discusses black unemployment with members of the Congressional Black Caucus: Representative Parren J. Mitchell of Maryland (left) and Representative Shirley Chisholm of New York (right).

label "Study Group" to avoid offending non-liberal representatives. Though not an official party entity, it collects dues from its members, raises funds through mailings and banquets, employs a large staff (about eighteen persons), and publishes weekly reports and other materials on pending legislation. It has over two hundred members, though it publishes no list of members for fear that some might be embarrassed if their constituents knew of their affiliation. The DSG does not take a stand on specific bills, in part to avoid alienating members who might oppose that position and in part because on some questions there is no clearly "liberal" position. (It has been deeply split, for example, on gun control.)

Democratic Research Organization. Composed of about seventy moderate-to-conservative House

Democrats, it is a counterweight to the DSG. It performs similar functions and has a staff of five.

Wednesday Group. An organization of moderately conservative and middle-of-the-road House Republicans, selected by secret ballot by the existing members. It meets every Wednesday to discuss legislation. It usually has about thirty members and a staff of three or four.

Republican Study Committee. A group of about seventy conservative Republicans who receive weekly reports prepared by a staff of ten.

State Delegations. Members from certain large states, such as California, New York, and Texas, meet together on matters of common interest. Some such delegations vote together on many issues owing to the power of the local party organization. The Democratic representatives from Illinois, for example, are apt to vote together, especially the members from Cook County (Chicago). The powerful Democratic party organization in Cook County, once led by Richard J. Daley, usually decisively influences who gets nominated for office.

Specialized Caucuses. Various groups exist to handle racial, ethnic, regional, and policy interests. There is an Environmental Policy Committee for ecology-minded representatives, a Northeast-Midwest Economic Advancement Coalition for congressmen from areas that seem to be sagging economically, and caucuses for women members, Spanish-speaking members, and blacks. The black caucus is one of the best known of these, and probably typical of many in its operations. There were, in 1979, sixteen blacks in the House of Representatives. Their organization, the Congressional Black Caucus, meets regularly and employs a staff. As with most caucuses, some members are very active, others only marginally so. On some issues it simply registers an opinion; on other issues it attempts to negotiate with leaders of other blocs so that votes can be traded in a mutually advantageous way. It keeps its members informed, and on occasion presses to have one of its members fill a vacancy on a regular congressional committee that has no blacks on it.

THE ORGANIZATION OF CONGRESS: COMMITTEES

The most important organizational feature of Congress is the set of legislative committees of the House and Senate. There the real work of Congress is done; in the chairmanship of these committees, and their subcommittees, most of the power in Congress is found. The number and jurisdiction of these committees are of the greatest interest to congressmen since decisions on these subjects determine what group of congressmen, with what political views, will pass on legislative proposals, oversee the workings of agencies in the executive branch, and conduct investigations.

The 96th Congress that began in January 1979 had a total of 314 committees and subcommittees, as follows:

House: 27 committees with 157 subcommittees
Senate: 20 committees with 101 subcommittees
Joint: 4 committees with 5 subcommittees

Periodically, efforts have been made to cut the number of committees to give each a broader jurisdiction and to reduce conflict between committees over a single bill. One such effort was the Legislative Reorganization Act of 1946. But as the number of committees declined, the number of subcommittees rose, leaving matters about as they once were.

There are three kinds of committees: *standing committees* (more or less permanent, continuing bodies with specified legislative responsibilities), *select committees* (groups appointed for a special, limited purpose, most of which last for only one

❝In the early 1970s Congress further decentralized and democratized its operations.❞

Congress), and *joint committees* (those on which both representatives and senators serve). An especially important kind of joint committee is the *conference committee,* made up of representatives and senators appointed to resolve differences in the Senate and House versions of the same piece of legislation before final passage.

Though members of the majority party could, in theory, occupy all the seats on all the committees, in practice they take the majority of the seats, name the chairman, and allow the minority party to have the remainder of the seats. The number of seats varies with the committee, from about a half dozen to over fifty. Usually the ratio of Democrats to Republicans on a committee roughly corresponds to their ratio in the House or Senate. (In 1978 the Democrats had a two-to-one advantage in most committees.) Standing committees are created under the rules of each house. Subcommittees can be created at the discretion of any committee, though a House rule requires that any committee of twenty or more members establish at least four subcommittees.

Standing committees are the important ones because, with a few exceptions, they are the only ones that can propose legislation by reporting a bill out to the full House or Senate. Each member of the House usually serves on two standing committees, unless he or she is on the Appropriations, Rules, or Ways and Means committees. In such a case the representative is limited to one. Each senator may serve on two "major" committees and one "minor" committee. (Major and minor senate committees are indicated on the next page.)

When party leaders were strong, as under Speakers Reed and Cannon, committee chairmen were picked on the basis of loyalty to the leader. Now that this leadership has been weakened, seniority on the committee governs the

STANDING COMMITTEES IN THE SENATE DURING THE 96th CONGRESS, 1979-1980

Major Committees

(no senator may serve on more than two)

Agriculture, Nutrition, and Forestry
    Chairman: Herman E. Talmadge (D, Ga.)
Appropriations
    Chairman: Warren G. Magnuson (D, Wash.)
Armed Services
    Chairman: John C. Stennis (D, Miss.)
Banking, Housing, and Urban Affairs
    Chairman: William Proxmire (D, Wisc.)
Budget
    Chairman: Edmund S. Muskie (D, Maine)
Commerce, Science, and Transportation
    Chairman: Howard W. Cannon (D, Nev.)
Energy and Natural Resources
    Chairman: Henry M. Jackson (D, Wash.)
Environment and Public Works
    Chairman: Jennings Randolph (D, W. Va.)
Finance
    Chairman: Russell B. Long (D, La.)
Foreign Relations
    Chairman: Frank Church (D, Idaho)
Governmental Affairs
    Chairman: Abraham Ribicoff (D, Conn.)
Human Resources
    Chairman: Harrison A. Williams, Jr. (D, N.J.)
Judiciary
    Chairman: Edward M. Kennedy (D, Mass.)

Minor Committees

(no senator may serve on more than one)

Aging
    Chairman: Lawton Chiles (D, Fla.)
Indian Affairs
    Chairman: John Melcher (D, Mont.)
Intelligence
    Chairman: Birch Bayh (D, Ind.)
Rules and Administration
    Chairman: Claiborne Pell (D, R.I.)
Small Business
    Chairman: Gaylord Nelson (D, Wisc.)
Veterans' Affairs
    Chairman: Alan Cranston (D, Calif.)

Ethics Committee (not subject to limitations on membership)
    Chairman: Adlai E. Stevenson III (D, Ill.)

selection of chairmen. Of late, however, even seniority has been under attack. In 1973 House Democrats decided in their caucus to elect committee chairmen by secret ballot; two years later they used that procedure to remove three committee chairmen who had held their positions by virtue of seniority: Wright Patman (Tex.), Banking Committee; F. Edward Hebert (La.), Armed Services Committee; and W. R. Poage (Tex.), Agriculture Committee.

Traditionally, the committees of Congress were dominated by the chairmen. They often did their most important work behind closed doors (though their hearings and reports were almost always published in full). In the early 1970s Congress further decentralized and democratized its operations by a series of changes that some members regarded as a "bill of rights" for representatives and senators, especially those with relatively little seniority. These changes were by and large made by the Democratic Caucus, but since the Democrats were in the majority, the changes, in effect, became the rules of Congress. The more important were these:

House

- Committee chairmen to be elected by secret ballot in party caucus.
- No member to chair more than one committee or more than one legislative subcommittee.
- Each member to receive one major committee assignment.
- Each committee to have written rules.
- All committees with more than twenty members to have at least four subcommittees.
- Subcommittee chairmen and ranking minority members to be allowed to hire one staff person each to work for subcommittee.
- All committee and subcommittee sessions to be open to the public unless members, in open session, vote to close the meeting.
- Minority (i.e., Republican) members of committees to be guaranteed the right to call witnesses.

Senate

- All committee and subcommittee meetings to be open to the public unless members, in open session, vote to close meetings for an authorized reason (e.g., to consider national defense secrets).
- Committee chairmen to be elected by secret ballot at request of one-fifth of party caucus.
- Junior senators to receive staff assistance on their committees.
- No senator to chair more than one committee.

Some of these changes, such as those governing the choice of committee chairmen, had an immediate effect in only a few cases. Others, such as those requiring open meetings, had a substantial impact. Whereas 44 percent of all House committee meetings were closed to the public in 1972, only 3 percent were closed in 1975.[7] For a long time committee meetings in the Senate—but not in the House—could be covered by television. As we have seen, that difference gave senators an enormous advantage in acquiring personal publicity and furthering policy positions of interest to them. Since 1971 television coverage of House committee hearings has also been permitted. When television cameras appear, it is usually to obtain short film clips for nightly news broadcasts, but occasionally, as with the deliberations of the House Judiciary Committee on the proposed impeachment of President Nixon, it is to televise the meetings live and in their entirety.

Americans tend to favor openness, democracy, and bills of rights, and therefore the changes in committee procedure described above are likely to strike most readers as desirable. Before endorsing such an opinion, however, one should consider the possible effects of these changes on the behavior of members of Congress and on the kinds of laws they adopt. Since the changes were made rather recently, their effects are not yet clear, but there are several possibilities. We may witness greater public accountability—or more congressional grandstanding; more thorough consideration of proposed laws—

STANDING COMMITTEES IN THE HOUSE OF REPRESENTATIVES DURING THE 96th CONGRESS, 1979–1980

Agriculture
Chairman: Thomas S. Foley (D, Wash.)
Appropriations
Chairman: Jaimie L. Whitten (D, Miss.)
Armed Services
Chairman: Melvin Price (D, Ill.)
Banking, Finance, and Urban Affairs
Chairman: Henry S. Reuss (D, Wisc.)
Budget
Chairman: Robert N. Giaimo (D, Conn.)
District of Columbia
Chairman: Ronald V. Dellums (D, Calif.)
Education and Labor
Chairman: Carl D. Perkins (D, Ky.)
Government Operations
Chairman: Jack Brooks (D, Tex.)
House Administration
Chairman: Frank Thompson, Jr. (D, N.J.)
Interior and Insular Affairs
Chairman: Morris K. Udall (D, Ariz.)
International Relations
Chairman: Clement J. Zablokci (D, Wisc.)
Interstate and Foreign Commerce
Chairman: Harley O. Staggers (D, W. Va.)
Judiciary
Chairman: Peter W. Rodino (D, N.J.)
Merchant Marine and Fisheries
Chairman: John M. Murphy (D, N.Y.)
Post Office and Civil Service
Chairman: James M. Hanley (D, N.Y.)
Public Works and Transportation
Chairman: Harold T. Johnson (D, Calif.)
Rules
Chairman: Richard Bolling (D, Mo.)
Science and Technology
Chairman: Don Fuqua (D, Fla.)
Small Business
Chairman: Neal Smith (D, Iowa)
Standards of Official Conduct
Chairman: Charles F. Bennett (D, Fla.)
Veterans' Affairs
Chairman: Ray Roberts (D, Tex.)
Ways and Means
Chairman: Al Ullman (D. Ore.)

Note: There are in addition five select committees—on aging, intelligence, narcotics abuse, the outer continental shelf, and the committee system.

Congressmen at work: Representative Jack Kemp (R, N.Y.) meets with members of his state's Republican party (top), and Representative Romano Mazzoli (D, Ky) watches his office computer.

or more obstructionism and delay. We may discern more power for rank-and-file members of Congress—or more power for lobbyists and reporters who attend the meetings; more public respect for Congress—or more public dismay at congressional confusion and delay. Only time, and some careful study, will tell.

No matter what rules they operate under, many key committees have, because of their membership or leadership, a distinctive political coloration that must be recognized if one is to understand why Congress acts as it does. For example, bills pertaining to civil rights and courts often got a very different reception from the Senate Judiciary Committee when it was chaired by James Eastland of Mississippi, a staunch conservative, than they did from the House Judiciary Committee, chaired by Peter Rodino of New Jersey, a liberal. When Eastland retired in 1978, however, Edward M. Kennedy of Massachusetts, a liberal, became the new chairman of the Senate Judiciary Committee. Should Rodino retire, the next in line for chairman of the House Judiciary Committee would be the more conservative Jack Brooks of Texas.

Not only are the political colorations of congressional committees different, so also are their functions and operating styles. Richard F. Fenno looked closely at six House and six Senate committees and found them to differ in subtle but important ways. Some, such as the House Appropriations and Ways and Means committees and the Senate Foreign Relations and Human Relations committees, were attractive to members who wanted to influence public policy, who liked to become experts on important issues, and who valued having influence with their colleagues in Congress. Others, such as the House Interior and Insular Affairs Committee, the House Post Office and Civil Service committees, and the Senate counterparts of those committees, were attractive to members who valued an opportunity to serve constituency groups and who worried more about solidifying their reelection prospects than about having influence with their congressional colleagues. Work on the first kind of committee—the Congress-oriented, policy-oriented type—does in fact give members more prestige and influence in Congress than work on the second kind, those that focus on external, constituency concerns. The committee to which he or she is assigned, thus, importantly determines what kind of role a representative or senator will play.[8]

THE ORGANIZATION OF CONGRESS: STAFFS AND SPECIALIZED OFFICES

At one time representatives and senators worked alone, unaided by assistants. Today Congress employs a large and rapidly growing bureaucracy. In 1976 over eighteen thousand persons worked for Congress, three times as many as worked for it only twenty years earlier. Some of these employees perform only clerical or housekeeping functions, but a growing number are professional persons who play a key role in shaping legislation, drafting bills, handling constituents, and maintaining the congressmen's political bases. In 1975 the average senator employed thirty-one persons. Some senators from the larger states had as many as seventy employees. Representatives typically had smaller, but still significant, staffs averaging, in 1977, about sixteen persons. This did not include staffs assigned to committees and subcommittees.

Tasks of Staff Members
Most of the time of staff members assigned to a senator or representative is spent servicing requests from constituents—answering mail, handling problems, sending out newsletters, and meeting with voters. In short, a major function of a congressman's staff is to help constituents solve problems and thereby help the congressman get reelected. Indeed, over the last two dec-

"A major function of a congressman's staff is to help constituents solve problems and thereby help the congressman get reelected."

These are staff workers in Senator Edward M. Kennedy's office in Washington.

ades, a larger and larger portion of congressional staffs have worked in the local (district or state) office of the congressman, rather than in Washington.[9] Almost all congressmen have such offices on a full-time basis; about half maintain two or more offices in their constituencies. Some scholars believe that this growth in constituency-serving staff helps explain why it is so hard to defeat an incumbent representative or senator.[10]

The legislative function of congressional staff members is also important. With each senator serving on an average of more than two committees and eleven subcommittees and each representative serving on an average of six com-

mittees and subcommittees, it is virtually impossible for congressmen to become familiar in
detail with all the proposals that come before
them or to write all the bills they feel ought to be
introduced.[11] As the workload of Congress has
grown (over 20,000 bills are introduced, 600 to
800 public laws are passed, and uncounted hearings and meetings are held during a typical Congress), the role of staff members in devising
proposals, negotiating agreements, organizing
hearings, writing questions for congressmen to
ask of witnesses, drafting reports, and meeting
with lobbyists and administrators has grown
correspondingly.

The orientation of committee staff members
differs. Some think of themselves as—and to a
substantial degree are—politically neutral professional persons. They see their jobs as assisting
the members of a committee, Democrats or
Republicans, to hold hearings or revise bills.
Others see themselves as partisan advocates, interested in promoting Democratic or Republican
causes depending on who hired them and what
their ambitions may be. (Some committee staff
members are appointed to important positions in
the executive branch or on regulatory commissions.)

Those who work for individual congressmen,
as opposed to committees, see themselves entirely
as advocates for their bosses. As the mass media
have supplanted political parties as ways of
communicating with voters, the advocacy role of
staff members has led them to find and promote
legislation for which a representative or senator
can take advantageous credit. This is the entrepreneurial function of the staff. While it is sometimes performed under the close supervision of
the congressman, just as often a staff member
takes the initiative, finds a policy, and then
"sells" it to his employer. Lobbyists and reporters
understand this completely and, therefore, spend
a lot of time cultivating congressional staffers,
both as sources of information and as consumers
of ideas.

One reason for the rapid growth in the size
and importance of congressional staffs is that a
large staff creates conditions that seem to require
an even larger staff. As the staff grows in size, it
generates more legislative work. Subcommittees
proliferate to handle all the issues with which
congressmen are concerned. But as the workload
increases, congressmen complain they cannot
keep up and need more help. Resolutions are
passed authorizing more staff for congressmen
and for committees. This larger staff, naturally,
produces even more proposals, circulates more
paper work, and calls for more hearings. Thus,
the staff is increased again to "keep up."

The impact of staffers on policy-making has
not been studied. Perhaps staffers do only what
congressmen would do if they had unlimited
time and expertise, but that seems improbable. It
is more likely that staffers impart, to a degree,
their own preferences to the content of legislation, but it is not clear what those preferences are
or what issues they chiefly affect.

Staff Agencies

In addition to increasing the number of staff
members, Congress has also created a set of staff
agencies that work for Congress as a whole.
These have come into being in large part to give
Congress specialized knowledge equivalent to
what the president has by virtue of his position as
chief of the executive branch of government.

Congressional Research Service (CRS). Formerly
the Legislative Reference Service, the CRS is
part of the Library of Congress. Since 1914 it has
responded to congressional requests for information and now employs nearly nine hundred persons, many with advanced academic training, to
respond to more than a quarter of a million
questions each year. As a politically neutral body
it does not recommend policy, but it will look up
facts and indicate the arguments for and against
a proposed policy. CRS also keeps track of the
status of every major bill before Congress and

produces a summary of each bill introduced. This information is instantly available to congressmen via computer terminals located in almost all Senate and most House offices. Because of its heavy workload and its need to be nonpartisan, CRS can rarely produce studies that have an important effect on the shaping of policy.

General Accounting Office (GAO). Created in 1921, this agency once performed primarily routine financial audits of the money spent by executive branch departments. Today it also investigates agencies and policies and makes recommendations on almost every aspect of government—defense contracting, drug enforcement policies, the domestic security investigations of the FBI, Medicare and Medicaid programs, water pollution programs, and so forth. Though the head of the GAO—the comptroller general—is appointed by the president (with the consent of the Senate), he serves for a fifteen-year term and is very much the servant of Congress rather than the president. The GAO employs nearly five thousand persons, many of whom are permanently assigned to work with various congressional committees.

Office of Technology Assessment (OTA). Established in 1972 to study and evaluate policies and programs with a significant use of or impact on technology, it has a staff of more than one hundred. Staff members look into matters as a plan to build a pipeline to transport coal slurry. A new agency, it as yet has had little impact.

Congressional Budget Office (CBO). Created in 1974, the CBO advises Congress on the likely economic effect of different spending programs and provides information on the cost of proposed policies. The latter task—estimating the cost of a new policy—has probably been more useful to Congress than the more ambitious and speculative job of guessing at the overall economic impact of the federal budget.

HOW A BILL BECOMES LAW

Some bills zip through Congress; others make their way slowly and painfully. Congress is like a crowd, moving either sluggishly or, when excited, with great speed. In 1977 a major bill outlawing the mandatory retirement of persons before the age of seventy was reported out of the House Committee on Education and Labor on July 25. It was passed (359 to 4) by the full House on September 23, reported out of the Senate Human Resources Committee two weeks later, and passed (88 to 7) by the full Senate one week after that. After a conference committee ironed out differences between the House and Senate versions, the final bill was passed within two weeks. All this happened despite intense protests by business groups and universities that the law was harmful and undesirable.

By contrast, after President Carter proposed an energy policy on April 29, 1977, eighteen months of the most complex political maneuvering were spent before a much-amended, barely recognizable version of the Carter program was obtained from Congress. And all along the way there were close votes and intense bargaining. What made the difference? In the case of the retirement bill, "helping old folks" seems to have been irresistibly appealing to almost all congressmen. The bill embodied a simple idea and, right or wrong, it elicited a sympathetic reaction. In addition, the groups that opposed it had difficulty showing just how they would be hurt. Adopting an energy policy, on the other hand, involved complex questions, pitted one interest (such as gas-producing states) against another (such as gas-consuming ones), and stimulated a major ideological debate on the facts and philosophy of energy management. When such conflicts appear, congressional rules and procedures provide ample opportunities for opponents to resist or block action.

The principal stages a bill passes through on

HOW A BILL BECOMES LAW

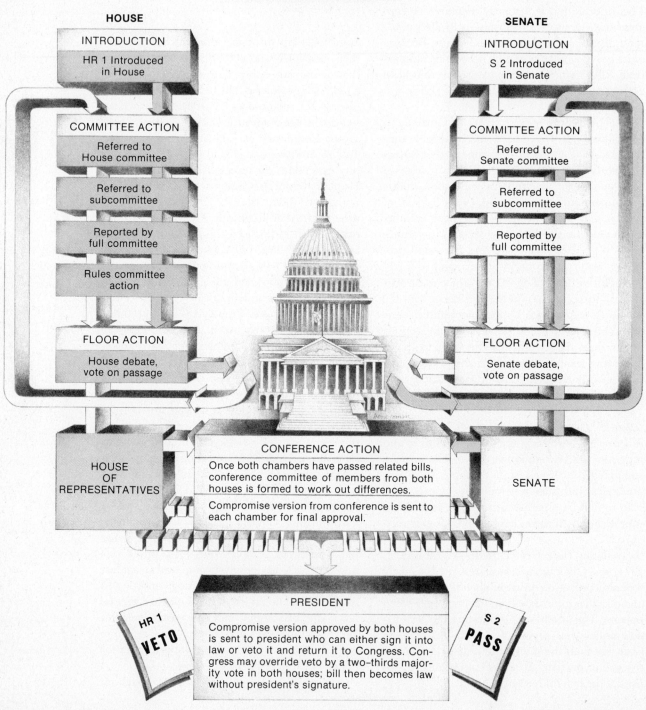

HOUSE

INTRODUCTION

HR 1 Introduced
in House

COMMITTEE ACTION

Referred to
House committee

Referred to
subcommittee

Reported by
full committee

Rules committee
action

FLOOR ACTION

House debate,
vote on passage

HOUSE
OF
REPRESENTATIVES

SENATE

INTRODUCTION

S 2 Introduced
in Senate

COMMITTEE ACTION

Referred to
Senate committee

Referred to
subcommittee

Reported by
full committee

FLOOR ACTION

Senate debate,
vote on passage

SENATE

CONFERENCE ACTION

Once both chambers have passed related bills,
conference committee of members from both
houses is formed to work out differences.

Compromise version from conference is sent to
each chamber for final approval.

HR 1
VETO

S 2
PASS

PRESIDENT

Compromise version approved by both houses
is sent to president who can either sign it into
law or veto it and return it to Congress. Congress may override veto by a two-thirds majority vote in both houses; bill then becomes law
without president's signature.

its way to becoming a law are shown in the accompanying chart. The rules governing each step in the House and the Senate differ and in some cases are quite complex. A simplified version of this process follows, with those rules especially noted that may importantly affect its outcome. Many of the technical terms are defined in a glossary at the end of this book.

Introducing a Bill

Any member of Congress may introduce a bill: in the House, simply by handing it to a clerk or dropping it in a box (the "hopper"); in the Senate, by being recognized by the presiding officer and announcing the bill's introduction. Bills are numbered and sent to the printer: a House bill bears the prefix HR, a Senate bill the prefix S. A bill can be either "public" (pertaining to affairs generally) or "private" (pertaining to a particular individual, such as a person pressing a financial claim against the government or seeking special permission to become a naturalized citizen). Once private bills were very numerous; today the matters addressed by many such bills have been delegated to administrative agencies or to the courts. If a bill is not passed by both houses and signed by the president within the life of one Congress, it is dead and must be reintroduced again during the next Congress. Pending legislation does not carry over from one Congress to the next.

We often hear that legislation is initiated by the president and enacted by Congress—the former proposes, the latter disposes. The reality is more complicated. Congress often initiates legislation—in fact, as we shall see in a later chapter, most of the consumer and environmental protection legislation passed since 1966 began in Congress, not in the executive branch. And even laws formally proposed by the president often represent presidential versions of proposals that have incubated in Congress. This was the case, for example, with some civil rights laws and with the proposal that eventually became Medicare.

Even when the president is the principal author of a bill, he usually submits it (if he is prudent) only after careful consultation with key congressional leaders. In any case, the president cannot himself introduce legislation; he must get a member of Congress to do it for him.

One study showed that of ninety major laws passed between 1880 and 1945, seventy-seven were introduced without presidential sponsorship. In shaping the final contents, congressional influence was dominant in thirty-five cases, presidential influence in nineteen, and influence was mixed in the remaining thirty-six.[12] Another study, covering the period 1940 to 1967, found that Congress was the major contributor to the contents of the laws passed in about half the cases.[13]

In addition to bills, Congress can pass resolutions. *Simple* resolutions (passed by either the House or the Senate) are used for such matters as establishing the rules under which each body will operate. *Concurrent* resolutions settle housekeeping and procedural matters that affect both houses. Simple and concurrent resolutions are not signed by the president and do not have the force of law. A *joint* resolution requires approval by both houses and the signature of the president; it is essentially the same as a law. A joint resolution is also used to propose a constitutional amendment. In this case it must be approved by a two-thirds vote of each house, but it does not require the signature of the president.

Study by Committees

A bill is referred to a committee for consideration by either the Speaker of the House or the presiding officer of the Senate. Rules govern which committee will get which bill, but sometimes a choice is possible; in the House the right of the Speaker to make such choices is an important component of his power. (His decisions can be appealed to the full House.) In 1963 a civil rights bill was referred by the presiding officer of the Senate to the Commerce Committee in order to

95TH CONGRESS
2D SESSION

H. R. 13931

IN THE HOUSE OF REPRESENTATIVES

AUGUST 17, 1978

Mr. MEEDS (for himself, Mr. ULLMAN, Mr. FOLEY, Mr. DUNCAN of Oregon, Mr. DICKS, Mr. MCCORMACK, Mr. CUNNINGHAM, Mr. HANSEN, and Mr. SYMMS), introduced the following bill; which was referred jointly to the Committees on Interior and Insular Affairs and Interstate and Foreign Commerce

A BILL

To assist the electrical consumers of the Pacific Northwest through use of the Federal Columbia River power system to achieve cost-effective energy conservation, to encourage the development of renewable energy resources, to establish a representative regional power planning process, to assure the region of an efficient and adequate power supply, and for other purposes.

Be it enacted by the Senate and House of Representa-

JOHN BRADEMAS
INDIANA
MAJORITY WHIP

CHIEF DEPUTY WHIP
DAN ROSTENKOWSKI
ILLINOIS
DEPUTY WHIPS
BENJAMIN S. ROSENTHAL
NEW YORK
BILL ALEXANDER
ARKANSAS
GEORGE E. DANIELSON
CALIFORNIA

Congress of the United States
House of Representatives
Office of the Majority Whip
Washington, D.C. 20515

225-5604

WHIP NOTICE INFORMATION
Legislative Program — 51600
Floor Information — 57400
Whip Information — 55606

My dear Colleague:

The program for the House of Representatives for the week of July 23, 1979, is as follows:

MONDAY
July 23

HOUSE MEETS AT NOON
District (No Bills)
Suspensions (6 Bills)

(ALL RECORDED VOTES WILL BE POSTPONED UNTIL TUESDAY, JULY 24, 1979)

1. S. 41 — Release of Contingent Interest in Land Owned by Bell County, Ky.
2. H.R. 3777 — To Incorporate into Law Provisions Concerning Congressional Use of Frank Mail
3. H.R. 3528 — Increase Coast Guard Enforcement of Laws on Importation of Controlled Substances and Other Items
4. H.R. 4591 — Technical Corrections to Education Amendments of 1978
5. H.R. 3807 — Codify Recent Law to U.S.C. Title 49
6. H.R. 4453 — Saccharin Extension

GENERAL DEBATE ONLY ON FOLLOWING BILLS (RULES ALREADY ADOPTED):

H.R. 4440 — Transporation Appropriations, FY'80
H.R. 4034 — Export Administration Act Amendments of 1979
H.R. 3633 — Nurses Training Amendments
H.R. 4040 — DOD FY'80 Authorizations

TUESDAY and the BALANCE OF THE WEEK
July 24, 25, 26, and 27

HOUSE MEETS AT 10 a.m.

H.J. Res. 74 — Constitutional Amendment to Prohibit School Busing

RECORDED VOTES ON SUSPENSION BILLS DEBATED MONDAY, JULY 23, 1979

H.R. 3996 — Amtrak Reorganization Act of 1979 (OPEN RULE, ONE HOUR)
S. 1030 — Gas Rationing Authority and Conservation (SUBJECT TO A RULE BEING GRANTED)
H.R. 3000 — DOE Authorizations, FY'80 (OPEN RULE, ONE AND ONE-HALF HOURS)
H.R. 3180 — DOE Authorizations, FY'79 (OPEN RULE, ONE HOUR)
H.R. 3920 — Unemployment Compensation Commission (RULE ALREADY ADOPTED)
H.R. 2462 — Maritime Authorizations, FY'80 (COMPLETE CONSIDERATION)
H.R. 3236 — Disability Insurance Amendments of 1979 (MODIFIED RULE, ONE HOUR)
H.R. 4473 — Foreign Assistance Appropriations, FY'80 (COMPLETE CONSIDERATION)

Shown above is a bill (H.R. 13931) as it looks after being introduced in the House. The Whip Notice informs party members (here, the Democrats) on matters scheduled for a vote.

keep it out of the hands of the chairman of the Judiciary Committee who was hostile to the bill. In the House the same piece of legislation was referred by the Speaker to the Judiciary Committee in order to keep it out of the grasp of the hostile chairman of the Interstate and Foreign Commerce Committee.

The Constitution requires that "all bills for raising revenue shall originate in the House of Representatives." The Senate can and does amend such bills, but only after the House has first acted. Bills that are not for raising revenue—that is, bills that do not change the tax laws—can originate in either house. In practice, the House originates appropriations bills as well. Because of the House's special position on revenue legislation, the committee that handles those bills—the Ways and Means Committee—is particularly powerful.

Most bills die in committee. They are often introduced only to get publicity for the congressman or to enable him to say to a constituent or pressure group that he "did something" on a matter concerning them. Bills of general interest—many of which will have been drafted in the executive branch even though introduced by a congressman—are assigned to a subcommittee for a hearing where witnesses appear, evidence is taken, and questions are asked. These hearings are used to inform congressmen, to permit interest groups to speak out (whether or not they have anything helpful to say), and to build public support for a measure favored by the majority on the committee.

Though committee hearings are necessary and valuable, they also fragment the process of considering bills dealing with complex matters. Both power and information are dispersed in Congress and thus it is difficult to take a comprehensive view of matters cutting across committee boundaries. When President Carter's energy plan went before Congress in 1977, this complex set of proposals was broken up into small sections for the consideration of the various committees that had jurisdiction.

Proposal	House Committee
Energy conservation plan for existing buildings	Commerce
Financial aid to home-owners for conservation	Banking
Federal pooling programs	Government Operations
Solar heating demonstrations	Public Works
Tax provisions for energy	Ways and Means
Economic effects of plan	Budget

To try to pull all these hearings and opinions together, the Speaker created an Ad Hoc Energy Committee. It was composed of leading members of the six committees listed above, and it managed to produce a more or less unified bill. After the House passed the bill, the process had to begin all over again in the Senate. Here six more committees—Finance, Energy and Natural Resources, Banking, Judiciary, Commerce, and Joint Economic—held hearings. In addition, staff studies were carried out by the Governmental Affairs Committee, the Congressional Budget Office, and the Office of Technology Assessment. Eighteen months after the president made his proposal, five bills embodying a much-revised version of his plan were passed and became law.

After the hearings the committee or subcommittee will "mark up" the bill—that is, make revisions and additions, some of which are extensive. These changes do not become part of the bill unless they are approved by the house of which the committee is a part. If a majority of the committee votes to report a bill out to the House or Senate, it goes forward. It is accompanied by a report that explains why the committee favors the bill and why it wishes to see its amendments, if any, adopted. Committee members who oppose the bill have an opportunity to include their dissenting opinions in the report.

"Both power and information are dispersed in Congress and thus it is difficult to take a comprehensive view of matters cutting across committee boundaries.**"**

If the committee does not report the bill out favorably, that ordinarily kills it. There is a procedure whereby the full House or Senate can get a bill that is stalled in committee out and onto the floor, but it is rarely used. In the House a "discharge petition" must be signed by 218 members; if the petition is approved by a vote of the House, the bill comes before it directly. In the Senate a member can move to discharge a committee of any bill and, if the motion passes, the bill comes before the Senate. During this century there have been over eight hundred efforts in the House to use discharge petitions; only two dozen have succeeded. Discharge is rarely tried in the Senate, in part because the opportunity for a filibuster virtually assures that any bill bottled up in committee can also be blocked on the floor.

For a bill to come before either house, it must first be placed on a calendar. There are five of these in the House and two in the Senate.

Though the bill goes onto a calendar, it is not necessarily considered in chronological order or even considered at all. In the House the Rules Committee reviews major bills and adopts a rule that governs the procedures under which they will be considered by the House. A "closed rule" sets a strict time limit on debate and forbids the introduction of any amendments from the floor, or forbids amendments except those offered by the sponsoring committee. Obviously, such a rule can make it very difficult for opponents to do anything but vote "yes" or "no" on the measure. An "open rule" permits amendments from the floor. Most routine bills do not go through the Rules Committee. But when a bill does come before it, the Committee can go so far as to block any House consideration of a measure at all, as it did in the early 1960s when it prevented civil rights bills from coming to the floor. Also, the Rules Committee can bargain with the legislative

Congressional Calendars

HOUSE

Union Calendar
Bills to raise revenue or spend money
Example: an appropriations bill

House Calendar
Nonmoney bills of major importance
Example: a civil rights bill

Private Calendar
Private bills
Example: a bill to waive the immigration laws so that a Philadelphia woman could be joined by her Greek husband

Consent Calendar
Noncontroversial bills
Example: a resolution creating National Stenographers' Week

Discharge Calendar
Discharge petitions

SENATE

Executive Calendar
Presidential nominations, proposed treaties

Calendar of Business
All legislation

NINETY-SIXTH CONGRESS

FIRST SESSION { CONVENED JANUARY 15, 1979
SECOND SESSION {

CALENDARS
OF THE UNITED STATES
HOUSE OF REPRESENTATIVES
AND
HISTORY OF LEGISLATION

LEGISLATIVE DAY 56   CALENDAR DAY 56

Monday, May 14, 1979

DISTRICT OF COLUMBIA—DISCHARGE CALENDAR—SUSPENSIONS

HOUSE MEETS AT 12 M.

SPECIAL ORDERS

---

committee, offering a helpful rule in exchange for alterations in the substance of the bill.

The Rules Committee is powerful but no longer as independent as it once was. It tends today to be dominated by the Speaker and the Democratic Caucus. But no matter who controls it, there is a need for some such "traffic cop." The House has 435 members, and without some limitations on debate and amendment nothing would ever get done. The House has at least three ways of bypassing the Rules Committee: (1) a member can move that the rules be suspended: this requires a two-thirds vote; (2) a discharge petition, as explained above, can be filed; or (3) the House can use the "Calendar Wednesday" procedure.* These methods are not used very often, but they are available if the Rules Committee departs too far from the sentiments of the House.

No such barriers to floor consideration exist in the Senate. There, bills may be considered in any order at any time whenever a majority of the Senate chooses. In practice, the majority leader in consultation with the minority leader schedules bills for consideration.

Floor Debate—The House
Once on the floor, the bills are debated. In the House all revenue and most other bills are discussed by the "Committee of the Whole," which is nothing more than whoever happens to be on the floor at the time. The quorum for the Committee of the Whole is only 100 members and thus easier to assemble than a quorum for the House itself, which the Constitution specifies as a majority, or 218 members. The Speaker does not preside but chooses another person to wield the gavel. The Committee of the Whole debates, amends, and generally decides the final shape of

---

*On Wednesdays the list of committees of the House is called more or less in alphabetical order and any committee can bring up for action a bill of its own already on a calendar. Action on a bill brought to the floor on Calendar Wednesday must be completed that day or the bill goes back to committee. Since major bills rarely can be voted on in one day, this procedure is not often used.

the bill, but technically cannot pass it. To do that, the Committee of the Whole reports the bill back to the House (that is, to itself!), which takes final action. During the debate in the Committee of the Whole, the committee sponsoring the bill guides the discussion, divides the time equally between proponents and opponents, and decides how long each member will be allowed to speak. If amendments are allowed under the rule, they must be germane to the purpose of the bill—extraneous matters ("riders") are not allowed—and no one may speak for more than five minutes on an amendment. During this process persons wishing to take time out to huddle about strategy or to delay action can demand a quorum call—a calling of the roll to find out if the necessary minimum number of members is present. If a quorum is not present, the House must either adjourn or dispatch the sergeant-at-arms to round up missing members. The sponsoring committee almost always wins: its bill, as amended by it, usually is the version the House passes.

Floor Debate—The Senate

Things are a good deal more casual in the Senate. Short of cloture (to be discussed below), there is no rule limiting debate, and any member can speak for as long as he can stay on his feet. A senator's remarks need not be relevant to the matter under consideration (some senators have read aloud from the Washington telephone directory), and anyone can offer an amendment at any time. There is no Committee of the Whole. Amendments need not be germane to the purposes of the bill, and thus the Senate often attaches "riders" to bills. In fact, the opportunity to offer nongermane amendments gives a senator a chance to get a bill onto the floor without regard to the calendar or the schedule of the majority leader—he or she need only offer a pet bill as an "amendment" to a bill already under discussion. (This cannot be done to an appropriations bill.) Indeed, the entire committee hearing process can be bypassed in the Senate if the House has already passed the bill. In that

---

"CHRISTMAS TREES":
Almost Anything Can Be Put Into a Senate Bill

The rule permitting the offering of nongermane amendments in the Senate can be used for a variety of purposes, good and bad, funny and serious.

In 1965 Senator Everett Dirksen of Illinois tried to add a constitutional amendment on reapportionment, an enormously important issue, to a joint resolution then before the Senate that would have created "National American Legion Baseball Month."

In 1966 the Foreign Investors Act, designed to help solve the balance of payments problem, had added to it amendments to give assistance to importers of scotch whiskey, hearse owners, the mineral ore business, and presidential candidates. Senator Russell Long of Louisiana, who floor-managed the bill, later referred to it, with pride, as his "Christmas Tree" bill, a name that has since been applied to all such bills.

In 1978 the "Christmas Tree" bill was one extending the life of the Export-Import Bank. Added to it were amendments to construct a dam on the Mississippi River, exclude textiles from tariff reduction talks, and set environmental requirements on nuclear energy.

---

case, a senator can get the House-passed measure put directly onto the Senate calendar without committee action. In 1957 and again in 1964 this was done with House-passed civil rights bills to make certain they would not be bottled up in the conservative Senate Judiciary Committee.

A Senate filibuster is difficult to break. The current cloture rule requires that sixteen senators sign a petition to move cloture. The motion is voted on two days after the petition is introduced; to pass, three-fifths of the entire Senate membership (sixty senators if there are no vacancies) must vote for it. If it passes, each senator is thereafter limited to one hour of debate on the bill under consideration. The total amount of debate, including roll calls and the introduction of amendments, cannot exceed 100 hours. From the first opportunity for invoking cloture in 1917 to the end of 1976, there have been 127 attempts to impose it; of these, only 38 were successful. Conservatives have used the filibuster to try to block civil rights laws; liberals have used it to try to block funds for the supersonic transport. Since both factions have found the filibuster useful, it seems most unlikely that it will ever be abolished or even sharply curtailed. Furthermore, some filibusters can be broken without invoking cloture—if only a few senators are filibustering, and if the Senate is willing to stay in session around the clock (with members napping on cots dragged into the cloak room), the filibusterers can sometimes be worn down to the point where they quit.

One rule is common to both houses: courtesy, often of the most exquisite nature, is required at all times. Members always refer to each other as "distinguished" even if they are mortal political enemies. Personal or ad hominem criticism is not tolerated, and there have been only a few cases of members taking a punch at each other, and most of those occurred in the nineteenth century.

The electronic voting system in the House of Representatives displays each member's name on the wall of the chamber. By inserting a plastic card in a box fastened to the chairs, a member can vote "Yea," "Nay," or "Present," and the result is shown opposite his or her name.

Methods of Voting

There are several methods of voting in Congress. They can be applied to amendments to a bill as well as to the question of final passage. Some observers of Congress make the mistake of deciding who was for and who against a bill by the final vote. This can be misleading—often, a congressman will vote for final passage of a bill after having supported amendments which, if they had passed, would have made the bill totally different. To keep track of a congressman's voting record, therefore, it is often more important to know how he voted on key amendments than how he voted on the bill itself.

Finding that out is not always easy, though it has become more so in recent years. There are four procedures for voting in the House. A *voice vote* consists of the members shouting "aye" or "no"; a *division* (or standing) *vote* involves the members standing and being counted. In neither a voice nor a standing vote are the names of persons recorded as having voted one way or another. To learn how an individual votes, there must either be a recorded *teller vote* or a *roll call.* In a teller vote, the members pass between two tellers, the ayes first and then the nays. Since 1971 a teller vote can be "recorded," which means that, at the request of twenty members, clerks write down the names of persons favoring or opposing a bill as they pass by the tellers. Since teller votes but not roll calls may be taken in the Committee of the Whole, the use of a recorded teller vote enables observers to find out how members voted in those important deliberations. A roll-call vote, of course, consists of persons answering aye or nay to their names. It can be done at the request of one-fifth of the representatives present in the House. When roll calls were done orally, it was a time-consuming process since the clerk had to drone through 435 names. Since 1973 an electronic voting system has been in operation that permits each member, by inserting a plastic card into a slot, to record his or her own vote and to learn the total automatically. Owing to the use of recorded teller votes and the advent of electronic roll-call votes, the

HOUSE-SENATE DIFFERENCES: A SUMMARY

House	Senate
Bills are introduced into the "hopper."	Bills may be introduced from the floor.
Speaker referral of bills to committee is hard to challenge.	Referral decisions may be appealed.
Speaker can create ad hoc panels to consider legislation.	No ad hoc panels may be created.
Committees almost always consider legislation first.	Committee consideration can easily be bypassed.
Rules Committee powerful; controls time of debate, admissibility of amendments.	Rules Committee weak; limits on debate and amendments controlled by full Senate.
Nongermane amendments may not be introduced on floor.	Nongermane amendments may be introduced.
Debate usually limited to one hour.	Debate usually unlimited unless shortened by unanimous consent or invoking of cloture.
Scheduling and rules tend to be controlled by majority party.	Scheduling and rules tend to be mutually agreed to by majority and minority leaders.
Uses teller votes, as well as voice, standing, and roll-call votes.	Does not use teller votes.

number of recorded votes has gone up sharply in the House—there were only 180 roll calls in the 86th Congress (1959–1961) but 810 in the 94th (1975–1977). Voting in the Senate is much the same, only simpler: there is no such thing as a teller vote, and no electronic counters are used.

If a bill passes the House and Senate in different forms, the differences must be reconciled if the bill is to become law. If they are minor, the last house to act may simply refer the bill back to the other house which then accepts the alterations. If the differences are major, it is often necessary to appoint a conference committee to iron them out. Only a minority of the bills requires a conference. Each house must vote to form such a committee. The members are picked by the chairmen of the House and Senate standing committees that have been handling the legislation, with representation given to the minority as well as the majority party. There are usually between three and fifteen members from each house. No decision can be made unless approved by a majority of *each* delegation.

Bargaining is long and hard; in the past it was also secret. Now, some conference sessions are open to the public. Often—as with President Carter's energy bill—the legislation is substantially rewritten in conference. Theoretically, the conferees are not supposed to change anything already agreed to by both the House and Senate, but in the inevitable give-and-take even matters already approved may be changed.

In most cases the conference reports tend to favor, slightly, the Senate version of the bill. Several studies have suggested that the Senate wins in from 57 to 65 percent of the cases.[14] Whoever wins (and both sides always claim they got everything out of the bargaining they possibly could), conferees report their agreement back to their respective houses, which usually consider the report immediately. The report can be accepted or rejected; it cannot be amended. In the great majority of cases, it is accepted—the alternative is to have no bill at all, at least for that Congress. The bill, now in final form, goes to the president for signature or veto. If a veto is cast, the bill returns to the house of origin. There, an effort can be made to override the veto. This requires that two-thirds of those present (provided there is a quorum) must vote to override; this vote must be a roll call. If both houses override in this manner, the bill becomes law without the president's approval.

EXPLAINING HOW CONGRESSMEN VOTE

Voting on bills is not the only thing a congressman does, but it is among the more important and is probably the most visible. Since leaders in Congress are not nearly so powerful as those in a typical parliament, since political parties have been declining in influence, and since Congress has gone to great lengths to protect the independence and power of the individual member, it is by no means obvious what factors will lead a representative or senator to vote for or against a bill or amendment.

There are at least three kinds of explanations: representational, organizational, and attitudinal. A representational explanation is based on the reasonable assumption that members want to get reelected, and therefore they vote to please their constituents. The organizational explanation is based on the equally reasonable assumption that since most constituents do not know how their congressman has voted it is not essential to please them. However it *is* important to please fellow congressmen whose goodwill is valuable in getting things done and in acquiring status and power in Congress. The attitudinal explanation is based on the assumption that there are so many conflicting pressures on a congressman that they cancel one another out, leaving him virtually free to vote on the basis of his own beliefs.

Political scientists have studied, tested, and argued about these (and other) explanations of voting in Congress for decades, and nothing like a consensus has emerged. Some facts have emerged, however.

Representational View

The representational view has some merit under certain circumstances, namely, when constituents have a clear view on some issue and a congressman's vote on that issue is likely to attract their attention. Such is often the case on civil rights laws. For example, representatives with significant numbers of black voters in their districts are not likely to oppose civil rights bills; representatives with few blacks in their districts, or with blacks who were prevented from voting (as was the case in much of the South until the late 1960s), are comparatively free to oppose such bills. (Many representatives without black constituents supported civil rights bills, partly out of personal belief and partly, perhaps, because certain white groups in their districts—organized liberals, for example—insisted on such support.)

One study of congressional roll-call votes and constituency opinion showed the correlation between the two was quite strong on civil rights bills. There was also a positive (though not as strong) correlation between roll-call votes and constituency opinion on social welfare measures. There was scarcely any correlation, however, between votes and opinion on foreign policy measures.[15] Foreign policy is generally remote from the daily interests of most Americans and, as we shall see later, public opinion about such matters can change rapidly. It is not surprising, therefore, that congressional votes and constituent opinion should be different on such questions.

From time to time an issue arouses deep passions among the voters, and no congressman can escape the need either to vote as his constituents want, whatever his views, or to anguish at length about which side of a divided constituency to support. Gun control has been one such question, the ratification of the Panama Canal treaties another, and using federal money to pay for abortions a third. Some fortunate congressmen get unambiguous cues from their constituents on these matters, and no hard decision is necessary; others get conflicting views, and they know that whichever way they vote it may cost them dearly in the next election. Occasionally, congressmen in this fix will try to be out of town when the matter comes up for a vote. One careful study found that constituency influences were an important factor in Senate votes,[16] but no comparable study has been done for the House.

You might think that congressmen who won a close race in the last election—who come, in short, from a "marginal" district—will be especially eager to vote the way their constituents want. Research so far has not shown that is generally the case. There seem to be about as many independent-minded congressmen from marginal as from safe districts. Perhaps it is because in a marginal seat, opinion is so divided that there is no way one can please everybody. As a result, the representative votes on other grounds.

In general, the problem with the representational explanation is that public opinion is not strong and clear on most measures on which congressmen must vote. Many representatives and senators face constituencies that are divided on key issues. Some constituents go to special pains to make their views known; these are called interest groups and were discussed in Chapter 8. But as indicated there, the power of interest groups to affect congressional votes depends, among other things, on whether a congressman sees them as united and powerful in his or her district or as divided and unrepresentative.

This does not mean that constituents rarely have a direct influence on voting. The influence they have probably comes from the fact that a congressman risks defeat should he steadfastly vote in ways that can be held against him by a rival in the next election. Even though most congressional votes are not known to most citizens, blunders (real or alleged) quickly become known when an electoral opponent exploits them.

Still, any congressman can choose the positions he or she takes on most roll-call votes (and on all voice or standing votes, where names are not recorded). Furthermore, even a series of recorded votes that are against constituency opinion need not be fatal: a congressman can win

❝ When voting on matters where constituency interests or opinion are not vitally at stake, congressmen respond primarily to cues provided by their colleagues.**❞**

votes in other ways—for example, by doing services for constituents or by appealing to the party loyalty of the voters.

Organizational View

When voting on matters where constituency interests or opinion are not vitally at stake, congressmen respond primarily to cues provided by their colleagues. This is the organizational explanation of their votes. The principal cue is party; as already noted, what party a congressman belongs to explains more of his or her voting record than any other single factor. Additional organizational cues come from the opinions of colleagues with whom the congressman feels a close ideological affinity: for liberals in the House, it is the Democratic Study Group; for conservatives, it has often been the Republican Study Committee or the Wednesday Club. But party and other organizations do not have clear positions on all matters. For the scores of votes that do not involve the "big questions," a representative or senator is especially likely to be influenced by the members of his party on the sponsoring committee.

It is easy to understand why. Suppose you are a Democratic representative from Michigan who is summoned to the floor of the House to vote on a bill to authorize a new weapons system. You haven't the faintest idea what issues might be at stake. There is no obvious "liberal" or "conservative" position on this matter. How do you vote? Simple. You note that there are several Democrats on the House Armed Services Committee that handled the bill. Some are liberal (such as Les Aspin of Wisconsin), others are conservative (such as Sonny Montgomery of Mississippi). If Aspin and Montgomery both support the bill, you vote for it unhesitatingly. If Aspin and Montgomery disagree, you vote with whichever Democrat is generally closest to your own political ideology. If the matter is one that affects your state, and you know nothing about the measure, you can take your cue from other members of your state's delegation to Congress.

Attitudinal View

Finally, the congressman's personal beliefs affect his or her vote. We do not know exactly what those beliefs are before a roll-call vote is taken—congressmen, unlike the rest of us, are not regularly surveyed by public opinion pollsters. We usually cannot say, therefore, whether, at the time they are elected, representatives and senators are like or unlike most Americans in their attitudes. One such study, however, was done in 1970 (see Table 10.3). It revealed that on five important questions the opinion of members of the House of Representatives was quite similar to the opinion of the average citizen. On only one issue—a guaranteed annual income—were representatives of a substantially different view (they were more favorable than the public to this plan). Senators, on the other hand, had opinions quite different from those of the citizenry on all these questions—on each of the five the senators were much more liberal than the public.[17]

These differences may exist in part because senators are elected from states, most of which are large and diverse, thereby freeing many senators from the need to conform too closely to any given segment of opinion. But the fact that senators may be freer of sharply focused, homogeneous constituency pressure does not explain why they should tend to be more liberal: they could as easily depart from public opinion in a conservative direction, and of course some do. Why the Senate should have a liberal tilt is an interesting question to which no clear answer can be given; it is something about which the student might wish to speculate.

In any event, the fact that senators are more liberal, as individuals, than representatives helps explain why the Senate version of bills passing through Congress tends, on the average, to be somewhat more liberal than the House version.[18] This is not always the case. During the 1950s and early 1960s conservative southern Democrats in the Senate were able, by use of the filibuster, to block civil rights bills that the House had passed by substantial majorities. And even without the filibuster, a "conservative coalition" of southern Democrats and Republicans has often been able to block liberal legislation. In 1978, as in most years, a majority of southern Democrats voted together with a majority of Republicans and against a majority of northern Democrats on about one-fifth of the recorded votes in the House and Senate. This conservative coalition won on about half the issues in 1978 (and on somewhat more in earlier years). The power of this coalition has weakened over the last twenty or thirty years, however, owing to changes in the composition of the Democratic party. Since the

TABLE 10.3   Comparison of Public and Congressional Opinion on Key Policy Issues, 1970

	Public	U.S. House Members	U.S. Senators
1. *Vietnam:* Percent say "speed up our withdrawal"	27%	30%	45%
2. *Defense:* Percent say "place less emphasis" on military weapons programs	30	37	45
3. *Guaranteed Income:* Percent approve at least "$1,600 for a family of four or more"	48	65	76
4. *Civil Rights:* Percent say government should go farther to improve blacks' conditions	53	58	76
5. *Supreme Court:* Percent deny it gives "too much consideration to rights of people suspected of crimes"	29	36	56

Source: Robert S. Erikson and Norman G. Luttbeg, *American Public Opinion* (New York: John Wiley, 1973), p. 257. Reprinted by permission of John Wiley & Sons, Inc.

Note: Except for question 5, the questions asked the public sample and the congressmen were not exactly identical, although close enough to each other to allow rough comparison.

emergence of black voters in large numbers in the South, an increasing number of southern Democrats (and Republicans) are more liberal than once was usual, especially on race and related questions. The regional cleavage in the Democratic party is thus becoming less significant. In 1969, for example, southern Democrats in the House and Senate were on opposite sides of the fence on 36 percent of all roll-call votes. In 1978, however, they were opposed only 24 percent of the time.[19]

ETHICS AND CONGRESS

The Framers of the Constitution hoped that congressmen would be virtuous citizens, but they feared some would not. They had, as stated earlier, a rather sober view of human nature and designed the system of checks and balances in part to minimize the chance that anybody, by gaining corrupt influence over one part of the government, would be able to impose his will on the other parts. It could be argued that this very separation of powers made corruption more, rather than less, likely. If power were concentrated in one set of hands—say, those of a prime minister—nobody would have any incentive to bribe or even influence any other political figure; there is little that subordinate officials could do for that person. And though a favor-seeker might try to influence the prime minister, the latter would have so much power that he could command a price few could pay. When bits and pieces of power are placed in many different hands, as in the United States, there are many opportunities to exercise influence—many officials have something they could sell, and few can exact a high price.

For example, the appointive power is shared by the president and the Senate. Since the Senate will not confirm anybody for appointment to federal office who is personally obnoxious to either senator from the candidate's state (the rule of "senatorial courtesy"), the opportunity exists for an office-seeker to try to influence a senator to

get the desired appointment. The stage is also set for a senator, who may want the president to nominate a certain person, to delay some piece of presidential legislation until the nomination is made, or for the president to try to get a piece of legislation passed by offering to appoint the senator's campaign manager, brother-in-law, or law partner to a lucrative federal post.

Some of these attempts at influence may involve money, some may not. The point is that divided power means divided responsibility, and divided responsibility creates the possibility for evaded responsibility. It also creates the need to use influence to assemble enough power to get anything done. What the Constitution has separated, men and women must pull together; sometimes the pulling together involves mere persuasion, sometimes an exchange of favors, occasionally the payment of money.

Not only the Senate, or only Congress, is vulnerable to undue influence; such vulnerability is a characteristic of the government as a whole. During much of the nineteenth century and well into the twentieth, influence-peddling of all sorts—from favor-trading to money-giving—existed. In all likelihood the more base forms of influence-wielding are much less common today than once was the case. There are a number of reasons: citizens are better educated and have higher standards of proper official conduct; party bosses have lost power; and the mass media have a strong incentive to find and expose instances of improper influence and corruption.

But scandals do occur, and each stimulates a new wave of reform. In 1963 former Representative Thomas F. Johnson of Maryland was convicted of charges of conflict of interest—intervening in a pending criminal case in exchange for a large "campaign contribution." In 1967 Senator Thomas J. Dodd of Connecticut was found to have diverted campaign funds to his personal use. In 1971 Representative John Dowdy of Texas was convicted of taking a $25,000 bribe, a conviction later overturned by an appeals court. In 1972 Representative Cornelius E. Gallagher of New Jersey went to prison

"Koreagate": Tongsun Park, a Korean businessman, testifies before a House committee investigating charges of influence-buying by Korea among members of Congress.

for income-tax evasion. In 1974 Representative Frank J. Brasco of New York went to jail for bribery. In 1975 Representative Bertram L. Podell of New York was sentenced to prison for conflict of interest.

In 1976 former Representative John F. Hastings of New York was sentenced to prison for taking kickbacks from congressional employees, and in 1977 Representative Richard A. Tonry of Louisiana went to prison for violating federal election laws. In 1978 Representative Richard T. Hanna of California went to prison, having pleaded guilty to charges of fraud in dealing with South Korean businessman Tongsun Park, and Representative Charles C. Diggs, Jr., of Michigan was convicted of padding his office payroll and diverting the money to his own use. During the 95th Congress alone, thirteen members or former members of the House were indicted or convicted on criminal charges.[20]

These cases, mostly involving violations of the ordinary criminal laws, are easy to judge: the behavior is obviously wrong and requires only

detection and prosecution. Far harder to judge and to control are the opportunities congressmen have for taking advantage of their position in ways that are not clearly illegal but may be questionable. For example, what other sources of employment or income should congressmen have? What kinds of campaign contributions should they be allowed to accept? From whom should they be allowed to accept contributions? What kinds of trips at public expense are useful, and what kinds are self-serving "junkets"? For what purposes should offices and official stationery be used? A congressman may approach a government agency on behalf of a constituent regulated or benefited by that agency; when does that contact become the exercise of improper influence?

When Congress moved toward the impeachment of President Nixon, some charged that Congress imposed standards of conduct on a president that it was not clearly willing to see imposed on itself. When it was then learned that a South Korean, Tongsun Park, had apparently made lavish financial gifts to congressmen, entertained them at parties, and otherwise endeavored to generate a sympathetic hearing for his and his country's interests, it was clear Congress would have to act more boldly than it ever had before. "Koreagate" was about to replace "Watergate" as a national scandal.

In 1977 the House and Senate each passed a new code of ethics. They differed in some details (each house, under the Constitution, can set its own rules and punish its own members), but in broad outlines they were the same. Some key provisions were these:

- Each congressman must file a financial disclosure statement each year listing income, gifts, financial holdings, and certain other transactions.
- No congressman may accept a gift valued at more than $100 from any lobbyist or lobbying organization during any year.
- No representative may earn extra income in excess of 15 percent of his congressional salary

(this does not include "unearned income" from stocks and bonds). No senator may earn more than $25,000 in outside fees.

- No representative may charge more than $750 and no senator more than $2,000 for making a speech or writing an article.

Other laws had already restricted the amount of money any individual may contribute to a congressman's election campaign and how those funds are to be handled. (See Chapter 7.)

The ethics code was based on the assumption that improper influence is associated with financial transactions, yet obviously that is not always the case. Many congressmen who in the past earned substantial incomes from speaking and writing did not have their votes corrupted by such activities; other congressmen who rarely take such fees may be heavily influenced, perhaps unduly so, by personal friendships and political alliances that have no direct monetary value at all. And no ethics code can address the bargaining among congressmen, or between congressmen and the president, involving the exchange of favors and votes.

Moreover, the ethics rules seem to favor persons with inherited wealth or those who earned large sums before entering Congress at the expense of persons of modest means who might want to take advantage, while in Congress, of legitimate opportunities to give speeches for large fees. Former Representative Otis G. Pike of New York decided not to seek reelection in part because of the new financial rules. Pike, an attorney, complained to a reporter: "If I get a hundred thousand dollars a year sitting on my —— and collecting dividends, interest, rents, and royalties, I am ethical. If I work and earn [that], I am unethical. Our new no-work ethic makes no sense to me."[21]

It might not have made sense to the Framers, either. Their object was not to create a simon-pure Congress, but one that was powerful, that would be composed of representatives who (at least in the lower house) could be closely checked by the voters, and that would offer manifold

How to Look Up Facts About Congress

To find out how Congress is organized, staffed, and run:

Congressional Quarterly. *Guide to Congress*, rev. ed. Washington, D.C.: Congressional Quarterly, 1976. One volume that covers almost everything.

Congressional Directory (published annually by Congress). Lists of members of Congress, committee assignments, telephone numbers, maps of districts.

Congressional Staff Directory. Lists all staffers and gives biographical sketches.

To find out about the political inclinations and constituency characteristics of congressmen:

Michael Barone et al. *The Almanac of American Politics.* New York: E. P. Dutton, 1977. Revised every two years, this is a candid description of districts, states, members of Congress, and how they vote.

Congressional District Data Book. Published by the Census Bureau, it compiles all relevant census data by congressional district.

To find out what is going on in Congress currently:

Congressional Quarterly Weekly Report. A weekly summary of issues, votes, politics. Commercially published.

Congressional Record. The official, verbatim account of what is said (after being revised by congressmen who do the saying). Published daily by the Government Printing Office while Congress is in session.

To find out what Congress did in the past:

Congressional Quarterly Almanac. Published each year as a summary of issues, votes, and politics.

Congressional Quarterly. *Congress and the Nation*, 4 volumes, 1945–1976. Convenient compilation of past *Almanacs*.

To find out the exact wording of laws passed:

United States Statutes at Large. Published by the Government Printing Office; the laws and volumes are chronologically arranged.

opportunities for competing interests and opinions to check each other. Their goal was liberty more than morality, though they knew that in the long run the latter was essential to the former.

SUMMARY

Congress differs from a parliament in that it does not choose the nation's chief executive and it is composed of members who attach greater importance to representing local constituencies than to supporting a national party leadership. Power in the American Congress is fragmented, specialized, and decentralized. Most of the important decisions are made in committees and subcommittees. Though there have been periods—such as during the late nineteenth century—when party leaders in Congress were powerful, the general tendency, particularly in the last twenty years, has been to enhance the independence and influence of the individual members of Congress.

The great majority of representatives and senators are secure in their seats, a security that has been acquired chiefly by serving local constituency interests and by developing a personal following. The ability of political parties to determine who shall become a candidate for Congress has declined. As a result, votes in Congress are less likely to follow strict party lines than votes in most European parliaments. Nonetheless, party affiliation remains an important influence on the behavior of congressmen. In part this is because party loyalties in Congress correspond, to a degree, to the personal political ideologies of members of Congress. On the whole, Democrats are much more liberal than Republicans. Senators are more liberal than representatives. The opinions of representatives seem to be closer to the opinions of the voters than are the opinions of senators.

The organization and procedures of the House are tightly structured to facilitate action and orderly debate. The committees, therefore, tend to dominate decisions made on the House floor. Senate procedures, on the other hand, permit lengthy debate and many floor amendments, with the result that individual senators have as much or more influence than senate committees.

Congress does not simply respond to presidential proposals for action; it initiates some proposals on its own and influences the kinds of proposals a president will offer. In shaping the policies of Congress, congressional staffs have become important. Though most of their time is spent on serving the constituency interests of congressmen, the multiple committee assignments and heavy workload of members of Congress mean that staffers often acquire substantial influence.

Suggested Readings

Dodd, Lawrence C., and Bruce I. Oppenheimer, eds. *Congress Reconsidered.* New York: Praeger, 1977. Good collection of recent studies of congressional politics.

Fenno, Richard F., Jr. *Congressmen in Committees.* Boston: Little, Brown, 1973. Study of the goals and styles of twelve standing committees.

———. *The Power of the Purse.* Boston: Little, Brown, 1966. Careful analysis of the appropriations process in Congress.

Mayhew, David R. *Congress: The Electoral Connection.* New Haven, Conn.: Yale University Press, 1974. Analyzes how a congressman's desire to win reelection influences his legislative behavior.

Oleszek, Walter J. *Congressional Procedures and the Policy Process.* Washington, D.C.: Congressional Quarterly Press, 1978. Brief factual account of the organization and procedures of Congress.

Orfield, Gary. *Congressional Power: Congress and Social Change.* New York: Harcourt Brace Jovanovich, 1975. Studies the impact on policy-making of congressional reforms; argues that a "reformed" Congress is not necessarily a liberal one.

Ornstein, Norman, ed. *Congress in Change: Evolution and Reform.* New York: Praeger, 1975. Essays on how Congress has changed over the years.

Peabody, Robert L., and Nelson W. Polsby, eds. *New Perspectives on the House of Representatives,* 3rd ed. Chicago: Rand McNally, 1969. Collection of important studies of House politics.

Political Symbols and Popular Beliefs

A nation as diverse as the United States has had a special need for—and a special difficulty in creating—symbols of national unity. At the time of the Revolutionary War, a distinctive sense of American nationhood had not yet formed; instead, people thought of themselves as Virginians or New Yorkers. Though a sense of national identity began to emerge with the War of Independence and the ratification of the Constitution, even as late as the 1850s many writers still referred to the United States in the plural ("the United States are . . ."), thereby implying no common bond except a legal agreement.

The earliest popular political symbols were not of the nation itself, but of the great statesmen who led it. George Washington became so revered that after his death in 1799 an artist painted him being transported into heaven. Jefferson and Jackson, though bitterly controversial while alive, were glorified soon after their deaths. Citizens were loyal to the various states but were willing to honor those few national leaders who had helped pull the states together.

SACRED
to the Memory of
WASHINGTON
ob. 14 Dec. A.D. 1799
Ætat 68.

PLURIBUS
UNUM

With the passing of the Founders, it became hard to find popular leaders (except for Lincoln, and then only after his death) worth celebrating. But there were many who could be exploited. Trade cards, one of the first forms of national advertising, were often collected and exchanged. President Grover Cleveland and his wife appeared on one touting a brand of cotton thread.

Folk art turned to more abstract symbols that conveyed an emerging sense of nationalism. At first the nation was personified as "Columbia" (a feminine version of Christopher Columbus), sometimes called "Miss Liberty." The American bald eagle became the official national emblem in 1782 and rivaled

Baker Library, Harvard University

Becker Collection, Division of Political History, Smithsonian Institution

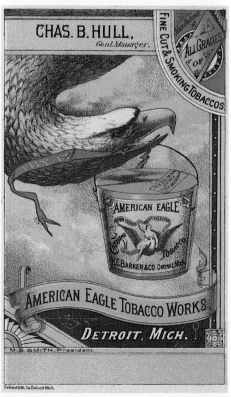

Baker Library, Harvard University

Miss Liberty as a popular symbol; here it is used to sell tobacco.

Both were eclipsed by Uncle Sam, a figure invented during the War of 1812 by troops who used the name to refer to meat casks stamped "U.S." and shipped to them by Sam Wilson. Uncle Sam—rough, unsophisticated, but smart and determined—became the cartoonists' symbol of the country. Thomas Nast drew him in his modern form, but James Montgomery Flagg provided the most memorable depiction in his famous World War I recruiting poster. The Statue of Liberty was erected in 1886, and Uncle Sam shared his popularity with this national image.

I WANT YOU
FOR U.S. ARMY
NEAREST RECRUITING STATION

During the Civil War Lincoln began referring to the country as a nation, and soon books began appearing that attempted to define the American nation as something above and more important than the states. But it was not pure devotion to nation, for the country remained fiercely proud of localism and its real and presumed connection with liberty. The Fourth of July celebration, a popular holiday almost from the beginning, was commemorated with growing enthusiasm. When these Philadelphians enjoyed it in 1819, the Revolution was already nearly half a century old: then, as now, the Fourth was as much a party as a ritual.

One aspect of American nationalism was a sense of mission, of having a special destiny, of Americans' being crusaders in some cause. *Westward-ho,* painted in 1872, showed the westward movement in almost mystical terms, with Miss Liberty hovering over prospectors and pioneers. The brutal conflict with the Indians had many motives, some quite base, but Americans justified it as an expression of manifest destiny. The same theme is captured in a poster for a World War I silent film, *Pershing's Crusaders.* The war was being fought "to make the world safe for democracy," with Pershing shown as a modern version of a medieval crusader. Dwight Eisenhower's book on the liberation of Europe during World War II echoed the same theme. It was called *Crusade in Europe.*

"Fourth of July Celebration in Center Square, Philadelphia, 1819," *by John Lewis Krimmel. Historical Society of Pennsylvania*

"Westward-ho (Manifest Destiny)," *by John Gast.*
Courtesy, Harry T. Peters, Jr.

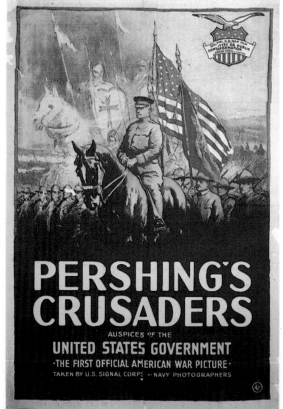

PERSHING'S CRUSADERS

AUSPICES OF THE

UNITED STATES GOVERNMENT

·THE FIRST OFFICIAL AMERICAN WAR PICTURE·

TAKEN BY U.S. SIGNAL CORPS AND NAVY PHOTOGRAPHERS

"Pershing's Crusaders." *Collection of*
George J. Goodstadt

Even when Americans disagree about issues of fundamental importance, each side tries to attach its cause to an existing symbol of national unity. The poster lamenting the lack of equal rights for blacks used the flag and the Pledge of Allegiance to suggest a promise only half-fulfilled. Marchers protesting the war in Vietnam used the American flag to make their point; their critics used the same flag to make theirs.

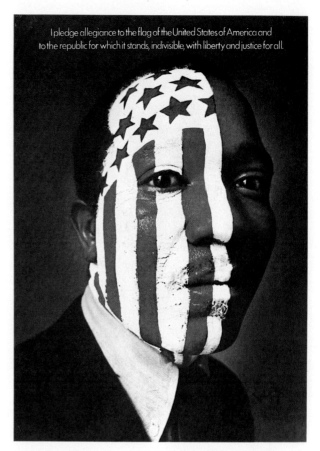

"I Pledge Allegiance..." *National Collection of Fine Arts, Smithsonian Institution. Poster owned by Gary Yanker*

"McCarthy Peace, 1968," *by Ben Shahn*
© *Cosmopress, Geneva; S.P.A.D.E.M., Paris*

If symbols can be so elastic as to support both war and peace, do they have any meaning at all? Most assuredly. They define a national existence and shared aspirations. It is all but impossible to listen to the Gettysburg Address or to hear "The Star-Spangled Banner" played during the Olympic Games without being moved. They evoke ambiguous but deeply felt sentiments. On July 4, 1976, after a decade or more of domestic turmoil, the nation pulled itself together for a festive bicentennial celebration at which the old, somewhat tattered symbols took on a renewed luster.

* * *

11 The Presidency

Happy times and lonely times for the president: Franklin D. Roosevelt in 1940 with advisers. President John F. Kennedy alone in the Oval Office (right).

The single most distinctive feature of national government in the United States is the popularly elected president. It is, in fact, a peculiarly American invention. Of the fifty-eight countries in which there is some degree of party competition and thus, presumably, some measure of free choice for the voters, only sixteen have a directly elected president, and thirteen of these are nations of North and South America. There is no purely presidential political system in Europe (France combines a directly elected president with a prime minister and parliament), and only three among the politically competitive nations of Africa and Southeast Asia.[1]

PRESIDENTS AND PRIME MINISTERS

The parliamentary system of government, described at the beginning of the previous chapter, is a democratic alternative to a presidential one.

Prime Minister Margaret Thatcher enters the British House of Commons. The House Chamber is small and crowded—there are not even enough seats for all members. The two parties sit on opposite sides of the aisle.

The parliamentary system is twice as common as the presidential system and can be found in almost all the democratic nations of Europe—in England, Sweden, Denmark, Norway, Italy, the Netherlands, West Germany—as well as in Japan and Israel. In a parliamentary system, the chief executive, called the "prime minister," is chosen, not by the voters, but by the legislature. The prime minister, in turn, selects the other ministers from the members of parliament. If the parliament has only two major parties, the ministers will usually be chosen from the majority party; if

there are many parties (as in Italy), several parties may participate in a coalition cabinet. The prime minister remains in power as long as his or her party has a majority of the seats in the legislature or as long as the coalition he or she has assembled holds together. The voters choose who is to be a member of parliament—usually by voting for one or another party—but cannot choose who is to be the chief executive officer.

One obvious result of the different ways presidents and prime ministers are chosen is that whereas the prime minister's party always has a majority in the parliament (if it did not, somebody else would be prime minister), the president's party may not have a majority in Congress. This, in fact, happens rather often. Since 1900 thirty-nine congresses have been elected; during ten of them, the president was a member of a party that was in the minority in one or both houses of Congress. This situation has been especially common in recent years. Of the seven presidents to hold office since Franklin D. Roosevelt, four had to deal with a "split government"—that is, an opposition party that was in control of either the House or the Senate or both. These presidents were Harry S. Truman (1947–1948), Dwight D. Eisenhower (1955–1960), Richard M. Nixon (1969–1974), and Gerald R. Ford (1974–1976).

Other differences are less obvious but just as important. A presidential candidate in the United States is nominated during an election year at a convention in which legislators, and even full-time professional politicians, are in a distinct minority. The person who will be prime minister, should his or her party come to power, is usually chosen during a nonelection year by a meeting—often a small, informal caucus—of veteran politicians, most of whom hold seats in the legislature. This means that a presidential candidate is usually selected with an eye toward who can win an election, and thus with an eye toward who is popular with the electorate. A prime minister is selected with a view toward who can hold the party together inside parliament. This difference is not always clear. In 1964 the Republican party in the United States selected Barry Goldwater as its presidential nominee, and in 1972 the Democratic party selected George McGovern as its nominee, despite substantial evidence that other candidates had a broader appeal to the voters. Usually, however, presidential nominees are much better known to the voters, when first selected, than prime ministers when they are first chosen.

Presidential candidates will not usually have had much high-level administrative experience in Washington. Generally, they will have been senators or governors; only rarely will they have been cabinet officers. Herbert Hoover was the last person elected president of the United States who had been in the cabinet (he was secretary of commerce from 1921 to 1929). The last one before Hoover was William Howard Taft (elected president in 1908, he had previously been secretary of war). Franklin Roosevelt had been in the "subcabinet" as an assistant secretary of the navy. Prime ministers, on the other hand, almost always have held important executive positions in national government. In Great Britain, for example, a person may well serve as foreign secretary, chancellor of the exchequer, or president of the board of trade before being chosen prime minister.

Once in office, a British prime minister will choose cabinet officers and advisers primarily from the members of his or her party who hold seats in Parliament. This means that the prime minister will be in close touch with the mind and mood of the legislature. This fact is reinforced by the obligation, in most parliamentary systems, for the prime minister to appear regularly in Parliament and personally defend his or her policies against opposition criticism. At the same time, however, the prime minister's power to select cabinet officers from the ranks of his or her own party in the legislature provides a great deal of influence over that party. If you are an ambi-

❝ Presidential appointments are made with an eye to public opinion; prime ministerial appointments, with an eye to parliamentary opinion and power. ❞

tious member of Parliament, desirous of becoming prime minister some day, and if you know that your only chance of realizing your ambition is to be appointed to a series of ever-more-important cabinet posts, then you are not likely to antagonize the person who does the appointing.

The president of the United States, on the other hand, selects his cabinet officers and advisers, not in order to control Congress—he cannot—but to reward personal followers (especially his key campaign workers), recognize important organized constituencies (blacks, women, farmers, unionists, businessmen), and mobilize nongovernmental expertise in the direction of public policy. To oversimplify, presidential appointments are made with an eye to public opinion; prime ministerial appointments, with an eye to parliamentary opinion and power.

The results of these differences are clear. In a two-party country with a parliamentary system—Great Britain, for example—a prime minister has very great power because he or she can dominate the cabinet and the legislature. This power exists even though the prime minister has little authority expressly granted by the constitution and may never have run in a nationwide election. (Where a parliamentary system operates in a country with many parties—such as Italy—the prime minister is ordinarily much weaker because the cabinet is composed of an unstable coalition of several parties.) Although the president of the United States is elected by the people at large and occupies an office with powers derived from the Constitution, he may have great difficulty in exercising any legislative leadership at all owing to his inability to control Congress.

This is true even when the presidency and Congress are controlled by the same political

❝The greatest source of presidential power, however, is not to be found in the Constitution at all but in politics and public opinion.**❞**

party. When John F. Kennedy was president, his Democrats held a substantial margin in the House of Representatives (263 seats to the Republicans' 174) and in the Senate (65 seats to the Republicans' 35). Yet Kennedy was frustrated in his efforts to obtain passage of legislation on civil rights, federal aid for school construction, the creation of a Department of Urban Affairs and Housing, and the establishment of a program of subsidized medical care for the elderly. During his last year in office he was able to get Congress to pass only about one-fourth of his proposals. In each case a majority of Democrats and some Republicans favored the plans, but enough Democrats opposed them, either in committee or in the final vote, to prevent their approval.

THE POWERS OF THE PRESIDENT

Though, unlike a prime minister, the president cannot command an automatic majority in the legislature, he does have some formidable, albeit vaguely defined, powers. These are mostly set forth in Article II of the Constitution, and are of two sorts: those he can exercise in his own right, without formal legislative approval, and those that require the consent of the Senate or of Congress as a whole.

Powers of the President Alone
- Commander-in-chief of the armed forces
- Commission officers of the armed forces
- Grant reprieves and pardons for federal offenses (except impeachment)
- Convene Congress in special sessions
- Receive ambassadors
- Take care that the laws be faithfully executed

- Wield the "executive power"
- Appoint officials to lesser offices

Powers of the President Shared with the Senate
- Make treaties
- Appoint ambassadors, judges, and high officials

Powers of the President Shared with Congress as a Whole
- Approve legislation

Taken alone and interpreted narrowly, this list of powers is not very impressive. Obviously, the president's authority as commander-in-chief is important, but, literally construed, most of the other constitutional grants seem to provide for little more than a president who is chief clerk of the country. A hundred years after the Founding, that is about how matters appeared to even the most astute observers. In 1884 Woodrow Wilson wrote a book about American politics entitled *Congressional Government* in which he described the business of the president as "usually not much above routine," mostly "*mere* administration." The president might as well be an officer of the civil service. To succeed, he need only obey Congress and stay alive.[2]

But even as Wilson wrote, he was overlooking some examples of enormously powerful presidents, such as Lincoln, and was not sufficiently attentive to the potential for presidential power to be found in the more ambiguous clauses of the Constitution as well as in the political realities of American life. In Chapter 20 we shall see how the president's authority as commander-in-chief has grown—especially, but not only, in wartime—to encompass not simply the direction of the military forces but the management of the economy and the direction of foreign affairs as well. A quietly dramatic reminder of the awesome implications of the president's military powers occurs at the precise instant a new president assumes office. An army officer carrying a locked briefcase moves from the side of the outgoing president to the side of the new one. In the briefcase are the secret codes and orders that permit the president to authorize the launching of American nuclear weapons.

The president's duty to "take care that the laws be faithfully executed" has become one of the most elastic phrases in the Constitution. By interpreting this broadly, Grover Cleveland was able to use federal troops to break a labor strike in the 1890s and Dwight Eisenhower to send troops to help integrate a public school in Little Rock, Arkansas, in 1957.

The greatest source of presidential power, however, is not to be found in the Constitution at all but in politics and public opinion. Increasingly since the 1930s, Congress has passed laws that confer on the executive branch broad grants of authority to achieve some general goals, leaving it up to the president and his deputies to define the regulations and programs that will actually be put into effect. In Chapter 12 we shall see how this delegation of legislative power to the president has contributed to the growth of the bureaucracy. Moreover, the American people— always in time of crisis, but increasingly as an everyday matter—look to the president for leadership and hold him responsible for a large and growing portion of our national affairs. In Chapters 16 and 17 we shall see how these popular expectations have shaped presidential authority and decisions in the areas of economic policy and social welfare legislation.

People argue about whether the president has become too powerful and whether his authority ought to be cut back to its constitutional grants. There is a good deal of sloppy and even hypocritical talk on this subject. Liberals and conservatives frequently switch positions on the power of the presidency depending on whether they like or dislike the policies a particular president is pursuing. (Conservatives thought President Carter was too powerful when he signed the Panama Canal treaty and abrogated our defense treaty with Taiwan, but they thought he

66 Liberals and conservatives frequently switch positions on the power of the presidency depending on whether they like or dislike the policies a particular president is pursuing. **99**

When he signed the Panama Canal treaties with General Omar Torrijos, President Carter was called "too powerful" by many of the same critics who on other issues called him "too weak."

was not acting powerfully enough in dealing with inflation. Liberals thought President Roosevelt was making rightful use of his power when he acted boldly to deal with the Depression and Nazi Germany, but thought President Johnson was too "imperious" when he heightened United States military involvement in Vietnam.) In this book we shall defer an assessment of presidential power until we have seen how presidents act in a number of policy areas over a long period of time (Part IV).

THE EVOLUTION OF THE PRESIDENCY

In 1787 few issues inspired as much debate or concern among the Framers of the Constitution as the problem of defining the chief executive. The delegates feared anarchy and monarchy in about equal measure. When the Constitutional Convention met, the existing state constitutions gave most, if not all, power to the legislatures. In eight states the governor was actually chosen by the legislature, and in ten states the governor could not serve more than one year. Only in New York, Massachusetts, and Connecticut did governors have much power or serve for any length of time. Some of the Framers proposed a plural national executive (i.e., several persons would each hold the executive power in different areas, or they would exercise the power as a committee). Others wanted the executive power checked, as it was in Massachusetts, by a council that would have to approve many of the chief executive's actions. Alexander Hamilton strongly urged the exact opposite—in a five-hour speech he called for something very much like an elective monarchy, patterned in some respects after the British kind. No one paid much attention to this plan, nor even, at first, to the more modest (and ultimately successful) suggestion of James Wilson for a single, elected president.

In time, those won out who believed that the governance of a large nation, especially one threatened by foreign enemies, required a single president with significant powers. Their cause was aided, no doubt, by the fact that everybody assumed that George Washington would be the first president, and confidence in him, and in his sense of self-restraint, was widely shared. Still, several delegates feared that the presidency would become, in the words of Edmund Randolph of Virginia, "the foetus of monarchy."

Concerns of the Founders

The delegates in Philadelphia, and later the critics of the new Constitution during the debate over its ratification, worried about aspects of the presidency that were quite different from those that concern us today. In 1787–1789 some Americans suspected that the president, by being able to command the state militia, would use the militia to overpower state governments. Others were worried that if the president were allowed to share treaty-making power with the Senate, he would be "directed by minions and favorites" and become a "tool of the Senate." But the most frequent concern was over the possibility of presidential reelection: Americans in the late eighteenth century were sufficiently suspicious of human nature and sufficiently experienced in the arts of mischievous government to believe that a president, once elected, would arrange to be in office in perpetuity by resorting to bribery, intrigue, and force. This would happen, for example, every time the presidential election was thrown into the House of Representatives because no candidate had received a majority of the votes in the Electoral College. Most persons expected that to happen frequently.

In retrospect, these concerns seem misplaced, even foolish. The power over the militia has had little significance; the election has gone to the House but twice (1800 and 1824); and though the Senate dominated the presidency off and on during the second half of the nineteenth century, it has not done so recently. The real sources of the expansion of presidential power—his role in foreign affairs, his ability to shape and lead public opinion, his position as head of the executive branch, and his claims to have certain "inherent" powers by virtue of his office—were hardly predictable in 1787. And not surprisingly. There was nowhere in the world at that time, nor had there been at any time in history, an example of an American-style presidency. It was a unique and unprecedented institution, and some of the Framers and their critics can easily be forgiven for not predicting accurately how it would evolve. At a more general level, however, they understood the issue quite clearly. Gouverneur Morris of New York put the problem of the presidency this way: "Make him too weak: the Legislature will usurp his power. Make him too strong: he will usurp on the Legislature."

The Framers knew very well that the relations between the president and Congress and the manner in which the president is elected were of profound importance, and they debated both at great length. The first plan was for the Congress to elect the president—in short, for the system to be quasi-parliamentary. But if that were done, some delegates pointed out, the Congress could dominate an honest or lazy president while a corrupt or scheming president might dominate Congress. After much discussion it was decided that the president should be chosen directly by voters. But by which voters? The emerging nation was large and diverse. It seemed unlikely that every citizen would be familiar enough with the candidates to cast an informed vote for a president directly. Worse, a direct popular election would give inordinate weight to the large, populous states, and no plan with that outcome had any chance of adoption by the smaller states. Thus, the Electoral College was invented whereby each of the states would select electors in whatever manner it wished. The electors would then meet, in each state capital, and vote for president and vice-president. Many Framers expected that this procedure would lead to the electors of each state voting for a favorite son, and thus no candidate would win a majority of the popular vote. In this event, it was decided, the House of Representatives should make the choice, with each state delegation casting one vote. The plan seemed to meet every test: large states would have their say, but small states would be protected by having a minimum of three electoral votes no matter how tiny their populations. The small states together could wield considerable influence in the House where, it was widely expected, most presidential elections would ultimately be decided. Of course, it did not work out quite this way—the Framers did

The first cabinet: left to right, Secretary of War Henry Knox, Secretary of State Thomas Jefferson, Attorney General Edmund Randolph, Secretary of the Treasury Alexander Hamilton, and President George Washington.

not foresee the role political parties would play in producing nationwide support for a slate of national candidates.

Once the manner of electing the president was settled, the question of his powers was much easier to decide. After all, if you believe the procedures are fair and balanced, then you are less reluctant to see larger powers managed by those procedures. Accordingly, the right to make treaties and the right to appoint lesser officials, originally reserved for the Senate, were given to the president "with the advice and consent of the Senate."

Another issue was put to rest soon thereafter. George Washington, the unanimous choice of the Electoral College to be the first president, firmly limited himself to two terms in office (1789–1796), and no president until Franklin D. Roosevelt (1933–1945) dared to run for more (though U. S. Grant tried). In 1951 the Twenty-Second Amendment to the Constitution was ratified, formally limiting all subsequent presidents to two terms. The remaining issues concerning the nature of the presidency, and especially the relations between the president and Congress, have been the subject of continuing dispute. The pattern of relationships that we see today is the result of an evolutionary process that has extended over nearly two centuries.

The first problem was to establish the legitimacy of the presidency itself: that is, to assure, if possible, public acceptance of the office, its incumbent, and its powers, and to establish an orderly transfer of power from one incumbent to the next.

Today we take this for granted. When Jimmy Carter was inaugurated in January 1977 as our thirty-ninth president, Gerald Ford, the thirty-eighth president, quietly left the White House and went home. In the world today, that is an unusual event. In many nations a new chief executive comes to power with the aid of military force or as a result of political intrigue; his predecessor often leaves office disgraced, exiled, or dead. At the time the Constitution was written, the Founders could only hope that an orderly transfer of power from one president to the next would occur. France had just undergone a bloody revolution; England in the not-too-distant past had beheaded a king; and in Poland the ruler was elected by a process so manifestly corrupt and so open to intrigue that Thomas Jefferson, in what may be the first example of ethnic humor in American politics, was led to refer to the proposed American presidency as a "bad edition of a Polish king."

Yet, by the time Abraham Lincoln found himself at the helm of a nation plunged into a

The Electoral College

Each state is allotted by the Constitution as many electoral votes as it has senators and representatives in Congress. Thus, no state has fewer than three electoral votes. (The District of Columbia also gets three even though it has no members of Congress.)

In each state, each party runs a slate of electors pledged to that party's presidential and vice-presidential candidates. The names of these electors usually do not appear on the ballots. The slate whose candidate wins more popular votes than any other is authorized to cast all the votes of that state in the Electoral College.

This results in a "winner-take-all" effect. Since it is up to the state legislatures to decide how electors are chosen, they could devise systems that would produce a split in the states' electoral votes. Michigan in 1892 and Maine in 1972 did this by allowing some or all electors to be chosen by congressional district rather than at large. A split electoral vote resulted in Michigan where the Republican candidate carried nine districts and the Democratic one carried five. In Maine, the Republican carried both congressional districts.

The winning slates of electors assemble in their state capitals about six weeks after the election to cast their ballots. Ordinarily, this is a pure formality. Occasionally, however, an elector will vote for a presidential candidate other than the one who carried the state. Such "faithless electors" have appeared in eight elections since 1796. The most recent case was in 1976 when a Washington elector pledged to Gerald Ford voted instead for Ronald Reagan.

The state electoral ballots are opened and counted before a joint session of Congress during the first week of January. The candidate with a majority of votes is declared elected.

If no candidate wins a majority, the House of Representatives chooses the president from among the three leading candidates, with each state casting one vote. By House

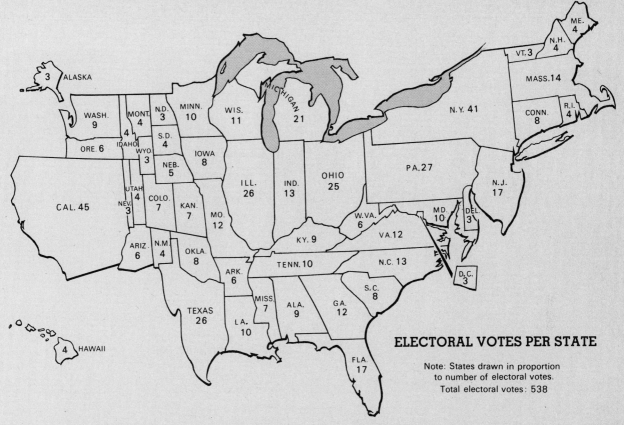

ELECTORAL VOTES PER STATE

Note: States drawn in proportion
to number of electoral votes.
Total electoral votes: 538

rule, each state's vote is allotted to the candidate pre-ferred by a majority of the state's House delegation. If there is a tie within a delegation, that state's vote is not counted. The House has had to decide two presidential contests. In 1800 Thomas Jefferson and Aaron Burr tied in the Electoral College because of a defect in the language of the Constitution—each state cast two electoral votes without indicating which was for president and which for vice-president. (Burr was supposed to be vice-pres-ident and, after much maneuvering, he was.) This problem was corrected by the Twelfth Amendment, ratified in 1804. The only House decision under the modern system was in 1824 when it chose John Quincy Adams over Andrew Jackson and William H. Crawford, even though Jackson had more electoral votes (and probably more popular votes) than his rivals.

The chief political effects of the Electoral College are these: The winner-take-all system probably discourages the emergence of serious third parties. The system en-courages candidates to focus their campaigns on states, especially states whose vote may be in doubt. It espe-cially encourages candidates to emphasize large, doubt-ful states. A candidate who carries the ten largest states wins 259 electoral votes, only 31 short of a majority. These states tend to be the most urbanized, industrialized, and politically competitive ones. A president seeking reelection has reason to be attentive to the needs of such states.

Proposals to alter or abolish the Electoral College have been made, but none has come close to adoption. Among these are plans to elect the president by direct, national, popular vote; to divide each state's electoral votes in proportion to the popular vote received by each candidate in that state; to have electors chosen by con-gressional district rather than at large; and to retain the electoral system but abolish the office of elector and thus the chance of a faithless elector.

The issues and arguments are complex. Those who want to preserve the Electoral College generally believe that it is important for the states to have a role in choosing the president and for the president to have an electoral reason to attend to state interests. Those favoring direct popular election argue that the states are irrelevant in presidential elections and that each person's vote should count the same as every other person's regardless of where he or she lives.

> "The first problem was to establish the legitimacy of the presidency . . . and to establish an orderly transfer of power from one incumbent to the next."

A military coup—as took place in Portugal in 1974—is not uncommon when the legitimacy of the government, and of opposition parties, is not well established. For nearly two centuries there has been an orderly transfer of power in the American government, not only

bitter, bloody civil war, fifteen presidents had been elected, served their time, and left office without a hint of force being used to facilitate the process and with the people accepting the process—if not admiring all the presidents. This orderly transfer of authority occurred despite passionate opposition and deeply divisive elections (such as that which brought Jefferson to power). It did not happen by accident.

The First Presidents

Those who first served as president were among the most prominent men in the new nation, all active either in the movement for independence or in the Founding or in both. Of the first five presidents, four (all but John Adams) served two full terms. Washington and Monroe were not even opposed. The first administration had at the highest levels the leading spokesmen for all of the major viewpoints: Alexander Hamilton was Washington's secretary of the treasury (and was sympathetic to the urban commercial interests),

and Thomas Jefferson was secretary of state (and more inclined toward rural, small-town, and farming views). Washington spoke out strongly against political parties and, though parties soon emerged, there was a stigma attached to them—many people believed that it was wrong to take advantage of divisions in the country, to organize deliberately to acquire political office, or to make legislation depend upon party advantage. As it turned out, this hostility to party (or "faction," as it was more commonly called) was unrealistic: parties are as natural to democracy as churches to religion.

Establishing the legitimacy of the presidency was made easier by the fact that the national government had relatively little to do. It had, of course, to establish a sound currency and to settle the debt accrued during the Revolutionary War. The Treasury Department inevitably became the principal federal office, especially under the strong leadership of Hamilton. Relations with England and France were important—and

between leaders of different parties (such as Woodrow Wilson and William Howard Taft in 1913), but even when a popular leader is assassinated and his vice-president is sworn in.

difficult—but otherwise government took little time and few resources.

In appointing persons to federal office, a general rule of "fitness" emerged: the persons appointed should have some standing in their communities and be well thought of by their neighbors. Appointments based on partisanship soon arose, but community stature could not be neglected.

The presidency was kept modest. Washington clearly had not sought the office and did not relish the exercise of its then modest powers. He traveled widely so that as many people as possible could see their new president. His efforts to establish a semi-regal court etiquette were quickly rebuffed; the presidency was to be kept simple. Congress decided that not until after a president was dead might his likeness appear on a coin or on currency; no president until Eisenhower was given a pension on his retirement.

The president's relations with Congress were correct but not close. Washington appeared before the Senate to ask its advice on a proposed treaty with some Indian tribes. He got none, and instead was politely told that the Senate would like to consider the matter in private. He declared that he would be "damned if he ever went there again," and he never did. Thus ended the responsibility of the Senate to "advise" the president. Alexander Hamilton tried to function like a prime minister, even to attempting to appear before the House of Representatives to exercise personal leadership over his legislative program. The House would not let him enter their chamber (he had to buttonhole members in the lobby instead). Vetoes were sometimes cast by a president, but sparingly and then only when the president believed the law was not simply unwise but unconstitutional. Washington cast only two vetoes; Jefferson and Adams none.

The Jacksonians

At a time roughly corresponding to the presidency of Andrew Jackson (1828–1836), broad changes began to occur in American politics which, together with the personality of Jackson himself, altered the relations between president and Congress and the nature of presidential leadership. As so often happens, few people at the time Jackson took office had much sense of what his presidency would be like. Though he had been a member of the House of Representatives and of the Senate, he was elected as a military hero, and an apparently doddering one at that. Sixty-one years old and seemingly frail, he nonetheless used the powers of his office as no one before him had. He vetoed twelve acts of Congress, more than all his predecessors combined and more than any subsequent president until Andrew Johnson thirty years later. His vetoes were not simply on constitutional grounds, but on policy ones: he saw himself as the only official elected by the entire voting citizenry, and thus as the "Tribune of the People." None of his vetoes was overridden. He did not initiate many new policies, but he struck out against the ones he did not like. He did so at a time when the size of the electorate was increasing rapidly, and new states,

Andrew Jackson used the powers of the presidency as had no one before him, vetoing many acts of Congress.

especially in the West, had entered the Union. (There were then twenty-four states in the Union; twice the original number.)

Jackson demonstrated what could be done by a popular president. He did not shrink from conflict with Congress, and the tension between the two branches of government that was intended by the Framers became intensified by the personalities of the men in government: Jackson in the White House, and Henry Clay, Daniel Webster, and John Calhoun in Congress. These powerful figures walked the political stage at a time when bitter sectional conflicts—over slavery and commercial policies—were beginning to split the country. Jackson, though he was opposed to a large and powerful federal government and wished to return somehow to the agrarian simplicities of Jefferson's time, was nonetheless a believer in a strong and independent presidency. This view, though obscured by nearly a century of subsequent congressional dominance of national politics, was ultimately to triumph—for better or for worse.

Abraham Lincoln, photographed here as he met with General George B. McClellan and other Union army officers at Antietam in 1862, met the challenge of the Civil War by making unprecedented use of the "inherent" powers of the presidency.

The Reemergence of Congress

With the end of Jackson's second term, Congress quickly reestablished its power and, except for the wartime presidency of Lincoln and brief flashes of presidential power under James Polk (1845–1849) and Grover Cleveland (1885–1889, 1893–1897), the presidency for a hundred years was the subordinate branch of the national government. Of the eight presidents who succeeded Jackson, two (William H. Harrison and Zachary Taylor) died in office, and none of the others served more than one term. Schoolchildren, trying to memorize the list of American presidents, always stumble in this era of the "no-name" presidents. This is hardly a coincidence: Congress was the leading institution, struggling, unsuccessfully, with slavery and sectionalism.

It was also an intensely partisan era, a legacy of Jackson that lasted well into the twentieth century. Public opinion was closely divided. Out of seventeen presidential elections between the end of Jackson's term in 1836 and Theodore Roosevelt's election in 1904, in nine cases the winning candidate received less than half the popular vote. Only two candidates (Lincoln in 1864 and Ulysses S. Grant in 1872) received more than 55 percent of the popular vote.

During this long period of congressional—and usually senatorial—dominance of national government, only Lincoln broke new ground for presidential power. Lincoln's expansive use of that power, like Jackson's, was totally unexpected. He was first elected in 1860 as a minority president, receiving less than 40 percent of the popular vote in a field of four candidates. Though a member of the new Republican party, he had been a member of the Whig party, a group that had stood for limiting presidential power. He had opposed America's entry into the Mexican War and had been critical of Jackson's use of executive authority. But as president during the Civil War, he made unprecedented use of the vague gift of powers in Article II of the Constitution, especially of those he felt were "implied" or were "inherent" in the phrase,

❝It had become abundantly clear that a national emergency could equip the president with great powers and that a popular and strong-willed president could expand his powers even without an emergency.**❞**

Theodore Roosevelt, here addressing a crowd in Evanston, Illinois, in 1903, became a powerful president not because of a national crisis but as a result of his forceful personality.

"take care that the laws be faithfully executed," and in the express authorization for him to act as commander-in-chief. Lincoln raised an army, spent money, blockaded southern ports, temporarily suspended the writ of habeas corpus, and issued an Emancipation Proclamation to free the slaves—all without prior congressional approval. He justified this, as most Americans probably would have, by the emergency conditions created by civil war. In this, he acted little differently from Thomas Jefferson who, while president, waged undeclared war against various North African pirates.

After Lincoln, Congress again reasserted its power and became, during the Reconstruction of the South and for many decades thereafter, the principal federal institution. But it had become

The President: Qualifications and Benefits

Qualifications

- A natural-born citizen (can be born abroad of parents who are American citizens).
- Thirty-five years of age.
- A resident of the United States for at least fourteen years (but not necessarily the fourteen years just preceding the election).

Benefits

- A nice house.
- A salary of $200,000 per year (taxable).
- Expense account of $50,000 per year (taxable).
- Travel expenses of $100,000 per year (tax-free).
- Pension, on retirement, of $63,000 per year (taxable).
- Staff support on leaving the presidency.
- A White House staff of 400–500 persons.

abundantly clear that a national emergency could equip the president with great powers and that a popular and strong-willed president could expand his powers even without an emergency. Except for the administrations of Theodore Roosevelt (1901–1909) and Woodrow Wilson (1913–1921), the president was, until the New Deal, at best a negative force—a source of opposition *to* Congress, not a source of initiative and leadership for it. Grover Cleveland was a strong personality, but for all his efforts he was able to do little more than veto bills he did not like. He cast 414 vetoes—more than any other president until Franklin Roosevelt. A frequent target of his vetoes were bills to confer special pensions on Civil War veterans.

Today we are accustomed to thinking that the president formulates a legislative program to which Congress then responds, but until the 1930s the opposite was more nearly the case. Congress ignored the initiatives of such presidents as Grover Cleveland, Rutherford Hayes, Chester Arthur, and Calvin Coolidge. Woodrow Wilson in 1913 was the first president since John Adams to deliver personally the State of the Union address, and one of the first to develop and argue for a presidential legislative program. The popular conception of the president as the central figure of national government, devising a legislative program and commanding a large staff of advisers, is very much a product of the modern era and of the enlarged role of government. In the past the presidency only became powerful during a national crisis (the Civil War, World War I) or because of an extraordinary personality (Andrew Jackson, Theodore Roosevelt, Woodrow Wilson). Since the 1930s, however, the presidency has been powerful no matter who occupied the office and whether or not there was a crisis. Because government now plays such an active role in our national life, the presidency is the natural focus of attention and the titular head (whether he is the real boss is another matter) of a huge federal administrative system.

THE OFFICE OF THE PRESIDENT

It was not until 1857 that the president was allowed to have a private secretary paid for with public funds, and it was not until after the assassination of President McKinley in 1901 that the president was given a Secret Service bodyguard. He was not able to submit a single presidential budget until after 1921, when the Budget and Accounting Act was passed and a Bureau of the Budget (now called the Office of Management and Budget) was created. Grover Cleveland personally answered the White House telephone, and Abraham Lincoln often answered his own mail.

Today, of course, the president has hundreds of persons assisting him, and the trappings of power—helicopters, guards, limousines—are plainly visible. The White House staff has grown enormously, as shown in Figure 11.1, from 51 persons in 1943 to 583 in 1971. Add to this the opportunities for presidential appointments to the cabinet, the courts, and various agencies, and the resources at the disposal of the president would appear to be awesome. That conclusion is partly true and partly false, or at least misleading, and for a simple reason. If the president was once helpless for lack of assistance, he now confronts an army of assistants so large that it constitutes a bureaucracy he has difficulty controlling.

The ability of a presidential assistant to affect the president is governed by the Rule of Propinquity: In general, power is wielded by persons who are in the room when a decision is made. Presidential appointments can thus be classified in terms of their proximity, physically and politically, to the president.

The White House Office

These are the men and women who have offices in the White House, usually in the West Wing of that building. Their titles often do not reveal the

❝The ability of a presidential assistant to affect the president is governed by the Rule of Propinquity: In general, power is wielded by persons who are in the room when a decision is made.❞

functions they actually perform: "counsel," "counsellor," "assistant to the president," "special assistant," "special consultant," and so forth. The actual titles vary from one administration to another, but in general the men and women who hold them oversee the political and policy interests of the president.

There are essentially two ways in which a president can organize his personal staff—what one observer called the "circular" and the "pyramid" methods.[3] In the former, used by Franklin Roosevelt and Carter, several assistants report directly to the president; in the latter, used by Eisenhower and Nixon, most assistants report

FIGURE 11.1 Growth of the White House Staff, 1943-1979

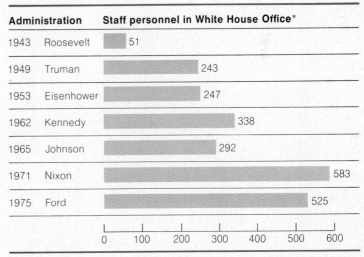

Administration		Staff personnel in White House Office*
1943	Roosevelt	51
1949	Truman	243
1953	Eisenhower	247
1962	Kennedy	338
1965	Johnson	292
1971	Nixon	583
1975	Ford	525

0   100   200   300   400   500   600

Source: Subcommittee on Employee Ethics and Utilization, Committee on Post Office and Civil Service, U.S. House of Representatives, *Presidential Staffing—A Brief Overview* (95th Congress, 2nd Session, July 25, 1978), p. 57.

*Comparable data for the Carter White House are not available.

THE WHITE HOUSE

West Wing

Mansion

East Wing

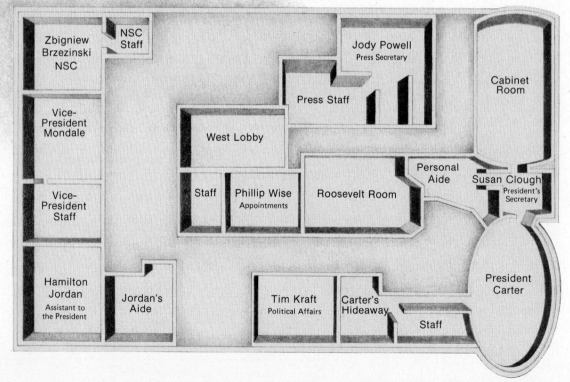

Zbigniew Brzezinski NSC

NSC Staff

Vice-President Mondale

Vice-President Staff

Hamilton Jordan
Assistant to the President

Jordan's Aide

West Lobby

Staff

Phillip Wise
Appointments

Roosevelt Room

Tim Kraft
Political Affairs

Carter's Hideaway

Staff

Jody Powell
Press Secretary

Press Staff

Personal Aide

Susan Clough
President's Secretary

Cabinet Room

President Carter

Having an office close to the president's own (the Oval Office) is important for an aide's power and status. The closer one is to the president, the easier it is to see him. In this drawing of the main floor of the West Wing, the key offices—as they were occupied by members of the Carter administration in 1979—are shown. In the basement and on the second floor of the West Wing are additional offices for slightly less important persons.

through a hierarchy to a chief of staff (Sherman Adams under Eisenhower, H. R. Haldeman under Nixon) who then deals with the president. The circular method has the virtue of giving the president a great deal of information but at the price of confusion and conflict among assistants. The pyramid method provides for an orderly flow of information and decisions but at the risk of isolating or misinforming the president.

All presidents claim they are open to many sources of advice, and some presidents try to guarantee that openness by using the circular method of staff organization. President Carter liked to describe his office as a wheel with himself as the hub and his several assistants as spokes. But most presidents discover, as did Carter, that the difficulty of managing the large White House bureaucracy and of conserving their own limited supply of time and energy makes it necessary for them to rely heavily on one or two key subordinates. Carter in July 1979 dramatically altered the White House staff organization by elevating Hamilton Jordan to the post of chief of staff with the job of coordinating the work of most of the other staff assistants. Though the press quickly compared this move—unfavorably —to the Richard Nixon style of management, in fact most presidents have found it necessary to rely on a pyramidlike structure. However much he may wish to make all the decisions himself, no president in fact can.

The key staff persons have titles such as "assistant to the president," "counsel to the president," and "press secretary." Each assistant has, of course, others working for him or her, sometimes a large number. There are, at a slightly lower level of status, "special assistants to the president" for various purposes. (Being "special" means, paradoxically, being less important.) As these aides are part of his personal staff, their appointments do not have to be confirmed by the Senate; the president can hire and fire them at will.

Typically, senior White House staff members are drawn from the ranks of the president's campaign staff—long-time associates in whom he

---

THE WHITE HOUSE OFFICE—SENIOR STAFF
(as of September 1978)

President Jimmy Carter
Personal Secretary
  Susan Clough

Counsel to the President
  Robert J. Lipshutz
  6 lawyers handling legal issues

Assistant to the President
  Hamilton Jordan
  7 political and policy advisers

Assistant to the President: Domestic Affairs
  Stuart E. Eizenstat
  supervises Domestic Policy staff of 29 persons

Assistant to the President: National Security Affairs
  Zbigniew Brzezinski
  supervises National Security Council staff of 33

Assistant to the President: Congressional Liaison
  Frank B. Moore
  14 persons who are the president's lobbyists
  with Congress

Assistant to the President: Intergovernmental Affairs
  Jack H. Watson, Jr.
  8 persons for liaison with states and cities; also,
  secretary to the cabinet

Assistant to the President: Public Liaison
  Anne Wexler
  7 persons who deal with civil rights, civic, ethnic, and
  other interest groups

Press Secretary
  Jody Powell
  supervises 17 press officers

Assistant to the President for Political Affairs
and Personnel
  Tim Kraft
  5 persons who handle politics

Assistant to the President for Communications
  Gerald M. Rafshoon
  18 persons who write speeches, handle public relations,
  and generally try to improve the president's image

has confidence. A few members, however, will be experts brought in after the campaign—such was the case, for example, with Henry Kissinger, a former Harvard professor who became President Nixon's assistant for national security affairs. The offices these men and women occupy are often small and crowded (Kissinger's was not much bigger than the one he had while a professor at Harvard), but their occupants willingly put up with any discomfort in exchange for the privilege (and the power) of being *in* the White House. The arrangement of offices—their size, and especially their proximity to the Oval Office in which the president sits—is a good measure of the relative influence of the persons in them.

To an outsider, the amount of jockeying among the top staff for access to the president

The ability to see the president frequently is a good measure of the power of a White House aide. Here Hamilton Jordan and Jody Powell confer with President Carter.

may seem comical or even perverse. The staff attaches enormous significance to whose office is closest to the president's, who can see him on a daily as opposed to a weekly basis, who can get an appointment with the president and who cannot, and who has a right to see documents and memoranda just before they go to the Oval Office. To be sure, there is ample grist here for Washington political novels. But there is also something important at stake—it is not simply a question of power plays and ego trips. Who can see the president and who sees and "signs off" on memoranda going to the president affect in important ways who influences policy and thus whose goals and beliefs become embedded in policy. For example, if a memo from a secretary of the treasury who believes in free trade can go directly to the president, the president may be more likely to support free trade (low tariffs). On the other hand, let us assume that the memo must be routed through the office of the assistant to the president for political matters. He (let us suppose) is worried about the adverse effects of foreign competition on jobs in the American steel industry because the votes of steelworkers are important to the president's reelection campaign. As a result, what the president sees may well reflect these political realities and argue for higher rather than lower tariffs.

Executive Office of the President

These agencies report directly to the president and perform staff services for him but are not located in the White House itself. Their members do not usually enjoy intimate contact with him; some are rather large bureaucracies. The top positions in these organizations are filled by presidential appointment, but unlike the White House staff positions, these appointments must be confirmed by the Senate.

Of all the agencies in the Executive Office of the President, perhaps the most important in terms of the president's need for advice and assistance in administering the federal government is the Office of Management and Budget (OMB). First called the Bureau of the Budget when it was created in 1921, it became OMB in 1970 to reflect its broader responsibilities. Today it does considerably more than assemble and analyze the figures that go each year into the national budget the president submits to Congress. It also studies the organization and operations of the executive branch, devises plans for reorganizing various departments and agencies, develops ways of getting better information about government programs, and reviews proposals that cabinet departments want included in the president's legislative program. OMB has a staff of over six hundred persons, almost all career civil servants, many of high professional skill and substantial experience. Traditionally, OMB has been a nonpartisan agency: experts serving all presidents, without regard to party or ideology. Under Presidents Nixon, Ford, and Carter, OMB has been expected to play a larger role in advocating, rather than simply analyzing, certain policies. Under any president OMB will depart in some measure from the ideal of neutral expertise—governmental policies rarely lend themselves to purely scientific analysis. In the Nixon administration, however, OMB was especially "political."

The Cabinet

The cabinet is a product of tradition and hope. There once was a time when the heads of the federal departments met regularly with the president to discuss matters, and some persons, especially those critical of strong presidents, would like to see this kind of collegial decision-making reestablished. But, in fact, the cabinet is largely a fiction. Indeed, the Constitution does not even mention the word, and when Washington tried to get his cabinet members to work together, the two strongest members of it—Alexander Hamilton and Thomas Jefferson—spent most of their time feuding. The cabinet, as a presidential committee, did not work any

> **KEY AGENCIES IN THE EXECUTIVE OFFICE OF THE PRESIDENT**
>
> Office of Management and Budget
>   *Director:* James T. McIntyre, Jr.
>
> Council of Economic Advisers
>   *Chairman:* Charles L. Schultze
>
> Central Intelligence Agency
>   *Director:* Admiral Stansfield Turner
>
> Office of the Special Representative for Trade Negotiations
>   *Special Representative:* Robert S. Strauss
>
> Council on Environmental Quality
>   *Chairman:* Charles H. Warren
>
> Office of Telecommunications Policy
>   *Director:* William J. Thaler
>
> Office of Science and Technology Policy
>   *Director:* Frank Press
>
> Office of Personnel Management
>   *Director:* Alan K. Campbell

better for John Adams or Abraham Lincoln, for Franklin Roosevelt or for John F. Kennedy. Dwight Eisenhower is almost the only modern president who came close to making the cabinet a truly deliberative body—he gave it a large staff, held regular meetings, and listened to opinions expressed there. But even under Eisenhower, the cabinet did not have much influence over presidential decisions, nor did it help him obtain more power over the government.

Cabinet officers are the heads of those administrative departments that, by custom, are considered part of the cabinet. These departments, together with the dates of their creation and the approximate number of their employees, are given in Table 11.1. The order of their creation is unimportant except in terms of protocol—where one sits at cabinet meetings is determined by the age of the department one heads. Thus,

The very size of the cabinet—here shown meeting with President Carter in 1978—is one reason why it cannot act as a policy-making body. Another is the fact that each member is interested in maintaining the power and policies of the departments he or she heads.

TABLE 11.1 The Cabinet

Department	Created	Approximate employment (January 1978)
State	1789	32,000
Treasury	1789	132,000
Defense[a]	1947	982,000
Justice	1789	93,000
Interior	1849	76,000
Agriculture[b]	1889	114,000
Commerce	1913	39,000
Labor	1913	17,000
Health, Education, and Welfare	1953	158,000
Housing and Urban Development	1965	18,000
Transportation	1966	74,000
Energy	1977	20,000

[a] Formerly the War Department, created in 1789. Figures are for civilians only.

[b] Agriculture Department created in 1862; made part of cabinet in 1889.

the secretary of state sits next to the president on one side and the secretary of the treasury next to him on the other. Down at the foot of the table are found the heads of the newer departments.

Though the president appoints, with the consent of the Senate, the heads of these cabinet departments, the power he obtains over them is sharply limited. One reason is that he cannot appoint more than a tiny fraction of all of a department's employees. For example, when he took office in 1977, President Carter could appoint persons of his own choosing to fewer than one hundred positions in the Treasury Department—less than 1 percent of its employees. In only one department—State—can the president appoint at his discretion more than 1 percent of the employees, and many of these are ambassadors. Table 11.2 shows the number of employees (and the percentage of all employees) presidentially chosen in each cabinet department. And even this number of presidential positions is an exaggeration, since many of the posts exempted from civil service are scientific or professional in nature and are occupied by persons who are not replaced by a new administration. A British prime minister has far fewer political appointments to make than an American president, but then a prime minister does not need so many because he or she does not have to compete with an independent Congress for influence over the bureaucracy.

But the main reason why the cabinet is a weak entity is the fact that its members are heads of vast organizations that they seek to defend, explain, and enlarge. The secretary of Housing and Urban Development (HUD), for example, spends 99 percent of his or her time on departmental business and perhaps 1 percent (or even less) of the time speaking to the president about his business. It is hardly surprising that the HUD secretary is more of a representative of HUD *to* the president than his representative to HUD. Under these circumstances, the HUD secretary is not especially interested in discussing policy at cabinet meetings with the secretary of the treasury—the latter probably wants the president to do things that are very different from what the former would like him to do. In the Carter administration, HUD Secretary Patricia Harris quarreled frequently with Treasury Secretary Michael Blumenthal over housing and mortgage policies.

Independent Agencies, Commissions, and Judgeships

The president also appoints persons to four dozen or so agencies and commissions that are not considered part of the cabinet and that, by law, must have a quasi-independent status. The difference between a "presidential" and an "independent" agency is not precise. In general it means that the heads of presidential agencies serve at the pleasure of the president and can be removed by him any time he wishes. On the other hand, the heads of independent agencies serve for fixed terms of office and can be removed only "for cause."

The president can also appoint federal judges, subject to the consent of the Senate. Judges serve for life unless they are removed by impeachment and conviction. The reason for the special barriers to the removal of judges is that they represent an independent branch of government, defined by the Constitution, and limits on presidential removal powers are necessary to preserve that independence. Thus, the president can usually appoint only a few judges at any given time unless Congress creates new posts. When President Carter took office in January 1977, there were no vacancies on the Supreme Court, only three vacancies on the courts of appeals, and sixteen vacancies in the district courts.[4]

TABLE 11.2　Number of "Political" or "Policy" Positions in Cabinet Departments (as of September 1976)

Department	Number of non–civil service positions	Percent of all positions in each department
State	554	1.80%
Treasury	99	0.07
Defense (civilians)	237	0.02
Justice	307	0.58
Interior	126	0.17
Agriculture	317	0.28
Commerce	192	0.50
Labor	81	0.47
Health, Education, and Welfare	142	0.09
Housing and Urban Development	102	0.58
Transportation	143	0.19
Energy	a	—

Source: Committee on Post Office and Civil Service, U.S. House of Representatives, *Policy and Supporting Positions* (94th Congress, 2nd Session, November 1976). This publication is known affectionately among politicians as the "Plum Book."

Note: Many of these positions are in fact not "political," but are exempt from civil service to make possible the appointment of persons with specialized (e.g., scientific, legal) backgrounds.

a Not available.

**FEDERAL AGENCIES CLASSIFIED BY WHETHER PRESIDENT
HAS UNLIMITED OR LIMITED RIGHT OF REMOVAL**

"Presidential" Agencies	"Independent or "Quasi-Independent" Agencies
(Head can be removed at any time)	*(Head serves for a fixed term)*
Action	Federal Reserve Board (14 years)
Arms Control and Disarmament Agency	Civil Aeronautics Board (6 years)
Commission on Civil Rights	Consumer Product Safety Commission (6 years)
Energy Research and Development Agency	Equal Employment Opportunity Commission (5 years)
Environmental Protection Agency	Federal Communications Commission (7 years)
Federal Mediation and Conciliation Service	Federal Deposit Insurance Corporation (6 years)
General Services Administration	Federal Maritime Commission (5 years)
National Aeronautics and Space Administration	Federal Energy Regulatory Commission (5 years)
Postal Service	Federal Trade Commission (7 years)
Small Business Administration	Interstate Commerce Commission (7 years)
Veterans' Administration	National Labor Relations Board (5 years)
All cabinet departments	National Science Foundation (6 years)
Executive Office of the President	Securities and Exchange Commission (5 years)
	Tennessee Valley Authority (9 years)

WHO GETS APPOINTED

Not only can a president make relatively few appointments, he rarely knows more than a few of the people he does appoint. Unlike cabinet members in a parliamentary system, the president's cabinet officers and their principal deputies usually have not served with the chief executive in the legislature. Instead, they come from private business, universities, "think tanks," foundations, law firms, labor unions, and the ranks of former and present congressmen as well as past state and local government officials. A president is fortunate if most cabinet members turn out to agree with him on major policy questions. After Richard Nixon appointed James Allen as commissioner of education, the president discovered that Allen, though a Republican, was an outspoken liberal who became publicly critical of Nixon's policies. After much controversy, Nixon fired Allen.

The men and women appointed to the cabinet and to the "subcabinet" (a loose term for persons holding posts as deputy secretary or assistant secretary in the cabinet departments) will usually have had some prior federal experience. One study of over a thousand such appointments made by five presidents (Franklin Roosevelt through Lyndon Johnson) found that about 85 percent of the cabinet, subcabinet, and independent agency appointees had some prior federal experience. In fact, most were in government service (at the federal, state, or local levels) just before they received their cabinet or subcabinet appointments.[5] Clearly, the executive branch is not, in general, run by novices.

Many of these appointees are what Richard Neustadt has called "in-and-outers": persons who alternate between jobs in the federal government and ones in the private sector, especially in law firms and in universities. Cyrus Vance, before becoming secretary of state to President Carter, had been general counsel in the Defense Department, secretary of the army, and deputy secretary of defense under President

Johnson. Before and after these federal jobs, he was a member of a large Wall Street law firm. This is a quite different pattern from that of parliamentary systems where all the cabinet officers come from the legislature and are typically full-time career politicians.

At one time the cabinet had in it many persons with strong political followings of their own—former senators and governors and powerful local party leaders. The postmaster general, for example, was, under Roosevelt, Truman, and Kennedy, the president's campaign manager. George Washington, Abraham Lincoln, and other presidents had to contend with cabinet members who were strong figures in their own right: Alexander Hamilton and Thomas Jefferson worked with Washington; Simon Cameron (a Pennsylvania political boss) and Salmon P. Chase (formerly a governor of Ohio) worked for—and against—Lincoln. Before 1824 the post of secretary of state was regarded as a stepping-stone to the presidency; and even after that, at least ten persons ran for president who had been either secretary of state or ambassador to a foreign country.[6]

Of late, however, there seems to have emerged a tendency for presidents to place in their cabinets persons known for their expertise or their administrative experience rather than for their political following. This has come about in part because political parties are now so weak that party leaders can no longer demand a place in the cabinet and in part because presidents want (or think they want) "experts." A remarkable illustration of this is the number of professors or persons with Ph.D. degrees who have entered the cabinet. President Nixon, who supposedly did not like Harvard professors, appointed two—Henry Kissinger and Daniel Patrick Moynihan—to important posts; Gerald Ford added a third, John Dunlop.

A president's desire to appoint experts who do not have independent political power is modified—but not supplanted—by his need to

A Government of Professors?

Professors and Holders of the Ph.D. Degree in the Nixon-Ford and Carter Administrations

Nixon-Ford Administration

Secretary of State: Henry Kissinger
Ambassador to the UN: Daniel Patrick Moynihan
Attorney General: Edward H. Levi
Secretary of Agriculture: Earl Butz
Secretary of the Treasury: George Schultz
Secretary of Defense/Director of the CIA: James R. Schlesinger
Chairman of the Federal Reserve Board: Arthur F. Burns
Secretary of Labor: John T. Dunlop
Secretary of HEW: F. David Matthews
Chairman, Council of Economic Advisers: Herbert Stein

Carter Administration

Assistant for National Security Affairs: Zbigniew Brzezinski
Secretary of Defense: Harold Brown
Secretary of Energy: James R. Schlesinger
Secretary of Commerce: Juanita Kreps
Secretary of Labor: Ray Marshall
Secretary of the Treasury: W. Michael Blumenthal
Chairman, Council of Economic Advisers: Charles L. Schultze
Chairman, Office of Personnel Management: Alan K. Campbell

Juanita Kreps

Daniel Patrick Moynihan

recognize various politically important groups, regions, and organizations. Since Robert Weaver became the first black to serve in the cabinet (as secretary of HUD under President Johnson), it is clear it would be quite costly for a president *not* to have one or more blacks in his cabinet. The secretary of labor must be acceptable to the AFL-CIO, the secretary of agriculture to at least some organized farmers. Women have been in several cabinets since Franklin Roosevelt's; with the growing importance of the feminist movement, it is now essential that they be in every cabinet. Traditionally, the interior secretary comes from the resource- and land-conscious West. And so on and on.

Because political considerations must be taken into account in making cabinet and agency appointments as well as the fact that any head of a large organization will tend to adopt the perspective of that organization, there is an inevitable tension—even a rivalry—between the White House staff and the department heads. Staff members see themselves as extensions of the president's personality and policies; department heads see themselves as repositories of expert knowledge (often knowledge of why something will *not* work as the president hopes). White House staffers, many of them young men and women in their twenties or early thirties with little executive experience, will call department heads, often persons in their fifties with substantial executive experience, and tell them "the president wants" this or that or "the president asked me to tell you" one thing or another. Department heads try to conceal their irritation, and then maneuver for some delay so they can develop their own counterproposals. On the other hand, when department heads call a White House staff person and ask to see the president, unless they are one of the privileged few in whom the president has special confidence, they are often told "the president can't be bothered with that" or "the president doesn't have time to see you."

Left, Secretary of Labor Frances Perkins, appointed by President Franklin Roosevelt, was the first woman cabinet member. Below, when Robert Weaver was made secretary of Housing and Urban Development by President Johnson, he became the first black to hold a cabinet post.

THE PRESIDENT AND PUBLIC OPINION

The president is not only chief executive of the federal government, he is also head of his party (or at least of the presidential wing of it), head of state (and thus responsible for performing many ceremonial duties), and candidate for reelection (unless he is already serving his second, and thus final, term). These other functions are always an intrusion on his time and resources, and they are often a source of threats and problems (as when an adverse news story appears about one of his decisions). But they are sometimes an opportunity for increasing presidential power.

Communicating

The president will try to use his party leadership, his executive function, his head-of-state ceremonies, and his value as an object of publicity to acquire power beyond that supplied by the Constitution. In doing so, he confronts at least three audiences. The first, and often the most important, is his Washington, D.C., audience of fellow politicians and leaders. As Richard Neustadt pointed out in his book *Presidential Power,* a president's reputation among his Washington colleagues is of very great importance in affecting how much deference his views receive and thus how much power he can wield.[7] If a president is thought to be "smart," "sure of himself," "cool," "on top of things," or "shrewd" and thus "effective," he *will* be effective. Roosevelt had that reputation, and so did Lyndon Johnson, at least for his first few years in office. Truman, Ford, and Carter often did not have that reputation, and they lost ground accordingly. Power, like beauty, exists largely in the eye of the beholder.

A second audience is composed of party activists and officeholders outside Washington—the partisan grass roots. These persons want the president to exemplify their principles, flourish their slogans, appeal to their fears and hopes, and help them get reelected. Since, as was ex-

❝The president will try to use his party leadership, his executive function, his head-of-state ceremonies, and his value as an object of publicity to acquire power beyond that supplied by the Constitution.**❞**

Traveling as head of state to foreign nations is always an opportunity for getting valuable publicity and sometimes an occasion for making historic decisions. President Richard Nixon's trip to Peking, China, in 1972 was both.

plained in Chapter 6 on political parties, partisan activists increasingly have an ideological orientation toward national politics, these people will expect "their" president to make fire-and-brimstone speeches that confirm in them a shared sense of purpose and, incidentally, help them raise money from contributors to state and local campaigns.

The third audience is "the public," but of course that audience is really many publics, each with a different view or set of interests. A president on the campaign trail speaks boldly of what he will accomplish; a president in office

▪ The shortest president	*James Madison*
▪ The tallest president	*Abraham Lincoln*
▪ The only bachelor president	*James Buchanan*
▪ Three presidents who died on the Fourth of July	*Thomas Jefferson (1826) John Adams (1826) James Monroe (1831)*
▪ The shortest presidential term	*William Henry Harrison (one month)*
▪ The longest presidential term	*Franklin D. Roosevelt (12 years and 1 month)*
▪ The youngest president when inaugurated	*Theodore Roosevelt (42)*
▪ The oldest president when inaugurated	*William Henry Harrison (68)*
▪ First president born in the twentieth century	*John F. Kennedy (1917)*
▪ First presidential automobile	*Owned by William Howard Taft*
▪ Smallest percentage of popular vote cast for a president	*John Quincy Adams, 30.5% (1824)*
▪ Largest percentage of popular vote cast for a president	*Lyndon B. Johnson, 61.7% (1964)*

PRESIDENTIAL
trivia

speaks quietly of the problems that must be overcome. Citizens are often irritated at the apparent tendency of officeholders, including the president, to sound mealy-mouthed and equivocal. But is is easy to criticize the cooking when you haven't been the cook. A president learns quickly that his every utterance will be scrutinized closely by the media and by organized groups here and abroad, and his errors of fact, judgment, timing, or even inflection will be immediately and forcefully pointed out. Given the risks of saying too much, it is a wonder presidents say anything at all.

In general, presidents have made fewer and fewer impromptu remarks in the years since Roosevelt and have relied more and more on prepared addresses (from which errors can be culled in advance). Table 11.3 shows the presidential use of press conferences since 1932. As is evident, there has been a more or less steady decline in the average number per year, though Carter has tried to surpass the number given by Nixon.

There is no comparable count of the number of prepared radio or television addresses given by presidents, but they have no doubt grown rapidly. Not only do they offer a president the

TABLE 11.3 Presidential Press Conferences

President	Number	Years in office	Average per year
Roosevelt	998	12	83
Truman	322	8	40
Eisenhower	193	8	24
Kennedy	64	3	21
Johnson	126	5	25
Nixon	37	5½	7
Ford	39	2½	16
Carter	41	2[a]	20

[a] Through 1978.

“Given the risks of saying too much, it is a wonder presidents say anything at all.”

Lyndon Johnson's great political skill was not his ability to make speeches but his knack for dealing effectively with people alone or in small groups. Left, his face shows the strain of making a public address; right, he relaxes while talking informally with reporters in the White House.

advantage of advance preparation, they also permit him to speak directly to citizens without the intervening filter of newspaper editors and reporters and television commentators. Speaking before organizational meetings is another way the president can build publicity—and perhaps power—for his program.

Whatever publicity methods the president employs, they are only of limited and diminishing value. If he speaks out too often, he will bore or irritate people, and if he constantly calls for support, he will receive criticism for sounding weak. Sometimes he can speak effectively and rally support, as when President Roosevelt, speaking on the radio on the day after the bombing of Pearl Harbor, called December 7, 1941, a "day that will live in infamy" and rallied

the nation to a war effort, or when President Kennedy announced on television the news that Soviet offensive missiles had been installed in Cuba. But the occasions on which support can be rallied dramatically are rare, as Gerald Ford learned when he tried to get citizens to fight inflation by urging them not to pay high prices, when Richard Nixon tried to dissociate himself from Watergate, or when Jimmy Carter tried to persuade the people that the country faced a grave energy crisis.

Popularity with the Public and Congress

The grim reality is that a president loses support more or less steadily and surely from the day he takes office. Figure 11.2 shows the standing of seven presidents in the Gallup Poll; all but Eisen-

FIGURE 11.2   Presidential Popularity

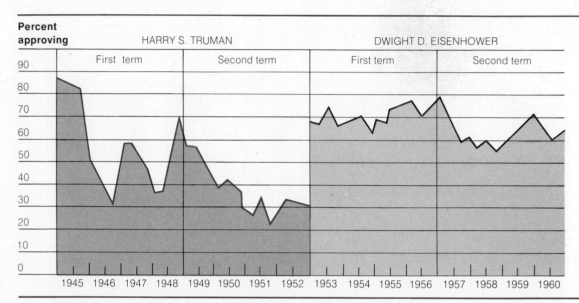

Note: Popularity was measured by asking every few months, "Do you approve of the way——is handling his job as president?"

hower lost support between their inauguration and the time they left office, except when their reelection gave them a brief burst of renewed popularity. Truman was hurt by scandals among his subordinates and by the protracted Korean War; Johnson was crippled by the increasingly unpopular war in Vietnam; Nixon was severely damaged by the Watergate crisis in his second term; and Ford was hurt when he pardoned Nixon for his part in Watergate. These are not very reassuring explanations; every president must expect to encounter scandal, foreign policy crises, and other problems.

Because a president's popularity tends to be highest immediately after his election, political commentators like to speak of a "honeymoon" period during which, presumably, the president's love affair with the people and with Congress can be consummated. Certainly Franklin D. Roosevelt enjoyed such a honeymoon. In the legend-

ary "first hundred days" of FDR's presidency, from March to June of 1933, he obtained from a willing Congress the passage of a large number of laws. Through these laws vast new powers were conferred on the federal government and several new agencies were created—the Federal Emergency Relief Administration, the Civilian Conservation Corps, the Tennessee Valley Authority, the Public Works Administration, the National Recovery Administration, and others. But those were extraordinary times: the most serious economic depression of this century had put millions out of work, banks were failing, farmers were insolvent, and the stock market was in shambles. It would have been political suicide for Congress to try to block, or even greatly delay, action on measures that appeared designed to help the nation out of the crisis.

Other presidents, serving in more normal times, have not enjoyed such a honeymoon.

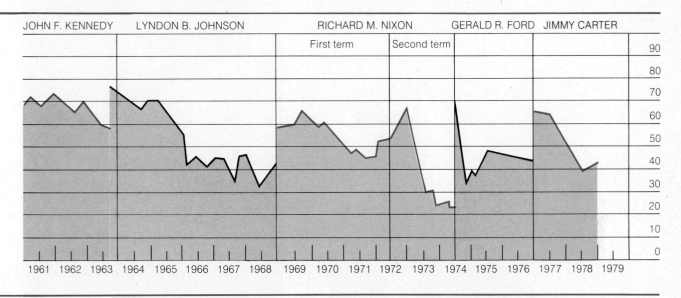

| JOHN F. KENNEDY | LYNDON B. JOHNSON | RICHARD M. NIXON | GERALD R. FORD | JIMMY CARTER |

Source: Thomas E. Cronin, *The State of the Presidency* (Boston: Little, Brown, 1975), pp. 110–111. Copyright © 1975 by Little, Brown and Company (Inc.). Reprinted by permission. Updated with Gallup Poll data, 1976–1979.

Harry Truman, though he aroused much sympathy when he was suddenly elevated to the presidency after the death of Roosevelt in 1945, was unable to persuade Congress to pass legislation on civil rights, health insurance, housing, or federal aid to schools. After his unexpected election victory in 1948 and a resurgence of his popularity, Truman was able to get his housing plan adopted but not his programs in education, civil rights, agriculture, or labor relations. Eisenhower did not propose a large domestic legislative program; his concerns were with foreign policy and with balancing the federal budget and cutting defense expenditures. Kennedy, Nixon, Ford, and Carter enjoyed some successes in their first year in office, but nothing that was remotely comparable to 1933 and little that would characterize their relations with Congress as a "honeymoon." Only Lyndon Johnson enjoyed a highly productive relationship with

Congress; perhaps because he came to the presidency after the shocking murder of Kennedy, perhaps because of his great legislative skill acquired by years of leadership experience in the Senate, perhaps because of the huge Democratic majorities he enjoyed after the 1964 election. In any event, during his first year or two in office, he obtained passage of important new bills regarding civil rights, aid to education, housing, poverty, economic development, highway beautification, and other subjects. Until the war in Vietnam sapped his political strength, Johnson rarely lost.

In short, no president can count on a honeymoon. Congress is a separate, independent institution, instinctively jealous of its prerogatives and suspicious of presidential pressure. Presidents often try to "take their case to the people" by the use of publicity, but only occasionally does that strategy work; often it backfires. Con-

A president's political reputation can change with startling speed. In 1964 a cartoonist portrayed President Johnson as a political maestro; three years later another cartoonist saw him being ground up by issues that he could not control.

gress resents a president who whips up public sentiment against it.

The president cannot make credible electoral threats against Congress. President Roosevelt attempted to "purge" congressmen who opposed his program by working for their defeat in the congressional elections, but he failed. Nor does presidential support help a congressional candidate. Presidents rarely endorse particular congressmen in primary elections because, should the congressman lose, a president would be embarrassed. Usually, a winning presidential candidate will sweep into office with him an increased number of congressmen of his party, as shown in Table 11.4.

But in recent decades presidents, especially Republican ones, have had remarkably short coattails on which legislators of the same party could ride into office. Eisenhower won 57.4 percent of the vote in 1956, but the Republicans lost seats in the House and the Senate. Kennedy won narrowly in 1960, but his party, the Democrats, lost seats in the House and gained only one in the Senate. Nixon saw his Republicans pick up a few seats in the 1968 election, but in 1972, when Nixon was reelected with one of the largest majorities in American history, the Republicans lost seats in the Senate and made only modest gains in the House.

During off-year elections—those in which congressmen are up for reelection but the president is not—the president's party fares even more poorly (see Table 11.5). Between 1934 and 1978, twelve off-year elections were held. The president's party lost seats in one or both houses of Congress in eleven of those elections.

THE POWER TO SAY "NO"

The Constitution gives the president the power to veto legislation. In addition, most presidents have asserted the right to "executive privilege" regarding information Congress may obtain from him or his subordinates, and some presidents have tried to impound funds appropriated by Congress. These efforts by the president to say "no" are not only a way of blocking action but also a way of forcing Congress to bargain with him over the substance of policies.

Veto

If a president disapproves of a bill passed by both houses of Congress, he may veto it in one of two ways. One is by a *veto message*. This is a statement that the president sends to Congress accompanying the bill, within ten days (not counting Sundays) after the bill has been passed. In it he sets forth his reasons for not signing the bill. The other is the *pocket veto*. If the president does not sign the bill within ten days *and* Congress has adjourned within that time, then the bill will not become law. Obviously, a pocket veto can only be used during a certain time of the year—just before Congress adjourns at the end of its second session. At times, presidents have pocket-vetoed a bill just before Congress recessed for a summer vacation or to permit its members to campaign during an off-year election. In 1972 Senator Edward M. Kennedy of Massachusetts protested that this was unconstitutional, since a recess is not the same thing as an adjournment. In a case brought to federal court, Kennedy was upheld, and it is now understood that the pocket veto can only be used just before the life of a given Congress expires.

A bill that is not signed or vetoed within ten days while Congress is still in session becomes law automatically without the president's approval. A bill that has been returned to Congress with a veto message can be passed over the president's objections if at least two-thirds of each house votes to override the veto. A bill that has received

TABLE 11.4   Partisan Gains or Losses in Congress in Presidential Elections

Year	President	Party	Gains or Losses of President's Party in House	Senate
1932	Roosevelt	Dem.	+90	+9
1936	Roosevelt	Dem.	+12	+7
1940	Roosevelt	Dem.	+7	−3
1944	Roosevelt	Dem.	+24	−2
1948	Truman	Dem.	+75	+9
1952	Eisenhower	Rep.	+22	+1
1956	Eisenhower	Rep.	−3	−1
1960	Kennedy	Dem.	−20	+1
1964	Johnson	Dem.	+37	+1
1968	Nixon	Rep.	+5	+7
1972	Nixon	Rep.	+12	−2
1976	Carter	Dem.	+1	+1

Source: Congressional Quarterly, *Guide to U.S. Elections,* p. 928; and *Congress and the Nation,* Vol. IV (1973–1976), p. 28.

TABLE 11.5   Partisan Gains or Losses in Congress in Off-Year Elections

Year	President	Party	Gains or Losses of President's Party in House	Senate
1934	Roosevelt	Dem.	+9	+9
1938	Roosevelt	Dem.	−70	−7
1942	Roosevelt	Dem.	−50	−8
1946	Truman	Dem.	−54	−11
1950	Truman	Dem.	−29	−5
1954	Eisenhower	Rep.	−18	−1
1958	Eisenhower	Rep.	−47	−13
1962	Kennedy	Dem.	−5	+2
1966	Johnson	Dem.	−48	−4
1970	Nixon	Rep.	−12	+1
1974	Ford	Rep.	−48	−5
1978	Carter	Dem.	−12	−3

Source: Congressional Quarterly, *Guide to U.S. Elections,* p. 928; and *Congress and the Nation,* Vol. IV (1973–1976), p. 28.

a pocket veto cannot be brought back to life by Congress (since Congress has adjourned), nor does such a bill carry over to the next session of Congress. If Congress wants to press the matter, it will have to start all over again by passing the bill anew in its next session, and then hope that the president will sign it or that, if he does not, they can override his veto.

The president must accept or reject the entire bill; he does not have, as some governors do, the right to exercise an item veto in which he approves of some provisions and disapproves of others. Congress can take advantage of this fact by putting provisions a president wants into a bill he does not like, thereby forcing him to sign the entire bill, objectionable parts and all, to get what he wants.

Nevertheless, the veto power is a substantial one because Congress rarely has the votes to override it. From George Washington to Gerald Ford, there have been 2,355 presidential vetoes cast; only 90, or less than 4 percent, have been overridden (see Table 11.6). Cleveland, Franklin Roosevelt, Truman, and Eisenhower made the most extensive use of vetoes, accounting for 70 percent of all vetoes ever cast. Often the vetoed legislation is revised by Congress and passed in a form suitable to the president. There is no tally of how often this happens, but it is frequent enough so that both branches of government recognize that the veto, or even the threat of it, is part of an elaborate process of political negotiation in which the president has substantial powers.

Executive Privilege

The Constitution says nothing about whether the president is obliged to divulge private communications between himself and his principal advisers, but presidents have acted as if they did have that privilege of confidentiality. The presidential claim is based on two grounds. First, the doctrine of the separation of powers means that one branch of government does not have the right to inquire into the internal workings of another branch headed by constitutionally named officers. Second, the principles of statecraft and of prudent administration require that the president have the right to obtain confidential and candid advice from subordinates; such advice could not be obtained if it would quickly be exposed to public scrutiny.

TABLE 11.6 Presidential Vetoes, 1789–1977

	Regular vetoes	Pocket vetoes	Total vetoes	Vetoes overridden
Washington	2	–	2	–
Madison	5	2	7	–
Monroe	1	–	1	–
Jackson	5	7	12	–
Tyler	6	3	9	1
Polk	2	1	3	–
Pierce	9	–	9	5
Buchanan	4	3	7	–
Lincoln	2	4	6	–
A. Johnson	21	8	29	15
Grant	45	49	94	4
Hayes	12	1	13	1
Arthur	4	8	12	1
Cleveland	304	109	413	2
Harrison	19	25	44	1
Cleveland	43	127	170	5
McKinley	6	36	42	–
T. Roosevelt	42	40	82	1
Taft	30	9	39	1
Wilson	33	11	44	6
Harding	5	1	6	–
Coolidge	20	30	50	4
Hoover	21	16	37	3
F. Roosevelt	372	261	633	9
Truman	180	70	250	12
Eisenhower	73	108	181	2
Kennedy	12	9	21	–
L. Johnson	16	14	30	–
Nixon	24	19	43	5
Ford	50	16	66	12
Carter[a]	6	13	19	0

Source: Senate Library, *Presidential Vetoes* (Washington, D.C.: Government Printing Office, 1969), p. 199; *Congressional Quarterly Almanac*, 1976.

[a] Through December 1977.

For almost two hundred years there was no serious challenge to the claim of presidential confidentiality. The Supreme Court did not require the disclosure of confidential communications to or from the president.[8] Congress was never happy with this claim but until 1973 did not seriously dispute it. Indeed, in 1962, a Senate committee explicitly accepted a claim by President Kennedy that his secretary of defense, Robert S. McNamara, was not obliged to divulge the identity of Defense Department officials who had censored certain speeches by generals and admirals.

In 1973 the Supreme Court for the first time met the issue directly. A federal special prosecutor had sought tape recordings of White House conversations between President Nixon and his advisers as part of his investigation of the Watergate scandal. In the case of *United States* v. *Nixon,* the Supreme Court, by a vote of eight to zero, held that while there may well be a sound

❝As a practical matter, it seems likely that presidential advisers will be able, except in unusual cases such as Watergate, to continue to give private advice to the president.❞

basis for the claim of executive privilege, especially where sensitive military or diplomatic matters are involved, there is no "absolute unqualified Presidential privilege of immunity from judicial process under all circumstances."[9] To admit otherwise would be to block the constitutionally defined function of the federal courts to decide criminal cases. Thus, Nixon was ordered to hand over the disputed tapes and papers to a federal judge so that the judge could decide which were relevant to the case at hand and allow those to be introduced into evidence. In the future, another president may well persuade the Court that a different set of records or papers are so sensitive as to require protection,

President Nixon justified his refusal to disclose tapes of conversations in the Oval Office by the argument that a president must have the private and candid views of his advisers, such as John Ehrlichman and Henry Kissinger (standing) and H. R. Haldeman (seated). The Supreme Court recognized this need but decided that tapes containing evidence bearing on possible criminal violations must be handed over to a judge.

especially if there is no allegation of criminal misconduct requiring the production of evidence in court. As a practical matter, it seems likely that presidential advisers will be able, except in unusual cases such as Watergate, to continue to give private advice to the president.

Impoundment of Funds

From time to time presidents have refused to spend money appropriated by Congress. Truman did not spend all that Congress wanted spent on the armed forces, and Johnson did not spend all that Congress made available for highway construction. Kennedy refused to spend money appropriated for new weapons systems that he did not like. Indeed, the precedent for impounding goes back at least to the administration of Thomas Jefferson.

But what has precedent is not by that fact constitutional. The Constitution is silent on whether the president *must* spend the money Congress appropriates; all it says is that the president cannot spend money Congress has *not* appropriated. The major test of presidential power in this respect occurred during the Nixon administration. Nixon wished to reduce federal spending. He proposed in 1972 that Congress give him the power to reduce federal spending so that it would not exceed $250 billion for the coming year. Congress, under Democratic control, refused. Nixon responded by pocket-vetoing twelve spending bills and then impounding funds appropriated under other laws he had not vetoed.

Congress responded by passing the Budget Reform Act of 1974 that, among other things, required the president to spend all appropriated funds unless he first tells Congress what funds he wishes not to spend and Congress, within forty-five days, agrees to delete the items. If he wishes simply to delay spending the money, he need only inform Congress, but Congress in turn can refuse the delay by passing a resolution requiring the immediate release of the money. It is not clear, however, that this will settle the matter. If a future president impounds funds, Congress will

have to find some way of enforcing its will—by impeachment (which is unlikely), by refusing to act on other items in the president's program, or by political and public pressure.

THE PRESIDENT'S PROGRAM

The authority a president has by virtue of his constitutional position, combined with the influence he can accumulate through appointments, public opinion, and political bargaining, are in theory put to the service of his policies and programs. Those policies, however, are not ready-made; someone must think them up. For a newly elected president, that is not as easy as it might appear.

A presidential candidate who is not an incumbent will spend at a minimum two years full time running for the presidency, and in some cases many more years. His campaign, of necessity, dwells on problems and proposals in general terms. With few exceptions, overly specific proposals are risky—they may lose more votes than they win. Campaigning, as explained in another chapter, is devoted chiefly to positioning oneself in a general way in the perceptions of voters: usually as a sincere, honest, attractive, middle-of-the-road leader who does not take extreme positions and who plays on certain discontents evident in the electorate.

Once elected, the new president discovers that he has no clear policies, no budget, no cabinet, and in many cases no notion of what the daily routine of the White House is like. Furthermore, deadlines are short. He has just two months from election to inauguration to fill hundreds of key posts. Additionally, he must prepare a State of the Union message that is required by the Constitution and that by custom is given two or three weeks after his inauguration, and annually thereafter. As a result of the shortness of time and lack of experience, most newly elected presidents only tinker with their predecessor's budget and policies. It takes a year at least for a new administration to get its feet firmly on the ground.

Putting Together a Program

Before the modern presidency with its large role in the nation's affairs, presidential policies were of little significance. A new president might mention two or three things important to him—tariffs, relations with England or France, veterans' pensions, or civil service reform—but he was not expected to have something to say (and to offer) to everybody. Today he is.

In formulating policies on short notice, he can draw on several sources, each with particular strengths and weaknesses:

His aides and campaign advisers
Strength: Will test new ideas for their political soundness.
Weakness: Will not have many ideas to test, being inexperienced in government.

Federal bureaus and agencies
Strength: Will know what is feasible in terms of governmental realities.
Weakness: Will propose plans that promote own agencies and will not have good information on whether plans will work.

Outside, academic, and other specialists and experts
Strength: Will have many general ideas and criticisms of existing programs.
Weakness: Will not know the details of policy or have good judgment as to what is feasible.

Interest groups
Strength: Will have specific plans and ideas.
Weakness: Will have narrow view of the public interest.

In formulating his policies, a president must piece together programs out of all these sources of advice, trying to use the strengths of one group to offset the weaknesses of another. One of his major problems is that he will not know more than a small fraction of the people on whom he must rely for advice. In this respect his experience is quite different from the British prime minister who will have served for a long time in the House of Commons with many of the men and women who later become cabinet officers, aides, and advisers. In short, a president takes risks when he devises a new policy. Therefore, he often will allow certain elements of his planned policy to be "leaked" to the press, or to be "floated" as a "trial balloon" to test public and congressional reaction before he commits himself fully to the policy. Members of the executive branch and of the permanent federal bureaucracy who do not like aspects of a president's program will, of course, do exactly the same thing, hoping for the opposite effect—they will leak unpopular parts of a presidential program in an effort to discredit the whole thing. This process of testing the winds by a president and his critics helps explain why so many news stories coming from Washington mention no person by name but only an anonymous "highly placed source."

In addition to the risks of adverse reaction, the president faces three other constraints on his ability to plan a program. One is the sheer limit of his time and attention span. Every president

A president must cope with a staggering workload. Here President Ford ponders one of countless documents that cross his desk.

works harder than he has ever worked before. A ninety-hour week is typical. Even so, he has great difficulty keeping up with all the things he is supposed to know and make decisions about. For example, Congress during an average year passes between 400 and 600 bills, each of which the president must sign, veto, or allow to take effect without his signature. Scores of persons wish to see him. Hundreds of phone calls must be made to congressmen and others in order to ask for help, to soothe ruffled feathers, or to get information. He must receive all newly appointed ambassadors and visiting heads of state and in addition have his picture taken with countless persons, from a Nobel Prize winner to a child whose likeness will appear on the Easter Seal.

The second constraint is the unexpected crisis. Roosevelt, obviously, had to respond to a depression and to the mounting risks of world war. But most presidents get their crises when they least expect them:

Truman
- Major strikes in the auto, steel, coal, railroad, and shipping industries
- Civil wars in Greece and Palestine
- South Korea invaded by North Korea
- Berlin put under siege by Soviet troops
- Truman's military aide charged with accepting improper gifts

Eisenhower
- Egypt seizes Suez Canal
- Revolts against Communist rule in East Berlin, Poland, Hungary
- Supreme Court outlaws school segregation
- USSR launches Sputnik satellite
- Presidential aide accused of accepting improper gifts

Kennedy
- Failure of Bay of Pigs invasion of Cuba
- Soviets put missiles in Cuba
- China invades India
- Federal troops sent to South to protect blacks

Johnson
- Vietnam War
- Black riots in major cities
- War between India and Pakistan
- Civil war in Dominican Republic
- Arab-Israeli war
- U.S. ship seized by North Korea
- Civil rights workers murdered in South
- Presidential aide arrested for immoral conduct

Nixon
- Watergate scandal
- Arab-Israeli war
- Value of dollar falls in foreign trade
- Arabs raise the price of oil

Carter
- OMB Director Bert Lance accused of improprieties
- Lengthy coal strike
- Collapse of the Shah of Iran

The third constraint is the fact that the federal government and most federal programs, as well as the federal budget, can only be changed, except in special circumstances, marginally. In ways that will be explained in later chapters, the vast bulk of federal expenditures are beyond control in any given year: the money must be spent whether the president likes it or not. Most federal programs have sufficiently strong congressional or public support that they must be left intact or modified only slightly. And this means that most federal employees can count on being secure in their jobs, whatever a president's views on whether the bureaucracy is or is not too large.

The result of these constraints is that the president, at least in ordinary times, will have to be selective about what he wants. He can be thought of as having a stock of influence and prestige the way he might have a supply of money. If he wants to get the most "return" on his resources, he must "invest" that influence and prestige carefully in enterprises that promise substantial gains—in public benefits and political support—at reasonable costs. Each president will tend to speak in terms of changing everything at once, calling his approach a "New Deal," a "New Frontier," a "Great Society," or the "New Federalism." But beneath the rhetoric, he must identify a few specific proposals on which he wishes to bet his resources, all the while mindful of the need to leave a substantial stock of resources in reserve to handle the inevitable crises and emergencies. In recent decades events have required every president to devote a substantial part of his time and resources to two key issues: the state of the economy and foreign affairs. What he manages to do in addition to this will depend on his personal views and his sense of what the nation, as well as his reelection, requires.

Measuring Success

His accomplishments are frequently measured in terms of his "legislative box score" based on the proportion of the measures he favors that are passed by Congress. It has only been in the last thirty years or so that the president has formally presented to Congress (or, more accurately, has had introduced on his behalf) a detailed, comprehensive package of legislative proposals. Once, cabinet departments could submit bills directly to Congress; now, all must first be "cleared" by the president, usually by way of OMB. Figure 11.3 shows how these bills fared year by year from Eisenhower to Carter. During this period Congress approved on the average a bit more than half of the president's proposals, ranging from a high under Lyndon Johnson in 1965 to a low under Richard Nixon in 1973. In

FIGURE 11.3   Presidential Success on Votes, 1953–1978

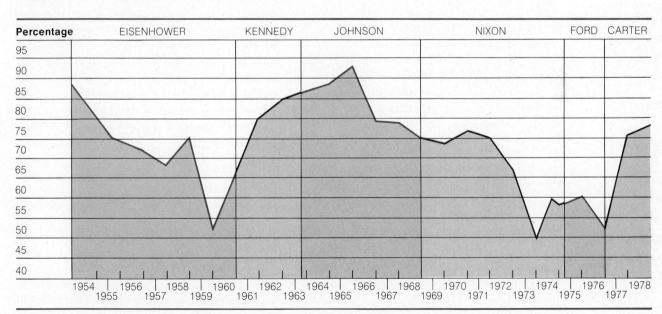

Note: Percentage of bills on which the president took a position with which Congress agreed.

Great Britain, by contrast, 96 percent of the prime minister's bills were approved by the House of Commons during the period 1957 to 1969.

Attempts to Reorganize

There is one item on the presidential agenda that has been the same for almost every president since Herbert Hoover: reorganizing the executive branch of government. With few exceptions, every president since 1928 has tried to change the structure of the staff, departments, and agencies which are theoretically subordinate to him. Every president has been appalled by the number of agencies that report to him and the apparently helter-skelter manner in which they have grown up. But this is only one—and often not the most important—reason for wanting to reorganize. If a president wants to get something done, or put new people in charge of a program, or recapture political support for a policy, it often proves easier to do so by creating a new agency, or reorganizing an old one, than by abolishing a program, firing a subordinate, or passing a new law. Reorganization serves many objectives, and thus is a recurring theme of presidential efforts at leadership.

Between 1948 and 1961 the agency in charge of foreign aid was reorganized eight times. Between 1968 and 1973 the federal agency charged with enforcing narcotics laws was reorganized twice, and in 1977 a third reorganization was proposed. Presidents Truman and Eisenhower each created a national commission to recommend wholesale reorganizations, both chaired by former President Hoover. President Roosevelt appointed a commission on administrative management; over thirty years later President Nixon created another one. President Carter made reorganization a priority concern of his staff. From 1949 to 1973 ninety-two separate reorganization plans, some calling for small changes, some for large ones, were sent to Congress. About two-thirds were approved, many

only after hard-fought battles. In modern times Presidents Johnson, Nixon, and Carter have been the most determined advocates of reorganization, though not necessarily the most successful.

Legally, the president can reorganize his personal White House staff any time he wishes. To reorganize in any important way the larger Executive Office of the President or any of the executive departments or agencies, however, Congress must first be consulted in one of two ways. The president can submit legislation that is considered by Congress in the normal manner and, if passed by both houses, signed into law. Or the president can submit a reorganization plan that automatically takes effect provided that the House and Senate do not pass within sixty days a concurrent resolution disapproving of the plan. A reorganization *plan* can change an agency but cannot abolish it or create a new one; a reorganization *law* can do any of these things. This procedure, called the "legislative veto," was first created by the Reorganization Act of 1939 and has been retained, with slight modifications, in subsequent versions of this law. Congress is quite reluctant to give broad authority to the president to reorganize. In 1973, when Congress was particularly distrustful of the president as a result of the Watergate scandal, his power to submit reorganization plans was allowed to lapse and was not renewed until after President Carter took office in 1977.

There have been many bitter fights over reorganization plans. At stake are differing beliefs as to what the agency should do, who should head it, and what congressional committee should have power over it. The Department of Health, Education, and Welfare was created by a reorganization plan in 1953, but to get the plan accepted, President Eisenhower had to promise to leave the Public Health Service and the Office of Education, nominally part of the new department, relatively autonomous. The first efforts to create a Department of Urban Affairs were blocked because key congressmen objected to the prospect of a black heading the agency (it was later created and a black did head it). The law designed to create a Department of Transportation, which finally passed in 1966, involved one of the most difficult legislative struggles of President Johnson's administration: his chief domestic policy aide later wrote that it took 15 percent of the aide's time and required daily presidential attention, and even then fell well short of a thorough restructuring of transportation agencies.[10]

What has been said so far may well give the reader the impression that the president is virtually helpless. That is not the case. The *actual* power of the president can only be measured in terms of what he can accomplish, and an analysis of that requires that we first consider a number of concrete policies. This we shall do in Part IV of this book. After that, we shall return to the question of presidential power with a summary assessment. What this chapter has described to this point has been the office as the president finds it—the burdens, restraints, demands, complexities, and resources that he encounters on entering the Oval Office for the first time. Every president since Truman has commented, feelingly, on how limited the powers of the president seem when seen from the inside compared to what they appear to be when viewed from the outside. Roosevelt spoke of his struggles with the bureaucracy in terms of punching a featherbed; Truman wrote that the power of the president was chiefly the power to persuade people to do what they ought to do anyway. After being in office a year or so, Kennedy spoke to interviewers about how much more complex the world appeared than he first supposed. Johnson and Nixon were broken by the office and the events that happened there.

Yet Roosevelt helped create the modern presidency with its vast organizational reach and directed a massive war effort. Truman ordered two atomic bombs dropped on Japanese cities.

"How limited the powers of the president seem when seen from the inside compared to what they appear to be when viewed from the outside."

President Kennedy sought the advice of former President Eisenhower at Camp David in April 1961, as Kennedy struggled with the failure of the Bay of Pigs landing by anti-Castro Cubans who were supported by the United States.

Eisenhower sent American troops to Lebanon, and Kennedy supported an effort to invade Cuba. Johnson sent troops to the Dominican Republic and to Vietnam; Nixon ordered an invasion of Cambodia; and Ford sent military forces to free a captured American merchant ship. Obviously, Europeans, Russians, Vietnamese, Cambodians, Cubans, Dominicans, and Japanese do not think of the American president as "helpless." In later chapters, especially Chapter 20 on foreign policy, we shall return to this apparent paradox.

PRESIDENTIAL TRANSITION

No president but Franklin Roosevelt has ever served more than two terms and, since the ratification of the Twenty-Second Amendment to the Constitution in 1951, no president may do so again. But more than tradition or the Constitution escorts presidents from office. Only thirteen of the thirty-eight presidents since George Washington have been elected to a second term. Of the twenty-six not reelected, four died in office during their first term. But the remainder either did not seek or, more usually, could not obtain, reelection.

Of the eight presidents who died in office, four were assassinated: Lincoln, Garfield, McKinley, and Kennedy. At least another five presidents were the objects of unsuccessful assassination attempts: Jackson, Theodore Roosevelt, Franklin Roosevelt, Truman, and Ford. (There may, of course, have been attempts on other presidents that never came to public notice; the attempts mentioned here involved public efforts to fire weapons at presidents.)

The presidents who served two or more terms fall into certain periods such as the Founding (Washington, Jefferson, Madison, Monroe) or wartime (Lincoln, Wilson, Roosevelt, Lyndon Johnson), or happened to be in office during especially tranquil times (Monroe, McKinley, Eisenhower), or some combination of the above. When the country was deeply divided, as during the years just before the Civil War and during the period of Reconstruction after it, it was the rare president who was reelected.

The Vice-President

Eight times a vice-president has become president because of the death of his predecessor. It first happened to John Tyler who became president when William Henry Harrison died, peacefully, after only one month in office. The problem for Tyler and for the country was substantial: Was Tyler simply to be the acting pres-

The tasks of a vice-president are largely ceremonial. Vice-President Walter Mondale here is greeted by West German Chancellor Helmut Schmidt in Bonn.

ident and a kind of caretaker until a new president was elected, or was he to be *president* in every sense of the word? Despite criticism, and despite what might have been the contrary intention of the Framers of the Constitution, Tyler decided on the latter course and was confirmed in that opinion by a decision of Congress. Ever since then, the vice-president has automatically become president, in title and in powers, when the occupant of the White House died or resigned.

But if vice-presidents frequently acquire office because of death, they rarely acquire it by election. Since the earliest period of the Founding, when John Adams and Thomas Jefferson were each elected president after having first served as vice-president under their predecessors, there have only been two occasions when a vice-president was later able to win the presidency without his president having died in office. One was 1836, when Martin Van Buren was elected president after having served as Andrew Jackson's vice-president; the second was in 1968 when Richard Nixon became president after having been vice-president to Dwight Eisenhower eight years earlier. Many vice-presidents who enter the Oval Office because their predecessors died are subsequently elected to terms in their own right—this happened to Theodore Roosevelt, Calvin Coolidge, Harry Truman, and Lyndon Johnson—but no one who wishes to become president should assume that to become vice-president first is the best way to get there.

The vice-presidency is just what so many vice-presidents have complained about its being: a rather empty job. John Adams described it as "the most insignificant office that ever the invention of man contrived or his imagination conceived," and most of his successors would agree. Thomas Jefferson, almost alone, had a good word to say for it: "The second office of the government is honorable and easy, the first is but a splendid misery."[11] Daniel Webster rejected a vice-presidential nomination in 1848 with the phrase, "I do not choose to be buried until I am really dead."[12] (Had he taken the job, he would have become president after Zachary Taylor died in office, thereby achieving a remarkable secular resurrection.) For all the good and bad jokes about the vice-presidency, however, candidates still struggle mightily for it. John Nance Garner gave up the Speakership of the House to become Franklin Roosevelt's vice-president (a job he valued as "not worth a pitcher of warm spit*"), and Lyndon Johnson gave up the majority leadership of the Senate to become Kennedy's. Harry Truman, Richard Nixon, Hubert Humphrey, and Walter Mondale all left reasonably secure Senate seats for the vice-presidency.

The only official task of the vice-president is to preside over the Senate and to vote in case of a tie. Even this is scarcely time-consuming, as the Senate chooses from among its members a president pro tempore, as required by the Constitution, who (along with others) presides in the absence of the vice-president. The vice-president's leadership powers in the Senate are weak, especially when the vice-president is of a different party than the majority of the senators. Presidents have from time to time found tasks for their vice-presidents—minor foreign missions, the chairmanship of governmental commissions, and the like—but there can be no escaping the fact that the vice-president can do little more than endorse whatever the president does, and wait.

Problems of Succession

If the president should die in office, the right of the vice-president to assume that office, and to be sworn in as president, has been clear since the time of John Tyler. But two questions remain: What if the president falls seriously ill, but does not die? And if, the vice-president steps up, who then becomes the new vice-president?

The first problem has arisen on a number of occasions. After President James A. Garfield was shot in 1881, he lingered through the summer before he died. President Woodrow Wilson col-

---

*The word he actually used was a good deal stronger than "spit," but historians are decorous.

"For the first time in history, the nation had as its two principal executive officers men who had not been elected to either the presidency or the vice-presidency.**"**

Gerald R. Ford, who assumed the presidency in 1974, nominated Nelson Rockefeller as his vice-president.

lapsed from a stroke and was a virtual recluse for seven months in 1919 and an invalid for the rest of his term. President Eisenhower had three serious illnesses while in office.

The second problem arose on eight occasions when the vice-president became president owing to the death of the incumbent. In these cases there was no elected person available to succeed the new president should he die in office. For many decades the problem was handled by law. The Succession Act of 1886, for example, designated the secretary of state as next in line for the presidency should the vice-president die, followed by the other cabinet officers in order of seniority. But this meant that a vice-president who becomes president could pick his own suc-

cessor by choosing his own secretary of state. In 1947 the law was changed to make the Speaker of the House and then the president pro tempore of the Senate next in line for the presidency. But that created still other problems: a Speaker or a president pro tempore is likely to be chosen because of his age, not his executive skill, and in any event might well be of the party opposite to that occupying the White House.

Finally, both problems were resolved in 1967 by the Twenty-Fifth Amendment to the Constitution. It deals with the disability problem by allowing the vice-president to serve as "acting president" whenever the president declares that he is unable to discharge the powers and duties of his office or whenever the vice-president and a majority of the cabinet declare that the president is incapacitated. If the president disagrees with the opinion of his vice-president and a majority of the cabinet, then Congress decides the issue. A two-thirds majority is necessary to confirm that the president is unable to serve.

The amendment deals with the succession problem by requiring a vice-president who assumes the presidency after a vacancy is created by death or resignation to nominate a new vice-president. This person takes office if the nomination is confirmed by a majority vote of both houses of Congress.

The disability problem has not arisen since the adoption of the amendment, but the succession problem has. In 1973 Vice-President Spiro Agnew resigned, having pleaded no contest to criminal charges. President Nixon nominated Gerald R. Ford as vice-president and, after extensive hearings, he was confirmed by both houses of Congress and sworn in. Then on August 9, 1974, Nixon resigned the presidency—the first man to do so—and Ford became president. He nominated as his vice-president Nelson Rockefeller who was confirmed by both houses of Congress—again, after extensive hearings—and was sworn in on December 19, 1974. For the first time in history, the nation had as its two principal executive officers men who had not been elected to either the presidency or the vice-presidency. It is a measure of the legitimacy of the Constitution that this arrangement caused no crisis in public opinion. Suggestions were made for a further constitutional amendment that would require a special presidential election in these cases, but nothing came of them.

Impeachment

There is one other way, besides death, disability, or resignation, by which a president can leave office before his term expires, and that is impeachment. Not only the president and vice-president, but also all "civil officers of the United States" can be removed by being impeached and convicted. As a practical matter, civil officers—cabinet secretaries, bureau chiefs, and the like—will not be subject to impeachment because the president can remove them at any time and usually will if their behavior makes them a serious political liability. Federal judges, who serve for life and who are constitutionally independent of the president and Congress, have been the most frequent objects of impeachment.

An impeachment is like an indictment in a criminal trial: a set of charges against somebody, voted by (in this case) the House of Representatives. To be removed from office, the impeached officer must be convicted by a two-thirds vote of the Senate which sits as a court, hears the evidence, and makes its decision under whatever rules it wishes to adopt. Twelve persons have been impeached by the House, and four have been convicted by the Senate. The last conviction was in 1936 when a federal judge was removed from office for lack of integrity.

Only one president has been impeached—Andrew Johnson in 1868—but Richard Nixon almost surely would have been had he not first resigned. Johnson was not convicted on the impeachment, the effort to do so falling one vote short of the necessary two-thirds majority. Many historians feel that the effort to remove Johnson was entirely partisan and ideological in nature, for he was not charged with anything that they would regard as "high crimes and misdemeanors" within the meaning of the Constitution.

The Congress detested Johnson's "soft" policy toward the defeated South after the Civil War and was determined to use any pretext to get him out of office. The charges against Nixon were far more grave, involving allegations of illegal acts arising out of his effort to cover up his subordinates' involvement in the burglary of the Democratic National Committee headquarters in the Watergate building.

Some Founders may have thought that impeachment would be frequently used against presidents, but as a practical matter it is so complex and serious an undertaking that we can probably expect it to be reserved in the future only for the gravest forms of presidential misconduct. No one quite knows what a high crime or misdemeanor is, but most scholars seem agreed that the charge must involve something illegal or unconstitutional, not just unpopular. Unless a president or vice-president is first impeached and convicted, many experts believe that he is not liable to prosecution as would be an ordinary citizen. (No one is certain, because the question has never arisen.) President Ford's pardon of Richard Nixon meant that he could not be prosecuted under federal law for things he may have done while in office.

Students may find the occasions of misconduct or disability remote and the details of succession or impeachment tedious. But the problem is not remote—succession has occurred nine times and disability at least twice—and what may appear tedious goes, in fact, to the heart of the presidency. The first and fundamental problem is to make the office legitimate. That was the great task George Washington set himself, and that was the substantial accomplishment of his successors. Despite bitter and sometimes violent partisan and sectional strife, beginning almost immediately after Washington stepped down, presidential succession has always occurred peacefully, without a military coup or a political plot. For centuries, in the bygone times of kings as well as in the present times of dictators and juntas, peaceful succession has been a rare phenomenon among the nations of the world. Many of the critics of the Constitution believed, in 1787, that it would not happen in the United States either: somehow, the president would connive to hold office for life or to hand-pick his successor. Their predictions were wrong, though their fears were understandable.

SUMMARY

A president, chosen by the people and with powers derived from a written constitution, has less power than does a British prime minister, even though the latter depends entirely on the support of his or her party in Parliament. The separation of powers between the executive and legislative branches, the distinguishing feature of the American system, means that the president must deal with a competitor—Congress—in setting policy and even in managing executive agencies.

Presidential power, though still sharply limited, has grown from its constitutional origins as a result of congressional delegation, the increased importance of foreign affairs, and public expectations. But if the president today has more power, more is also demanded of him. As a result, how effective he is depends, not on any general grant of authority, but on the nature of the issue he confronts and the extent to which he can mobilize informal sources of power (public opinion, congressional support).

Though the president seemingly stands at the head of a vast executive branch apparatus, in fact he appoints but a small portion of the officials and the behavior of even these is often beyond his easy control. Moreover, public support, high at the beginning of any new presidency, usually tends to decline as the term proceeds. As a result, each president must conserve his power (and his energy and time), concentrating these scarce resources to deal with a few matters of major importance. Virtually every president since Franklin Roosevelt has tried to enlarge his ability to manage the executive branch—by reorganization, by appointing White House aides, by creating specialized staff agencies—but no president has been satisfied with the results.

The president, in dealing with Congress, can rely to some degree on party loyalty; thus presidents of the same party as that controlling Congress tend to have more of their proposals approved. But such loyalty is insufficient; every president must in addition employ cajolery, the awarding of favors, and the threat of vetoes to influence legislation. Few presidents can count on a honeymoon; most discover that their own plans are at the mercy of unexpected crises.

The extent to which a president will be weak or powerful will vary with the kind of issue and the circumstances of the moment. It is a mistake to speak of an "imperial presidency" or of an ineffectual one. A president's power is better assessed by considering how he behaves in regard to specific issues.

Suggested Readings

General

Corwin, Edward S. *The President: Office and Powers,* 4th ed. New York: Oxford University Press, 1957. Historical, constitutional, and legal development of the office.

Cronin, Thomas E. *The State of the Presidency.* Boston: Little, Brown, 1975. Analyzes the political position of the presidency, with special emphasis on the constraints on the office.

Cunliffe, Marcus. *American Presidents and the Presidency.* New York: American Heritage Press/McGraw-Hill, 1972. Readable history of the presidency, with shrewd insights and ample anecdotes.

Hess, Stephen. *Organizing the Presidency.* Washington, D.C.: Brookings Institution, 1976. How presidents from Roosevelt to Nixon organized the White House Office.

Neustadt, Richard E. *Presidential Power: The Politics of Leadership,* rev. ed. New York: John Wiley, 1976. How presidents try to acquire and hold political power in the competitive world of official Washington, by a man who has been both a scholar and an insider.

Pious, Richard M. *The American Presidency.* New York: Basic Books, 1979. A comprehensive, up-to-date treatment of the presidency in all its aspects.

On Particular Presidents

FRANKLIN D. ROOSEVELT

—Burns, James MacGregor. *Roosevelt: The Lion and the Fox.* New York: Harcourt Brace, 1956.

—Leuchtenberg, William E. *Franklin D. Roosevelt and the New Deal, 1932–1940.* New York: Harper & Row, 1963.

HARRY S. TRUMAN

—Hamby, A. L. *Beyond the New Deal: Harry S. Truman and American Liberalism.* New York: Columbia University Press, 1973.

—Truman, Harry S. *Memoirs,* 2 vols. Garden City, N.Y.: Doubleday, 1958.

DWIGHT D. EISENHOWER

—Donovan, R. J. *Eisenhower: The Inside Story.* New York: Harper & Row, 1956.

JOHN F. KENNEDY

—Paper, Lewis J. *The Promise and the Performance: The Leadership of John F. Kennedy.* New York: Crown, 1975.

—Sorenson, Theodore M. *Kennedy.* New York: Harper & Row, 1965.

LYNDON B. JOHNSON

—Kearns, Doris. *Lyndon Johnson and the American Dream.* New York: Harper & Row, 1976.

—Evans, Rowland, and Robert Novak. *Lyndon B. Johnson: The Exercise of Power.* New York: New American Library, 1968.

12 The Bureaucracy

Comparison with other countries · Growth of
the bureaucracy · Change in role · Hiring
and firing · Scope of power · Agency point of
view · A bureaucratic personality? ·
Agency–interest group relations · Relationship
to Congress and the president · The problem
of bureaucracy

The visible struggles for political power occur
within and between the presidency and Congress, but the invisible struggles take place in and
among the myriad departments, agencies, commissions, and offices of government—in short,
within the bureaucracy. Moreover, it is in the
actions of bureaucratic organizations that one
finds the concrete expression of the policies that
emerge from these struggles. The bureaucracy is
a key element in both the struggle for power and
the definition of values government is to serve.

"Bureaucracy" was once simply a pejorative
term, implying red tape, rigidity, confusion, or
arrogance. People who criticize government still
use the word in that sense—during the 1976 election campaign, Jimmy Carter and Gerald Ford
seemed to agree on little other than their oft-ex-
pressed distaste for "the bureaucracy." But the
word also has a technical meaning, and that is
how we will use it here. A bureaucracy is a large,

The U.S. Post Office, was for long the only sizable
federal bureaucracy (left). Today there are millions
of persons who receive money and services from
Washington (right).

complex organization composed of appointed officials. By "complex" we mean that authority in the organization is divided among several managers; no one person is able to make all the decisions (see Figure 12.1). A large corporation is a bureaucracy; so is a government agency. Increasingly, people who work in or attempt to run government organizations call themselves bureaucrats without any embarrassment.

FIGURE 12.1   How Bureaucracy Grows: The Increasing Division of Managerial Authority

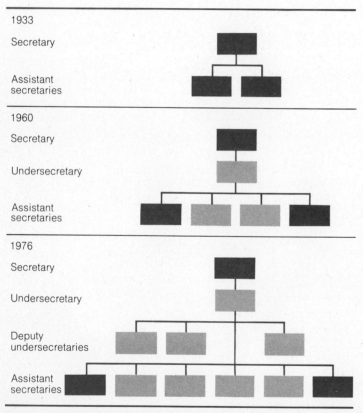

1933

Secretary

Assistant secretaries

1960

Secretary

Undersecretary

Assistant secretaries

1976

Secretary

Undersecretary

Deputy undersecretaries

Assistant secretaries

Source: Hugh Heclo, "Issue Networks and the Executive Establishment," in Anthony King, ed., *The New American Political System* (Washington, D.C.: American Enterprise Institute, 1978), p. 114. Copyright © 1978 by the American Enterprise Institute. Reprinted by permission.

Note: Charts show political appointees above the level of bureau heads, U.S. Department of Labor, 1933, 1960, and 1976.

DISTINCTIVENESS OF THE U.S. BUREAUCRACY

Bureaucratic government has become an obvious feature of all modern societies, democratic and nondemocratic. In the United States, however, three aspects of our constitutional system and political traditions give to the bureaucracy and its operations a distinctive character. First, political authority over the bureaucracy is not in one set of hands, but shared among several institutions. In a parliamentary regime, such as in Great Britain, the appointed officials of the national government work for the cabinet ministers who are in turn dominated by the prime minister. In theory and to a considerable extent in practice, British bureaucrats report to and take orders from the ministers in charge of their departments, do not deal directly with Parliament, and rarely give interviews to the press. In the United States, the Constitution permits both the president and Congress to exercise authority over the bureaucracy. Every senior appointed official has at least two masters: one in the executive branch and the other in the legislative. Often there are many more than two—Congress, after all, is not a single organization but a collection of committees, subcommittees, and individuals. This divided authority encourages bureaucrats to play one branch of government off against the other and to make heavy use of the media.

Second, most of the agencies of the federal government share their functions with related agencies in state and local government. Though some federal agencies deal directly with American citizens—the Internal Revenue Service collects taxes from them, the Federal Bureau of Investigation looks into crimes that may have been committed by them, the Postal Service delivers mail to them—many agencies work with other organizations at other levels of government. For example: the Office of Education gives money to local school systems; the Health Care Financing Administration in the Department of Health,

Education, and Welfare reimburses states for money spent on health care for the poor; the Department of Housing and Urban Development gives grants to cities for community development; and the Employment and Training Administration in the Department of Labor supplies funds to local governments so they can run job training programs. In France, by contrast, government programs dealing with education, health, housing, and employment are centrally run with little or no control exercised by local governments.

Third, the institutions and traditions of American life have contributed to the growth of what was called in Chapter 4 an "adversary culture" in which the definition and expansion of personal rights, and the defense of rights and claims through lawsuits as well as political action, are given central importance. A government agency in this country operates under closer public scrutiny and with a greater prospect of court challenges to its authority than is true in almost any other nation. Virtually every important decision of the Occupational Safety and Health Administration or of the Environmental Protection Agency is likely to be challenged in the courts or attacked by an affected party; in Sweden, by contrast, comparable decisions by similar agencies go largely uncontested.

The scope as well as the style of bureaucratic government differs. In most Western European nations, the government owns and operates large parts of the economy—the French government operates the railroads and owns companies that make automobiles and cigarettes; the British government owns and operates the electric power system, the coal mines, the steel industry, the airlines, and one of the major television networks; the Italian government owns many similar enterprises and also the nation's oil refineries. In just about every large nation except the United States, the telephone system is government owned. Publicly operated enterprises account for about 12 percent of all employment in France and England but less than 3

66 A government agency in this country operates under closer public scrutiny and with a greater prospect of court challenges to its authority than is true in almost any other nation. **99**

percent in the United States.[1] As we shall see in another chapter, however, the United States government regulates privately owned enterprises to a degree not found in many other countries. Why we should have preferred regulation to ownership as the proper government approach to the economy is an interesting question to which we shall later return.

THE GROWTH OF THE BUREAUCRACY

The Constitution made scarcely any provision for an administrative system other than to allow the president to appoint, with the advice and consent of the Senate, "ambassadors, other public ministers and consuls, judges of the Supreme Court, and all other officers of the United States whose appointments are not herein otherwise provided for, and which shall be established by law."[2] Departments and bureaus are not mentioned.

In the First Congress in 1789, James Madison introduced a bill to create a Department of State to assist the new secretary of state, Thomas Jefferson, in carrying out his duties. Persons appointed to this department were to be nominated by the president and approved by the Senate, but they were "to be removable by the president" alone. These six words, which would confer the right to fire government officials, occasioned six days of debate in the House. At stake was the locus of power over what was to become the bureaucracy. Madison's opponents argued that the Senate should consent to the removal of officials as well as their appointments. Madison responded that, without the unfettered right of removal, the president would not be able to control his subordinates, and without this control he would not be able to discharge his constitutional obligation to "take care that the laws be faithfully executed."[3] Madison won, 29 votes to 22. When the issue went to the Senate, another debate ensued, resulting in a tie vote that was broken, in favor of the president, by Vice-President John Adams. The Department of State, and all subsequent cabinet departments created, would be run by persons removable by the president.

That did not resolve the question of who would really control the bureaucracy, however. Congress retained the right to appropriate money, to investigate the administration, and to shape the laws that would be executed by that administration—more than ample power to challenge any president who claimed to have sole authority over his subordinates. And many congressmen expected the cabinet departments, even though headed by persons removable by the president, to report to Congress.

The government in Washington was at first minute. The State Department started with only nine employees; the War Department did not have eighty civilian employees until 1801. Only the Treasury Department, concerned with collecting taxes and finding ways to pay the public debt, had much power, and only the Post Office Department provided any significant service.

The Appointment of Officials

Small as the bureaucracy was, men struggled, often bitterly, over who would be appointed to it. From George Washington's day to modern times, presidents have found appointment to be one of their most important and difficult tasks. The officials they select affect how the laws are interpreted (thus the political ideology of the jobholders is important), what tone the administration will display (thus character is important), how effectively the public business is discharged (thus competence is important), and how strong will be the political party or faction in power (and thus party affiliation is important). Presidents trying to balance the competing needs of

ideology, character, fitness, and partisanship have rarely pleased most people. As John Adams and others were later to remark, every appointment creates one ingrate and ten enemies.

Because Congress during most of the nineteenth century and much of the twentieth was the dominant branch of government, congressional preferences often dominated the appointment of officials. And since Congress was, in turn, a collection of representatives and senators who represented local interests, appointments were made with an eye to rewarding the local supporters of congressmen or building up local party organizations. These appointments made on the basis of political considerations—patronage—were later to become a major issue. They galvanized various reform efforts that sought to purify politics and to raise the level of competence of the public service. Many of the abuses the reformers complained about were real enough, but patronage served some useful purposes as well. It gave to the president a way of ensuring that his subordinates were reasonably supportive of his policies; it provided a currency that the president could use to induce recalcitrant congressmen to vote for his programs; and it enabled party organizations to be built up to perform the necessary functions of nominating candidates and getting out the vote.

Though at first there were not many jobs to fight over, by the middle of the nineteenth century there were a lot. From 1816 to 1861 the number of federal employees increased eightfold. This was not, however, the result of the government taking on new functions but simply a result of the increased demands on its traditional functions. The Post Office alone accounted for 86 percent of this growth.[4]

The Civil War was a great watershed in bureaucratic development. Fighting the war led, naturally, to hiring many new officials and creating many new offices. Just as important, the Civil War revealed the administrative weakness of the federal government and led to demands by the civil service reform movement for an improvement in the quality and organization of federal employees. And finally, the war was followed by a period of rapid industrialization and the emergence of a national economy. The effects of these developments could no longer be managed by state governments acting alone. With the development of a nationwide network of railroads, commerce among the states became increasingly important. The constitutional powers of the federal government to regulate interstate commerce, long dormant for want of much commerce to regulate, now became an important source of controversy.

A Service Role

From 1861 to 1901 new agencies were created, many to deal with particular sectors of society and the economy. Over two hundred thousand new federal employees were added, with only about half of this increase in the Post Office. A rapidly growing Pension Office began paying benefits to Civil War veterans; a Department of Agriculture was created in 1862 to help farmers;

a Department of Labor was founded in 1882 to serve workers; and a Department of Commerce was organized in 1903 to assist businessmen. Many more specialized agencies, such as the National Bureau of Standards, also came into being.

These agencies had one thing in common: their role was primarily to serve, not to regulate. Most did research, gathered statistics, dispensed federal lands, or passed out benefits. Not until the Interstate Commerce Commission was created in 1887 did the federal government begin to regulate the economy (other than by managing the currency) in any large way. Even the ICC, the creation of which will be described in Chapter 15, had, at first, relatively few powers.

There were several reasons why federal officials primarily performed a service role. The values that shaped the Constitution were still strong: these included a belief in limited government, the importance of states' rights, and the fear of concentrated discretionary power. The proper role of government in the economy was

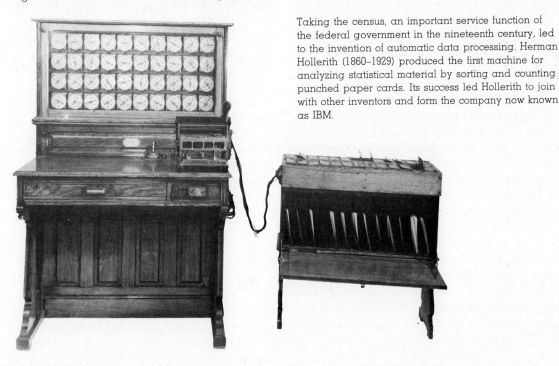

Taking the census, an important service function of the federal government in the nineteenth century, led to the invention of automatic data processing. Herman Hollerith (1860–1929) produced the first machine for analyzing statistical material by sorting and counting punched paper cards. Its success led Hollerith to join with other inventors and form the company now known as IBM.

"The bureaucracy as we know it today is largely a product of two events: the Depression of the 1930s (and the concomitant New Deal program of President Roosevelt) and the Second World War."

thought to be promotional, not regulatory, and a commitment to *laissez-faire*—a freely competitive economy—was strongly held. But just as important was the fact that the Constitution said nothing about giving any regulatory powers to bureaucrats. It gave to Congress the power to regulate commerce among the states. Now, obviously, Congress could not make the necessary day-to-day decisions to regulate, for example, the rates that interstate railroads charged to farmers and other shippers. Some agency or commission composed of appointed officials and experts would have to be created to do that. For a long time, however, the prevailing interpretation of the Constitution was that no such agency could exercise such regulatory powers unless Congress first set down clear standards that would govern the agency's decisions. As late as 1935 the Supreme Court held that a regulatory agency could not make rules on its own; it could only apply the standards enacted by Congress.[5] The Court's view was that the legislature may not delegate its powers to the president or to an administrative agency.[6]

These restrictions on what administrators could do were set aside during wartime. During World War I, for example, President Woodrow Wilson was authorized by Congress to fix prices, take over and operate the railroads, manage the communications system, and even control the distribution of food.[7] This kind of extraordinary grant of power usually ended with the war.

Some changes in the bureaucracy did not end with the end of the war. During the Civil War, World War I, World War II, the Korean War, and the war in Vietnam, the number of civilian (as well as military) employees of the government rose sharply. These increases were not simply in the number of civilians needed to help serve the war effort; many of the additional people were hired by agencies, such as the Treasury Department, not obviously connected with the war. Furthermore, the number of federal officials did not return to prewar levels after each war. Though there was some reduction, each war left the number of federal employees larger than before.[8]

It is not hard to understand how this happens. During wartime there is scarcely a government agency that cannot argue that its activities have *some* relation to the war effort, and there is rarely any legislator who wants to be caught voting against something that may help that effort. Hence, in 1944 the Reindeer Service in Alaska, an agency of the Interior Department, asked for more employees because reindeer are "a valued asset in military planning."

A Change in Role

The bureaucracy as we know it today is largely a product of two events: the Depression of the 1930s (and the concomitant New Deal program of President Roosevelt) and the Second World War. Though many agencies have been added since then, the basic features of the bureaucracy were set mainly as a result of changes in public attitudes and constitutional interpretation that occurred during these periods. The government was now expected to play an active role in dealing with economic and social problems. The Supreme Court reversed its earlier decisions (see Chapter 13) on the question of delegating legislative powers to administrative agencies and upheld laws by which Congress merely instructs agencies to make decisions that serve "the public interest" in some area.[9] As a result, it was possible for President Nixon to set up in 1971 a system of price and wage controls based on a statute that simply authorized the president "to issue such orders and regulations as he may deem appropriate to stabilize prices, rents, wages, and salaries."[10] The Cost of Living Council and other agencies that Nixon established to carry out this order were composed of appointed officials who had the legal authority to make sweeping decisions based on general statutory language.

World War II was the first occasion during which the government made heavy use of federal income taxes—on individuals and corporations—to finance its activities. Between 1940 and 1945 total federal tax collections increased from about $5 billion to nearly $44 billion. The end of the war brought no substantial tax reduction—the country believed that a high level of military preparedness continued to be necessary and that various social programs begun before the war should enjoy the heavy funding made possible by the wartime taxes. Tax receipts continued, by and large, to grow. Before 1913, when the Sixteenth Amendment to the Constitution was passed, the federal government could not collect income taxes at all (it financed itself largely from customs duties and excise taxes). From 1913 to 1940 income taxes were small (in 1940 the average American paid only $7 in federal income taxes). World War II created the first great financial boom for the government, permitting the sustained expansion of a great variety of programs and, thus, the support of a large number of administrators.[11]

THE FEDERAL BUREAUCRACY TODAY

About 2.8 million civilians work for the federal government, most as members of the nonpolitical civil service. Contrary to general opinion, the size of the federal bureaucracy has not increased greatly in recent years. Indeed, federal employment was about the same in 1979 as it was in 1970 and less than it was during World War II. In fact, the federal government employed in 1979 a smaller percentage of the civilian work force (3.1 percent) than it did in 1955 (3.9 percent).[12] The great majority of these employees work, not in Washington, D.C., but throughout the country in various local and regional offices. The largest growth in public employment has occurred, not in the federal agencies, but among state and local governments. But in addition to the employees on the federal government payroll, there are another 6 to 8 million persons who work indirectly for Washington because their jobs—at the local level or in private industry—are paid for with federal dollars.

The power of the bureaucracy cannot be measured by the number of employees, however. A bureaucracy of 5 million persons would have little power if each employee did nothing but type letters or file documents; a bureaucracy of only 100 persons would have awesome power if

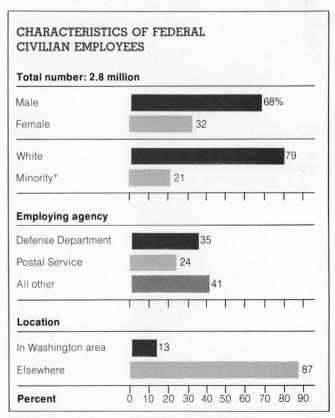

CHARACTERISTICS OF FEDERAL CIVILIAN EMPLOYEES

Total number: 2.8 million

Male	68%
Female	32
White	79
Minority*	21

Employing agency

Defense Department	35
Postal Service	24
All other	41

Location

In Washington area	13
Elsewhere	87

Percent   0 10 20 30 40 50 60 70 80 90

Source: *Statistical Abstract of the United States,* 1978.

* Black, Oriental, Native American, and Hispanic.

"The power of the bureaucracy depends on the extent to which appointed officials have discretionary authority—that is, on their ability to choose courses of action and to make policies that are not spelled out in advance by laws."

The Nuclear Regulatory Commission is one of the many federal agencies with discretionary authority.

each member were able to make arbitrary life-and-death decisions affecting the rest of us. The power of the bureaucracy depends on the extent to which appointed officials have discretionary authority—that is, on their ability to choose courses of action and to make policies that are not spelled out in advance by laws. In Figure 12.2 we see how the volume of regulations issued and the amount of money spent have risen much faster than the number of employees who write the regulations and spend the money.

By this test, the power of the federal bureaucracy has grown enormously. Congress has delegated substantial authority to administrative agencies in three areas: (1) paying subsidies to particular groups and organizations in society (farmers, veterans, scientists, schools, universities, hospitals); (2) transferring money from the federal government to state and local governments (the grant-in-aid programs described in Chapter 3); and (3) devising and enforcing regulations for various sectors of society and the economy. Some of these administrative functions, such as grants-in-aid to states, are closely monitored by Congress; others, such as the regulatory programs, usually operate with a large degree of independence. These delegations of power, especially in the areas of paying subsidies and regulating the economy, did not become commonplace until the 1930s and then only after the Supreme Court decided that such delegations were constitutional. In Chapter 15 we shall discuss how this power is used. For now it is enough to know that appointed officials can decide, within rather broad limits, who shall own a television station, which airlines shall fly between any two cities, what safety features automobiles shall have, what kinds of scientific research shall be specially encouraged, what drugs shall appear on the market, which dissident groups shall be investigated, what fumes an industrial smokestack may emit, which corporate mergers shall be allowed, what use shall be made of national forests, and what price farmers and dairymen shall receive for their products.

If appointed officials have this kind of power, then how they use it is a question of paramount importance in understanding modern government. There are, broadly, four factors that explain the behavior of these officials:

1. The manner in which they are recruited and rewarded.

2. Their personal attributes, such as their socioeconomic backgrounds and their political attitudes.

3. The nature of the jobs they have.

4. The way in which outside forces—political superiors, legislators, interest groups, journalists—influence how bureaucrats behave.

Recruitment and Retention

About 61 percent of all appointed officials are part of the "competitive service." This means that they are initially appointed only after they have passed a written examination administered by the Office of Personnel Management (OPM) or have met certain selection criteria (such as training, educational attainments, or prior experience) devised by the hiring agency and approved by OPM. Where competition for a job exists and candidates can be ranked by their scores or records, the agency must usually appoint one of the three top-ranking candidates.

The other 39 percent of the civilian employees are part of the "excepted" service—that is, they are not appointed on the basis of qualifications designed or approved by the Office of Personnel Management. Most of these, however, are also appointed on a nonpartisan basis but by various agencies that have merit-based appointment systems independent of the one run by the OPM. These include Postal Service employees, FBI agents, intelligence agents, foreign service officers in the State Department, and doctors in the Public Health Service and the Veterans' Administration.

Some of the excepted employees—probably no more than 3 percent—are appointed on grounds other than or in addition to merit, narrowly defined. These legal exceptions exist to permit the president and his staff to select, for policy-making and politically sensitive posts, persons who are in agreement with their policy views. These appointees are generally of three kinds:

1. Presidential appointments authorized by statute (cabinet and subcabinet officers, judges, U.S. marshals and U.S. attorneys, ambassadors, and members of various boards and commissions).

2. "Schedule C" jobs that are described as having a "confidential or policy-determining character" below the level of cabinet or subcabinet posts (including executive assistants, special aides, and confidential secretaries).

3. Noncareer Executive Assignments (NEA jobs) given to high-ranking members of the regular competitive civil service, or to persons brought into the civil service at these high levels, who are deeply involved in the advocacy of presidential programs or who participate in policy-making.

These three groups of excepted appointments constitute the patronage available to a president and his administration. In the nineteenth century, practically every job was a patronage job.

FIGURE 12.2 Federal Government Growth: Money, Rules, and People

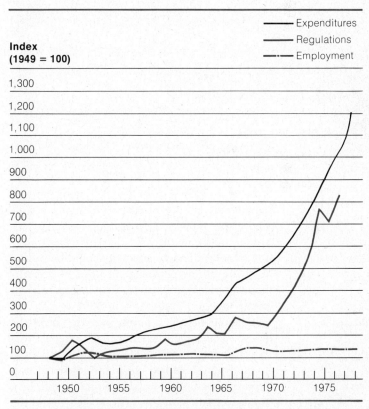

Source: Hugh Heclo, "Issue Networks and the Executive Establishment," in Anthony King, ed., *The New American Political System* (Washington, D.C.: American Enterprise Institute, 1978), p. 90. Copyright © 1978 by the American Enterprise Institute. Reprinted by permission.

Most, but not all, federal civil servants are hired on the basis of competitive examinations. These technicians are part of a "sniffing team" that checks gases for pollution.

For example, when Grover Cleveland, a Democrat, became president in 1885, he replaced some forty thousand Republican postal employees with Democrats. In 1883, with the passage of the Pendleton Act, there began a slow but steady transfer of federal jobs from the patronage to the merit system. It may seem strange that a political party in power should be willing to relinquish its patronage in favor of a merit-based appointment system. Two factors made it easier for the Republicans in 1883 to pass the Pendleton Act: (1) public outrage over the abuses of the spoils system, highlighted by the assassination of President James Garfield by a man always described in the history books as a "disappointed office-seeker" (lunatic would be a more accurate term); and (2) the fear that if the Democrats came to power on a wave of antispoils sentiment, existing Republican officeholders would be fired. (The Democrats won anyway.)

The merit system spread to encompass most of the federal bureaucracy, generally with presidential support. Though presidents may have liked in theory the idea of hiring and firing subordinates at will, most felt that the demands for patronage made on them were impossible either to satisfy or ignore. Furthermore, by increasing the coverage of the merit system a president could "blanket in" patronage appointees already holding office, thus making it difficult or impossible for the next administration to fire them.

The Buddy System. The actual recruitment of civil servants, especially in middle- and upper-level jobs, is somewhat more complicated, and slightly more political, than the laws and rules might suggest. Though many persons enter the federal bureaucracy by learning of a job, filling out an application, perhaps taking a test, and being hired, many also enter on a "name-request" basis. A "name-request" job is one that is filled by a person whom an agency has already identified. In this respect, the federal government is not so different from private business. A person learns of a job from somebody who already has one, or the head of a bureau decides in advance whom he or she wishes to hire. The agency must still send a form describing the job to the OPM, but it also names the person it wants to get it. Sometimes the job is even described in such a way that the person named is the only one who can qualify for it. Occasionally, this tailor-made, name-request job is offered to a person at the insistence of a congressman who wants a political supporter taken care of; more often, it is made available because the bureaucracy itself knows whom it wishes to hire and wants to circumvent an elaborate search. This is the "buddy system."

The buddy system does not necessarily produce poor employees. Indeed, it is often a way of hiring able persons who are unwilling to fill out an application and then wait around hoping somebody will hire them. But it also opens up the possibility of hiring persons whose policy views are congenial to those already in office. Hugh Heclo refers to these recruitment patterns as "issue networks." Such networks are based on shared policy views, not (as once was the case) on narrow partisan affiliations. Bureaucrats in consumer protection agencies, for example, recruit new bureaucrats from private groups with an interest in consumer protection, such as the various organizations associated with Ralph Nader, or from academics who have a pro-consumer inclination. As we shall see in Chapter 20, the attitudes of the higher level officials who deal with foreign affairs shift with changes in administrations and in elite opinion about foreign policy. There has always been an informal "old boys' network" among those who move in and out of high-level government posts; with the increasing appointment of women to these jobs, there has emerged the ladies' auxiliary of the old boys' network.[13] In the next section we will consider whether, or in what ways, these recruitment patterns make a difference.

Senior Executive Service. With the passage of the Civil Service Reform Act of 1978, Congress recognized that many high-level positions in the civil service have important policy-making responsibilities and that the president and his cabinet officers ought to have more flexibility in recruiting, assigning, and paying such persons. Accordingly, the law created a Senior Executive Service (SES) of about eight thousand top federal managers who could be hired, fired, and transferred more easily than ordinary civil servants. Moreover, members of the SES would be eligible for substantial cash bonuses if they were judged to have performed their duties well. (To protect the rights of SES members, anyone who is removed from the SES is guaranteed a job elsewhere in the government.)

This flexibility was requested by the proposers of the Reform Act because of the great difficulty government executives ordinarily have in firing, transferring, or demoting civil servants. Most persons holding a presidential appointment can

Firing a Bureaucrat

To fire or demote a member of the competitive civil service, the following procedures must be followed:

1. The employee must be given written notice at least thirty days in advance that he or she is to be fired or demoted for incompetence or misconduct.

2. The written notice must contain a statement of reasons, including specific examples of unacceptable performance.

3. The employee has the right to an attorney and to reply, orally or in writing, to the charges.

4. The employee has the right to appeal any adverse action to the Merit Systems Protection Board, a three-person, bipartisan body appointed by the president with the consent of the Senate.

5. The MSPB must grant the employee a hearing and the right to an attorney.

6. The employee has the right to appeal the MSPB decision to the United States Court of Appeals, which can hold new hearings.

How to Get Rid of
a Career Civil Servant

Without Going Through the System

1. **The frontal assault**
   Tell him he is no longer wanted and that if he quits, he will get a nice letter of recommendation and a farewell luncheon. If he won't quit but later wants to leave for a better job, he will get a nasty letter of recommendation.

2. **The transfer technique**
   Find out where in the country the civil servant does *not* want to live and threaten to transfer him there. Send Bostonians to Texas and Texans to Maine.

3. **The special assignment technique**
   Useful for a family person who does not like to travel. Tell him that to keep his job he must inspect all the agency's offices in cities with less than 20,000 population and bad motels. Even if he doesn't quit, at least you will have him out of the office.

4. **The layering technique**
   Put loyal subordinates in charge of disloyal ones or put the objectionable civil servant into an out-of-the-way post where you can ignore him.

Source: Adapted from the "Federal Political Personnel Manual" printed in "Presidential Campaign Activities of 1972," *Hearings* before the Select Committee on Presidential Campaign Activities, 93rd Congress, 2nd Session, Vol 19 (1974). This manual was produced by members of the Nixon administration but in some version its principles have been applied by all administrations.

be fired by the president at any time. But there are limits even here. The members of independent regulatory commissions or persons serving for fixed terms of office cannot be summarily discharged; they can only be removed "for cause." And even a person legally removable at the president's pleasure is sometimes immune to being fired if the political costs—in terms of adverse publicity or interest group opposition—are too high. When President Carter in 1979 fired Bella Abzug from an unpaid position on a commission, many other women members resigned in protest in an effort to portray the president as "anti-women."

The great majority of bureaucrats who are part of the civil service and do not hold presidential appointments have jobs that are, for all practical purposes, beyond reach. There are elaborate steps that an executive must go through to fire, demote, or suspend a civil servant. Realistically, what this means is that no one is fired or demoted unless his or her superior is prepared to invest a great deal of time and effort in the attempt. In 1976 only six out of 71,000 tenured employees of the Internal Revenue Service were dismissed for inefficiency. The Office of Education, an agency with nearly three thousand employees, tried during a four-year period to fire only three employees; of the three cases, two were still under appeal one year later and the third had resigned because he had been indicted by a federal grand jury. It is hard to believe that in a private organization of comparable size there would be no more than three dismissals. And it is impossible to imagine that any dismissal effort would take a year or more. To cope, political executives devise a number of stratagems for bypassing or forcing out civil servants with whom they cannot work effectively.

Agency Point of View. When one realizes that most agencies are staffed by persons who were recruited by that agency, sometimes on a name-request basis, and who are virtually immune from dismissal, it becomes clear that the recruitment and retention policies of the civil service work to ensure that most bureaucrats will have an "agency" point of view. In 1975 over 92 percent of the persons appointed to the top three federal civil service grades came from within the agency; less than 5 percent were transfers from other agencies, and less than 3 percent came in from outside the government.[14]

The Senior Executive Service may in time change this pattern, but for now most government agencies are dominated by persons who have grown up in that agency, have not served in any other agency, and who have been in government service most of their lives. This fact has some advantages—it means that most bureaucrats are expert in the procedures and policies of their agencies and that there will be a substantial degree of continuity in agency behavior no matter which political party happens to be in power. But it has costs as well. A political executive entering an agency with responsibility for shaping its direction will discover that he must carefully win the support of his career subordinates. They have an infinite capacity for discreet sabotage and can make life miserable for a political superior by delaying action, withholding information, following the rulebook with literal exactness, or making an "end run" around their superior to mobilize congressmen sympathetic to the bureaucrats' point of view. When one political executive wanted to downgrade a bureau in his department, he found, naturally, that the bureau chief was opposed. The opponent spoke to friendly lobbyists and a key congressman. When the political executive asked the congressman if he had any problem with the contemplated reorganization, the congressman replied, "No, you have the problem, because if you touch that bureau I'll cut your job out of the budget."[15]

Personal Attributes

A second factor that might shape the way bureaucrats use their power is their personal attributes. These include their social class, education, and personal political beliefs. The federal civil service as a whole looks very much like a

66 It becomes clear that the recruitment and retention policies of the civil service work to ensure that most bureaucrats will have an 'agency' point of view. 99

cross section of American society in the education, sex, race, and social origins of its members. But at the higher-ranking levels where the most power is found—say, in the supergrade ranks of GS-16 through GS-18—the typical civil servant is very different from the typical American. In the great majority of cases, he is a middle-aged white male with a college degree whose father was somewhat more advantaged than the average citizen.

Because the higher civil service is unrepresentative of the average American, some people speculate that persons holding these top jobs think and act in ways very different from most Americans. Depending on their politics, these critics have concluded that the bureaucracy is either more conservative or more liberal than the country it helps govern. Some critics believe that the upper-middle-class bureaucrats will defend their class privileges.[16] Other critics, such as former President Richard M. Nixon, argue that, since the higher civil service was appointed by Democratic presidents and since it was trained by liberal faculty members in prestigious universities, it will favor liberal or leftist causes.[17]

These arguments are based on an assumption that requires careful examination. The assumption is that a person's age, sex, skin color, education, and political party membership will significantly affect how that person goes about his or her job. It may seem like a plausible assumption, but so far there is not a lot of evidence to support it. In one study, for example, federal bureaucrats in the supergrades were interviewed to find out their political beliefs. The relationship between these beliefs and the bureaucrats' race and social origins was then calculated. Virtually no correlation was found between social background and political attitudes—bureaucrats from highly privileged backgrounds were not any more or less likely than those from less

One barrier to improving presidential control of the federal bureaucracy is that even the White House has become a large bureaucracy.

privileged backgrounds to have liberal or conservative opinions. There was one small exception to this: blacks were found, not surprisingly, to have more favorable attitudes toward programs designed to improve welfare and minority rights than were whites, but even this correlation was quite weak.[18]

What *does* seem to be associated with bureaucratic attitudes is the agency for which a civil servant works. Persons working for the Defense Department have quite different political beliefs from those working for environmental protection organizations, even though the social backgrounds of the two sets of bureaucrats are quite similar. In another study a scholar found that persons holding foreign service jobs in the State Department tended to be more liberal, and were more likely to think of themselves as Democrats, than those doing similar tasks (i.e., managing foreign affairs) in the Department of

Defense.[19] Here also, the social backgrounds of the two groups of bureaucrats were quite similar. It is not clear whether their differences in attitudes were produced by the jobs they held or whether these jobs attracted as applicants persons who had different political beliefs. Probably both forces were at work.

Whatever the mechanism that causes it, there seems little doubt that different agencies display different political ideologies. A study done in 1976 revealed that Democrats and persons with liberal views tended to be overrepresented in social service agencies, whereas Republicans and persons with conservative views tended to be overrepresented in defense agencies.[20]

But we have only fragmentary evidence of the extent to which these differences in attitudes affect bureaucratic behavior. It may seem obvious that a person will act in accordance with his or her beliefs, but that common-sense observation is only true when the nature of the job allows people to make decisions based on their beliefs. If you are a voter at the polls, your beliefs will clearly affect how you vote (see Chapter 5). But if you are the second baseman for the Boston Red Sox, your political beliefs, social background, and education will have nothing to do with how you field ground balls. Sociologists like to call the different things people do in their lives "roles" and to distinguish between roles that are loosely structured (such as the role of voter) and those that are highly structured (such as that of second baseman). Personal attitudes greatly affect loosely structured roles and only slightly affect highly structured ones. Applied to the federal bureaucracy, this suggests that civil servants performing tasks that are routinized (such as filling out forms), tasks that are closely defined by laws and rules (such as issuing welfare checks), or tasks that are closely monitored by other persons (such as supervisors, special interest groups, or the media) will probably perform them in ways that can only partially be explained, if at all, by their personal attitudes. Civil servants performing complex, loosely defined tasks that are not closely monitored may carry out their work in ways powerfully influenced by their attitudes.

One personal attribute has been shown to have a clear effect on bureaucratic behavior: the professional values of a civil servant. An increasing number of bureaucrats are employed because they are lawyers, economists, engineers, and physicians. These men and women have received extensive training that produces, not only a set of skills, but also a set of attitudes as to what is important and valuable. For example, the Federal Trade Commission (FTC), charged with preventing unfair methods of competition among businesses, employs two kinds of professionals—lawyers, organized into a Bureau of Competition, and economists, organized as a Bureau of Economics. Lawyers are trained to draw up briefs and argue cases in court and are taught the legal standards by which they will

66 The tasks people are given often explain more of their behavior than the attitudes they have or the way in which they are hired and fired. **99**

know whether they have a chance of winning a case or not. Economists are trained to analyze how a competitive economy is supposed to work and what costs consumers must bear if the goods and services are produced by a monopoly (one firm controlling the market) or an oligopoly (a small number of firms dominating the market).

Because of their training and attitudes, lawyers in the FTC prefer to bring cases against a business firm that does something clearly and demonstrably illegal, such as attending secret meetings with competitors to rig the prices that will be charged to a purchaser. These cases appeal to lawyers because there is usually a victim (the purchaser or a rival company) who complains to the government, the illegal behavior can be proved in a court of law, and the case can be completed rather quickly. Economists, on the other hand, are trained to measure the value of a case, not by how easily or quickly it can be proved in court, but by whether the illegal practice imposes large or small costs on the consumer. FTC economists often dislike the cases that appeal to the lawyers. The economists feel that the amount of money such cases save the consumer is often small and the cases are a distraction from the big issues—such as whether IBM unfairly dominates the office-machine business or whether General Motors is too large to be efficient. Lawyers, in turn, are leery of big cases because the facts are hard to prove and take forever to decide (one big case can drag through the courts for ten years). In many federal agencies, professional values such as these help explain how power is used.

Roles and Mission
The tasks people are given often explain more of their behavior than the attitudes they have or the way in which they are hired and fired. We have

Learning to Speak and Write in Bureaucratese

A few simple rules, if remembered, will enable you to speak and write in the style of a government official.

1. **Use nouns as if they were verbs.**
   Don't say, "*We gave the department this task*"; say instead, "*We tasked the department.*"

2. **Use adjectives as if they were verbs.**
   Don't say, "*We put the report in final form*"; say instead, "*We finalized the report.*"

3. **Use several words where one word would do.**
   Don't say, "*at this point*"; say instead, "*at this point in time.*"

4. **Never use ordinary words where unusual ones can be found.**
   Don't say you "*made a choice*"; say you "*selected an option.*"

5. **No matter what subject you are discussing, employ the language of sports and war.**
   Never say "*progress*"; say "*breakthrough.*" Never speak of a "*compromise*"; instead, consider "*adopting a fallback position.*"

6. **Avoid active verbs.**
   Never say, "*Study the problem*"; say instead, "*It is felt that the problem should be subjected to further study.*"

already seen how a highly structured role can powerfully affect behavior, notwithstanding personal attitudes. But even a loosely structured one will make a difference because, though how the job is done is not precisely spelled out in a manual of instructions, it is nonetheless shaped by forces inside the bureaucracy that the civil servant cannot easily ignore.

Consider the job of a forest ranger. A ranger is in charge of a national forest, often one remote from Washington (indeed, remote from anywhere). There he must reconcile the many different purposes for which a forest can be used—as a recreational area, a source of lumber, a haven for wildlife, and a scenic wilderness. Because the ranger can choose among these uses and still act within the law, he has discretion. The question is, How will he use it? The Forest Service has gone to great lengths to ensure that this discretion will be used in ways the chief of the Forest Service wants and in ways he thinks Congress and the public would approve. The Service cannot tell each ranger in advance how to act in every case because the needs and problems of every forest differ. The person on the scene must use his judgment. The Forest Service does a number of things to make certain that a ranger takes into account every possibility and does not act irresponsibly. It requires him to keep

© Jefferson Communications, Inc. 1979
Distributed by C.T.N.Y.N.S.

Panel 1: OUR GUEST TODAY ON "PRESS THE MEAT" IS J. DAVIS BRATWURST, DIRECTOR OF THE OFFICE OF GOVERNMENT SIMPLIFICATION.

Panel 2: WELCOME TO "PRESS THE MEAT," MR. BRATWURST...

Panel 3: THANK YOU... AND LET ME RETROJECT AT THIS POINT MY EXPRESSION OF INTROFUSED PLEASEDNESS... IN TERMS OF MY PRESENCE.

a detailed record of every decision he makes; it subjects his office to frequent inspections; it transfers him frequently from one forest to another to prevent him from developing overly strong attachments to local interests; and above all it puts him in a training program to instill doctrines and attitudes about the principles of good forestry. These doctrines may not always be what an outsider would regard as entirely correct—for a long time, for example, rangers were taught not to practice controlled burning in forests, even though some scientists believed that occasional fires would benefit forests by eliminating undergrowth and diseased trees.[21] What is important, however, is that a far-flung organization made up of employees exercising discretionary authority must have *some* doctrine if it is to be managed at all.

When an organization has a clear doctrine that is widely shared by its members, we say it has a sense of *mission*. Some federal agencies have a sense of mission; some do not. The Forest Service, the Federal Bureau of Investigation, and the Public Health Service are examples of agencies that have, or have had, a powerful sense of mission.[22] This leads to easier management, higher morale, and tighter controls on behavior. But it also makes such organizations hard to change and sometimes resistant to political direction. This dilemma—whether to indoctrinate organizational members with a sense of mission or to keep them accountable to the public—is one of the central problems of bureaucratic government.

In addition to a consciously developed sense of mission, constraints are imposed on bureaucrats by governmentwide rules and laws. Civil service regulations, already discussed, are one example of these. There are many others.

- The Freedom of Information Act gives citizens the right to inspect most of the files and records of agencies.
- Various laws require careful accounting of all money spent.

"When an organization has a clear doctrine that is widely shared by its members, we say it has a sense of *mission*."

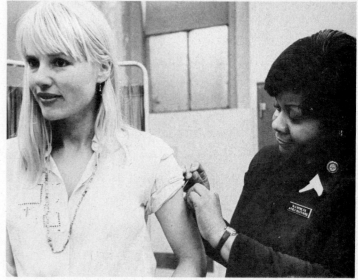

The Federal Bureau of Investigation and the Public Health Service are agencies with a sense of mission.

- Laws and orders oblige agencies to provide equal opportunity to minorities and women in hiring employees.
- Environmental impact statements must be compiled before certain construction projects are undertaken.
- The Administrative Procedure Act requires that interested people be given ample notice of, and a chance to comment on, proposed new rules as well as an opportunity to introduce evidence at hearings that must be held before certain rules can be enforced.

Perhaps the most important constraint on bureaucratic power is the fact that agencies are complicated organizations, the component parts of which do not always see things the same way. Before action can be taken, one part of an agency must consult with another part and get its agreement, and sometimes that agency must then consult with other agencies. This is called the process of obtaining "concurrences" and reflects the fragmentation of power in our government. Action requires persuading—rather than ordering—other persons to go along. These constraints do not mean the bureaucracy is feeble, but they do mean that it is often easier to block an action than to implement one. Decisive action is likely only in those areas where just a few persons need agree or where the action has little public visibility.

These limits on bureaucratic power are not obvious to persons who object to how that power is used. An electric utility will be furious at the "all-powerful bureaucracy" if it fails to get a license from the Nuclear Regulatory Commission to build a nuclear power plant. On the other hand, environmental organizations will be furious at the "all-powerful bureaucracy" if the utility *does* get the license. Nor are these limits obvious to a citizen who has an income-tax return audited, a son drafted into the army, or a business enterprise found to be in violation of the occupational safety and health laws.

But these limits will be all too obvious to persons who enter government eager to take power and use it for what they regard as good ends. Business executives who came to Washington during the Republican administrations of Dwight Eisenhower and Richard Nixon soon discovered that the bureaucracy they were supposed to run could ignore, undercut, or defeat them. Consumer advocates who came to power in the administration of Jimmy Carter discovered that to bring about change within the government is much harder than to attack it from outside. When Joan Claybrook, formerly head of Congress Watch, a Ralph Nader organization, became administrator of the National Highway Traffic Safety Administration, she discovered that she could not make by herself the kinds of decisions she would have liked. Experts in her agency had views that could not be ignored, and her superior (Secretary of Transpor-

Joan Claybrook, formerly head of a Ralph Nader organization, was criticized by Nader after she joined the government as head of the National Highway Traffic Safety Administration in 1977.

tation Brock Adams) had the right to review her decisions. The result, of course, was that whereas she was able to do enough to make the automobile industry mad at her, she was not able to do enough to keep Nader from being mad at her also. He demanded that she resign. (She refused.)

External Forces

Bureaucracies do not operate in a vacuum. They exist in a constellation of political forces, in and out of the government, that affect agency behavior. There are at least seven external forces with which a government bureau must cope.

- Executive branch superiors (cabinet officers, etc.)
- The White House, especially the president's staff
- Congressional committees
- Interest groups
- The media
- The courts
- Other, rival government agencies.

Not every agency is equally exposed to these external sources of influence. Much depends on the task the agency performs, the degree of public or political interest in it, and the extent to which those affected by its actions are organized, knowledgeable, and effective.

At the most general level, one can distinguish between those agencies that are more oriented toward presidential control and those that are more sensitive to congressional control. All of these agencies are nominally subordinate to the president; the difference in orientation is the result of political forces. "Presidential" agencies include those that carry out policies that do not distribute benefits among significant groups, regions, or localities within the United States. Thus they do not (usually) affect important congressional constituencies, or at least do not affect them differently in different places. "Congressional" agencies are those whose actions

have a more pronounced distributional effect within the country. Examples of each follow:

"Presidential" Agencies
State Department
Treasury Department
Central Intelligence Agency
Office of the Secretary of Defense
Justice Department
Arms Control and Disarmament Agency

"Congressional" Agencies
Department of Agriculture
Interior Department
Department of Housing and Urban Development
Army Corps of Engineers
Small Business Administration
Veterans' Administration

There are also many agencies that have neither a presidential nor a congressional orientation and which can act somewhat independently of either institution.

Of course, both the president and Congress have authority over all the agencies on this list, and from time to time an agency will change its sensitivity to one institution or the other. But generally, the government bureaus that receive the closest attention of Congress are those that do things that affect directly the constituents of a congressman—as when the Interior Department manages public lands in the western states, or HUD gives community development grants to cities, or the Army Corps of Engineers builds dams and levees on various rivers. This is an inevitable result of the fact, explained in Chapter 10, that Congress is an assemblage of *representatives of localities*, not a parliament of debaters. The foreign and monetary policies of the president tend to affect the entire country without (in most cases) special local significance. Thus agencies charged with responsibilities in these areas tend to be more alert to presidential directives and less subject to congressional intervention.

❝The government bureaus that receive the closest attention of Congress are those that do things that affect directly the constituents of a congressman.**❞**

Building a dam, such as this one at Glen Canyon in Utah, is an example of a federal program with great impact on a locality and which thus receives close congressional attention.

Desire for Autonomy. Though the divided authority the agencies face can sometimes give them the freedom to play off one superior against another, in general most agencies would prefer a political environment that had less conflict and uncertainty. Government bureaucrats, like people generally, prefer to be left alone so they can do their work as they wish. When they are left more or less alone, free of bureaucratic rivals and without close political supervision, we say an agency has "autonomy." All agencies would like more autonomy than they have, and some have managed to get a great deal. The FBI, by the skillful use of publicity, by preventing its agents from acting in corrupt or brutal ways, and by some striking investigative successes, was able to develop such strong public support during its first forty-five years that it was virtually immune to criticism, and thus to serious presidential or congressional supervision. It had acquired autonomy to an enviable degree. When the National Aeronautics and Space Administration (NASA) succeeded in landing a man on the moon, it was at the crest of a wave of popular support that conferred upon it substantial autonomy. But autonomy, like beauty, invariably fades. When the FBI was publicly shown to have exceeded its powers by investigating persons because of their political opinions and by engaging in illegal investigative methods (break-ins or "black-bag" jobs), it lost much of its autonomy and came under the most searching congressional inspection and supervision. After the moon landing, NASA lost much of its claim on the popular imagination and its budget declined.

Most agencies cannot depend on favorable publicity to produce strong support because most do rather prosaic things that, while important, are rarely soul-stirring. Indeed, given the power of the press and its interest in conflict and scandal (see Chapter 9), many agency heads would probably be happier if they were never mentioned in the media at all. But there is another source of power and autonomy: alliances with influential interest groups.

Agency Allies. Since many federal agencies were created explicitly to promote some sector of society—agriculture, business, the labor movement, environmentalism, minority groups—it is hardly surprising that organizations representing those sectors should take a keen interest in, and have substantial influence over, the agency designed to serve them. Thus, the American Legion and other veterans' groups closely monitor the work of the Veterans' Administration; the AFL-CIO watches over the Department of Labor; the NAACP is supportive of the Equal Employment Opportunity Commission; and the Environmental Defense Fund gets involved with the Environmental Protection Agency. These interest groups are both allies and critics: lobbying to ensure that their favored agency has adequate funds and legal powers, protesting when the agency acts contrary to what the group prefers.

Given the uncertain or conflict-ridden political environment that most government agencies face, these bureaucracies have a powerful incentive to develop strong allies in the private sector. They must often pay a price for that alliance, however, by deferring to the policy preferences of the ally.

Some scholars view these agency–interest group relations as so close that they speak of the agency as having been "captured" by the interest group and thus the interest group as having become the agency's "client." This, indeed, happens. It is inconceivable, for example, that the Department of Labor would ever recommend to Congress a decrease in the minimum wage even though many economists believe that a high minimum wage increases unemployment. The AFL-CIO would not tolerate such a position. For similar reasons, the Maritime Administration in the Department of Commerce would never question whether the government should continue to pay large subsidies to American shipping companies, even though such subsidies increase the cost to the consumer of goods shipped by sea. For many years the Federal Communications Commission discouraged the introduction of cable television systems that would have threatened the established television broadcasters.

Conflict Among Interest Groups. Important as these interest group relations are, in many cases their significance can be exaggerated. Many agencies, such as the Maritime Administration, would take the position they did whether or not an organized interest group influenced them. The simple reason is that Congress requires them, by law, to take that position. And many agencies face, not a single, powerful ally, but an array of competing organizations. A secretary of agriculture, for example, must certainly be sensitive to the demands of farmers—but *which* farmers? If the secretary cultivates the support of farmers in the National Farmers' Union (NFU), he will favor, as they do, high government subsidies to farmers to compensate them for the uncertainties

of the competitive market. If, on the other hand, he seeks the support of the farmers in the American Farm Bureau Federation (AFBF), he will support a phasing out of farm subsidies and a greater reliance on the market to set farm prices. Because a choice of interest group allies is possible, we have had secretaries of agriculture who have opposed high subsidies (Ezra Taft Benson, secretary of agriculture under President Eisenhower, and Earl Butz, the secretary under Presidents Nixon and Ford); we have had secretaries who have favored high subsidies (such as Orville Freeman, secretary under President Kennedy); and we have had secretaries who tried to take a middle-of-the-road position (such as Clifford Hardin, Nixon's first secretary of agriculture).[23]

In some agencies the conflict among interest groups is even sharper. The Occupational Safety and Health Administration must deal with corporations that oppose strict or expensive safety standards and labor unions that favor them; the Office for Civil Rights will hear from women's groups that want strong pressure placed on universities to hire more women professors and from universities that believe their hiring practices are already fair.

In short, no simple description of agency–interest group relations will suffice: some may be pluralist, some elitist; some may be desirable, others may be corrupting. There is not always an "iron triangle" or "triple alliance" between an agency, a congressional committee, and an interest group. In Chapter 14, we shall set forth an explanation of why these relations are sometimes of one kind and sometimes of another. Whatever the pattern, there are few agencies that can afford to ignore entirely the interest group environment in which they operate.

CONGRESSIONAL OVERSIGHT

The main reason why some interest groups are important to agencies is that they are important to Congress. Not every interest group in the country has substantial access to Congress, but those that do and that are taken seriously by the relevant committees or subcommittees must also, for that reason, be taken seriously by the agency. Furthermore, even apart from interest groups, congressmen have constitutional powers over agencies and policy interests in how agencies function.

Congressional supervision of the bureaucracy takes several forms. First, no agency may exist (except for a few presidential offices and commissions) without congressional approval. Congress influences—and sometimes determines precisely—agency behavior by the statutes it enacts. Lately, however, Congress has passed statutes, especially in the regulatory and subsidy areas, that give broad discretion to agencies.

Second, no money may be spent unless it has first been both authorized and appropriated by Congress. *Authorization* legislation originates in a legislative committee (such as Agriculture, Education and Labor, or Public Works) and states the maximum amount of money an agency may spend on a given program. This authorization may be permanent, it may be for a fixed number of years, or it may be annual (i.e., it must be renewed each year or the program or agency goes out of business). Today most federal spending is done on the basis of permanent authorizations, especially the funds used to pay social security benefits and hire military personnel. Increasingly, however, there has been a trend toward multiyear or annual authorizations to enable Congress to strengthen its control over certain executive agencies. Foreign aid, the State Department, the National Aeronautics and Space Administration, and the procurement of military aircraft, missiles, and ships by the Defense Department are now subject to annual authorizations.

Third, even funds that have been authorized by Congress cannot be spent unless (in most cases) they are also *appropriated*. Appropriations are usually made annually, and they originate, not with the legislative committees, but with the House Appropriations Committee and its various (and influential) subcommittees. An ap-

propriation may be, and often is, for less than the amount authorized. The Appropriations Committee's action, thus, tends to have a budget-cutting effect. There are some funds that can be spent without an appropriation, but in virtually every part of the bureaucracy each agency is keenly sensitive to congressional wishes and concerns at the time that the annual appropriations process is going on.

The Appropriations Committee and Legislative Committees

The fact that an agency budget must be both authorized and appropriated means that each agency serves, not one congressional master, but several, and that these masters may be in conflict. The real power over an agency's budget is that exercised by the Appropriations Committee; the legislative committees are especially important only when the substantive law is first passed or the agency first created or when an agency is subject to annual authorization.

The power of the Appropriations Committee has rarely been challenged: from 1947 through 1962, for example, 90 percent of the House Appropriations Committee recommendations on expenditures were approved by the full House without change.[24] Furthermore, the Appropriations Committee tends to recommend less money than an agency requests (though some specially favored agencies, such as the FBI, the Soil Conservation Service, and the Forest Service, have tended to get almost everything they've asked for). Finally, the process of "marking up" (revising, amending, and approving) an agency's budget request gives to the Appropriations Committee, or one of its subcommittees, substantial influence over the policies the agency follows.

Of late, the legislative committees have begun to reclaim some of the power over agencies exercised by the Appropriations Committee. They have done this by approving laws that entitle persons to certain benefits (for example, social security or retirement payments) and creating "trust funds" to pay for them. These funds are not subject to annual appropriations. Legislative committees have also gained in influence by making their annual authorizations more detailed. Instead of simply authorizing the military, for example, to spend some lump sum next year, the Armed Services Committee will now specify in detail how much will be authorized for what purpose (construction, procurement). This limits substantially the discretion of the Appropriations Committee.[25]

There are many less formal ways by which Congress can affect bureaucratic decision-making. For example, an individual congressman can call an agency head on behalf of a constituent. The great majority of such calls are merely to obtain information but some result in, or attempt to secure, special privileges for particular persons. Congressional committees may also obtain the right to pass on certain agency decisions. This is called "committee clearance," and though it is usually not legally binding on the agency, few agency heads will ignore the expressed wish of a committee chairman that he be consulted before certain actions (such as transferring funds or closing a military base) are taken.

Of late, Congress has made great use of the *legislative veto* as a way of controlling specific details of presidential or bureaucratic decisions. A legislative veto is a legal requirement that a presidential or agency decision must lie before Congress for a specified period (usually thirty or sixty days) before it can take effect. If *either* house adopts a resolution opposing the executive action, that decision is vetoed. Between 1932 and 1975 nearly two hundred statutes requiring a legislative veto were enacted. Most of them are of recent origin and many are in the field of foreign affairs, especially arms sales (see Chapter 20). Every president has opposed this enlargement of congressional power over the bureaucracy but, not surprisingly, many congressmen like it. Congress, for example, has the right to veto the president's choice of a route for a natural gas pipeline from Alaska. From 1960 to 1975, 351 resolutions were filed in Congress to veto some

> **❝** Each agency serves, not one congressional master, but several, and . . . these masters may be in conflict. **❞**

Warren G. Magnuson (D, Wash.) chairs the Senate Appropriations Committee, one of the many congressional masters of the bureaucracy.

executive branch action; 77 passed one house or the other, thereby making the veto effective. There have been efforts to make the decisions of nearly all federal regulatory agencies subject to legislative vetoes. A policy such as this, if adopted, would substantially reverse the tendency of Congress since the 1930s to authorize bureaucratic decision-making on the basis of general and even vague guidelines.[26] It is possible that the Supreme Court may someday decide that the legislative veto is unconstitutional.

Congressional Investigations

Perhaps the most visible and dramatic form of congressional supervision of an agency is the investigation. Since 1792 when Congress investigated an army defeat by an Indian tribe, congressional investigations of the bureaucracy have been a regular feature—sometimes constructive, sometimes debasing—of legislative-executive relations. The investigative power is not men-

The "Laws" of Bureaucratic Procedure

Acheson's Rule
"A memorandum is written not to inform the reader but to protect the writer."

Boren's Laws
"When in doubt, mumble."
"When in trouble, delegate."
"When in charge, ponder."

Robertson's Rule
"The more directives you issue to solve a problem, the worse it gets."

Murphy's Law
"If anything can go wrong, it will."

O'Toole's Corollary to Murphy's Law
"Murphy was an optimist."

Meskimen's Law
"There's never time to do it right but always time to do it over."

Parkinson's First Law
"Work expands to fill the time available for its completion."

Parkinson's Second Law
"Expenditure rises to meet income."

Peter Principle
"In every hierarchy, each employee tends to rise to his level of incompetence; thus, every post tends to be filled by an incompetent employee."

Smith's Principle
"Never do anything for the first time."

Chapman's Rules of Committees
"Never arrive on time, or you will be stamped a beginner."
"Don't say anything until the meeting is half over; this stamps you as being wise."
"Be as vague as possible; this prevents irritating others."
"When in doubt, suggest that a subcommittee be appointed."

Source: Discovered by persons with great experience in bureaucratic organizations, public and private. The best compilation of these and other laws is Paul Dickson, *The Official Rules* (New York: Delacorte Press, 1978).

tioned in the Constitution but has been inferred from the power to legislate. The Supreme Court has consistently upheld this interpretation, though it has also said that such investigations should not be solely for the purpose of exposing the purely personal affairs of private individuals and must not operate to deprive citizens of their basic rights.[27] Congress may compel a person to attend an investigation by issuing a subpoena; anyone who ignores the subpoena may be punished for contempt—Congress can vote to send the person to jail or can refer the matter to a court for further action. As explained in Chapter 11, the president and his principal subordinates have refused to answer certain congressional inquiries on grounds of "executive privilege."

Although many areas of congressional oversight—budgetary review, personnel controls, investigations—are designed to control the exercise of bureaucratic discretion, other areas are intended to ensure the freedom of certain agencies from effective coordination and control, especially by the president. In dozens of cases Congress has given authority to department heads and bureau chiefs to operate independently of presidential preferences. Congress has resisted, for example, presidential efforts to ensure that policies to regulate pollution do not impose excessive costs on the economy, and interest groups have brought suit to prevent presidential coordination of various regulatory agencies. If the bureaucracy sometimes works at cross-purposes, it is usually because Congress—or competing committees in Congress—wants it that way.

BUREAUCRATIC "PATHOLOGIES"

Everyone complains about bureaucracy in general (though rarely about bureaucratic agencies that one believes are desirable). This chapter should persuade you that it is difficult to say anything about bureaucracy "in general"; there are too many different kinds of agencies, kinds of bureaucrats, and kinds of programs to label the entire enterprise with some single adjective. Nevertheless, many people who recognize the enormous variety among government agencies still believe that they all have some general features in common and suffer from certain shared problems or pathologies.

This is true enough, but the reasons for it—and the solutions, if any—are not often understood. There are four major (or at least frequently mentioned) problems with bureaucracies: red tape, conflict, duplication, and imperialism. By "red tape" is meant the existence of complex rules and procedures that must be followed to get something done. Conflict exists because some agencies seem to be working at cross-purposes with other agencies. (For example, the Agricultural Research Service tells farmers how to grow crops more efficiently, while the Agricultural Stabilization and Conservation Service pays farmers to grow fewer crops or to produce less.) Duplication (usually called "wasteful duplication") occurs when two government agencies seem to be doing the same thing, as when the Customs Service and the Drug Enforcement Administration both attempt to intercept illegal drugs being smuggled into the country. "Imperialism" refers to the tendency of agencies to grow without regard to the benefits their programs confer or the costs they entail.

These problems all exist, but they do not necessarily exist because bureaucrats are incompetent or power-hungry. Most exist because of the very nature of government itself. Take red tape: partly, we encounter cumbersome rules and procedures because any large organization, governmental or not, must have some way of ensuring that one part of the organization does not operate out of step with another. Business corporations have red tape also; it is in part a consequence of bigness. But a great amount of governmental red tape is also the result of the need to satisfy legal and political requirements. Government agencies must hire on the basis of "merit," must observe strict accounting rules, must supply Congress with detailed information on their programs, and must allow for citizen

66 Government exists in part to achieve precisely those goals that are least measurable. **99**

access in countless ways. To meet each need, rules are necessary; to ensure that rules are obeyed, forms must be filled out.

Or take conflict and duplication: they do not occur because bureaucrats enjoy conflict or duplication. (Quite the contrary!) They exist because Congress, in setting up agencies and programs, often wants to achieve a number of different, partially inconsistent, goals or finds that it cannot decide which goal it values the most. Congress has 535 members and little strong leadership; it should not be surprising that 535 people will want different things and will sometimes succeed in getting them.

Finally, imperialism results in large part from the fact that government agencies seek goals that are so vague and so difficult or impossible to measure that it is hard to tell when they have

Customs inspection at O'Hare Airport in Chicago is "red tape" to a returning passenger. But a failure to carry out such inspections would be "irresponsibility" to a citizen worried about smuggling.

The federal government has employed as bureaucrats persons who were later to become famous in other careers.

• Clara Barton, founder of the American Red Cross	*Clerk in the U.S. Patent Office, 1854–1861*
• Alexander Graham Bell, inventor of the telephone	*Special agent of the U.S. Census Bureau, 1890*
• Nathaniel Hawthorne, author	*Weigher in the Boston Custom House, 1839–1841, and surveyor of the Port of Salem, Mass., 1845–1849*
• Washington Irving, author	*U.S. foreign service*
• Abraham Lincoln, president	*Postmaster of New Salem, Ill., 1833–1836*
• Knute Rockne, football coach	*Clerk in Chicago Post Office, 1907–1910*
• James Thurber, humorist	*Code clerk in State Department*
• James Whistler, painter	*Draftsman, U.S. Coast Survey, 1854–1855*
• Walt Whitman, poet	*Clerk, U.S. Department of the Interior, 1865*

Clara Barton

BUREAUCRATIC
tr1v1a

Alexander Graham Bell

been attained. A business firm knows when it has made a profit, but the State Department cannot say when it has produced a good foreign policy, the Office for Civil Rights is hard-pressed to explain what is meant by "equal opportunity," and the Occupational Safety and Health Administration cannot readily demonstrate that what it does is resulting in safer and more healthful workplaces. When these agencies, and many others like them, argue that they ought to be bigger, more powerful, and more amply endowed with funds, it is hard to refute them. Because their goals are elusive and progress toward them is in large part a matter of opinion, such agencies can always make a plausible case that more is better.

From this explanation, it should be easy to see why these bureaucratic problems are so hard to correct. To end conflicts and duplication, Congress would have to make some policy choices and set some clear priorities, but with all the competing demands it faces Congress finds it difficult to do that. You make more friends by helping people than by hurting them, and so Congress is more inclined to add new programs than to cut old ones, whether or not the new programs are in conflict with existing ones. To check imperialism, some way would have to be found to measure the benefits of government, but that is often impossible; government exists in part to achieve precisely those goals that are least measurable. Furthermore, what might be done to remedy some problems would make other problems worse: if you simplify rules and procedures to cut red tape, you are likely also to reduce the coordination among agencies and thus to increase the extent to which there is duplication or conflict. In short, the problem of bureaucracy is inseparable from the problem of government generally.

Just as people are likely to say they dislike Congress but like their own congressman, so also are they inclined to express hostility toward "the bureaucracy" but goodwill for that part of the bureaucracy with which they have dealt personally. In 1973 a survey of Americans found that over half had had some contact with one or more kinds of government agencies, most of which were either run directly or funded indirectly by the federal government. The great majority of people were satisfied with these contacts and felt they had been treated fairly and given useful assistance. When these people were asked their feelings about government officials in general, however, they expressed attitudes that were much less favorable. Whereas about 80 percent liked the officials with whom they had dealt, only 42 percent liked officials in general.[28] This finding helps explain why government agencies are rarely reduced in size or budget: whatever popular feelings about the bureaucracy, any given agency tends to have many friends.

SUMMARY

Bureaucracy is characteristic of almost all aspects of modern life, not simply the government. Government bureaucracies, however, pose special problems because they are subject to competing sources of political authority, must function in a constitutional system of divided powers and federalism, and often have vague goals. The power of bureaucracy should be measured by its discretionary authority, not by the number of its employees or the size of its budget.

War and depression have been the principal sources of bureaucratic growth, aided by important changes in constitutional interpretation in the 1930s that permitted Congress to delegate broad grants of authority to administrative agencies. Congress seeks to check or recover those grants by controlling budgets, personnel, and policy decisions and by the exercise of legislative vetoes, with only partial success. The uses to which bureaucrats put their authority can be explained in part by their recruitment and security (they have an agency orientation), their personal political views, and the nature of the tasks their agencies are performing.

Many of the popular solutions for the problems of bureaucratic rule—red tape, duplication, conflict, and agency imperialism—fail to take into account the fact that these problems are to a degree inherent in any government that serves competing goals and is supervised by rival elective officials.

Suggested Readings

Downs, Anthony. *Inside Bureaucracy.* Boston: Little, Brown, 1967. An economist's explanation of why bureaucrats and bureaus behave as they do.

Halperin, Morton H. *Bureaucratic Politics and Foreign Policy.* Washington, D.C.: Brookings Institution, 1974. Insightful account of the strategies by which diplomatic and military bureaucracies defend their interests.

Heclo, Hugh. *A Government of Strangers.* Washington, D.C.: Brookings Institution, 1977. Analyzes how political appointees attempt to gain control of the Washington bureaucracy and how bureaucrats resist those efforts.

Kaufman, Herbert. *The Forest Ranger.* Baltimore, Md.: Johns Hopkins University Press, 1960. Detailed study of the relations between top executives in Washington and their subordinates in the field.

Parkinson, C. Northcote. *Parkinson's Law.* Boston: Houghton Mifflin, 1957. Half-serious, half-joking explanation of why government agencies tend to grow.

Rourke, Francis E. *Bureaucracy, Politics, and Public Policy,* 2nd ed. Boston: Little, Brown, 1976. Overview of bureaucratic influences on public policy.

Seidman, Harold. *Politics, Position, and Power.* New York: Oxford University Press, 1975. Perceptive account by a former insider of relations between the White House and the bureaucracy.

Wilson, James Q. *The Investigators: Managing FBI and Narcotics Agents.* New York: Basic Books, 1978. What "bureaucracy" is and means in two federal agencies, the FBI and the Drug Enforcement Administration.

Note: Two important magazines regularly cover the workings of the Washington bureaucracy: the *National Journal* (which appears weekly and has a frequently published index to its articles) and *The Washington Monthly,* which is more irreverent.

13 The Judiciary

In no country in the world do the courts play as large a role in making public policy as they do in the United States. One aspect of this power is "judicial review"—the right to declare laws of Congress and acts of the executive branch void and unenforceable if they are judged to be in conflict with the Constitution. Since 1789 the Supreme Court has declared over one hundred federal laws to be unconstitutional. In Britain, by contrast, Parliament is supreme, and no court may strike down a law it passes. As Walter Bagehot, a nineteenth-century British journalist, put it, "There is nothing the British Parliament cannot do except transform a man into a woman and a woman into a man." All that prevents Parliament from acting contrary to the (unwritten) constitution of England are the consciences of its members and the opinion of the citizens. There are about sixty nations that do have something resembling judicial review, but in only a few cases does this power mean much in practice. In

John Marshall, chief justice of the United States, 1801–1835 (left), and Warren E. Burger, chief justice since 1969 (right).

almost all of these cases—in Australia, Canada, West Germany, India, and some other nations—there is a stable, federal system of government with a strong tradition of an independent judiciary.[1] (Some other nations—France, for example—have special councils, rather than courts, that can, under certain circumstances, decide that a law is not authorized by the constitution.)

But if reviewing acts of Congress were the only special power that American federal courts had, their role in policy-making would not be nearly so large as it is. As we shall see, relatively few federal laws that the Supreme Court has declared unconstitutional have been of major significance. Of those that have, many have been repassed (often with only trivial changes) in ways that met the Court's approval. It is the courts' activist stance that has been their major source of influence in policy-making. They have been increasingly willing to open their doors to individuals and organizations wishing to block, change, or stimulate governmental action for a wide variety of purposes. The courts have, for example:

Required the Federal Power Commission to regulate the prices of natural gas shipped in interstate commerce;

Decided what rules shall govern police investigations;

Assigned pupils to schools in various cities;

Prevented states from regulating certain businesses within their borders;

Instructed the Department of Health, Education, and Welfare on how to administer its Office for Civil Rights;

Decided that blacks are not American citizens (and later decided they were);

Specified detailed standards for the operation of prisons and mental hospitals;

Required some communities to build fewer roads (because they hurt the environment) and ordered others to build more (because the people need them);

Set down requirements for how much teachers shall be paid and what kinds of tests can be used to select firemen.

There is scarcely a feature of American life, public or private, that has not been touched, even shaped, by a court decision.

THE DEVELOPMENT OF THE FEDERAL COURTS

Most Founders probably expected the Supreme Court to have the power of judicial review (though they did not say that in so many words in the Constitution), but they did not expect federal courts to play so large a role in making public policy. The traditional view of civil courts was that they judged disputes between people who had direct dealings with each other—they had entered into a contract, for example, or one had dropped a load of bricks on the other's toe—and decided which of the two parties was right. The court then supplied "relief" to the wronged party, usually by requiring the other person to pay him money ("damages").

Sometimes one person sought, not damages for a wrongful act that had already occurred, but a judicial order to prevent some harm that was about to occur. Perhaps no one had dropped a load of bricks on his toe, but he noticed that his neighbor was planning to deposit those bricks on his property in a way that would ruin his rose bushes. He would ask the judge for an "injunction"—a court order—to prevent this.

Given this traditional understanding of what courts did and the fact that American society in 1787 was not very complicated—corporations, labor unions, and government agencies were all in the future—the defenders of the new Constitution thought of the courts as relatively weak and passive. Alexander Hamilton, writing in *Federalist* No. 78, described the judiciary as the branch "least dangerous" to individual rights.

The president is commander-in-chief and thus holds the "sword of the community"; Congress appropriates money and thus "commands the purse," as well as decides what laws shall govern. But the judiciary "has no influence over either the sword or the purse" and "can take no active resolution whatever." It has "neither force nor will but merely judgment," and thus is "beyond comparison the weakest of the three departments of power." As a result, "liberty can have nothing to fear from the judiciary alone." Hamilton went on to state clearly that the Constitution intended to give to the courts the right to decide whether a law is contrary to the Constitution. But this authority, he explained, was not designed to enlarge the power of the courts but to confine that of the legislature.

Obviously, things have changed since Hamilton's time. The evolution of the federal courts, especially the Supreme Court, toward the present level of activism and influence has been shaped by the political, economic, and ideological forces of three historical eras. From 1787 to 1865, nation-building, the legitimacy of the federal government, and slavery were the great issues; from 1865 to 1937, the dominant issue was the relationship between government and the economy; from 1938 to the present, the major issues confronting the Court have involved personal liberty and social equality and the potential conflict between the two. In the first period the Court asserted the supremacy of the federal government; in the second it placed important restrictions on the powers of that government; and in the third it enlarged the scope of personal freedom and narrowed that of economic freedom.

National Supremacy and Slavery

"From 1789 until the Civil War, the dominant interest of the Supreme Court was in that greatest of all the questions left unresolved by the Founders—the nation-state relationship."[2] The answer the Court gave, under the leadership of

CHIEF JUSTICES OF THE UNITED STATES

Chief Justice	Appointed by President	Years of Service
John Jay	Washington	1789–1795
Oliver Ellsworth	Washington	1796–1800
John Marshall	Adams	1801–1835
Roger B. Taney	Jackson	1836–1864
Salmon P. Chase	Lincoln	1864–1873
Morrison R. Waite	Grant	1874–1888
Melville W. Fuller	Cleveland	1888–1910
Edward D. White	Taft	1910–1921
William Howard Taft	Harding	1921–1930
Charles Evans Hughes	Hoover	1930–1941
Harlan Fiske Stone	Roosevelt	1941–1946
Fred M. Vinson	Truman	1946–1953
Earl Warren	Eisenhower	1953–1969
Warren E. Burger	Nixon	1969–present

Note: Omitted is John Rutledge, who only served for a few months in 1795 and who was not confirmed by the Senate.

Chief Justice John Marshall, was that national law was in all instances the supreme law, with state law having to give way, and that the Supreme Court had the power to decide what the Constitution meant. In two cases of enormous importance—*Marbury* v. *Madison* in 1803 and *McCulloch* v. *Maryland* in 1819—the Court, speaking through decisions written by Marshall, held that the Supreme Court could declare an act of Congress unconstitutional, that the power granted to the federal government flows from the people and should be generously construed so that any laws "necessary and proper" to the attainment of constitutional ends would be permissible, and that federal law is supreme over state law even to the point that the state may not tax an enterprise (such as a bank) created by the federal government.[3]

The supremacy of the federal government was

Marbury Versus Madison

The story of *Marbury v. Madison* is oft told, but deserves another telling because it illustrates so many features of the role of the Supreme Court—how apparently small cases can have large results, how the power of the Court depends not simply on its constitutional authority but on its acting in ways that avoid a clear confrontation with other branches of government, and how the climate of opinion affects how the Court goes about its task.

When President John Adams lost his bid for reelection to Thomas Jefferson in 1800, he—and all members of his party, the Federalists—feared that Jefferson and the Republicans would weaken the federal government and turn its powers to what the Federalists believed were wrong ends (states' rights, an alliance with the French, hostility to business). Feverishly, as his hours in office came to an end, Adams worked to pack the judiciary with fifty-nine loyal Federalists by giving them so-called "midnight" appointments before Jefferson took office.

John Marshall, as Adams's secretary of state, had the task of certifying and delivering these new judicial commissions. In the press of business, he delivered all but seventeen; these he left on his desk for the incoming secretary of state, James Madison, to send out. Jefferson and Madison, however, were furious at Adams's behavior and refused to deliver the seventeen. William Marbury and three other Federalists who had been promised these commissions hired a lawyer and brought suit against Madison to force him to produce the documents. The suit requested the Supreme Court to issue a writ of mandamus (from the Latin, "we command") ordering Madison to do his duty. The right to issue such writs had been given to the Supreme Court by the Judiciary Act of 1789.

Marshall, the man who had failed to deliver the commissions to Marbury and his friends in the first place, had become the chief justice and was now in a position to decide the case. These days, a justice who had been involved in an issue before it came to the Court would probably disqualify himself, but Marshall had no intention of letting others decide this question. He faced, however, not simply a partisan dispute over jobs, but what was very nearly a constitutional crisis. If he ordered the commissions delivered, Madison might still refuse and the Court had no way—if Madison was determined to resist—to compel him. The Court had no police force, whereas Madison had the support of the president of the United States. And if the order were given, whether or not Madison complied, the Jeffersonian Republicans in Con-

John Adams

James Madison

gress would probably try to impeach Marshall. Indeed, after the case was decided they made an unsuccessful attempt to impeach and remove another Supreme Court justice, Samuel Chase, in part on the grounds that they disliked his policies. On the other hand, if Marshall allowed Madison to do as he wished, the power of the Supreme Court would be seriously reduced.

Marshall's solution was ingenious. Speaking for a unanimous Court, he announced that Madison was wrong to withhold the commissions, that courts could issue writs to compel public officials to do their prescribed duty—*but*, that the Supreme Court had no power to issue such writs in this case because the law giving it that power was unconstitutional. The law said that the Supreme Court could issue such writs as part of its "original jurisdiction"—that is, persons seeking such writs could go *directly* to the Supreme Court with their request (rather than to a lower federal court and then, if dissatisfied, appeal to the Supreme Court). Article III of the Constitution, Marshall pointed out, spelled out precisely the Supreme Court's original jurisdiction; it did not mention issuing writs of this sort and plainly indicated that on all matters not mentioned in the Constitution, the Court would have only appellate jurisdiction. Congress may not change what the Constitution says; hence, the part of the Judiciary Act attempting to do this was null and void.

The result was that a showdown with the Jeffersonians was avoided—Madison was not ordered to deliver the commission—but the power of the Supreme Court was unmistakably clarified and enlarged. As Marshall wrote, "It is emphatically the province and duty of the judicial department to say what the law is." Furthermore, "A law repugnant to the Constitution is void," and all other branches of government must be bound by the Court's decisions on such matters.

further enhanced by other decisions. In one, decided in 1816, the Supreme Court rejected the claim of the Virginia courts that the Supreme Court could not review the decisions of state courts. The Virginia courts were ready to acknowledge the supremacy of the United States Constitution but believed they had as much right as the United States Supreme Court to decide what that Constitution meant. The Supreme Court felt otherwise, and in this case and another like it the Court asserted its own broad powers to review any state court decision if that decision seem to violate federal law or the federal Constitution.[4]

The power of the federal government to regulate commerce among the states was also established. When New York gave to Robert Fulton, the inventor of the steamboat, the monopoly right to operate his steamboats on the rivers of that state, the Marshall Court overturned the license because the rivers connected New York and New Jersey and thus commerce *on* those rivers would involve people and goods going to and from other states. This meant it was *inter*state commerce, and federal law in that area was supreme. Since there was a conflicting federal law on the books, the state law was void.[5]

All of this may sound rather obvious to us today, when the supremacy of the federal government is largely unquestioned. In the early nineteenth century, however, these were almost revolutionary decisions. The Jeffersonian Republicans were in power, and had become increasingly devoted to states' rights; they were aghast at the Marshall decisions. President Andrew Jackson attacked the Court bitterly for defending the right of the federal government to create a national bank and for siding with the Cherokee Indians in a dispute with Georgia. In speaking of the latter case, Jackson is supposed to have remarked, "John Marshall has made his decision:—now let him enforce it!"[6]

Though Marshall seemed to have made secure the supremacy of the federal government,

Robert Fulton's steamboats led to a major Supreme Court decision that defined the meaning of "interstate commerce." The Supreme Court did not allow New York state to give Fulton a monopoly license to operate his boats on that state's rivers.

another issue had arisen even more divisive than national power; that, of course, was slavery. Roger B. Taney succeeded Marshall as chief justice in 1836. He was deliberately chosen by President Jackson because he was an advocate of states' rights, and he began to chip away at federal supremacy, upholding state claims that Marshall would have set aside. But the decision for which he is famous—or infamous—came in 1857 when, in the *Dred Scott* case, he wrote perhaps the most disastrous judicial opinion ever issued. A slave had been brought by his owner to a northern state where slavery was illegal and then returned to Missouri, where slavery was permitted. The slave sued, claiming that his residence in a free state had made him free. Taney held that under the Constitution, Negroes were not citizens of the United States, could not become so no matter where they lived, and a

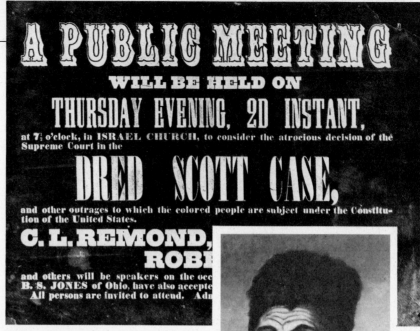

Roger B. Taney, chief justice from 1836 to 1864, wrote the *Dred Scott* decision, which asserted that blacks were not citizens of the United States. Dred Scott claimed that when his master brought him north to a free state he ceased to be a slave. The public outcry against the decision, at least in the North, was intense, as evident from this poster announcing a mass meeting "to consider the atrocious decision."

federal law giving them their freedom if they lived in the North was unconstitutional.[7] The public outcry against this view was enormous, and the Court and Taney were discredited in (at least) northern opinion. A civil war was fought over what the Court, mistakenly, had assumed it could treat as a purely legal question.

Government and the Economy

The supremacy of the federal government may have been established by John Marshall and a civil war, but the scope of the powers of that government or even of the state governments was still to be defined. During the period from the end of the Civil War to the early years of the New Deal, the dominant issue the Court faced was to decide under what circumstances

the economy could be regulated by state or nation.

The Court revealed a strong though not inflexible attachment to private property. In fact, that attachment had always been there—the Founders thought that political and property rights were inextricably linked, and Marshall certainly supported the sanctity of contracts. But now, with the muting of the federal supremacy issue and the rise of a national economy with important unanticipated effects, the property question became the dominant one. In general, the Court developed the view that the Fourteenth Amendment, adopted in 1868 primarily to protect black claims to citizenship from hostile state action, also protected private property and the corporation from at least unreasonable state action. The crucial phrase was this: no state shall "deprive any person of life, liberty, or property, without due process of law." Once it became clear to businessmen and craftsmen that a "person" could be a firm or a corporation as well as an individual, they began to flood the courts with cases challenging various government regulations of these enterprises.

The Court quickly found itself in a thicket: it began passing on the legality and constitutionality of virtually every effort by any government to regulate any aspect of business or labor, and its workload rose sharply. The "activism" of the courts was established in this period as the Court set itself up as the arbiter of what kind of regulation was permissible. In the first seventy-five years of this country's history, only 2 federal laws were held unconstitutional; in the next seventy-five years, 71 were.[8] Of the roughly 900 state laws held to be in conflict with the federal Constitution since 1789, about 800 were overturned after 1870. In one decade alone—the 1880s—5 federal and 48 state laws were declared unconstitutional.

Many of these decisions gave clear evidence of the Court's desire to protect private property—it upheld the use of injunctions to prevent labor strikes,[9] struck down the federal income tax,[10] sharply limited the reach of the antitrust law,[11] restricted the powers of the Interstate Commerce Commission to set railroad rates,[12] prohibited the federal government from eliminating child labor,[13] and prevented the states from setting maximum hours of work.[14] In 184 cases between 1899 and 1937, the Supreme Court struck down state laws for violating the Fourteenth Amendment, usually by economic regulation.[15]

But the Court also rendered decisions that authorized various kinds of regulation. It allowed states to regulate businessess "affected with a public interest,"[16] changed its mind about the Interstate Commerce Commission and allowed it to regulate railroad rates,[17] upheld rules requiring railroads to improve their safety,[18] approved

❝The 'activism' of the courts was established in this period as the Court set itself up as the arbiter of what kind of regulation was permissible.**❞**

state antiliquor laws,[19] approved state mine safety laws,[20] supported state workmen's compensation laws,[21] allowed states to regulate railroad rates within their borders,[22] and came, in time, to uphold a number of state laws regulating wages and hours. Indeed, between 1887 and 1910, in 558 cases involving the Fourteenth Amendment the Supreme Court upheld state regulations over 80 percent of the time.[23]

To characterize the Court as "pro-business" or "anti-regulation" is both simplistic and inexact. More accurate, perhaps, is a characterization of it as supportive of the rights of private property but unsure how to draw the lines that would distinguish "reasonable" from "unreasonable" regulation. There was nothing in the Constitution that clearly differentiated "reasonable" from "unreasonable" regulation and the Court could invent no consistent principle of its own to make this determination. For example, what kinds of businesses are "affected with a public interest"? Grain elevators and railroads are, but are bakeries? Sugar refiners? Saloons? And how much of commerce is "interstate"—anything that moves? Or only something that actually crosses a state line? The Court found itself trying to make detailed judgments it was not always competent to make and to invent legal rules where no clear legal rules were possible.

In one area the Court's judgments were clear however—the Fourteenth and Fifteenth amendments were construed so narrowly as to give blacks only the most limited benefits of their provisions. In a long series of decisions, the Court upheld segregation in schools and on railroad cars and permitted blacks to be excluded from voting in many states (see Chapter 19).

The Protection of Political Liberty and Economic Regulation

After 1936 the Supreme Court stopped imposing any serious restrictions on state or federal power to regulate the economy, leaving such matters in the hands of the legislatures. From 1937 to 1974 the Supreme Court did not overturn a single federal law designed to regulate business but did overturn thirty-six congressional enactments that violated personal political liberties. It voided as unconstitutional laws that restricted freedom of speech,[24] denied passports to Communists,[25] permitted the government to revoke a person's citizenship,[26] withheld a person's mail,[27] or restricted the availability of government benefits.[28]

This new direction began when one justice changed his mind, and continued as the composition of the Court changed. At the outset of the

The "Nine Old Men": The Supreme Court in 1937, not long after President Franklin D. Roosevelt tried, unsuccessfully, to "pack" it by appointing six additional justices who would have supported his New Deal legislation. Justice Owen J. Roberts (standing at the left) changed his vote on these matters, and the Court ceased to be a barrier to the delegation of power to the bureaucracy.

New Deal, the Court was, by a narrow margin, dominated by justices who opposed the welfare state and federal regulation based on broad grants of discretionary authority to administrative agencies. President Franklin Roosevelt, who was determined to get just such legislation implemented, found himself powerless to alter the composition of the Court during his first term (1932–1936): because no justice died or retired, he had no vacancies to fill. After his overwhelming reelection in 1936, he moved to remedy this problem by "packing" the Court. He proposed a bill that would have allowed him to appoint one new justice for every one over the age of seventy who refused to retire up to a total membership of fifteen. Since there were six men in this category then on the Supreme Court, he would have been able to appoint six new justices, enough to ensure a comfortable majority supportive of his economic policies. A bitter controversy ensued, but before the bill could be voted on, the Supreme Court astonished everyone by changing its mind. Whereas it had been turning down New Deal measures by votes of five to four, now it started approving them by the same vote. One justice, Owen Roberts, had switched his position—the famous "switch in time that saved nine."

The "court-packing" bill was not passed, but it was no longer necessary. Justice Roberts had yielded before public opinion in a way that Chief Justice Taney, a century earlier, had not, thus forestalling an assault on the Court by the other branches of government. Shortly thereafter, several justices stepped down, and Roosevelt was able to make his own appointments (he made nine in all during his four terms in office). From then on, the Court turned its attention to new issues—political liberties and, in time, civil rights. With the arrival in office of Chief Justice Earl Warren in 1953, the Court began its most active period yet. No longer, however, was the Court's activity concentrated on establishing national supremacy or defining the boundaries of permissible economic regulation; now, activism arose to redefine the relationship of the citizen to the government, and especially to protect the rights and liberties of citizens from governmental trespass. In a large measure, the Court has always seen itself as protecting citizens from arbitrary government. Before 1937 that protection was of a sort that conservatives preferred; after 1937 it was of a kind that liberals preferred.

THE STRUCTURE OF THE FEDERAL COURTS

The only federal court that must exist is the Supreme Court, required by Article III of the Constitution. All other federal courts, and their jurisdictions, are creations of Congress. Nor does the Constitution indicate how many justices shall be on the Supreme Court (there were originally six, now there are nine) nor what its appellate jurisdiction shall be.

Congress has created two kinds of lower federal courts to handle cases that need not be decided by the Supreme Court: "constitutional" and "legislative" courts. A constitutional court is one exercising the judicial powers found in Article III of the Constitution and, because of that, its judges are given constitutional protection—they may not be fired (they serve during "good behavior") nor may their salaries be reduced while they are in office. The most important of the constitutional courts are the district courts (a total of ninety-four, with at least one in each state, the District of Columbia, and the Commonwealth of Puerto Rico) and the courts of appeals (one in each of eleven regions or "circuits"). There are also four specialized courts that have constitutional status—the Court of Claims, the Tax Court, the Customs Court, and the Court of Customs and Patent Appeals—but we shall not be concerned with them.

A "legislative" court is one set up by Congress for some specialized purpose and staffed with persons who have fixed terms of office and can be removed or have their salaries reduced. Legislative courts include the Court of Military Appeals and the territorial courts.

The main federal constitutional courts are the only ones important for understanding how public policy is made and how the Constitution and laws are interpreted. Since the judges of these courts serve for life, how they are appointed and the attitudes they bring to the bench are obviously important. All are nominated by the president and confirmed by the Senate; almost invariably, the president nominates as a federal judge a member of his own political party (see Table 13.1). It is not clear, however, that whether a judge is a Democrat or a Republican profoundly affects his decisions—some Democrats turn out to be conservative or to interpret the Constitution strictly; some Republicans turn

TABLE 13.1 Percentages of Federal Judicial Appointments Adhering to the Same Political Party as the President, 1888–1979

President	Party	Percentage
Cleveland	Democrat	97.3%
B. Harrison	Republican	87.9
McKinley	Republican	95.7
T. Roosevelt	Republican	95.8
Taft	Republican	82.8
Wilson	Democrat	98.6
Harding	Republican	97.7
Coolidge	Republican	94.1
Hoover	Republican	85.7
F. D. Roosevelt	Democrat	96.4
Truman	Democrat	90.1
Eisenhower	Republican	94.1
Kennedy	Democrat	90.9
L. B. Johnson	Democrat	93.2
Nixon	Republican	93.7
Ford	Republican	81.2
Carter	Democrat	98.2[a]

Source: Henry J. Abraham, *Justices and Presidents: A Political History of Appointments to the Supreme Court* (New York: Oxford University Press, 1974), p. 60. Copyright © 1974 by Oxford University Press, Inc. Reprinted by permission. Percentages for Ford and Carter supplied by Abraham.

[a] As of February 1979.

SUPREME COURT JUSTICES, 1978 (in order of seniority)

Name	Year of Birth	Home State	Law School	Prior Experience	Appointed By	Year of Appointment
Warren E. Burger Chief Justice	1907	Minnesota	St. Paul College of Law	Assistant Attorney General, Federal Judge	Nixon	1969
William J. Brennan, Jr.	1906	New Jersey	Harvard	State Judge	Eisenhower	1956
Potter Stewart	1915	Ohio	Yale	Federal Judge	Eisenhower	1958
Byron R. White	1918	Colorado	Yale	Deputy Attorney General	Kennedy	1962
Thurgood Marshall	1908	Maryland	Howard	Counsel to NAACP, Federal Judge	Johnson	1967
Harry A. Blackmun	1908	Minnesota	Harvard	Federal Judge	Nixon	1970
Lewis F. Powell, Jr.	1907	Virginia	Washington & Lee	President, American Bar Association	Nixon	1972
William H. Rehnquist	1924	Arizona	Stanford	Assistant Attorney General	Nixon	1972
John Paul Stevens	1916	Illinois	Chicago	Federal Judge	Ford	1975

The Supreme Court in 1979 in a rare informal pose, left to right: John Paul Stevens, Lewis F. Powell, Jr., Harry A. Blackmun, William H. Rehnquist, Thurgood Marshall, William J. Brennan, Jr., Chief Justice Warren E. Burger, Potter Stewart, and Byron R. White.

out to be and do the opposite. One Supreme Court appointee, Hugo Black, had been briefly a member of the Ku Klux Klan, but few judges rendered more liberal opinions than he. Felix Frankfurter was a liberal professor at the Harvard Law School when Franklin Roosevelt put him on the Supreme Court; once there, he promptly became an opponent of judicial activism. When Theodore Roosevelt was upset by a decision rendered by Oliver Wendell Holmes, Jr., whom he had appointed to the Supreme Court, he raged: "I could carve out of a banana a judge with more backbone than that!" Later, Holmes was heard to say that he did not "give a damn" what Roosevelt wanted.[29]

Nonetheless, all presidents give careful thought to the political views of judicial candidates, at least for the highest court. Richard Nixon sought to appoint conservative strict constructionists, and by and large he succeeded, just as Franklin Roosevelt by and large succeeded in appointing liberal judicial activists. But in the lower courts, no president can have much of an idea as to how his appointees will behave. For one thing, there are too many—Franklin Roosevelt appointed over two hundred federal judges, and Richard Nixon appointed even more. Moreover, who gets to be a federal judge is heavily influenced by the preferences of the senators from the state where the vacancy occurs. By a tradition called "senatorial courtesy," the Senate will not confirm the appointment of any judge—or any other presidential nominee—if the senator from the candidate's state and of the president's party objects. Senators have long regarded their ability to influence the choice of, or even to select personally, the federal judges and United States attorneys from their areas as an important kind of political patronage with which to reward their supporters. Of late, some senators have begun to make their choices on the basis of recommendations from nonpartisan, "blue-ribbon" screening panels, but the practice is not yet general.

Of the 136 Supreme Court nominees pre-

TABLE 13.2 Senate Rejections of Supreme Court Nominations in This Century

Nominee	Year	President	Action
John J. Parker	1930	Hoover	Rejected
Abe Fortas*	1968	Johnson	Withdrawn
Clement F. Haynsworth, Jr.	1969	Nixon	Rejected
G. Harrold Carswell	1970	Nixon	Rejected

* Already on the Supreme Court; was nominated to be chief justice; when his nomination failed, he resigned from the Court.

sented to it, the Senate has rejected 26, though only 4 in this century.[30] These four cases are described in Table 13.2. The reasons for rejecting a Supreme Court nominee are complex—each senator may have a different reason—but have involved such matters as a record of hostility to civil rights, questionable personal financial dealings, poor records as lower court judges, and Senate opposition to the nominee's political or legal philosophy. Nominations of district court judges are rarely defeated because, typically, no nomination is made unless the key senators approve in advance.

THE JURISDICTION OF THE FEDERAL COURTS

We have a dual court system—one state, one federal—and this complicates enormously the task of describing what kinds of cases federal courts may hear and how cases beginning in the state courts may end up before the Supreme Court. The Constitution lists the kinds of cases over which federal courts have jurisdiction (in Article III and the Eleventh Amendment); by implication, all other matters are left to state courts. Federal courts can hear all cases "arising under the Constitution, the laws of the United States, and treaties" (these are "federal question" cases), and cases involving citizens of different states (these are called "diversity" cases).

**THE JURISDICTION OF
THE FEDERAL COURTS**

Supreme Court of the United States (1 court with 9 justices)
Original jurisdiction (cases begin in the Supreme
Court) over controversies involving:
1. Two or more states
2. The United States and a state
3. Foreign ambassadors and other diplomats
4. A state and a citizen of a different state (if begun by
   the state)
Appellate jurisdiction (cases begin in another, lower
court)
Hears appeals, under certain circumstances, from:
1. Lower federal courts
2. Highest state court

United States Courts of Appeals (1 in each of 11 "circuits"
or regions)
Hear only appeals; no original jurisdiction
Appeals from:
1. Federal district courts
2. U.S. regulatory commissions
3. Certain other federal courts

United States District Courts (1 in each of 94 districts)
Have only original jurisdiction; do not hear appeals
Original jurisdiction over cases involving:
1. Federal crimes
2. Civil suits under federal law where the amount exceeds $10,000
3. Civil suits between citizens of different states where
   the amount exceeds $10,000
4. Admiralty and maritime cases
5. Bankruptcy cases
6. Review of actions of certain federal administrative
   agencies
7. Other matters assigned to them by Congress

Some kinds of cases can be heard in either federal or state courts. For example, if citizens of different states wish to sue one another and the matter involves more than $10,000, they can do so in either a federal or a state court. Similarly, if a man robs a federally insured bank, he has broken both state and federal law and thus he can be prosecuted in either state or federal courts. Lawyers have become quite sophisticated in deciding whether, in a given civil case, their clients will get better treatment in state or federal court. Prosecutors often refer a person who has broken both federal and state law to whichever court system is likely to give the toughest penalty.

Furthermore, a matter that is exclusively in the province of a state court—for example, a criminal case in which the defendant is charged with violating only a state law—can be appealed to the Supreme Court of the United States under certain circumstances to be described below. Thus, federal judges can supervise state court rulings even when they have no jurisdiction over the original matter. Under what circumstances this should occur is the subject of long-standing controversy between the state and federal systems.

Some matters however, are exclusively under the jurisdiction of federal courts. When a federal criminal law is broken—but not a state one—the case is heard in federal district court. If you wish to appeal the decision of a federal regulatory agency, such as the Federal Communications Commission, you can only do so before a federal court of appeals. And if you wish to declare bankruptcy, you do so in federal court. If there is a controversy between two state governments— say, California and Arizona sue each other over which state is to use how much water from the Colorado River—the case can only be heard by the Supreme Court.

The vast majority of all cases heard by federal courts begin in the district courts. The volume of business there is tremendous. In 1975 the 400 district court judges were presented with 117,320 civil cases (almost 300 per judge) and over 43,000 criminal cases (over 100 per judge). Most of these

In The Supreme Court of The United States
Washington D.C.
Clarence Earl Gideon
Petitioner
vs.
H.G. Cochran, Jr., as
Director, Divisions
of corrections state
of Florida.

Petition for a writ
of Certiorari Directed
to the Supreme Court
State of Florida.

No. 890 Misc.
OCT. TERM 1961
U. S. Supreme Court

> **A major broadening of the Bill of Rights . . . began when impoverished Clarence Earl Gideon, imprisoned in Florida, wrote in pencil on prison stationery an appeal and sent it to the Supreme Court.**

Clarence Earl Gideon studied law books while in prison so that he could write an appeal to the Supreme Court. His handwritten appeal asked that his conviction be set aside because he had not been provided with an attorney.

cases involve rather straightforward applications of the law, and few lead to the making of new public policy. Those that do affect the interpretation of the law or the Constitution can begin with seemingly minor events. For example, a major broadening of the Bill of Rights—requiring for the first time that all accused persons in *state* as well as federal criminal trials be supplied with a lawyer, free if necessary—began when impoverished Clarence Earl Gideon, imprisoned in Florida, wrote in pencil on prison stationery an appeal and sent it to the Supreme Court.[31]

The law governing what matters may reach the Supreme Court is complicated. At one time a large number of matters could be appealed directly from district courts to the Supreme Court, but as the latter became overloaded with work, Congress passed laws giving the Court the power to control its workload by selecting, in most instances, the kinds of cases it wanted to hear. There are now essentially two routes to the Supreme Court (other than by starting there with a case that falls under its original jurisdiction).

One is by means of an *appeal*, which the Court technically must hear (though there are ways it can avoid hearing some appeals). There are only a few matters that qualify for an appeal. In general, they involve clear constitutional issues, such as when a lower federal court or the highest state

KINDS OF LAW

The differences between *civil* and *criminal* law are not precise. Generally speaking:

- *Civil law* is the body of rules defining relationships among citizens ("private law") and consists of both statutes and the accumulated customary law embodied in judicial decisions (the "common law").

- *Criminal law* is the body of rules defining offenses which, though they harm an individual (e.g., murder, rape, robbery), are considered to be offenses against society as a whole and as a consequence warrant punishment by and in the name of society.

HOW CASES GET TO THE SUPREME COURT

1. They may begin there (original jurisdiction)

2. They may arrive there on appeal

   a. From the highest state court, if the state court has declared a federal law or treaty to be unconstitutional or upheld a state law despite a claim that it violates federal law or the federal Constitution

   b. From a federal court of appeals, if a state law or federal law has been found unconstitutional

   c. From a federal district court, if a federal law has been held unconstitutional and the United States was a party to the suit

   d. Certain other limited cases

3. They may arrive by writ of certiorari

   a. From the highest state court where the case raises a "substantial federal question"

   b. From the federal courts of appeals

Note: As a practical matter, there is very little difference between cases being heard via an appeal and those being heard via a writ of certiorari. In both instances the Supreme Court has great discretion to select the cases it wants to hear.

court has found a federal law to be unconstitutional or has found a state law to be in conflict with federal laws or the Constitution, or when the highest state court has upheld a state law against the claim that it was in violation of federal law or the Constitution. Only about 10 percent of the Supreme Court's cases arrive by appeal.

The main route is by a writ of certiorari. *Certiorari* is a Latin term that means, roughly, "made more certain," and describes a procedure the Supreme Court can use whenever, in the opinion of at least *four* of its members, the decision of the highest state court involves a "substantial federal question" (the Supreme Court decides what that is). This procedure is also invoked when the decision of a federal court of appeals involves the interpretation of a federal law or the Constitution. Either side in a case may ask the Supreme Court for certiorari (or "cert," as the lawyers call it), and the Court can decide whether or not to grant it without divulging its reasons.

In exercising its discretion in granting certiorari, the Supreme Court is on the horns of a dilemma. If it grants it frequently, it will be inundated with cases. As it is, the workload of the Court has tripled in the last twenty-five years, from fewer than 900 cases in 1930 to about 4,000 in 1975. If, on the other hand, the Court grants certiorari only rarely, then the federal courts of appeals have the last word on the interpretation of the Constitution and federal laws, and since there are eleven of these staffed by ninety-seven judges, they may well be in disagreement. In fact, this diversity of constitutional interpretation has happened: because the Supreme Court reviews only about 1 percent of appeals court cases, applicable federal law may be different in different parts of the country.[32] One way proposed to deal with this dilemma is to devote the Supreme Court's time entirely to major questions of constitutional interpretation and to create a national court of appeals that would ensure that the eleven circuit courts of appeals are producing uniform decisions.[33]

GETTING TO COURT

In theory, the courts are the great equalizer in the federal government. To use the courts to settle a question, or even to alter fundamentally the accepted interpretation of the Constitution, one need not be elected to any office, have access to the mass media, be a member of an interest group, or be otherwise powerful or rich. Once the contending parties are before the court, they are legally equal.

It is too easy to believe this theory uncritically or to reject it cynically. In fact, it is hard to get before the Supreme Court—it rejects about 95 percent of the applications for certiorari it receives. And the costs involved in getting to the Court can be high. To apply for certiorari costs only $100 (plus forty copies of the petition), but if certiorari is granted and the case heard, the costs—for lawyers and for copies of the lower court records in the case—can be very large. And by then one has already paid for the cost of the first hearing in the district court and probably one appeal to the circuit court of appeals. Furthermore, the time it takes in federal court to settle a matter can be quite long.

But there are ways to make these costs lower. If you are indigent—without funds—you can file and be heard as a pauper for nothing; about half the petitions arriving before the Supreme Court are *in forma pauperis*, such as that from Gideon described earlier. If your case began as a criminal trial in the district courts and you are poor, the government supplies a lawyer at no charge. If the matter is not a criminal case and you cannot afford to hire a lawyer, there are interest groups representing a wide spectrum of opinion that sometimes are willing, if the issue in the case seems sufficiently important, to take up the cause. The American Civil Liberties Union (ACLU) represents some persons who believe their freedom of speech or press has been abridged or that their constitutional rights in criminal proceedings have been violated. The NAACP brought many of the decisive civil rights cases on behalf of various individuals, some of whom had sought it out for help and others of whom it had sought out in order to have a test case. Environmentalist, consumer, and labor organizations have of late become especially active in the courts, partially offsetting the advantage enjoyed by corporations and corporate law firms. Finally, many important issues are raised by state and local governments that, of course, have their own attorneys. Several price-fixing cases have been won by state attorneys general going to federal court on behalf of consumers in their states.

Each party to a lawsuit in the United States must pay its own way, but this is not a common practice around the world (in Europe, only Belgium has a similar requirement). American practice in this regard is changing, however. Congress has passed a number of laws that permit the plaintiff (i.e., the party that initiates the suit) to collect its lawyers' fee from the defendant if the defendant loses. For example, if a corporation is found to have violated the antitrust laws, it must pay the legal fees incurred by the side that brought the charge. Similarly, if a corporation or a government agency is found to have violated the Civil Rights Act of 1964, the court may require it to reimburse the plaintiff for attorneys' fees. Environmentalist groups that sue the Environmental Protection Agency may also get reimbursed for their costs. Of late, the Court has refused to award legal fees except where authorized by Congress.[34] Bills have been introduced that would allow courts to award fees to private parties in practically any kind of case. The matter is not yet settled, but it seems clear that the drift of public policy is to make it easier and cheaper to go into court.

Standing

There is another, nonfinancial restriction on getting into federal court. To sue, one must have "standing." Standing is a legal concept that refers to who is entitled to bring a case. It is especially important in determining who can challenge the laws or actions of government itself. A complex and changing set of rules govern standing: some of the more important ones are these:

1. There must be an actual controversy between real adversaries. (You cannot bring a "friendly" suit against someone, hoping to lose in order to prove your friend right. You cannot ask a federal court for an opinion on a hypothetical or imaginary case, or ask it to render an advisory opinion.)

2. You must show that you have been harmed by the law or practice about which you are complaining. (It is not enough to dislike what the government or a corporation or a labor union does; you must show that you were actually harmed by that action.)

3. Merely being a taxpayer does not ordinarily entitle you to challenge the constitutionality of a federal governmental action. (You may not want your tax money to be spent in certain ways, but your remedy for that is to vote against the politicians doing the spending; the federal courts will generally require that you show some other personal harm before you can sue.)

Congress and the courts in recent years have made it easier to acquire standing. It has always been the rule that a citizen could ask the courts to order a federal official to carry out some act that he was under a legal obligation to perform or to refrain from some action that was contrary to law. A citizen can also sue a government official personally in order to collect damages if the official acted contrary to law. For example, it was for long the case that if an FBI agent broke into your office without a search warrant, you could sue the agent and, if you won, collect money. However, you cannot sue the government itself without its consent. This is the doctrine of "sovereign immunity." For instance, if the army accidentally kills your cow while testing a new cannon, you cannot sue the government to recover the cost of the cow unless the government agrees to be sued. (Since testing cannons is legal, you cannot sue the army officer who fired the cannon.) By statute, Congress has given its con-

sent for the government to be sued in many cases involving a dispute over a contract or damage done as a result of negligence (e.g., the dead cow). Over the years these statutes have made it easier and easier to take the government into court as a defendant.

Even some of the oldest rules defining standing have been liberalized. The rule that merely being a taxpayer does not entitle you to challenge in court a government decision has been relaxed where the citizen claims that a right guaranteed under the First Amendment is being violated. The Supreme Court allowed a taxpayer to challenge a federal law that would have given financial aid to parochial (i.e., church-related) schools on the grounds that this aid violated the constitutional requirement of separation between church and state. On the other hand, another taxpayer suit to force the CIA to make public its budget failed because the Court decided the taxpayer did not have standing in matters of this sort.[35]

Class-Action Suits

Under certain circumstances a citizen can benefit directly from a court decision even though he has not gone into court himself. This can happen by means of a "class-action" suit: a case brought into court by a person on behalf, not only of himself, but of all other persons in the country under similar circumstances. Among the most famous such cases is the school desegregation decision of the Supreme Court in 1954 when it found that Linda Brown, a black girl attending the fifth grade in the Topeka, Kansas, public schools, was denied the equal protection of the laws (guaranteed under the Fourteenth Amendment) because the schools in Topeka were segregated. The Court did not limit its decision to Linda Brown's right to attend an unsegregated school, but extended it—as Brown's lawyers from the NAACP had asked—to cover all "others similarly situated."[36] As we shall see in Chapter 19, it was not easy to design a court order that would eliminate segregation for black children, but the principle was clearly established in this class action.

Many other groups have been quick to take advantage of the opportunity created by class-action suits. By this means, the courts could be used to give relief, not simply to a particular person, but to all those represented in the suit. Another landmark class-action case was that which challenged the malapportionment of state legislatures (see Chapter 10).[37] In 1975 there were nearly eight thousand class-action suits in the federal courts involving civil rights, the rights of prisoners, antitrust suits against corporations, and other matters. These suits became more common partly because people were beginning to have new concerns that were not being met by Congress but also because some class-action suits became quite profitable. The NAACP got no money from Linda Brown or from the Topeka Board of Education in compensation for its long and expensive labors, but beginning in the 1960s court rules were changed to make it financially attractive for lawyers to bring certain kinds of class-action suits.

Suppose, for example, you think your telephone company overcharged you by $75. You could try to hire a lawyer to get a refund, but not many lawyers would take the case because there is no money in it. Even if you were to win, the lawyer would stand to earn no more than perhaps one-third of the settlement, or $25. Now suppose that you bring a class action against the company on behalf of everybody who was overcharged. Millions of dollars might be at stake; lawyers would line up eagerly to take the case because their share of the settlement, if they win, could be huge. The opportunity to win a profitable class-action suit, combined with the possibility (discussed above) of having the losing corporation pay attorneys' fees even when the damages awarded were not large, led to a proliferation of such cases.

In response to this increase in its workload, the Supreme Court decided in 1974 to tighten drastically the rules governing these suits. It held that

66 The Court did not limit its decision to Linda Brown's right to attend an unsegregated school, but extended it . . . to cover all 'others similarly situated.' **99**

Linda Brown was refused admission to a white elementary school in Topeka, Kansas. On her behalf the NAACP brought a class-action suit that resulted in the 1954 landmark Supreme Court decision, *Brown v. Board of Education.*

it would no longer hear (except in certain kinds of cases defined by Congress, such as civil rights matters) class-action suits seeking money damages unless each and every ascertainable member of the class was individually notified of the case. To do this is often prohibitively expensive (imagine trying to find and send a letter to every customer that may have been overcharged by the telephone company!), and so the number of such cases declined and the number of lawyers seeking them out dropped.[38]

In sum, getting into court depends on having standing and having resources. The rules governing standing are complex and changing,

THE SUPREME COURT

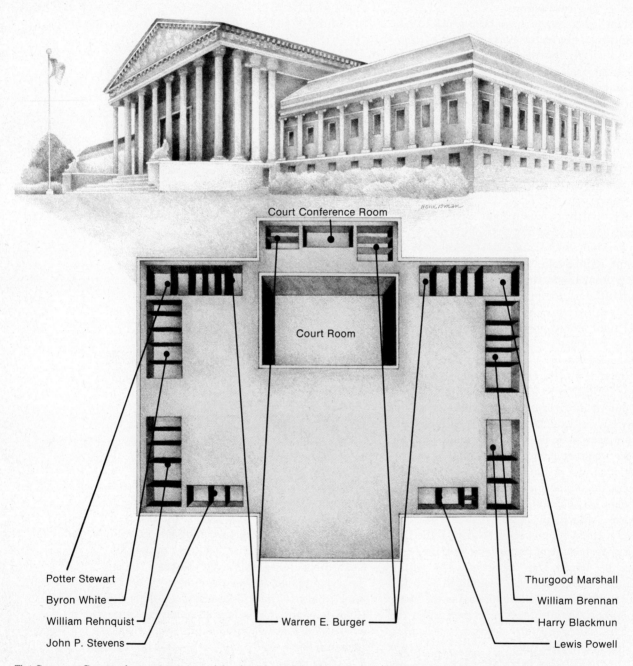

Court Conference Room

Court Room

Potter Stewart
Byron White
William Rehnquist
John P. Stevens

Warren E. Burger

Thurgood Marshall
William Brennan
Harry Blackmun
Lewis Powell

The Supreme Court is the most intimate of the three branches of government. Each justice has an office along the outer wall, with three or four small adjoining offices for his law clerks. The justices work alone with their clerks but meet as a group in the court room to hear cases and in the adjoining court conference room to decide them.

but generally have been broadened to make it easier to enter the federal courts, especially for the purpose of challenging the actions of the government. Obtaining the resources is not easy, but has become easier because laws in some cases now provide for "fee-shifting" (getting the loser to pay the costs), because private interest groups are willing to finance cases, and because it was possible—for a while—to bring inexpensively a class-action suit that lawyers would find lucrative.

THE SUPREME COURT IN ACTION

If your case should find its way to the Supreme Court—and of course the odds are that it will not—you will be able to participate in one of the more impressive, sometimes dramatic ceremonies of American public life. The Court is in session in its white marble building for thirty-six weeks out of each year, from early October until the end of June. The nine justices read briefs in their individual offices, hear oral arguments in the large stately courtroom, and discuss their decisions with each other in a conference room where no outsider is ever allowed.

Most cases, as we have seen, come to the Court on a writ of certiorari. The lawyers for each side may then submit their briefs, documents that set forth the facts, summarize the lower court decision, give the arguments for the side represented by the lawyer, and discuss the other cases the Court has decided that seem to bear on the issue. Then the lawyers are allowed to present their oral arguments in open court. These usually summarize the briefs or emphasize particular points in them, and are strictly limited in time—usually to no more than a half hour. (The lawyer speaks from a lectern that has two lights on it. When the white light goes on, the attorney has five minutes remaining; when the red flashes, he must stop—instantly.) The oral arguments give the justices a chance to question the lawyers, sometimes searchingly.

❝The rules governing standing are complex and changing, but generally have been broadened to make it easier to enter the federal courts, especially for the purpose of challenging the actions of the government.❞

Since the federal government is a party—as either plaintiff or defendant—to about half the cases the Supreme Court hears, the government's top trial lawyer, the solicitor general of the United States, makes frequent appearances before the Court. The solicitor general is the third-ranking officer of the Department of Justice, right after the attorney general and deputy attorney general. (When Attorney General Elliot Richardson was fired by President Nixon during

Wade H. McCree as solicitor general of the United States represents the United States in cases before the Supreme Court. By tradition he wears formal attire—frock coat and striped pants—during these Court appearances.

the Watergate controversy, Deputy Attorney General William Ruckelshaus resigned also, thus making Solicitor General Robert Bork the acting attorney general.) The solicitor general decides what cases the government will appeal from lower courts and personally approves or disapproves every case the government presents to the Supreme Court. In recent years he has often been selected from the ranks of distinguished law school professors.

In addition to the arguments made by lawyers for the two sides in a case, written briefs and even oral arguments may also be offered by "friends of the court," or *amicus curiae*. An amicus brief is from an interested party not directly involved in the suit. For example, when Allan Bakke complained that he had been the victim of "reverse discrimination" when he was denied admission to a

Allan Bakke was admitted to the Medical School at the University of California at Davis after the Supreme Court found that he had been unreasonably denied admission because of racial quotas favoring minority groups.

University of California medical school, fifty-eight amicus briefs were filed supporting or opposing his position. Before such briefs can be filed, both parties must agree or the Court must grant permission. These documents are a kind of polite lobbying of the Court which, though they sometimes offer new arguments, generally are a declaration of what interests are on which side. The ACLU, the NAACP, the AFL-CIO, and the United States government itself have been among the leading sources of such briefs.

These briefs are not the only source of influence on the justices' views, however. Legal periodicals such as the *Harvard Law Review* and the *Yale Law Journal* are frequently consulted, and citations to them often appear in the Court's decisions. Thus, the outside world of lawyers and law professors can help shape, or at least supply arguments for, the conclusions of the justices.

The justices retire to their conference room every Friday where, in complete secrecy, they debate the cases they have heard. The chief justice speaks first, followed by the other justices in order of seniority. After the arguments they vote, traditionally in reverse order of seniority—the newest justice votes first, the chief justice last. In this process an able chief justice can exercise considerable influence—in guiding or limiting debate, in setting forth the issues, and in handling the sometimes temperamental personalities of his colleagues. In deciding a case, a majority of the justices must be in agreement—if there is a tie, the lower court decision is left standing. (There can be a tie among nine justices if one is ill or disqualifies himself because of prior involvement in the case.)

Though the vote is what counts, by tradition the Court usually issues a written opinion explaining its decision. Sometimes this opinion is brief and unsigned (called a *per curiam* opinion); sometimes it is quite long and signed by the justices agreeing with it. If the chief justice is in the majority, he will either write the opinion or assign its writing to a justice who agrees with him. If he is in the minority, the senior justice on the winning side will decide who writes the Court's

The law clerks of the United States Supreme Court are young men and women who are picked every year by the justices from among the highest-ranking law school graduates.

opinion. There are four kinds of opinions: *unanimous* (obviously, when all justices have voted the same way), *majority* (the opinion of the Court when it is divided), *concurring* (an opinion by one or more justices who agree with the majority's conclusion but for different reasons that they wish to express), and *dissenting* (the opinion of the justices on the losing side). Each justice has three law clerks (bright, young graduates of leading law schools) to help him study cases and write drafts of opinions. The influence of the law clerks on the Court has not been systematically studied.

Scholars have made elaborate and ingenious efforts to explain the pattern of voting of Supreme Court justices. The intricacies of these inquiries are best left to specialists, but the results can be summarized in general terms. They show that justices, like any group of men or women in politics, tend to take more or less consistent positions at least on those issues they have carefully studied. There are, in short, "blocs" on the

Court, though they are not hard-and-fast. Casual observers may suppose that these are simply "liberal" and "conservative" blocs, but the reality is more complicated. Several scholars agree that justices tend to differ consistently along at least two distinct dimensions: those involving *civil liberties* (such as free speech, obscenity, and police practices) and those pertinent to *economic issues* (such as regulation of business and labor-management conflicts). During 1973, for example, there was one bloc (made up of Justices William O. Douglas, William Brennan, and Thurgood Marshall) that regularly took "liberal" positions on both civil liberties and economic issues, and another bloc (made up of Chief Justice Warren Burger and Justice William Rehnquist) that just as regularly took "conservative" positions on these two kinds of questions. In between there were some justices (such as Justice Byron White) who were liberal on economic questions, but much less so on civil

liberties, and still others (such as Justice Harry Blackmun) who were conservative on civil liberties matters but in the middle on economic ones.[39]

When the Court is deeply divided (as it has been of late), justices who are not regularly members of either the liberal or conservative bloc can have great influence by casting the swing votes. Justices such as White, Blackmun, and—more recently—John Paul Stevens can decide an issue, depending on whether they vote with the very liberal Marshall-Brennan bloc or the very conservative Burger-Rehnquist group. Of late, Brennan and Marshall have lost frequently. During 1975–1976 they dissented a total of 125 times, almost twice as often as any other pair of justices.[40]

Voting blocs are only tendencies, clearest in the extreme cases but not always decisive. Jus-

tices have strong attitudes, but they also must deal with complex cases, participate in private discussions with their colleagues, and react to the research of their law clerks.

THE POWER OF THE COURTS

The great majority of the cases in federal courts have little or nothing to do with changes in public policy: persons accused of bank robbery are tried, disputes over contracts are settled, personal injury cases are heard, and the patent law is applied. Though there is no way to measure it, in most cases the courts are simply applying a relatively settled body of law to a controversy.

The Power to Make Policy

The courts make policy whenever they reinterpret the law or the Constitution in significant ways, extend the reach of existing laws to cover matters not previously thought to be covered, or design remedies for problems that involve the judges acting in administrative or legislative ways. By any of these tests, the courts have become exceptionally powerful.

One measure of that power is that over 110 federal laws have been declared unconstitutional, though since 1937 relatively few of these had broad national significance. And as we shall see, on matters where Congress feels strongly, it can often get its way by passing slightly revised versions of the voided law.

Another measure, and perhaps a more revealing one, is the frequency with which the Court changes its mind. An informal rule of judicial decision-making has been *stare decisis*, meaning "let the decision stand." It is the principle of precedent—a court case today should be settled in accordance with prior decisions on similar cases. (What constitutes a similar case is not always clear; lawyers are especially gifted at finding ways of showing that two cases are different in some relevant way.) The reason for the importance of precedent should be obvious:

if the meaning of the law continually changes, if the decisions of judges become wholly unpredictable, then human affairs affected by those laws and decisions become chaotic. A contract signed today might be invalid tomorrow; what once one was free to do one could no longer do. On the other hand, if times so change that an old precedent becomes a straightjacket, then it might be foolish to persist in its application to contemporary affairs. And the Court can make mistakes; it should not be afraid to admit them. As Justice Felix Frankfurter once said, "Wisdom too often never comes, and so one ought not to reject it merely because it comes late."[41]

However compelling the arguments for flexibility, the pace of change can become dizzying. By one count, the Court between 1810 and 1974 overruled its own previous decisions in at least 105 cases.[42] In fact, it may have done it more often, because sometimes the Court does not say it is abandoning a precedent, claiming instead that it is merely distinguishing the present case from a previous one.

A third measure of judicial power is the degree to which courts are willing to handle matters once left to the legislature. For example, the Court refused, for a long time, to hear a case about the size of congressional districts no matter how unequal their populations.[43] The determination of congressional district boundaries was regarded as a "political question"—that is, as a matter that the Constitution left entirely to another branch of government (in this case, the Congress) to decide for itself. Then, in 1962, the Court decided that it was competent after all to handle this matter, and the notion of a "political question" became a much less important (but by no means absent) barrier to judicial power.[44]

By all odds the most powerful indicator of judicial power can be found in the kinds of remedies the courts will impose. A "remedy" is a judicial order setting forth what must be done to correct a situation that a judge believes to be wrong. In ordinary cases, such as one person suing another, the remedy is straightforward—the

❝By all odds the most powerful indicator of judicial power can be found in the kinds of remedies the courts will impose.❞

Federal court decisions have had a sweeping impact on the administration of prison systems in several states.

loser must pay the winner for some injury he has caused, or he must agree to abide by the terms of a contract he has broken, or he must promise not to do some unpleasant thing (such as dumping garbage on his neighbor's lawn). Today, however, judges design remedies that go far beyond what is required to do justice to the parties who actually appear in court. The remedies now imposed often apply to large groups and affect the circumstances under which thousands or even millions of persons work, study, or live. For example, when a federal district judge in Alabama

JUDICIAL ACTIVISM IN ACTION

heard a case brought by a prison inmate in that state, he issued an order, not simply to improve the lot of that prisoner, but to revamp the administration of the entire prison system. The result was an improvement in the living conditions of many prisoners at a cost to the state of an estimated $40 million a year. Similarly, a person thinking herself entitled to welfare payments that have been denied her may sue in court to get the money; the court order, however, will in all likelihood affect all welfare recipients. In one case, certain court orders made an additional one hundred thousand persons eligible for welfare.[45]

The basis for these sweeping court orders can sometimes be found in the Constitution; the Alabama prison decision, for example, was based on the judge's interpretation of the Eighth Amendment which prohibits "cruel and unusual punishments."[46] Others are based on court interpretations of federal laws. The Civil Rights Act of 1964 forbids discrimination on grounds of "race, color, or national origin" in any program receiving federal financial assistance. The Supreme Court interpreted that as meaning that the San Francisco school system was obliged to teach English to Chinese students unable to speak it.[47] Since a Supreme Court decision is the

law of the land, the impact of that ruling was not limited to San Francisco. Local courts and legislatures elsewhere decided that that decision meant that classes must be taught in Spanish for Hispanic children. Whether that is what Congress meant by the Civil Rights Act is not clear; it may or may not have believed that teaching Hispanic children in English rather than Spanish was a form of discrimination. What is important is that it was the Court, not Congress, that decided what Congress meant.

Views of Judicial Activism

Judicial activism has, of course, been controversial. Those who support it argue that the federal courts must correct injustices when the other branches of government, or the states, refuse to do so. The courts are the institution of last resort for those without the votes or the influence to obtain new laws, and especially for the poor and powerless. State legislatures and the Congress, after all, tolerated segregated public schools for decades. If the Supreme Court had not declared segregation unconstitutional in 1954, it might still be law today.

Those who criticize the activist courts rejoin that judges usually have no special expertise in matters of school administration, prison management, or environmental protection; they are lawyers, expert in defining rights and duties but not in designing and managing complex institutions. Furthermore, however desirable court-declared rights and principles may be, implementing those principles means balancing the conflicting needs of various interest groups, raising and spending tax monies, and assessing the costs and benefits of complicated alternatives. Finally, judges are not elected; they are appointed, and are thus immune to popular control. As a result, if they depart from their traditional role of making careful and cautious interpretations of what a law or the Constitution means and instead begin formulating wholly new policies, they become unelected legislators.

We shall not judge this argument; in any case it would be premature to do so before we have seen in greater detail (as we shall in Part IV) how the courts have behaved in various policy areas—civil liberties, civil rights, environmental protection, and economic regulation. Here we shall simply try to explain why activism has developed and what checks on it exist.

Some people think that we have activist courts because we have so many lawyers. The more we take matters to courts for resolution, the more likely it is that the courts will become powerful. It is true we have more lawyers, in proportion to our population, than most other nations. In 1973 there was one lawyer for every 475 Americans, but only one for every 1,800 Britons, every 2,000 West Germans, and every 5,000 French.[48] But that may well be a symptom, not a cause, of court activity. As was suggested in Chapter 4, we have an adversary culture based on an emphasis on individual rights and an implicit antagonism between people and government. Generally speaking, lawyers do not create cases, contending interests do, thereby generating a demand for lawyers. Furthermore, there were more lawyers in relation to our population in 1900 than there were in 1970, yet the courts seventy years ago were far less active in public affairs. In fact, in

"Generally speaking, lawyers do not create cases; contending interests do, thereby generating a demand for lawyers."

Our adversary culture leads us to bring many of the problems of daily life into court.

1932 there were more court cases (per 100,000 people) than in 1972.[49]

Another, more plausible reason has been the developments, discussed earlier in this chapter, that have made it easier for persons to get standing in courts, to pay for the costs of litigation, and to bring class-action claims. The courts and Congress have gone a long way toward allowing private citizens to become "private attorneys general." Making it easier to get into court increases the number of cases being heard. For example, in 1961 civil rights cases, prisoner rights cases, and cases under the Social Security laws were relatively uncommon in federal court. Between 1961 and 1975 the increase in the number of such matters was phenomenal—civil rights cases rose by 3,410 percent and prisoner

TABLE 13.3   Civil Cases Filed in U.S. District Courts

Nature of suit	1961	1975	Percent increase
All civil cases	58,293	117,320	101.3%
Civil rights	296	10,392	3,410.8
State prisoner petitions	1,020	14,260	1,298.0
Social Security	537	5,846	988.6

Source: Annual Report of the Director of the Administrative Office of the United States Courts, 1975 (Table 17).

petitions by nearly 1,300 percent (see Table 13.3). Such matters are the fastest-growing portion of the courts' civil workload.

Legislation and the Courts

More cases will not by themselves lead to sweeping remedies. For that to occur, the law must be sufficiently vague to permit judges wide latitude in interpreting it, and the judges must want to exercise that opportunity to the fullest. The Constitution is filled with words of seemingly ambiguous meaning—"due process of law," the "equal protection of the laws," the "privileges or immunities of citizens." Such phrases may have been clear to the Framers, but to the Court they have become equivocal or elastic. How the Court has chosen to interpret such phrases has changed greatly over the last 190 years in ways that can be explained in part by the personal political beliefs of the justices.

Increasingly, Congress has passed laws that also contain vague language, thereby adding immeasurably to the courts' opportunities for designing remedies. Various civil rights acts outlaw discrimination but do not say how one is to know whether discrimination has occurred or what should be done to correct it if it does occur. That is left to the courts and the bureaucracy. Various regulatory laws empower administrative agencies to do what the "public interest" requires but say little about how the public interest is to

be defined. Laws intended to alleviate poverty or rebuild neighborhoods speak of "citizen participation" or "maximum feasible participation" but do not explain who the citizens are that should participate, or how much power they should have.

In addition to laws that require interpretation, other laws induce litigation. Almost every agency that regulates business will make decisions that cause the agency to be challenged in court—by business firms if the regulations go too far, by consumer or labor organizations if they do not go far enough. In 1974 the federal courts of appeal heard 506 cases in which they had to review the decision of a regulatory agency. In two-thirds of them the agency's position was supported; in the other third the agency was overruled.[50] Perhaps one-fifth of these cases arose out of agencies or programs that did not even exist in 1960. The federal government today is much more likely to be on the defensive in court than was true twenty or thirty years ago.

Finally, the attitudes of the judges powerfully affect what they will do, especially when the law gives them wide latitude. There have been very few studies of the attitudes of federal judges, but their decisions and opinions have been extensively analyzed—well enough, at least, to know that different judges often decide the same case in different ways. Conservative southern federal judges in the 1950s, for example, often resisted plans to desegregate public schools while judges with a different background authorized bold plans.[51] Some of the greatest disparities in judicial behavior can be found in the area of sentencing criminals.[52]

CHECKS ON JUDICIAL POWER

No institution of government, including the courts, operates without restraint. The fact that judges are not elected does not make them immune to public opinion or to the views of the other branches of government. How important these restraints are will vary from case to case, but in the broad course of history they have been significant.

One restraint occurs because of the very nature of courts. A judge has no police force or army; decisions he makes can sometimes be resisted or ignored *if* the person or organization resisting is not highly visible and *if* the resister is willing to run the risk of being caught and charged with contempt of court. For example, long after the Supreme Court had decided that praying and Bible-reading could not take place in public schools,[53] schools all over the country were still allowing prayers and Bible-reading.[54] Years after the Court declared segregated schools to be unconstitutional, scores of school systems remained segregated. On the other hand, when a failure to comply is easily detected and punished, the courts' power is usually unchallenged. When the Supreme Court declared the income tax to be unconstitutional in 1895, income-tax collections promptly ceased. When the Court in 1952 declared illegal President Truman's effort to seize the steel mills in order to stop a strike, the management of the mills was immediately returned to their owners.

Congress and the Courts

Congress has a number of ways of checking the judiciary. It can alter gradually the composition of the judiciary by the kinds of appointments the Senate is willing to confirm or by impeaching judges it does not like. (Ten federal judges have been the object of impeachment proceedings in our history, and nine others have resigned when such proceedings seemed likely. Of the ten who were impeached, five were acquitted, four convicted, and one resigned.)[55] In practice, however, confirmation and impeachment proceedings can rarely be used to make much of an impact on the federal courts because simple policy disagreements are not generally regarded as adequate grounds for voting against a judicial

The Government
Goes on the Defensive

At one time lawsuits involving the federal government were mostly brought by the government itself—it was the plaintiff, and somebody else (an individual, organization, or corporation) was the defendant. Today the government is the defendant in the great majority of civil cases in which it is involved.

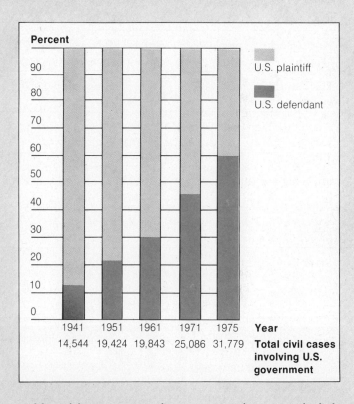

Most of this increase in the proportion of cases in which the government is a defendant has come about because of the greater ease with which the decisions of federal administrative agencies can be challenged.

Source: Annual Reports of the Director of the Administrative Office of the United States Courts.

■ Supreme Court justice who served the longest	*William O. Douglas: 36 years (1939–1975)*
■ Only Supreme Court justice to run for president	*Charles Evans Hughes (resigned from Court in 1916 to seek presidency; lost to Woodrow Wilson)*
■ Only president to become Supreme Court justice	*William Howard Taft (president, 1909–1913; chief justice of the Supreme Court, 1921–1930)*
■ First Catholic Supreme Court justice	*Roger B. Taney (1836–1864) (six Catholics have served)*
■ First Jewish Supreme Court justice	*Louis Brandeis (1916–1939) (five Jews have served)*
■ First black Supreme Court justice	*Thurgood Marshall (1967 to present) (the only black)*
■ Only Supreme Court justice to have been impeached	*Samuel Chase (impeached by House in 1804; acquitted by Senate)*
■ State that has produced most Supreme Court justices	*New York (15)*
■ State that has had the most laws declared unconstitutional by federal courts	*Louisiana*

William Howard Taft

COURT
trivia

Charles Evans Hughes

nominee or starting an impeachment effort.

The Congress can alter the number of judges, however, and by increasing the number sharply, it can give a president a chance to appoint persons to his liking. This was proposed by Roosevelt in his "court-packing" plan in 1937 specifically to change the political persuasion of the Supreme Court. In 1979 Congress passed a bill creating 152 new federal district and appellate judges to help ease the workload. This bill, combined with normal judicial retirements and deaths, gave President Carter a chance to appoint over 40 percent of the federal bench. During and after the Civil War, Congress expressed its dislike of Supreme Court decisions by changing the size of the Court three times in six years: raising it from nine to ten in 1863, lowering it from ten to seven in 1866, and raising it again from seven to nine in 1869.

Congress and the states can also react to a Supreme Court decision interpreting the Constitution by amending that document. They have done just that in perhaps nine cases: the Eleventh Amendment was ratified to prevent a citizen from suing a state in federal court; the Sixteenth Amendment was passed to make the income tax constitutional; the Thirteenth, Fourteenth, and Fifteenth Amendments were passed to undo the *Dred Scott* decision on slavery; and the Twenty-Sixth Amendment was approved, giving the vote in state elections to eighteen-year-olds. This is obviously, however, a difficult and time-consuming process.

Sometimes Congress merely repasses a law that the Court has declared unconstitutional. This has occurred over thirty times, as when a bill to aid farmers, voided in 1935, was accepted by the Court in slightly revised form three years later.[56] (In the meantime, of course, the Court had changed its collective mind about the New Deal.)

One of the most powerful potential sources of control over the federal courts, however, is the authority of Congress to decide what the entire jurisdiction of the lower courts and the appellate jurisdiction of the Supreme Court shall be. In theory, Congress could prevent matters on which it did not want federal courts to act from ever coming before the courts. In 1868 just this happened. A Mississippi newspaper editor named McCardle was jailed by federal military authorities who had occupied the defeated South. McCardle asked the federal district court for a writ of habeas corpus to get him out of custody; when the district court rejected his plea, he appealed to the Supreme Court. Congress at that time was fearful that the Court might find the laws on which its Reconstruction policy was based (and under which McCardle was in jail) unconstitutional. To prevent that from happening, it passed a bill withdrawing from the Supreme Court appellate jurisdiction in cases of this sort. The Court conceded that Congress could do this and thus dismissed the case because it no longer had jurisdiction.[57]

Congress has threatened to do this on other occasions, and the mere existence of the threat may have influenced the nature of Court decisions. In the 1950s, for example, congressional opinion was hostile to Court decisions in the field of civil liberties and civil rights, and legislation was proposed that would have curtailed the Court's jurisdiction in these areas. It did not pass, but the Court may have allowed the threat to temper its decisions.[58] On the other hand, as congressional resistance to the court-packing plan shows, the Supreme Court enjoys a good deal of prestige in the nation, even among people who disagree with some of its decisions; and passing laws that would frontally attack it would not be easy except, perhaps, in times of national crisis (war or depression).

Furthermore, laws changing jurisdiction or restricting the kinds of remedies a court can impose are often blunt instruments that might not achieve the purposes of their proponents. Suppose you, as a congressman, would like to prevent the federal courts from ordering schoolchildren to be bused in order to achieve racial balance in the schools. If you denied the Supreme Court appellate jurisdiction in this matter, you would leave the lower federal courts and all state courts

No federal court decisions in recent years have been as controversial as those ordering schoolchildren to be bused in order to integrate schools. The police escorted school buses in Boston, the scene of periodic school violence.

free to do as they wish, and many of them would go on ordering busing. If you wanted to attack that problem, you could propose a law that would deny to all federal courts the right to order busing as a remedy for racial imbalance. But the courts would still be free to order busing (and, of course, a lot of busing goes on even without court orders), provided that they did not say it was for the purpose of achieving racial balance. (It could be for the purpose of "facilitating desegregation" or making possible "redistricting.") Of course, you could always make it illegal for children to enter a school bus for any reason, but then many children would not be able to get to school at all. Finally, the Supreme Court might well decide that, if busing is essential to achieve a constitutional right, then any congressional law prohibiting such busing would itself be unconstitutional. Trying to think through how *that* dilemma would be resolved is like trying to visualize two kangaroos simultaneously jumping into each other's pouches.

"An overly simple but useful generalization is that the Supreme Court has been most powerful when the political parties were either weak, deeply divided, or undergoing a realignment.**"**

Public Opinion and the Courts

Though not elected, judges read the same newspapers as congressmen, and thus they too are aware of public opinion, especially elite opinion. Though it may be going too far to say that the Supreme Court follows the election returns, it is nonetheless true that the Court is sensitive to certain bodies of opinion, especially of those elites—liberal or conservative—to which its members happen to be attuned. The justices will recall cases when, by defying opinion frontally, their predecessors very nearly destroyed the legitimacy of the Court itself. This was the case with the *Dred Scott* decision which infuriated the North and was widely disobeyed. No such crisis exists today, but it is altogether possible that changing political moods affect the kinds of remedies judges will think appropriate.

Opinion not only restrains the courts; it may also energize them. The most activist periods in Supreme Court history have coincided with times when the political system was undergoing profound and lasting changes. The assertion by the Supreme Court, under John Marshall's leadership, of the principles of national supremacy and judicial review occurred at the time when the Jeffersonian Republicans were coming to power and their opponents, the Federalists, were collapsing as an organized party. The pro-slavery decisions of the Taney Court came when the nation was so divided along sectional and ideological lines as to make almost any Court decision on this matter unpopular. Supreme Court review of economic regulation in the 1890s and 1900s came at a time when the political parties were realigning and the Republicans acquiring dominance that was to last for several decades. The Court decisions of the 1930s corresponded to another period of partisan realignment. (The meaning of a realigning election was discussed in Chapter 7.)

An overly simple but useful generalization is that the Supreme Court has been most powerful when the political parties were either weak, deeply divided, or undergoing a realignment. The Court has rarely struck out in new directions, or used its powers most actively, when there was a broad public consensus as to the correct course of action. (When it tried to violate such a consensus in 1935–1936, it quickly discovered how weak its support was.)

An obvious exception to this generalization would appear to be the Court's activism in the period since the 1950s. There was no partisan realignment, no deep crisis, and yet the Court, starting with Chief Justice Warren and continuing to the present, has presided over an extraordinary amount of law-making. Some of the reasons for this have already been discussed—rising caseloads, class-action suits, broad grants of legislative authority to administrative agencies. But another reason is perhaps even more important: the courts have become more powerful for the same reason that the president, the bureaucracy, and Congress have become more powerful—government has come to play, permanently, a large role in our lives, thereby enhancing the power of *all* of its components. In 1890 hardly anybody would have thought of asking the president, the Congress, the bureaucracy—or the courts—to make rules governing the participation of women in college sports, the hiring policies of an electric utility, or the district boundaries of state legislatures. As the scope of government activity widens, the scope of court activity widens as well. How this widening occurs will be discussed in Part IV.

SUMMARY

An independent judiciary with the power of judicial review—the right to decide the constitutionality of acts of Congress, the executive branch, and state governments—can be a potent political force in American life. That influence has been realized from the earliest days of the nation, when Marshall and Taney put the Supreme Court at the center of the most important issues of the time. From 1787 to 1865 the Supreme Court was preoccupied with the establishment of national supremacy. From 1865 to 1937 it struggled with defining the scope of political power over the economy. In the present era it has sought to expand the range of personal liberties.

The scope of the courts' political influence has increasingly widened as various groups and interests have acquired access to the courts, as the judges serving on them have developed a more activist stance, and as Congress has passed more laws containing vague or equivocal language. Whereas in other political arenas (the electorate, Congress, the bureaucracy) the influence of contending groups is largely dependent on their size, intensity, prestige, and political resources, before the courts the influence of contending groups depends chiefly on their arguments and the attitudes of the judges.

Though the Supreme Court is the pinnacle of the federal judiciary, most decisions, including many important ones, are made by the eleven circuit courts of appeals and the ninety-four district courts. The Supreme Court can control its own workload by deciding when to grant certiorari. It has become easier for citizens and groups to gain access to the federal courts (through class-action suits, by amicus curiae briefs, by laws that require government agencies to pay fees, and because of the activities of private groups such as the NAACP and the ACLU).

At the same time, the courts have widened the reach of their decisions by issuing orders that cover whole classes of citizens or affect the management of major public and private institutions. However, the courts can overstep the bounds of their authority and bring upon themselves a counterattack from public opinion and from Congress. Congress has the right to control much of the courts' jurisdiction, but it rarely does so. As a result, the ability of judges to make law is only infrequently challenged directly.

Suggested Readings

Abraham, Henry J. *The Judicial Process*, 3rd ed. New York: Oxford University Press, 1975. An excellent, comprehensive survey of how the federal courts are organized and function.

Cardozo, Benjamin N. *The Nature of the Judicial Process*. New Haven, Conn.: Yale University Press, 1921. Important statement of how judges make decisions, by a former Supreme Court justice.

Corwin, Edward S. *The Constitution and What It Means Today,* 14th ed. Rev. by Harold W. Chase and Craig R. Ducat. Princeton, N.J.: Princeton University Press, 1978. A line-by-line interpretation of the Constitution in the light of the most recent court decisions; kept up to date by annual supplements.

Horowitz, Donald L. *The Courts and Social Policy*. Washington, D.C.: Brookings Institution, 1977. Study of the way activist courts make policy.

Lewis, Anthony. *Gideon's Trumpet*. New York: Random House, 1964. Fascinating account of how a pauper in jail persuaded the Supreme Court to change the rules governing criminal trials.

McCloskey, Robert G. *The American Supreme Court*. Chicago: University of Chicago Press, 1960. Superb brief history of the Court and its role in American politics and thought.

Murphy, Walter F. *Elements of Judicial Strategy*. Chicago: University of Chicago Press, 1964. An effort to explain why Supreme Court justices behave as they do.

Peltason, Jack W. *Fifty-Eight Lonely Men: Southern Federal Judges and School Desegregation*. New York: Harcourt, Brace, 1961. Revealing account of federal district judges as they grappled with school desegregation in the South.

Pritchett, C. Herman. *The American Constitution,* 2nd ed. New York: McGraw-Hill, 1968. Authoritative exposition of constitutional law.

PART IV
The Politics of Public Policy

"In the extended republic of the United States, and among the great variety of interests, parties, and sects which it embraces, a coalition of a majority of the whole society could seldom take place on any other principles than those of justice and the general good."

FEDERALIST NO. 51

409

14 The Policy-Making Process

Deciding what goes on the political agenda ·
A model for explaining the politics of different
policy issues · Perceived costs and benefits ·
Their distribution

If our political system handled all issues in the same way, this study of American government would be at an end. Now that we have seen how Congress, the presidency, the courts, the parties, the mass media, and other interest groups operate, we should be able to explain how policies get made (or not made). Some observers do argue that the system always operates more or less the same way—to serve corporate interests (the Marxist view), to manage conflict among organized groups (the pluralist view), to sustain the dominance of a pervasive bureaucracy (the Weberian view), and so on. In this part we shall look at how policies are actually made to see if any of these generalizations are correct.

Consider some examples of the variety of outcomes that need to be explained if we are to understand the political influence wielded by just one kind of institution—the business corpo-

Two views of policy-making: Uncle Sam ensnared in bureaucratic agencies and red tape (left), and the dignity of the president's annual State of the Union address (right).

"He who decides what politics is about runs the country."

ration. Certain oil companies were once able to persuade the government to restrict sharply the amount of foreign oil imported into the United States, to allow preferential tax treatment of their incomes, and to permit them to drill for new oil about anywhere they liked. Today the restrictions on foreign oil imports have ended, the tax break the oil companies enjoy has been reduced somewhat (though it still exists), and their right to drill in certain places—offshore—has been sharply curtailed. Automobile manufacturers once faced virtually no federal controls on the kind of product they manufactured; now they face many. Businessmen have been able to obtain favorable tax treatment of the investments they make (increases in the value of their capital are taxed at a lower rate than ordinary income), but they have not been able to avoid having their corporate profits taxed at a high rate (about half of what they earn goes to the federal government) or to prevent the dividends they pay from being taxed twice (once when they are earned as profits, a second time after they are paid out to stockholders). Some corporations have been regulated in ways that have increased their profitability (the airlines); others in ways that have reduced their profitability (the railroads); and still others in ways that may not have affected their profits much one way or another (electric utilities). These outcomes of government action or inaction are complicated. To understand why they happen, we need some theory of policy-making. This chapter will provide one; subsequent chapters will apply it.

SETTING THE AGENDA

The most important decision that affects policy-making is also the least noticed: deciding what to make policy *about* or, in the language of political science, deciding what goes on the political agenda. This is little noticed because we take for granted that politics is about certain familiar issues such as taxes, energy, welfare, and civil rights. We forget that there is nothing inevitable about these issues, rather than some other ones, being on our agenda. At one time it was unconstitutional for the federal government to levy income taxes, energy was a nonissue because everybody (or at least everybody who could chop down trees for a fireplace) had enough, welfare was something for cities and towns to handle, and civil rights was supposed to be a matter of private choice rather than governmental action. Until the 1930s, the national political agenda was quite short, and even in the 1950s many persons would have been astonished or upset to be told that the federal government was supposed to worry about the environment, consumerism, or civil rights.

"He who decides what politics is about runs the country."[1] This is a statement of profound significance, though it exaggerates the extent to which somebody—some "he"—actually "decides" what politics is all about. What it correctly suggests is that at any given time there exist beliefs that determine what it is legitimate (proper, right) for the government to do. This legitimacy is affected by several forces: shared political values (if many people believe that poverty is the result of individual failure rather than social forces, then there is no reason for a government program to combat poverty), the weight of custom and tradition (people will usually accept what the government has customarily done even if they are leery of what it proposes to do), the impact of events (wars and depressions alter our sense of the proper role of government), and changes in the way political elites think and talk about politics.

The Legitimate Scope of Government Action
Because many people believe that whatever the government now does, it ought to do, and because changes in attitudes and the impact of events tend to increase the number of things

Popular views as to the legitimate scope of government action, and thus as to the kinds of issues that ought to be on the political agenda, are changed by the impact of events.

Two events that changed the political agenda: An oil spill on a California beach and the gasoline shortage.

government does, the scope of legitimate government action is always getting larger. As a result, the scope of what it is illegitimate for government to do steadily gets smaller. This means that today we hear far fewer debates about the legitimacy of a proposed government policy than we heard in the 1920s or the 1930s. The rise of "big government" is a result of this process of expanded beliefs about legitimacy—which are, in turn, the result of popular expectations—and not the consequence of some sinister power grab by politicians or bureaucrats. When President Gerald Ford, a Republican, ran for election in 1976, a favorite slogan of his was that a government big enough to give you everything you want is also big enough to take away everything you have. No doubt he thought he was criticizing liberal Democrats. But it was his immediate predecessor, Presi-

dent Richard M. Nixon, also a Republican, who had imposed peacetime wage and price controls and proposed a guaranteed annual income for every family, working or not working. And it was another Republican president, Dwight Eisenhower, who had sent federal troops to Little Rock, Arkansas, to enforce a school desegregation order. For better or worse, the expansion of government has been the result, fundamentally, of a nonpartisan process.

Popular views as to the legitimate scope of government action, and thus as to the kinds of issues that ought to be on the political agenda, are changed by the impact of events. During wartime, especially during a war in which the United States has been attacked, the people expect the government to do whatever is necessary to win, whether or not such actions are clearly authorized by the Constitution. (As we saw in

Chapter 12, the federal bureaucracy enjoys its most rapid growth in wartime.) A depression, such as the one that began in 1929, also leads people to expect the government to do something. As we shall see in Chapter 17, public opinion favored federal action to deal with the problems of the unemployed, the elderly, and the poor well in advance of the actual decisions of the government to take action. A coal mine disaster leads to an enlarged role for the government in promoting mine safety. A series of airplane hijackings leads to a change in public opinion so great that what once would have been unthinkable—requiring all passengers at airports to be searched before boarding their flights—becomes routine. Most citizens probably oppose rationing; but let there be long lines at the corner gasoline station because of a fuel shortage, and the demands for rationing become loud.

But sometimes, often dramatically, the government enlarges its agenda of policy issues without any widespread public demand. This may happen even at a time when the conditions

at which a policy is directed are improving. There was no public demand for government action to make automobiles safer before 1966 when a law was passed imposing safety standards on cars. Though the number of auto fatalities (per 100 million miles driven) had gone up slightly just before the law was passed, the long-term trend in highway deaths had been more or less steadily downward. The Occupational Safety and Health Act was passed in 1970 at a time when the number of industrial deaths (per 100,000 workers) had been steadily dropping for almost twenty years.[2] Programs to combat urban poverty and unemployment were adopted in the mid-1960s at a time when the number of persons, black as well as white, living below the poverty line was declining, not rising, and when the adult unemployment rate—for blacks as well as whites—was lower than it had been at any time in the preceding ten years.[3]

Pressure Groups

It is not an easy matter to explain why the government adds new issues to its agenda and adopts new programs when there is little public demand and when, in fact, there has been an improvement in the conditions to which the policies are addressed. In general, the explanation may be found in the behavior of groups, the workings of institutions, and the opinions of political elites. Many policies are the result of small groups of persons enlarging the scope of government by their demands. Sometimes these are organized interests (corporations, unions); sometimes they are intense but unorganized groups. The organized groups often work quietly, behind the scenes; the intense, disorganized ones may take their causes to the streets.

Organized labor favored a tough federal safety law governing factories and other workplaces, not because it was unaware that factory conditions had been improving, but because the standards by which union leaders and members judged working conditions had risen even faster. As people became better off, conditions that once were thought normal suddenly became intolera-

Perceptions—and fears—are as important as facts in determining what goes on the political agenda. The nuclear accident at Three Mile Island in Pennsylvania had unknown effects but a powerful political impact.

ble. When Alexis de Tocqueville sought to explain the French Revolution, he observed that citizens are most restless and easily aroused, not when they are living in abject poverty or under grinding repression, but when they have started to become better off.[4] Social scientists sometimes refer to this as a sense of "relative deprivation."

On occasion, a group expresses in violent ways its dissatisfaction with what it judges to be intolerable conditions. The black riots in American cities during the mid-1960s had a variety of causes, and persons participated out of a variety of motives. For many, riots were a way of expressing pent-up anger at what they regarded as an unresponsive and unfair society. This sense of relative deprivation—of being worse off than one thinks one *ought* to be—helps explain why so large a proportion of the rioters were not uneducated, unemployed recent migrants to the city, but rather young men and women born in the North, educated in its schools, and employed in its factories.[5] Life under these conditions turned out to be not what they had come to expect nor what they were prepared to tolerate.

The new demands of such groups need not result in an enlarged political agenda and do not when society and its governing institutions are confident of the rightness of the existing state of affairs. Unions could have been voted down on the occupational safety bill; rioting blacks could have been jailed and ignored. At one time exactly this would have happened. But society itself had changed: many persons who were not workers sympathized with the plight of an injured worker and were distrustful of the good intentions of businessmen in this matter. Many whites felt that a constructive as well as a punitive response was required to the urban riots and thus urged the formation of commissions to study—and the passage of laws to deal with—the problems of inner city life. These changes in the values and beliefs of persons generally, or at least of persons in key governmental positions, are an essential part of any explanation of why policies not demanded by public opinion nonetheless become part of the political agenda.

❝Among the institutions whose role in agenda-setting has become especially important are the courts, the bureaucracy, the United States Senate, and the mass media.**❞**

Washington, D.C., 1968: Black riots in American cities profoundly affected public policy toward cities.

Among the institutions whose role in agenda-setting has become especially important are the courts, the bureaucracy, the United States Senate, and the mass media (or at least the part of it that was called, in Chapter 9, the national press). The courts, because of their power to set new standards for the operation of public and private institutions, can by their decisions put in motion events that force the hand of other governing institutions. It was a court order, and local resistance to it, that led President Eisenhower to send troops to Little Rock. Eisenhower personally was not much in sympathy with some aspects of the school desegregation orders and may have disliked intensely the idea of using force against a local government. His alternative, however, was to do nothing while a lawful court order was

A crisis in the "Great Society": President Lyndon Johnson conferred with some of his advisers (Cyrus Vance seated, right, and Robert S. McNamara, standing, right) during the ghetto riots in Detroit in 1967.

violated. The costs of having the legitimacy of the government successfully challenged were to him (and to any president) far graver than the costs of following a court order about which he may have had reservations. The courts, in this and similar cases, are like trip-wires—when activated, they set off a chain reaction of events that results in a revised governmental agenda and a new constellation of political forces.

The bureaucracy has acquired a new significance in American politics, not simply because of its size or power, but also because it is now a source of political innovation. At one time the federal government reacted to events in society and demands from segments of society; ordinarily, it did not, itself, propose changes and new ideas. Today the bureaucracy is so large, and includes within it so great a variety of experts and advocates, that it becomes a *source* of policy proposals as well as an implementer of those that become law. Daniel Patrick Moynihan called this the "professionalization of reform," by which he meant, in part, that the

government bureaucracy had begun to think up problems for government to solve rather than simply to respond to the problems identified by others.[6] In the 1930s many of the key elements of the New Deal—social security, unemployment compensation, public housing, old-age benefits— were ideas devised by nongovernmental experts and intellectuals here and abroad and then, as the crisis of the Depression deepened, sold to the federal government. In the 1960s, by contrast, most of the measures that became known as part of Lyndon Johnson's "Great Society"— federal aid to education, manpower development and training, Medicare and Medicaid, the "War on Poverty," the "safe streets" act providing federal aid to local law enforcement agencies—were developed, designed, and advocated by government officials, bureaucrats, and their political allies.

Chief among these political allies are United States senators and their staffs. Once the Senate was best described as a club that moved slowly, debated endlessly, and resisted, under the leadership of conservative southern Democrats, the plans of liberal presidents. With the collapse of the one-party South and the increase in the number of activist liberal senators from all parts of the country, the Senate has become an incubator for developing new policies and building national constituencies.[7] Increasingly, young, mostly liberal, senators have seized the initiative in the Senate and made it, less the brake on the government that the Founders anticipated, and more the engine.[8] This change is related to the fact that most presidential candidates in recent years—and thus most politicians interested in developing a national following—have been senators.

Finally, the national press can either help place new matters on the agenda or publicize those matters placed there by others. There was a close correlation between the political attention given in the Senate to proposals for new safety standards for industry, coal mines, and automobiles and the amount of space devoted to these questions in the pages of the *New York*

Times. Newspaper interest in the matter, low before the issue was placed on the agenda, peaked at about the time the bill was passed.[9] It is hard, of course, to decide which is cause and which effect. The press may have stimulated congressional interest in the matter or merely reported on what Congress had already decided it was interested in. Nonetheless, the press must choose which of thousands of proposals it will cover. The beliefs of editors and reporters led it to select the safety issue. In later chapters we shall discuss the kinds of issues in which the national press is important.

In short, the political agenda can change because of changes in popular attitudes, elite interest, critical events, or governmental actions. An overly simple but not incorrect generalization might be this: popular attitudes usually change slowly, often in response to critical events; elite attitudes and government actions are more volatile and interdependent—they change more quickly, often in response to each other.

MAKING A DECISION

Once an issue is on the political agenda, its nature will affect the kind of politicking that will ensue. Some issues will provoke intense interest group conflict; others will allow one group to get its way almost unchallenged. Some issues will involve ideological appeals to broad national constituencies; others will involve quiet bargaining in congressional offices. We all know that private groups try to influence governmental policies; we often forget that the nature of the issues with which government is dealing influences the kinds of groups that will become politically active.

One way to understand how an issue affects the distribution of political power is to examine what appear to be the costs and benefits of the proposed policy. By "cost" is meant any burden, monetary or nonmonetary, that someone must bear, or thinks he must bear, if the policy is adopted. The costs of a government spending

&&The Senate has become an incubator for developing new policies and building national constituencies.&&

Senator Edmund Muskie (D, Maine) was a presidential contender in 1972.

program are the taxes it entails; the costs of a school desegregation plan may include the need to have children bused to schools away from home; the cost of a foreign policy initiative may be the increased chance of having the nation drawn into war. By "benefit" is meant any satisfaction, monetary or nonmonetary, that persons believe they will enjoy if the policy is adopted. The benefits of a spending program are the payments, subsidies, or contracts received by some persons; the benefits of a school desegregation plan include any improvement in educa-

66 Costs and benefits are what people *believe* them to be. . . . In politics, perceptions are everything.**99**

tional opportunity, attainment, or motivation; the benefits of a foreign policy initiative may include the enhanced security of the nation, the protection of a valued ally, or the vindication of some important principle such as human rights.

Note that costs and benefits are what people *believe* them to be. These beliefs may be accurate or inaccurate, and they are likely to change from time to time. In politics, perceptions are everything. This is especially the case where the costs and benefits are symbolic rather than material. At one time the wide distribution of magazines containing pictures of nude women would have been regarded by many persons as deeply objectionable and thus as a serious cost of allowing such distribution without government interference. Today *Playboy* and similar magazines are available almost everywhere. Though some people still find the magazines offensive, most do not think the cost (to society and its values) of allowing their distribution is very high, or at least not high enough to make them want to do much about it.

Perceptions also change quickly in the area of foreign policy. As we shall see in Chapter 20, public opinion tends to oppose American military intervention abroad before it occurs (the benefits do not seem to be worth the obvious costs); to support such intervention should the president decide to order it (the costs of *not* supporting our troops when they are actually in combat seem very great); and to question or even oppose the actual intervention if the benefits of the war (in terms of military victories or aid to worthy allies) do not seem forthcoming.

The costs and benefits of public policy, like those of work and leisure, may be high or low. Most persons do not care very much one way or another about many policies, which is to say they do not experience the costs or benefits as being very great. In this, of course, they may be wrong. Few Americans think about this nation's commitment to the defense of Western Europe by means of the NATO alliance. Should a land war develop there, however, they may suddenly discover that we were long ago committed to a course of action that has very important consequences for every citizen.

Though perceptions about costs and benefits change and may on occasion be wrong, it is not unreasonable to assume that most people prefer government programs that provide substantial benefits to them at low cost. This rather obvious fact can have important implications for how politics is carried out. In a political system based on some measure of popular rule, public officials have a strong incentive to offer programs that confer—or appear to confer—benefits on people with costs that are either small in amount, remote in time, or borne by "somebody else." Policies that seem to impose high, immediate costs in return for small or remote benefits will be avoided, or enacted with a minimum of publicity, or proposed only in response to a real or apparent crisis. Ordinarily, no president would propose a policy that would raise immediately the cost of fuel even if he were convinced that future supplies of oil and gasoline are likely to be exhausted unless higher prices reduce current consumption. When a crisis occurs, such as the Arab oil price increases beginning in 1973, it becomes possible for the president to offer such proposals—as, in varying ways, did Nixon, Ford, and Carter. Even then, however, people are reluctant to see the price of fuel go up, and thus many are led to dispute the president's claim that an emergency actually exists.

These entirely human responses to the perceived costs and benefits of proposed policies can be organized into a simple theory of politics.[10] It is based on the observation that the costs and benefits of a policy may be *widely distributed* (spread over many, most, or even all citizens) or *narrowly concentrated* (limited to a relatively small number of citizens, or to some identifiable, organized group). For instance, a widely distributed cost would include an income tax, a social security tax, or a high rate of crime; a widely distributed benefit might include retirement benefits for all citizens, clean air, national security, or low crime rates. Examples of narrowly concentrated costs include the expenditures by a factory to reduce the pollution it produces, government regulations imposed on doctors and hospitals participating in the Medicare program, or restrictions on freedom of speech imposed on a dissident political group. Examples of narrowly concentrated benefits include subsidies to farmers or merchant ship companies, the enlarged freedom to speak and protest afforded a dissident group, or protection against competition given to an industry because of the way in which the government regulates it.

The cases will become clearer in the following chapters where detailed attention will be given to several of the policies mentioned briefly above. What the reader should grasp now is a sense of how the distribution of costs and benefits—whether concentrated or distributed—affects the way politics usually (though not always) is carried out.

"MAJORITARIAN POLITICS": DISTRIBUTED BENEFITS, DISTRIBUTED COSTS

Some policies promise benefits to large numbers of persons at a cost that large numbers of persons will have to bear. (Figure 14.1.) Almost everybody will receive, at some point in their lives, social security benefits, and everybody who works has to pay social security taxes. Large numbers of people may benefit from government-sponsored research on heart disease or cancer, and everybody pays for this through income taxes. National defense offers the prospect of a distributed benefit that all pay for through taxes (though some young men pay more when they are drafted into military service).

FIGURE 14.1 A Way of Classifying and Explaining the Politics of Different Policy Issues

	If the perceived **costs** *are:*	
If the perceived **benefits** *are:*	*Distributed*	*Concentrated*
Distributed	Majoritarian politics	Entrepreneurial politics
Concentrated	Client politics	Interest group politics

The outcome of issues of this sort usually depends, not on the pulling and hauling among interest groups, but on appealing successfully to popular majorities. For this reason the politics of these issues is called "majoritarian." As we saw in Chapter 8, citizens rarely have much of an incentive to join interest groups that support policies that will benefit everyone whether or not they are members of the group. They will, however, vote for or against politicians depending on the positions the politicians take on these highly visible issues. Such issues get on the national political agenda because they are visible or even dramatic; they are resolved by a process in which the congressional majority usually has public opinion on its side.

Initially, such issues are often debated in ideological terms—that is, persons who are left-liberal take one side and persons who are right-conservative take the other. When social security was first enacted in 1935, the debate was between those who thought it was the duty of the federal government to remedy social ills and those who thought that it was wrong for government to interfere in the marketplace or to supplant existing state, local, and private welfare organizations. When the United States decided to rearm in 1940, just before we were drawn into World War II, there was an emotional debate between "internationalists" who thought we

Smog in Los Angeles creates a political dilemma: How do you persuade citizens to reduce doing things they enjoy as individuals (driving cars) in order to provide benefits for them as a group (cleaner air)?

"INTEREST GROUP POLITICS": CONCENTRATED BENEFITS, CONCENTRATED COSTS

In this case a proposal will confer benefits on one relatively small, identifiable group and impose costs on a different equally identifiable group. A tariff (i.e., tax) placed on imported bicycle chains will benefit American companies that make bicycle chains, but it will hurt American companies that make bicycles and want to use imported chains in building them. Similarly, most of the decisions made by the National Labor Relations Board will either help labor and hurt management or vice versa. When the Federal Communications Commission makes a decision about what a cable television company can broadcast, it will create benefits for either the cable companies or the regular television networks and corresponding costs for the other side.

Issues of this type are almost entirely dominated by interest group activity. Each side sees the policy as hurting or helping it. Each side is small enough to make it worthwhile and relatively easy to get organized, raise money, and hire lobbyists and lawyers.

Though many issues of this type involve money costs and benefits, that need not always be the case. If the American Nazi party wants to march through a predominantly Jewish community carrying flags with swastikas on them, the community is likely to resist strenuously out of revulsion against the disgraceful treatment of Jews by Nazi Germany. Each side organizes and hires lawyers who fight the issue out in the courts.

"CLIENT POLITICS": CONCENTRATED BENEFITS, DISTRIBUTED COSTS

Here, some identifiable group will benefit, but everybody—or at least a substantial portion of society—will pay whatever cost is incurred.

had a role to play in the world, especially in resisting Hitler's Germany, and "isolationists" or "American Firsters" who thought we should stay home and let the Europeans fight it out alone.

If there is anything to argue about in majoritarian politics, it is usually whether it is legitimate for the government to take any action at all on the matter in dispute. If the new policy is adopted, however, and the proposed benefits turn out (in the people's minds) to be real, then the issue loses its ideological significance and the program continues, often growing in size. Today, when both parties support social security and regularly vote for increases in its benefits, it is hard to remember that in 1935 it was an intensely partisan issue with almost all Democrats on one side and almost all Republicans on the other. In 1935 majority sentiment prevailed; within a decade or two, that had become almost unanimous sentiment.

Because the benefits are concentrated, the group that is to benefit has a strong incentive to organize and work for it, but because the costs are widely distributed, affecting everybody slightly, those who are to pay have little incentive to organize and may be either ignorant of or indifferent to the proposal. Farmers benefit substantially from agricultural price supports; each consumer, however, pays only a small amount of the costs of these subsidies in the form of higher taxes and higher food prices. Furthermore, the average consumer is unaware of how much, if any, of his costs are the result of what farmers are paid. Similarly, when oil prices were low, oil companies found it relatively easy to get Congress to restrict the importation of foreign oil even though the result of the restriction was to increase fuel costs for many citizens. The increase was too slight to be noticed. (After oil prices skyrocketed in the 1970s, of course, people became very sensitive to these costs, and the oil importation restrictions or quotas had to be repealed.) For a long time airlines benefited substantially from the restrictions imposed by the Civil Aeronautics Board on the licensing of new airlines and by rulings that kept prices up, but most citizens did not mind or even notice. And when, in 1978, steps were taken to reduce the protection given by the CAB to the airlines, it was not because of pressure from the customers.

When an unopposed group becomes the beneficiary of government policies, it becomes a "client" of the government, and we call this "client politics" (or "clientele politics"). Usually, such policies win the lopsided approval of Congress or the agency. When a law was passed in 1970 increasing government subsidies to the merchant marine industry (at a sizable cost to the consumer), the vote in the House was 307 to 1 and in the Senate, 68 to 1.[11] The clients or beneficiaries—the shipping companies and maritime unions—were well organized; consumers were not heard from.

Not all such clients are economic interests. Localities can benefit also, as when a city, county,

❝Client politics does not always involve material benefits. Certain groups may enjoy special legal protections from the government or have their values specially honored.❞

or region gets a substantial benefit with the cost spread over the entire country. Regularly, Congress passes a "rivers and harbors" bill that provides various communities with new dams, deeper river channels, better harbors, and improved drainage and irrigation systems. Some of the projects may be entirely justified, some may not; by custom, however, they are referred to as "pork barrel" projects. Usually, several pieces of "pork" are put into one barrel—that is, several projects are passed as part of the same piece of legislation. This attracts to the bill the support of the congressmen from each area to be benefited; with enough projects, a majority coalition is formed. This process is called "logrolling."

Client politics does not always involve material benefits. Certain groups may enjoy special legal protections from the government or have their values specially honored. Virtually every ethnic group in the country has some day or event officially celebrated by presidential proclamation, such as Columbus Day (which particularly honors Italian-Americans) or St. Patrick's Day (which recognizes Irish-Americans). Members of a religious sect, Jehovah's Witnesses, have sometimes refused to recite the pledge of allegiance in school. Some communities have attempted to force them to recite the pledge or to punish them for not doing so. These "flag salute" cases went all the way to the Supreme Court. At first the Court upheld the right of the state to require the pledge, but later it decided to uphold the right to disobey the requirement.[12] The politics of symbolic issues is far more complex than that of economic ones, and occasionally a group asserting a right encounters far more opposition than one claiming a subsidy. As we shall see, however, the general direction of American

❝ Policy entrepreneurs . . . find ways of pulling together a legislative majority on behalf of interests not directly represented in the government.**❞**

A policy entrepreneur in action: Howard Jarvis celebrating the passage of Proposition 13 to cut local property taxes in California (June 1978).

politics has been to allow more and more freedom to groups demanding symbolic or expressive benefits.

"ENTREPRENEURIAL POLITICS": DISTRIBUTED BENEFITS, CONCENTRATED COSTS

Here, society as a whole or some large part of it will benefit (or is led to believe it will benefit) from a policy that imposes a substantial cost on some small, identifiable segment of society. Antipollution and safety requirements for automobiles were proposed as ways of improving the health and well-being of all persons at the expense of the automobile manufacturers. Compulsory national health insurance has been proposed with the claim that it will benefit everybody, but many doctors see it as harming substantially their interests.

It is remarkable that policies of this kind should ever be passed. After all, the American political system creates manifold opportunities for checking and blocking policies that threaten an organized interest. If the beneficiaries are supposed to be the public at large, and if the public at large has little incentive and no mechanism for organizing to press for what it thinks are its interests, then one would suppose that the organized opponents would ususally win. And, indeed, this is what has often happened. During certain periods, however, the political system changes in ways that make it much easier for these policies to get adopted. Just what those changes are and how they work will be discussed in detail in later chapters, especially in the ones dealing with business regulation and civil liberties. Much of the explanation lies in those institutions and processes—changing values, the national press, the new role of the Senate—that are important in altering the political agenda. A key element in these processes is the fact that, since the public is not organized to act for itself, somebody must find a way of acting on its behalf. Such persons are called "policy entrepreneurs"—persons, in or out of the government, who find ways of pulling together a legislative majority on behalf of interests not directly represented in the government. Politics of this kind is "entrepreneurial."

These policy entrepreneurs may or may not represent accurately the interests and wishes of the public at large, but they at least have the ability to persuade others that they are faithful representatives. Ralph Nader is perhaps the best-known example of a policy entrepreneur—or, as he might describe himself, a "watchdog." But there are other examples that can be found at both ends of the political spectrum, conservative as well as liberal. Senator Joseph R. McCarthy in the 1950s mobilized large numbers of citizens in opposition to certain public officials and college professors whom he tried to portray as Communists. Howard Jarvis led a taxpayers' revolt in California over the opposition of organized groups that stood to lose benefits they were receiving from government spending programs. Policy entrepreneurs may act for selfish as well as for selfless reasons and may seek good or bad objectives; what is distinctive about them is their ability to devise political strategies by which costs can be imposed on small, organized groups as the result of dramatic appeals to large numbers of unorganized citizens.

SUMMARY

Policy-making involves two stages—placing an issue on the governmental agenda and reaching a decision about that issue once it is on the agenda. The political agenda steadily expands as the result of group activity, historical crises, and the operations of key institutions, especially the courts, the bureaucracy, the Senate, and the mass media. Decision-making can be understood by examining the distribution of the perceived costs and benefits of a policy proposal and the relation between those costs and benefits and the organization of political activity. Four types of politics have been identified: majoritarian, client, interest group, and entrepreneurial.

This simplified perspective on politics will be applied, in the chapters that follow, to seven policy areas. As will quickly become evident, not every policy will fit neatly into one or another category. The "theory" outlined in this chapter is, of necessity, rather crude. But it will help the reader make some useful distinctions among kinds of policies. Such distinctions are essential if we are to answer, in any serious way, the question, "Who governs?".

In the remaining chapters we shall discuss the politics, not the merits, of various policies. If the politics of one issue is "majoritarian" and that of another is "clientelist," one should not assume that the former policy is good and the latter bad (or vice versa). The worth of a policy depends on its results, not on the motives of its supporters, and that would be the subject of a different book.

The policy chapters are arranged in a particular sequence, though they can be read in any order. Business regulation is discussed first because it illustrates each of the four kinds of policy-making. The next two chapters, on economic policy and social welfare, involve primarily monetary costs and benefits. In Chapters 18 and 19, we take up civil liberties and civil rights, two domestic issues that involve essentially nonmonetary costs and benefits (and, for that reason, are especially difficult to analyze). Finally, in Chapters 20 and 21, we take up issues—foreign policy and defense spending—in which perceptions about forces operating outside the United States are potentially important in explaining how our government behaves. In Part V the analysis will be summarized and that summary will be used to evaluate the competing theories of political power set forth in Chapter 1.

Suggested Readings

Lowi, Theodore J. "American Business, Public Policy, Case Studies, and Political Theory," *World Politics*, Vol. 16 (July 1964). A theory of policy-making somewhat different from that offered in this book.

Walker, Jack L. "Setting the Agenda in the U.S. Senate: A Theory of Problem Selection," *British Journal of Political Science*, Vol. 7 (1977), pp. 423–445. Explores the enlarged role of the Senate in putting new issues on the governmental agenda.

Wilson, James Q. *Political Organizations*. New York: Basic Books, 1973, Ch. 15. An earlier and fuller statement of the theory presented in this chapter.

15 Business Regulation

Different forms of business-government relations · Client politics: dairy and maritime industries, airlines, occupational licensing · Interest group politics: labor vs. business, Interstate Commerce Commission · Majoritarian politics: antitrust laws · Entrepreneurial politics: consumer and environmental protection laws · Perceptions of costs and benefits

The Grange sought to arouse farmers to the dangers of a railroad monopoly (left). Senator Edward M. Kennedy leads efforts to deregulate the transportation industry.

No aspect of public policy raises more profound questions about the nature of politics or more fully illustrates the variety of political processes than the relations between business and government. To some persons, the very existence of business enterprise, especially the large corporation, is a threat to popular rule. Economic power will dominate political power, they believe, because wealth can be used to buy influence, or because elected officials must defer to the wishes of business leaders if the economy is to grow at a rate sufficient to ensure the continued reelection of those officials. Some see a threat to popular rule in the fact that politicians and businessmen share a common class background and thus a common set of beliefs about public policy, or worry that business influence can be used to prevent the rise of potential political rivals. The most sweeping version of the view

that economics controls politics was, of course, that of Karl Marx, for whom the state was nothing more than the executive committee of the propertied classes. But there are other, non-Marxian versions of the same concern.[1]

To other persons, politics, especially democratic politics, is a threat to the existence of a private economy and the values—economic growth, private property, personal freedom—that they believe such an economy embodies. Politicians, in the competitive struggle for votes, will, these persons feel, find it to their advantage to take the side of the nonbusiness majority against that of the business minority. Since the heads of large corporations are few in number but great in wealth, they fear that they will be portrayed as a sinister elite on whom politicians can blame war, inflation, unemployment, or pollution. Defenders of business worry that it will be taxed excessively to pay for social welfare programs that in turn will produce electoral majorities. Moreover, the modern corporation requires for its management a technical and intellectual elite that, trained in universities, will acquire attitudes hostile to essential business values.[2]

In fact, the political relations between government and business take so many forms that some examples could be found to support either of these two theories, and practically any theory in between. But the question need not be left with the statement that the world is complicated. The simplified theory (or, more accurately, categorization) of the politics of public policy outlined in Chapter 14 can be used to understand the circumstances under which business-government relations will take one form or another. To the extent this theory fits the facts, it will help us make more precise statements about politics—instead of asserting that "big corporations run the government" or "self-seeking politicians are ruining business," we can say, "If certain conditions exist, then business-government relations will take certain forms."

CLIENT POLITICS

Client politics tends to exist when a proposal is made that would confer substantial benefits on a relatively small group (say, a particular industry) with the costs of the proposal spread over so large a number of persons that no one person feels especially aggrieved (if, indeed, he or she notices it at all). Usually, the benefit enjoyed by the small group is recognized as such, and is called by its right name—a subsidy, tax-break, legal protection, or whatever. But sometimes the benefit appears at first glance to be a regulation: a casual observer would suppose that the government is imposing its will on some segment of society. Then, when an enterprising journalist or scholar discovers that the regulation, far from making life worse for the group, is actually making it better, we are told that the regulated group must have "captured" the regulatory agency. Usually, nothing of the sort has happened—the policy was intended from the first to benefit the group, and nobody had to be "captured" in order to realize that intent.

In the early 1930s the American dairy industry was suffering from rapidly declining prices for milk. As the farmers' incomes fell, many could no longer pay their bills and were forced out of business. Some lost their farms. Congress responded with the Agricultural Adjustment Act that set up a complicated procedure whereby the federal government would, in effect, determine the minimum price at which Grade A milk could be sold. The government did this by empowering the Dairy Division of the Agricultural Marketing Service, a part of the United States Department of Agriculture (USDA), to issue "market orders" that regulate all milk handlers in various regions of the country. These market orders control several aspects of the fluid milk business, but their principal purpose was and is to prevent competition among dairymen from driving down the price of milk. If the existence of a guaranteed minimum price leads to the production of more milk than people want to drink, another part of the USDA—the Commodity Credit Corporation—stands ready to buy up the surplus using tax dollars.[3] The result is that consumers pay higher prices for milk than they would if market orders were not issued. But consumers do not object to this, at least in any politically significant way, because most are unaware that prices are kept artificially high and because the cost to any given consumer is relatively small (economists have tried to measure the difference between the regulated and unregulated price of fluid milk, and find it to be on the order of 5 cents to 21 cents per gallon).[4] Not many people are going to make a political issue out of paying a few pennies extra on a quart of milk.

There are many other examples of client politics of this sort. The Maritime Administration in the Department of Commerce pays subsidies to the operators of American merchant ships, primarily to make up the difference between what the American ship-owners have to pay in wages to American merchant seamen and the lower wages that foreign competitors pay to their seamen.[5] These subsidies cost the taxpayers about a quarter of a billion dollars a year. In addition, the builders of American merchant ships receive a governmental subsidy to permit them to lower their prices so that they can compete with ships built more cheaply in foreign shipyards. And finally, federal law requires that a large proportion of all American goods transported by sea be carried in American-built and American-registered ships. The total cost of the economic benefits of these subsidies and regulations is very large—several billions of dollars—but the share of this cost paid by the average taxpayer or the average shipper is either not noticeable or, in the case of the shipper, is readily passed on to the ultimate consumer.

Federal regulation of the maritime industry is, in ordinary times, noncontroversial. All the par-

A tank truck hauls fresh milk away from a dairy farm. The milk will be sold at a government-fixed minimum price in order to reduce competition.

ties immediately involved—the seamen and their unions, the ship-builders, and the ship-owners—benefit substantially, while those on whom the costs fall are sufficiently numerous, uninformed, or indifferent as to create no effective political opposition. As we shall see, that can change.

For many years the Civil Aeronautics Board (CAB) that set air fares was also an example of client politics. The major airlines regulated by the CAB did not always agree with its decisions, and there were struggles over which airline should win the right to serve various routes. However, the net effect of CAB regulation—to keep airfares higher than they would be under a system of free competition—was usually not controversial. The airlines benefited from the absence of price competition and from fares high enough, especially on the longer routes, to permit them to buy and maintain advanced

The Airline Deregulation Act of 1978 allowed this airline, once restricted to intrastate flights, to acquire a new route from Miami to Washington, D.C. Previously, CAB rulings had sharply limited such competitive efforts.

aircraft and to serve smaller cities. Many of these smaller cities might not have had airline service at all had flights to them not been subsidized by the revenues obtained from the high fares charged to persons going long distances to larger cities.[6] Usually, the airline passengers did not complain, either because they were not aware that the prices they paid on many flights were higher than they need be or because they were reimbursed for their fares by the business firms or other organizations for which they worked. Changing conditions in the airline industry did lead to challenges to these high fares.

In 1978 Congress enacted a law that would substantially increase competition in the airline industry.

Such client-oriented regulation can also be observed in state and city politics. State law regulates not only the practice of medicine and law, but many other occupations as well, including beauticians, barbers, plumbers, and undertakers. These regulations are in part designed, and always defended, as ways to ensure against fraud, malpractice, and safety hazards. But they tend also to have the effect of restricting entry into the protected occupation, thereby keeping the prices charged by members of it higher than they would otherwise be.[7] Ordinarily, citizens do not object to this, in part because they believe the regulations in fact protect them (whether they are right to think this is not always clear) and in part because the higher prices are spread over a large number of customers and generally not noticed.

Most cases of client-oriented government regulation of business arise, not out of shadowy "deals" made by unscrupulous politicians and self-seeking economic interests, but out of the fact that certain kinds of issues facilitate the organization and representation of one set of interests and impede the organization and representation of a competing set. A regulatory policy may be client-oriented at the outset (as when one interest presses for a law that no one opposes) or become so in the course of its administration (as when a regulatory commission or agency discovers that it receives information and arguments from only one interest). Because only one interest is effectively involved in a particular regulation, the actions of the responsible agency often receive little or no publicity. (To the mass media, something becomes newsworthy when there is conflict involved—no conflict, no attention.) The regulated party often prefers this lack of publicity for, should publicity arise, latent political opposition might be aroused.

Nevertheless, when one group stands to benefit greatly from regulatory decisions made by a government official and that official receives little scrutiny from the public or from rival interest groups, there exists a strong incentive to use money to influence that decision. Although there have been few cases of a federal government regulator receiving a money bribe, there have been many cases of the elected officials to whom that regulator reports receiving generous campaign contributions from regulated industries. The maritime unions and shippers have contributed heavily to presidential and congressional campaigns (the maritime unions gave well over three-quarters of a million dollars to congressional candidates in 1974 and 1978),[8] as have many other groups whose welfare depends on government decisions.

The dairy interests have made massive contributions to Democrats and Republicans alike; in 1971–1972 those contributions were clearly illegal in form and probably corrupt in purpose. The secretary of agriculture had decided on March 12, 1971, not to raise federal price supports for milk. On March 23 several key aides met with President Nixon to discuss the importance of the farm vote and in particular the large amount of money dairy organizations had given and were prepared to give to the 1972 presidential campaign. The Associated Milk Producers, Inc., had already secretly and illegally given $100,000 to White House fund raisers, and this organization, together with others, had pledged a total of $2 million (only about a quarter of which was actually delivered). By the end of the day on March 23, the White House had promised to support higher milk prices; the next day the dairymen renewed their campaign finance pledge; and on March 25 the Department of Agriculture reversed its earlier decision and announced higher milk prices. (The dairymen also made large gifts to two Democrats, Wilbur Mills and Hubert Humphrey.) Several dairy organizations and their principal officers were convicted in 1974 of having made illegal campaign contributions.[9]

It is not always clear in these cases what is

> **❝**Whenever government has the power to issue orders that can affect the level of business profits or the number of jobs, it has the power to attract or compel payoffs.**❞**

cause and what effect: an economic interest may try to influence regulators by money payments (a case of bribery), or regulators may use their power to extract such payments with an implicit threat of hostile action (a case of extortion), or money may be contributed without any specific expectation of a policy change but simply in order to build or retain goodwill (an instance of politics as usual). As we saw in Chapter 7, important restrictions were placed in 1974 on the ability of corporations, unions, and interest groups to contribute to federal election campaigns.

Laws restricting how much money a firm or union may contribute to a political campaign are efforts to reduce opportunities for bribery or extortion created by other laws that regulate business or labor. Whenever government has the power to issue orders that can affect the level of business profits or the number of jobs, it has the power to attract or compel payoffs. As we saw in Chapter 7, the Watergate scandal revealed that businessmen had made large illegal contributions to the Nixon reelection campaign (as they had made them to the campaigns of many prior presidents) *and* Nixon campaign workers had solicited such contributions by threatening, explicitly or implicitly, to allow the regulatory powers of government to be used in ways that were hostile to business.

INTEREST GROUP POLITICS

Where an economic condition or a proposed policy will not only confer benefits on a small organized group but will also impose costs on another small organized group, both groups will struggle over the enactment and administration

" In each of these cases the struggle was highly publicized. The winners and losers were determined by the partisan composition of Congress and the existence of economic conditions that affected opinion on the matter. **"**

of any government regulation that affects them. This is interest group politics.

In 1935 labor unions sought government protection for their right to organize and to compel workers in unionized industries to join the unions. Business firms opposed these efforts. The struggle was fought out in Congress, and the unions won. The Wagner Act, passed that year, created the National Labor Relations Board (NLRB) to regulate the conduct of union organizing drives and to decide complaints of unfair labor practices between union members and their employers. In 1947 labor and management again fought an interest group battle, this time over a bill (the Taft-Hartley Act) that would make illegal certain union practices (such as the closed shop and secondary boycotts) and would authorize the president to obtain a court order to block for up to eighty days any strike that imperiled the "national health or safety." Business won.

In 1959 there was another struggle, over a bill (the Landrum-Griffin Act) intended to prevent corruption in labor unions, to change the way in which union organizing drives were carried on, and to prohibit certain kinds of strikes and picket lines. Business won.

In each of these cases the struggle was highly publicized. The winners and losers were determined by the partisan composition of Congress (Republicans and southern Democrats tended to support the business view, northern Democrats to support the labor position) and the existence of economic conditions (a depression in 1935, revelations of labor racketeering in 1959) that affected opinion on the matter.

But the interest group struggle did not end with the passage of the laws; it continued

Interest group politics is vividly illustrated by labor-management disputes. West Virginia coal miners protest against the Taft-Hartley Act, and schoolteachers in Washington, D.C., demonstrate against the school board over violence in the schools.

throughout their administration. The National Labor Relations Board, composed of five members appointed by the president, had to adjudicate countless disputes between labor and management over the interpretation of the laws. Nor did matters end there. The losing party often appealed the NLRB decision to the federal courts, where the issue was fought out again. Moreover, each president has sought to "tilt" the NLRB in one direction or another by the kinds of appointments he makes. Democratic presidents favor labor, and thus tend to appoint pro-union board members; Republican presidents often favor business, and thus tend to appoint pro-management board members. Since the term of an NLRB board member is five years, a new president cannot immediately appoint all of its members, and thus there is often a split on the board between pro-union and pro-management members.

The Occupational Safety and Health Act, passed in 1970, is another example of business regulation dominated by interest group politics. Labor unions wanted a strict bill with tough standards set by a single administrator; business organizations wanted a more flexible bill with standards set by a commission that would include some representatives of business. After a long struggle labor won, and an Occupational Safety and Health Administration (OSHA), headed by a single administrator, was created as part of the Department of Labor. Again, conflict did not end with the passage of the law. As the administrator began to formulate safety and health standards for workplaces, he had to preside over protracted disputes between labor and industry as to whether the standards would be effective, reasonable, and economical. Many of these disputes were later carried into the federal courts.[10]

Scholars disagree as to whether some regulatory politics should be described as interest-group or client-oriented. A major dispute, for example, has existed over the origins of the Interstate Commerce Act of 1887. This law created the first major federal regulatory agency, the Interstate Commerce Commission (ICC), charged with applying rules to interstate railroads (and later to interstate barges, trucks, and pipelines). In one view, this regulation was the result of a conflict between various interests in which some groups (for example, farmers shipping their produce to market) won out over other interests (for example, railroads charging exorbitant prices to carry farm produce).[11] In another view, the Commerce Act was the result of client politics in which the railroads helped create a commission, designed not to regulate but to protect them.[12]

The details of this legislation are so complex and the evidence produced by historians on various sides of this issue is so voluminous that no brief summary of the issues is possible here. The preponderance of evidence suggests, however, that it is wrong to conclude, as do Gabriel Kolko and others, that the Interstate Commerce Commission was created and endorsed by the railroads in order to protect the railroads. While it is true that the railroads in 1887 got out of the law some things they wanted, such as a ban on rebates that big shippers had been extracting from railroads before they would give them their business, they did not get the things they most wanted. They did not get the right to fix rates in order to reduce the intense competition among the major cross-country railroads, and as a result rates on these lines continued to fall. (By the time of World War I, many railroads were losing money rapidly.) Worst of all from the railroads' point of view, the 1887 law contained a provision making it illegal to charge greater prices on short-haul lines (that usually had no competition) than on long-haul lines (where competition usually was intense). As a result, the prices farmers paid to get their goods to the market on these short-haul lines were cut by the railroads in order to conform to the law. In sum, the evidence is consistent with the view that the Interstate Commerce Act was the result of the demands of many different, competing groups, each of which got something.[13]

The subsequent history of the ICC reveals quite clearly the extent to which interest group politics has dominated it. Railroads have attempted to use the ICC to prevent competition from trucks; truckers have tried to use the ICC to weaken the position of the railroads; and the ICC has asserted its power over both.[14] If any group has won more power, it has been the ICC itself rather than any of the continuing interests it regulates. (Interest group politics often has this effect: by surrounding an agency with competing interests, it allows the agency freedom to choose its own course of action.)

MAJORITARIAN POLITICS

A third form of business regulation occurs when there is a broad popular sentiment that a law is needed to obtain benefits that will be widely shared, with the costs, if any, to be small and to be paid by all. No small organized group of beneficiaries takes the leadership in arguing for the law; similarly, there is no group that clearly sees itself as the target of the law and thus the likely bearer of its costs. This is majoritarian politics.

Much of the antitrust legislation passed in this country, including the Sherman Act (1890) and various provisions of the Federal Trade Commission Act (1914) and the Clayton Act (1914), is the result of majoritarian politics. Toward the end of the nineteenth century, there arose a broadly based criticism of business monopolies (then called "trusts") and, to a lesser extent, of large corporations whether or not they monopolized trade. The Grange, an organization of farmers, was outspoken in its criticism, and popular opinion generally—insofar as we can know what it was in an era without pollsters—seems to have been indignant about trusts and in favor of "trust-busting." Newspaper editorials and magazine articles frequently dwelt on the problem.[15]

But though the antitrust feeling was strong, it was also vague—no single industry was selected as the special target of this feeling (the Standard Oil Company probably came as close as any), and no specific regulation was proposed. Different spokesmen supporting antitrust legislation referred to different problems: for some, monopoly was the problem; for others, sheer bigness was the problem; for still others, the modern corporation itself was the issue. And the bill that was proposed by Senator John Sherman was aimed, not at creating a specific kind of regulation or a new regulatory agency, but at making it a crime to do certain things ("restrain" or "monopolize" trade), leaving the enforcement of that law to the regular courts. Though some large corporations must have worried about what all this would mean, few felt sufficently threatened to try hard to defeat the bill. It passed the Senate by a voice vote and the House by a vote of 242 to 0.

Laws are not self-executing, and vague laws are especially likely to lie dormant unless political leaders invest energy in bringing them to life. For the first decade or so, only one or two cases a year were filed charging violations of the Sherman Act.[16] In 1904 President Theodore Roosevelt persuaded Congress to appropriate enough money to hire five full-time lawyers, and the number of prosecutions increased to about seven a year until 1938. In that year President Franklin Roosevelt appointed as head of the Antitrust Division (a part of the Justice Department) a vigorous lawyer named Thurman Arnold, and soon fifty cases a year were being brought.[17] Today over four hundred lawyers in the division sift through complaints alleging monopolistic practices and other restraints of trade. The American effort to enforce competition, however successful or unsuccessful it may be in the abstract, is the strongest to be found in any industrial nation.

Additional resources were mobilized and new legal tools created to handle anticompetitive business activities by the Federal Trade

Commission Act and the Clayton Act, both passed in 1914. The former created the Federal Trade Commission, and the latter made illegal certain specific forms of competition (such as price discrimination). As with the earlier Sherman Act, the supporters of these measures had a variety of motives. Some wanted the new laws because the Supreme Court had weakened the effect of the Sherman Act by interpreting it to mean that only "unreasonable," rather than all, restraints on trade were illegal.[18] Others believed that the Sherman Act was inadequate because it did not permit the government to attack certain objectionable business practices until a monopoly in fact existed. By this time, they felt, the prosecution would be too late to do any good for a competitor who had been squeezed out of business. And there were also some businessmen who wanted the government to pass laws restricting certain forms of competition, not because they were ethically objectionable, but because competition itself hurt profits.[19] In short, whereas some proponents of these laws saw them as helping consumers (by ensuring that competition would not be hampered by the use of unfair practices), others saw them as helping business (by protecting firms against certain tactics that rivals might employ).

President Woodrow Wilson supported both bills and embraced, to a degree, all the various motives of their proponents. He helped forge a broad coalition on behalf of the legislation, with the result that the votes in favor of the two bills were by lopsided majorities.[20]

The administration of these laws has followed somewhat the same path as that of the Sherman Act, with much depending on who is in charge and how the courts choose to interpret the language of the statutes and the merits of the cases. The essential fact, however, is that neither the bursts of administrative energy nor the periods of quiescence can be explained by the influence of organized interest groups.[21] The reason for the relative absence of interest group activity is that the laws do not divide society into permanent

> "Laws do not divide society into permanent and identifiable blocs of proponents and opponents. Any given business firm can be either benefited or burdened by the enforcement of the antitrust laws."

John D. Rockefeller, founder of Standard Oil, walks to court with his lawyers and messenger boys to hear the government's case brought against him under the Sherman Antitrust Act. Standard Oil had controlled 95 percent of the nation's oil. The government won, and in 1911 Standard Oil was broken up into a number of smaller companies.

and identifiable blocs of proponents and opponents. Any given business firm can be either benefited or burdened by the enforcement of the antitrust laws. At one time the XYZ Widget Company may be sued by the government to prevent it from unfairly advertising its widgets, and at another time the company may ask the government to prosecute its competitor for trying to drive it out of business by selling widgets at prices that are below cost. Antitrust laws apply to virtually all firms, not to certain industries, and thus any firm can, depending on the circumstances, be either a complainant or a defendant. Individual firms frequently use the antitrust laws against each other, as when the Berkey company sued the Kodak company and won a large sum of money. The antitrust laws are enforceable chiefly because rival firms are willing to file complaints; the passage of these laws and the general level of resources spent on their enforcement are not, however, the product of interest group pressures.

This is not to say that there are no efforts made by outsiders to influence the decisions of the Antitrust Division of the Federal Trade Commission. There are, and a book produced by a Ralph Nader study project listed thirty-two such cases involving the division.[22] But three things should be noted about these efforts at influence: first, many were unsuccessful; second, many that were successful could be explained as much by the merits of the arguments advanced by the outside parties as by their political "clout"; and third, and most important, these

efforts typically represented the actions, not of interest groups or trade associations, but of *individual* firms (both those wanting stronger prosecution of rivals as well as those wanting less prosecution of themselves).[23]

ENTREPRENEURIAL POLITICS

Each of the preceding three types of business regulation has had a rather obvious political explanation—either the issue led to the formation of an interest group with a strong stake in regulation (client politics and interest group politics) or was of the sort that produced no organized opponent of regulation (majoritarian politics). The fourth case is another matter: here, a proposed policy will impose serious costs on a small organized segment of the economy (say, a particular industry) but supply benefits (if any) to people generally. This means that, for the proposal to become law, it must be enacted on behalf of an unorganized majority over the objections of an organized minority that stands to lose money if the bill passes. Since the American political system provides so many points at which a proposal can be defeated (in subcommittee, in committee, in either house of Congress, in the White House) and so many ways by which opposition can be carried on (by lobbying, by court action, by filibusters), it is astonishing that any proposal imposing concentrated costs and supplying diffuse benefits ever passes.

Yet they do, and of late at an increasing rate. In 1906 Congress passed the Pure Food and Drug Act, which barred from interstate commerce any misbranded or adulterated food or drug, and the Meat Inspection Act, which required government inspection of meat products sold in interstate commerce. In 1934 the Securities and Exchange Act was passed, creating the Securities and Exchange Commission to regulate the stock markets. Four years later the Food and Drug Act was strengthened. And in the 1960s and early

Federal meat inspection began in 1906 and is carried out by employees of the U.S. Department of Agriculture.

1970s, about two dozen laws in the consumer and environmental protection area were passed, including ones that regulated the automobile industry (the Motor Vehicle Air Pollution Control Act of 1965, the National Traffic and Motor Vehicle Safety Act of 1966, and the Clean Air Act of 1970), the oil industry (the Water Quality Improvement Act of 1970, fixing liability for oil spills), the toy industry (the Children Protection and Toy Safety Act of 1969), pharmaceutical companies (the 1962 amendments to drug laws), poultry companies (the Wholesome Poultry Act of 1968), and the chemical industry (the Toxic Substances Control Act of 1976).

When measures such as these become law, it is often the result of entrepreneurial politics. Someone must galvanize public opinion, mobilize congressional supporters, and mount a vigorous effort to enact a law that will have strong interest group opposition and little or no interest group support. Sometimes that entrepreneur is in the government (a senator or, just as important, a key aide to a senator); sometimes that entrepreneur is a private person (the best known, of course, is Ralph Nader). The motives of such an entrepreneur can either be self-serving or public-serving—he or she can be in search of a good issue with which to win votes or attract publicity, or be selflessly concerned about the public well-being. In most cases the motives are probably mixed.

Dr. Harvey Wiley, a chemist in the Department of Agriculture, actively campaigned for what was to become the Pure Food and Drug Act of 1906. Senator Estes Kefauver held hearings that built support for the 1962 drug laws (and for his presidential campaign). Senator Edmund S. Muskie was the chief architect of many of the air and water pollution control bills, partly out of a genuine interest in the issue and partly to formulate a public reputation that would enhance his presidential ambitions in 1972. One study of the origins of the auto safety bill concluded that the senators responsible for it—Abraham Ribi-

❝The task of the policy entrepreneur can be made easier if there is a crisis or scandal that focuses public attention on a problem.❞

coff and Warren Magnuson—were actively searching for an issue with which they could become identified at the same time that Ralph Nader was actively looking for congressional sponsors for his proposals.[24]

The Congress, and especially the Senate, has often been the source of consumer and environmental protection laws. The Senate can provide national publicity for policies by means of well-managed committee hearings, especially those covered by television. Since the Senate has become an incubator for presidential candidates, there are always senators on the lookout for popular issues with which their names can be linked. (The fact that self-serving motives help explain why some causes are taken up does not make those causes any less deserving, any more than the fact that public-spirited persons endorse such policies makes them necessarily beneficial. Good policies can arise from base motives, and bad policies from altruistic ones.)

The task of the policy entrepreneur can be made easier if there is a crisis or scandal that focuses public attention on a problem. Upton Sinclair's book *The Jungle*[25] dramatized the frightful conditions in meat-packing plants and helped build support for the Meat Inspection Act of 1906. The deaths of some persons from taking a patent medicine, elixir of sulfanilamide, led to the passage of the 1938 drug laws. Costly oil spills off the Santa Barbara, California, coast made easier the job of passing the Water Quality Improvement Act of 1970. Highway fatalities were not a major item of popular concern when the auto safety act was under consideration in 1965–1966. Support for that act grew, however, when it was revealed that General Motors had hired a private detective who made a clumsy effort to collect (or manufacture) gossip harmful to Ralph Nader whose book, *Unsafe at Any Speed*, had criticized the safety of certain GM cars. The economic collapse of the early 1930s helped develop support for the Securities and Exchange Act of 1934.

But a crisis or scandal is not essential to the passage of such laws. Most of the air and water pollution control bills were adopted despite the absence of any disaster, as was the truth-in-lending bill.[26] Carefully planned committee hearings can build support for a policy without the aid of a scandal. For example, by drawing attention to the profits of pharmaceutical companies or the small sums spent (in 1966) by auto companies on safety devices, the hearings can persuade people that the firms in question are insensitive to the public welfare. In this process it is essential that the sponsor of the measure have at least a few allies in the media who can produce frequent and graphic stories that dramatize a problem (such as highway accidents or deaths from unsafe drugs) and convey the belief that an efficacious solution (a law or regulation) is readily available.[27]

If a policy entrepreneur manages to convert a new proposal into law, he or she creates a strong impetus for additional legislation of the same kind. A successful innovator produces imitators, in politics as well as in art or entertainment. Once the auto safety law was passed in 1966, it became easier to pass a coal mine safety bill in 1969 and an occupational safety and health bill in 1970.

Because political resistance must be overcome without the aid of a powerful economic interest group, entrepreneurial politics often takes on a moralistic tone, with opponents portrayed as devils and compromises fiercely resisted. In this process outside groups often keep intense pressure focused on their allies within the government. This is a reversal of the usual process of lobbying, in which an interest group works closely and comfortably with its congressional supporters. When Senator Muskie was drafting an air pollution bill, Ralph Nader issued a highly publicized report *attacking* Muskie, his nominal ally, for not being tough enough.[28] This forced Muskie, who wanted public acclaim, not criticism, for his efforts to deal with pollution, to revise the bill so that it imposed more stringent standards. Dr. William Haddon, Jr., the first administrator of the National Traffic Safety Agency, got the same treatment. He came under attack not only from the auto industry for devising rules it claimed were too strict but also from Ralph Nader for devising ones he thought too weak.[29]

A regulatory agency created as a result of a scandal or some other form of entrepreneurial politics is obviously more vulnerable to being captured by the industry it is supposed to regulate than one created by a process of interest group conflict in which each organized party keeps a watchful eye on its rival. The Food and Drug Administration (FDA), which administers the various laws governing the pharmaceutical industry, fell victim during much of its history to precisely this kind of influence. Once the enthusiasm of the founders had waned and public attention turned elsewhere, the FDA seemed to develop a comfortable and uncritical attitude toward the pharmaceutical industry. (In 1958 the head of the FDA received an award from the Pharmaceutical Manufacturers' Association.)[30] In the mid-1960s, under the spur of renewed congressional and White House attention, the agency was revitalized.

It is not clear, however, whether the newer agencies that administer the consumer and environmental protection laws of the 1960s and 1970s will be equally vulnerable to "capture." For one thing, these newer agencies are organized differently: most are headed by a single administrator rather than a commission, and thus responsibility for decisions is less easily evaded. (Influencing one or two votes on a multimember commission is easier than capturing a single administrator who is accountable for his or her decisions.) For another, the laws conferring authority on these newer agencies often impose specific standards and strict timetables that leave little room for discretion. (The Environmental Protection Agency, for example, is required by law to reduce pollutants by a fixed percentage within a certain number of years. Congress, in 1977, was persuaded to change some of these rules, but they still give relatively little choice to the EPA.) Still another difference is found in the political environments of these agencies. Whereas the CAB deals with a single industry (the airlines), the Occupational Safety and Health Administration deals with virtually every kind of industry. As a result, it rarely confronts a unified business opponent. And even those agencies that do deal with one industry (such as the National Highway Traffic Safety Administration) face competing pressures—the auto manufacturers may resist rules governing the location and shape of bumpers, but the bumper manufacturers are delighted to see such rules enforced, because it means more expensive bumpers will be sold. And finally and perhaps most important, the laws and rules governing "standing" often make it easier to use the federal courts to put competing pressure on an agency. If the Environmental Protection Agency issues a rule disliked by a chemical company, the company naturally will sue; if it issues one that pleases the company, the recent rules on standing and fee-shifting permit an association of nature lovers to sue. (See Chapter 13.)

POLITICS, INTERESTS, AND PERCEPTIONS

It may seem easy, from the examples given, to classify the costs and benefits of a proposed policy and thus to put into the correct pigeonhole the political process that is likely to ensue. But reality, of course, is a good deal more complicated than this. What constitutes a cost or a benefit is often a matter of opinion, and the magni-

tude as well as the distribution of costs and benefits may change over time.

People often disagree as to whether a program will confer a cost or a benefit, and if so, to whom and when. The Federal Energy Regulatory Commission has regulated the maximum price at which natural gas can be sold in interstate commerce. To some, this may seem like a benefit conferred on millions of persons who use natural gas, and so it is—in the short run. But if, as others believe, these price controls discourage exploration for new gas fields, in the long run there will be a shortage of natural gas and sharply increased prices. The oil industry has enjoyed certain tax advantages (called the "oil depletion allowance") that made it cheaper and more attractive than it otherwise would be to drill new oil wells. This seemed like a benefit to the oil industry (and it was) and possibly also a benefit to the consumer (because it helped keep down the price of oil). But it was also a cost to the consumer, for it depleted the treasury of tax revenues that would otherwise be available. In addition, it may have discouraged investment in alternative sources of energy, with the result that these other sources are still scarce and costly.[31] Laws to ensure that new drugs are carefully tested before being used seem clearly intended to protect the consumer, and so they are, but there are hidden costs—these laws postpone for long periods the introduction of some drugs that are helpful in treating serious diseases.

A political conflict is in large measure a struggle to make one definition of the costs and benefits of a proposal prevail over others. In carrying on that conflict, certain points of view enjoy a natural advantage over others. What happens immediately or in the near future is more important to most people than what happens in the distant future. (Economists refer to this as the human tendency to "discount the future.") As a result, in a legislative debate as well as in the popular mind, the definition of who benefits and who loses, and by how much, will be based, in

❝The definition of who benefits and who loses, and by how much, will be based, in large measure, on perceptions of *present* costs and benefits.**❞**

large measure, on perceptions of *present* costs and benefits. Thus, people will think of drug laws as making existing drugs safer, not as making future ones more expensive; they will view the oil depletion allowance as a short-term tax loophole for oil companies, and not as a long-term deterrent to energy development; and they will prefer cheaper natural gas today to more abundant natural gas tomorrow.

But perceptions can change, either because reality changes, or because people acquire more knowledge about a policy, or because future costs and benefits eventually become present ones. Initially, the idea of making the atmosphere cleaner by removing pollutants from automo-

bile exhaust commanded widespread popular assent. That support diminished somewhat (though it remains high) when the passage of time revealed that many auto-emission control devices were costly in terms of money and engine performance and that these costs might lead to reduced employment in the auto industry if auto sales were to drop. In 1977 the United Auto Workers union decided that pollution-control costs were too high and joined with industry in persuading Congress to relax somewhat the auto-emission standards. Another example: protecting endangered species seemed to many a virtually costless benefit until a court order halted the completion of a multimillion-dollar dam in order to spare the snail darter, a fish that few had seen and even fewer loved.

Perceptions can change because the regulations begin to produce costs that fall on groups that have the capacity to organize. In 1977 maritime policy ceased being a pure case of client-

Electricity was once so cheap we used it without thinking about its cost. Today it costs much more to produce. Politicians are in a dilemma: how to get people to conserve energy without being blamed for raising prices.

oriented politics because of a new law that would have required that a certain portion of all imported oil be shipped in American tankers. American oil companies had been importing oil in their own ships, which were registered under foreign flags and thus cheaper to operate than American-registered ships. The new law would have meant that these oil companies would have seen a part of their imported oil shifted to more expensive American-registered tankers, thereby increasing the cost of doing business. Maritime policy had suddenly become a case of interest group politics, with one economic lobby fighting another. The issue was also joined by Common Cause, an entrepreneurial organization, that claimed the new maritime legislation was a political payoff for the heavy campaign contributions made by the maritime industry and unions.[32]

Just as perceptions change, the structure of the economy can change in ways that alter the distribution of costs and benefits. When the Interstate Commerce Commission was formed, farmers transported their produce to distant markets by train or not at all. The advent of the truck and the paved highway put the train at a competitive disadvantage and created a rival political interest. Instead of dealing with one industry, the ICC found itself (in fact, eagerly sought out the chance for) adjudicating the competitive demands of railroaders and truckers. The Federal Communications Commission, in setting long-distance communications rates, was for a long time regulating but one firm—the American Telephone and Telegraph Company, which owned all the long-distance phone lines. But with the advent of microwave transmission systems and other new techniques, companies were formed that could compete with AT&T. Then the FCC found itself adjudicating between competing interests rather than dealing with one monopoly interest.

The most interesting and perhaps the most important changes in the politics of business regulation occur when important segments of

The Endangered Species Act, which was passed in 1973, protected the snail darter, a three-inch-long fish, and prevented the completion of a multimillion-dollar dam at Tellico, Tennessee.

elite opinion revise their views as to the value and nature of regulatory legislation. *Mass* opinion does not change; the structure of the economy does not change; but the theories that policymakers have about the relationship between business and government change. In the 1930s political elites believed that multimember regulatory commissions with broad discretionary authority ought to be created to regulate business competition. In the 1960s a new generation of political elites, perhaps believing it had learned from the mistakes of the old, argued for regulatory agencies headed by single administrators and equipped with specific, narrowly drawn grants of authority. These agencies would presumably avoid the problem of "capture" that had supposedly afflicted the older commissions. Now, in the late 1970s, yet another view has acquired influence: competition can produce more efficient and less costly services in certain industries, such as transportation and communication, that were once thought to require regulation. Under the influence of lawyers and economists who share this view, important steps have been taken to deregulate air transportation, and proposals have been made to deregulate surface transportation. These changing elite opinions about regulation remind us of an important fact—politics is not a stable system of "forces" acting on each other. The forces are people, and people change; they even learn from experience.

SUMMARY

Changing interests as well as changing perceptions alter the politics of business regulation, transforming what once may have been a pattern of clientele politics to an interest group or entrepreneurial pattern or vice versa. Such changes make it difficult to predict accurately how a given issue will arise or be resolved at different times. (Who, in 1964, would have guessed that the automobile industry would be placed under federal regulation within two years?) But one can explain many of the relations between business activity and government regulation by observing the distribution of costs and benefits of the proposed policy (or of the state of affairs a policy is designed to alter).

Client-oriented politics arise when substantial benefits are available to a small organized segment of society, with the costs spread over large numbers of persons. The issue is developed with little public attention; the policy and its administration will tend to conform to the desires of the "regulated" (i.e., benefited) group or industry; and a major goal of the regulation will be reducing or eliminating competition, especially in prices.

Interest group politics arise when an issue will confer benefits on one organized economic sector and corresponding costs on another. The argument over the legislation will be heated and lengthy; periodic efforts will be made to amend the law or to alter the leadership of the administering agency; court appeals will be frequent; who wins and who loses will be influenced by the partisan and ideological composition of the legislature or the agency.

Majoritarian politics occurs when apparent general benefits are to be obtained without threatening the vital interests of any organized segment of the economy. The proposed regulation will apply to business generally rather than to a specific segment, and will either contain language so vague that differing interpretations are possible as to what is intended or impose rules whose general thrust (if not specific application) will enlist support among large parts (if not all) of the business community.

Entrepreneurial politics requires exceptional leadership to mobilize an interested but inactive majority against a group or industry that will bear the costs of a regulation. This mobilization strategy tends to involve entrepreneurs skilled in using publicity or in taking advantage of a crisis or scandal. Unlike in majoritarian politics, public opinion must be developed rather than followed, and a rationale must be found to justify imposing burdens on a firm or industry.

It must be remembered that one cannot decide whether a policy is good or bad from knowing the political process that led to its adoption. Deciding whether milk marketing orders, auto-emission control systems, environmental impact statements, antitrust prosecutions, union organizing rules, or drug testing programs are desirable or undesirable requires one to evaluate their *actual* costs and benefits; explaining the political process by which they are created can, up to a point, be done by examining their *perceived* costs and benefits.

Suggested Readings

Davies, J. Clarence,III, and Barbara S. Davies. *The Politics of Pollution*, 2nd ed. Indianapolis, Ind.: Bobbs-Merrill, 1975. A pro-regulation account of the development of environmental protection legislation.

Nadel, Mark V. *The Politics of Consumer Protection*. Indianapolis, Ind.: Bobbs-Merrill, 1971. An analysis on the sources and uses of political influence in consumer legislation.

Noll, Roger G. *Reforming Regulation*. Washington, D.C.: Brookings Institution, 1971. A useful summary of the criticisms economists make of many regulatory laws.

Stigler, George J. *The Citizen and the State: Essays on Regulation*. Chicago: University of Chicago Press, 1975. A trenchant, often witty analysis of the politics and economics of regulation by a defender of the free market.

Stone, Alan. *Economic Regulation and the Public Interest: The Federal Trade Commission in Theory and Practice*. Ithaca, N.Y.: Cornell University Press, 1977. A study of the origins and behavior of an important regulatory agency by a political scientist who once worked for the FTC.

Weaver, Suzanne. *Decision to Prosecute: Organization and Public Policy in the Antitrust Division*. Cambridge, Mass.: MIT Press, 1977. Explains how antitrust lawyers in the Justice Department make their decisions.

Wilson, James Q. "The Politics of Regulation," in James W. McKie, ed., *Social Responsibility and the Business Predicament*. Washington, D.C.: Brookings Institution, 1974, pp. 135-168. A fuller statement of the theory presented in this text.

16 Economic Policy

Influence of income, ideology, and party on economic goals · Policies most easily enacted · Governmental tools: fiscal policy, monetary policy, wage-price controls · Decentralization of policy decisions · Budget-making · Getting reelected

The making of economic policy is a clear case of majoritarian politics. The benefits of a healthy economy are widespread, if not universal; the costs of producing such an economy, in terms of effort and taxes, are broadly shared. Moreover, the great majority of citizens are well informed about the condition of the economy, at least as it affects them—they know when jobs are easy or hard to find and when prices are rising or stable. As we shall see, citizens cast their votes in part on the basis of their assessment of economic conditions, and politicians know they vote in this way. The political party occupying the White House always worries, as election day draws near, about the state of the economy and does what it can to make that economy as vigorous as possible during the period when voters are making up their minds.

Despite the central importance of economic conditions to democratic politics, this nation, like every other, has been wracked over its history

The presidential campaign of 1900, like that of 1896, pitted "hard-money" Republicans against "soft-money" Democrats (left). The Federal Reserve Board meets (right).

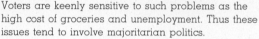

Voters are keenly sensitive to such problems as the high cost of groceries and unemployment. Thus these issues tend to involve majoritarian politics.

with cycles of prosperity followed by recession followed by recovery. Since the Second World War, in a period when the government has devoted the most sophisticated and complex methods of forecasting and control to the economy, the United States has had at least seven recessions (though none as serious as the Great Depression that began in 1929). Since the mid-1960s it has experienced a prolonged period of relatively high rates of both unemployment and inflation, and our rate of economic growth, though significant, has been less than that of some other industrial nations, such as Japan and West Germany. And despite the acknowledged importance of economic factors in winning elections, the incumbent party has frequently lost control of the White House, or suffered a larger-than-normal drop in the number of its congressional seats, because of economic reversals. Richard Nixon was convinced, and with good reason, that his defeat in 1960 was the result, in large part, of the weakened condition of the economy

brought on by his Republican predecessor in the White House, Dwight Eisenhower. In the 1976 election Gerald Ford was unsuccessful in part because both unemployment and inflation were major problems.

In short, no one needs to look for interest group activity or skillful political entrepreneurs to explain the attention that politicians give to the larger questions of economic and tax policy. Elected officials have ample incentive to worry about the state of the economy. What does need to be explained is why one policy rather than another is pursued in order to serve the evident common interest of officials and citizens.

As with most majoritarian policies, ideology plays at least as important a role as material interests in that explanation. What people believe about the goals that ought to be served and how they can best be attained powerfully influences the shape of the debate over the economy.

Few topics in American political history have

produced debates as intense, as widespread, and as long-lasting as those concerned with how the federal government should deal with the economy. Almost the first issue to be taken up by the newly formed government in 1790 was a series of reports by Secretary of the Treasury Alexander Hamilton, calling for the creation of a national bank and the full funding of the state governments' Revolutionary War debts, levying custom duties and excise taxes to pay off that debt and support essential services, and raising tariffs to protect American industries. Thomas Jefferson and James Madison led the opposition to the idea of a national bank and federal assumption of state debts. The question of a national bank erupted again during Andrew Jackson's presidency.

Throughout much of the nineteenth century, especially after the Civil War, a major dividing line between Democrats and Republicans was the tariff—most Democrats wanted low tariffs so that the South and West could import manufactured equipment from abroad; most Republicans wanted high tariffs so that American industry in the Northeast would be protected against foreign competition. The periodic depressions and financial panics of the late nineteenth and early twentieth centuries gave rise to major popular debates over how the national currency should be managed. And they led to the formation of political parties that sought either a more abundant currency (the Greenbackers) or a reorganization of the economy (the Socialists). Franklin D. Roosevelt and the New Deal not only put in place increased government regulation of business (see Chapter 15) but also began, in a tentative and uncertain manner, to experiment with ways of shaping the federal budget to affect the level of economic activity.

In short, economic policy has been one of the oldest sources of national political issues. Though many of the tools for making and implementing various policies are quite modern, the cleavages of opinion within both the public and the political elite on the subject of the economy are of long standing.

THE GOALS OF ECONOMIC POLICY

People emphasize different things when they speak of economic well-being. Though scarcely anybody likes unemployment or inflation, economic liberals tend to worry more about unemployment whereas economic conservatives tend to worry more about inflation.[1] In 1976, for example, citizens were asked in an opinion poll which they thought was more important—that jobs be available or that inflation be controlled. A majority thought both were equally important, but of those earning less than $5,000 a year, 35 percent said that jobs was a more important issue, and only 19 percent said inflation was more important. Among those earning over $25,000 a year, only 13 percent mentioned jobs first, and 29 percent mentioned inflation first (see Table 16.1). In a 1975 opinion survey, persons holding managerial or professional jobs were more likely to be worried about inflation than laborers or unemployed persons (though even the unemployed attached a good deal of importance to inflation).[2]

TABLE 16.1 Attitudes of Americans Toward Goals of Economic Policy, 1976

	Family income less than $5,000	*Family income more than $25,000*
Jobs more important	35%	13%
Inflation more important	19	29
Both equally important	42	57
Not sure	4	1
	100%	100%

Source: Edward R. Tufte, *Political Control of the Economy,* p. 84. Copyright © 1978 by Princeton University Press. Reprinted by permission of Princeton University Press.

" Even if citizens agreed on the goals of economic policy, it is by no means clear that the government and its experts know how to attain those goals. **"**

Halt Inflation or Decrease Unemployment?

Some of these differences in opinion are obviously the result of differences in economic circumstances. Understandably, unemployed or low-income persons worry more about jobs than prices. Even though doctors or lawyers are rarely out of work, they may well worry about what their dollars can buy. But attitudes toward economic issues are not a simple expression of economic class. During periods of high unemployment, the proportion of persons concerned about unemployment is much larger than the proportion actually out of work. In 1971 and 1972 a majority of citizens felt that unemployment was the major problem even though about 94 percent of the work force was employed.[3] Views on economic goals also seem to follow party lines. Elected officials belonging to different political parties tend to have different goals for economic policy even though they have quite similar social and economic backgrounds. In their party platforms, their high-level government documents, and their policy proposals, Democrats, especially liberal ones, are chiefly concerned with unemployment; Republicans, especially conservative ones, worry most about inflation.[4]

In addition, people disagree as to the long-term effects of short-term conditions. Many persons, for example, believe that in the long run inflation will increase unemployment because inflation discourages saving and investing and thus inhibits economic growth. Others argue that unemployment is the greater risk because consumer demand is reduced when large numbers of people are out of work and, without that demand, new investment will be reduced whatever the rate of inflation. Adding to the confusion are those persons (a minority, but a

vocal one) who object to economic growth because of what they take to be the costs of that growth, such as pollution, the more rapid depletion of resources, and congestion. To complicate matters still further, a majority of the American public has always believed that the federal budget should be balanced.[5] Most economists, on the other hand, are convinced that if unemployment is to be reduced (something else that most people want), the government will have to run deficits in some years. Indeed, in the twenty-four years from 1954 to 1978, there were only two years (1960 and 1969) when Washington managed to take in as much money as it spent.[6]

Prediction and Control

But even if citizens agreed on the goals of economic policy, it is by no means clear that the government and its experts know how to attain those goals. Even predicting what the economy will be like next year is difficult, to say nothing of making it behave in accordance with one's prediction. What Paul Samuelson, the Nobel Prize–winning economist, once said of stock market prices might also be said of economists: they have predicted nine of the last five recessions. Economists have learned a great deal about how the economy operates, at least in the aggregate, and have become quite sophisticated about measuring its behavior and the relations among its components. (By contrast, President Herbert Hoover in 1929 did not even have reasonably reliable information about how many people were unemployed or the size and distribution of national income.) But even the most carefully tested theories that prescribe ways of increasing employment or cutting inflation run the risk of being outdated by changing circumstances. For example, a common economic generalization is that there is a "trade-off" between unemployment and inflation so that as you get more of one you get less of the other. This may have been true in the past, but since the late 1960s we have had high levels of unemployment *and* high rates of inflation—so-called "stagflation." The reasons for stagflation are complex (and controversial), and include events that have occurred abroad, such as the Arab nations' quadrupling the price of oil virtually overnight.

Finally, and most important from the point of view of one seeking to understand politics, the government is not a neutral, easily controlled instrument for implementing economic policy. Politically, certain policies are much easier to enact than others, and thus certain policies are more likely to occur than others almost regardless of economic circumstances.

Likely Occurrences

First, it is always easier to increase than to decrease government expenditures. Increasing expenditures on a program makes the beneficiaries of that program happy, and the additional costs are scarcely noticed by taxpayers generally; cutting expenditures on a program makes those beneficiaries angry, but the cuts are hardly noticed, and thus rarely appreciated, by the public at large. The political system tends to be especially sensitive to *intense* opinion. Moreover, conflicts among organized interests and localities are easier to manage when all parties to the dispute can be offered something. Dividing a large pie is easier than dividing a small one. To put this into the language of Chapter 14, client and interest group politics exert a relentless upward pressure on government expenditures.

Second, it is easier to cut taxes than to raise them; the reasons should be obvious. (This does not mean, by the way, that citizens always prefer a tax cut to any other economic policy. Regularly, opinion polls show that people prefer controlling inflation to reducing taxes.)[7] Between 1948 and 1976, Congress enacted sixteen major tax laws and dozens of lesser ones; six of the major ones increased taxes, nine reduced them, and one left rates pretty much unchanged.[8] Of the six that raised taxes, four were enacted during times of obvious national emergency—three

in the period 1950–1951, when we were at war in Korea, and one in 1968, when we were at war in Vietnam. One of the other tax increases was a special case (it raised federal taxes on gasoline to pay for the interstate highway program). There has been, since World War II, only one peacetime tax increase, and that law (the Tax Reform Act of 1976) chiefly raised the tax liability of well-off individuals while it provided cuts for average citizens. Six of the nine laws that reduced taxes were passed in election years, and a seventh, adopted on December 30, 1969, missed by only two days being enacted in an election year. The greater ease of passing tax cuts than tax increases becomes important, as we shall see, because of the view among most economists that raising taxes is one way to curb inflation.

Third, and complicating the point just made, is that there is rarely any such thing as a simple tax cut or tax increase, and thus any new tax legislation is likely to be time-consuming and controversial. There are two reasons for this: taxes do not fall evenly on all persons, and tax laws are used to accomplish a variety of objectives. Since the federal income tax is "progressive"—that is, higher income persons generally pay a larger proportion of their earnings in taxes than lower income persons—and since the total amount one pays is a result of deductions and exemptions as well as tax rates, any proposal to raise or lower taxes will precipitate a fight over who should benefit from or be burdened by the change. Both ideology and self-interest play a role in this fight. Some people will favor reducing taxes on higher incomes both because they will benefit from such reductions and because they believe that, since higher income persons save and invest more than lower income ones, a tax cut in the upper brackets will produce investment and economic growth.

Others will want lower brackets cut both because they are moderate-income people who will benefit and because they believe that such persons, being so numerous, will spend their tax

❝The tax laws . . . are heavily shaped by client and interest group politics, and thus changing taxes to serve majoritarian interests in economic stability and growth is rarely easy.**❞**

STOP INFLATION
END HIGH PRICES
END UNEQUAL,
UNFAIR TAXES
COALITION FOR JOBS AND
ECONOMIC JUSTICE
PHONE: 373-3550

Tax reform is easier to support in the abstract than in the concrete owing to the large number of people who are benefited by various "loopholes."

savings on consumer purchases in ways that will stimulate the economy in the short run.

The hundreds of pages of the Internal Revenue Code contain provisions designed to achieve a bewildering variety of objectives—helping charitable and educational organizations by making contributions to them tax-exempt, fostering business by giving special tax treatment to investment, facilitating home ownership by allowing persons to deduct mortgage interest and taxes on owner-occupied homes, helping the elderly by excluding social security benefits from taxable income, and encouraging oil exploration by keeping tax rates on oil and gas production low. Any debate over tax rates is also a debate over these purposes and over abstract considerations of fairness—who should pay, and how much. Everybody, of course, is in favor of closing "tax loopholes," but that agreement tends to evaporate when the question becomes, "Whose loophole?" The tax laws, in short, are heavily shaped by client and interest group politics, and thus changing taxes to serve majoritarian interests in economic stability and growth is rarely easy.

The reason why closing tax loopholes is difficult if not impossible becomes apparent from Table 16.2. There are listed, in descending order of importance, the twenty largest loopholes and the amounts by which individuals and corporations benefit from them. (These twenty accounted for 84 percent of the value of all tax loopholes in 1975.) As is evident, the principal beneficiaries are individuals, not corporations, and ordinary individuals at that. The tax exemptions allowed for mortgage interest paid by homeowners, pension contributions, property taxes, medical insurance premiums, charitable contributions, social security income, and unemployment insurance benefits, taken together, benefit the vast majority of all citizens. It is hard to imagine a Congress willing to close all or even most of these loopholes; indeed, to the typical citizen, these are not loopholes at all but rather the proper exclusion of certain kinds of income and expenses from the reach of the tax collectors.

Fourth, elected officials may, as thoughtful men and women, have the long-term interests of the American economy at heart but, as practicing politicians, they must keep the short-term problem of getting reelected clearly in view. Since the House of Representatives is up for election every two years and the president every

TABLE 16.2 Who Gets What from Federal Tax "Loopholes"
(The twenty largest tax exemptions* and the amounts by which individuals and corporations benefited as of January 1, 1975)

"Loophole"*	Amount saved (in millions)		
	Total	By individuals	By corporations
State and local tax deduction	$9,950	$9,950	0
Mortgage interest on homes	6,500	6,500	0
Pension contributions	5,740	5,740	0
Investment credit	5,370	950	$4,420
Property tax deduction	5,270	5,270	0
Charitable contributions	5,125	4,840	285
Interest on state and local bonds	4,765	1,260	3,505
Capital gains	4,165	4,165	0
Unemployment insurance benefits	3,830	3,830	0
Medical insurance premiums	3,745	3,745	0
Corporate surtax exemption	3,570	0	3,570
Deduction of interest paid on consumer credit	3,460	3,460	0
Depletion allowance	3,055	445	2,610
Social security (OASDI) benefits	2,940	2,940	0
Medical expenses	2,630	2,630	0
Interest on life insurance savings	1,820	1,820	0
Standard deductions	1,420	1,420	0
Oil exploration	1,365	130	1,235
Deferred income of domestic international sales corporations	1,320	0	1,320
Exemption for being age 65 or over	1,250	1,250	0

Source: Adapted from George F. Break and Joseph A. Pechman, *Federal Tax Reform: The Impossible Dream?* (Washington, D.C.: Brookings Institution, 1975), pp. 14–15. Reprinted by permission.

* These "loopholes" are the exemptions, exclusions, and deductions permitted by law. The table does not include revenue lost from income splitting, assets transferred by gift or death, deferred taxes on foreign corporate income, the asset depreciation system, and the maximum tax limits on earned income.

" Any economic policy likely to command much political support will tend to provide for immediate benefits even at the expense of long-term stability. **"**

four, any economic policy likely to command much political support will tend to provide for immediate benefits even at the expense of long-term stability. From the politicians' point of view, if expenditures are to be increased or taxes cut, this should happen soon, and visibly; if taxes are to be raised or programs curtailed, the effective date of such decisions, or even the decisions themselves, should be postponed. Politicians are not wholly preoccupied with their immediate electoral interests as is evident from the fact that not all expenditures are increased every year and that tax increases are sometimes voted. Moreover, congressmen from similar constituencies will often see economic issues in different ways: a conservative may worry more

about inflation and a liberal more about unemployment, even though the voters to which each is responsive think pretty much alike. But all other things being equal, the political importance of economic conditions will lead elected officials to prefer policies that are popular in the short run.

THE METHODS AND MACHINERY OF ECONOMIC POLICY-MAKING

The government has, broadly speaking, three methods for influencing the economy: fiscal policy, monetary policy, and wage-price controls.

Fiscal Policy

Fiscal policy involves the size, and relationship one to the other, of what the government takes in (taxes) and what it spends (expenditures). These taxing and spending decisions may be

Most politicians promise more, but Jerry Brown became governor of California by promising less—a cutback in the expansion of government.

made with a view to their *"macro*economic" effect (i.e., their effect on the total level of national income, employment, production, and investment) or with a view to their *"micro*economic" effect (i.e., their effect on particular groups, localities, individuals, or businesses).

For a long time, most government taxes and expenditures were judged almost entirely in terms of their microeconomic effect: Should we have bigger or smaller pensions for veterans, build many or few flood control projects, levy high or low taxes on various kinds of imported goods? There were two reasons for this emphasis. One was that the federal government was too small to have much of an effect on the economy as a whole. (In 1929 federal expenditures amounted to less than 3 percnt of the gross national product, and only the very well-to-do paid any significant amount of income taxes.) (See Figure 16.1) The other reason was that most officials, like the public generally, believed that it is important for the government to have a balanced budget—that is, to spend no more than it takes in. This was not a hard-and-fast rule (during every war the government spent more than it took in and borrowed the rest), but it was a general goal. If the budget is balanced, the federal government will ordinarily not have much of an effect on the level of economic activity—whatever it takes out in taxes, it puts back in expenditures.

Today the federal government plays a large role in the economy (it now spends over one-fifth of the gross national product, and most people pay a steep tax bill), and very few officials any longer believe that the budget must always be balanced. Under these new conditions, the *macro*economic effects of federal policy can be quite significant.

Monetary Policy

A second tool for influencing the economy is monetary policy. By this is meant the decisions affecting the amount of money available (in

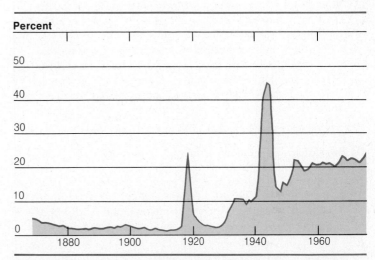

FIGURE 16.1 Federal Outlays as a Percentage of Gross National Product, 1869–1975

Source: Reprinted from David J. Ott and Attiat F. Ott, *Federal Budget Policy*, 3rd ed. (Washington, D.C.: Brookings Institution, 1977), p. 58. Reprinted by permission.

bank deposits as well as cash) and the price of money (the interest rate and other terms that affect the cost of borrowing funds). Unlike fiscal policy, which is of relatively recent origin, the government has always worried about monetary policy. From the very beginning, the federal government has had a monopoly over minting coins and printing currency and intermittently since the early nineteenth century it has run a central bank, first the Bank of the United States and now the Federal Reserve System. Throughout the nineteenth century and well into the twentieth, an important, often dominant political issue has been the size and value of the currency. "Cheap money" groups have advocated increasing the supply of money (hoping to make it easier to pay off debts), and "hard money" groups have advocated restricting the money supply (hoping to avoid inflation). Since 1914

The Federal Reserve Board

The Tools by Which the Fed Implements Its Monetary Policy

1. **Buying and selling federal government securities** (bonds, Treasury notes, and other pieces of paper that constitute government IOUs). When the Fed buys securities, it in effect puts more money into circulation and takes securities out of circulation. With more money around, interest rates tend to drop, and more money is borrowed and spent. When the Fed sells government securities, it in effect takes money out of circulation, causing interest rates to rise and making borrowing more difficult.

2. **Regulating the amount of money a member bank must keep on hand as reserves** to back up the customer deposits it is holding. A bank lends out most of the money deposited with it. If the Fed says it must keep in reserve a larger fraction of its deposits, then the amount it can lend drops, loans become harder to obtain, and interest rates rise.

3. **Changing the interest charged banks** that want to borrow money from the Federal Reserve System. Banks borrow from the Fed to cover short-term needs. The interest the Fed charges for this is called the "discount rate." The Fed can raise or lower that rate; this will have an effect, though usually rather small, on how much money the banks will lend.

THE FEDERAL RESERVE SYSTEM

Federal Reserve Board (7 members)
- Determines how many government securities will be bought or sold by regional and member banks.
- Determines interest rates to be charged by regional banks and amount of money member banks must keep in reserve in regional banks.

Regional Federal Reserve Banks (12)
- Buy and sell government securities.
- Loan money to member banks.
- Keep percentage of holdings for member banks.

Member Banks (6,000)
- Buy and sell government securities.
- May borrow money from regional banks.
- Must keep percentage of holdings in regional banks.
- Interest rates paid to regional banks determine interest rates charged for business and personal loans and influence all bank interest rates.

monetary policy has been principally the province of bureaucratic rather than legislative or electoral politics. In that year the Federal Reserve System was created, headed by the semi-independent Federal Reserve Board (the "Fed"). The Fed has various tools with which it tries to expand or contract the supply of money and the ease (or cost) with which individuals and businesses can borrow money.

Wage-Price Controls

A third tool of economic policy is regulation of prices and wages. The most obvious form this regulation may take are controls: orders and regulations about how much businesses can charge and workers can earn. Such controls are often put into effect during wartime (they were used in World War II and the Korean War but not during Vietnam), but only once have they been employed in peacetime. President Nixon, acting under congressional authority, froze prices and wages in August 1971, and then put in place government controls of slowly diminishing stringency ("Phase II" and then "Phase III") that lasted until 1974, when the authorizing legislation expired.

The government also employs routinely many other, far less obvious forms of price and wage regulation. The White House may announce "guideposts" for judging "acceptable" price increases or wage settlements and then try to use persuasion and publicity, usually called "jawboning," to get at least the larger corporations and unions to abide by them.

Sometimes the jawbone is more than just words: a firm can be threatened with an antitrust investigation if it does not follow the guideposts or promised government contracts if it does. In 1978 President Carter threatened to withhold government contracts from firms that did not comply with his price guidelines. The government may create labor-management committees to try to minimize inflationary contract negotiations. And almost all of the government's efforts to regulate business and labor—requiring licenses, mandating safety procedures and pollution controls, influencing hiring decisions, raising the minimum wage, authorizing quotas on imported goods, and restricting entry into certain industries—often have the effect, whether intended or not, of raising prices and wages.

Who Makes the Decision?

The machinery by which these various policy instruments may be used is highly decentralized. Within the executive branch, three agencies are of special importance: the Council of Economic Advisers, the Office of Management and Budget (OMB), and the Treasury Department. Each new president gives careful thought to the leadership of these groups because he knows that the political predilections of these officials will powerfully affect the kind of advice he gets. Democratic presidents tend to give these posts to liberal academic economists and businessmen; Republican presidents tend to award them to conservative economists and businessmen.

Though all professional economists share certain ways of thinking about the economy—they agree that every course of action has a cost, that economic efficiency is desirable, that people respond rationally to incentives—they also differ ideologically about what will make the economy work better. Democratic and liberal economists tend to be Keynesians, to favor a large role for the government in providing services to people, and to worry more about unemployment than inflation; Republican and conservative economists tend to be monetarists, to favor a larger role for the private market, and to worry more about inflation and federal deficits than about unemployment or slack demand. Paul Samuelson, James Tobin, Walter Heller, and Charles Schultze are liberal economists who have played important roles in Democratic administrations; Milton Friedman, Paul McCracken, Arthur Burns, and Alan Greenspan are conservative

❝Sometimes the jawbone is more than just words: a firm can be threatened with an antitrust investigation if it does not follow the guideposts or promised government contracts if it does.**❞**

Though a conservative, President Nixon imposed price and wage controls in 1971. Subsequently, Presidents Ford and Carter used a variety of voluntary "guideposts," presidential "jawboning," and threats of withholding government contracts to try to moderate the rate of inflation.

economists who have been involved with Republican administrations.

Despite their tendency to select advisers with the same general outlook, presidents will often get competing words of advice—the Council of Economic Advisers may worry about getting the

The Debate
Over Economic Policy

How the government ought to behave with respect to the economy is a subject of passionate debate among economists. To oversimplify, one school, dominant in public affairs in recent years, can be called "Keynesians" (after the late British economist John Maynard Keynes), and the other can be called "monetarists" (because of their belief in the importance of the money supply) or sometimes "Friedmanites" (after the American economist Milton Friedman).

Keynesians: Keynes taught that the level of employment in society depends on the total level of demand for goods and services and that demand, in turn, will depend on what fractions of their incomes people spend and save. If people save too much, there will be too little demand, employment will fall, and a recession will occur. If they save too little, demand will rise faster than the nation's capacity to produce, shortages will develop, and inflation will result. The economy will not automatically operate at a full-employment, low-inflation level. The task of government is to maintain demand at a high level (by public spending and public works) and to keep interest rates low (by increasing the supply of money when necessary). There is no need for the government's budget to be balanced on a year-to-year basis; what counts is the performance of the economy.

Monetarists: Monetarists such as Milton Friedman believe that the money supply is the major determinant of demand in the economy. They argue that government spending programs create stop-and-start economic fluctuations and interfere with the free workings of the market by regulating or distorting voluntary transactions. Moreover, manipulating the money supply to deal with booms and busts will make these fluctuations worse because policy-makers can rarely act in a timely, rational manner. Since inflation is caused, they believe, by a too-rapid growth in the money supply and recessions by a too-small growth, the principal responsibility of government should be to maintain a steady, predictable growth in the money supply at a rate about equal to the increase in the economy's productivity; beyond that, it should as much as possible keep its hands off the market.

These are much-simplified accounts that neglect debates within each school and many refinements in each doctrine. But the central core of these ideas exerts a powerful influence on government and officials. Keynesians tend to have confidence in government and want it to play a large role in society; monetarists tend to have little faith in it and want it to play a small role.

economy moving, the head of OMB may be concerned about problems of efficiency and waste, and the secretary of the treasury may be especially sensitive to the value of the dollar in foreign trade. Getting agreement on fiscal policy often involves a good deal of pulling and hauling among these agencies.

Congress, of course, must approve any proposals for expenditures or taxes, and within Congress that approval depends very heavily on the attitude of the House and Senate Appropriations Committees and of the House Ways and Means Committee and the Senate Finance Committee.

John Maynard Keynes

Milton
Friedman

The Board of Governors of the Federal Reserve System is by law an independent agency: its seven members are appointed by the president with the consent of the Senate. Members serve for fourteen-year terms (nonrenewable), and may not be removed except "for cause." (No member has ever been removed since the Board's creation in 1913.) The most important decisions of the Fed are made by its Open Market Committee, the group that buys and sells government securities and thus most directly affects the money supply. Most of the regulatory decisions of the government that affect prices (and sometimes wages) are made by quasi-independent boards and commissions or by government bureaus over which the president has only weak control.

Image vs. Reality

Though decentralized in fact, the making of economic policy is centralized in perception. The public tends to hold the president and his party accountable for economic conditions even though he cannot always coordinate the efforts of the government to improve those conditions and even though those efforts under the best of circumstances might not have any visible short-term effect on the economy. Whether he likes it or not, the president is inescapably cast in the central role in the economic policy drama, to stand or fall on his own in public esteem even though the other important actors may forget their lines, ignore his words, or fail to show up on time.

The central position of the president—as initiator of action and as focus of public attention—is characteristic of majoritarian politics. In later chapters we shall see how he plays a prominent role in other examples of this kind of politics, such as social welfare and foreign policy. Over the years Congress has added a bit of substance to this role by making the Office of Management and Budget a staff arm of the president (since 1939), equipping him with a Council of

"Whether he likes it or not, the president is inescapably cast in the central role in the economic policy drama."

President Carter confers with Charles Schultze, chairman of the Council of Economic Advisers, in the unhappy knowledge that he cannot manage the economy as people would like.

Economic Advisers (since 1946), and allowing him to have substantial influence over the Treasury Department (an especially "presidential" agency since its creation in the eighteenth century). The Constitution requires the president to give a State of the Union address to Congress (by custom he does it every January), and in this he usually announces his economic priorities for the coming year. This address is soon followed by a Budget Message (which contains his compilation of, and decisions about, the thousands of different expenditure items of the government) and by an Economic Report. This latter document usually comes in two parts: a brief

Economic Report of the President, signed by him and containing his personal views, and a longer Annual Report of the Council of Economic Advisers, which contains a somewhat less partisan, more scholarly examination of economic trends and policies. The Economic Report is reviewed in Congress by the Joint Economic Committee, which does not recommend legislation but does hold hearings and frame some of the issues.

TRYING TO MAKE ECONOMIC POLICY MEMORABLE

Not only citizens, but presidents of the United States find it difficult to think clearly about economic policy. John F. Kennedy supposedly had so much trouble remembering the difference between fiscal and monetary policy and who was responsible for what that he relied on the fact that the word "monetary" and the name of the chairman of the Federal Reserve Board (then William McChesney Martin) both began with an "M."

Richard Nixon was reputedly so bored with lengthy discussions of foreign economic matters that his aides began looking for signs of what they called his "MEGO" (My Eyes Glaze Over) reaction.

The Budget-Making Process

The actual budget is the end product of a long, complicated process. The process begins in early spring when each agency and bureau formulates its requests for funds. After review by the relevant cabinet departments (where appropriate), these requests go to the Office of Management and Budget (OMB). The director of OMB takes the first set of figures to the president and his other principal economic advisers, the secretary of the treasury and the chairman of the Council of Economic Advisers. At this time the president must decide two things, at least in preliminary fashion. First, he must decide what his overall fiscal strategy is: Does he wish to run a deficit in order to pump extra federal dollars (above and beyond what is collected in taxes) into the economy to stimulate it and encourage growth and employment? Or, does he wish to reduce or eliminate the deficit, or even run a surplus, in order to reduce purchasing power and thus help control inflation? Second (and contingent upon his first decision), the president must decide what programs he feels must be increased (because of campaign pledges, personal views, or perceived public demands) or may be cut in a way that will minimize damage to the economy and political harm to him and his party.

The president's freedom of action in making these two decisions is usually small. He may wish to have a budget surplus but know that he cannot raise taxes or cut expenditures by enough to achieve it. He may have inherited a deficit from his predecessor (as did President Carter from President Ford, in 1977) so large that it cannot be eliminated in less than four or five years, if then. Or he may want a surplus for economic reasons but fear that his opponent will be able to charge him with ignoring "urgent needs" or with failing to lower taxes. Moreover, the federal budget is a vast accumulation of prior commitments and programs, many of which are legally or politically immune to cuts. In Figure 16.2 we see the percentages of total budget outlays that are uncontrollable because they involve contracts and commitments already made, payments to individuals (such as social security) that are guaranteed by law, and interest on the national debt. They accounted in 1978 for about three-fourths of all expenditures (nearly $334 billion). The proportion that is relatively controllable is only slightly more than a fourth, heavily concentrated in national defense items. This fact helps explain why, as we shall see in Chapter 21, there is a greater variation from year to year in the defense budget—and a greater likelihood in most years of cuts—than in the nondefense budget.

Presidential decisions on these matters are sent back to the agencies by OMB as guidelines for the preparation of final budget requests. Intensive haggling between OMB and the agencies goes on during this period.

The resulting executive budget is given final review by the president during the fall and transmitted to Congress in January. It contains spending plans for the fiscal year that begins the following October first. Within Congress, the process begins all over again. The House and Senate Budget Committees review the fiscal—that is, the macroeconomic—aspects of the president's proposals. They then submit to Congress by April 15 a "first budget resolution" that sets forth a tentative ceiling on total expenditures. This ceiling is voted by Congress by May 15 of each year; until it is adopted neither house can pass any new spending bills. This procedure ensures that Congress will take a look at the total cost of government before it starts deciding on the costs of parts of it. Then Congress takes up the appropriations bills sent to it from the Appropriations Committees, with action first in the House, completing work on them by early September. After this it adopts the "second budget resolution" that sets forth the final total spending figure and the final revenue figure. Both of these figures may be different from those in the first resolution. Once the second budget resolution has been set, Congress is not supposed to pass

spending bills that exceed the amounts specified—until the process starts over again in January. (Congress can, of course, make exceptions to this and, indeed, to any other self-imposed rule.) Throughout this process, presidential aides defend White House spending proposals while congressmen, interest groups, and the media criticize them. Other members of the executive branch, despite their nominal

---

FIGURE 16.2 Controllable and Uncontrollable Parts of the Federal Budget, 1978

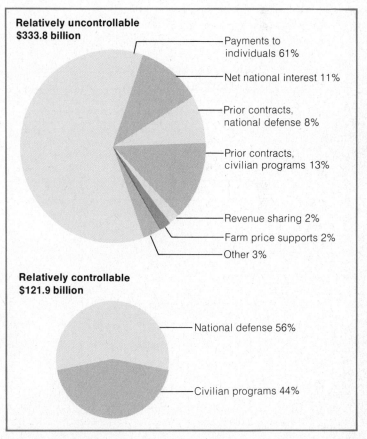

Source: The Budget of the United States Government, Fiscal Year 1980, pp. 560–561.

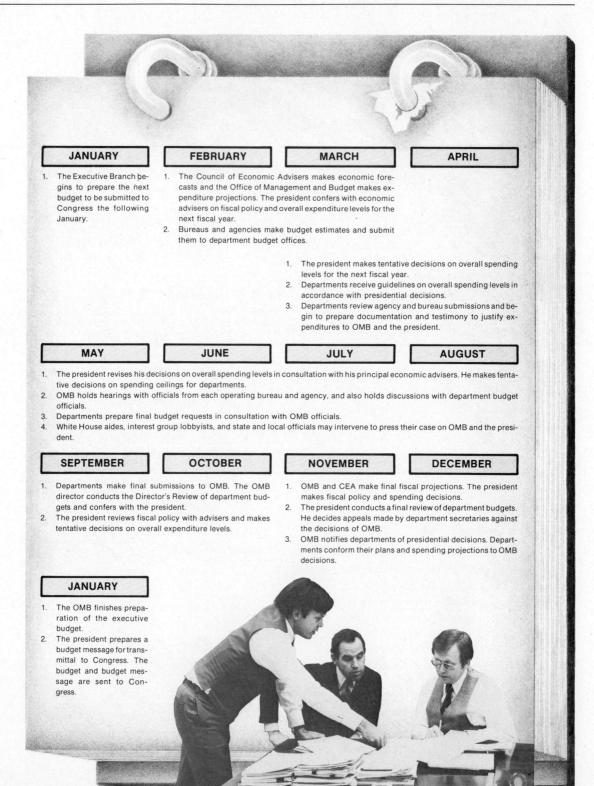

JANUARY

1. The Executive Branch begins to prepare the next budget to be submitted to Congress the following January.

FEBRUARY

1. The Council of Economic Advisers makes economic forecasts and the Office of Management and Budget makes expenditure projections. The president confers with economic advisers on fiscal policy and overall expenditure levels for the next fiscal year.
2. Bureaus and agencies make budget estimates and submit them to department budget offices.

MARCH   **APRIL**

1. The president makes tentative decisions on overall spending levels for the next fiscal year.
2. Departments receive guidelines on overall spending levels in accordance with presidential decisions.
3. Departments review agency and bureau submissions and begin to prepare documentation and testimony to justify expenditures to OMB and the president.

MAY   **JUNE**   **JULY**   **AUGUST**

1. The president revises his decisions on overall spending levels in consultation with his principal economic advisers. He makes tentative decisions on spending ceilings for departments.
2. OMB holds hearings with officials from each operating bureau and agency, and also holds discussions with department budget officials.
3. Departments prepare final budget requests in consultation with OMB officials.
4. White House aides, interest group lobbyists, and state and local officials may intervene to press their case on OMB and the president.

SEPTEMBER   **OCTOBER**

1. Departments make final submissions to OMB. The OMB director conducts the Director's Review of department budgets and confers with the president.
2. The president reviews fiscal policy with advisers and makes tentative decisions on overall expenditure levels.

NOVEMBER   **DECEMBER**

1. OMB and CEA make final fiscal projections. The president makes fiscal policy and spending decisions.
2. The president conducts a final review of department budgets. He decides appeals made by department secretaries against the decisions of OMB.
3. OMB notifies departments of presidential decisions. Departments conform their plans and spending projections to OMB decisions.

JANUARY

1. The OMB finishes preparation of the executive budget.
2. The president prepares a budget message for transmittal to Congress. The budget and budget message are sent to Congress.

loyalty to the president, will often try an "end run" around him in order to get his or OMB's cuts restored by Congress.

What results from this elaborate process is a budget that tends to look pretty much like the budget of the year before, only slightly larger. Though the grand totals, and even the totals for particular departments, may be only incrementally different from prior budgets, there are often a host of major policy decisions buried deep in the budget at the level of particular bureaus and specific programs. During some years, for example, spending on space exploration and health research skyrocketed, even though the total federal budget increased only marginally. The decisions made by the president and Congress are rarely evident in the totals, but show up only in the particular items that happen to exert, for political or public-spirited reasons, a special lure for elected officials.[9]

While all this is going on, proposals to raise, cut, or revise taxes may be working their way through Congress by way of entirely different committees. Most tax bills, like most spending ones, originate with the president, usually after a prolonged debate within the executive branch. In 1954 and again in 1961, the Council of Economic Advisers proposed tax cuts to stimulate the economy; the Treasury Department opposed these moves; eventually the president (Eisenhower in 1954, Kennedy in 1961) sided with the Council. In 1966 the Council proposed a tax increase to help pay for the war in Vietnam and to curb inflationary pressures generated by spending on that war; President Johnson refused to go along. (Two years later he accepted the arguments for a tax hike, and a surcharge was enacted.) Many economists who believe the federal government should be able to raise and lower taxes easily and quickly in order to counteract tendencies toward recession or inflation in the economy have argued in favor of laws that would give the president standby authority to change taxes, within limits, at his discretion.[10] Congress has never approved such proposals.

Most major changes in the tax laws take many months to become law (over a year in the case of the 1976 bill), and thus the fiscal impact, if any, of tax changes may be slow in coming.

While Congress and the president argue about spending and taxing, the Federal Reserve Board is taking steps to increase or decrease the money supply independently of Congress and the president. This independence is not total, however: Congress can threaten the Fed with investigations and changes in its legislative charter, and the president can select (with the consent of the Senate) the chairman of the Fed who serves as chairman for a four-year term. (Arthur F. Burns, appointed by President Nixon in 1974, came up for reappointment in 1978. President Carter, seeking to influence Burn's decisions, held out the prospect to him of being reappointed chairman, but, when Burns persisted in policies Carter did not like, he was replaced as chairman by G. William Miller.) The independence of the Fed is great enough, however, so that it has "leaned against the wind," tightening the money supply to curb inflation at times when other officials were increasing expenditures in order to reduce unemployment. Democratic Presidents Truman, Johnson, and Carter have all, at various times, complained of the Fed, while Republican presidents have tended to be supportive of it and critical of the spending programs enacted by Congress.

POLITICS AND ECONOMIC POLICY

The uncertain state of economic knowledge, the conflict over different economic goals, and the bewildering and uncoordinated complexity of the machinery that makes economic decision, taken together, make it difficult to produce an economic policy that is well suited to economic reality. But these difficulties do not mean that such policies as emerge are not adapted to any reality. Though the president cannot, in fact, meet the public expectation that he "manage"

Source: From a table in *The American Presidency,* by Richard M. Pious, p. 268. © 1979 by Richard M. Pious, Basic Books, Inc., Publishers, New York.

the economy, he can do two things. First, he can tip those few major policy decisions that are his to make in one direction or another depending on their presumed economic effect. He can, for example, cut or increase the controllable part of the federal budget by some amount (perhaps a few billion dollars one way or another), depending on whether he wants to stimulate or cool off economic activity. What Congress does with his budget, of course, is another matter. Or he can try to put pressure on corporations and labor unions to restrain price and wage increases.

Second, he can shape his policies to suit his reelection needs. Since the nineteenth century the government has used money to affect the electoral prospects of its elected leaders. At first, this took the form of patronage to the party faithful and money benefits to significant blocs of voters. (The massive system that dispensed pensions to Union army veterans of the Civil War was operated in ways that did no harm to the political fortunes of the Republican party.) Though the importance of patronage has been much reduced with the spread of civil service, spending on the clientele of various federal programs to increase their support for the party in power continues on an even larger scale. And to this has been added an array of new, more broadly based programs that can be used, within limits, to stimulate the economy as a whole.

Stimulating the Economy in Election Years

There is evidence, not only in the United States but in most major democratic nations, of a clear tendency on the part of politicians in office to stimulate the economy just before elections in order to enhance their prospects for being returned to office. During the period 1961 to 1972, real disposable income (that is, the amount of money the average person receives, after taxes and adjusted for inflation) increased faster in election years than in nonelection years in nineteen out of twenty-seven democratic countries.[11] In this country, the rate of change in real disposable income increased in eight of the eleven election years but in only two of the ten

nonelection years that occurred during the administrations of Presidents Truman, Kennedy, Johnson, Nixon, and Ford. (Only during the Eisenhower years was this clear relationship between income and elections absent. This was in part because Eisenhower and his advisers believed in the desirability of a balanced, and small, federal budget.) Moreover, the unemployment rate tends to be lower just before presidential elections in the United States (and before comparable elections in several other countries).[12] Except during the Eisenhower years, the unemployment rate in this country has been, on the average, one percentage point lower on the day of a presidential election than it was a year or a year and a half earlier.

Adlai Stevenson, twice a Democratic presidential nominee, referred to preelection economic stimulation as the "liberal hour" when all but the sternest believers in fiscal restraint and balanced budgets embrace, for the moment, the need to spend more on things they believe the voters want. Ironically, it was Stevenson's opponent, Dwight Eisenhower, who was the notable exception to this. Richard Nixon, who was trying in 1960 to succeed Eisenhower in the White House, never forgot that his predecessor had allowed personal economic beliefs to prevail over electoral necessities. Nixon blamed his defeat at the hands of John F. Kennedy in part on the fact that just before the election a sluggish economy delivered the "pocketbook issue" to the Democrats.

There is nothing very mysterious about how a party in power produces short-run economic expansion. It is done, in an election year, chiefly by accelerating the amount of money spent on payments to individuals (such as social security and veterans' benefits) and on aid to states and cities. The amount of money involved in these transfer payments is large, but even more important, it is visible. Social security benefits were increased or coverage broadened in 1950, 1952, 1954, 1956, 1958, 1960, 1970, 1972, 1974, and 1976—all election years—as well as in a few nonelection years. Seven of the ten major increases in social security benefits since 1950 were enacted in election years.[13] Moreover, when benefits are increased, they usually become effective immediately—typically, between June and October of an election year—whereas increased taxes to pay (in part) for these benefits usually do not take effect until the following January. Finally, to make certain the voters get the message, social security beneficiaries receive with their larger checks a printed notice that mentions the name of the incumbent president.

The same holds true for veterans' benefits: they have increased at an average annual rate of $660 million in the third quarter of years with elections but by only one-third as much in years without elections.[14] Grants to states and localities in the last quarter of 1972 (an election year) were more than 50 percent higher than they were in the last quarter of 1971.[15]

Some of these election-year increases in spending can be accomplished by the president acting alone, as when President Nixon in 1972 ordered a speed-up of payments on programs already approved by Congress in order to get the money out before the votes were counted.[16] Indeed, in preparing for that election, economists in OMB developed and tested elaborate statistical models to show the effect on votes of changes in per capita income and transmitted these results to the political staff of the White House.[17]

But many of the changes in spending plans require the consent of Congress, and often (as between 1968 and 1976) Congress and the presidency are controlled by different political parties. This party split does not prevent agreement on election-year spending plans, however, because incumbents, whether Democrats or Republicans, have a common interest in reelection. Both Republican President Nixon and Democratic congressmen could and did take credit for spending increases in 1972 (even on occasion for increases that they had opposed).

The political strategy of economic stimulus in election years seems to work, though the evidence on this is not entirely consistent. A number of

❝ To make certain the voters get the message, social security beneficiaries receive with their larger checks a printed notice that mentions the name of the incumbent president.**❞**

Higher social security payments

Your social security payment has been increased by 20 percent, starting with this month's check, by a new statute enacted by the Congress and signed into law by President Richard Nixon on July 1, 1972.

The President also signed into law a provision which will allow your social security benefits to increase automatically if the cost of living goes up. Automatic benefit increases will be added to your check in future years according to the conditions set out in that law.

Taken from Edward R. Tufte, *Political Control of the Economy* (Princeton, N.J.: Princeton University Press, 1978), p. 32.

This statement was in the envelopes in which social security checks were mailed to recipients in October 1972.

studies suggest that increases in real disposable income lead to increases in the percentage of votes won by incumbents. It has been estimated that a 1 percent increase in real disposable income produces a 1.3 percent increase in an incumbent president's popular vote. The party in control of Congress will usually lose seats in off-year (i.e., nonpresidential) elections, but when disposable income is rising, that loss is much less than ordinarily.[18]

Democrats and Republicans Agree on the "Pocketbook Issue"

Richard Nixon explained his defeat in 1960, and earlier Republican party reversals in the elections of 1954 and 1958, by the Eisenhower administration's failure to stimulate the economy:

I knew from bitter experience how, in both 1954 and 1958, slumps which hit bottom early in October contributed to substantial Republican losses in the House and Senate. The power of the "pocket-book" issue was shown more clearly perhaps in 1958 than in any off-year election in history. . . . The bottom of the 1960 dip did come in October and the economy started to move up in November—after it was too late to affect the election returns. In October, usually a month of rising employment, the jobless rolls increased by 452,000. All the speeches, television broadcasts, and precinct work in the world could not counteract that one hard fact.[1]

After the Democrats took office in 1961, Paul Samuelson, an economic adviser to President John F. Kennedy, wrote to him as follows:

When my grandchildren ask me: "Daddy, what did you do for the New Frontier?", I shall sadly reply: "I kept telling them down at the office, in December, January, and April that, *What this country needs is an across the board rise in disposable income to lower the level of unemployment, speed up the recovery and the return to healthy growth, promote capital formation and the general welfare, insure domestic tranquility and the triumph of the Democratic party at the polls.*"[2]

[1] Richard M. Nixon, *Six Crises* (Garden City, N.Y.: Doubleday, 1962), pp. 309–311.

[2] Paul Samuelson, "Memorandum for the President and the Council of Economic Advisers: That 'April Second Look' at the Economy," March 21, 1961 (John F. Kennedy Presidential Library).

Source: Based on Edward R. Tufte, *Political Control of the Economy* (Princeton, N.J.: Princeton University Press, 1978), pp. 6–7.

Other Electoral Forces

The process of stimulating the economy does not go on continuously, however, because other needs must be met. Increased spending before an election may well contribute to inflation, and inflation, in turn, worries business leaders who are trying to decide how much money to borrow and invest in new plant capacity and who are engaged in international trade. Investment becomes much riskier if investors believe they will be repaid a few years from now in dollars that are worth only a fraction of their present value. International trade is harder to carry on if inflation pushes up the cost of American-made goods compared to the cost of those goods made abroad. Large federal budget deficits weaken the international value of the dollar. (In the long run, of course, a devalued dollar may compensate for domestic inflation to some degree, but that tendency affects different firms differently and, as John Maynard Keynes once said, in the long run we are dead.) A president after an election will try to deal with these concerns, partly because he wants the support of business for political as well as other reasons, and partly because he shares these concerns and knows that inflation harms many groups in society. Thus, after an election, the president tends to be restrained in his spending proposals (unless the economy happens to be in a slump) and devotes some of his efforts to "restoring business confidence."

If all this is true, how is it that the party in power ever loses an election? One obvious reason is that the economy cannot be easily managed. Even a president determined to increase his reelection chances by stimulating economic activity and passing out money benefits may discover that his stimulus policies do not work or his money benefits go unnoticed or unappreciated.

A second reason is that not all elections are decided on economic issues. War, crime, corruption, and civil rights have all exercised an important influence on voter preferences; so have traditional party loyalties and assessments of the candidates' personalities.

A third reason is that some elected officials have sufficiently strong views about the proper policy for long-term economic well-being that they are willing to sacrifice short-term political benefits. President Eisenhower avoided stimulating the economy precisely because he was convinced that fiscal restraint was better for the country. Such a policy was a bit easier for him to pursue than for many other presidents owing to his personal popularity. His would-be successor, Richard Nixon, paid the price for this policy. Key congressmen, especially the chairman of those committees with important influence of fiscal legislation, may come from sufficiently secure seats that they can afford to take unpopular positions on tax and spending laws. For example, in 1964 Congressman Wilbur Mills, then the powerful and politically unbeatable chairman of the House Ways and Means Committee, and Senator Harry F. Byrd, the equally formidable chairman of the Senate Finance Committee, wanted any tax cut to be accompanied by a cut in government expenditures. Sometimes such antispending congressmen prevail, and when they do, they may jeopardize their *party's* electoral chances without jeopardizing their own.

Fourth, the internal politics of the two parties affects how their presidents, and presidential hopefuls, will behave. As we saw in Chapter 6, the national nominating conventions of the two parties have increasingly been influenced by delegates with strong ideological convictions. Candidates respond to these preferences by moving (among Democrats) further left and (among Republicans) further right. But whereas liberals in the Democratic party favor government spending programs, conservatives in the Republican party do not. Thus, a Republican candidate may have to be opposed to such spending in order to get the nomination even though he may discover that favoring spending is necessary to win the election. Just such a dilemma was faced by President Ford in 1976. He vetoed many spending measures during an election year, partly out of conviction but partly also

Richard Nixon believed that his defeat in 1960 was in part the result of the conservative economic policies of his fellow Republican, President Eisenhower.

out of the realization that if he did not his party might well have given the nomination to his rival, Ronald Reagan. Ford's attempt to block Reagan may have led him to adopt policies that cost him the election.

Finally, external events can tie a president's hands. For several years, the United States has had a deficit in its balance of trade—that is, it has imported more goods than it has exported—and foreign confidence in the dollar has been declining. All this raises the price of what we must import, and thus contributes to inflation at home. To maintain the value of the dollar in international trade, a president may have to take steps unpopular at home, such as raising the price of oil and gasoline. Or he may have to take political responsibility for unpopular actions by the Federal Reserve Board, such as raising interest rates. Because the state of our economy is in part beyond the president's control and since his actions must take into account foreign pressures, his reelection prospects may suffer beyond what he can recapture by short-run increases in spending.

One unanswered question is whether popular dislike of high taxes and high rates of inflation will ultimately lead to the defeat of a president or his party regardless of how skillfully they pump money into the economy. In 1978 when California voters adopted Proposition 13, a measure that cut local property taxes sharply, some commentators saw in it the beginnings of a national "tax revolt." Similar measures quickly appeared on the ballot in several other states. Two Republican congressmen, Representative Jack F. Kemp and Senator William V. Roth, Jr., proposed a bill that would cut federal income-tax rates by 30 percent over a three-year period.

There is as yet little or no evidence that taxes and inflation significantly affect the reelection prospects of incumbents. Federal income taxes, unlike California property taxes, have not increased by much in recent years. In any event they are mostly paid by money withheld from paychecks so that income taxpayers never experience, as do property taxpayers, the painful process of handing over to the government money they have already received (and, most likely, spent). The federal government, unlike most states, can finance current programs by borrowing rather than by higher taxes, and the size and growth in the federal debt has rarely been an important political issue. National tax revolts have erupted in Denmark and Sweden, but tax levels are much higher there than in the United States (see Figure 16.3) and, in any event, it is not clear that the "revolt" lasted very long. While it is possible that taxes and inflation will begin to exert a greater effect on elections than short-term changes in disposable income, the best evidence so far suggests that politicians who are worried only about reelection will be inclined to stimulate the economy and raise incomes rather than cut taxes or inflation.

FIGURE 16.3   Tax Burdens in Twelve Nations

Country	Total tax revenues as percentage of gross national product, 1973
Norway	45.9%
Netherlands	43.8
Sweden	43.5
West Germany	37.3
France	36.9
Canada	33.9
United Kingdom	32.8
Italy	29.2
UNITED STATES	28.0
Switzerland	26.4
Australia	23.8
Japan	22.6

0   5   10   15   20   25   30   35   40   45   50%

Source: From a table in Joseph A. Pechman, *Federal Tax Policy*, 3rd ed. (Washington, D.C.: Brookings Institution, 1977), p. 342.

SUMMARY

Economic policy-making reflects strong majoritarian interests in economic conditions. It is reinforced, to some degree, by the fact that officeholders who stimulate the economy and increase real disposable income in the short run are usually reelected. The mechanisms for making this policy are highly decentralized and involve instruments, such as tax and spending laws, that are shaped by client and interest group politics.

The president is the key figure in economic policy and tends to be held accountable by the public for economic performance. This holds true even though he cannot control all the relevant institutions (such as the Federal Reserve System), faces disagreement within the executive branch (usually between the Treasury Department and the Council of Economic Advisers), and must obtain the consent of Congress to any tax or spending policy. Democratic nations, including the United States, tend to adopt measures aimed at increasing income and lower unemployment just before elections and at restoring business confidence just after elections. Public and elite opinion favors policies aimed at both unemployment and inflation, but liberals tend to emphasize the former and conservatives the latter.

Suggested Readings

Fisher, Louis. *Presidential Spending Power*. Princeton, N.J.: Princeton University Press, 1975. An exposition of the struggle between presidents and the Congress over impoundment—the refusal to spend appropriated money.

Maisel, Sherman J. *Managing the Dollar*. New York: W. W. Norton, 1973. Nontechnical discussion of how the Federal Reserve Board works, by a former member.

Ott, David J., and Attiat F. Ott. *Federal Budget Policy*, 3rd ed. Washington, D.C.: Brookings Institution, 1977. Factual discussion of how the budget is devised and enacted, but with little attention to political factors.

Pechman, Joseph A. *Federal Tax Policy*, 3rd ed. Washington, D.C.: Brookings Institution, 1977. Description of federal tax policy and a discussion of the desirability and feasibility of proposed changes.

———."Making Economic Policy: The Role of the Economist," in Fred I. Greenstein and Nelson W. Polsby, eds., *Handbook of Political Science*. Reading, Mass.: Addison-Wesley, 1975. See Vol. 6, Ch. 2. Good introductory discussion of the main elements of economic policy-making with an emphasis on the role economists play.

Pious, Richard M. *The American Presidency*. New York: Basic Books, 1979. See Chs. 8, 9. The role of the president in making the budget and in fiscal policy, with special attention to the role of advisers.

Tufte, Edward R. *Political Control of the Economy*. Princeton, N.J.: Princeton University Press, 1978. Analyzes the relationship between economic policy-making and the electoral needs of politicians.

17 Social Welfare

Like every modern government, the United States has scores of programs that affect in varying ways the welfare of its citizens. Four are of special significance: the Social Security Act of 1935, the Economic Opportunity Act (or "War on Poverty") of 1964, the Medicare Act of 1965, and the Family Assistance Plan (proposed in 1969 but not passed). At their inception these laws were among the most controversial social welfare policies that Congress had ever considered, and parts of some of them remain controversial today. Moreover, Social Security and Medicare account for about two-thirds of all the money spent by the federal government on social welfare programs. In this chapter we shall look at the politics of these four proposals, not to acquire a comprehensive understanding of

Welfare, once a local responsibility, has become a federal one. On the left is a visiting nurse in a city slum around 1910; right, President Lyndon Johnson signs the Medicare Act in 1965 in the company of Senator Hubert Humphrey (standing) and former President Harry S. Truman (seated).

all forms of welfare politics, but because these proposals illustrate to varying degrees what was called, in Chapter 14, majoritarian politics. There are other social welfare programs, such as those providing benefits to veterans, that have quite different political origins (they tend to be more client-oriented).

Every nation, rich or poor, has welfare problems of some sort. Broadly speaking, these take one of two forms. First, some persons in every society face special disabilities in earning a living because they are old, handicapped, sick, blind, or members of a group (such as a racial minority) that is denied access to jobs. Second, even among persons able and willing to work, substantial differences in income result from differences in skill, education, intelligence, luck, energy, family connections, or whatever. Every Western industrial nation has programs aimed at aiding persons with disabilities. Some governments also attempt, deliberately, to narrow the differences in income by (for example) taxing the rich more heavily than the poor or taking money from the well-off and giving it to the less-well-off. In addition to these efforts to alter the distribution of income, many government policies have the incidental and perhaps unintended effect of changing that distribution, making it either more or less than equal.

HISTORY OF WELFARE IN THE UNITED STATES

By and large, welfare policies in the United States have been aimed at helping people with disabilities, not at redistributing income.[1] Some redistribution may occur, of course. After all, the money given to the disabled is taken from people paying taxes, and the net effect may be to lessen (or increase) differences in income. But American policy has not had income redistribution as its principal or explicit goal. As we shall see, one major reason for this is that

whereas helping the disabled has had a great deal of popular support, redistributing income has not.

Compared to the welfare policies of most other Western democratic nations, those of the United States display two striking features. First, they were adopted here much later than in other nations, and, second, their origins and much of their administration reflect the important role played by the states.

By 1935, when Congress passed the Social Security Act, at least twenty-two European nations already had similar programs on the books, as did a number of countries elsewhere, including Australia and Japan.[2] Germany was perhaps the first to create a nationwide social security program when it developed sickness and maternity insurance in 1883. Six years later it added old-age insurance, and, in 1927, unemployment insurance.

England offers perhaps the clearest contrast with the United States. In 1906 a national system of old-age pensions was set up, followed five years later by a plan for nationwide health and unemployment insurance.[3] England had a parliamentary regime in which a political party with liberal sentiments and a large majority had come to power. With authority concentrated in the hands of the prime minister and his cabinet, there was virtually no obstacle to carrying into effect measures, such as welfare programs, that commended themselves to party leaders on grounds of either principle or party advantage. Moreover, the British Labour party was then beginning to emerge. Though still small (it had only thirty seats in Parliament in 1906), it numbered among its leaders people who had been influential in formulating welfare programs that the leaders of the dominant Liberal party backed. And once these programs were approved, they were in almost all cases nationally run. There were no state governments to whom authority had to be delegated or whose different experiences had to be accommodated.

Moreover, the British in 1906 were beginning

to think in terms of social class, to accept the notion of an activist government, and to make welfare the central political issue. Americans in 1906 also had an activist leader, Theodore Roosevelt; there was a Progressive movement; and labor was well along in its organizing drives. But the issues were defined differently in the United States. Progressives, or at least most of them, emphasized the reform of the political process—by eliminating corruption, weakening the parties, and improving the civil service—and attacked bigness by breaking up industrial trusts. Though some Progressives favored the creation of a welfare state, they were a distinct minority. They had few allies in organized labor (which in any case was skeptical of public welfare programs) and could not overcome the general distrust of big government and the strong preference for leaving matters of welfare in state hands. In sum, what ordinary politics brought to England in 1906–1911, only the crisis politics of 1935 would bring to the United States.

Federalism powerfully influenced the development of a national welfare program. Since the Constitution was silent on whether Congress had the power to spend money on welfare and since powers not delegated to Congress were reserved to the states, it was not until the constitutional reinterpretation of the 1930s (see Chapter 13) that it became clear that the federal government could do anything in the area of social policy. At the same time, federalism meant that any state so inclined could experiment with welfare programs. Between 1923 and 1933 thirty states enacted some form of an old-age pension. By 1935 all but two states had adopted a "mother's pension"—a program whereby a widow with children was given financial assistance, provided she was a "fit mother" who ran a "suitable home." Paupers were given small doles by local governments, helped by private charities, or placed in "almshouses." Only one state, Wisconsin, had an unemployment insurance program.

Politically, the state programs had a double-

66 What ordinary politics brought to England in 1906–1911, only the crisis politics of 1935 would bring to the United States. **99**

The Great Depression: A bread line forms in a New York City street in December 1931.

edged effect: they provided opponents of a federal welfare system with an argument (the states were already providing welfare assistance), but they also supplied a lobby for federal financial assistance (state authorities would campaign for national legislation to help them out). Some were later to say that the states were the "laboratories" for experimentation in welfare policy. As we shall see, when the federal government entered the field in 1935, it did so in part by spending money

Senator Huey P. Long of Louisiana formed a "Share Our Wealth" movement that threatened the unity of the Democratic party. Left, in May 1935 he greets supporters of his effort to override President Roosevelt's veto of a veterans' bonus. Right, President Roosevelt meets with members of the Civilian Conservation Corps that put unemployed young men to work; he feared that Long might challenge him in the 1936 election.

through the states, thereby encouraging the formation in the states of a strong welfare bureaucracy whose later claims would be difficult to ignore.

THE FOUR LAWS IN BRIEF

Social Security Act of 1935

At the time the Great Depression began in 1929, the job of providing relief to needy persons fell to state and local governments or to private charities, and even these sources were primarily concerned with widows, orphans, and the elderly.[4] Hardly any state had a systematic program for supporting unemployed persons, though many states provided some kind of help if it was clear the person was out of work through no fault of his own. When the economy suddenly ground to a near standstill and the unemployment rate rose

to include one-fourth of the work force, private charities and city relief programs were nearly bankrupted.

The election of 1932 produced an overwhelming congressional majority for the Democrats and placed Franklin D. Roosevelt in the White House. Almost immediately a number of emergency measures were adopted to cope with the Depression by supplying federal cash to bail out state and local relief agencies and by creating public works jobs under federal auspices. These measures were recognized as temporary expedients, however, and were unsatisfactory to those who believed that the federal government had a permanent and major responsibility for welfare. Roosevelt created a Cabinet Committee on Economic Security to consider long-term policies. It drew heavily on the experience of European nations and on the ideas of various

American scholars and social workers, but understood that it would have to adapt these proposals to the realities of American politics. Chief among these was the widespread belief that any direct federal welfare program might be unconstitutional. The Constitution nowhere explicitly gave to Congress the authority to set up an unemployment compensation or old-age retirement program. And even if a welfare program was constitutional, it would be wrong because it violated the individualistic creed that persons should help themselves unless they were physically unable to do so.

Failure by the Roosevelt administration to produce a comprehensive social security program, it was thought, might well make the president vulnerable, in the election of 1936, to the leaders of various radical social movements. Huey Long of Louisiana was proposing a "Share Our Wealth" plan; Upton Sinclair was running for governor of California on a platform calling for programs to "End Poverty in California"; and Dr. Francis E. Townsend was leading an organization of hundreds of thousands of elderly persons on whose behalf he demanded government pensions of $200 a month.

The plan that emerged from the cabinet committee was carefully designed to meet popular demands within the framework of popular beliefs and constitutional understandings. It called for two kinds of programs: (1) an "insurance" program for unemployed and elderly persons to which workers would contribute and from which they would benefit when unemployed or upon retirement and (2) an "assistance" program for the blind, dependent children, and the aged. (Giving assistance as well as providing "insurance" for the aged was necessary because for the first few years the insurance program would not pay out any benefits.) The federal government would use its taxing power to provide the funds, but all of the programs (except for old-age insurance) would be administered by the states. Everybody, rich or poor, would be eligible for the insurance programs. Only the

Major Social Security Programs

(excluding Medicare)

There are two kinds of programs that are part of the Social Security system: those to which individual beneficiaries contribute and those paid for out of general revenues.

Contributory or "insurance" programs

1. **Old Age and Survivors Disability Insurance (OASDI):**

   Monthly payments to retired or disabled workers and their dependents and to the survivors of deceased workers

   Run entirely by the federal government through a trust fund

   Paid for by a payroll tax on employees and employers

2. **Unemployment Insurance:**

   Weekly payments, up to a limit, to persons out of work and looking for work

   State governments run program and set size of benefits

   Paid for by state and federal tax on employers, with money going to states

Noncontributory or "public assistance" programs

1. **Old-Age Assistance and Aid to the Blind and the Disabled:**

   Until 1974 payments were made to the aged, blind, and disabled even if not covered by an "insurance" program; run by states with federal funds

   Since 1974 this program has become the Supplementary Security Income (SSI) program, run and paid for entirely by the federal government on the basis of uniform national eligibility and payment standards

2. **Aid to Families with Dependent Children (AFDC):**

   Payments to families with dependent children, either one-parent families without a breadwinner or (in some states) two-parent families with an unemployed breadwinner

   Run by states that set own benefit and eligibility rules

   Paid for partly by states and partly by federal government

"Though bitterly opposed by some, the Social Security Act . . . passed swiftly and virtually unchanged through Congress.**"**

poor, as measured by a means test, would be eligible for the assistance programs. Though bitterly opposed by some, the Social Security Act, embodying these proposals, passed swiftly and virtually unchanged through Congress. It was introduced in January 1935 and signed by President Roosevelt in August of that year.

Economic Opportunity Act of 1964

When President Lyndon Johnson declared a War on Poverty, he did so, not in the midst of a depression, but at a time of prosperity. The program was aimed at a minority of the population—especially, but not exclusively, a black minority—that seemed not to be sharing in the general affluence.[5]

These "pockets of poverty" had recently been "discovered" by various writers and scholars. Books, such as Michael Harrington's *The Other America*,[6] and studies, such as those of the economist Robert Lampman,[7] had called attention to poverty amidst plenty. In both the Kennedy and Johnson administrations, key officials devised programs aimed at one or another part of what some felt amounted to a crisis—unemployment, inadequate schooling, juvenile delinquency, and urban squalor. Other persons in and out of the government felt that, in addition to conventional job-training and job-creation programs, there ought to be a concerted effort to mobilize poor persons so they could use their collective power to enlarge the opportunities open to them. Dozens of different (and sometimes inconsistent) ideas were proposed by presidential assistants in response to a presidential directive that a new approach to poverty be made ready for the 1964 State of the Union address.

The proposals might never have acquired any special sense of urgency save for two events. One was the civil rights movement, which was steadily becoming stronger, with demonstrations in hundreds of American cities climaxed in August 1963 by a "March on Washington" of some 200,000 persons, mostly black. The march drew attention to black demands for jobs as well as for civil rights. The second event, two and a half months later, was the murder of President Kennedy in Dallas. It led many legislators to rally behind President Johnson and to treat favorably those Kennedy proposals that had become part of the Johnson program.

Unlike the Social Security Act, the Economic Opportunity Act provided services rather than money to its beneficiaries. It called for:

- A Job Corps to train in camps young persons who were chronically unemployed;
- Literacy programs to teach English to adults not able to read or write;

The march on Washington of nearly a quarter million blacks and whites in August 1963 demanded a civil rights bill and a jobs program.

- A Neighborhood Youth Corps to provide work experience to young persons in cities;
- A work-study program to subsidize the part-time employment of college students from poor families; and
- A Community Action Program (CAP) to fund organizations that were to give residents in poor neighborhoods an opportunity for "maximum feasible participation" in planning and implementing service programs intended for their benefit.

The bill passed Congress in the summer of 1964 on a nearly party-line vote, with most Democrats in favor and most Republicans opposed. But this vote was only the beginning of the political struggle. Unlike the Social Security Act, which authorized cash transfers that could be handled by relatively simple administrative arrangements, the Economic Opportunity Act authorized the provision of a complex, poorly understood, incredibly difficult set of services (training, teaching, organizing, counseling) that led to the creation of hundreds of complicated and often controversial organizations in hundreds of American communities.

Much of the controversy arose because of the efforts in many cities to use the community action programs as mechanisms for transferring political power from city halls or established agencies (such as schools and welfare offices) to neighborhood-based organizations of poor persons or of leaders claiming to represent the poor. Mayors and school superintendents were frequently confronted by protest marches, sit-ins, and political campaigns organized by CAPs and paid for with federal funds. Not surprisingly, the officials complained to their congressmen, and efforts—many successful—were made to amend the Economic Opportunity Act to bring local CAPs more under the control of city hall.

Medicare Act of 1965

The idea of having the government pay the medical and hospital bills of the elderly and the poor had been discussed in Washington since the Social Security Act was being drafted in the 1930s. President Roosevelt and his Committee on Economic Security sensed that medical care would be very controversial, and so health programs were left out of the 1935 bill in order not to jeopardize its chances of passage.[8]

The proponents of the idea did not abandon it, however. Working mostly within the executive branch, they continued to press, sometimes publicly, sometimes behind the scenes, for a national health care plan. Democratic presidents, including Truman, Kennedy, and Johnson, favored it; Republican President Eisenhower opposed it; Congress was deeply divided on it. The American Medical Association attacked it as "socialized medicine." For thirty years, key policy entrepreneurs, such as Wilbur Cohen, worked to find a formula that would produce a congressional majority.

The first and highest hurdle to be overcome, however, was not Congress as a whole but the House Ways and Means Committee, and especially the man who was its powerful chairman from 1958 to 1975, Wilbur Mills of Arkansas. A majority of the committee members opposed a national health care program. Some members believed it wrong in principle; others feared that adding a costly health component to the social security system would jeopardize the financial solvency and administrative integrity of one of the most popular government programs. By the early 1960s a majority of the House favored a health care plan, but without the approval of Ways and Means it would never reach the floor.

The 1964 elections changed all that. The Johnson landslide produced such large Democratic majorities in Congress that the composition of the committees changed. In particular, the membership of the Ways and Means Committee was altered. Whereas before it had three Democrats for every two Republicans, after 1964 it had two Democrats for every one Republican. The House leadership saw to it that

Representative Wilbur Mills (D, Ark.), then the powerful chairman of the House Ways and Means Committee, changed his mind in 1965 and became a key supporter of the Medicare plan.

the new Democrats on the committee were strongly committed to a health care program. Suddenly, the committee had a majority favorable to such a plan, and Mills, realizing that a bill would pass and wanting to help shape its form, changed his position and became a supporter of what was to become Medicare.

The policy entrepreneurs in and out of the government who drafted the Medicare plan attempted to anticipate the major objections to it. First, the bill would apply only to the aged —those eligible for social security retirement benefits. This would reassure legislators worried about the cost of providing tax-supported health care for everybody. Second, the plan would only cover hospital expenses, not doctors' bills. Since doctors were not to be paid by the government, they would not be regulated by it; thus, presumably, the opposition of the American Medical Association would be blunted.

Unexpectedly, however, the Ways and Means Committee broadened the coverage of the plan beyond what the administration had thought was politically feasible. It added sections providing medical assistance, called Medicaid, for the poor (defined as those already getting public assistance payments) and public payment of doctors' bills for the aged (a new part of Medicare). The new, much-enlarged bill passed both houses of Congress with ease. The key votes pitted a majority of the Democrats against a majority of the Republicans.

Family Assistance Plan of 1969

Though most of the programs created by the Social Security Act proved quite popular, one—that providing public assistance to families with dependent children, or AFDC—became controversial as the number of "welfare mothers" grew rapidly in the 1960s. Between 1964 and 1969 the number of AFDC recipients increased by more than 60 percent while the costs more than doubled. This happened during a time of low and generally declining unemployment.[9]

AFDC was criticized for different reasons by different groups. Some objected to paying persons public money if they were able to work and to subsidizing the families of men who were unwilling to support them. Others felt that the women needed the money but that in many states the benefit levels were too low. (The states ran the program with federal financial assistance and decided how large the payments should be.) Others objected to the fact that intact poor families—that is, those with a mother and father both present in the home—were often excluded from any assistance, even though their incomes might be lower than those of single-parent families who were eligible for welfare payments. They thought that the program might even encourage families to break up. Still others felt that AFDC discouraged recipients from looking for jobs, since they lost their benefits if they went to work. And still others believed that the means tests used to find out if a person was eligible were demeaning.

For some time economists and others had been advocating a "guaranteed annual income" or "negative income tax" to replace AFDC that would put a floor under the incomes of all families, working and nonworking, single-parent and two-parent. President Nixon, at the urging of his urban affairs adviser, Daniel Patrick Moynihan, endorsed the concept, though he preferred calling it by a different name—the Family Assistance Plan, or FAP. It was a bold step, and if it had been passed, it would have meant a radical departure from traditional American welfare concepts. Instead of helping only persons who were disabled, retired, or unemployed, it would redistribute income by establishing a national minimum income below which no family, whether working or not working, would be allowed to fall. To minimize its boldness, one early proponent half-seriously suggested calling the bill the "Honest Christian Anti-Communist Working Man's Family Allowance National Defense Human Resources Rivers and Harbors Act of 1969."[10]

The plan was complicated, a fact that did not help it. Every family with children would receive a guaranteed minimum income. All able-bodied recipients would be required to work or enter a job-training program. Any money they earned would be offset against their FAP benefits, but at a rate less than dollar-for-dollar. Thus, as their job incomes rose, they would be able to keep some part of their FAP income as well, to a point (around $3,000 a year in job earnings) at which the FAP income would stop.

With the support of Wilbur Mills and other conservatives, FAP passed in the House. What appealed to conservatives was the hope that FAP would reduce "welfare cheating," the knowledge that the federal government would assume a bigger share of the costs of welfare now borne by states and cities, and the belief that FAP would provide stronger incentives for welfare recipients to find and hold jobs. (A penalty of several hundred dollars was to be deducted from the FAP payment of anyone refusing a suitable job or job training.) The fact that a conservative president had proposed FAP also reassured many Republicans. The ranking minority member of Ways and Means, John Byrnes of Wisconsin, worked as hard as Mills for the plan's passage.

Daniel Patrick Moynihan (left), a Democrat, became urban affairs adviser to Republican President Nixon, and persuaded him to propose a Family Assistance Plan that would provide a guaranteed minimum income for all families.

A majority of both Democrats and Republicans supported it.

It was a different story in the Senate. The bill was referred to the Finance Committee whose key members saw things very differently from Mills and Byrnes. Chairman Russell Long of Louisiana and ranking Republican member John Williams of Delaware thought FAP would make the "welfare mess" even worse by adding a large number (some said as many as 14 million) of persons to the welfare rolls, increasing welfare costs, and providing inadequate work incentives. By now, some liberal senators were also becoming skeptical. Their objections were precisely the opposite of the conservatives: FAP would not increase welfare benefits enough, too many persons would be left in poverty, and the work incentives were too severe. Moreover, liberal senators were suspicious of any welfare plan put forth by Nixon. Senator Fred Harris of Oklahoma, a liberal member of the Finance Committee,

66Three of the four proposals—Social Security, Economic Opportunity, and Medicare—found the great majority of Democrats pitted against the great majority of Republicans.**99**

offered an amendment to raise substantially the level of benefits (and, of course, of costs).

By 1972, not only was the bill dead but the idea underlying it was very nearly dead as well. (In the presidential campaign that year, Senator George McGovern offered a version of a guaranteed annual income that was poorly presented, quickly attacked, and hastily withdrawn.) In part the bill was defeated because there is no "welfare reform" capable of simultaneously keeping costs down, benefits high, and work incentives strong. President Carter discovered this when he introduced his own version of a guaranteed income plan (the "Program for Better Jobs and Income"), only to encounter many of the same objections as those made against FAP.

THE POLITICS OF WELFARE

Presidential Initiative

These four examples suggest five generalizations about the politics of welfare policy-making. First, the initiative in welfare politics—at least when a new policy is proposed—comes from the president. Presidential ideas—not those of interest groups or congressmen—dominate the legislative politics of welfare. In developing their proposals, the presidents rely heavily on specialists and experts in and out of the government. Roosevelt in 1935, Johnson in 1964 and 1965, and Nixon in 1969 turned to professionals and academics to help formulate their proposals.

Ideological Debate

Second, the debate on three of the four policies was heavily ideological. At issue in Social Security, Medicare, and Family Assistance were profound differences of opinion over whether it was proper for the government to take this action at all and whether the action was compatible

with fundamental American values. In 1935 Congress debated the legitimacy of the federal government assuming responsibility for supporting people in their old age and the constitutionality of creating any federal program at all in an area, welfare, that traditionally had been left to the states and localities. In the years leading up to 1965, Congress argued heatedly over whether the government should intervene in private medical and hospital practice, with doctors fearing red tape and government controls and their opponents pointing to the unmet health needs of the poor and the aged. In 1969 the propriety of a guaranteed annual income for every family, whether working or not, was at issue, as well as the more practical questions of costs and administration.

Social Security and Medicare divided liberals from conservatives in fairly clear fashion. FAP produced so much intellectual and political confusion that a curious coalition of liberals and conservatives supported it in the House and defeated it in the Senate. Only the Economic Opportunity Act—the War on Poverty of 1964—escaped an ideological debate, largely because it seemed to involve providing disadvantaged persons with services rather than incomes. In the American value system, many people find it easier to accept the idea of the government helping people overcome disabilities (by education or training) rather than transferring money from one group to another. As the act was implemented, however, it became clear that it raised a major ideological question—whether, and how, political power in the cities should be given to persons claiming to represent the poor.

Party Preferences

Third, the vote on new welfare policies tends to follow party lines rather closely. Table 17.1 shows the key votes in the House on each of the four welfare measures. To a larger degree than is true of most items of congressional business, three of the four proposals—Social Security, Economic Opportunity, and Medicare—found the great majority of Democrats pitted against the great majority of Republicans. If one were to remove the votes of southern Democrats from the figures, the partisan nature of this issue would be even clearer. (Conservative southern Democrats were more likely to oppose each of the four welfare measures than were the more liberal northern Democrats.)

Because conservative southern Democrats have frequently voted with Republicans against welfare measures (at least when they were initially proposed), and since southern Democrats and Republicans taken together have frequently constituted a majority of the House and the Senate, the passage of a controversial new welfare plan often required the existence in Congress of Democratic majorities so large that northern Democrats outnumbered southern Democrats and Republicans combined. Such extraordinary majorities did in fact exist in 1935 and 1965 when the two most important welfare programs were adopted. The election of 1932 had brought in a huge Democratic majority, and the congressional election of 1934 made that majority even larger, so that by 1935 Democrats outnumbered Republicans by three to one in the House and by better than two to one in the Senate. No conservative coalition could block Social Security in 1935.

The 1964 Johnson landslide also produced extraordinary Democratic majorities in Congress, with Democrats outnumbering Republicans by better than two to one in the House and Senate. Thus, conservative Democrats allied with Republicans were too few to defeat Medicare. No such extraordinary majorities existed in 1964 when the Economic Opportunity Act was passed, but other special circumstances prevailed to overcome opposition: it was a service-providing rather than an income-transferring program, the murder of President Kennedy had made many legislators desirous of honoring his memory by supporting his policies, and President Johnson was at the time exceptionally popular in the country as well as skillful in dealing with Congress.

TABLE 17.1   Key Votes on Four Major Welfare Proposals in the House of Representatives

Proposals	Democrats	Republicans
Social Security[1]		
Yes	252	1
No	45	95
Economic Opportunity[2]		
Yes	204	22
No	40	145
Medicare[3]		
Yes	226	10
No	63	128
Family Assistance Plan[4]		
Yes	141	102
No	83	72

[1] Vote April 19, 1935, on motion to recommit HR 7260. A "yes" vote was *against* Social Security. To clarify the intent, these are counted as "no" votes in the table.
[2] Vote August 8, 1964, on S 2642.
[3] Vote April 8, 1965, on motion to recommit HR 6675. A "yes" vote was a vote *against* Medicare. To clarify the intent, these are counted as "no" votes in the table.
[4] Vote April 16, 1970, on HR 16311.

Societal Values

Fourth, public opinion supported Social Security and Medicare (the two largest and most intensely debated welfare initiatives), but was at best closely divided over FAP. (At the time of its passage, the War on Poverty had no clear status in public opinion, probably because it was a complicated collection of different and poorly understood programs.) Though the art of surveying public opinion was in its infancy in 1935, it seems clear that large majorities favored government pensions for old people and that somewhat smaller majorities also favored unemployment compensation.[11] In the early 1960s popular majorities supported the Medicare concept well in advance of the passage of the act.[12] In short, Congress followed the general outlines of public opinion on these matters.

Attitudes Toward Welfare

Americans have ambivalent attitudes toward welfare programs. They want the government to help those who cannot help themselves or who have genuine needs, but they think that there are many persons on welfare who do not deserve it. The answers citizens gave to a Harris Survey in 1976 reveal this ambivalence.

The following year a New York Times/CBS Poll showed that a majority of citizens were opposed to a guaranteed minimum income for all persons and were critical of most welfare programs, but strongly favored a national health care program, food stamps, and aid to poor families with dependent children.

The reason why opinions were more deeply divided on FAP is suggestive of the political limitations on welfare reform. Politically successful welfare programs have been those that seemed to provide assistance to persons unable to help themselves rather than those that involved redistributing income. From the earliest days of social security, the public seems to have preferred the concept of "insurance" over "relief" as a way of helping those unable to work and

The Harris Survey

	AGREE	DISAGREE	NOT SURE
It is not right to let people who need welfare go hungry.	94%	4%	2%
Too many people on welfare could be working.	89	6	5
Too many people on welfare cheat by getting money they are not entitled to.	85	9	6
Many women whose husbands have left them with several children have no choice but to go on welfare.	74	22	4
Criteria for getting on welfare are not tough enough.	64	23	13
The welfare system allows no dignity for the poor.	45	46	9
Most people go on welfare only as a last resort.	39	54	7
People on welfare should just be given the money and end all the red tape.	16	77	7

The New York Times/CBS Poll

	NEED HELP	COULD GET ALONG	NO OPINION
Do you think that most people who receive money from welfare could get along without it if they tried, or do you think they really need this help?	31%	54%	15%

	YES	NO	
Do you approve of most government-sponsored welfare programs?	32	58	10
Do you approve of a guaranteed minimum income?	44	50	6
Do you approve of a national health care program?	60	33	7
Do you approve of food stamps for the poor?	81	13	6
Do you approve of aid to poor families with dependent children?	81	13	6
Do you approve of health care for the poor?	82	13	5

Source: The Harris Survey, February 1976. Reprinted by permission of the Chicago Tribune–New York Syndicate, Inc.

Source: *The New York Times*, August 3, 1977. © 1977 by The New York Times Company. Reprinted by permission.

job-creation over cash-payment programs as ways of helping those able to work but lacking jobs.[13] Moreover, though opinion has always supported a major role for the federal government in dealing with poverty, those holding that opinion have also believed that welfare has undesirable effects by reducing the incentive to work and by stimulating cheating, and that much (though not all) poverty is the result of individual failings rather than social circumstances.[14] Some of these apparently inconsistent attitudes can be understood as popular reactions to words that have become symbols. "The poor" and "the needy" are words that evoke sympathy and concern, and "insurance" is a term that suggests self-help and pay-as-you-go. On the other hand, "welfare" is a term that conjures up images of "chiselers," and "relief" is a term that implies a "dole." These attitudes express a genuine tension in popular thought: citizens want the government to help the poor but fear the consequences of many of the programs that supply that help.

When FAP was proposed, the idea of giving money to the working poor to bring them up to some minimum income level received mixed reactions from the public. Though some surveys found strong support for the idea of "welfare reform," that term was too general to mean much. When the question was stated more precisely—"putting a floor under every family's income"—people split almost evenly.[15] Opposition was strongest in the South, and it was southern senators who led the fight against FAP.

Interest Group Participation

Fifth, and finally, interest groups played a role in some of the bills, but not by and large on behalf of their own members. Welfare politics does not usually involve groups of welfare recipients fighting it out with groups of taxpayers: welfare recipients and taxpayers are rarely organized for lobbying purposes, for reasons explained in Chapter 8. Rather, most of the interest groups active on these issues expressed views based on the ideas and beliefs, rather than the material interests, of their leaders. There was scarcely any interest group activity at all in the fight over Social Security. Even organized labor, whose members stood to benefit from unemployment compensation, by and large remained on the sidelines. Nor were interest groups decisive in the Economic Opportunity Act. They were of great importance in Medicare and FAP, however. Clubs of senior citizens became active on behalf of Medicare, as did the AFL-CIO. The American Medical Association was a key opponent.

The mixed feelings of citizens about the good and bad features of welfare were reflected in the curious mixture of interest groups supporting and opposing FAP. The National Association of Manufacturers favored it, but the Chamber of Commerce opposed it. Various Jewish and Catholic welfare organizations generally favored it, but some key Protestant ones opposed it. The AFL-CIO was sympathetic but had reservations, as did several religious groups. Social workers were opposed as were the National Welfare Rights Organization, a group of militant welfare recipients, and several civil rights organizations. The clear, liberal-versus-conservative split that characterized earlier welfare proposals, which offered relatively simple choices (for or against old-age pensions, for or against unemployment compensation, for or against federal payment of hospital bills for the elderly), was replaced, in the case of FAP, by complex and apparently inconsistent alliances because what people wanted out of "welfare reform" was itself complex and inconsistent.

TWO KINDS OF WELFARE POLITICS

Majoritarian Politics

Certain welfare programs have offered widely distributed benefits paid for by widely distributed tax burdens. The old-age pensions created in 1935 and the Medicare plan created in 1965 were preeminently policies of this sort. Almost everybody will reach the age of sixty-five; almost everybody will become eligible for social security pensions and Medicare; and almost everybody helps pay for this through payroll deductions. The development of these policies displays the features of what was called earlier "majoritarian politics."

At the outset, the debate in Washington was not whether the welfare policies were popular—they clearly were—but whether it was legitimate for the government to provide such benefits. After an intense, often ideological controversy, the measures were approved by a Congress that, in each instance, happened to have large liberal majorities in power. Once the issue of legitimacy of government action was settled and the benefits began to flow, it quickly became good politics to support frequent increases in the scope of the program and the size of the benefits. From 1950 to 1975 there was only one occasion (1959–1965) when Congress allowed more than two years to pass without either increasing the level of benefits paid out to the elderly and their survivors, broadening the list of occupations covered by the plan, or both.[16] It is not hard to see why. The House comes up for reelection every two years. Though many members no doubt voted for larger social security benefits out of a sincere

belief that the elderly needed more help, few could have been unaware of the fact that it was a political asset to be able to say during one's reelection campaign that one had voted to provide more of a highly popular program. The legislation expanding social security was always immensely complex and some provisions remained highly controversial. However, by 1954 the program was so well established that a Republican president proposed to a Republican-controlled Congress that benefits and coverage be enlarged. The vote in the House was 356 to 8 in favor.

Majoritarian politics remains good politics unless costs to the individual begin to go up faster than his or her benefits. Though Social Security and Medicare were supposed to be "insurance" programs, in fact they were not. What a retired or ill person took out in benefits bore little relationship to what he or she had earlier contributed in payments. In effect, the benefits received by the present generation of elderly persons is paid for by taxes on the present generation of workers. This was not a problem so long as there were plenty of workers to contribute for every eligible retired person, and thus the payroll taxes for each worker remained small. By the 1970s, however, the proportion of elderly persons in the population had begun to grow so that there were fewer and fewer workers to support every retired person. In addition, inflation led to sharp increases in benefit levels. In 1950, for example, there were fourteen persons paying social security taxes for every one person drawing retirement benefits. By 1970, however, there were only four workers for every one beneficiary, and by the end of this century there may only be two workers for every retiree.[17] (See Table 17.2.)

Moreover, the social security tax must now pay for Medicare as well as for retirement and disability. With the growth in programs and benefits and the increase in the proportion of persons retired, the social security tax—once so small as to be scarcely noticed—has become sufficiently large to generate political com-

TABLE 17.2   Increasing Social Welfare Spending

Year	Federal expenditures		
	In billions of dollars	As percent of federal outlays	As percent of gross national product
1950	$ 10.5	26.2%	4.0%
1960	25.0	28.1	5.0
1965	37.7	32.6	5.7
1970	77.3	40.1	8.1
1976	198.3	56.0	12.3

Source: U.S. Bureau of the Census, Statistical Abstract of the United States, 1978, p. 327

Note: Includes all federal expenditures, from trust funds and from general revenues, for social insurance, public assistance, health, veterans' programs, education, and housing.

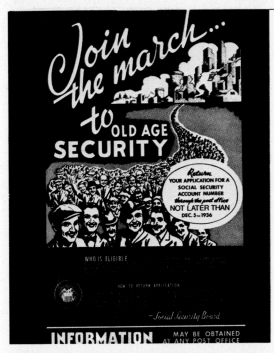

Though controversial at first, Social Security became a highly popular program that Congress continually expanded. By the mid-1970s, however, senior citizens were becoming so numerous as to threaten the solvency of the system.

❝Though Social Security and Medicare were supposed to be 'insurance' programs, in fact they were not. What a retired or ill person took out in benefits bore little relationship to what he or she had earlier contributed in payments.**❞**

plaints. In 1937 the combined tax was only 2 percent on a worker and his employer; in 1950 it had risen only slightly, to 3 percent. But by 1978 it was 10 percent and scheduled to go much higher. Even so, the social security trust fund was starting to run a deficit. Congress, for almost the first time, had to face some painful political choices. A policy amply supported by public opinion as long as current taxes were low and future benefits were high became less popular when present taxes became high.

Since everybody, the wealthy as well as the poor, receives retirement and Medicare benefits from the social security system, one might suppose that Congress would ease the tax burden by making these benefits available only to those in need. But there is not much chance of that happening because the plan was initially sold to Congress and the public as an "insurance"

program, one from which everybody who contributed was entitled to benefit. (A plan designed only for the needy and employing a means test would have been labeled a "dole" and encountered much tougher political opposition.) However, if everybody now contributing to social security taxes thinks of the program as "insurance" (though in fact it is not), they will expect to benefit from it and thus be ill-disposed to allow Congress to reduce or eliminate their benefits.

In 1977 Congress faced up to these problems by raising social security taxes over the next few years. It felt trapped by its own program. For the first time it had to raise taxes without raising benefits. The final bill carried the House by only twenty-six votes, a far cry from the near unanimous votes by which social security bills once passed. The political effects of the "insurance"

66Whereas for forty years it was thought to be good politics to enlarge old-age insurance benefits, it became increasingly 'bad politics' to do anything other than investigate, curtail, and attack the 'welfare' program.**99**

approach to retirement, unemployment, and disability benefits were accurately predicted by President Roosevelt when he first proposed it: "We put those payroll contributions there so as to give the contributors a legal, moral, and political right to collect their pensions and their employment benefits. With those taxes in there, no damn politician can ever scrap my social security program."[18]

Client Politics

Certain other welfare programs, especially Aid to Families with Dependent Children (AFDC) and the Community Action Program of the War on Poverty, were increasingly perceived by Congress and the public as examples of "client politics." The benefits seemed to be concentrated in a relatively small group of beneficiaries (welfare mothers, the inner city poor), while the costs were paid by all in the form of higher taxes. These programs followed a political history almost exactly the opposite of that of old-age pensions and Medicare. They were initially enacted with virtually no controversy, in part because both seemed to be supplying help to a small number of deserving persons, in part because the cost originally seemed negligible. There were relatively few unwed mothers with dependent children in 1935, and in 1964 the phrase "community action" seemed harmless. Welfare mothers and the inner city poor were, at first, small groups receiving modest benefits that cost the average taxpayer little.

As the number of families using AFDC grew dramatically and as some community action groups began using protest marches, sit-ins, and other forms of public display to advance their goals, public sentiment changed. Moreover, both programs became increasingly identified in the public mind as "black" programs. (In fact, a

majority of welfare mothers were white during the 1960s.) A program apparently (though not in fact) designed to provide money to black unwed mothers inevitably attracted the suspicion and hostility of a large proportion of the white majority. As a result, whereas for forty years it was thought to be good politics to enlarge old-age insurance benefits, it became increasingly "bad politics" to do anything other than investigate, curtail, and attack the "welfare" (that is, the AFDC) program.

When the AFDC program was first adopted as part of the Social Security Act, a mother needing assistance was perceived as a white woman with children living in a small town. Her husband had been killed in World War I or a mining accident. Thirty years later, a welfare mother was perceived as a black woman in a big-city public housing project whose children had been deserted by their father. This change in perceptions, which corresponded only partially with changes in reality, made "welfare" a controversial issue.

Between the majoritarian politics of old-age pensions and the client politics of AFDC, there are any number of intermediate cases. Unemployment compensation was more controversial than old-age pensions (though less so than AFDC). While most citizens knew they would someday be old but would never be mothers of deserted children, they were not sure whether they would be unemployed. Hence, they had mixed feelings about unemployment compensation. They knew some people genuinely needed it and worried that someday they might need it themselves, but they also suspected that some persons were abusing it by taking it though they were able to work. Similarly with FAP: most citizens wanted to reduce poverty, but few were confident it could be done without creating other problems.

Despite the unpopularity of the AFDC program in many quarters, the federal government does not cut it. This is not because its ultimate clients—welfare mothers—are well organized or politically powerful. Quite the contrary: owing to their large numbers and low-income status, welfare mothers are difficult to organize (see Chapter 8). There are, however, other intermediate "clients" to defend this and other public assistance programs directed at particular groups in society. These are the government officials, especially at the state and local levels, who run the programs and distribute the benefits. The "welfare bureaucracy," like the military bureaucracy or the school bureaucracy, is not inclined to endorse efforts to reduce its ranks or trim its programs. And since the welfare bureaucracy is chiefly part of state and local government, it is strategically situated to lobby in Congress against any effort to curtail federal grants to the states (for welfare as for any other purpose). Federalism, thus, was a factor both in delaying the introduction of a national social welfare program and in making fundamental changes in that program difficult. In addition, state administration of such programs as AFDC and unemployment insurance means that the level of benefits will vary greatly from one state to another (see Chapter 3).

SUMMARY

If this interpretation is correct, welfare politics in America can principally be explained by two factors: who benefits and who pays, and the beliefs citizens have about the nature of social justice. Neither factor is static: gainers and losers vary as the composition of society and the workings of the economy change, and beliefs about who deserves what are modified as attitudes toward work, the family, and the obligations of government change.

The benefits and costs of the policies help explain the popularity of two social welfare programs and the controversy surrounding a third. Social Security and Medicare provide widely distributed benefits and impose widely distributed costs. The politics surrounding their enactment and expansion have been majoritarian. The Aid to Families with Dependent Children (AFDC) program provided benefits to some at a cost to many. It has experienced a form of client politics, made especially controversial by the public perception of the program as one that served an "undeserving" group.

Popular beliefs about the meaning of social justice—and thus about who "deserves" public aid—not only help us understand why AFDC has become controversial but why the Family Assistance Plan failed to be enacted. It appeared to many to give money to persons who were able to work.

The congressional (as opposed to the parliamentary) system of government means that greater political effort and more time are required for the adoption of a new welfare policy. Finally, federalism means that the states will play a large role in determining how any welfare program is administered and at what level benefits shall be set.

Suggested Readings

Heclo, Hugh. *Modern Social Politics in Britain and Sweden*. New Haven, Conn.: Yale University Press, 1974. Comparative analysis of how social welfare programs came to Britain and Sweden.

Moynihan, Daniel Patrick. *Maximum Feasible Misunderstanding*. New York: The Free Press, 1969. Lively account of the intellectual and political origins of the Community Action Program of the War on Poverty.

————. *The Politics of a Guaranteed Income*. New York: Random House, 1973. Account, by a key participant, of the abortive effort to pass the Family Assistance Plan in 1969.

Piven, Frances Fox, and Richard A. Cloward. *Regulating the Poor*. New York: Pantheon, 1971. A neo-Marxist account of the adoption of the social security program and later welfare plans.

Sundquist, James. *Politics and Policy*. Washington, D.C.: Brookings Institution, 1968. Political history of the passage of the Economic Opportunity and Medicare acts in the 1960s.

Witte, Edwin E. *The Development of the Social Security Act*. Madison: University of Wisconsin Press, 1962. An account of the 1935 act by one of its principal architects.

18 Civil Liberties

Purpose of the Bill of Rights • Freedom of expression • Restrictions on free speech • The "clear and present danger" test • The states and the Bill of Rights • What kinds of expression are not protected • Crime and due process

MR. PRESIDENT
REMEMBER THE CONSTITUTION
"CONGRESS SHALL MAKE NO LAW----
ABRIDGING THE FREEDOM OF SPEECH.
OR OF THE PRESS---" THE POLITICAL
PRISONERS WHO BELEIVED IN THIS
GUARANTEE. ARE NOW SERVING 20
YEARS IN PRISON

The Framers of the Constitution believed they were creating a national government of strictly limited powers, and therefore they did not feel it was necessary to make a special list of those things that government could *not* do about speech or press. It would be enough, for example, that the Constitution did not authorize the government to censor newspapers; a Bill of Rights prohibiting censorship would be superfluous. The persons who gathered in the various states to consider ratifying that Constitution were not so optimistic. They suspected—rightly, as it turned out—that the government might well try to do things it was not expressly authorized to do, and they insisted that a list of things it should not do become part of that document. Hence, the Bill of Rights was added shortly after the Constitution was ratified. Until the Fourteenth Amendment was passed, the Bill of Rights applied only to the acts of the federal government.

Women picketed in front of the White House urging President Warren Harding to release political radicals arrested during his administration (left). Chicago police protected American Nazi party speakers in 1978.

That Bill of Rights is an important restriction on popular rule. It says that there are things a government cannot do even if a majority wants them done. But why would the government, to say nothing of a popular majority, ever want to do these things? In our review of the politics of policy-making, we have repeatedly observed the ability of small but intensely motivated minorities to block action that would impose heavy costs on them. Milk producers have successfully resisted efforts that would reduce government subsidies for their products, and trucking companies and truck drivers have been able to block efforts to introduce more competition (and presumably lower prices) into their industry. The political system has facilitated this kind of "client politics."

If a largely indifferent public permits various economic, occupational, or professional minorities to safeguard their own interests, why should other kinds of minorities—religious or ideological ones—require special constitutional protection? Just as the average citizen bears only slight costs created by the advantages enjoyed by milk producers or truck drivers, presumably the average citizen only bears slight (if any) costs from the publication and distribution of a Communist party newspaper or from the refusal of a member of Jehovah's Witnesses to recite the pledge of allegiance to the flag. If costs are small and widely distributed, then one would expect political activity to reduce those costs would be infrequent and often ineffective. Moreover, some of these "costs"—such as the consequences of people reading a Communist party newspaper—will occur in the distant future, if at all. Ordinarily, people are not politically sensitive to such distant or hypothetical burdens.

RIGHTS IN CONFLICT

There are at least two ways in which a minority can find itself vulnerable to government actions that restrict its freedom. One occurs when the issue involves a conflict between two persons or small groups, one of which stands to lose whatever the other stands to gain. Usually we think of "civil liberties" as rather abstract guarantees of the rights of everyone, all of which can be observed all of the time. In fact, the Constitution contains a list of *competing* rights and liberties, and sometimes that competition is crystalized in a struggle between two distinct interests, each of which asserts the primacy of the right it favors.

For example:
- Dr. Samuel H. Sheppard of Cleveland, Ohio, asserted his right to have a fair trial on the charge of having murdered his wife. Bob Considine and Walter Winchell, two radio commentators, as well as other reporters, asserted their right to broadcast whatever facts and rumors they heard about Dr. Sheppard and his love life. Two rights in conflict.
- The United States government has an obligation to "provide for the common defense" and, in pursuit of that duty, has claimed the right to keep secret certain military and diplomatic information. The *New York Times* claimed the right to publish such secrets as the "Pentagon Papers" without censorship in exercise of the freedom of the press. A duty and a right in conflict.
- Carl Jacob Kunz delivered inflammatory anti-Jewish speeches on the street corners of a Jewish neighborhood in New York City, suggesting, among other things, that Jews be "burnt in incinerators." The Jewish people living in that area were outraged. In view of this, the New York police commissioner revoked Kunz's license to hold public meetings on the streets. When he continued to air his views on the public streets, Kunz was arrested for speaking without a permit. Freedom of speech versus the preservation of public order.

These struggles over rights follow much the same pattern as interest group politics of the sort found in economic issues, even though the claims in question are those of individuals. Indeed, formal interest groups organize even in the field of civil liberties. The Fraternal Order of the Police complains of restrictions on police powers; the American Civil Liberties Union defends and seeks to enlarge those restrictions. Groups of Catholics have pressed for public support of parochial schools; groups of Protestants and Jews have argued against it. Sometimes the opposed groups are entirely private; sometimes one or both are government agencies. (When the Supreme Court decided the cases given above, Sheppard, the *New York Times*, and Kunz all won.)[1]

There is a second way whereby civil liberties become an issue. A political entrepreneur can mobilize large numbers of normally indifferent citizens and legislators to support restrictions on the freedom of minorities. We saw in Chapter 15 how this was done with respect to consumer and environmental protection legislation; an analogous process can be found in civil liberties cases. In entrepreneurial politics, someone in or out of the government is able to dramatize, usually in highly moralistic terms, the real or imagined threat to widely shared values posed by the activities of some sinister force in order to mobilize a temporary majority on behalf of legislation that will curb the evil. Often this mobilization has required the existence of a crisis or scandal.

There have been several periods in American history when the politics of civil liberties became a mass issue rather than a contest between opposed parties who were directly affected by the outcome: the sedition laws of the late eighteenth century, the "red scare" of the period 1917–1920, the relocation of Japanese-Americans from California during the Second World War, the anti-Communist agitation of the late 1940s and early 1950s, and the debate over secrecy in government in the early 1970s. In each case, either war (World War I, World War II, the Korean War, the war in Vietnam) or the threat of war (tension between France and the United States in 1795–1800 and between the Soviet Union and the United States in 1945–1955) provided the

The conflict of rights: A bookstore sells pornography across the street from a family restaurant. Should the government protect those who wish to patronize the bookstore or those who wish to keep stores away from areas frequented by children?

political backdrop and much of the emotional energy for the issue. In each case, the issue arose suddenly and disappeared just as suddenly within a few years. And in most cases, the extent of the restrictions on civil liberties tended to be less than in the previous instance, with the result that the scope of those liberties tended to be larger after the issue subsided than it had been before it erupted.

NATIONAL SECURITY AND CIVIL LIBERTIES

The Sedition Act

Though the First Amendment to the Constitution had been adopted in 1791, it was not until 1798 that a serious debate developed over its meaning. That debate was precipitated by the bitter partisan quarrel between the Federalists, then in power in Washington, and the Jeffersonian Republicans, who were hoping to come to power in the 1800 presidential election. But more was at stake than the usual bickering between the "ins" and the "outs": the United

❝Smoldering popular passions often require the spark of a dramatic event before they burst into political flame.**❞**

States was engaged in what President John Adams called a "half war" with France. French ships were seizing American merchant vessels en route to England in order to prevent American supplies from reaching a country with which France was at war. Americans were outraged, and a special session of Congress in 1797 authorized the calling to arms of eighty thousand militia and the building of new warships.

The country was not, however, united in its attitudes toward France. To the Federalists, France was the symbol of the excesses of mob rule. The French Revolution of 1789 had led to the Reign of Terror of 1793–1794, when hundreds of real and imagined opponents of the Revolution were put to death, to the abolition of the worship of God, and to military campaigns against other nations. To the Jeffersonian Republicans, the French Revolution, however deplorable its excesses, represented an enlargement of popular rule and thus ought to be supported by Americans. The philosophical differences between Federalists and Jeffersonians that had been growing since the first administration of George Washington were symbolized, perhaps in exaggerated form, by the issue of our relations with France. Federalists were concerned about the maintenance of public order and the development of a national economy and felt that a strong federal government was essential to these tasks; Jeffersonians were concerned about the maintenance of personal liberties and believed that the preservation of states' rights was essential to that end. To Federalists, pro-French sentiment was tantamount to an endorsement of anarchy; to Jeffersonians, anti-French feeling was tantamount to an opposition to liberty.

Smoldering popular passions often require the spark of a dramatic event before they burst into political flame. That spark was the XYZ affair, a shabby incident involving the refusal of the French foreign minister, Talleyrand, to meet with American envoys to discuss ways of ending the "half war" unless he was first paid a bribe of a quarter of a million dollars. ("X, Y, and Z" referred to the then-anonymous intermediaries whom Talleyrand used to solicit the bribe.) When news of this affair was revealed to the United States, the nation was galvanized into anti-French feeling, and war preparations began.

During this period newspapers were becoming a major political force. There were over 230 of them in the country by 1800, and few were models of moderation or objectivity.[2] They were partisan in outlook and vituperative in tone, printing rumors as if they were facts, publishing scurrilous but anonymous essays, and in general making life miserable for public officials they disliked.

The Federalist party struck back by introducing a series of bills in 1798, the most important of which was the Sedition Act that would make it a crime, punishable by fine and imprisonment, to write, utter, or publish "any false, scandalous, and malicious writing" against the president, the Congress, or the government "with intent to defame" the government or to "excite against [the government] the hatred of the people." Persons charged with this crime—seditious libel—could offer in their defense evidence showing that their assertions were true and were entitled to a trial by jury.

The debate over the Sedition Act was the first effort by the new Republic to define the acceptable limits of public critcism of government. The Federalist position was that the First Amendment, while it prohibited censorship (i.e., the government preventing a newspaper from publishing a story), did not prohibit punishing a newspaper for having printed a false and malicious story. Just as individual citizens had the right to sue a newspaper for publishing a libelous story about them, so also the government had the right to sue a newspaper for libeling it. Contrary to what is often supposed, the Jeffersonian Republicans did not argue in response that the press should be free from any government controls. Instead, they argued chiefly that the First Amendment did not authorize the *federal* government to punish the press for seditious libel. Punishing what Jefferson called "the overwhelming torrent of slander" was "the exclusive right" of the states.[3] In short, the first major debate over the meaning of the constitutional freedoms conferred on those who wrote and spoke was in large measure a debate over states' rights.

The Sedition Act passed the House by a vote of 44 to 41 (it had already passed in the Senate on, ironically, the Fourth of July), and President Adams signed it. About two dozen persons were prosecuted, and ten were convicted for violating the law; all were editors of Republican (i.e., Jeffersonian) newspapers. Fines and jail sentences were imposed. The law expired on March 3, 1801, the day Jefferson assumed the presidency. In his inaugural address he made an argument for freedom of speech and press— "Error may be tolerated where reason is left free to combat it"—and followed it with pardons for all those convicted under the Sedition Act. At about the same time, however, he wrote to the governor of Pennsylvania that, though the Sedition Act had been a deplorable "gag law," the "licentiousness" and "lying" of the press remained a problem. For this, he recommended that the state libel laws be put to use: "A few prosecutions of the most prominent offenders would have a wholesome effect in restoring the integrity of the press."[4]

The Sedition Act convictions were never reviewed by the Supreme Court, and thus we have no final determination of their constitutionality. But the political verdict on the act was clear. Its author, the Federalist party, was defeated in 1800 and shortly thereafter virtually disappeared as an organized entity. Though state criminal libel laws remained on the books, the federal government abandoned for over a

hundred years any claim that it could punish an editor or writer for having been maliciously or even falsely critical of it. As a matter of law, however, the scope of the First Amendment remained unsettled.

The Espionage Act and the "Red Scare"

It was not until the twentieth century that the Supreme Court spoke on the issue of free speech and press. When it did, it had to decide how far one could go in relying on reason to combat error. Suppose, for example, that certain words bring about conditions that suppress freedom so that reason never has a chance. This might occur if speeches and pamphlets produce an armed revolution, assure the success of foreign enemies, or cause the commission of a crime.

In 1917 that possibility seemed quite real. The United States was being drawn into World War I. Espionage and sabotage by Germans and Austrians in the United States were feared. Labor unions had become more militant, and a wave of strikes and violence (committed both by and against labor) erupted. A revolution in Russia had been successful, which by October of 1917 would bring to power in that country a Bolshevik regime with ideological allies in many other nations. There was a generalized fear that hostile groups—anarchists, labor leaders, Germans, Russians, Communists—were conspiring to commit illegal acts in the United States and to overthrow the government. After Germany began unrestricted submarine warfare that resulted in the sinking of a number of American ships, the United States declared war.

Two months after the declaration, the Congress passed, in June 1917, an espionage act that contained two provisions directly bearing on free speech. One made it a crime to make false statements with the intent of interfering with American military forces or to "attempt to cause insubordination, disloyalty, mutiny, or refusal of duty" among the military forces. The other section made it a crime to send through the mails any material violating the law or "advocating or

During the "red scare" of 1919, police seized literature at Communist party headquarters in Cambridge, Massachusetts.

urging treason, insurrection, or forcible resistance to any law of the United States." (A provision authorizing censorship of the press was defeated in Congress.)

Meanwhile, many states (by 1920, thirty-six of them) were adopting laws forbidding seditious speech and the display of the red flag. In 1918 the federal Espionage Act was broadened by the passage of amendments (the Sedition Act) that made it a crime to utter, print, write, or publish any disloyal, profane, scurrilous, or abusive language intended to incite resistance to the United States, promote the cause of its enemies, or curtail war production.

The Espionage and Sedition Acts were supposed to be wartime measures, and in this sense they were different from the peacetime Sedition Act of 1798. But the laws continued in effect after the end of World War I in November 1918; as late as May 1920 President Woodrow Wilson vetoed a bill that would have terminated them.[5]

Indeed, the Espionage Act remains on the books today.

The end of the war did not end the concern; it only intensified it. In 1919 the "red scare" reached its peak. Beginning in November of that year, federal agents under the direction of Attorney General A. Mitchell Palmer (who may have had presidential ambitions) raided the homes and offices of various groups of political radicals and labor leaders, especially aliens. Anybody who had opposed American entry into World War I or the drafting of troops was fair game. Some of the persons arrested may have been trying to interfere with the war effort or to stir up revolutionary action, but many, probably most, were simply expressing unpopular opinions. Over two thousand persons were prosecuted under federal law; about half were convicted. Many more were prosecuted under various state sedition laws. Thousands of aliens were deported. By the spring of 1920, the national hysteria was over, having died almost as quickly as it arose. The Sedition Act was repealed in 1921, without protest.[6]

Six major cases involving the sedition prosecutions reached the Supreme Court. At issue was whether, or under what circumstances, speaking and writing could be punished. The first of these cases set the tone for the rest. A socialist named Charles T. Schenck had mailed circulars to young men urging them to resist being drafted into the army during World War I. He was convicted of inciting resistance to the recruitment of soldiers in violation of the Espionage Act. When his case reached the Supreme Court, Justice Oliver Wendell Holmes, Jr., wrote the opinion of the unanimous Court. He distinguished between language that was merely critical of the government and that which directly caused an illegal act (he noted that the First Amendment does not protect a person who had been "falsely shouting fire in a theatre and causing a panic"). To decide what kind of speech was subject to punishment, he advanced the "clear and present danger" test: "The question in every case is whether the words used are used in such circumstances and are of such a nature as to create a clear and present danger that they will bring about the substantive evils that Congress has a right to prevent."[7] Using this test, the Court decided that Schenck had been properly convicted.

Shortly thereafter, two more prosecutions were sustained by the Court, again employing the clear and present danger test.[8] But six months later, Holmes, joined by Justice Louis Brandeis, decided that this test had not been met when the government prosecuted Jacob Abrams and five associates for tossing from the rooftops leaflets which denounced American military intervention in Russia and urged the "workers of the world" to resist by engaging in a "general strike." Holmes criticized the government for prosecuting a man for passing out a "silly leaflet" whose contents in no way created an imminent danger of some immediate interference with the war effort. But Holmes and Brandeis were this time in the minority, and the conviction of Abrams was upheld, seven to two.[9]

Throughout the 1920s the majority of the Court tended to uphold federal and state prosecutions of radical pamphleteers, while Holmes and Brandeis continued to refine, sometimes in dissenting opinions, their clear and present danger test. They stressed that the danger must be both imminent and serious, that it must be a danger to the state and not merely to property, and that the speech leading to the danger must involve actual incitement rather than mere advocacy.[10]

The Smith Act

Once again war, or the the threat of war, led to fears of domestic subversion and seditious speech. In 1939 Nazi Germany began its war of European conquest after signing a nonaggression treaty with the Soviet Union. Americans worried about Nazi and Communist subversion in the United States, though Communists became less of a worry after Germany invaded Russia in 1941

❝One response to these fears was the Smith Act of 1940. . . . It punished, not those who speak critically of the government, but those who willfully advocate the overthrow of the government by force or violence.❞

and the latter turned to the United States for assistance. One response to these fears was the Smith Act of 1940, the first peacetime sedition law since that of 1798. Its language, however, was considerably narrower than that of its predecessor. It punished, not those who speak critically of the government, but those who willfully advocate the overthrow of the government by force or violence. This provision was designed to meet the tests evolved by the Supreme Court during the 1920s: speech was to be judged by its intended effect, not by its content alone. (Whether the language would have met the stricter test of "imminent danger" developed by Holmes and Brandeis was far from clear.) In addition, the Smith Act made it a crime to organize, or to be a member of, a group that advocated the forceful overthrow of the government (the "membership" clause).

During World War II only a handful of cases were brought under the Smith Act, probably because Attorney General Francis Biddle, unlike his predecessor during World War I, A. Mitchell Palmer, was reluctant to enforce any laws that might tend to curb the free expression of opinion.[11] After the war, however, the law became an important weapon directed at the Communist party in the United States.

The defeat of Germany ended the alliance between the Soviet Union and the United States; the actions of the Soviet Union, especially its military domination of formerly independent nations of Eastern Europe, contributed to the rise of the Cold War. Fear of Communist espionage (which was not misplaced, since Soviet spies were operating in the United States) fueled a more general fear of communism and led to heavily publicized investigations into the loyalties of Americans working for the government. It was a

Senator Joseph R. McCarthy appears at congressional hearings held in 1954 to consider his attacks against an alleged "Communist cover-up" in the United States Army. Joseph N. Welch, seated, was the special counsel for the army, who denounced McCarthy as a "cruelly reckless character assassin." Shortly thereafter, the Senate voted to condemn McCarthy and he faded into obscurity.

situation ripe for exploitation by demagogues, and they soon arose. Chief among them was Senator Joseph R. McCarthy of Wisconsin who, beginning in 1950, branded various public officials as Communists on the basis of little or no evidence. Until the mid-1950s partisan passions on this issue ran high: many liberal Democrats accused McCarthy and his followers of character assassination and "witch hunts"; many conservatives in the Democratic and Republican parties charged that President Harry Truman and his aides were "covering up" or "coddling" known Communists in federal offices.

To the Smith Act of 1940 were added the Internal Security Act of 1950 (which required the Communist party to register and make public its membership lists and barred party mem-

bers from holding federal appointive office) and the Communist Control Act of 1954 (which declared the Communist party to be part of a conspiracy to overthrow the United States government and denied to it those legal rights to which a political party was ordinarily entitled). Both acts, as well as others in the same vein, passed by large majorities. (A provision, offered by Senator Hubert Humphrey, to have membership in the Communist party declared a crime was defeated.)

The issues raised by these measures came to the Supreme Court as a result of federal prosecutions of Communist party leaders, first under the "advocacy" clause of the Smith Act and later under its "membership" clause. The government charged that these men and women were teaching and advocating the forceful overthrow of the government or were members of an organization that they knew to be advocating that overthrow. The Court had to decide whether advocating the overthrow of the government could be punished without violating the First Amendment. (Nobody disagreed that actually *trying* to overthrow the government, or organizing a conspiracy that took steps to overthrow it, was a crime; such behavior had been illegal at least since 1861.)

Its first look at the matter was the *Dennis* case in 1951, in which the Court modified the clear and present danger test while applying it to the conviction of eleven Communist leaders. It decided, six to two, that the (revised) test had been met and that conviction of the men did not violate the First Amendment. The government did not have to wait, the Court said, "until the *putsch* is about to be executed, the plans have been laid and the signal is awaited." Even if the Communist party leaders were not likely to be successful in overthrowing the government, their advocacy of that overthrow could be punished. "In each case," the opinion read, the courts "must ask whether the gravity of the 'evil,' discounted by its improbability, justifies such invasion of free speech as is necessary to avoid the danger."[12]

Over the next six years, eighty-nine persons were convicted of violating the Smith Act.[13] But then the Court started to change its mind. The composition of the Court had altered; public furor against Communists had somewhat abated; and a majority of the Court was now more worried about unreasonable restrictions on speech than they were about the unlikely possibility of the government being overthrown. In the *Yates* case, the majority of the Court went to great pains to distinguish between the expression of a philosophical belief ("the government should be overthrown") and the advocacy of an illegal act ("meet tomorrow night to plan that overthrow"). Persons could be punished for the second but not for the first. From now on, the government would have to prove that a person actually intended to overthrow the government and that the words he or she spoke were in fact "calculated to incite" that overthrow. Though the Court did not say it had changed its mind, or that the *Dennis* decision was overruled, or that the Smith Act was unconstitutional, the *Yates* decision made the further prosecution of Communists under the advocacy clause all but impossible.[14] (Communists could still be prosecuted under the membership clause. In 1961 the Supreme Court upheld the convictions of persons for being "knowing, active" party members.)[15]

The subsequent history of the effort to balance freedom of speech against the government's right to protect itself from a hostile and violent conspiracy became so complex that it defies quick summary. The Court upheld the right of the government to require the Communist party to register but refused to overrule a lower court decision that said that such a requirement was unconstitutional because it amounted to self-incrimination.[16] The Court also held that a Communist could not be denied a passport[17] nor be compelled to register with the government.[18] The Smith Act had become a dead letter and, as of 1979, is likely to be repealed; the Subversive Activities Control Board, created by the Internal Security Act of 1950, became defunct in 1973.

Urban Riots and Vietnam

The Vietnam War, almost alone among the major wars in which this country has been involved, produced no significant new legislation that sought to combat or restrict political speech. Perhaps this was because our participation in the war was so controversial that "respectable" persons, as well as unpopular political sects and various Communist party functionaries, were in opposition to it. The absence of new restrictions was also the result of the Court having developed, in reaction to the legislation produced at the time of World Wars I and II, such strict tests of constitutionality that there was little opportunity for legislative invention that would pass scrutiny.

Moreover, the mood of Congress and of the public was more tolerant of speech and advocacy than it had been in past cases, despite the fact that Vietnam produced mass demonstrations, bombings of offices, and campus insurrections. While the overwhelming majority of citizens wanted to see illegal actions punished, a majority (unlike in the 1950s and presumably in the 1920s) were willing to hear unpopular causes espoused. In Table 18.1 we see the rising proportion of persons who said they were willing to allow admitted Communists and advocates of other unpopular views to speak. Whereas in 1954 only a quarter would let a Communist and only a third would let an atheist speak in their communities, by 1974 those proportions had risen to well over one-half.

The closest the federal government came to extending the legal regulation of speech came in 1968. In response to the wave of urban riots that had swept the country, a civil rights bill included an antirioting provision that made it a federal crime to cross state lines or to use interstate communications in order to incite or organize a riot. The law stipulated that expressions of belief would not constitute incitement unless the remarks advocated violence. Seven persons were tried and convicted in Chicago (the Chicago Seven) for inciting riots at the Democratic convention in that city in 1968, but the convictions were overturned on appeal on grounds that the trial was unfairly conducted.[19]

The clearest example of the new mood of the Court came in 1969, when Clarence Brandenburg, a leader of the Ku Klux Klan, was convicted in Ohio of violating that state's criminal syndicalism law. Brandenburg staged a cross-burning ceremony at which he reviled blacks and Jews. The police charged him with being disorderly and told him to clear the street; as he left, he said, "We'll take the [expletive] street later." The conviction was based on the view that by this remark he was attempting to incite further lawless action by the mob. The Supreme Court disagreed: the constitutional guarantee of free speech does not permit a state to forbid advocacy of force or the violation of a law except where such advocacy is likely to incite imminent lawless action.[20] This represented a substantial change from the view of the Court in the 1920s and even the 1950s when the clear and present danger test was being developed. By the standard of the *Brandenburg* case, it is hard to imagine how any form of political speech could be punished unless it led immediately and directly to some harm, or had a very high probability of doing so. Merely advocating a course of action, however dangerous, can no longer be punished.[21]

The political climate of the 1970s was generally supportive of such interpretations. Despite the fact—or perhaps because of the fact—that the war in Vietnam was deeply controversial, the end of the war brought no significant legislative effort to detect and punish radicals or critics of the war—no "red scare," no witch hunt. The closest was, by the standards of the 1920s, a mild example. After Daniel Ellsberg, a critic of the war, made public some confidential government documents about the history of our involvement in that war—the so-called Pentagon Papers—a bill was introduced in 1975 that would have made it a crime knowingly to communicate information about national defense or other secret documents to a person not authorized to receive them, or to a foreign power. Various groups, including the American Civil Liberties Union and organizations of reporters and broadcasters, objected strenuously. They claimed that the bill—a part of a general codification of federal criminal law known as "S.1"—would prevent the press from publishing anything the government deemed secret and would make it easier for politicians to cover up misdeeds, as some had attempted to do after Watergate. Supporters of the bill rejoined that the government had a right to punish persons who willfully handed over its confidential documents to outsiders. The authors of S.1 deleted the controversial provision.

Efforts to restrict by federal law opportunities to speak and publish occur, not regularly, but

TABLE 18.1   Willingness to Grant First Amendment Rights

Type of freedom	Year	Admitted Communist	Against religion	For governmental ownership
To speak	1954	27	37	58
	1972	52	65	77
	1974	58	62	75
To have book in library	1954	27	35	52
	1972	53	60	67
	1974	58	60	69
To teach	1954	6	12	33
	1972	32	40	56
	1974	42	42	57

Source: Hazel Erskine and Richard L. Siegel, "Civil Liberties and the American Public," *Journal of Social Issues,* Vol. 31, No. 2 (1975). Reprinted by permission.

Note: The questions were as follows: "There are always some people whose ideas are considered bad or dangerous by other people. For instance, somebody who is against all churches and religion. If such a person wanted to make a speech in your city (town, community) against churches and religion, should he be allowed to speak, or not? Should such a person be allowed to teach in a college or university, or not? If some people in your community suggested that a book he wrote against churches and religion be taken out of your public library, would you favor removing this book, or not?" The same questions were asked about the other "extremists."

The war in Vietnam produced a wave of antiwar protests, especially among college students.

episodically, usually in connection with a national crisis in which a group once thought harmless is seen as sinister. This was apparent in the foregoing history of efforts to reconcile national security and civil liberties but can also be seen in other policy areas—government programs to combat crime, for example, or to deal with drugs.

The Supreme Court acts as a kind of delayed-action brake on these efforts. Initially, the Court tends to defer to the popular and political majority, in part out of the belief that the legislature is entitled to make reasonable judgments about threats to the national security. It accepted these judgments initially after World War I (the *Schenck* decision) and again after World War II (the

Dennis decision). In time, however, the Court begins to apply its own standards for judging the reasonableness of a restriction, as it did when it evolved the "clear and present danger" test and later the test of "imminence."

In consequence, one might almost say that legislative efforts to restrict civil liberties have, over the long run, tended to enlarge them. Each effort has presented new issues to the Court which, once political calm was restored, has been inclined to confer ever greater protection on these liberties.

THE PREFERRED POSITION OF CIVIL LIBERTIES

The course charted by the Supreme Court over its history, while not always clear or free of reversals, has in general tended to expand the scope of civil liberties. This has applied especially to those liberties granted by the First Amendment, but also to the liberties of citizens involved with the police and the criminal courts. One result of this has been that the United States is among those few nations, perhaps no more than two dozen in all, that afford the greatest protection to personal liberty.[22] To some people, of course, that is not enough: further protections are thought necessary. To others, the balance between liberty and order has already been tipped too far in favor of individual self-expression and against community protection.

Our purpose here is less to evaluate the Court's position than to explain how it was reached. It is important to realize that the Court has had to interpret a written Constitution in the context of a federal system of government by settling actual cases. The results of this process are likely to differ from what might ensue if, instead, one tried to outline the permissible scope of personal freedom by writing a philosophical treatise or drafting legislation. Defining liberty in the abstract is far easier than balancing competing rights in an actual case. At the same time, the

66Defining liberty in the abstract is far easier than balancing competing rights in an actual case.99

very difficulty of the cases that reach the Court often leads to mischievous results: as Oliver Wendell Holmes once said, "Great cases like hard cases make bad law."[23] The tendency of the legal and judicial mind to formulate a rule or principle by which to settle a case can produce, where the case is especially complex, a rule that leads to unreasonable results or new difficulties when applied to other cases.

In interpreting the First Amendment, the Court has had to resolve three major issues. First, does the First Amendment, and the Bill of Rights generally, apply to the states or only to the federal government? Second, what constitutes "speech" within the meaning of the First Amendment? Third, by what tests shall restrictions on speech be judged?

The States and the Bill of Rights

When the Bill of Rights was being debated in Congress in 1790, the Senate refused to accept one amendment that would have protected

RANKING OF NATIONS BY CIVIL LIBERTIES

MOST FREE ———————————————————————————————————→ LEAST FREE

1	2	3	4	5	6	7
Australia	Bahamas	Bolivia	Bahrain	Argentina	Algeria	Afghanistan
Austria	Dominican	Botswana	Bangladesh	Bhutan	Burma	Albania
Barbados	Republic	Colombia	Brazil	Chile	Cameroon	Angola
Belgium	Fiji	Dominica	Cyprus	Egypt	Cape Verde Is.	Benin
Canada	Finland	Grenada	Djibouti	El Salvador	Chad	Bulgaria
Costa Rica	France	Honduras	Ecuador	Hungary	China (Mainland)	Burundi
Denmark	Gambia	Jamaica	Ghana	Indonesia	Cuba	Central African
Iceland	Germany (West)	Nigeria	Guatemala	Iran	Czechoslovakia	Emp.
Ireland	Greece	Senegal	Guyana	Ivory Coast	Gabon	Congo
Japan	India	Sri Lanka	Kenya	Korea (South)	Germany (East)	Equatorial Guinea
Luxembourg	Israel	Tonga	Kuwait	Lesotho	Guinea-Bissau	Ethiopia
Netherlands	Italy	Turkey	Lebanon	Liberia	Haiti	Guinea
New Zealand	Malta	Upper Volta	Malaysia	Maldives	Iraq	Kampuchea
Norway	Nauru		Mauritius	Nepal	Jordan	Korea (North)
Sweden	Papua		Mexico	Nicaragua	Libya	Laos
Switzerland	New Guinea		Morocco	Pakistan	Madagascar	Malawi
United Kingdom	Portugal		Peru	Panama	Mali	Mongolia
United States	Solomon Is.		Thailand	Paraguay	Mauritania	Mozambique
	Spain			Philippines	Niger	Somalia
	Surinam			Poland	Oman	Uganda
	Trinidad &			Qatar	Rumania	Vietnam
	Tobago			Rhodesia	Rwanda	Yemen (South)
	Tuvalu			Seychelles	Sao Tome &	
	Venezuela			Sierra Leone	Principe	
	Western Samoa			Singapore	Saudi Arabia	
				Sudan	South Africa	
				Swaziland	Syria	
				Taiwan	Tanzania	
				Transkei	Togo	
				Tunisia	USSR	
				United Arab	Uruguay	
				Emirates	Zaire	
				Yemen (North)		
				Yugoslavia		
				Zambia		

Source: Raymond D. Gastil, *Freedom in the World, 1979* (New York: Freedom House, 1979). Reprinted by permission.

freedom of speech, press, and religion, and the right to a trial by jury from infringement by *state* governments. Faced with this clear indication of congressional intent, the Supreme Court had little choice but to rule, as it did in 1833, that the Bill of Rights applied only to the actions of the federal government and not to those of the states.[24] The adoption in 1868 of the Fourteenth Amendment, however, brought into the Constitution language that created for the first time the possibility that the Bill of Rights might now restrict state action. The phrase on which the argument turned was the "due process" clause: "No state shall ... deprive any person of life, liberty, or property, without due process of law." The issue that arose was whether this clause was intended to "incorporate" the Bill of Rights into the phrase "due process of law" so that guarantees of free speech and free press would constitute restrictions on what state governments could do.

For over half a century the Supreme Court steadfastly denied that the due process clause made the Bill of Rights applicable to the states. Then, in 1925, Benjamin Gitlow was convicted of violating the New York sedition law, a law similar to the federal Sedition Act of 1918. When Gitlow appealed, the Supreme Court upheld his conviction but added the statement that the Court assumed that freedom of speech and of the press were among the "fundamental personal rights" that are protected by the due process clause from state infringement.[25] This was the first time that the Court had explicitly proclaimed this principle. Not long thereafter, state laws involving speech,[26] the press,[27] and peaceful assembly[28] were struck down by the Supreme Court as violating the due process clause of the Fourteenth Amendment.

An "Honor Roll" of Fundamental Liberties. Soon confusion reigned. Did the due process clause incorporate the entire Bill of Rights, or just part of it? And if part, what part? In 1937 the Court tried to answer that question in a case involving a man, Frank Palko, who claimed that when Con-

necticut twice convicted him of first-degree murder it had violated his right under the federal Constitution not to be "twice put in jeopardy" for the same offense. Justice Benjamin Cardozo tried, in writing the Court's opinion, to sort out which rights were and which were not part of the due process clause. Those "fundamental principles of liberty and justice which lie at the base of all our civil and political institutions" were, he wrote, part of the due process clause; those rights which, though they are valuable and important, are "not of the essence of a scheme of ordered liberty" were not part of that clause. The so-called "Honor Roll" of fundamental liberties mentioned by Cardozo included freedom of speech, of the press, of peaceable assembly, and of the exercise of religion, and the right to counsel in a criminal trial. Those important but not essential rights that were excluded from the due process clause included the prohibition against double jeopardy and self-incrimination, and against unreasonable searches and the right to a jury trial.[29] Palko lost his appeal, and was electrocuted.

No division of rights into "fundamental" and "nonfundamental" categories, nor any other judicial rule interpreting a phrase such as "due process of law," is likely to last much longer than the justices who formulate it. The *Palko* rule lasted for a quarter of a century with only minor changes, but then, in the 1960s, a more activist and liberal Supreme Court began to expand dramatically the list of rights that were made applicable to the states by the due process clause.

Further Restrictions. The Court held that the states:

- Could not conduct unreasonable searches and seizures;[30]
- Could not introduce into court evidence obtained by an illegal search even if that evidence was relevant to the case;[31]
- Must provide an accused person with a lawyer (if necessary at state expense) in all cases where imprisonment might result;[32]

The Supreme Court during the 1960s greatly expanded the rights of citizens who are stopped, questioned, searched, or arrested by the police.

- Cannot require a person to testify against himself;[33]
- Must allow an accused person a chance to confront witnesses against him;[34]
- Must provide a speedy trial by jury in criminal cases;[35]
- Could not impose "cruel and unusual" punishment;[36]
- Cannot try a person twice for the same offense;[37] and
- Must allow an arrested person to remain silent, to have an attorney present (if necessary, at government expense) when he or she is questioned, and to be warned in advance of these rights.[38]

After all this one might wonder whether there is anything in the Bill of Rights that does *not* now apply to the states. No one is certain, but the answer seems to be, "very little." The Court has not required the states to provide jury trials in civil cases nor grand jury indictments in criminal cases, and those are about the only exclusions of any importance.[39]

Indeed, some justices have argued that the due process clause not only incorporates everything in the Bill of Rights, it also makes applicable to the states other restrictions not found in the Bill of Rights or anywhere in the Constitution. For example, when Estelle T. Griswold and Dr. C. Lee Buxton were convicted in Connecticut of giving birth-control advice to persons in violation of that state's anti-birth-control statute, the Supreme Court reversed the conviction on the grounds that the state law was unconstitutional. Since the Bill of Rights nowhere mentions freedom to receive or make use of birth-control methods, one may wonder on what grounds the Connecticut statute, silly as it may have been, was a violation of the federal Constitution.

The justices made varied use of three arguments. First, the specific liberties mentioned in the Bill of Rights have "penumbras"—or "emanations"—that create "zones of privacy" for individuals that include the right to practice birth control. Second, the Ninth Amendment refers to other, unnamed, rights, not specifically enumerated in the Constitution, that are "retained by the people"; arguably, these include a "right to privacy." Finally, punishing people for giving advice was thought to be on its face a denial of due process without any need to find a specific right that this clause incorporated.[40] The Court also relied on a Court-created "right to privacy" in overturning state laws that restrict the opportunity of women to have abortions.[41]

Judicial Policy-Making.   The abortion and birth-control cases are among the clearest examples of judges making law. The substance of these decisions may be good policy or bad, but it is hard to argue that they are based on any explicit constitutional provisions. As Justice Hugo Black put it, the "right to privacy" is not found in the Constitution, and the phrase is an "ambiguous concept" that judges can expand or shrink to fit their own views.[42] If judges are to base decisions on "penumbras" and "emanations," then the decisions of the Court will "emanate" from the personal political philosophy of the judges. Even where the Court interprets specific constitutional language, meanings will change. We saw this in Chapter 13 with respect to governmental power to regulate business; we see it in this chapter with regard to the definition of permissible speech; we shall see it again in Chapter 20 on the military powers of the president.

Though judicial philosophies shape judicial decisions, judges rarely act without any regard to public opinion. The Court allowed legal restrictions on speech and press during and after World War I and World War II when the public believed that subversives posed a threat; it permits fewer such restrictions today when the public is much less worried about radical political movements. But the Court is not simply a barometer of mass opinion. Popular moods may set the outer limits within which the Court feels comfortable in acting, but within those limits elite opinion—the views of those persons and groups to whom judges are especially attuned—is much more important. Elite opinion, as we saw in Chapters 4 and 5, is today strikingly libertarian (i.e., valuing personal liberty above other considerations) on a wide range of issues, including freedom to speak, publish, demonstrate, have abortions, and use certain kinds of drugs. Since the 1950s the Court has moved more or less steadily in this direction, in part because its members (being drawn from this elite) believe such principles to be correct and in part because they see the special role of the Court as protecting unpopular or controversial matters from the constraints of mass opinion.

The Meaning of "Speech" and "Press"

The movement toward libertarianism can be seen by examining the standards the Court has

> **"**Popular moods may set the outer limits within which the Court feels comfortable in acting, but within those limits elite opinion—the views of those persons and groups to whom judges are especially attuned—is much more important.**"**

evolved in its effort to define the forms of speaking and writing that ought to be given constitutional protection. There is little doubt the Founders meant that religious and political speech were to be protected, but great doubt as to what else they might have meant.

How big an issue this might be can be seen by comparing the sorts of motion pictures one may see in New York today with those permitted to be shown two or three decades ago. In 1957 New York State banned the showing of *Lady Chatterley's Lover* on the grounds that the "theme" of the movie encouraged adultery. Today, as any visit to Times Square will quickly confirm, there is no form of sexual behavior that is not presented, in print or in film, in the most precise clinical detail. Nor is New York an extreme case: in the 1950s Maryland banned the movie *The Moon Is Blue*, because actors in it uttered the words "pregnant" and "virginity";[43] today pornographic movies are readily available in Baltimore and elsewhere in the state.

In deciding on the meaning of "speech" and "press," the Supreme Court has held that virtually any form of visual, printed, or auditory communication—newspapers, books, magazines, pamphlets, motion pictures, and speeches—are "speech" or "the press." In fact, money expended in support of a political candidate is a form of speech. But not all the content of these forms of communication are equally entitled to First Amendment protections. The exceptions seem to be the following.

First, libel is not protected speech. If you harm another person by writing or publishing statements that defame his or her character, you can be sued by the injured party and cannot claim in defense that your freedom to speak and write

"Symbolic speech": When young men burnt their draft cards during the 1960s to protest the Vietnam War, the Supreme Court ruled that it was an illegal act for which they could be punished.

is constitutionally guaranteed. However, the Court, as we saw in Chapter 9, has limited this restriction on libelous statements to those aimed at private persons. Public officials (and even "public figures" or celebrities) are excluded from protection, making them fair game for even false and defamatory statements provided they were not uttered with "actual malice"—that is, uttered with reckless disregard of their accuracy or while knowing them to be false.[44]

Second, you cannot ordinarily claim that illegal *action* should go unpunished because that action is meant to convey a political or social message. For example, if you burn your draft card to protest the foreign policy of the United States, you can be punished for the illegal act (burning the draft card) even if your intent was to communicate your political beliefs. The Court felt that if "symbolic speech" were given the same constitutional protection as actual speech or writing, then virtually any action—murder,

arson, rioting—could be excused on grounds that its perpetrator meant to send a message.[45] But here, as elsewhere, the Court finds it difficult to draw a clear line: when some students in Des Moines wore black armbands to class, their punishment by the school authorities was overruled on grounds that the armbands were a form of protected speech and wearing them was not illegal.[46]

Third, you cannot freely use words that incite others to commit illegal acts or that directly and immediately provoke another person to violent behavior. As we have already seen, the Court has steadily expanded the protection afforded to persons who advocate illegal actions so long as that incitement to action is not immediate and direct. But the Court has sustained state laws that make it illegal to insult a person to his or her face in a way that provokes a fight; it has insisted, however, that laws prohibiting "fighting words" be carefully drawn and narrowly applied.[47] The provocation would probably have to be severe, face-to-face, and person-to-person before the Court would allow it to be punished. When a group of American Nazis in 1977 wanted to parade through Skokie, Illinois, a community with a large Jewish population, lower courts (acting after Supreme Court prodding) held that, noxious and provocative as their anti-Semitic slogans might be, the Nazis had a constitutional right to speak and parade peacefully.[48]

Fourth, obscenity is not protected by the First Amendment. The Court has always held that obscene materials, because they have no redeeming social value or are calculated chiefly to appeal to one's sexual rather than political or literary interests, can be regulated by the state. The problem, of course, arises with the meaning of "obscene." In one eleven-year period, 1957 to 1968, the Court decided thirteen major cases involving the definition of obscenity which resulted in fifty-five separate opinions.[49] Some justices, such as Hugo Black, believed that the First Amendment protected all publications, even wholly obscene ones. Others believed that obscenity deserved no protection and struggled heroically to define the term. Still others shared the view of Justice Potter Stewart who objected to "hard-core pornography" but admitted that the best definition he could offer was "I know it when I see it."[50]

It is unnecessary to review in detail the many attempts by the Court at defining obscenity. The justices have made it clear that nudity and sex are not, by definition, obscene and that they will provide First Amendment protection to anything that has any arguable political, literary, or artistic merit, allowing the government to punish only the distribution of "hard-core pornography." Their most recent (1973) definition of this is as follows: To be obscene, the work, taken as a whole, must be judged by "the average person applying contemporary community standards" to appeal to the "prurient interest" or to depict "in a patently offensive way, sexual conduct specifically defined by applicable state law" and to lack "serious literary, artistic, political, or scientific value."[51]

A year later, after Albany, Georgia, had decided that the movie *Carnal Knowledge* was obscene by contemporary local standards, the Supreme Court overturned the conviction of the distributor on the grounds that the authorities in Albany had failed to show that the film depicted "patently offensive hard-core sexual conduct."[52]

It is easy to make sport of the problems the Court has faced in trying to decide obscenity cases (one conjures up images of black-robed justices leafing through the pages of *Hustler* magazine, taking notes), but these problems reveal, as do other civil liberties cases, the continuing problem of balancing competing claims. One part of the community wants to read or see whatever it wishes; another part wants to protect private acts from public degradation. The first part cherishes liberty above all; the second values decency as well. The former fears that any restriction on literature will lead to pervasive restriction; the latter believes that reasonable persons can distinguish (or reasonable laws can

When American Nazis in 1977 wished to march through Skokie, Illinois, a largely Jewish suburb of Chicago, many residents protested, and the town denied a parade permit. In the ensuing legal dispute, the courts held that, noxious as the Nazi philosophy may be, the party had a right to parade peacefully.

require them to distinguish) between patently offensive and artistically serious work.

Anyone strolling today through an "adult" bookstore must suppose that there exist no restrictions at all on the distribution of pornographic works. This condition does not arise simply from the doctrines of the Court. Other factors operate as well, including the priorities of local law enforcement officials, the political climate of the community, the procedures that must be followed to bring a viable court case, the clarity and workability of state and local laws on the subject, and the difficulty of changing the

Testing Restrictions on Expression

The Supreme Court has employed various tests to decide whether a restriction on freedom of expression is constitutionally permissible. These include:

1. **Preferred position:** The right of free expression, though not absolute, occupies a higher, or more preferred, position than many other constitutional rights, such as property rights. This is still a controversial rule; nonetheless, the Court always approaches a restriction on expression skeptically.

2. **Prior restraint:** With scarcely any exceptions, the Court will not tolerate a prior restraint on expression, such as censorship, even when it will allow subsequent punishment of improper expressions (such as libel).

3. **Imminent danger:** Punishment for uttering inflammatory sentiments will only be allowed if there is an imminent danger that the utterances will incite an unlawful act.

4. **Neutrality:** Any restriction on speech, such as a requirement that parades or demonstrations not disrupt other persons in the exercise of their rights, must be neutral—that is, not favor one group more than another.

5. **Clarity:** If you must obtain a permit to hold a parade, the law must set forth clear (as well as neutral) standards to guide administrators in issuing that permit. Similarly, a law punishing obscenity must have a clear definition of obscenity.

6. **Least means:** If it is necessary to restrict the exercise of one right to protect the exercise of another, the restriction should employ the least means to achieve its end. For example, if press coverage threatens a person's right to a fair trial, the judge may only do what is minimally necessary to that end, such as transferring the case to another town rather than issuing a "gag order."

Cases cited, by item: (1) United States v. Carolene Products, 304 U.S. 144 (1938). (2) Near v. Minnesota, 283 U.S. 697 (1931). (3) Brandenburg v. Ohio, 395 U.S. 444 (1969). (4) Kunz v. New York, 340 U.S. 290 (1951). (5) Hynes v. Mayor and Council of Oradell, 425 U.S. 610 (1976). (6) Nebraska Press Association v. Stuart, 427 U.S. 539 (1976).

behavior of many persons by prosecuting one person. The current view of the Court is that localities can decide for themselves whether to tolerate pornography; but if they choose not to, they must meet some fairly strict constitutional tests.

CRIME AND DUE PROCESS

Much the same evolution of Court doctrines can be seen with regard to the rights afforded persons accused of breaking the law. These rights are often referred to as "procedural due process," because they involve definitions of what constitutes unfair, arbitrary, or unreasonable government *procedures* in attaining some legitimate goal, such as controlling crime. (If the goal itself is deemed improper, the Court is said to be applying a concept of *substantive* due process.)

Controversial Cases

The politics of procedural due process in the area of crime has been quite different from the politics of interpreting the First Amendment. The Supreme Court has been sensitive to public moods when it has defined the constitutional guarantees afforded to speech and press. It has permitted significant restrictions when the public was deeply concerned about domestic security and allowed only a few restrictions when the popular mood was less concerned. In the area of criminal due process, however, the Court has broadened the protections afforded to accused persons in the teeth of strenuous opposition. The landmark cases of the 1960s that enlarged the right to counsel, restricted police powers to search and question, increased the rights of prisoners, and limited the scope of death-penalty statutes were met with widespread criticism from many quarters and led to efforts in Congress to overturn some of them. For example, when the Supreme Court ruled in 1966 that a person arrested for a crime could not be questioned without his or her consent unless a defense attorney was present, a bitter public debate ensued.[53] Law enforcement agencies denounced the ruling; civil libertarians praised it; and Congress passed a law (the Omnibus Crime Control and Safe Streets Act of 1968), sections of which were designed to limit or block the applicability of the ruling in federal prosecutions. Many other rulings in the same vein produced a similar reaction, and the Court found itself embroiled in more controversy than it had experienced with any issues other than the New Deal in 1935 and the school desegregation cases of 1954 (see Chapter 19).

The 1966 decision illustrates the way the Court operates in most such due process cases. Ernesto A. Miranda was convicted in the Arizona courts for the rape-kidnapping of an eighteen-year-old woman. The conviction was based on a written confession that Miranda signed after two hours of police questioning. (The woman also identified him.) Miranda appealed his conviction. For many decades the Supreme Court had held that the Fifth Amendment to the Constitution prohibited the use of involuntary confessions in *federal* criminal trials but had not held that the Fifth Amendment was applicable to *state* trials. Two years before Miranda's appeal came before the Court, however, it decided in another case that the due process clause of the Fourteenth Amendment "incorporated" the rule against self-incrimination contained in the Fifth Amendment; henceforth, involuntary confessions could not be used in state or federal prosecutions.[54] Now the question was, what constitutes an "involuntary" confession? The Court decided that a confession would be presumed involuntary unless the person in custody had been fully and clearly informed of his or her right to be silent, to have an attorney present during any questioning, and to have an attorney provided free of charge if he or she could not afford one. The accused may waive these rights and voluntarily offer to talk, but the waiver must be truly voluntary. Otherwise, there must be either no questioning or questioning only with a lawyer present. Since Miranda did

How Would You Decide?

Suppose you are on the Supreme Court. In each of the actual cases summarized below, you are asked to decide whether the First Amendment to the Constitution permits or prohibits a particular action. What would be your decision? (How the Supreme Court actually decided is given on page 504.)

CASE 1. A girl in Georgia was raped and died. A local television station broadcast the name of the girl, having obtained it from court records. Her father sued, claiming that his family's right to privacy had been violated, and pointed to a Georgia law that made it a crime to broadcast the name of a rape victim. The television station claimed it had a right under the First Amendment to broadcast the name. Who is correct?

CASE 2. Jacksonville, Florida, passed a city ordinance prohibiting drive-in movies from showing films containing nudity if the screen was visible to passers-by on the street. A movie theater manager protested, claiming he had a First Amendment right to show such films even if they could be seen·from the street. Who is correct?

CASE 3. Florida passed a law giving a political candidate the right to equal space in a newspaper that had published attacks on him. A newspaper claimed that this violated the freedom of the press to publish what it wants. Who is correct?

CASE 4. Zacchini is a "human cannonball" whose entire fifteen-second act was filmed and broadcast by an Ohio television station. Zacchini sued the station, claiming that his earning power had been reduced by the film because the station showed for free what he charges people to see at county fairs. The station replied that it had a First Amendment right to broadcast such events. Who is correct?

CASE 5. Dr. Benjamin Spock wanted to enter Fort Dix Military Reservation in New Jersey to pass out campaign literature and discuss issues with service personnel. The military denied him access on grounds that regulations prohibit partisan campaigning on military bases. Who is correct?

CASE 6. A town passed an ordinance forbidding the placing of "For Sale" or "Sold" signs in front of homes in racially changing neighborhoods. The purpose was to reduce "white flight" and panic selling. A realty firm protested, claiming its freedom of speech was being abridged. Who is correct?

not have a lawyer present when he was questioned and since there was no clear evidence that he had knowingly waived the right to a lawyer, his confession could not be admitted as evidence in court. By a vote of five to four, the Court overturned his conviction.

Two things are important to remember about this and other due process decisions. First, the relevant part of the Bill of Rights is applied by the Court to state action only after the Court has decided that that part has been "incorporated" by the due process clause of the Fourteenth Amendment (see p. 497). Second, the Court implements its decisions in these matters by the so-called "exclusionary rule"—it orders that evidence unconstitutionally obtained be excluded from the trial. It could do things differently. In England and other European countries, any relevant and important evidence pertaining to guilt or innocence can be introduced at a trial, but the court then punishes (with civil or criminal penalties) the officers who collected it for doing so illegally. The almost uniform practice in this country, however, has been to try to control police misconduct by suppressing or excluding improperly collected evidence.

To make clear what the Court expected, it listed the things the police should do when arresting someone. These have become known as the "Miranda Rules." After the Court upset Miranda's conviction because the police had not followed these rules, he was tried again in the Arizona courts and convicted, this time on the basis of the evidence of his girl friend who testified that he had admitted to her that he was guilty. His appeal this time was refused, and he went back to prison. Nine years later he was released; four years after that he was killed in a barroom quarrel. When the Phoenix police arrested the prime suspect, they read him his rights from a "Miranda card."[55]

The exclusionary rule has been applied to the results of illegal searches as well as to confessions. In 1961 the Fourth Amendment ban on "unreasonable searches and seizures" was incorporated into the Fourteenth Amendment, and thus made applicable to state and local police actions. The Cleveland, Ohio, police had entered

---

HOW THE COURT DECIDED

The United States Supreme Court answered the questions on page 503 in the following way:

CASE 1. The television station won. The Court, 8-1, decided the First Amendment protects the right to broadcast the names of rape victims obtained from public (i.e., court) records.
 Cox Broadcasting Corp. v. *Cohn*, 420 U.S. 469 (1975)

CASE 2. The drive-in movie won. The Supreme Court, 6-3, decided that the First Amendment protects the right to show nudity; it is up to the unwilling viewer on the public streets to avert his or her eyes.
 Erznoznik v. *Jacksonville*, 422 U.S. 205 (1975)

CASE 3. The newspaper won. The Supreme Court decided, unanimously, that the First Amendment prohibits the state from intruding into the function of editors.
 Miami Herald Publishing Co. v. *Tornillo*, 418 U.S. 241 (1974)

CASE 4. Zacchini, the human cannonball, won. The Supreme Court, 5-4, decided that broadcasting the entire act without the performer's consent jeopardized his means of livelihood even

though the First Amendment would guarantee the right of the station to broadcast newsworthy facts about the act.
 Zacchini v. *Scripps-Howard Broadcasting Co.*, 433 U.S. 562 (1977)

CASE 5. The military won. The Supreme Court, 6-2, decided that military reservations are not like public streets or parks, and thus civilians can be excluded from them, especially if such exclusion prevents the military from appearing to be the handmaiden of various political causes.
 Greer v. *Spock*, 424 U.S. 828 (1976)

CASE 6. The realtor won. The Supreme Court, 8-0, decided that the First Amendment prohibits the banning of signs, even of a commercial nature, without a strong, legitimate state interest. Banning the signs would not obviously reduce "white flight," and the government has no right to withhold information from citizens for fear they will act unwisely.
 Linmark Associates, Inc. v. *Willingboro*, 431 U.S. 85 (1977)

the home of Dollree Mapp in search of drugs and, finding none, took some obscene pictures from among her effects and arrested her. The Supreme Court held that the police had engaged in an illegal search and seizure because they had not obtained a search warrant though they had ample time to do so and, by virtue of the Fourteenth Amendment, this was unconstitutional. Beginning with this case of *Mapp* v. *Ohio*,[56] the Court has broadened the requirement that warrants be obtained before searches can be made. It has not, however, barred all searches without a warrant. For example, your home can be searched if you consent to it, you can be searched if the search is incident to a lawful arrest, your baggage (and you) can be searched by Customs officers when you enter the country or by security officers when you board an airplane, and your automobile can be searched if you are stopped by an officer who has good reason ("probable cause") to believe that you have committed a crime.[57]

Crime Control or Due Process?

The reason why the *Miranda, Mapp,* and other Court decisions should have been so controversial is not hard to understand. The Supreme Court issued many of these decisions at a time when crime rates were rising, thereby revealing an important split in public beliefs about the police and courts. To some people, and certainly to most police officers and many citizens worried about crime, the purpose of the criminal justice system is to "control crime." To others, and certainly to many appellate court judges and legal scholars, the purpose of the system is to "do justice." In fact, most people want the system to do both. But when an issue, such as the exclusionary rule, arises that forces one to choose which goal one is willing to sacrifice, some people prefer to give up some crime control effectiveness and other people prefer to give up some due process. (How much crime control you do give up by following these exclusionary rules is itself controversial.) This conflict was evident even among members of the Supreme Court. Many of its key

The Miranda Rules

The Supreme Court has interpreted the due process clause to require that local police departments issue warnings, of the sort shown below, to persons they are arresting.

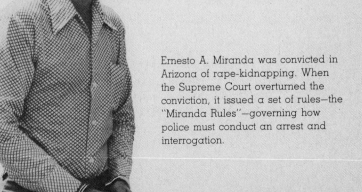

> PHILADELPHIA POLICE DEPARTMENT
> STANDARD POLICE INTERROGATION CARD
>
> WARNINGS TO BE GIVEN ACCUSED
>
> We are questioning you concerning the crime of (state specific crime).
>
> We have a duty to explain to you and to warn you that you have the following legal rights:
>
> A. You have a right to remain silent and do not have to say anything at all.
>
> B. Anything you say can and will be used against you in Court.
>
> C. You have a right to talk to a lawyer of your own choice before we ask you any questions, and also to have a lawyer here with you while we ask questions.
>
> D. If you cannot afford to hire a lawyer, and you want one, we will see that you have one provided to you free of charge before we ask you any questions.
>
> E. If you are willing to give us a statement, you have a right to stop any time you wish.
>
> 75-Misc.-3   (Over)
> (6-24-70)

Ernesto A. Miranda was convicted in Arizona of rape-kidnapping. When the Supreme Court overturned the conviction, it issued a set of rules—the "Miranda Rules"—governing how police must conduct an arrest and interrogation.

decisions were reached on close votes, with the minority often arguing for greater attention to crime control objectives.

The Court majority during the 1960s was able to maintain its position in the face of hostile reactions because, at the time of the free speech cases, there was no national crisis that influenced the Court to defer to congressional opinion. Crime was a serious problem, but not, to the Court, a "crisis." As the composition of the Court began to change in the 1970s, its decisions started to strike a slightly different balance between the crime control and due process objectives. The Court under Chief Justice Warren Burger did not by any means repeal or even drastically modify the due process rules of the Warren Court, but a new emphasis became clearly evident. The Burger Court began to restrict somewhat the opportunity afforded persons being prosecuted in state courts to raise procedural issues in federal courts.[58] Moreover, some members of the Court raised questions about the value of the exclusionary rule as a way of controlling police misconduct and hinted rather clearly that they might, under certain circumstances, be prepared to allow improperly obtained evidence to be admitted in criminal trials if the evidence were important.[59] These shifts in emphasis reflect the consequences of the changing ideological orientation of the Court as well, perhaps, as the Court's sensitivity to shifts in elite opinion. By the mid-1970s, the exclusionary rule had come to be regarded as a disappointment by many legal scholars who in the 1960s had staunchly defended it.

SUMMARY

We tend to think of civil liberties, and the Bill of Rights generally, as matters of such weighty philosophical importance as to be radically different from "ordinary" political issues. The fact is, however, that questions of civil liberties come to the fore in much the same way as any political issue: people disagree over what ought to be done, or how it ought to be done, and they fight out their disagreement by enlisting the support of various parts of the government. One person wants a trial free of publicity; another person wants to write newspaper stories without interference. One group wishes to live in a community free of raucous loudspeakers or pornographic bookstores; another group wants to broadcast over those loudspeakers or patronize those bookstores. In these cases interest group politics occurs. The rival groups could take their quarrel to the legislature, and often they do, but they also can take it (and increasingly do) to the courts.

Minorities with unusual or extreme political or religious beliefs are usually ignored, at least by the law if not by the customs of the people. But on occasion, especially in times of national crisis, intense (though usually short-lived) majorities are mobilized against such groups, and new laws are passed restricting their behavior for better or for worse. This is often a case of entrepreneurial politics. The affected minority, or a group speaking on its behalf, asks the courts to overrule the legislature.

The resolution of these issues by the courts is political, in the sense that differing opinions about what is right or desirable compete, with one side or another prevailing (often by a small majority). In this competition of ideas, federal judges, though not elected, are aware of and often keenly sensitive to strong currents of popular opinion. When entrepreneurial politics has produced new action against apparently threatening minorities, judges are inclined, at least for a while, to give serious consideration to popular fears and legislative majorities. And when no strong national mood is discernible, the opinions of elites influence judicial thinking, in ways that we reviewed in Chapter 13.

At the same time, courts resolve political conflicts in a manner that differs in important respects from the resolution of conflicts by legislatures or executives. First, the very existence of the courts, and the relative ease with which one may enter them to advance a claim, facilitates challenges to accepted values. An unpopular political or religious group may have little or no access to a legislature, but it will have substantial access to the courts. Second, judges often settle controversies about rights, not simply by deciding the case at hand, but by formulating a general rule to cover like cases elsewhere. This has an advantage (the law tends to become more consistent and better known) but a disadvantage as well: a rule suitable for one case may be unworkable in another. Judges reason by analogy and sometimes assume that two cases are similar when in fact there are important differences. A definition of obscenity or of "fighting words" may suit one situation but be inadequate in another. Third, judges interpret the Constitution, whereas legislatures often consult popular preferences or personal convictions. However much their own beliefs influence what judges read into the Constitution, almost all of them are constrained by its language.

The desire to find and announce rules, the language of the Constitution, and the personal beliefs of judges taken together have led to a general expansion of civil liberties. As a result, even allowing for temporary reversals and frequent redefinitions, any value thought to be competitive with freedom of expression and the rights of the accused has generally lost ground to the claims of the First, Fourth, Fifth, and Sixth Amendments.

Suggested Readings

Abraham, Henry J. *Freedom and the Court,* 3rd ed. New York: Oxford University Press, 1977. Up-to-date analysis of leading Supreme Court cases on civil liberties and civil rights.

Berns, Walter. *The First Amendment and the Future of American Democracy.* New York: Basic Books, 1976. A fresh look at what the Founders intended by the First Amendment that takes issue with contemporary Supreme Court interpretations of it.

Clor, Harry M. *Obscenity and Public Morality.* Chicago: University of Chicago Press, 1969. Argues for the legitimacy of legal restrictions on obscenity.

Corwin, Edward S. *The Constitution and What It Means Today,* 14th ed. Revised by Harold W. Chase and Craig R. Ducat. Princeton, N.J.: Princeton University Press, 1978. A frequently updated analysis, section by section, of what the Constitution means in light of Court interpretations. A valuable reference.

Emerson, Thomas I. *Toward a General Theory of the First Amendment.* New York: Random House, 1966. Argues, contrary to Walter Berns (cited above), that the First Amendment confers an absolute protection on speech.

Levy, Leonard W. *Legacy of Suppression: Freedom of Speech and Press in Early American History.* Cambridge, Mass.: Harvard University Press, 1960. Careful study of what the Founders and the early leaders meant by freedom of speech and press.

Shapiro, Martin. *Freedom of Speech: The Supreme Court and Judicial Review.* Englewood Cliffs, N.J.: Prentice-Hall, 1966. Studies the Supreme Court from a political perspective.

19 Civil Rights

When can the government treat people differently · Blacks and the political system · Role of NAACP · Role of the courts · Testing of "separate but equal" education · Recruiting white support · Getting civil rights on the national political agenda · Civil disobedience and violence · How legislation was passed · Equality of opportunity or equality of result?

A segregated bus station in Durham, North Carolina, in 1940 (left). President Lyndon Johnson signing the 1965 Civil Rights Act in the company of the Reverend Martin Luther King, Jr. (right).

In 1830 Congress passed a law requiring all Indians east of the Mississippi River to move to the "Indian Territory" west of the river, and the army set about implementing it. In the 1850s a major political fight broke out in Boston over whether the Boston Police Department should be obliged to hire an Irish officer. Until 1920 women could not vote in most elections. In the 1930s the Cornell University Medical School had a strict quota to limit the number of Jewish students who could enroll. In the 1940s the army, with the approval of President Franklin D. Roosevelt, removed all Japanese-Americans from their homes in California and placed them in "relocation centers" in the interior.

In all these cases and others, some group, usually defined along racial or ethnic lines, was denied access to facilities, opportunities, or services that were available to other groups. Such

cases raise the issue of civil rights. That issue is not whether the government has the authority to treat different people differently, but only whether such differences in treatment are "reasonable." All laws and policies make distinctions—for example, the tax laws require higher income people to pay taxes at a higher rate than lower income ones—but not all distinctions are defensible. The courts have long held that classifying people on the basis of their income and taxing different classes at different rates is quite permissible, because such classifications are not arbitrary or unreasonable, and they are related to a legitimate public policy (i.e., raising revenue). Increasingly, however, the courts have said that classifying persons on the basis of their sex, race, or ethnicity is unreasonable—these are "suspect classifications"—and while not every law making such classifications will be ruled unconstitutional, they all will be subjected to especially strict scrutiny.[1]

Given the theory of policy-making developed so far in this book, it may seem surprising that certain groups, particularly those that constitute only a small minority of the population, should require any special protection at all. We have seen how easy it is for many small groups—businesses, occupations, unions—to practice "client politics." They can obtain some special advantage (a grant, a license, a subsidy) or avoid some threatened regulation because, being small, they find it easy to organize and to escape general public notice. Yet American Indians, blacks, Japanese-Americans, and Mexican-Americans are also relatively small groups whose presence or demands seemingly place little burden on the majority population. Despite this, they have been more the victims than the clients of the policy-making process.

Rather than deal with the political and legal processes involved in the claims made by all groups that have raised civil rights issues, this chapter will look only at the case of black Americans. Blacks have had perhaps the longest history of trying to overcome arbitrary public and private action to become full-fledged citizens. Most of the major civil rights laws and landmark court cases have involved black claims. However, the political and legal strategies employed by or on behalf of blacks are similar to—indeed, have often set the pattern for—the strategies employed by Mexican-Americans, Indians, and even feminists.

THE BLACK PREDICAMENT

Though constituting less than 12 percent of the population, blacks until fairly recently could not in many parts of the country vote, attend integrated schools, ride in the front seats of buses, or buy homes in white neighborhoods. And some restrictions along these lines persist even today.

One reason is that the perceived costs of granting these demands were not widely distributed among the public at large but instead were concentrated on some relatively small, readily organized, immediately affected group. Citizens generally may not feel threatened if a black moves into Cicero, Illinois, goes to school at Little Rock Central High School, or votes in Neshoba County, Mississippi, but at one time most whites (and even now, some whites) in Cicero, Little Rock, and Neshoba County felt deeply threatened. In the language of this book, civil rights in these places were not a matter of client politics, but of competitive or interest group politics. This was especially the case in those parts of the country, notably in the Deep South, where blacks were often in a majority. There the politically dominant white minority felt keenly the potential competition for jobs, land, public services, and living space posed by large numbers of persons of another race. But even in the North, black gains often appeared to be at the expense of lower income whites who lived or worked near them, not at the expense of upper status whites who lived in suburbs.

The interest group component of racial politics put blacks at a decided disadvantage: they were not allowed to vote at all in many areas, could vote only with great difficulty in others, and in those places where voting was easy they often lacked the material and institutional support for effective political organization. If your opponent feels deeply threatened by your demands and in addition can deny to you the means of access to the political system that will decide those demands, you are, to put it mildly, at a disadvantage. Yet from the end of Reconstruction down to the 1960s—for nearly a century—that was the position in which many blacks in the South found themselves.

A second reason is that majoritarian politics worked to the disadvantage of blacks. Because of white attitudes this was the case even when white and black interests were not directly in competition. To the dismay of those who prefer to explain political action by economic motives, people often attach greater importance to the intangible costs and benefits of policies than to the tangible ones. Thus, even though the average black represented no threat to the average white, antiblack attitudes—racism—produced some appalling actions. Between 1882 and 1946, 4,715 people, about three-fourths of them blacks, were lynched in the United States.[2] Some lynchings were carried out by small groups of vigilantes acting with much ceremony, but others were the actions of frenzied mobs. In the summer of 1911 a black charged with murdering a white man in Livermore, Kentucky, was dragged by a mob to the local theater where he was hanged. The audience, which had been charged admission, was invited to shoot the swaying body (those in the orchestra seats could empty their revolvers, those in the balcony were limited to a single shot).[3]

Though public opinion in other parts of the country was often shocked by such events, little was done: lynching was a local, not a federal, crime. It obviously would not require many lynchings to convince blacks in these localities that it would be foolhardy to do such things as vote or enroll in a white school. And in those

❝In the language of this book, civil rights in these places were not a matter of client politics, but of competitive or interest group politics.**❞**

In many parts of the Deep South where segregation was the strongest, blacks were a majority of the population but, because they often could not vote, they lacked political power.

states where blacks could and did vote, popular attitudes were not conducive to blacks' buying homes or taking jobs on an equal basis with whites. Even among those professing to support equal rights, a substantial proportion opposed black efforts to obtain them and federal action to secure them. In 1942 a national poll showed that only 30 percent of whites thought that black and white children should attend the same schools; in 1956 the proportion had risen to 49 percent, still

❝Civil rights became less a matter of gaining entry into the political system and more one of waging interest group politics within that system.❞

less than a majority. (In the South, of course, white support for school integration was even lower—14 percent favored it in 1956, about 31 percent in 1963.) As late as 1956, a majority of southern whites were opposed to integrated public transportation facilities. Even among whites who generally favored integration, there was in 1963 (*before* the ghetto riots) considerable opposition to the black civil rights movement: nearly half of the whites who were classified in a survey as moderate integrationists thought that demonstrations hurt the black cause, nearly two-thirds disapproved of actions taken by the civil rights movement, and over a third felt that civil rights should be left to the states.[4]

In short, the political position in which blacks found themselves until the 1960s was one which made it difficult for them to advance their own interests with any feasible legislative strategy: their opponents were aroused, organized, and powerful. Thus, if those interests were to be championed in Congress or state legislatures, blacks would have to make use of white allies. Though some such allies could be found, they were too few to make a difference in a political system, such as the one found in Congress, that gives a substantial advantage to strongly motivated opponents of any new policy. For that to change, one or both of two things would have to happen: additional allies would have to be recruited (a delicate problem given the fact that many white integrationists disapproved of aspects of the civil rights movement), or the struggle would have to be shifted to a policy-making arena in which the opposition enjoyed less of an advantage.

Partly by plan, partly by accident, black leaders followed both strategies simultaneously. By publicizing their grievances, but above all by developing a civil rights movement that (at least

in its early stages) dramatized the denial of essential and widely accepted liberties, blacks were able to broaden their base of support in elite and public opinion and thereby to raise civil rights matters from a low to a high position on the political agenda. By waging a patient, prolonged, but carefully planned legal struggle, black leaders were able to shift the key civil rights decisions out of the Congress, where they had been stymied for generations, and into the federal courts.

After this strategy had achieved some substantial successes—after blacks had been enfranchised and legal barriers to equal participation in political and economic affairs had been lowered—the politics of civil rights became more conventional. Blacks were able to assert their demands directly in the legislative and executive branches of government with reasonable (though scarcely certain) prospects of success. Civil rights became less a matter of gaining entry into the political system and more one of waging interest group politics within that system. At the same time, and not by accident, the goals of civil rights politics were broadened: whereas the struggle to gain entry into the system had been focused on the denial of fundamental rights (to vote, to organize, to obtain equal access to schools and public facilities), since that entry the dominant issues have been ones of manpower development, economic progress, and the improvement of housing and neighborhoods.

THE CAMPAIGN IN THE COURTS

The Fourteenth Amendment was both the opportunity and the problem. Adopted in 1868, it *seemed* to guarantee equal rights for all: "No state shall make or enforce any law which shall abridge the privileges or immunities of citizens of the United States; nor shall any state deprive any person of life, liberty, or property, without due process of law; nor deny to any person within its jurisdiction the equal protection of the laws."

But what are these "privileges and immunities," and what constitutes this "liberty" of which persons could not be deprived without due process of law? Unfortunately, the congressmen who drafted and voted for the amendment said very little about exactly what rights it was supposed to protect. For example, at the time it was debated, schools were scarcely mentioned, and when they were (in discussing a civil rights act that was under discussion at the same time) it was to assert that civil rights did not include a right to attend integrated schools.[5] On the other hand, broad constitutional language has frequently been interpreted by the courts in accordance with its general thrust rather than in strict observance of the intentions of its authors; recall, from Chapter 18, how the First Amendment grew in scope and power. Whatever it had been meant to accomplish, the Fourteenth Amendment gave the courts ample opportunity, if they wished to exercise it, to use its language to attack segregation.

It was not to be. The Supreme Court, in a series of decisions interpreting the Fourteenth Amendment, so limited its meaning and so narrowed its application that it removed almost every legal barrier to Jim Crow laws that guaranteed the segregation of Negroes. In the *Slaughterhouse Cases* (1873), in which no claim of black rights was at issue, the Court interpreted the "privileges and immunities" clause into near-oblivion.[6] Ten years later, in the *Civil Rights Cases,* the Court declared unconstitutional an act of Congress prohibiting racial discrimination in the use of public accommodations (hotels, conveyances, and the like) on the grounds that the Fourteenth Amendment applied only to *state* action and did not authorize Congress to forbid discrimination by *private* individuals.[7]

But the tombstone was the case of *Plessy* v. *Ferguson,* in which the Court upheld a Louisiana law that required whites and blacks to occupy separate cars on railroad trains in that state. When Adolph Plessy, who by parentage was seven-eighths white and one-eighth Negro, refused to obey the law, he was arrested. On appeal, the Supreme Court decided that separate-

ORIGIN OF "JIM CROW"

Thomas D. ("Daddy") Rice, a white entertainer, began around 1828 to employ a vaudeville sketch in which he blacked his face with burnt cork and sang a ditty that acquired the title, "Wheel About and Turn About and Jump, Jim Crow." Thus was born what later became the immensely popular minstrel shows, a burlesque by whites of black songs and speech mannerisms. The phrase "Jim Crow" from Rice's song soon came to be a slang expression for blacks and later for laws and practices that segregated blacks from whites.

but-equal facilities were constitutional because such separation does not by itself stamp "the colored race with a badge of inferiority" unless "the colored race chooses to put that construction on it."[8] (The insincerity of this interpretation became evident a few lines later in the opinion when the Court added, "If one race be inferior to the other socially, the Constitution of the United States cannot put them on the same plane.")

To make crystal clear that the separate-but-equal doctrine applied to everything and not just railroad cars, the Court, three years after *Plessy,* held that the existence of segregated public schools in Georgia was not a violation of the Constitution. Indeed, it went even farther: in Richmond County, where the case began, there

THE CRISIS

A RECORD OF THE DARKER RACES

Volume One	NOVEMBER, 1910	Number One

Edited by W. E. BURGHARDT DU BOIS, with the co-operation of Oswald Garrison Villard, J. Max Barber, Charles Edward Russell, Kelly Miller, W. S. Braithwaite and M. D. Maclean.

CONTENTS

Along the Color Line   3

Opinion   7

Editorial   10

The N. A. A. C. P.   12

Athens and Brownsville . . .   13
By MOORFIELD STOREY

The Burden . . .   14

What to Read . .   15

PUBLISHED MONTHLY BY THE

National Association for the Advancement of Colored People
AT TWENTY VESEY STREET   NEW YORK CITY

ONE DOLLAR A YEAR   TEN CENTS A COPY

Shown above is the cover of the first issue of *The Crisis*, the magazine started by the NAACP in 1910 to raise black consciousness and publicize racist acts.

was a public high school for whites but not one for blacks. (The school board told the blacks they could go to private schools.) The Court refused to find that unequal public facilities, to say nothing of separate ones, violated the Constitution.[9]

What a court has made, a court can unmake. But to get it to change its mind requires a long, expensive series of lawsuits, and that in turn requires organizational support. Such support was to come from the National Association for the Advancement of Colored People (NAACP), founded in 1909 by a small group of whites and blacks in the aftermath of an antiblack riot. The NAACP performed several roles—lobbying in

Washington and publicizing black grievances, especially through the pages of *The Crisis*, a magazine edited by W. E. B. Du Bois—but its chief role, and ultimately its most influential one, was to hire lawyers to develop and press court challenges to segregationist practices. The NAACP's strategy was well suited to its political circumstances: waging court cases in defense of essential rights did not require the formation of a broad legislative alliance, focused attention on the clearest abuses of civil rights, did not confront white opinion with economic demands, and allowed the association to remain nonpartisan. Though the NAACP formed local branches all over the country, and though some of these branches carried on campaigns of their own, the major function of these branches was to raise funds to support the national office and its small cadre of attorneys, many drawn from the faculty and graduates of the all-black Howard University Law School in Washington, D.C.

Though a sound strategy, it was also a slow and difficult one. If the Supreme Court were to be persuaded to broaden the meaning of the equal protection clause, the cases brought to it would have to be selected to present the clearest possible violation of an essential right. Additionally, the arguments supporting each case would have to be carefully drawn to permit the Court either to distinguish it from earlier cases in which the decision had gone against black claims or to move, gradually, toward a reversal of those earlier cases.

The NAACP pursued several broad lines of attack, but two were of special importance: one involved voting rights (reviewed in Chapter 7) and the other concerned black access to public schools and universities. In the case of schools, with which the remainder of this section will be concerned, the NAACP had to coax the Court to move step by step: first, to declare unconstitutional those laws creating schools that were separate but obviously *un*equal; next, to declare unconstitutional laws creating schools that were separate but unequal in not-so-obvious ways;

A 1916 issue of *The Crisis* carried this cartoon. Even then blacks saw the Constitution as the best weapon to use against Jim Crow laws and segregation.

and finally, to rule that separate schools were inherently unequal and that laws requiring separate schooling for blacks and whites were unconstitutional. That effort lasted from 1938 to 1954. It was followed by what some see as the continuation of the earlier strategy and what others argue is a reversal of it—namely, persuading the Court, not simply to overturn laws that forbid blacks from attending white schools, but to require that blacks and whites attend the same schools.

Phase I: Obtaining Equal-Though-Separate Schools

In 1935 Lloyd Gaines graduated from the all-black Lincoln University in Missouri and wanted to go on to law school. There was, however, no black law school in the state and the all-white law school at the University of Missouri refused to admit him because of his race. It instead offered to reimburse him for any extra charges he might incur if he went to an out-of-state law school. Alternatively, the state promised to build a law school for blacks at Lincoln. In 1938 the issue reached the United States Supreme Court, which by then had acquired two liberal justices (Hugo Black and Stanley Reed) to replace two retired conservatives who earlier had helped overturn New Deal legislation. In a five-to-three decision, the Court held that the "separate-but-equal" doctrine required Missouri to admit Gaines into its all-white law school because no equal facility for blacks was then available in that state.[10]

Ten years later Ada Lois Sipuel complained to the Supreme Court that she could not get into the University of Oklahoma Law School because of her race. Oklahoma rejoined that it would soon open a law school for blacks, but "soon" was not good enough. The Court, this time unanimously, said that the state had to supply a legal education to Sipuel as soon as it did for whites.[11] Faced with the threat of seeing its white law school closed down until a black one could be built, the state ordered a small section of the state capitol building roped off and assigned three law professors to teach her there. Though white students and faculty at the university protested this within-school segregation and though another lawsuit objecting to this scheme was begun, the Court was not yet ready to go farther and upheld the state plan.[12]

Now the problem for the NAACP was to persuade the Court that a separate facility had to be equal in more than a token sense. In Texas the association found a black postman, Heman Sweatt, who had been denied admission to the University of Texas Law School. Sweatt got a lower court order requiring the state to supply him with a black law school he could attend. This the state did by renting a few rooms in Houston, hiring two black lawyers to be professors, and telling Sweatt to go there. Sweatt

"That September, Thurgood Marshall, the black law-yer who headed the NAACP legal staff, began five suits challenging segregated schools in carefully selected locales around the country.**"**

The team of NAACP lawyers who brought the school desegregation cases. Standing in front of the Supreme Court, left to right: George Hayes, Thurgood Marshall, and James Nabritt, Jr.

refused, and the case went to the Supreme Court. At the same time, back in Oklahoma, George W. McLaurin was trying to get into the graduate school of the University of Oklahoma to work for his Ph.D. He was refused on grounds of race. After a federal district court ordered him admitted, the state complied by allowing him to attend the University of Oklahoma but only in a special "colored" section of the classrooms and library. McLaurin's case also went to the Supreme Court.

On June 5, 1950, the Court ruled on the *Sweatt* and *McLaurin* cases. Unanimously, it decided that the separate law school provided Sweatt was not equal to that provided whites at the University of Texas—it lacked not only the facilities of the white school, but its faculty, ex-

perience, alumni, traditions, and prestige as well. Sweatt had to be admitted into the white school. And, unanimously, the Court decided that McLaurin could not be kept in a segregated part of an all-white school because such separation creates handicaps to effective learning that would make his education inferior to that provided whites.[13]

Phase II: Making Separation Inherently Unequal

In the 1950 cases the Court had stopped short of overturning the separate-but-equal doctrine. It had, however, struck down so many ways of creating a separate education that the NAACP began to hope that a case could be found that would induce the Court to decide that no form of separate schooling could provide equality of opportunity. On the other hand, many southern states were trying to prevent this from happening by launching extensive building programs to bring black schools up to white standards. The NAACP was in a quandary: Should it forge ahead with challenges to separateness, even at the risk of blocking, by court order, the building of new, all-black schools and colleges? Or should it settle for the improvement in black schooling that might well result from southern efforts to meet the Supreme Court standards as to what constituted equal facilities?[14]

At a major conference in the summer of 1950, the NAACP decided to go for integration. That September, Thurgood Marshall, the black law-yer who headed the NAACP legal staff, began five suits challenging segregated schools in care-fully selected locales around the country: Clar-endon County, South Carolina; Prince Ed-ward County, Virginia; Delaware; the District of Columbia; and Topeka, Kansas. In Topeka, Oliver Brown had tried to enroll his daughter, Linda, in an all-white school, and was refused on grounds of race. The lower federal court that heard Brown's complaint concluded that, from the evidence, the black school that Linda could attend was substantially equal in quality to the white school; therefore, following *Plessy* v. *Ferguson*, the segregated system was constitutional. Brown appealed to the Supreme Court, and the crucial test of the separate-but-equal doctrine was ready.

On May 17, 1954, after two sets of oral arguments before the Court, the unanimous justices, in an opinion written and delivered by Chief Justice Earl Warren, found that "in the field of public education the doctrine of 'separate but equal' has no place" because "separate educational facilities are inherently unequal." Thus, laws requiring segregated schools were a violation of the equal protection clause of the Fourteenth Amendment. The Court's reason for overruling *Plessy* was *not* that the Framers of the Fourteenth Amendment had intended to bar school segregation and *not* that the language of the Fourteenth Amendment requires state laws to be color-blind. The reason was that segregation in schools on the basis of race "has a detrimental effect upon the colored children" by generating "a feeling of inferiority as to their status in the community" which may "affect their hearts and minds in a way unlikely ever to be undone."[15] This conclusion was supported by a footnote referring to a number of social science studies of the apparent impact of segregation on black children.

Phase III: Implementation and Resistance

A court order of this magnitude is not self-enforcing. Schools all over the country, and not just in Topeka, that were segregated by law would have to be desegregated. The Court was prepared to allow time for this. In 1955 it decided that local federal courts would oversee the transition to nondiscriminatory school systems. Local plans, adapted to local conditions, should be prepared and implemented "with all deliberate speed."[16]

That speed, except in a few places, turned out to be a snail's pace. Massive resistance to desegregation broke out in many southern states. Some communities simply defied the Court

decision; others sought to evade it by closing the public schools and enrolling the white pupils in "private" schools. President Dwight Eisenhower was not a warm or vocal supporter of the Court ruling. Over one hundred southern congressmen and senators of both parties signed, in 1956, a "Southern Manifesto" that condemned the Court decision as "an abuse of judicial power" and pledged to "use all lawful means to bring about a reversal of this decision." Violence erupted when some black parents tried to enroll their children in white schools.

Despite Eisenhower's misgivings about the decision, he could not ignore the direct challenge to federal authority made by Governor Orval Faubus of Arkansas when in 1957 he used that state's National Guard to prevent nine black children from entering Little Rock Central High School. Eisenhower put the National Guard under federal authority and ordered it to prevent violence and protect the black students. Five years later, in 1962, President John Kennedy had to send paratroopers to protect a black seeking admission to the University of Mississippi. He later deployed the Alabama National Guard, brought under federal control, to overcome Governor George Wallace's effort to block the admission of black students into the University of Alabama.

In 1964, ten years after the *Brown* decision, only about 2 percent of the black pupils in the eleven states of the Old Confederacy were attending schools with whites, and most of those were in Texas and Virginia.[17] Massive resistance or token integration endured until well into the 1960s, but then it collapsed. There were several reasons. The federal courts held firm, striking down one evasive expedient after another. The show of armed federal force convinced many that resistance was futile. Southern extremists began to alienate more moderate Southerners who saw in massive resistance a destruction of orderly political and economic life. The number of black voters in the South was beginning to increase (by 1964 over a third of voting-age blacks were

In 1962 Governor George Wallace of Alabama stood in the doorway of the University of Alabama to block the entry of black students. Facing him is United States Attorney General Nicholas Katzenbach.

registered) as a result of voter education campaigns and, in time, federal civil rights laws that overturned efforts to maintain lily-white ballot boxes. Finally, in the 1970s, federal laws provided financial aid to desegregated districts and withheld such aid from segregated ones.

By the fall of 1970, the dual school system of the South was, except for pockets of resistance, a thing of the past. Of the roughly 2,700 school districts in the eleven southern states, over 97 percent had been desegregated by 1970. The number of desegregated *schools* was smaller than the number of desegregated *systems*, but it was still large: by 1970, 39 percent of southern black children attended schools where a majority of the pupils were white, and only 14 percent attended schools that were still all-black.[18]

Phase IV: From Desegregation to Integration

The *Brown* decision, for all its importance, was ambiguous on many key issues. Though it said that racially separate schools were inherently unequal, it did not say what a racially "unseparate" school might be. Was it one that any pupil was free to attend without regard to race? Or was it one that whites and blacks in fact attended? If the former, then simply repealing laws and administrative practices that kept blacks from enrolling in the school of their choice would be sufficient, even if blacks chose not to attend white schools and whites chose not to attend black ones. But if it was the latter, then nothing would suffice short of actually mixing black and white children in schools.

During the decade or more that the issue was being fought out in the South, this problem did not arise because there segregated schools were maintained by law (*"de jure"* segregation); the problem was to get the laws changed. But in the North, laws did not keep the races apart; that was the result of the pattern of residential settlement, discrimination in the housing market, the manipulation of neighborhood school boundaries, the preferences of parents, and a host of other factors (*"de facto"* segregation). And in many areas of both the North and the South, especially in the heavily black areas of the larger cities, many schools remained virtually all-black because no whites lived within walking distance of them.

Congress expressed its view on this matter in the Civil Rights Act of 1964: desegregation means assigning children to school without regard to race, but it does not mean assigning children so as to achieve any particular racial balance in those schools. The federal courts, however, thought differently. In 1966 the Court of Appeals for the Fifth Circuit held that the words "desegregation" and "integration" meant the same thing and that schools had an absolute duty to "integrate," by which it meant the "racial mixing of students."[19] The Supreme Court declined to review the lower court's interpretation. Two years later, however, it made clear its thinking in a pivotal decision. The New Kent County, Virginia, school board had created a "freedom of choice" plan under which no student would be assigned to school on the basis of race. Rather, every pupil would be allowed to choose which school to attend. After three years, all of the white children had chosen to remain in an all-white school, and 85 percent of the black children had chosen to remain in an all-black school. The Supreme Court rejected this plan because the "ultimate end to be brought about" was a "unitary, nonracial system of public education."[20] What the Court seemed to be saying was that it would judge the *results* of a desegregation plan, not just the absence of discrimination in the design of the plan.

Three years later, in 1971, the Court confirmed that impression in its first case of court-ordered busing. In Mecklenburg County, North Carolina—which includes Charlotte—pupils had been assigned to the nearest school without regard to race. As a result, about half the black children now attended formerly all-white schools, but the other half were still going to all-black schools. The federal district court felt that more integration was necessary, and ordered some busing of children to achieve greater racial balance. When the school board appealed, the Supreme Court upheld the busing as well as other features of the plan because it was designed to achieve a "unitary school system" and eliminate "all vestiges of state-imposed segregation."[21] The Court, now speaking through Chief Justice Warren Burger, said that though not every school must reflect the racial balance of the community and though some one-race schools might be permissible, any school system that had once practiced deliberate segregation could be ordered to use racial quotas, redistricted schools, and mandatory busing in order to remedy past discrimination even if such requirements were "administratively awkward, inconvenient, or even bizarre."

Court-ordered busing to achieve racial balance in the schools quickly became an explosive political issue. There were violent demonstrations in many communities where it was at-

Many schools and classrooms remained all black long after the 1954 school desegregation decision.

tempted and calm acceptance in some others, bitter academic debates over the effect (if any) of busing on educational attainment, and various congressional efforts to block or limit busing orders. The Court tried to pick its way carefully through the mine field. It upheld a citywide busing plan in Denver,[22] but struck down one cutting across city lines in Detroit.[23] In the Detroit case, the Court majority (it was a five-to-four vote) argued that a city-suburb integration plan could not be ordered unless the lower court found that the suburbs had intentionally acted so as to contribute significantly to the segregation in the city. Following this rule, city-suburb busing plans have been upheld in Louisville, Kentucky, and Wilmington, Delaware, but not in Indianapolis, Indiana.[24] But Supreme Court rules are not the whole of the matter, for the Court has left substantial discretion in the hands of local federal district judges.

On the face of it, the history of Court action since 1954 seems paradoxical. In 1954 the Court held, in effect, that state and local governments

> "Court-ordered busing to achieve racial balance in the schools quickly became an explosive political issue."

White parents protested the court-ordered busing to integrate schools in Louisville, Kentucky. Other anti-busing protesters buried a school bus (unoccupied) to dramatize their cause.

could *not* use race as a factor in assigning children to school. In 1971 and again in 1973, it held that state and local governments *must* use race as a factor in assigning children to school. There are several possible explanations for this apparently inconsistent view. One is that it is not in fact inconsistent. The Court did not, in 1954, say that the Fourteenth Amendment forbids the use of racial classifications; it said instead that racially segregated schools were "inherently unequal" and produced harmful effects on black children. Thus, to the extent the Court was announcing in 1954 its desire to achieve a certain result (i.e., better treatment of black children) rather than to apply a racially neutral rule (i.e., the Constitution is color-blind), it could later say, consistently, that schools should be racially balanced.

A second explanation, one preferred by the Court itself, is that producing racially balanced schools is a remedy for past discrimination. If the state does something illegal, the victims of that illegality are entitled to corrective action. On the other hand, if racially separate schools are entirely the result of "natural" forces and not government action, or if schools that are once balanced become later unbalanced as a result of population movements, then (according to Court doctrine so far) no judicial remedy is available.[25]

Finally, the courts, like other agencies with the task of enforcing nondiscrimination laws, seek some way of measuring whether or not discrimination exists. Now, calculating the percentage of blacks and whites in schools (or on faculties, or in unions, or in companies) cannot by itself prove the presence or absence of discrimination, but judges and administrators understandably employ it as a guide in the absence of any other easily collectible facts. As a result, they often make the attainment of some percentage the object of their orders.

Critics of these arguments rejoin that the language of the Fourteenth Amendment requires equality of opportunity but not equality of result; thus, children should be free to attend a school of their choice without regard to race but not compelled to attend a school because of their race in order to achieve some social objective. Moreover, if racial balancing is a remedy for past discrimination, the burdens of it should not fall on those members of the present generation who may not be guilty of that discrimination. As we shall see in the next section, Congress, as well as the courts, has had to face this controversy. But a legislative body finds it easier than a court to duck hard questions or to take both sides of such questions simultaneously as a way of coping with seemingly irreconcilable points of view.

These issues, the merits of which are beyond the scope of this book, illustrate the consequences of a court-oriented rather than a legislative strategy: (1) social change becomes possible despite the political advantages of its opponents; (2) the change takes the form of attempts to establish general rules for the management of complex enterprises; (3) the implementation of these rules must be left to other agencies which may not endorse them; and (4) there are few means for accommodating popular opposition to the enforcement of the rules.

THE CAMPAIGN IN CONGRESS

The campaign in the courts, though slow and costly, could be centrally directed, carefully managed, and nationally planned. The effort to get new civil rights laws from Congress, on the other hand, required a far more difficult, decentralized, and uncertain strategy. It would first be necessary to get civil rights on the national political agenda. That in turn would require dramatizing the problems of blacks in ways that

❝ To get civil rights on the national political agenda . . . would require dramatizing the problems of blacks in ways that shocked the consciences of those whites who were not racists but who were ordinarily indifferent to black problems. **❞**

Whites harassed blacks and others who participated in a sit-in at a Jackson, Mississippi, lunch counter in 1963 to protest the refusal to serve blacks. A bus used by black "freedom riders" who sought to integrate the buses was set afire in Anniston, Alabama, in 1961.

shocked the consciences of those whites who were not racists but who were ordinarily indifferent to black problems. The incidents that might provide this agenda-setting drama were not ordinarily within the power of black leaders to create or control. Brutal lynchings of blacks would generate brief waves of sympathy and concern, but such emotions were hard to sustain and in any case lynchings became less frequent in the 1950s.

There were some things blacks could do, however, and beginning in the late 1950s, they began to happen—sit-in demonstrations at segregated lunch counters, "freedom rides" to attempt to integrate public transportation, boycotts by blacks of segregated facilities, and protest marches aimed at ending segregation and obtaining equal employment opportunities. Some of these events were carefully planned, others occurred spontaneously, and most involved different local groups that acknowledged no central leadership.

The early civil rights demonstrations, especially those led by Martin Luther King, Jr., were based on a philosophy of nonviolent civil disobedience. But the momentum of protest, once unleashed, could not be led or directed—a rising tide of anger, especially among younger

---

CHRONOLOGY OF MAJOR EVENTS IN THE CIVIL RIGHTS MOVEMENT, 1955–1968

Dec. 5, 1955	Blacks in Montgomery, Alabama, begin year-long boycott of bus company; the Reverend Martin Luther King, Jr., emerges as leader.
Feb. 1, 1960	First sit-in demonstration. Black students at North Carolina Agricultural and Technical College sit in at dime-store lunch counter in Greensboro.
May 4, 1961	Freedom rides begin as blacks attempt to ride in white sections of interstate buses. Violence erupts, a bus burned, U.S. marshals dispatched to restore order.
Sept. 30, 1962	Violence greets effort of James Meredith, a black, to enroll in University of Mississippi.
April 3, 1963	Demonstrations by blacks begin in Birmingham, Alabama; police retaliation.
June 12, 1963	Medgar Evers, Mississippi state chairman of NAACP, murdered in Jackson.
Aug. 28, 1963	March on Washington by 250,000 whites and blacks.
Fall 1963	Blacks boycott schools in several northern cities to protest *de facto* segregation.
June 1964	Three civil rights workers killed in Neshoba County, Mississippi.
Summer 1964	First ghetto riots by blacks in northern cities, beginning in Harlem on July 18.
Jan 2, 1965	King begins protest marches in Selma, Alabama; police attack marchers in February and March.
Aug. 11, 1965	Black riots in Watts section of Los Angeles and on West Side of Chicago.
June 6, 1966	James Meredith shot (but not killed) while on protest march in Mississippi.
Summer 1966	Black ghetto riots in Chicago, Cleveland, New York, and other cities; King leads protest marches in Chicago.
Summer 1967	Riots or violent demonstrations in 67 cities.
April 4, 1968	Martin Luther King, Jr., murdered in Memphis, Tennessee.

The Reverend Martin Luther King, Jr. (fourth from right) led a civil rights march at Selma, Alabama, in 1963.

blacks, resulted in the proliferation of new organizations and the occurrence in dozens of cities of black riots that erupted without leadership or organization of any kind. From 1964 to 1968 there were, in the North as well as the South, four "long, hot summers" of racial violence.

The rapid escalation of demonstrations, confrontations, and rioting unquestionably succeeded in putting civil rights high on the public agenda. But that very success created a problem with the second requirement of any legislative campaign—the need to build a broadly based coalition in Congress to pass new civil rights laws in the face of determined opposition from strategically placed southern legislators. The civil rights movement simultaneously mobilized white supporters and alienated white opponents. In 1964 and again in 1968, over two-thirds of the whites interviewed in national opinion polls said they thought the civil rights movement was pushing "too fast," had "hurt" the black cause,

and was predominantly violent in nature.[26] But white opinion was by no means united on this—some whites not only approved of the civil rights movement, they joined in it by participating in freedom rides and protest marches.

The conflict between the agenda-setting and coalition-building aspects of the civil rights movement was not easily reconciled, but certain factors helped dampen it. The black leadership group was becoming large and diverse. As a result, the more moderate leaders (such as Roy Wilkins of the NAACP, Whitney Young of the Urban League, and Martin Luther King of the Southern Christian Leadership Conference) could form alliances with liberal and moderate white groups by describing themselves as alternatives to the more militant black activists in the Student Nonviolent Coordinating Committee (SNCC), the Congress of Racial Equality (CORE), and the Black Panther Party.

Though no black leaders instigated the urban

riots of 1964–1968, the threat of such distur-
bances enhanced the bargaining power of black
leaders opposed to rioting. Moreover, despite
white criticism of the civil rights movement,
sentiment favoring integration was increasing
among whites generally. As is evident in Figure
19.1, the upward trend, beginning in the 1950s,
in the proportion of whites favoring integrated
schools, housing, and transportation continued—
in fact, accelerated—in the 1960s. At the leading
edge of this growth in integrationist views was
the "New Class" (see Chapter 5) of upper middle
class whites who were prepared to support directly the black cause. But perhaps most impor-

tant, the early civil rights protest demonstrations
in some southern cities precipitated violent reactions from local authorities. When these were
vividly portrayed by television to the nation
at large, they gave to the black cause a powerful moral force that its critics found hard to
discredit.

Birmingham, Neshoba, and Selma
The three most dramatic incidents occurred in
Birmingham, Alabama, Neshoba County, Mis-
sissippi, and Selma, Alabama. In Birmingham
and Selma, marches led by Martin Luther King,
Jr., were met by force; in Neshoba County, three

FIGURE 19.1   The Increasing Acceptance of Integrationist Beliefs, 1963–1976 (percent giving pro-integration answers)

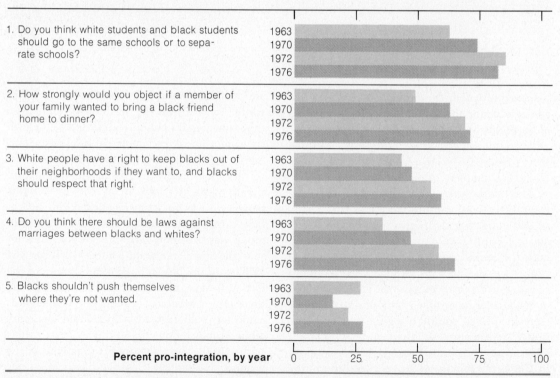

Source: D. Garth Taylor, Paul B. Sheatsley, and Andrew M. Greeley, "Attitudes Toward Racial Integration," *Scientific American*, Vol. 238 (June 1978), p. 43. Copyright © 1978 by Scientific American, Inc. All rights reserved.

Note: Questions on racial attitudes were administered to a nationwide sample of about 1,350 whites in 1963, 1970, 1972, and 1976. The bars show for each year the percentage of respondents giving what is considered to be a pro-integration response to each question.

civil rights workers, two white and one black, were murdered. There were other protest marches and other acts of violence, but these three captured the nation's attention and contributed directly to breaking the legislative logjam that had stalled civil rights legislation.

The nonviolent civil disobedience movement led by King and the Southern Christian Leadership Conference had grown out of a boycott in 1955–1956 of the city bus lines in Montgomery, Alabama. The city had arrested a black woman, Rosa Parks, for refusing to move to the colored section at the back of the bus. The boycott itself did not succeed, though a suit in federal court brought against the city did lead to an order that the buses be desegregated. In 1961 and again in 1962, King led demonstrations in Albany, Georgia, but they achieved little except the jailing of the protesters. The failure in Albany resulted from the restraint of the local police: though they arrested hundreds, they did not use excessive force.[27] In 1963 King led marches in Birmingham aimed at desegregating public facilities and increasing job opportunities. For several days the police did little more than make arrests. But on May 3–4, Public Safety Commissioner Eugene "Bull" Connor ordered his police to repulse the marchers with police dogs and high-pressure fire hoses. Television and newspaper accounts of the ensuing scene created a national sensation. That summer, a nationwide "March on Washington" was organized that brought about 250,000 persons, white and black, to the Lincoln Memorial where King gave a stirring and widely hailed address.

In the summer of 1964, hundreds of white and black civil rights workers, mostly students, went to Mississippi for a "Summer Project" aimed chiefly at getting more blacks registered to vote. But there was for some of the project leaders another goal—to provoke a violent white reaction that would require massive and direct federal intervention in the state. The Ku Klux Klan, aware of this possibility, instructed its members not to engage in violence.[28] But a segregationist movement is no more easily controlled than an

❝The three most dramatic incidents . . . captured the nation's attention and contributed directly to breaking the legislative logjam that had stalled civil rights legislation.**❞**

This picture of a police dog lunging at a black during a racial demonstration in Birmingham, Alabama, in May 1963 was one of the most influential news photographs ever published. It was widely reprinted throughout the world and frequently referred to in congressional debates on the civil rights bill of 1964.

integrationist one. In June 1964 three civil rights workers—James Earl Chaney, Andrew Goodman, and Michael Schwerner—were brutally murdered by Klansmen, aided by a local sheriff and a deputy sheriff. The FBI soon arrested the persons involved. Black leaders later complained that more attention was given to a few murdered white students than to many murdered southern blacks, and they may have been right. But the effect of the Chaney-Goodman-Schwerner killings on public opinion was galvanic: the possibility that any white southern leader could offer respectable or persuasive opposition to federal laws protecting black voting rights was powerfully diminished.

Early in 1965, Selma, Alabama, became the target of demonstrations aimed at obtaining voting rights for blacks. Off and on for a month there were marches followed by arrests. Then again, as in Birmingham, the police resorted to violence: in a nearby town, club-swinging state troopers charged a black crowd. A few days later, an effort to march from Selma to Montgomery was broken up by police using nightsticks and teargas. And again, as in Neshoba County, some whites tried to take matters into their own hands—a white minister was beaten to death by a mob; a white woman, Mrs. Viola Liuzzo, was shot to death while driving a car used to transport demonstrators to Selma. Another rally in Washington ensued, this one of clergymen protesting the government's failure to protect the demonstrators. More rallies occurred in other cities in memory of Mrs. Liuzzo. Her funeral was attended by high-ranking national figures; her home was visited by the vice-president of the United States; her death was the subject of a presidential television address.

National attention to dramatic incidents of violence and death became the crucial ingredient for building a legislative coalition for new civil rights legislation. But that coalition had first to surmount the complexities of the legislative process.

Legislative Politics

Opponents of civil rights legislation had three major defensive positions: (1) the Senate Judiciary Committee, long dominated by a coalition of southern Democrats and Republicans critical of civil rights bills; (2) the House Rules Committee, until the 1960s under conservative southern control and able to delay or block the introduction of civil rights legislation in the House; and (3) the filibuster, whereby a minority of senators could talk an unpopular bill to death. And parliamentary roadblocks

were not the only problem: until well into the 1960s, presidents were rarely ardent champions of civil rights legislation. Woodrow Wilson had been hostile to it; Franklin Roosevelt had signed, under pressure, executive orders to facilitate integration in defense employment during World War II. Dwight Eisenhower had supported the Supreme Court's school desegregation decision as federal law but was hardly enthusiastic about its substance; John F. Kennedy during 1961 and 1962 resisted demands that he submit general civil rights legislation. And Richard Nixon and Gerald Ford were cool to new civil rights initiatives. Other than Lyndon Johnson, only Harry Truman steadfastly submitted strong civil rights bills (to ban poll taxes, make lynching a federal crime, and require equal opportunity in employment), but his proposals, made in the 1940s and 1950s, got nowhere in Congress.

Between 1957 and 1968 five major pieces of civil rights legislation were passed by Congress. (There have been additional laws since 1968, but these five were the breakthroughs.) Three (in 1957, 1960, and 1965) were chiefly directed at the right to vote; one (1968) was aimed at preventing discrimination in housing; and one (1964), the most comprehensive and far-reaching of the lot, dealt with voting, employment, schools, and public accommodations. All five were passed by a majority of northern Democrats and a majority of Republicans joining together against the opposition of a majority of southern Democrats; all five required elaborate parliamentary maneuvers to avoid or overcome the defensive advantages enjoyed by the opponents.

The first two—in 1957 and 1960—were, by today's standards, rather mild pieces of legislation. They were limited to protecting the right to vote in elections, a principle with which it was difficult to argue. The 1957 bill provided sufficiently weak enforcement machinery that it was able to get through the House Rules Committee and to pass the Senate without an organized filibuster (though one senator, Strom Thurmond, did speak against it for 24 hours and 18 minutes). Even so, to ensure that it would not be bottled up in the Senate Judiciary Committee, the House-passed version was brought directly to the Senate floor without committee consideration. The 1960 bill had tougher enforcement machinery—it authorized the appointment of federal "referees" to help blacks to register in areas where there was a "pattern or practice" of depriving citizens of the right to vote. That was sufficiently threatening to lead the House Rules Committee to try to bottle it up and southern senators to mount a filibuster. The Rules Com-

mittee changed its mind when a discharge petition (see Chapter 10) was about to succeed; the filibuster was broken when Majority Leader Lyndon Johnson kept the Senate in around-the-clock, nonstop sessions for over a week. In both cases, the bill was the result of a compromise between what liberals and moderates wanted, with the latter generally prevailing.

1964 Civil Rights Bill. The decisive legislative struggle occurred over the 1964 bill. It was sweeping in its breadth, covering hotels, restaurants, and other privately owned facilities as well

---

KEY PROVISIONS OF MAJOR CIVIL RIGHTS LAWS

1957 Made it a federal crime to try to prevent a person from voting in a federal election. Created the Civil Rights Commission.

1960 Authorized the attorney general to appoint federal referees to gather evidence and make findings about allegations that blacks were being deprived of their right to vote. Made it a federal crime to use interstae commerce to threaten or carry out a bombing.

1964 *Voting:* Made it more difficult to use administrative devices or literacy tests to bar blacks from voting.
　　　Public accommodations: Barred discrimination on grounds of race, color, religion, or national origin in restaurants, hotels, lunch counters, gasoline stations, movie theaters, stadiums, arenas, and lodging houses with more than five rooms.
　　　Schools: Authorized the attorney general to bring suit to force the desegregation of public schools on behalf of citizens. Did not authorize issuing orders to achieve racial balance in schools by busing.
　　　Employment: Outlawed discrimination in hiring, firing, or paying employees on grounds of race, color, religion, national origin, or sex. Eventually covered all firms employing twenty-five workers or more.
　　　Federal funds: Barred discrimination in any activity receiving federal assistance. Authorized cutting off federal funds to activities where discrimination practiced.

1965 Authorized appointment by the Civil Service Commission of voting examiners who would require registration of all eligible voters in federal, state, and local elections, general or primary, in areas where discrimination was found to be practiced or where less than 50 percent of voting-age residents were registered to vote in 1964 election. Suspended use of literacy tests or other devices to prevent blacks from voting. Directed the attorney general to bring suit challenging the constitutionality of poll taxes.

1968 *Housing:* Banned, by stages, discrimination in sale or rental of most housing (excluding private owners who sell or rent their homes without the services of a real estate broker).
　　　Riots: Made it a federal crime to use interstate commerce to organize or incite a riot.

❝The decisive legislative struggle occurred over the 1964 bill. . . . The passage of this bill and of the 1965 civil rights law . . . profoundly altered the politics of civil rights and the political position of southern blacks.**❞**

One key to the passage of the Civil Rights Act of 1964 was the agreement President Johnson obtained from Senate Minority Leader Everett Dirksen not to oppose the imposition of cloture in order to end the Senate filibuster.

as public facilities such as schools; it authorized potentially important new enforcement machinery, including cutting off federal funds to any federally assisted program that practiced discrimination; and it outlawed discrimination on the basis of race, religion, or sex in all business firms and labor unions above a certain small size. (It did not, as we saw in the preceding discussion on the campaign in the courts, authorize racially balancing schools.) The passage of this bill and of the 1965 civil rights law the following year profoundly altered the politics of civil rights and the political position of southern blacks.

Though the 1960 platforms of both parties promised many more changes in civil rights than either party had promised before, the Kennedy

administration—elected with a bare plurality of the popular vote and facing a Congress in which the cooperation of key Southerners was essential to any legislative program—made scarcely any civil rights proposals. The violence in Birmingham in May 1963, the subsequent demonstrations in other cities, and the March on Washington in the summer of 1963 began to change that. When President Kennedy left for a speaking engagement in Dallas in November, a bipartisan civil rights bill had just reached the House Rules Committee. Kennedy's murder in Dallas (initially, but wrongly, believed by many to be the work of a right-wing conspiracy) left the nation in shock. On assuming the presidency, Lyndon Johnson, a Texan, moved quickly to bring the bill to a vote. A discharge petition to get it out of the Rules Committee received administration support. The Committee, however, reported the bill out without waiting for the petition, and it passed the House overwhelmingly.

The major struggle was in the Senate. A bill this strong was sure to precipitate a filibuster, and it did; defeating a filibuster would require both Republican and northern Democratic votes. The key to the former was Senate Minority Leader Everett Dirksen of Illinois. The object of intense lobbying pressure and of lavish (but private) presidential attention, Dirksen finally agreed to support a cloture motion in exchange for certain amendments, none of major significance. After fifty-seven days of debate, the Senate voted 71–29 to end the filibuster (67 votes were needed). Cloture was imposed on a civil rights bill for the first time in history. (It was imposed again in debates on the 1965 and 1968 civil rights bills.) A few days after the manhunt began for the killers of the three civil rights workers, the bill was passed in final form and signed by President Johnson.

The Power of Public Opinion.   The debate over the 1965 bill was much shorter. No filibuster was attempted. (The Senate imposed cloture anyway, just to make certain.) There were two reasons for this accelerated progress: the 1964 elections had produced a large increase in the size of the Democratic majority in the House as well as an overwhelming victory for Johnson, and the national reaction to the violence in Selma provided a strong impetus to action. The 1965 law, passed in only five months, greatly enhanced the legal protection of the right to vote. It authorized the attorney general to appoint federal examiners who would actually direct the registration of qualified black voters in areas where there was legal or statistical evidence of racial groups being denied the right to vote. The law also suspended the use of literacy tests or other devices that were used to exclude blacks from voting and directed the attorney general to bring suit challenging the constitutionality of poll taxes. (In 1966 the Supreme Court decided such a suit, holding that poll taxes in state elections were a violation of the Fourteenth Amendment.[29] Poll taxes in federal elections had already been outlawed by the Twenty-Fourth Amendment, ratified in 1964.)

The combined effect of these laws, but especially of the 1964 and 1965 ones, was twofold. First, the number of blacks able to vote in the South rose dramatically between 1960 and 1970. Whereas less than 30 percent of the voting-age blacks in eleven southern states were registered in 1960, by 1971 over 58 percent were. (From 1960 to 1964, the number of blacks on the voting rolls in the South increased by 48 percent; from 1964 to 1970, it increased by another 55 percent.)[30] White politicians who were once able to ignore black voters with impunity were now required—and soon became eager—to court that vote. The consequences of their change in attitude soon became apparent in congressional votes on civil rights measures. Whereas in 1957 not one southern Democrat in the House voted in favor of the relatively mild voting rights act, a bill in 1970 to extend the duration of the stringent voting rights act of 1965 attracted the support of thirty-four southern Democrats in the House. (Fifty were opposed.) (See Tables 19.1 and 19.2.)

The second consequence is harder to measure

The number of black voters has increased dramatically.

TABLE 19.1   Increase in Number of Black Elected Officials

Office	1970	1978
Congress and state legislatures	182	316
City and county offices	715	2,595
Judges and sheriffs	213	454
Boards of education	362	1,138
Total	1,472	4,503[a]

Source: Statistical Abstract of the United States, 1978, p. 519.

[a] Of this total, 2,733 are in the South.

TABLE 19.2   Votes in Congress on Passage of Major Civil Rights Acts, 1957–1970

	House			Senate		
	No. Dem.	Rep.	So. Dem.	No. Dem.	Rep.	So. Dem.
1957 Civil Rights Act						
Yes	119	167	0	26	43	3
No	16	19	91	1	0	17
1960 Civil Rights Act						
Yes	175	131	5	40	29	2
No	11	15	83	0	0	18
1964 Civil Rights Act						
Yes	141	136	12	43	27	3
No	3	35	88	1	6	20
1965 Civil Rights Act						
Yes	180	111	37	43	30	6
No	0	20	54	1	1	16
1968 Civil Rights Act						
Yes	137	100	13	39	29	3
No	13	84	75	0	3	17
1970 Voting Rights Act						
Yes	138	100	34	27	33	4
No	6	76	50	1	1	10

Source: Congressional Quarterly, *Congress and the Nation,* Vols. I, II, III.

but perhaps of even greater significance. The mood of the Congress on civil rights had shifted markedly and, apparently, permanently, so that in the late 1960s, when the civil rights movement had taken a turn that was, to most whites, ugly and threatening, there was no serious effort to repeal or weaken the civil rights laws or, with few exceptions, to pass punitive legislation. By 1968 the headlines were dominated by black riots in northern cities instead of police violence in Birmingham or Selma, the nonviolent posture of Martin Luther King had been partially eclipsed by the calls for revolution by younger leaders, and the integrationist philosophy of the NAACP had to share the spotlight with the separatist philosophy of CORE and the Black Panthers. Congress responded by passing another civil rights act that barred discrimination in the sale or rental of private housing, despite the fact that only 35 percent of the public favored such a law.[31] (The law also contained a provision making it illegal to use interstate commerce for the purpose of inciting or organizing a riot.)

IMPLEMENTATION: THE UNRESOLVED ISSUE

By the 1970s the major issues surrounding civil rights for blacks involved matters of implementation rather than legislation. (Women, American Indians, and Hispanic-Americans, among other groups, were continuing to campaign for legislation. One notable effort was the attempt by feminists to secure congressional approval

In the mid-1970s the focus of civil rights attention shifted from blacks to women (here, right, a group demonstrates on the Capitol steps on behalf of the Equal Rights Amendment) and to the claims of other ethnic groups (left, Mexican-American farm workers make a flag in Salinas, California).

and state ratification of an equal rights amendment to the Constitution.) One of the most important implementation issues involved the meaning of "equal protection of the laws."

Just as the Supreme Court rulings on school desegregation gave rise in time to the controversy over busing, so also the various civil rights acts gave rise to a controversy over "affirmative action" or "reverse discrimination." Both the busing and the affirmative action questions reflected a common philosophical and political problem: Does "desegregation" mean simply removing barriers, legal or administrative, to the enjoyment of equal opportunities in schooling, jobs, housing, or college admissions? Or does it mean taking steps to ensure that blacks and whites actually enroll in the same schools, work in the same jobs, and live in the same housing projects?

Measuring Compliance

The matter is not, of course, quite as simple as a choice between equality of opportunity and

equality of result. For example, the government might well regard the absence of any blacks on a college faculty or in a building-trades union as evidence that the college or the union is discriminating, perhaps in subtle and hard-to-prove ways, against blacks. Similarly, the government might well view an increase in the proportion of blacks on the faculty or in the union as evidence that discrimination does not exist. In both cases, the agency implementing civil rights laws might use numerical information as an important, though not conclusive, administrative test of compliance with those laws. But such numbers can also become an end in themselves: a "quota" for the admission or employment of particular groups, and thus a quota for the denial of such admission or employment to other groups.

Though this is not the only problem facing agencies that implement civil rights laws, it is surely the most explosive one. Public opinion, black and white, strongly endorses equality of treatment in jobs and schooling; civil rights

Compensatory Action Versus Preferential Treatment

Americans are sensitive to the distinction between *compensatory action* and *preferential treatment*. Compensatory action means measures to help disadvantaged groups catch up to the standards of competition set by the larger society. Preferential treatment means suspending those standards. Americans will accept the argument that race and sex are disadvantages which justify some degree of compensation. But every attempt to introduce a reference to preferential treatment meets stiff opposition from a vast majority of Americans. Whites in a 1972 survey by the University of Michigan Survey Research Center favored "government job training programs for Negroes" by 77 to 16 percent, but opposed "giving Negroes a chance ahead of whites in promotions where they have equal ability" by 82 to 12 percent. In 1974 Gallup asked whether "a black person who is qualified should be given a job or a promotion instead of a white person even if the white person is somewhat better qualified." Predictably, Americans were almost unanimous—96 percent—in saying that the job or promotion should go to the best qualified person regardless of race. Even 83 percent of blacks agreed. Because of the heavily weighted wording, the 1974 Gallup question should be taken as a test of one "extreme" end of the scale of affirmative action: promoting a black over a better qualified white. Question wording does have a significant effect on the public's response, but even the "softest" wording cannot generate a plurality of Americans who accept "preferential treatment" in hiring or in university admissions. In March 1977 Gallup asked people to choose between "preferential treatment" for women and minorities in getting jobs and college admission, and "ability, as determined by test scores," as "the main consideration." Eighty-three percent chose "ability," and only 10 percent favored "preferential treatment." Women favored "ability" by a margin of 71 points, and even blacks endorsed the meritocratic standard by a margin of 37 points, 64 to 27 percent.

The Gallup and other surveys contrast quotas or preferential treatment with "merit" or "ability." A 1976 survey by Pat Caddell's Cambridge Survey Research eliminated these code words and so provides the "softest" test of public opinion on this issue: "Some large corporations are required to practice what is called affirmative action. This sometimes requires employers to give special preference to minorities or women when hiring. Do you approve or disapprove of affirmative action?" Caddell did not give his respondents a contrasting "meritocratic" option, and he limited the application of affirmative action to "some large corporations." Still, 51 percent disapproved of such policies, compared with 35 percent who approved, a margin of 16 points. Women disapproved of affirmative action by 12 points. In this case, blacks endorsed affirmative action by 58 to 24 percent. People describing themselves as "liberals" were evenly divided, 43 percent approving and 45 percent disapproving.

leaders, on the other hand, are also willing to support "quotas," somehow defined. (As with opinion on all complex public issues, much depends on the exact wording of the question, but however phrased, the difference between mass and elite opinion seems clear.) To civil rights leaders, changing the status quo is the crucial objective; to the public at large, applying a meritocratic principle is the proper course. The civil rights leaders point to evidence that substantial disparities continue to exist between blacks and whites in schooling and earnings; the public rejects preferential treatment as the correct way to change social conditions.

The Congress and Busing

Congress has clearly found itself in a dilemma: it has been torn between the desire to maintain the momentum in favor of civil rights and the desire to support the principle of equality of opportunity rather than equality of result. To a substantial degree, it has managed to occupy both positions simultaneously, a phenomenon characteristic of many policy areas where competing values are at stake. The school busing question provides one example of this.

Over several years, especially after 1971 when the Supreme Court approved busing to integrate schools, the House adopted, by growing majorities, amendments to various appropriations bills designed to prevent or sharply limit busing. During this period the Senate changed the House amendments in ways that would avoid a direct challenge to court-ordered busing plans. In 1974, for instance, the House adopted an amendment that would prevent spending HEW funds to assign teachers or students to schools or classes for reasons of race. The Senate added to this language a clause permitting federal funds to be spent to achieve racially based assignments if "required to enforce nondiscrimination provisions of federal law."[32] The House eventually

Source: Seymour Martin Lipset and William Schneider, "An Emerging National Consensus," *The New Republic,* October 15, 1977, pp. 8–9. Reprinted by permission of *The New Republic,* © 1978, The New Republic, Inc.

agreed to the Senate version. In another instance, the House passed an amendment to an educational appropriations bill that would limit busing for integration purposes to the school nearest (or next nearest) the pupil's home and restricted the courts' ability to order busing in the future. The Senate rejected, by one vote, the House language. It adopted instead a provision that would confine busing to nearby schools but without restricting the right of courts to enforce the Fourteenth Amendment, by busing if necessary.[33]

In the busing controversy, the traditional political roles of the House and the Senate were reversed. Before the 1960s the House had always passed civil rights bills by large majorities only to see them die of neglect or filibuster in the Senate. After the 1960s the House passed by large majorities bills restricting the use of busing to achieve civil rights objectives only to see them amended out of existence in the Senate, sometimes with the aid of a filibuster. Much of this change reflects the greater sensitivity of the House to public opinion (a result of the small size of its districts and the frequency with which its members face election). In the early 1960s the House reflected northern beliefs that civil rights laws ought to be passed and, owing to its procedures, no determined minority could block this (except in the House Rules Committee). In the late 1960s and early 1970s, national opinion turned sharply against busing, and the House changed accordingly. The Senate contained Northerners less keenly exposed to public opinion and thus more willing to take risks in supporting busing; the Senate also provided liberals with the same means (the filibuster) to block action that had once been used by conservatives.

The Court and Quotas

The Supreme Court showed that it, too, recognized the importance of straddling a deeply controversial issue. Though it supported busing for reasons already discussed, it found itself deeply split on the questions of affirmative action and quotas for admission to universities. When

"Congress has clearly found itself in a dilemma: it has been torn between the desire to maintain the momentum in favor of civil rights and the desire to support the principle of equality of opportunity rather than equality of result."

Allan Bakke, a thirty-eight-year-old white engineer, was twice denied entrance into the medical school of the University of California at Davis, he brought suit, charging that the university had unconstitutionally set aside sixteen places in the entering class for minority applicants and awarded these places to candidates substantially inferior to him in qualifications. The California Supreme Court agreed with Bakke, and ordered the university to admit him. The university appealed to the United States Supreme Court, which rendered its decision on June 28, 1978.

The Court split into three groups. One, made up of Justices Stevens, Rehnquist, and Stewart, and Chief Justice Burger, found the university's quota system to be a violation of the 1964 Civil Rights Act, which says, among other things, that "no person shall, on the ground of race, color, or national origin, be excluded from participation in . . . any program or activity receiving federal financial assistance." (The medical school was receiving such assistance.)

A second group, made up of Justices Brennan, Blackmun, Marshall, and White, argued that the Constitution permitted the government to take race into account in order to redress the continuing effects of past discrimination, that the 1964 Civil Rights Act did not change this, and that the use of racial quotas for remedial rather than harmful purposes was proper. The Court has never said the Constitution is color-blind, they stated, but rather permits the use of racial classifications for legitimate purposes such as ensuring that racial minorities obtain access to schools.

The third "group" was made up of Justice Powell. He agreed with the Stevens group that an explicit racial quota system was a violation of the equal protection clause of the Fourteenth Amendment and thus unlawful. (That produced a five-to-four majority in favor of letting Bakke into the school and outlawing explicit quotas.) But Powell also agreed with the Brennan group that a university may take race into account in its admission process provided it is one of several factors and does not become the single decisive factor. (That produced a five-to-four majority upholding the constitutionality of "affirmative action" programs not involving explicit quotas.)[34] Obviously, a host of issues remain unresolved, and more court cases will follow, in which the permissible scope of affirmative action plans and the meaning of terms such as "quota" are debated.

RACE AND INTEREST GROUP POLITICS

The issue of civil rights of blacks could not, for a hundred years after the Civil War, find its way onto the national legislative agenda in any meaningful way. Race politics existed, but was limited for the most part to those northern cities with large black populations. Southern whites were a determined minority that could keep a rival minority, southern blacks, from entering into the bargaining relationship of interest group politics by excluding them from political participation in all but a few southern communities. To change that situation required using the courts to outflank a blocked legislative system and, simultaneously, converting an indifferent

Susan B. Anthony (standing) and Elizabeth Cady Stanton were early leaders of the women's rights movement. One of the tactics used by the women who sought to gain the right to vote was picketing in front of the White House.

W. E. B. Du Bois was a founder of the NAACP and editor of its magazine. In the 1960s blacks staged nonviolent sit-ins to dramatize their plight.

Blacks and Feminists

Civil rights movements on behalf of blacks and women have been intertwined at many points in their history and display many parallels, suggesting how different groups employ similar protest tactics.

Origins: The campaign against slavery stimulated the formation of a campaign for women's rights. When the Antislavery Society was founded in 1833, it excluded women. Four years later women abolitionists formed their own National Female Antislavery Society. Early female opponents of black slavery—Lucy Stone, Susan B. Anthony, Sarah and Angelina Grimké—later became active in the women's rights movement.

Conflict: When Congress was considering the Fourteenth and Fifteenth Amendments to the Constitution, many female abolitionists opposed the amendments because the Fifteenth gave the right to vote to blacks but not to women and the Fourteenth added the word "male" to the Constitution for the first time (with a provision that penalized states that denied the franchise to men). The feminist movement split into two organizations—the American Woman Suffrage Association, led by Lucy Stone, sought voting rights for women but did not oppose black enfranchisement, while the National Woman Suffrage Association, led by Susan B. Anthony, sought women's rights but opposed the Fifteenth Amendment because it was limited to blacks.

Tactics: Black leaders eventually formed a variety of civil rights organizations, each specializing in a different tactic and each appealing to a somewhat different constituency. The NAACP followed a legal strategy; the Urban League negotiated with white businessmen; SNCC led sit-in demonstrations; and CORE began as an integrationist-pacifist group that later advocated "Black Power" and separatist goals. Feminists in the early twentieth century formed the National American Woman Suffrage Association, which followed a legislative strategy aimed at getting a constitutional amendment enfranchising women, and to that end entered into many alliances with moderate and even conservative male political groups. At the same time, the National Woman's Party was formed by more militant feminists to engage in direct action—picketing, hunger strikes, and demonstrations. The success of militant tactics by both black and feminist groups depended in large part on provoking a violent reaction by the opposition—physical attacks by police on blacks, the forced feeding of women who were on hunger strikes while in jail.

Goals: Blacks and feminists initially focused on clear, easily understood goals with broad appeal—and especially on obtaining the right to vote. When they were successful in that, the goals became broader, involving economic opportunity and affirmative action programs.

Many blacks have made economic progress since 1964. But for young black males in urban ghettos there are few jobs available, and sometimes government programs do not benefit them.

northern public into an active ally of southern blacks. The latter was done chiefly by a civil rights movement that combined a lofty moral purpose with a shrewdly planned capacity to provoke violent reactions from some southern officials. Moreover, court victories had political consequences: when the Supreme Court decided *Brown* v. *Board of Education* in 1954, it set in motion events that inevitably drew a reluctant president and a divided Congress into the school desegregation issue. The Court's decision made it impossible for the political parties any longer to pretend that race was not a significant national issue.

Once the basic legal framework for the protection of civil rights had been put into place and blacks had been enfranchised in the South, the politics of civil rights began to assume a conventional interest group form. Government agencies were created to administer the new laws—the Civil Rights Division of the Department of Jus-

tice, the United States Civil Rights Commission, the Office for Civil Rights in HEW, the Office of Federal Contract Compliance in the Department of Labor, and the Equal Employment Opportunity Commission—and these agencies acquired clientele groups that supported them. Though civil rights groups have been critical of what they felt were the inadequate powers or weak leadership of some of these agencies, by and large they have defended them. There are also, of course, interest groups that actively oppose some civil rights demands: employers and labor unions dispute with black groups the rulings of the Equal Employment Opportunity Commission and the Office of Federal Contract Compliance; universities and feminist organizations argue over the decisions of the Office for Civil Rights. Though principles are at stake (in politics, they almost always are), much of the argument involves not issues, but the pace of progress—more or less, faster or slower.

In this competition, civil rights groups have tended to enjoy an advantage for the same reason that any group that has espoused the formation of a government agency enjoys an initial advantage: such an agency typically has a "tilt" toward whatever interest is most closely identified with the agency's creation, even though the nominal task of the agency is to resolve disputes or hear competing claims. At least in its early years, an Equal Employment Opportunity Commission will define its task as increasing the number of blacks and other minorities in business, just as in its formative years a National Labor Relations Board will see its job as protecting workers who want to unionize. In time, of course, such agencies may lose that tilt or may come under leadership hostile to the demands of the formative interest. (President Nixon tried, with some success, to get civil rights agencies in HEW and the Justice Department to ease up on pressing local school systems to desegregate.)

The Economic Position of Blacks

There is evidence that a combination of civil rights laws, changed public attitudes, and government manpower programs helped many blacks make economic progress after 1964. Though blacks had gained—relative to whites—in the 1950s, the gains were much greater after 1964 and have continued into the 1970s. Whereas black males earned, on the average, 50 percent of white wages and salaries in 1950, they earned 73 percent by 1975. (The wages of black females increased even more: from 40 percent of white female wages in 1950 to 97 percent in 1975.)

But many blacks did not participate in this change, especially young black males from broken or disadvantaged homes who lived in urban ghettos. Whereas the median weekly earnings of black men with five years of college are, on the average, 94 percent of the earnings of white men with similar educations, over 38 percent of black teenagers in 1977 were unemployed.

Part of the difference between the earnings of blacks making economic progress and those not making it is geographic—there are few jobs in the largest urban ghettos where the poorest live. (Jobs, like people, have migrated to the suburbs.) Part of the difference is also the result of family background: blacks from intact families with educated parents are much more likely than blacks without these advantages to participate in economic progress. (Blacks from two-parent families earn 75 percent of what whites earn; blacks from one-parent homes earn only 64 percent.) And part of the difference is the result of government programs that are often more accessible or more advantageous to blacks (and others) who are already well-off.

The growing cleavage between blacks who are making progress and those who are not is a major social problem. Unlike the problems of the 1950s, however, civil rights laws are not likely to make much of a difference. Thus, the kinds of black issues with which the political system now must cope are more complex, less easily dramatized, and less suited to protest strategies than those of the 1950s.

Among the programs that seek to cope with these employment problems are *CETA* (the Comprehensive Employment and Training Act) programs that provide public service jobs; the *Job Corps* that provides training and counseling in camps to the hard-core unemployed; *summer youth jobs* for students during school vacation; and *entitlement projects* that seek to guarantee postgraduate jobs to disadvantaged youths who remain in school.

Congress, if it wishes, can intervene in interest group conflict in executive agencies, but it often does not wish to, especially if the competing interests are strong and politically important. Just as few congressmen are eager to take sides between business and labor in the affairs of the Occupational Safety and Health Administration, so also few are eager to take sides between civil rights groups and private employers in the disputes before the Office for Civil Rights. Particular congressional *committees* may happen to favor one side or the other, and intervene accordingly, but Congress as a whole will ordinarily be loathe to pass legislation clearly hostile to one party or another in an agency dispute. This is true especially if (as is the case in civil rights matters) such legislation may run afoul of court rulings. But there are limits to congressional disinclination to take clear stands on hotly disputed questions. When HEW ruled in 1976 that father-son and mother-daughter dinners in public schools were a violation of civil rights laws, as were American Legion "Boys' State" and "Girls' State" programs, Congress passed a law exempting such activities from antidiscrimination regulations. While they were at it, the congressmen added another proviso allowing scholarships to be given to beauty pageant winners without violating federal regulations saying that schools must treat boys and girls equally.

SUMMARY

The civil rights movement in the courts and in Congress profoundly changed the nature of black participation in politics by bringing southern blacks into the political system so that they could become an effective interest group. The decisive move was to enlist northern opinion in this cause, a job made easier by the northern perception that civil rights involved simply an unfair contest between two minorities—southern whites and southern blacks. That perception changed when it became evident that the court rulings and legislative decisions would apply to the North as well as to the South, leading to the emergence of northern opposition to court-ordered busing and affirmative action programs.

By the time this reaction developed, however, the legal and political system had been changed sufficiently to make it difficult if not impossible to limit the application of civil rights laws to the special circumstances of the South or to alter by legislative means the decisions of federal courts. Though the courts can accomplish little when they have no political allies (as revealed by the massive resistance to the early school desegregation decisions), they can accomplish a great deal, even in the face of adverse public opinion, when they have some organized allies (as revealed by their ability to withstand antibusing moves). In some segments of policy-making, blacks have acquired clientele relations with the relevant government agencies, and the focus of policy initiatives has shifted in large measure to more complex economic issues.

Suggested Readings

Abraham, Henry J. *Freedom and the Court,* 3rd ed. New York: Oxford University Press, 1977. See Chapter 7. A brief summary of the leading court cases on school desegregation.

Franklin, John Hope. *From Slavery to Freedom,* 4th ed. New York: Alfred A. Knopf, 1974. A survey of black history in the United States.

Kluger, Richard. *Simple Justice.* New York: Random House/Vintage Books, 1977. Detailed and absorbing account of the school desegregation issue, from the Fourteenth Amendment to the *Brown* case.

Orfield, Gary. *Congressional Power: Congress and Social Change.* New York: Harcourt Brace Jovanovich, 1975. Analysis of the legislative politics of the major civil rights laws.

Sindler, Allan P. *Bakke, DeFunis, and Minority Admissions.* New York: Longman, 1978. History and analysis of the landmark Supreme Court case on affirmative action and quotas in college admissions.

Wilhoit, Francis M. *The Politics of Massive Resistance.* New York: George Braziller, 1973. The methods—and ultimate collapse—of all-out southern resistance to school desegregation.

Woodward, C. Vann. *The Strange Career of Jim Crow.* New York: Oxford University Press, 1957. Brief, lucid account of the evolution of Jim Crow practices in the South.

20 Foreign Policy

Focus on war, peace, and global diplomacy—
majoritarian issues • Preeminence of the
president • Relationship of White House and
State Department • Relationship of president
and Senate • Checks on presidential power •
Impact of public opinion • Origins of elite
opinion • Isolationism vs. internationalism •
Vietnam paradigm • Revisionist debate

Isolationism to world power: Charles A. Lindbergh,
the hero aviator, at an America First rally around
1939–1940 (left), and former Ambassador Andrew
Young at the United Nations (right).

Foreign policy has always had an ambiguous relationship with democratic politics. To some, such as Tocqueville, the proper conduct of foreign affairs requires precisely those qualities most lacking in a democratic nation: "A democracy can only with great difficulty regulate the details of an important undertaking, persevere in a fixed design, and work out its execution in spite of serious obstacles. It cannot combine its measures with secrecy or await their consequences with patience."[1] This view is often held—privately—by secretaries of state who would like to be free of the restraints of what they take to be an impatient and uncomprehending public. A similar view is sometimes voiced publicly by those who believe that domestic politics is interfering with the development of a sound foreign policy. During the 1930s and again in the 1970s, for example, many persons argued that

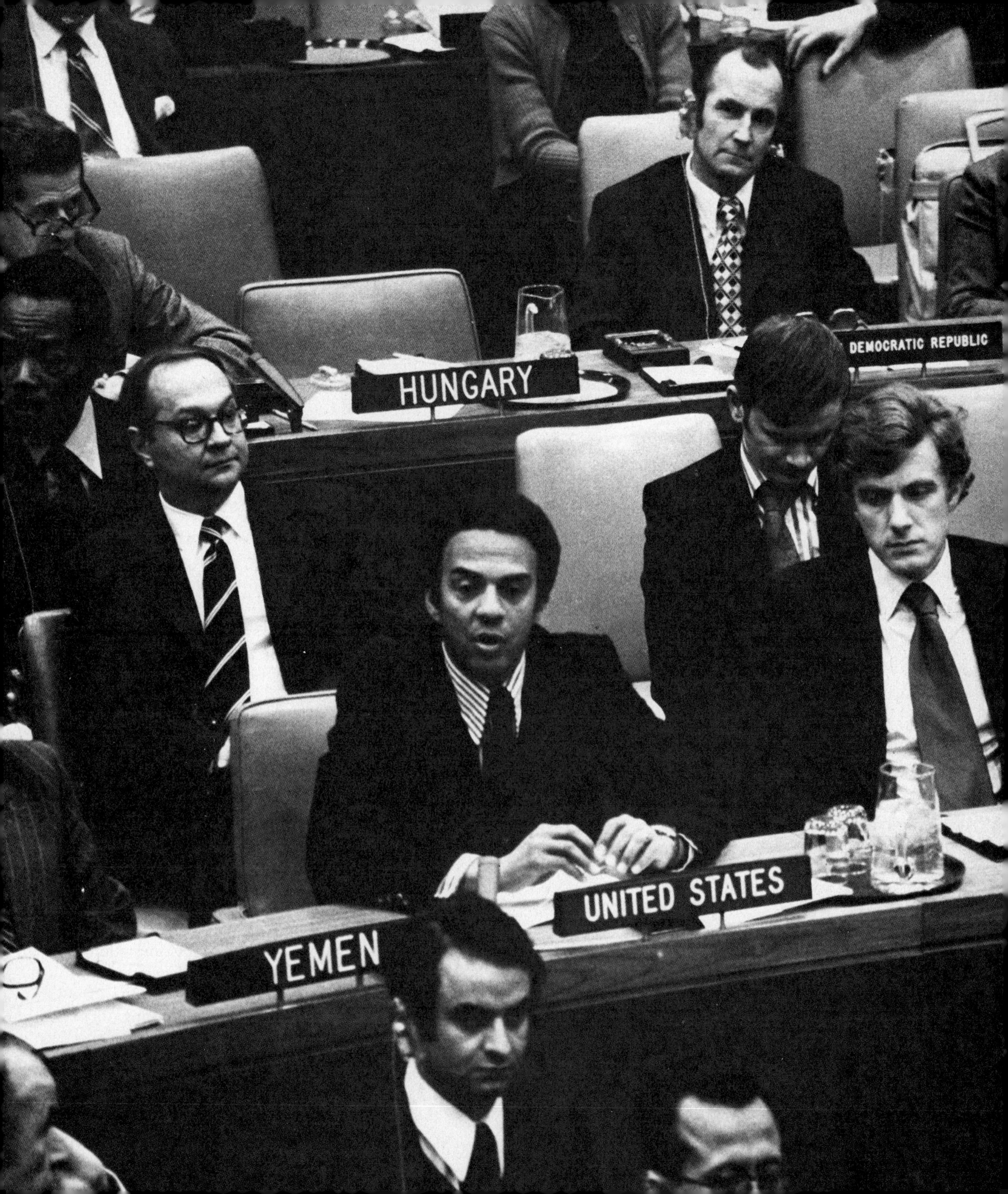
DEMOCRATIC REPUBLIC
HUNGARY
UNITED STATES
YEMEN

the isolationist tendencies of the American people prevented making or keeping military alliances that would have checked foreign aggressors bent on threatening the country's interests.

Others, however, find fault, not with popular influence on foreign policy, but with those officials who make policy without regard to popular wishes. During the 1960s, for example, many critics of our policy in Vietnam claimed that this policy was worked out in secret, without consultation with Congress or exposure to public debate, and as a result sought goals and employed means that were impractical, improper, or immoral.

KINDS OF FOREIGN POLICY

People arrive at such contradictory judgments in part because they seek different things but in part also because foreign policy is not a single thing but rather a collection of many different things, each with a distinctive political structure. "Foreign policy," in short, is too broad a term. (Imagine trying to analyze the politics of "domestic policy" without regard to the differences among welfare policy, civil rights policy, and economic policy.) In the terminology of Chapter 14, some parts of foreign policy are characterized by majoritarian politics, some kinds reveal the workings of interest group politics, and still other aspects are akin to client politics.

The majoritarian component of foreign policy includes those decisions (and nondecisions) that are perceived to confer widely distributed benefits and impose widely distributed costs. The decision to go to war is an obvious example of this. So, too, are the establishment of military alliances with Western Europe, the negotiation of a nuclear test–ban treaty or a strategic arms limitation agreement, the response to the crisis posed by the Soviet blockade of West Berlin or the placement of Soviet offensive missiles in Cuba, the decision to carry out covert CIA oper-

ations in another country, and the opening up of diplomatic relations with the People's Republic of China. These may be good or bad policies, but such benefits as they have and such costs as they entail accrue to the nation generally. Some persons argue that the costs of many of these policies are in fact highly concentrated—for example, when soldiers bear the burden of a military operation—but that argument is not for our purposes very important. For one thing, any sizable military operation affects not only the military personnel directly involved, but their families, relatives, and friends as well, and imposes financial costs, in the form of inflation or higher taxes or both, on almost everybody. For another, what counts is the perception people have of costs, and in wartime these perceptions are that everybody is affected to some degree.

Foreign policy decisions may also reflect interest group politics. Government policy toward Cyprus will be powerfully affected (though not wholly determined) by the rival claims of Turks and Greeks living on that island and by organized groups of Greek-Americans and Turkish-Americans in this country. Tariff decisions confer benefits on certain business firms and labor unions and impose costs on other firms and unions. If the price of Japanese steel imported into this country is increased by tariffs, quotas, or other devices, this helps the American steel industry and the United Steelworkers of America. On the other hand, it hurts those firms (and associated unions) that had been purchasing the once-cheap Japanese steel. After the president proposed to build an antiballistic missile (ABM) defense system, the military was soon pitted against the communities in which ABM units were to be located. Even the most important issues of war and peace may activate interest groups, especially ethnic ones. Americans of German and Italian origin were, during the 1930s, opposed to American intervention in Europe, in part because they feared American hostility to Hitler or Mussolini abroad might lead to discrimination directed at German-Americans

Domestic interest groups powerfully affect foreign policy. Arab-Americans support the Palestinian movement. Jewish-Americans denounce the Palestinian Liberation Organization and support Israel.

and Italo-Americans at home. In the 1950s Americans of East European origin took the opposite stance: they saw their native countries overrun by Soviet armies and wanted the United States actively to resist this domination.

There are even examples of client politics in foreign affairs. Washington will often provide assistance to American corporations doing business abroad because it benefits those firms directly without imposing any apparent costs on an equally distinct group in society. Our policy toward Israel has in part reflected the fact that Jews in this country feel strongly about the need to support a Jewish state abroad and are well organized to make those concerns felt. (Other factors also help explain our support of Israel; it is by no means a pure case of client politics.) Of late, our policy toward Israel has begun to change as Arab nations have retaliated against the United States by raising the price of the oil we import. Also, Arab-Americans have begun to organize and press a set of concerns very different

from the pro-Israel arguments on the government. We may, in fact, be witnessing a transformation of our policy toward Israel from one chiefly influenced by client politics to one that is more subject to interest group politics.

Who has power in foreign policy depends very much on what kind of foreign policy we have in mind. Where it is of a majoritarian nature, the president is clearly the dominant figure and much, if not everything, depends on his beliefs and skills and those of his chief advisers. Public opinion will ordinarily support this presidential leadership, but it will not guide it. As we shall see, public opinion on majoritarian foreign policy issues will usually reflect a disposition to trust the president, but woe to the president who by his actions forfeits that trust.

When interest group or client politics are involved, Congress plays a much larger role. Although Congress, by choice or necessity, plays a subsidiary role in the conduct of Soviet-American diplomacy, the decision to send troops

❝Who has power in foreign policy depends very much on what kind of foreign policy we have in mind. Where it is of a majoritarian nature, the president is clearly the dominant figure.❞

The president dominates the politics of grand diplomacy, as did President Carter when he announced the signing of the Camp David agreement between Egyptian President Anwar Sadat and Israeli Prime Minister Menachem Begin.

overseas, or the direction of intelligence operations, it plays quite a large role in decisions involving foreign economic aid, the structure of the tariff system, the shipment of weapons to Greece and Turkey, the placing of ABM sites in various communities, and the support of Israel.

And Congress is the central political arena on those occasions when entrepreneurial politics shapes foreign policy. If a multinational corporation, such as International Telephone and Telegraph (ITT) is caught in a scandal, congressional investigations shake the usual indifference of politicians to the foreign conduct of such

corporations. If presidential policies abroad lead to reversals, as when China fell to the Communists in 1949, then Congress becomes the forum for charges and countercharges by those seeking to affix blame.

This chapter will be chiefly concerned with foreign policy insofar as it displays the characteristics of majoritarian politics. Limiting the discussion in this way permits us to focus on the "grand issues" of foreign affairs—war, peace, and global diplomacy. It allows us to see how choices are made in a situation in which public majorities support without directing policy, in which opinion tends to react to events, and in which interest groups are relatively unimportant.

THE CONSTITUTIONAL AND LEGAL CONTEXT

The Constitution defines the authority of the president and of Congress in foreign affairs in a way that, as Edward Corwin put it, is an "invitation to struggle."[2] The president is commander-in-chief of the armed forces, but Congress must authorize and appropriate money for those forces. The president appoints ambassadors, but they must be confirmed by the Senate. The president may negotiate treaties, but the Senate must ratify these by a two-thirds vote. Only Congress may regulate commerce with other nations and "declare" war. (The Framers in an early draft had given to Congress the power to "make" war but changed this to "declare" in order, it appears, to leave open the possibility that the president acting without Congress might have to take military measures to repel a sudden attack.) Because powers over foreign affairs are shared by the president and Congress and thus conflict between them is to be expected, a naive reading of the Constitution would lead one to suppose that the president's role in these matters would be quite subordinate to that of Congress.

With respect to most military and diplomatic matters, the exact opposite is more nearly the case. Almost every American thinks instinctively of the president as being in charge of foreign affairs, and what popular opinion supposes the historical record confirms. Presidents have asserted the right to send troops abroad on their own authority in more than 125 instances.[3] Only five of the eleven major wars in which this country has been involved have followed a formal declaration of war by Congress.[4] The State Department, the Central Intelligence Agency, and the National Security Agency are almost entirely "presidential" agencies, with only modest congressional oversight. The Defense Department, though keenly sensitive to congressional views on issues of weapons procurement and the location of military bases (see Chapter 21), is very much under the control of the president on matters of military strategy. While the Senate has, since 1789, ratified well over a thousand treaties signed by the president, the president during this period has also signed around seven thousand executive agreements with other countries that do not require Senate ratification but yet have the force of law.[5]

Presidential Box Score

When the president seeks congressional approval for foreign policy matters, he tends to win more often than when he asks for support on domestic matters. Between 1948 and 1964 Congress approved 73 percent of the president's defense measures, 71 percent of his treaty and foreign aid proposals, 59 percent of his other foreign policy measures, but only 40 percent of his domestic programs.[6] This has led one student of the presidency, Aaron Wildavsky, to conclude that the American political system has "two presidencies"—one, in domestic affairs, that is relatively weak and closely checked and another, in foreign affairs, that is quite powerful.[7] As we shall see, this view considerably overstates presidential power in some ways.

By the standards of American government (limiting our attention to majoritarian issues of diplomacy and military deployment), the president is indeed strong, much stronger than the

A wise president will consult on foreign affairs with congressional leaders such as Senate Minority Leader Howard H. Baker, Jr. (left) and Majority Leader Robert C. Byrd (right).

Framers in 1789 may have intended and certainly stronger than many congressmen would like. Examples abound:

- In 1801 Thomas Jefferson sent the navy to deal with the Barbary pirates.
- In 1845 James K. Polk sent troops into Mexico to defend newly acquired Texas.
- In 1861 Abraham Lincoln blockaded southern ports and declared martial law.
- In 1940 Franklin D. Roosevelt sent fifty destroyers to England to be used against Germany with whom we were then technically at peace.
- In 1950 Harry S. Truman sent American troops into South Korea to help repulse a North Korean attack on that country.

Shifting Patterns of Leadership in Foreign Policy

Depending on the personalities, skills, and interests of those involved, leadership in making American foreign policy may be found centered in the White House (the president and his national security adviser) or in the State Department (the secretary of state).

Periods of White House dominance

President	Secretary of State
Franklin D. Roosevelt	Cordell Hull (1933–1944)
John F. Kennedy and National Security Adviser McGeorge Bundy	Dean Rusk (1961–1969)
Richard M. Nixon and National Security Adviser Henry A. Kissinger	William P. Rogers (1969–1973)

John F. Kennedy with Dean Rusk

Periods of leadership by the secretary of state

Secretary of State	President
George C. Marshall (1947–1949) and Dean Acheson (1949–1953)	Harry S. Truman
John Foster Dulles (1953–1959)	Dwight D. Eisenhower
Henry A. Kissinger (1973–1977)	Gerald R. Ford

- In the 1960s John F. Kennedy and Lyndon Johnson sent American forces into South Vietnam without a declaration of war.
- In the 1970s Richard M. Nixon extended the war into Laos and Cambodia without congressional approval or, for a while, knowledge.

However, by the standards of other nations, even other democratic ones, the ability of an American president to act decisively often appears rather modest. England was dismayed at the inability of Woodrow Wilson in 1914–1915 and Franklin Roosevelt in 1939–1940 to enter into an alliance at times when England was engaged in a major war with Germany. Wilson was unable to bring this country into the League of Nations. Gerald Ford could not intervene covertly in Angola in support of an anti-Marxist faction. And Jimmy Carter was barely able to persuade the Senate to return control of the Canal Zone to Panama.

By contrast, totalitarian nations such as China and the Soviet Union have supported military intervention or guerrilla warfare in countries around the globe seemingly uncon-

Gerald Ford with Henry Kissinger

strained by domestic political considerations. The prime minister of Britain was able, by command of his automatic parliamentary majority, to make that country part of the European Common Market over the strenuous objection of many, perhaps most, citizens of that country and in the teeth of well-organized interest-group opposition. Indeed, in Britain—democratic nation though it is—not even a declaration of war needs the assent of Parliament.[8] Charles de Gaulle brought France into the Common Market over the explicit opposition of a majority of the French Assembly and granted independence to Algeria, then a French colony, without seriously consulting the Assembly.[9] Treaties signed by most European prime ministers become binding on their countries almost automatically; a treaty signed by an American president is little more than a commitment by him to attempt to obtain Senate approval. Though American presidents have signed thousands of executive agreements, the vast majority of these (by one recent count, over 87 percent of those signed between 1946 and 1972) have been made pursuant to explicit congressional authorization.[10]

Lyndon Johnson with Senator J. William Fulbright

Rivalry vs. Cooperation Between the President and the Senate

Because the Senate must ratify treaties and consent to the appointment of ambassadors and other high foreign policy officials, it has the opportunity to play a large role in the conduct of foreign affairs. The key figure in the Senate is usually the chairman of the Senate Foreign Relations Committee. Depending on personalities and circumstances, the president and the chairman have sometimes been able to work together closely and at other times have been bitter, outspoken rivals.

In general, cooperation occurs when there is a widely shared foreign policy world view; rivalry erupts when one world view is being challenged by another.

Periods of shared world views and political cooperation

President	Chairman of Foreign Relations Committee
Franklin D. Roosevelt	Tom Connally (1941–1947, 1949–1953)
Harry S. Truman	Arthur H. Vandenberg (1947–1949)

Harry S. Truman with Senator Arthur Vandenberg

Periods of competing world views and political rivalry

President	Chairman of Foreign Relations Committee
Woodrow Wilson	Henry Cabot Lodge (1919–1924)
Lyndon B. Johnson Richard M. Nixon	J. William Fulbright (1959–1975)

> **"** A president strong enough to do something one thinks proper is also strong enough to do something one finds wrong. **"**

President Kennedy forced the Soviet Union to withdraw the ballistic missiles it had placed in Cuba in 1962, as shown in this Defense Department aerial photograph (left). In 1965 President Johnson ordered the buildup of American troops in Vietnam.

Evaluating the Power of the President

Whether one thinks the president too strong or too weak in foreign affairs depends not only on whether one holds a domestic or international point of view, but also on whether one agrees or disagrees with his policies. Historian Arthur M. Schlesinger, Jr., thought President Kennedy skillfully exercised commendable presidential discretion when he made a unilateral decision to impose a naval blockade on Cuba to induce the Soviets to remove missiles installed there. However, he viewed President Nixon's decision to extend United States military action in Vietnam into neighboring Cambodia as a deplorable example of the "imperial presidency."[11] To be sure, there were important differences between these

two actions, but that is precisely the point: a president strong enough to do something one thinks proper is also strong enough to do something one finds wrong.

The Supreme Court has fairly consistently supported the view that the federal government, in the conduct of foreign and military policy, has powers above and beyond those specifically mentioned in the Constitution. The leading decision, rendered in 1936, holds that the right to carry out a foreign policy is an inherent attribute of any sovereign nation: "The power to declare and wage war, to conclude peace, to make treaties, to maintain diplomatic relations with other sovereignties, if they had never been mentioned in the Constitution, would have vested in the

Federal Government as necessary concomitants of nationality."[12] The individual states have few rights in foreign affairs.

Moreover, the Supreme Court has been most reluctant to intervene in disputes over the conduct of foreign affairs. When various congressmen brought suit challenging the right of President Nixon to enlarge the war in Vietnam without congressional approval, the court of appeals handled the issue, as one scholar was later to describe it, with all the care of porcupines making love. It said that the matter was a "political question" for the president and Congress to decide and that if Congress was unwilling to cut off the money to pay for the war it should not expect the courts to do the job for it.[13]

Because the president is commander-in-chief, because diplomacy involves negotiations among heads of state or their personal representatives, and because the president is expected by public opinion and historical experience to respond to emergency situations, the Supreme Court has rarely interfered with presidential conduct of foreign affairs or even domestic matters that touch on foreign affairs. The Court upheld the extraordinary measures taken by President Lincoln during the Civil War[14] and refused to overrule the decision of Presidents Johnson and Nixon to wage war in Vietnam.[15]

How great that deference to presidential power may be is vividly illustrated by the actions of President Roosevelt in ordering the army to remove over one hundred thousand Japanese, the great majority of them born in this country and citizens of the United States, from their homes on the West Coast and to confine them in "relocation centers" for the duration of World War II. Though this action was manifestly a wholesale violation of the constitutional rights of citizens unprecedented in American history, the Supreme Court decided that in time of war with Japan and with the defenses of the West Coast weak, the president was within his rights to decide that persons of Japanese ancestry might pose a threat to internal security; the relocation

Japanese-Americans awaiting transportation under military guard from their homes on the West Coast to relocation camps in the interior, where they remained for the duration of World War II.

order was upheld.[16] (No Japanese-American was ever found guilty of espionage or sabotage.) One of the few cases in which the Court denied the president broad wartime powers occurred in 1952. It decided, by a five-to-four vote, to reverse President Truman's seizure of the steel mills—a move he had made in order to avert a strike that, in his view, would have imperiled the war effort in Korea.[17]

Checks on Presidential Power

If there is a check on the powers of the federal government in foreign affairs or on the president in the exercise of those powers, it is chiefly political rather than constitutional. The most important check is Congress's control of the purse-strings. In addition, Congress has passed laws placing more than seventy limitations on the president's freedom of action. While some of these are of minor significance (for example, foreign aid money may not be used to pay for abortions), some are of substantial importance. Most restrict the president's freedom to give military or economic aid to certain countries, such as Cuba. From 1974 to 1978 the president could not sell arms to Turkey because of the dispute between that country and Greece over the future of Cyprus. In retaliation, Turkey closed down almost all American military and intelligence-gathering bases within its borders. Relations between the two countries, both members of NATO, were severely strained as a result. After a prolonged debate, Congress finally lifted the restriction. Whenever the president wishes to sell arms worth more than $25 million to any country, Congress may block the sale if it adopts a concurrent resolution to that effect within thirty days. An especially significant restriction, adopted in 1976, prevented President Ford from giving aid to the pro-Western faction in the Angolan civil war.

Outside the area of foreign aid, the two most significant restrictions on a president relate to covert intelligence operations and the commitment of American troops. Since 1974 the president must advise eight congressional committees of any CIA operations (other than intelligence-gathering) he proposes to undertake abroad. Presumably, a committee could block that plan by either argument or the threat of exposure. In 1973 Congress passed, over President Nixon's veto, a War Powers Resolution that requires the president to consult with Congress before sending American troops into hostile situations. After these forces are sent, the president must report to Congress within forty-eight hours. Sixty days after that, the forces must be withdrawn from hostilities unless Congress has in the meantime passed a declaration of war, extended the sixty-day time limit, or is unable to meet because the nation is under attack.

Both these pieces of restrictive legislation were passed at a time when the political stock of the presidency was low as a result of reaction against the war in Vietnam, the revelations of illegal CIA operations within the United States, and especially the daily headlines about Watergate. It is far from clear that they would have become law in any other circumstances or that, being law, they will have much effect. No one knows how CIA operations have been affected, if at all, by the reporting requirements of the 1974 law, since all such reports are secret and the congressional committees involved are sworn to secrecy. The War Powers Resolution has led to the president's reporting to Congress on the use of troops on at least four occasions—when President Ford sent armed forces to assist in evacuating personnel from Danang, Phnom Penh, and Saigon as Communist forces overran Cambodia and South Vietnam, and when he directed the navy and marine corps to free the crew of the American merchant ship *Mayaguez* that had been captured at sea by Cambodia.

Each of these four episodes was brief and relatively noncontroversial. No one knows, however, what effect the War Powers Resolution would have if a president committed American forces to a protracted engagement of the Vietnam kind, or even to a conflict that was shorter and less costly. Hardly any congressman would challenge a military operation that was swift and successful; some might rebuke a president, but only after the fact, for engaging in one that was swift but unsuccessful. A protracted military operation requires the support of congressional appropriations; in the Vietnam case they were forthcoming from Congress even after the war had become unpopular. It is not clear that the War Powers Resolution would change much of this. What is clear is that it creates a more explicit congressional claim to be consulted, though every president has recognized that such consultation is politically essential even when not legally required. The blunt truth is that, as we shall see, public opinion tends to support the president in times of military crisis whatever its views beforehand about the merits of becoming involved in the crisis. For Congress to ignore this public support and undercut the president and American military forces engaged in combat would be risky in the extreme. Nor is it clear that crises could be effectively managed by 535 congressmen, or even twenty or thirty.

This fact is clearly shown by the Vietnam experience. Between 1966 and 1973 Congress took 113 roll-call or teller votes on various measures designed to limit or end American involvement in combat in Vietnam. Virtually all failed to pass; those that did become law proved innocuous. Not once did Congress cut off funds for military operations in Vietnam; not once did it require the withdrawal of American troops by any certain date. The only law effectively restricting the use of funds in Southeast Asia was passed *after* the United States had signed a peace agreement with North Vietnam.[18]

FOREIGN POLICY AND PUBLIC OPINION

The Second World War was the great watershed in the politics of foreign policy. Before that time, insofar as we can judge by the limited opinion polls of the time, a clear majority of the American public was opposed to an active involvement in world affairs by the United States. The public saw the costs of such involvement as substantially in excess of the benefits, and only determined, skillful leaders were able, as was President Roosevelt during 1939–1940, to affect in even a limited fashion the diplomatic and military struggles then convulsing Europe and Asia.

Our participation in the war produced a dramatic shift in popular opinion that endured for three decades, supplying broad (though thin and often ambiguous) public support for an internationalist foreign policy. The reason why World War II had this effect, alone among all wars we have fought, is not entirely clear. Per-

❝Public opinion tends to support the president in times of military crisis whatever its views beforehand about the merits of becoming involved in the crisis.❞

The battleship *West Virginia* burning after being hit by Japanese warplanes at Pearl Harbor on December 7, 1941.

haps it was because it was almost the only universally popular war in which we have been engaged, one that produced few, if any, recriminations afterward. Perhaps it was because that war seemed successful: an unmitigated evil (the Nazi regime) was utterly destroyed; an attack on our own land and people (by Japan at Pearl Harbor) was thoroughly avenged. And perhaps also it was because that war ended with the United States, owing to its sole possession of the atomic bomb and its enormous military and economic productivity, recognized as the dominant power on earth.

In 1937, 94 percent of the American public preferred the policy of doing "everything possible to keep out of foreign wars" to the policy of doing "everything possible to prevent war, even if it means threatening to fight countries that fight wars." In 1939, after World War II had begun in Europe but before Pearl Harbor was attacked, only 13 percent of Americans polled thought we should enter the war against Germany. Just a month before Pearl Harbor, only 19 percent felt the United States should take steps, even at the risk of war, to prevent Japan from becoming too powerful.[19] Congress reflected the noninterventionist mood of the country: in the summer of 1941, with war breaking out almost everywhere, the proposal to continue the draft passed the House of Representatives by only one vote.

The Japanese attack on Pearl Harbor on December 7 changed all that. Not only was the American war effort supported almost unanimously, not only did Congress approve the declaration of war with only one dissenting vote, but World War II—unlike World War I—produced popular support for an active assumption of international responsibilities that continued after the war had ended.[20] Whereas a majority after World War I opposed American entry in the League of Nations, a clear majority after World War II favored our entry into the United Nations.[21]

This willingness to see the United States remain a world force persisted into the 1960s when the inconclusive war in Vietnam led an increasing proportion of citizens to return to isolationist sentiments. The number of persons thinking we should "keep independent" in world affairs as opposed to "working closely with other nations" rose from 10 percent in 1963 to 22 percent in 1969.[22] Even so, as late as 1967, after more than two years of war in Vietnam, 44 percent of Americans believed this country had an obligation to "defend other Vietnams if they are threatened by communism."[23]

But the support for an internationalist American foreign policy was, and is, highly general, heavily dependent on the phrasing of the question, the opinions expressed by popular leaders, and the impact of world events. Public opinion, while more internationalist than once was the case, is nonetheless quite volatile. Just prior to President Nixon's decision to send troops into Cambodia, only 7 percent of the people said they supported such a move. After the troops were sent and Nixon made a speech explaining his move, 50 percent of the public said they supported it.[24] Similarly, only 40 percent of the people favored a halt in American bombing of North Vietnam before President Johnson, in 1968, ordered such a halt; afterward, 60 percent of the public said it supported such a policy.[25]

Backing the President

Much of this volatility in specific opinions (as opposed to general mood) reflects the already-mentioned deference to presidential leadership and a desire to support the United States when it confronts other nations. Table 20.1 shows the proportion of people saying they approve of the way the president is doing his job before and after various major foreign policy events. Each foreign crisis increased the level of public approval of the president, often dramatically. The most vivid illustration of this was the Bay of Pigs fiasco: an American-supported, American-directed invasion of Cuba by anti-Castro Cuban emigrés was driven back into the sea. President Kennedy publicly accepted responsibility for the aborted project. His popularity *rose*. (Comparable data for domestic crises tend to show no comparable effect.)

This tendency to "rally round the flag" has been carefully studied and seems to operate on behalf of any president engaged in any foreign policy initiative whether force is used or not. One analysis of the standing of presidents in public opinion from Truman through Johnson (1945–1968) found that, even allowing for the effects of ups and downs in the economy and the decay in presidential popularity that almost always occurs during the course of a presidential term of office, every president enjoys a boost in popularity immediately after an international crisis or major diplomatic event.[26]

If presidents derive more political rewards from playing a foreign policy role rather than a domestic one, then we would expect that most presidents would prefer the foreign policy role and that some presidents might even deliberately manufacture diplomatic "successes" to bolster their sagging popularity. Most presidents since 1941 have, in fact, felt that their most important tasks were in the field of foreign affairs (though the realities of international problems probably have as much to do with that pattern as the political rewards of playing the diplomatic role). President Carter's trip abroad in 1978 may have been designed as much for domestic political consumption as for any substantive effect. Since the rewards are so great, one wonders why any president would shun even risky international ventures.

One reason is that, though the president wins popular support during the early stages of an international crisis, that support tends to deteriorate if the crisis is not soon resolved or if a protracted and costly stalemate seems to ensue. World War II is the only major war about which we have opinion data in which public support remained high throughout. World War I, though it commanded popular support at the time, led to bitter recriminations afterward; by 1937 nearly two-thirds of the American people thought it was a mistake for the United States to have entered it.[27] Support for Truman's decision to send troops to Korea declined as the war went on; whereas initially about two-thirds of the people backed the decision, two years later only a bit more than a third thought it had been a good idea.[28] Support for the decision of President Johnson to send troops to Vietnam followed almost exactly the same pattern: initial support, giving way to mounting skepticism as the war dragged on inconclusively.[29] Though in retrospect we think of Vietnam as bitterly controversial and Korea as much less so, in fact *public* opinion was pretty much the same in both cases.

What was different is that *elite* opinion protested our involvement in Vietnam but not our participation in Korea.

The clearest lesson history can offer a president on the exercise of his war-making powers is this: either fight a vastly popular crusade or fight only short wars that you win quickly. Given the great edge enjoyed by Democrats in party identification, it is noteworthy that the only times since 1945 that a Republican has won the presidency have been in the midst of an un-

TABLE 20.1   Popular Reactions to Foreign Policy Crises

	Foreign Policy Crisis	Percent of public saying they approve of the way the president is handling his job	
		Before	*After*
1950	United States entry into Korean War	37%	46%
1958	United States lands Marines in Lebanon	52	58
1960	American U-2 spy plane shot down over Soviet Union	62	68
1961	Abortive landing at Bay of Pigs in Cuba	73	83
1962	Cuban missile crisis	61	74
1967	President Johnson meets with Soviet leader in Glassboro	44	52
1969	President Nixon announces plan to withdraw U.S. troops from Vietnam	53	68
1975	President Ford sends Marines to rescue the *Mayaguez*	40	51

Source: Adapted from Theodore J. Lowi, *The End of Liberalism* (New York: W. W. Norton, 1969), p. 184. Poll data are from Gallup Poll. Time lapse between "before" and "after" samplings of opinion was in no case more than one month.

66 The clearest lesson history can offer a president on the exercise of his war-making powers is this: either fight a vastly popular crusade or fight only short wars that you win quickly. 99

popular war—Eisenhower in 1952 and Nixon in 1968. (This is *not* the same thing as saying that Democrats start wars and Republicans end them. That bit of political demagoguery misreads history entirely, for it neglects the role that world events and sincere ideas played in our decisions to go to war.)

Reasons for Public Support

To divide the public into supporters and opponents of foreign policy, especially of military interventions, suggests the existence of a simple split between "hawks" and "doves." Though these are favorite journalistic labels, they are quite misleading. There are several different kinds of support, and motives for support, of a military action. One can support it because one trusts and follows the president, especially the president of one's own party; one can support it because one believes it is beneficial to the narrow national interests of the United States; or one can support it because one believes that international well-being or the interests of allies requires it. Opponents can have one or the other of a parallel set of motives. And given these different motives, one can have a complex mix of opinions about war. For example, "I think it was a grave mistake ever to get involved in Vietnam, but as long as we are fighting there I support our president and the armed forces." Or, "It may have been all right to intervene in the first place, but things haven't gone as we hoped and we ought to pull out now." Or, "The whole war from beginning to end was immoral, unwise, and impolitic." Or, "We should not be fighting there, but since we are, we should go all-out to win." Classifying these and other attitudes as simply "hawk" or "dove" is not very illuminating.

Opinion polls suggest that there were at least three kinds of critics of our participation in Vietnam. The first group consisted disproportionately of older citizens and persons with little schooling. From the beginning they were skeptical about the war, and their skepticism increased somewhat as the war continued. Moreover, they were not much more likely to favor escalation than were college-educated professional persons. However, they saw the war in terms of national interest and the obligation to support men in combat and would have nothing to do with protesters who wanted to use militant tactics to obtain an immediate withdrawal.[30] Ironically, the fact that some opponents of the war engaged in campus riots and public demonstrations may well have prolonged the war, for such tactics deeply offended most citizens including those opposed to the war but disinclined to abandon the president or the armed forces. For example, when the Chicago police roughed up antiwar demonstrators at the 1968 Democratic convention, popular reaction was overwhelmingly on the side of the police, even among people opposed to the war.[31]

The second kind of opponent consisted of those who initially supported the war, or were indifferent to it, but gradually came to oppose it because it seemed pointless or endless. Included in this group were some college students and upper status college graduates. Contrary to popular impression at the time, support for the war was greatest among younger persons and college graduates, at least until near the very end.[32] (See Figures 20.1 and 20.2.) Though we recall the protests on college campuses against the war, these opponents were not representative of most young persons or even of most college-educated persons.

The third kind of opponent were those persons, small in number, who always opposed the war, not on grounds of national self-interest as did many citizens, but because it violated their political ideology (pacifism, Marxism, or whatever). One reason for the increased attention

FIGURE 20.1 Trends in Support for the War in Vietnam, by Education

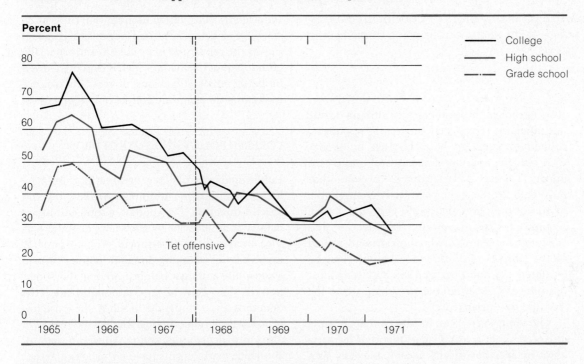

FIGURE 20.2 Trends in Support for the War in Vietnam, by Age

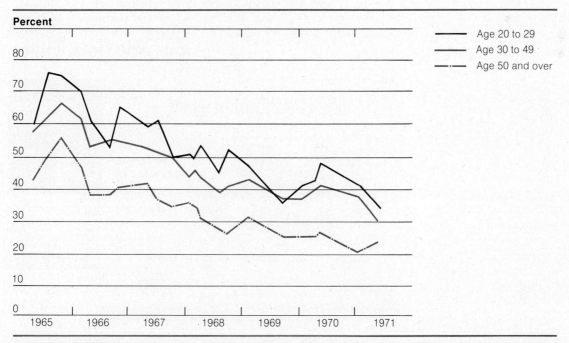

Source: John E. Mueller, *War, Presidents, and Public Opinion* (New York: John Wiley, 1973), pp. 125, 139. Reprinted by permission of John Wiley & Sons, Inc.

"Elite beliefs are probably more important in explaining foreign policy than in accounting for decisions in other policy areas."

paid to radical publications and authors during and after the war is that their early opposition seemed to many to be vindicated by events.

It was the opinion of the second group—the upper status, college-trained persons—that proved to be the most volatile. It changed the most, not only over the course of events, but in response to specific events. It was the well educated, for example, who most strongly rallied to the support of President Johnson when he escalated the bombing in 1966 and who most dramatically deserted the president when the Tet offensive occurred.[33]

The same pattern can be observed at the time of Korea: more or less steady support of the president by average citizens, accompanied by substantial, and somewhat increasing, skepticism about the merits of the war; sharp initial support

followed by sharp fluctuations in that support on the part of better educated persons.[34] This fact makes the role of the mass media, and especially of that part of the media which is closely followed by better educated persons, of great importance in shaping the domestic politics of foreign policy.

FOREIGN POLICY AND ELITE OPINION

Public opinion provides general support for presidential initiatives in foreign policy, but no specific direction. The content of those initiatives is heavily influenced by the views of those persons, in and out of government, who are actively involved in shaping foreign policy. World events—the military balance among the superpowers, the flow of international trade, the demands and complaints of allies, the existence of military conflict among smaller nations—will also, to a degree, determine American actions. But since world events have no meaning except as they are perceived and interpreted by persons who must react to them, the attitudes and beliefs

The reading matter of the foreign-policy political elite.

of the foreign policy elite often assume decisive importance.

That elite consists not only of those persons with administrative positions in the foreign policy field—the senior officials of the State Department and the staff of the National Security Council—but also the members and staffs of the key congressional committees concerned with foreign affairs (chiefly, the Senate Foreign Relations Committee and the House Foreign Affairs Committee) and various private organizations that help shape elite opinion, such as the members of the Council on Foreign Relations and the editors of two important publications, *Foreign Affairs* and *Foreign Policy*. To these must be added influential columnists and editorial writers whose work appears regularly in the national press. One could extend the list by adding ever-wider circles of persons with some influence (lobbyists, professors, leaders of veterans' organizations); this would complicate without changing the central point—elite beliefs are probably more important in explaining foreign policy than in accounting for decisions in other policy areas.

Important as elite opinion may be, it has rarely been studied in any systematic fashion. Nonetheless, one can infer a great deal about that opinion from the policies that are adopted and the public statements of those who adopt them. Foreign policy specialists write and speak a great deal, and though the art of diplomacy consists in part in using words to conceal rather than reveal one's true state of mind, the vast published output of what journalists like to refer to as the "Foreign Policy Establishment" provides important clues to, and often explicit statements of, the attitudes of those shaping policy.

How a World View Shapes Foreign Policy

These attitudes can be described, in simplified terms, as "world views" (or, as some social scientists like to put it, as "paradigms")—more or less comprehensive mental pictures of the critical problems facing the United States in the world

The Influence of the National Media

Between 1964 and 1968 the position taken on the war in Vietnam by the major national magazines and the principal newspapers changed. In 1964 they tended to support the war effort; by 1968 they tended to oppose it.

During the same time the Survey Research Center (SRC) of the University of Michigan asked citizens for their positions on the war—once in 1964, and again in 1968.

As the table below shows, between 1964 and 1968 opinion of upper middle class persons on the war effort changed much more than that of working-class persons *and*, among the former, opinions changed the most among those who regularly read several magazines and newspapers.

For example: in 1964, 78 percent of those upper middle class persons who regularly read many magazines and newspapers felt we should take a stronger stand in Vietnam, even if it meant invading North Vietnam. By 1968 only 40 percent of this group felt that way, a shift of 38 percent. By contrast, upper middle class persons who do not regularly read several magazines and newspapers changed by only half as much—from 59 percent favoring a stronger stand in 1964 to 41 percent favoring it in 1958, an 18 percent shift. And among working-class persons, there was scarcely any media effect at all—a decline of 7 percent in the proportion favoring a stronger stand for both those who read a lot and those who do not.

Decline in Support for a Stronger Stand in Vietnam, by Social Class and Media Readership

	Read several magazines and newspapers regularly			Do not read several magazines or newspapers		
	UMC	LMC	WC	UMC	LMC	WC
1964	78%	50%	55%	59%	41%	45%
1968	40	19	48	41	33	38
Change	−38	−31	−7	−18	−8	−7

Source: James D. Wright, "Life, Time and the Fortunes of War," TRANS-ACTION, Vol. 9, No. 3 (January 1972), pp. 42–52. Copyright © 1972 by Transaction, Inc. Reprinted by permission.

Note: UMC = white-collar workers earning over $10,000; LMC = white-collar workers earning under $10,000; WC = blue-collar workers. Omitted are nonwhites, Southerners, and persons with no opinion on the war.

and of the appropriate and inappropriate ways of responding to these problems. The clearest, most concise, and one of the most influential statements of one world view that held sway for many years was an article, published in 1947 in *Foreign Affairs*, entitled "The Sources of Soviet Conduct."[35] Written by a Mr. "X" (later revealed to be George F. Kennan, director of the Policy Planning Staff of the State Department and thereafter ambassador to Moscow), the article argued that the Soviet Union was pursuing a policy of expansion that could only be met by the United States applying "unalterable counterforce at every point where they show signs of encroaching upon the interests of a peaceful and stable world." This he called the strategy of "containment," and it became the governing principle of American foreign policy for at least two decades.

No single world view ever holds unanimous sway over the minds of any large group of men and women. There were critics of the containment policy at the time—Walter Lippmann, in his book *The Cold War*, argued against it in 1947[36]—but the criticisms were less influential than the doctrine. A world view is important precisely because it prevails over alternative views. One reason it prevails is that it is broadly consistent with the public's mood—in 1947, when Kennan wrote, popular attitudes toward the Soviet Union, which had been favorable during World War II when Russia and America were allies, had turned quite hostile. By 1946 less than one-fourth of the American people believed Russia could be trusted to cooperate with this country,[37] and by 1948 over three-fourths were convinced that the Soviet Union was trying, not simply to defend itself, but to become the dominant world power.[38] Such a world view was also influential because it was consistent with events as they were seen at the time. Russia had occupied most of the previously independent countries of Eastern Europe and was turning them into puppet regimes. When governments independent of both the United States and the

Appeasement at Munich: British Prime Minister Neville Chamberlain attempted to satisfy the territorial ambitions of Adolf Hitler in 1938.

Soviet Union attempted to rule in Hungary and Czechoslovakia, they were overthrown by Soviet-backed coups. Finally, a world view becomes dominant because it is consistent with the prior experiences of the persons holding it.

Lessons of Munich and Pearl Harbor. Those formative experiences typically involve a situation in which a foreign policy disaster occurs as the result, so it is thought, of applying an erroneous world view. "Appeasement" was discredited in the 1930s when, at a Munich conference, the efforts of British and French leaders to satisfy Adolf Hitler's territorial demands in Europe led, not to "peace in our time" as Prime Minister Neville Chamberlain had claimed, but to ever-greater territorial demands and ultimately to world war. This crisis brought to power men determined not to repeat their predecessors' mistakes—"Munich" became a synonym for weakness, and leaders such as Winston Churchill made antiappeasement the basis of their postwar policy of resisting Soviet expansionism. Churchill summed up the world view he had acquired from the Munich era in a famous speech delivered in 1946 in Fulton, Missouri, in which he coined the term "Iron Curtain" to describe Soviet policy in Eastern Europe.

For Americans, the lessons of Munich were reinforced by the experience of Pearl Harbor. The Japanese attack there discredited the previous world view of those American leaders who had argued that the United States could successfully remain aloof from foreign entanglements. These isolationist leaders were numerous and influential. The America First Committee, which spearheaded the drive to prevent American involvement in the war against Hitler, was led or assisted by Robert E. Wood (chairman of the board of Sears, Roebuck), Charles A. Lindbergh, Kingman Brewster (later president of Yale University), and Chester Bowles (later ambassador to India).[39] Pearl Harbor was the death knell for isolationism. Senator Arthur H. Vandenberg of Michigan, a staunch isolationist before the attack, became an ardent internationalist not only during but after the war. He later wrote of the Japanese attack on December 7, 1941: "That day ended isolationism for any realist."[40]

Every generation of political leaders comes to power with a foreign policy world view shaped, in large measure, by the real or apparent mistakes of the previous generation.[41] This pattern can be traced back, some have argued, to the very beginnings of the nation. Frank L. Klingberg traces the alteration since 1776 of national "moods" (what are here called world views) that favored first "extroversion" (or an active, internationalist policy) and then "introversion" (a less active, even isolationist posture).[42]

American Imperialism. A vivid illustration of how rapidly the prevailing world view can change is provided by the era of American imperialism. Within an eighteen-month period in 1898–1899, the United States fought a war in Cuba, became a colonial power by annexing the Hawaiian Islands, acquired Puerto Rico and the Philippines from Spain, and took control of Guam and part of Samoa. But as historian Ernest R. May notes, there was little sign before that of any interest in empire and little activity toward that end afterwards.[43] From the 1870s to the 1890s, America was in an introverted phase, so much so that when in 1873 Spain seized an American ship and executed fifty-three alleged pirates on board, the United States made only a mild diplomatic response. After 1900 it reverted to that mood, making no further effort to acquire more colonies even though it would have not been difficult to add Haiti and the Dominican Republic to the list or to have maintained control of Cuba. (The acquisition of the Panama Canal Zone in 1903 was virtually the only exception to this new introverted phase.)

Some of the reasons for this short-lived burst of colonial acquisition were economic: some businessmen saw an opportunity for new markets.[44] But economics alone provides an inadequate explanation; presumably there were advantages to be had from new overseas markets before 1898 and after 1900, yet during these periods colonial opportunities were spurned. The missing ingredient was a set of ideas that became dominant in the late 1890s, among them the views of Admiral Alfred T. Mahan. Mahan's book *The Influence of Sea Power Upon History*, published in 1890, argued a new world view based on what the author saw as past mistakes.[45] In the war of 1812 and in the Civil War, the nation had been harmed, almost fatally, by its inability to control the sea. To that idea was added the view of others that America had an obligation to improve the lot of persons, such as the Filipinos, who had been under Spanish rule. The anti-imperialists were the older generation, initially including President William McKinley and industrialist Andrew Carnegie, who had been raised on an

President Theodore Roosevelt sat at the controls of a giant earth-moving machine at the site of the Panama Canal in 1906. Roosevelt was a strong supporter of the Canal and of an interventionist American foreign policy.

isolationist philosophy. The younger imperialists—Theodore Roosevelt, Mahan, and others—felt that this older world view was discredited. In time, the imperialist passion became suspect as contrary to the libertarian impulses of American constitutional philosophy and the principles of self-rule set down in the Declaration of Independence. New leaders arose to campaign against further expansion and in favor of colonial independence movements.

Post-World War II Foreign Policy

The events leading up to the Second World War were the formative experiences of those leaders who came to power in the 1940s, 1950s, and 1960s. What they took to be the lessons of Munich and Pearl Harbor were applied repeatedly—in building a network of defensive alliances in Europe and Asia during the late 1940s and 1950s, in operating an airlift to aid West Berlin when road access to it was cut off by the Russians, in landing troops in Lebanon and the Dominican Republic, in coming to the aid of South Korea, and, finally, in intervening in Vietnam. Most of these applications of the Munich–Pearl Harbor world view were successful in the sense that they did not harm American interests (the alliances), they provided welcome help to allies (West Berlin, Lebanon), or they prevented a military conquest (Korea).

Vietnam was the formative experience for the younger foreign policy elite that came to power in the 1970s. Unlike previous applications of the Munich–Pearl Harbor view, our entry into Vietnam led to a military defeat and a domestic political disaster. There were three ways of interpreting that crisis: (1) we applied the correct world view in the right place but did not try hard enough; (2) we had the correct world view but tried to apply it in the wrong place under the wrong circumstances; (3) the world view itself was wrong. By and large, the critics of our Vietnam policy tended to draw the third lesson, and thus when they supplanted in office the architects of our Vietnam policy, they inclined toward a new world view, the "Vietnam paradigm."

The transfer of power occurred with the 1976 elections, when newly elected Jimmy Carter appointed to the highest foreign policy posts older persons (such as Secretary of State Cyrus Vance and Defense Secretary Harold Brown) who, though involved in making Vietnam policy during the 1960s, now felt guilty about it and appointed to the more numerous second echelon younger persons who had been governmental or academic critics of our Vietnam intervention. This new elite acts on a world view quite different from that of its predecessors: the United States should minimize rather than maximize its interventions abroad, slow down rather than increase the rate of military preparedness, negotiate with the Soviet Union on arms limitations rather than assume such negotiated treaties will work to our disadvantage, and show greater tolerance rather than greater resistance to attacks on American interests by other nations (especially in the Third World). Whereas in 1964 the foreign policy elite that shared the Munich world view intervened with American military aid (though no troops) to support an anti-Marxist regime in the Congo (now Zaire), in 1976 the foreign policy elite that held the Vietnam world view cut off United States aid to an anti-Marxist group in Angola.

Evaluating the correctness of these competing views of foreign policy is beyond the scope of this book. All that is being asserted is their importance in explaining foreign policy. But a prevailing world view cannot explain all important diplomatic or military decisions. Though

urged to do so, President Eisenhower did not intervene in Vietnam in 1954 at a time when the French were being driven out; Presidents Kennedy and Johnson did intervene there in the 1960s after the French had left. When the U.S. Navy ship *Pueblo* was seized by North Korea in 1968, President Johnson resorted to diplomacy and negotiated the release of the crew (but not of the ship); when the U.S. merchant ship *Mayaguez* was seized by Cambodia in 1975, President Ford sent in the marines. The particular circumstances of time and place, the anticipated response of public opinion, and judgments about what will succeed and what will fail all contribute to the way in which any world view is applied.

Moreover, elite opinions may or may not correspond to the military and economic realities of the world. When those opinions are dramatically refuted by events—as was isolationist opinion by the attack on Pearl Harbor—the

Vietnam split the country—and the youth—between those who thought the war immoral and those who thought it important to support our armed forces, whatever the value of the war.

The Sources of the Foreign Policy Elites

Several organizations with an interest in foreign affairs provide employment, meeting places, and platforms to foreign policy elites. This pattern of association is not a "conspiracy"—though sometimes it is viewed as such—but rather a set of linkages useful in understanding foreign policy. Who talks to whom makes a difference.

The older, largely displaced foreign policy elite that shared the "containment" paradigm came from prestigious law firms (Dean Acheson, George Ball, John Foster Dulles, John J. McCloy), "think tanks" such as the RAND Corporation (James A. Schlesinger, Fred Iklé), retired military officers (Maxwell Taylor), universities (W. W. Rostow from MIT, Henry Kissinger from Harvard), and business (Robert S. McNamara from Ford). Many were members of the Council on Foreign Relations, based in New York City, and wrote articles for the magazine *Foreign Affairs*.

The younger elite in power in the Carter administration rejects the containment paradigm. This elite group has few connections with law firms, the military, or corporations. The participants are often former members of the State Department (Anthony Lake, Richard C. Holbrooke, Richard Moose) who have served as congressional staff persons (Moose) or in the Peace Corps (Holbrooke). Some are former newspaper reporters for the national press (Leslie Gelb), and several have come from foundations such as Brookings (Henry Owen) or the Carnegie Endowment for International Peace (Thomas L. Hughes). The newer elite is likely to publish its views in the magazine *Foreign Policy* (once edited by Holbrooke).

There are, of course, many persons who do not quite fit either pattern of association, and some persons who have a foot in each camp. One can find similar sets of linkages among other kinds of political elites, but few are as conspicuous, or important, as those characteristic of foreign policy makers.

opinions are discredited. But short of some such crisis, competing beliefs can and do coexist. For example, the Soviet Union obviously has vast military power at its disposal. Those members of the foreign policy elite who wish to portray the USSR as benign or open to accommodation can point to the fact that the Soviets have not of late used their own armed forces, that the Soviet leaders speak favorably of "détente" and of the need for a strategic arms limitation treaty, and that the Russians no longer can lead a monolithic bloc of Communist nations. Those who believe the containment policy is still desirable can point instead to Soviet support for revolutionary movements in Africa, the Middle East, and Southeast Asia, the deployment of Russian forces along the Chinese border, and the high level of Soviet military spending and arms manufacture.

When one world view is under attack or is sharply in conflict with another, Congress is likely to play an especially large role in the conduct of foreign policy. It did so in the 1930s when isolationists and internationalists were contending for influence and Pearl Harbor had not yet settled the argument decisively in favor of the internationalists; it did so again in the late 1960s and early 1970s when the Munich–Pearl Harbor view was beginning to yield to a perspective that had been formed by our defeat in Vietnam.

ELITE INTERESTS VERSUS ELITE OPINIONS

A major challenge to the view just presented is offered by those who argue that it is material interests, not ideas and formative experiences, that explain American foreign policy. This argument is often referred to as a "revisionist" or radical theory of American foreign policy.

The Revisionist Debate

As with any important intellectual dispute, there are more than just two sides. There are many

ALTERNATIVE WORLD VIEWS OF UNITED STATES' RELATIONS WITH THE WORLD

Munich–Pearl Harbor View	Post-Vietnam View
Communism is a monolithic threat.	Communism is a divided spastic.
If we don't intervene overseas, we may get dragged into war.	If we do intervene overseas, we are sure to get into a war.
We must nip aggression in the bud.	We are not the world's policeman.
Only American military superiority will contain Soviet expansionism and preserve peace.	Only arms limitations treaties and force reductions will preserve peace.

President John F. Kennedy,
Inaugural Address, 1960:

"Let every nation know that we shall pay any price, bear any burden, meet any hardship, support any friend, oppose any foe to assure the survival and success of liberty."

John Kenneth Galbraith,
writing in *Esquire*, March 1972:

"[It means] an even more positive commitment to coexistence with the Communist countries. It means a much more determined effort to get military competition with the Soviets under control. . . . It means abandoning the Sub-Imperial ambitions in the Third World and recognizing instead that there is little we can do to influence political development in this part of the world and less that we need to do now."

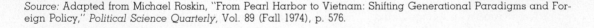

Source: Adapted from Michael Roskin, "From Pearl Harbor to Vietnam: Shifting Generational Paradigms and Foreign Policy," *Political Science Quarterly*, Vol. 89 (Fall 1974), p. 576.

variants of the revisionist interpretation of American diplomacy. Some argue that the world view based on the idea of containment and the fear of appeasement was an error—though ideas governed our actions, they were the wrong ideas. In this view, America overreacted to the legitimate security needs of Stalinist Russia by attempting to block Russia's desire to have "friendly" regimes along its western borders and sought to overawe the nation by using the atomic bomb, not simply to defeat Japan, on whose soil it was dropped, but to discourage the Soviet Union from making any military moves in the Far East or in Europe.[46] Others argue that American national security managers have sought, not peace, but American world dominance and the enlargement of their own bureaucratic empires.[47] These interpretations are at odds with orthodox historical accounts of World War II, the Cold War, and American military activities abroad, but they do not challenge the notion that elite ideas are important in explaining foreign policy. The debate over which ideas are correct or in this country's best interests is not the subject of this book.

The more radical version of the revisionist argument is that economic interests, not ideas or political systems, determine American foreign policy. Gabriel Kolko, for example, claims that events since 1945 are but a continuation of the basic thrust of American society since its beginnings—namely, to make government policy serve the conservative economic interests of business. Kolko applies to foreign policy the same perspective he and others have applied to the politics of economic regulation (see Chapter 15) and of military spending (see Chapter 21): the important political decisions are made in order to rationalize, enlarge, and protect corporate capitalism.[48]

A capitalist economy, the argument goes, requires expanding markets for its health. If these markets are limited to the United States, expansion (and thus profits) will be limited. Only by enlarging American political and military influence abroad can a larger share of the world market be obtained for American business. Moreover, many countries are important sources of vital raw materials, especially those of the underdeveloped Third World. Maintaining in those nations regimes friendly to the United States, even if (perhaps *especially* if) such regimes are reactionary and unpopular, is an important objective of American foreign policy. The multinational corporation—the large firm that makes investments and does business as both producer and seller in several nations simultaneously—is only the most recent and sophisticated form of international exploitation; one which, like all previous forms, requires governmental protection.[49] The United States has regularly, it is claimed, pursued such business-oriented policies—by making imperialist conquests in 1898–1899, by insisting on an "open door" trade policy in China and elsewhere, by supporting pro-Western

and anti-Marxist leaders in such places as copper-rich Katanga (a province of the Congo) and banana-rich Guatemala, and by giving economic and military aid to "client" states.

One does not require a full-scale Marxist interpretation of history to be aware that economic considerations play a part in many aspects of foreign policy. As suggested earlier in this chapter, the demands of economic groups (as well as of ethnic ones) are central to foreign policy issues that evoke interest group or client politics. Even the diplomatic and military decisions that reflect majoritarian politics often take economics into account—the struggle between the United States and the Soviet Union proceeds on the economic as well as on the military and diplomatic fronts. Trade agreements can be used as a tool to foster détente or to penalize aggression, to enhance goodwill or to extract concessions. When American corporations are expropriated abroad, American diplomats go to their aid (they are required to do so by an act of Congress), and on occasion corporations can be made the direct instruments of foreign policy. (This may well have been the case with ITT in Chile.) By the same token, however, corporations often push for liberalizing the rules governing trade with Communist regimes.

But all that is very different from saying that economic considerations, or the capitalist order, determine the major diplomatic and military moves of American foreign policy any more than they determine the moves of socialist or Communist countries. Apart from the factual inaccuracies that appear in many of the leading revisionist works,[50] the central difficulty of these arguments is that they do not prove that a cause-and-effect relationship exists between a given economic system (of this or any other country) and a given foreign policy.[51]

Korea, Vietnam, Israel

Three of the most important decisions in postwar American foreign policy—to intervene in Korea and Vietnam and to support Israel against its Arab neighbors—simply cannot be explained by economic imperialism. There were only trivial American investments in South Korea at the time war broke out there in 1950, and that country had neither provided the United States with an important market nor received significant American economic or military aid. Though Korea is next door to Japan, a nation of great economic importance, the military security of Japan depends far less on what happens in Korea than on Japan's own military capabilities. Yet the United States had concluded in 1945 a peace treaty with Japan that in effect forbade it to have a military establishment of any consequence. A far simpler explanation of the Korean decision is one that is in accord with all that was said and written at the time. The explanation is that the world view of American leaders in 1950, as well as domestic political opposition to communism, made them feel that it was essential to resist aggression in Korea if future aggressors elsewhere were to be deterred. When President Truman said in October 1952 that "we are fighting in Korea so we won't have to fight . . . on San Francisco Bay," it was no doubt campaign hyperbole, but it was hyperbole based on genuine conviction.[52]

The case was similar in Vietnam. American investments there—even in the whole region—were small, and though important raw materials and markets were available in some parts of Southeast Asia, such as Singapore, there were none of any consequence in Vietnam, Laos, or Cambodia. Scarcely anyone believed enough in the "domino theory" to predict that the economically important countries of Asia, notably Japan and the Philippines, would be powerfully affected by who won in Vietnam. Many accounts of our rationale for intervening in Vietnam were written by people who were close to the decision but who, because they disagreed, had little stake in defending it. They explain our intervention in Vietnam in almost exactly the same terms as they explain our earlier involvement in Korea: American leaders believed that an ally had been

❝Three of the most important decisions in postwar American foreign policy—to intervene in Korea and Vietnam and to support Israel against its Arab neighbors—simply cannot be explained by economic imperialism.❞

The United States fought on behalf of South Korea even though it had few investments there. It has also taken the Israeli side against the Arab nations despite the presence of giant American investments in the Arab world.

threatened by a Communist regime that invaded across a political boundary. If the United States did not help resist that aggression, these leaders felt, the credibility of our commitments elsewhere would be seriously eroded and Communist regimes in other parts of the world would be encouraged to attempt similar guerrilla "wars of liberation." Finally, Presidents Kennedy and Johnson had seen the domestic political consequences suffered by President Truman when China went Communist in 1949: bitter investigations and recriminations, political attacks from conservative opponents, and defeat at the polls at the hands of a public that would not support officials who appeared to be "soft on communism."[53] It is not clear whether American leaders believed they could win in Vietnam; it was clear that they believed, for public-spirited as well as for political reasons, that they could not afford to lose.

In the Middle East, the United States has vast investments, chiefly through the American (and allied) international oil companies. A resource on which we are vitally dependent is found in great abundance there, and our dependence on it has been growing steadily. Moreover, the tens of millions of people of the Arab world constitute a large potential market, especially the emergent Arab middle class that has grown affluent on oil revenues. Lastly, an Arab nation, Egypt, controls the Suez Canal, which is still important, even in the age of the supertanker, as a world trade route. Yet with all this, the United States has supported the state of Israel, since its creation, over the sustained, vociferous, and often violent objections of its Arab neighbors, and has persisted in that support even when oil shipments were cut off. Some of this support no doubt reflects the client politics arising out of the presence in this country of a sizable and well-organized Jewish population, but much of that support comes from politicians who have few or no Jewish constituents.[54] Again, ideas and beliefs are of decisive significance. In the case of Israel, more is involved than simply helping a small nation to resist aggression (though Soviet opposition to Israel is evident and important); also at stake is a sense of identification with an embattled democratic state with whom we share many religious and cultural affinities.

IDEOLOGY, INFORMATION, AND BUREAUCRACY

This chapter has drawn attention to alternative ways of explaining major diplomatic and military decisions that implicate the interests of the nation as a whole. It has suggested why—and how—the prevailing world view of the foreign

policy elite is of decisive importance. This is not the whole story of foreign policy making, however. Events (an oil embargo, a war in the Middle East, the declining value of the dollar abroad) are obviously important; so also is information (such as intelligence reports) about what is happening or about to happen. And so also is the behavior of the governmental bureaucracies charged with managing various aspects of foreign policy. An adequate account of these requires another book, or several books, and is the proper subject of a course on American foreign policy.

Though important, these other aspects of policy-making are less important than the beliefs of leaders: our most significant foreign policy decisions—to go to war, to negotiate security treaties, to intervene or not on behalf of various factions in civil wars abroad—are not the result of good or bad information or internecine struggles among rival bureaucracies. These decisions are the result of beliefs about the nature of the threats and opportunities that confront the United States as a nation preoccupied with its own security and freedom of action.

Within the limits set by these world views, significant conflicts among leaders and bureaucracies occur:

Vital information can be garbled or ignored. In 1941 we had every reason to believe that Japan was preparing military moves in the Pacific, but on the morning of December 7 the military forces in Honolulu were not on alert, aerial reconnaissance of the approaches to the city was haphazard, radar surveillance was not fully operational, and evidence that hostile forces were approaching got lost in the shuffle.[55]

Important strategic choices can reflect organizational routines. When American troops went to Vietnam, they followed prevailing army doctrine of searching out and attempting to destroy enemy combat units. This tactic was probably not well suited to a conflict in which the enemy was a guerrilla force that could fight from ambushes, blend in with the civilian population, and avoid any confrontation with superior American firepower.[56]

Organizational interests can influence how information is evaluated. The bombing of North Vietnam was evaluated by several intelligence agencies. Those connected with the organizations doing the bombing—the air force and the navy—tended to rate the bombing as effective in weakening the enemy, while those connected with organizations not doing the bombing, such as the Central Intelligence Agency, tended to be skeptical of the value of the aerial attacks. (By 1969 it was evident to all that the bombing policy had, in fact, not achieved its objectives.)[57] Because of the importance of information and organization in the conduct of foreign policy, conflicts frequently occur over how information should be gathered or government agencies reorganized.

SUMMARY

No single political explanation accounts for all foreign policy decisions since foreign policy covers a range of matters almost as diverse as domestic policy. Foreign affairs can follow an interest group pattern (especially where domestic economic or ethnic groups are in conflict) or a clientele pattern (when a domestic group is unopposed in seeking government protection for its overseas interests). This chapter has focused primarily on foreign policy decisions that implicate the interests of the nation as a whole (war and peace, relations with the Soviet Union) and evoke a variant of majoritarian politics. These decisions are constrained by the isolationist or internationalist opinion of the general public but directed in detail by the world views of a foreign policy elite.

The influence of such an elite arises from popular deference to the president and his advisers and is supported by the reluctance of the Supreme Court to challenge presidential authority. Congressional limitations on the president

tend to be weak in time of crisis but great when the dominant world views are being challenged or a new policy elite is rising to power. Elite world views are shaped by prior crises in which older views appear to have been discredited. There is little evidence that they primarily reflect economic or business imperatives.

Suggested Readings

Allison, Graham T. *Essence of Decision: Explaining the Cuban Missile Crises.* Boston: Little, Brown, 1971. Shows how the decision made by a president during a major crisis was shaped by bureaucratic and organizational factors.

Cohen, Benjamin J. *The Question of Imperialism.* New York: Basic Books, 1973. Careful analysis of theories claiming that economic motives control American foreign policy.

Destler, I. M. *Presidents, Bureaucrats, and Foreign Policy.* Princeton, N.J.: Princeton University Press, 1972. Analyzes the perennial struggle between the White House and the State Department.

Halberstam, David. *The Best and the Brightest.* New York: Random House, 1972. Readable, detailed account of the foreign policy elite—McGeorge Bundy, Robert S. McNamara, and others—that led the American involvement in Vietnam.

Henkin, Louis. *Foreign Affairs and the Constitution.* New York: W. W. Norton, 1972. How the Supreme Court has interpreted the constitutional sources of the war and foreign affairs powers.

Mueller, John E. *War, Presidents, and Public Opinion.* New York: John Wiley, 1973. Best summary of the relationship between presidential foreign policy decisions and public opinion.

Pious, Richard M. *The American Presidency.* New York: Basic Books, 1979. See Chapters 10 and 11. Up-to-date account of the relations between the president and Congress on foreign policy issues.

Spanier, John, and Eric M. Uslaner. *How American Foreign Policy Is Made.* New York: Praeger, 1974. Good brief overview of the politics of foreign policy.

Note: Two magazines regularly publish articles on both the substance and politics of foreign policy: *Foreign Affairs* (a more traditional, older journal) and *Foreign Policy* (much favored by the Carter administration policy-makers).

21 Military Spending

Who makes the decisions • The size of the
military establishment • Interservice rivalry and
allocations • Congressional voting • Profits of
defense firms • Cost overruns

The conventional view of national defense
policy-making is that it is an example, perhaps the clearest example, of "majoritarian politics." Both the benefits and the costs of national
defense are widely distributed—every American
citizen is protected by the military forces; every
taxpayer shares in the cost of these forces. During
most of our peacetime history, the size and cost of
the military establishment was quite small and
thus political controversy about it was low-key.
During wartime that size and cost became very
large, but these burdens were willingly accepted
by most citizens (except for some unpopular
wars, such as Vietnam). Public debates about the
proper size and cost of national defense have
been intense during times when people disagreed
about the magnitude of the threat the nation
faced and whether or not we should enter a
"foreign" or "European" war. The periods just

President Roosevelt reviewing the Pacific Fleet in San
Francisco, 1938 (left), and President Kennedy at his
inaugural parade in 1961 (right).

before World War I and World War II had just such debates. After each war there has been a sharp reduction in military spending and in the size of the armed forces. A substantial military force remained in existence only after World War II, and that was the result, in this view, of the persistent threat of Soviet expansion.

In the last twenty years or so, a competing theory of the politics of military policy has arisen. Usually called the theory of the "military-industrial complex," it is based on the assertion that much, if not all, spending for national defense is the result of client politics. A small group—military officers, corporations that receive military contracts, and congressmen that represent districts with high concentrations of military spending—receives most of the benefits, while the public at large pays the bill. Though there may be national benefits from a large defense establishment, the size of that establishment and the major weapons systems on which it depends are not the result of a reasonable judgment about the magnitude and nature of any foreign threat. They are the result of the organized demands of military leaders trying to enlarge the status of their services, of defense contractors seeking greater profits, and of key congressmen obtaining money for (and thus votes from) their districts. The public at large, and most of their elected representatives, have little control over the increasing military spending generated by this pattern of client politics. Because military spending benefits the few rather than the many, there is little pressure to make it efficient, and massive cost overruns for new weapons are commonplace.

There are several different versions of the theory of the military-industrial complex; persons subscribing to one do not necessarily accept others. One version is Marxist: a capitalist economy will spend heavily on the military establishment to sustain itself, to ensure high profits, and to provide the military force to protect American international trade and access to international markets and resources.[1] A second version is based on the belief, not that corporations run the country for their own benefit, but that military leaders have acquired undue power. The generals and admirals can undermine civilian control of the armed forces, giving them the ability to increase military spending, to enlarge the role and importance of their services, and to award defense contracts in a wasteful or self-serving manner.[2] A third version, related to the second, is that Congress has become progressively unable or unwilling to make sound judgments on military spending and defense policy. This is so partly because Congress lacks information and expertise and partly because its individual members feel the need to vote for high defense budgets to keep money flowing to the military bases and defense contractors in their districts. A fourth is that a strong national defense is in fact supported by public opinion, but that opinion has been created or manipulated by small groups of "Cold Warriors" who exaggerate the threat posed by the Soviet Union and other hostile nations.[3]

Though the specific theories differ, all have in common a mood expressed by former President Dwight Eisenhower. Upon leaving the White House in 1961, he cautioned Americans against "the acquisition of unwarranted influence, whether sought or unsought, by the military-industrial complex" made up of an "immense military establishment and a large arms industry." Though the caution, especially when uttered by a former army general, is worth remembering, it is also important to remember that the various theories to which it has given a common name are only theories, each of which must be tested with evidence before it can be accepted. Fortunately, evidence in these matters has been gathered, and though many issues remain unresolved, some things can be said about the degree to which defense politics more nearly approximates the majoritarian or the client model.

THE STRUCTURE OF DEFENSE DECISION-MAKING

The formal structure within which decisions about national defense are made was in large part created after the Second World War, but it reflects concerns that go back at least to the time of the Founding. Chief among these is the persistent desire by citizens to ensure civilian control over the military.

The National Security Act of 1947 and its subsequent amendments created a Department of Defense. It is headed by the secretary of defense, under whom serve the secretaries of the army, the air force, and the navy as well as the Joint Chiefs of Staff. The secretary of defense must be a civilian (though one former general, George C. Marshall, was allowed by Congress to be the secretary), and he exercises, on behalf of the president, command authority over the defense establishment. The secretary of the army, the secretary of the navy,* and the secretary of the air force are subordinate to the secretary of defense. Unlike him, they do not attend cabinet meetings or sit on the National Security Council. In essence, they manage the "housekeeping" functions of the various armed services under the general direction of the secretary of defense and his deputy and assistant secretaries of defense.

The four armed services are separate entities; by law, they cannot be merged or commanded by a single military officer, and each has the right to communicate directly with Congress. There are two reasons for having separate uniformed services functioning within a single department: the fear of many citizens that a unified military force might become too powerful politically and the desire of each service to preserve its traditional independence and autonomy.

---

*The secretary of the navy manages two services: the navy and the marine corps.

> **"**The result . . . is a good deal of interservice rivalry and bickering, but this is precisely what was intended by Congress when it created the Department of Defense.**"**

The result, of course, is a good deal of interservice rivalry and bickering, but this is precisely what was intended by Congress when it created the Department of Defense—rivalry and bickering, it was felt, would ensure that Congress would receive the maximum amount of information about military affairs and would enjoy the largest opportunity to affect military decisions.

Interservice rivalry has provided just this kind of opportunity to Congress. In 1948 the air force wanted to take over naval aviation; the navy counterattacked by criticizing the effectiveness of air force bombers and argued instead for building large aircraft carriers. When the navy was refused permission to build the "supercarriers" it

The Joint Chiefs of Staff, left to right: General Edward Meyer, Army Chief of Staff; Admiral Thomas B. Hayward, Chief of Naval Operations; General David C. Jones, chairman of the Joint Chiefs; General Lew Allen, Air Force Chief of Staff; and General Robert Barrow, Marine Corps Commandant.

DEPARTMENT OF DEFENSE, 1978

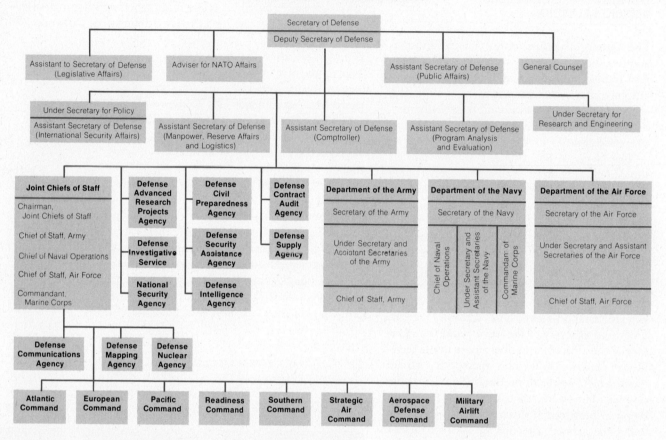

had in mind, several admirals resigned in protest. In the 1960s the navy and air force argued again, this time over a new fighter aircraft (the TFX), only one type of which was to be built. The air force wanted a plane to fly over long distances and carry nuclear weapons; the navy wanted one to take off and land from aircraft carriers and to fly at high speed for short distances. The air force was seeking to enlarge the role of manned aircraft as a major part of our deterrent forces; the navy wanted to preserve the role of the carrier as a strategic force.

In the 1970s another debate erupted, this time over whether the navy should build more large, nuclear-powered aircraft carriers or shift to smaller, oil-fueled ones. Though disputes like these often employ the usual techniques of bureaucratic in-fighting—leaking information to the press, mobilizing sympathetic congressmen, hiring rival civilian "experts"—they are not *merely* in-fighting, for they focus attention on major issues of national defense policy.

The Joint Chiefs of Staff, a committee composed of five senior officers, does not command the armed services, nor is the chairman of the joint chiefs the "head" of the military. Rather, this committee of equals (the chairman has only one vote) is the principal military adviser to the secretary of defense. It is charged with formulating plans and recommendations for the secretary and transmitting his orders to the various major military commands in the field. It also has the right to communicate directly with the president and Congress. The joint chiefs are assisted in their planning function by a joint staff of about four hundred officers drawn more or less equally from each military service. Since each member (other than the chairman) of the joint chiefs is also the highest-ranking uniformed officer in his own service, these men wear two hats and thus play potentially conflicting roles. The chief of naval operations (CNO), for example, is the senior officer of the navy who is responsible for training and equipping the navy's operating forces. At the same time he is a member of the joint chiefs where he is supposed to help formulate recommendations as to what is good for the national defense as a whole. Obviously, the CNO is likely to function on the joint chiefs as a representative of the navy point of view rather than of a national point of view (though the two may from time to time coincide).

Under the Constitution the president is commander-in-chief of the armed forces. He has, as we saw in Chapter 20, used that authority to order American military forces into combat on many occasions. During peacetime, however, his most important military powers are those he exercises through the secretary of defense in managing the defense establishment. To a large degree, his powers as manager depend on his ability to decide which service will be allowed to ask Congress for how much money and for what. In theory, a president and secretary of defense can make important decisions regarding the maximum size of the military budget that will be requested, the strategic plans that will be used to guide the allocation of these funds, the distribution of funds among the four services, and the nature of any new weapons systems that will be proposed. Congress, in turn, has the authority to approve, disapprove, or revise any of these spending requests and may be able to influence the strategic plans on which these requests are based. That, at least, is the theory.

THE SIZE OF THE MILITARY ESTABLISHMENT

The United States, from its Founding until rather recently, has sought to avoid having a large standing peacetime army. Because the United States is geographically isolated from Europe and other arenas of frequent conflict, it was possible to mobilize only when war was imminent and demobilize almost entirely when war was over. Hence, the percentage of the gross national product devoted to defense in 1935 was about what it had been in 1870.[4] After the Second World War, however, the advent of the long-range airplane and the intercontinental missile made the United States seem much less remote. World events, too, had an effect. The Soviet Union continued to dominate the Eastern European countries that it had occupied during the war, confrontations took place between Soviet and American military forces (as in the Soviet blockade of West Berlin), a Soviet-backed coup in Czechoslovakia was successful and a Soviet-backed insurgent movement in Greece was nearly so, and the Communist regime in North Korea invaded South Korea. All these events led the United States during the period 1948–1950 to stop short of complete demobilization and to begin instead to maintain a large peacetime military force. The United States' participation in the war in Korea raised military spending substantially; after a brief decline spending rose again during the war in Vietnam.

In general, however, the total amount of money spent on defense (measured in constant dollars*), as well as the total number of military personnel, declined more or less steadily from 1956 to 1976 (see Table 21.1). In 1955 we spent about 10 percent of the gross national product on defense; in 1978 we spent about 5 percent. (In the

---

*"Constant dollars" means dollars adjusted for inflation. It is a way of measuring costs that holds constant the purchasing power of the dollar. If one were to measure costs in "current dollars," they would seem to go up whenever the number of dollars in circulation went up.

TABLE 21.1   Money Spent on National Defense

Year	Current dollars*	Constant (1978) dollars*	As percentage of federal budget	As percentage of GNP
1950	$ 12.4	$ 45.9	29.1%	4.7%
1955	39.9	119.6	58.2	10.5
1960	45.2	115.4	49.0	9.1
1965	47.5	108.4	40.1	7.2
1970	78.6	141.1	40.0	8.2
1973	74.5	109.4	30.1	6.0
1975	85.6	104.9	26.2	5.9
1977	97.5	103.8	24.2	5.3
1978 (est.)	107.6	107.6	23.3	5.3

Source: Statistical Abstract of the United States, 1978, p. 370.

* In billions. "Constant dollars" are dollars adjusted for inflation.

1960s spending went up because of the Vietnam War.) Of late, defense has taken one-fourth or less of the total federal budget.

Civilian Control

The central political fact about these total defense expenditures is that the president can, within broad limits, decide what they are to be. President Truman decided in the late 1940s that the military was to get no more than one-third of the federal budget. Despite impassioned pleas by the secretary of defense and the joint chiefs of staff, proposals to exceed that limit were rejected. President Eisenhower in the 1950s used a different kind of ceiling: defense was not to consume more than 10 percent of the gross national product. Again the joint chiefs proposed spending more than this ceiling; again they were overruled by the president. President Kennedy in the early 1960s did not utilize a budget ceiling strategy. He left the budget instead to his energetic secretary of defense, Robert McNamara, who sought to evaluate personally each service proposal in the light of its potential contribution to national defense. Defense spending rose, in

constant dollars, but the decisions were almost always McNamara's, not the result of allowing the three services to have whatever they wanted. President Nixon returned to the practice of imposing budget ceilings as he moved to cut back on the size of the military following our gradual withdrawal from Vietnam.[5]

Nor are the president and the secretary of defense the only civilians whose views importantly affect defense decisions. Beginning with Secretary McNamara, a large contingent of civilian intellectuals—policy analysts, authors of books on strategy, professorial consultants—entered the Defense Department at the highest levels, bringing with them views as to the proper level and kind of defense expenditures. Their views were very different from those of the uniformed military officers. Because they were specifically recruited to assist the secretary of defense in evaluating military spending and

Secretary of Defense Robert S. McNamara exercised detailed control of military budgets and strategy. Here he described the targets of U.S. bombing missions in North Vietnam.

weapons proposals, they have had an influence out of proportion to their numbers. Military and civilian specialists often disagree over the assumptions, purposes, and requirements of military doctrine; the tension between these two groups has been a significant feature of defense policy-making since the 1960s.

Defense Spending and National Resources

Those theories of a military-industrial complex that claim that defense expenditures and the size of the armed forces increase steadily and autonomously are simply not consistent with the facts. Whether measured by the number of men and women in uniform, the number of aircraft and ships in service, or the number of constant dollars spent, resources committed to national defense fall in peacetime. Ceilings on total expenditures and total personnel are decided by the president (whether wisely or foolishly is another matter) and not by military leaders who are able to overcome presidential preferences. Of late (1976–1978), Presidents Ford and Carter have decided to authorize military budget requests that would increase the defense budget (in constant dollars), even though the nation was not at war. All the evidence suggests that this reflected a judgment, right or wrong, about the Soviet arms buildup and was not a concession to the special pleading of a small sector of the economy.[6]

Nor have defense expenditures obviously curtailed expenditures on other—especially social—programs. In 1955 federal expenditures for all social welfare programs took 3.9 percent of the gross national product (GNP) while national defense took 10.5 percent. In 1975 social welfare expenditures had risen to consume 19 percent of GNP, and defense expenditures had fallen to 5.9 percent. Stated another way, whereas human resources programs took one-quarter and national defense took one-half the 1960 federal budget, by 1976 these proportions had been nearly reversed—human resources took half, defense took one-quarter (see Figure 21.1).

Nor can the total amount of resources devoted

> **“**Those theories of a military-industrial complex that claim that defense expenditures and the size of the armed forces increase steadily and autonomously are simply not consistent with the facts.**”**

to national defense be explained by knowing the economic system of a country. The nations with the largest and most costly military forces include capitalist countries (the United States, South Korea, and Taiwan), Communist countries (the Soviet Union and the People's Republic of China), and socialist and social-democratic countries (Egypt, Israel). The size of the military establishment is determined by the nature of the military threats a country believes it faces or the scope of the military ambitions it entertains and not by the organization of its economic system.

FIGURE 21.1   Distribution of Federal Expenditures, by Category

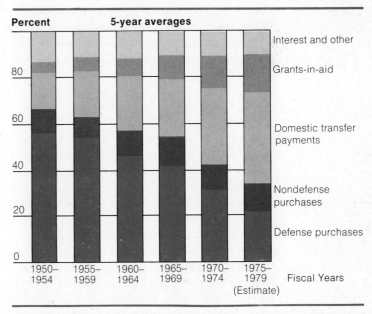

Source: Budget of the United States Government, Fiscal Year 1979, Special Analyses, p. 50.

THE ALLOCATION OF THE DEFENSE BUDGET

It is much more difficult for elected officials, such as the president, to alter substantially the allocation of defense expenditures among the military services than it is to change significantly the total level of those expenditures. In the United States—and probably in every nation—the army, the navy, the marine corps, and the air force can each mobilize important political allies if it is threatened with a loss of resources relative to the other services. It is, thus, much easier for a president or secretary of defense to require that all services accept an across-the-board cut in budgets, equally applicable to all, than to compel one service to accept a cut while another service enjoys an increase.

Support for Each Service

The Joint Chiefs of Staff, composed as it is of representatives of each service, usually will recommend unanimously policies that benefit all services equally and will accept (reluctantly) policies that penalize all equally. It is obviously incapable of making choices that would favor one service over another. In any coordinating committee, each member will tacitly agree to support the favored positions of every other member in exchange for the promise from the others to support his favored position. Though there have been exceptions when the joint chiefs split on major issues, in general they follow this pattern.

This support for each service is reinforced by members of the congressional committees who handle its authorizations and appropriations. At one time each military service was overseen by a committee in the House and one in the Senate, but after the Second World War these committees were merged into a single House Armed Services Committee and a single Senate Armed Services Committee. There remain within these committees strong congressional advocates of one or the other service. There is, for example,

within the House Armed Services Committee a Subcommittee on Seapower whose members, especially its chairman (Representative Charles E. Bennett of Florida), regularly support larger budget authorizations for the navy than even the Pentagon requests. In 1978 the subcommittee proposed a 68 percent increase in the Carter administration's request for funds with which to build navy ships.[7]

As a result of these factors, the share of the total defense budget going to each service changes very slowly. Each major service usually receives roughly a third of the defense budget. In peacetime the army share will be somewhat lower as the number of soldiers tends to fluctuate between wartime and peacetime more than the number of sailors or airmen.

The key allocative decisions, thus, become incremental ones—decisions about what new things to add to a service's existing budget rather than decisions about transferring a function from one service to another. Usually, these involve the purchase of major new weapons. About one-third of the total defense budget is devoted to

"The key allocative decisions, thus, become incremental ones—decisions about what new things to add to a service's existing budget rather than decisions about transferring a function from one service to another.**"**

The Pentagon in Washington, D.C.
The B-1 bomber on a test flight.
A rally in 1978 to ban production of the B-1 bomber.

weapons research, development, and procurement. The more expensive of these weapons systems, such as the B-1 bomber, the Trident nuclear submarine, the antiballistic missile (ABM) program, and the new main battle tank, become the subject of intense political debate involving the Pentagon, the White House, the Congress, and various interest groups. Interest groups include not only weapons manufacturers but organized groups of scientists and private defense budget analysts in such "think tanks" as RAND, the Brookings Institution, and the American Enterprise Institute.

In these debates many factors—strategic, economic, and political—come to the fore. A proposal to build the B-1 bomber, for example, involved arguments over whether we needed a supersonic intercontinental bomber or whether such a bomber, even if valuable, would cost too much and whether making such an investment would have desirable effects on the economy of those states in which major components would be produced. Each year that funds were requested for developing the B-1, a prolonged discussion occurred, with frequently close votes in Congress. Eventually, President Carter decided to terminate the program.

Congressional Influence

The congressional role in deciding on weapons systems has changed somewhat over the years. Before World War II, Congress often made, on military advice, the most detailed decisions as to what equipment to buy, what bases to open, and where ships and army units were to be located. During the war, it retreated from this activist stance in deference to military opinion; the all-out nature of the war effort, and the popularity of the cause, dissuaded congressmen from acting in a way that might have been interpreted as hindering the fighting forces. After the war Congress once again became assertive, but typically in favor of different or larger military programs than those proposed by the president. For example, Congress favored a larger marine corps and a larger air force than did President Truman. (When Congress appropriated more money for these purposes than Truman wanted, he refused to spend it.)

Congress was also deeply involved in postwar decisions regarding the B-36 bomber, the navy's "supercarriers," the choice among competing missile systems, and the building of new fighter aircraft such as the TFX. While a senator, John F. Kennedy criticized President Eisenhower's emphasis on strategic weapons (bombers and missiles armed with nuclear bombs) at the expense of conventional ground forces. After he became president in 1961, Kennedy began to

The national mood has changed with regard to military affairs. An enthusiastic parade celebrated the end of World War II and the role of the armed forces; twenty years later, pickets in front of the White House protested a plan to build an antiballistic missile (ABM) system.

build up these ground forces and encouraged the creation of the "Green Beret" special forces units. Throughout this period Congress was expanding its power to affect certain military decisions. In the 1950s it made military construction appropriations subject to an annual authorization; in the 1960s it made the procurement of weapons systems subject to annual authorization (see Chapter 12).

During the latter part of the 1960s congressional interest in these matters sharpened and

alone without extensive congressional debate, since the late 1960s almost every new weapons system is subjected to intensive discussion.

For example, in 1969 the proposed antiballistic missile system barely survived congressional and interest group opposition (in the Senate a motion to defeat the plan lost in a tie vote, 50 to 50). Ultimately, the president scaled down the plan to just one installation, and in 1975 Congress voted to close down even that facility.

During the 1960s Congress frequently made major changes in that portion of the Pentagon's budget requests having to do with research, development, and procurement. In the early 1960s these changes were usually in the direction of increasing the size of the budget; between 1964 and 1977 they involved substantial reductions in procurement and research.[8] After 1977 Congress seemed once again to have become receptive to increases in military procurement.

The decisive factors accounting for these shifts in congressional sentiment were not the economic interests of defense contractors or the public-relations skills of military leaders, but rather changes in the beliefs of congressmen about the nature of international conflict. In the 1940s and 1950s liberals generally believed that the United States should play a major role in international affairs and should restrict Soviet expansion. In the late 1960s and early 1970s many congressmen had changed their views. They now felt that the United States should play a more limited role overseas and should deal with the Soviet Union by negotiating treaties that limited armament programs. By the end of the 1970s, still another change seemed to take place as evidence appeared that the Soviet Union was supporting expansionist regimes in Africa and certain liberation movements hostile to Israel, substantially enlarging its military strength and budget (see Table 21.2), and violating some provisions of the arms limitation treaties.

For example, in the debate over the antiballistic missile (ABM) mentioned earlier, the votes cast by senators are best explained by their personal political ideologies rather than by the eco-

shifted its tone. Congress began to take a more critical stance toward the military. This reflected the growing unpopularity of the war in Vietnam, the increase in the influence of interest groups (such as liberal scientists with experience in weapons research) that opposed various new weapons systems, and a lessened popular confidence in military expertise. Unlike in the late 1940s and early 1950s, when a decision to go ahead with the development of the hydrogen bomb could be made by the president acting

TABLE 21.2 Strategic Forces of the U.S. and USSR, Selected Years

Category	1965 U.S.	1965 USSR	1977 U.S.	1977 USSR	1982 U.S.	1982 USSR	Difference U.S.–USSR 1982 N	Difference U.S.–USSR 1982 (%)
Delivery vehicles								
ICBM[a]	854	224	1,054	1,450	1,054	1,400	−346	(−24.7)
SLBM[b]	464	24	656	880	720	950	−230	(−24.2)
Strategic bombers	807	155	418	210	425	100	+325	(+325.0)
Total	2,125	403	2,128	2,540	2,199	2,450	−251	(−10.2)
Total missiles	1,318	248	1,710	2,330	1,774	2,350	−576	(−24.5)
Warheads								
Total	6,230	450	8,500	4,000	11,275	9,640	+1,635	(+16.9)
Missile warheads	1,670	248	6,700	2,900	7,700	7,150	+550	(+7.7)
Throw-weight[c]								
Total	10.0	2.6	7.5	10.2	9.9	11.1	−1.2	(−10.8)
Missile payload	2.2	1.1	3.9	8.2	4.5	10.1	−5.6	(−55.4)
Equivalent megatonnage								
Total	8,600	1,100	4,200	6,200	5,300	6,850	−1,550	(−22.6)
Total missile	1,400	600	2,200	4,800	2,500	5,850	−3,350	(−57.3)

Source: FY 1978 Defense Report, p. 61; Henry Owen and Charles Schultze, eds., *Setting National Priorities* (Washington, D.C.: Brookings Institution, 1976), p. 86. Reprinted by permission.

[a] Intercontinental ballistic missiles.
[b] Submarine-launched ballistic missiles.
[c] In millions of pounds.

nomic interests of their states or even by their political party affiliations. Liberal senators were against the ABM; conservative senators were for it.[9]

CONGRESSIONAL VOTING AND DEFENSE INTERESTS

A number of attempts have been made to discover whether congressmen from states or districts with high levels of defense-related activity vote differently on military and foreign policy issues than those from areas without such ac-

tivity. Though not all studies are in agreement, the preponderance of evidence is that the relationship between congressional votes and defense activity in states and districts is weak or nonexistent. One study compared levels of defense spending in congressional districts with the votes of the representatives from those districts on defense and foreign policy issues considered by the House in 1967–1968. It found no relationship except among a few very senior congressmen, and in those cases the direction of causality is far from clear. Such persons may not have voted for a strong military posture because there were a lot of defense-related jobs and contracts in their districts; rather, their districts may have received those jobs and contracts because, being very senior congressmen, they had substantial influence on their committees.[10]

Several persons have investigated the pattern of votes in the Senate on defense and foreign policy matters. Employing various measures of defense spending and the distribution of defense contracts, they either find weak and inconclusive relationships between votes and spending or no relationship at all.[11]

In short, there is no systematic evidence that congressional voting on national defense issues is influenced by the existence in districts or states of a defense-related economy. Other forms of congressional behavior, however, are quite sensitive to these considerations. This occurs, not when policy is being set, but when decisions are being made over whether to close or leave open a particular military base, naval shipyard, or aircraft facility. Such highly localistic issues are clear examples of "client politics"—the client in this case being the community that stands to lose the jobs if the base is closed. A senator or representative known for his opposition to high levels of defense spending in general, or who has argued against new weapons systems, will often behave just like a pro-defense congressman by protesting the planned closing of bases in his or her district.

When Congress approved the 1977 military construction authorization bill, it added a provision whereby Congress would have to be informed of any decision to close a military base in the United States employing more than five hundred civilians or to cut civilian employment at such a base by 50 percent or one thousand workers, whichever was larger. To make certain that the secretary of defense would take congressional interest in this matter seriously, the law requires that an "environmental impact statement" accompany the report. The secretary would then have to wait sixty days before implementing a decision.

❝A senator or representative known for his opposition to high levels of defense spending . . . will often behave just like a pro-defense congressman by protesting the planned closing of bases in his or her district.❞

The local impact of military policy: residents of Rhode Island protest a plan to close naval bases in that state.

CORPORATIONS AND DEFENSE

Though some corporations depend heavily on defense contracts, most of the largest ones do not. General Dynamics, like most aircraft companies, receives most of its income from defense-related activities, but the great majority of the largest industrial corporations—about three-fourths of the one hundred biggest firms—receive less than 5 percent of their sales from military contracts.[12] Naturally, those firms heavily dependent on defense spending will argue in favor of that spending, just as will labor unions whose members work in defense-related industries. Such arguments will come, not from industry and labor generally, but from a highly concentrated segment of it.

Defense contracting is, on the whole, no more profitable than serving the civilian market. In one study six large defense contracts were compared with six commercial firms of similar size. The percentage of profits on sales of the defense firms was less than that of the nondefense firms, a fact clearly recognized by the stock market. Investors will pay less for the stocks of defense firms than for the stocks of comparable nondefense firms* and have less confidence in the bonds issued by the former than those issued by the latter.[13] The General Accounting Office analyzed the profits of the seventy-four largest defense contractors and found that those with the highest volume of government business generally earned a smaller profit on their capital than did those that were least dependent on government sales.[14]

Defense Facilities as a National Resource

Because the defense industry is no more profitable, more heavily in debt, and less appealing to investors than nondefense firms of comparable size, the executives of defense firms worry greatly about obtaining new government contracts. They have little margin for error, enjoy few alternative sources of corporate income, and face serious problems if government spending is reduced. By the same token, Defense Department officials must worry about finding ways of supplying such contracts since the failure of a firm such as Lockheed or General Dynamics can lead to the dismantling of one of the few industrial facilities in the country capable of producing aircraft or ships.

This leads to what one scholar has called the

"follow-on imperative"—a tendency to distribute contracts for such things as airplanes and missiles so that as one contract nears completion at a particular plant another contract is available to keep the facility and its workers intact. For example, there were in 1972 eight major production lines for aircraft and missiles in the United States. The existence of these facilities is regarded by the Defense Department as a national resource that would be difficult, if not impossible, to create on short notice should war suddenly make necessary a high level of production. Hence, as McDonnell-Douglas finishes building F-4 fighter aircraft, both it and the government have an interest in finding a new contract for it (in this case to build the F-15 fighter).[15]

Cost Overruns

It is not this close relationship between a defense contractor and the government, however, that explains the cost overruns that have become so familiar a feature of military spending. During the 1950s the actual cost of the average new weapons system was three times the estimated cost; by the 1960s there had been only a marginal improvement—now final costs were running only twice estimated costs.[16] The vast increase in the cost of the F-111 fighter and the C-5A transport between what was proposed in the budget and what was actually paid out became headline stories. Some find in this evidence of incompetence, collusion, or "war profiteering."[17]

The correct explanation for cost overruns, however, is not political but bureaucratic. They occur, not because businessmen and military officers wield influence on each other and on Congress to obtain new weapons regardless of cost, but because the system by which weapons have been purchased has caused even well-meaning persons to buy expensive equipment in ways that virtually guarantee that costs will be higher than predicted.

A new aircraft, tank, or ship must be invented before it can be built or purchased. Unlike an automobile, a house, or a suit of clothes, all of

---

*More technically, the ratio of stock price to stock earnings is lower for defense than for nondefense firms.

which have been produced for years in well-understood ways and sold at known prices in competitive markets, an F-4 fighter or a C-5A transport plane begins as a concept in the minds of military officers who need something (a very high speed fighter, a very large transport plane) that does not yet exist. It cannot be purchased "off the shelf." Indeed, it cannot even be described very accurately, since no one knows (until it is built) exactly how to build it. In this, new weapons are no different from other unique, not-yet-tried things one might want to buy. It always costs more to remodel your house than you expect because, until the remodeling starts, you are not quite sure what is involved. The cost overruns of the new subway systems in Washington, D.C., and San Francisco were enormous. A congressional committee set up to investigate the cost of overruns of the military will itself experience cost overruns because no one can know in advance what such an investigation will cost until it is carried out. In fact, the hearings by the House Judiciary Committee to decide whether to recommend the impeachment of President Nixon exceeded their original estimated costs by 200 percent.[18]

Because one cannot know the cost of something that does not yet exist and because of the way military contracts are often awarded, everybody involved in producing a new weapons system has an incentive to act in ways that lead to inefficiency. Military officers, naturally, want the best new airplane or ship that modern technology can devise. As Air Force General Carl "Tooey" Spaatz once put it: "A second-best airplane is like a second-best poker hand. No damn good."[19] Hence, officers write contracts that are filled with detailed performance requirements and that call for new designs and techniques that may exist only in an inventor's imagination. The executives of defense industries, naturally, want to get the new contract, and hence they have every reason to underestimate the costs of, and overestimate their ability to produce, the new airplane or ship. Under this system they will

66The correct explanation for cost overruns . . . is not political but bureaucratic.**99**

The C-5A military transport proved far more costly to build than originally estimated, but it enabled the United States to support Israel during the Yom Kippur War.

make unrealistically low bids in order to get the business. Congress has good reason for not letting the American defense industry go bankrupt; thus when final costs turn out to be much higher than estimated costs, it will appropriate, however reluctantly, the money to make up the difference.[20]

These results are not unique to America, or to American politics, or to the American economic system. They occur in any country or economic order whenever someone makes a decision to buy some complex piece of technology that does not yet exist.

There are ways of reducing the problem, not by altering the political power of either buyers or sellers—power is not the problem—but by changing the purchasing system. One of the most important changes, instituted during the 1970s, is to "fly before you buy." Previously, the government would provide a written description of a new, sophisticated airplane and then award a contract to produce several hundred of them to whichever firm made the most plausible proposal. Under the "fly before you buy" procedure, the government commissions several firms to produce a small number of competing versions of the airplane and then, after testing, awards a contract for quantity production to whichever firm has built the most promising prototype. This does not necessarily mean that the product will be better or the cost lower, only that performance and cost will be known more accurately in advance. In this way a more rational decision can be made as to whether it is worth buying the airplane at all.

Whether changes in the purchasing system will be adopted extensively depends in part on how willing the participants in the system are to give up some of their autonomy and security. Military officers must be willing to forgo the writing of detailed specifications for new weapons and to avoid the overly rigid supervision of contractors. Understandably, some officers are so eager to have the "best" weapon that they may be reluctant to allow contractors to solve these problems themselves. Contractors, no doubt, would prefer less competition, not more, with guarantees that the government will reimburse them for any cost overruns. As explained in Chapter 12, bureaucrats, public or private, tend to be preoccupied with their jobs, not with larger issues of national policy, and thus more interested in solving immediate problems than in achieving long-run efficiencies.

SUMMARY

Simplistic notions of a "military-industrial complex" are not very helpful in analyzing the politics of issues as complicated as those involved in defense spending. To understand how power is distributed and used in this policy area, one must separate the issues into different categories.

What the total amount of defense spending will be and thus what the size of the armed forces as a whole will be are decisions that are made primarily, if not entirely, by civilian officials, chiefly the president. These decisions tend to follow the pattern of majoritarian politics, with both costs and benefits seen as widely distributed. Interest groups are not especially important in determining total spending levels; changing perceptions of international threats to American security and of public willingness to pay for defense are of crucial importance.

The allocation of the defense budget among the separate armed services takes the form of interest group politics: each service, and its allies in Congress, is keenly sensitive to its position relative to its rivals. Reallocating the defense budget among the four services would confer specific benefits on one and clear costs on another, and hence all affected parties are well organized to resist (usually successfully) any reallocation.

The opening of military bases and facilities in particular localities takes the form of client politics: one specific sector of society stands to gain substantially, with society as a whole bearing the (usually small) cost. Representatives of affected localities will work hard to keep specific facilities located in their districts and to attract new ones there, but the existence of such facilities or lack of them and the level of defense spending in these districts do not significantly affect the votes cast by congressmen and senators on matters of general foreign and military policy.

Congress controls defense policy chiefly by making decisions, not on the total size of the military budget, but on proposed new weapons systems. Since the 1960s Congress has become more assertive in reviewing these proposals and has shaped significantly the country's general defense posture. In addition, Congress plays an important role in those military matters that come to it in the form of treaties, such as the Strategic Arms Limitation Treaty (SALT).

Defense contracting, and in particular its efficiency and quality, is less a matter of political influence than of the bureaucratic arrangements for designing and acquiring new weapons systems. The military officers interested in detailed control over the characteristics of the new systems are more resistant to altering present purchasing arrangements than are the corporations that receive the contracts.

Suggested Readings

Art, Robert J. *The TFX Decision: McNamara and the Military.* Boston: Little, Brown, 1968. An interesting case study of how the decision was made to acquire a controversial new fighter aircraft.

Borklund, C. W. *The Department of Defense.* New York: Praeger, 1968. Factual account of the organization of the Defense Department.

Fox, J. Ronald. *Arming America.* Cambridge, Mass.: Harvard University School of Business Administration, 1974. Study of the weapons acquisition process, with suggestions for change.

Halperin, Morton H. *Bureaucratic Politics and Foreign Policy.* Washington, D.C.: Brookings Institution, 1974. Analysis of how the tasks and missions of military and intelligence agencies affect the kind of positions they take and political strategies they employ.

Rosen, Steven, ed. *Testing the Theory of the Military-Industrial Complex.* Lexington, Mass.: D.C. Heath/Lexington Books, 1973. Articles from different points of view on military-industry relations.

Sarkesian, Sam C., ed. *The Military-Industrial Complex: A Reassessment.* Beverly Hills, Calif.: Sage Publications, 1972. Studies testing various aspects of the military-industrial complex theory.

PART V

The Nature
of American Democracy

" Justice is the end of government. It is the end of civil society.
It ever has been and ever will be pursued until it be obtained, or until
liberty be lost in the pursuit. "

22 Who Governs?

What policies the government adopts • The politics of various policies • Evaluating the traditional theories of political power: Marxist theory, elitist theory, bureaucratic theory, pluralist theory

It is time to try to answer the questions with which this book began. We want to know who governs and to what ends. In this chapter we shall try to answer the first question; in the next, we shall say something about the second.

Describing, however closely, government institutions and political organizations is a necessary but not sufficient condition for deciding who governs. Simply by choosing what to emphasize and what to leave out, one can write an account of the presidency that makes that institution seem "imperialistic" or a "pitiful, helpless giant" (to use the contrasting imagery of Arthur Schlesinger and Richard Nixon). And depending on what issues one happens to pick, one can characterize Congress as a gathering of zealots that whoops new legislation through to passage in record time (as it did when it adopted a social security bill or a law outlawing mandatory retirement practices in business) or depict it as an

A disputatious New England town meeting (left), and a decorous meeting of the Vermont state legislature (right).

elephantine institution bogged down in its own convoluted procedures and internal quarrels (as it was when it labored for months over an energy bill and a tax-cut plan).

Since we want to know who governs largely because our lives are affected by the distribution of political power, it seems only reasonable to try to answer the question of governance by examining, as systematically as we can, what policies the government adopts (or fails to adopt). A scheme for classifying public policies was presented in Chapter 14. It does not deserve to be called a theory, for there are many policies that do not fit well into the classification, and the distinctions it suggests are crude and oversimplified. It does have at least two advantages: it requires us to look at a comprehensive list of policies (or nonpolicies) rather than permitting us to generalize about politics on the basis of a few issues in which we happen to be interested at the moment, and it calls attention to important ways in which those policies are thought to affect people (the distribution of perceived costs and benefits). Let us begin by summarizing what we have learned about the politics of making four kinds of policies and then use that information as evidence to evaluate the competing theories of political power described in Chapter 1.

FOUR KINDS OF POLITICS

Majoritarian Politics
The costs and benefits of a proposed course of action are sometimes seen by people as being widely distributed: everybody, or most everybody, or very broad groups of people stand to gain or lose in roughly the same way. We have seen several examples: the old-age and survivors' insurance provided under the 1935 Social Security Act, the medical benefits offered under the 1965 Medicare Act, the fair business competition requirements of the Sherman Antitrust Act of 1890 and the Federal Trade Commission Act of 1914, the general foreign policy posture of the United States (internationalist or isolationist), the particular decisions to go to war in 1941, 1950, and the 1960s (or *not* to go to war in 1914 or 1954), those features of macroeconomic policy that seem to contribute toward price stability and reasonably full employment, and the overall size and shape of our defense expenditures. All these policies, though greatly different in substance, have in common the fact that similar political institutions and actors tend to play the leading roles.

Public Opinion.   Because matters like those listed above are highly visible and seem to affect the country as a whole, there usually is a discernible *public* opinion about them. Sometimes that opinion is quite specific, as when polls showed that a majority of Americans wanted something very much like what the Social Security and Medicare Acts ultimately provided. Sometimes that opinion only provides a general direction but no particular details to policy-makers, as when the nation inclines toward internationalism and anticommunism or toward isolationism and indifference. And sometimes that opinion may want things that turn out to be inconsistent, as when people want stable prices, full employment, and high levels of government spending—all at the same time. But policy-makers are aware that public opinion does exist and that, even when it is lacking in detail or consistency, it is ignored only at a politician's peril. Citizens expect leadership and are willing to tolerate both delays and gambles in its exercise, but in the long run officials who ignore the thrust of opinion or devise policies that supply more costs than benefits are likely to suffer at the polls. The Republicans who opposed much of the New Deal misread public opinion or thought they could defy it; they learned differently in the Democratic sweep of 1936. Democratic politicians were supported for a while in their military policy in Vietnam, but by 1968 a majority of people had decided the policy was (at a min-

President Ford in the White House Rose Garden announced his WIN ("Whip Inflation Now") program. He didn't win. President Johnson could not win either—broken by the Vietnam War, he announced that he would not seek reelection.

imum) more burden than benefit and wanted a change. As this is written, pundits are wondering whether popular resentment over inflation will lead citizens to punish the incumbents in 1980.

Because these policies are shaped by public opinion, the president and his principal advisers tend to play a leading, if not the dominant, role in their development. People hold the president responsible for the economy, for national defense, for social welfare, and for foreign policy. Sometimes, as with foreign policy and military spending, that accountability is well taken, for the president, constitutionally and institutionally, plays the dominant role in these decisions. Sometimes, as with the state of the economy, the president may be as much victim as architect of the current state of affairs, but no matter: he must act as if he can control things because people believe that he should be able to control them.

Ideological Debate. A proposal to adopt a wholly new program that applies to many people often precipitates an intense, sometimes ideological debate. Social Security and Medicare were enacted after just such a debate; the Family Assistance Plan failed of enactment in consequence of such a debate. The struggles over neutrality versus interventionism in world affairs in 1939–1941, over strategic military doctrine in the 1960s and again in the 1970s, over whether the nation should have a balanced budget or follow Keynesian fiscal policy, and over whether to ratify the Panama Canal treaties—all these were genuine debates in which ideas as much as interests played a decisive role.

World View. The outcome of such debates is often the institutionalization of a new world view. The interventionists won out over the isolationists; the advocates of a federal social welfare policy defeated the supporters of private charity and local relief programs; the critics of big business won at least a rhetorical advantage over the defenders of large industrial trusts. In these struggles a crisis often provided the decisive leverage: what the depression of 1929–1940 did for welfare policy, the attack on Pearl Harbor in 1941 did for foreign policy, and the Second World War did for fiscal policy. When the constraints of public opinion are loose, as they are in foreign policy, the world view that is significant is that of policy elites who operate in or close to government. When the constraints are tighter, as they are in macroeconomic policy, elected officials discover that their freedom of action is narrow. Incumbent politicians must balance national interests as they define them against the need to get reelected, which often leads them to try to buy votes in the short term (as with biennial changes in social security and veterans' benefits).

But a crisis is not the only force that alters a popular or elite world view. Higher education among the general population, the influence of the mass media, changing perceptions of the causes and consequences of various human problems—all have had an effect on people's ideas of what is desirable public policy. The history of welfare legislation provides a good example of how a world view changes and evolves. It shows how a nation committed to a belief in self-reliance and the value of work has slowly modified (but not abandoned) those ideas as it came first to accept aid to the elderly and infirm on an "insurance" basis, then to endorse aid to the unemployed and the indigent, and then to accept some limited forms of direct income support for the poor (whatever their age or work experience) in the form of food stamps. But thus far this changing popular definition of social justice does not include large-scale income redistribution (as under a Family Assistance Plan or a negative income tax). And one particular form of welfare—aid to families with dependent children—is not seen to be a majoritarian policy

at all, but one in which a client group ("them") benefits at the expense of society at large ("us").

Political Parties. When Congress is adopting new majoritarian policies, political parties tend to be relatively important. Many of the key issues in social welfare, economic policy, and foreign affairs pit a substantial majority of Democrats against a substantial majority of Republicans. In policies of this sort, Congress has acted more like a parliament than an assemblage of independent legislators, debating broad issues in partisan and even ideological terms. Often no new policy can win if the parties are relatively evenly balanced in Congress, because, though Congress may debate in a parliamentary style, it lacks the parliamentary discipline to prevent a few defectors from one party or the other from blocking change. As a result, the victory of a new idea often requires an election that gives one party an extraordinary majority.

A majoritarian policy once adopted *and* proved popular tends to lose its ideological significance and to attract bipartisan support, especially when government can readily increase the level of benefits to the public (as with social security and Medicare). However, if costs become very high—as they may be for social security—the "easy politics" of continual benefit increases may end.

Interest Group Politics

When the costs of a policy are perceived to be concentrated in one distinct, relatively small group, and the benefits are seen as concentrated in a different, equally distinct and small group, interest group politics dominates the policy-making process. Interest groups, of course, are active to some degree in almost all policies, but in policies of this sort they are the dominant political forces. Labor legislation—the National Labor Relations Act, the Taft-Hartley Act, the Landrum-Griffin Act, and other bills—are obvious examples of this. So also are the struggles between cable and over-the-air television broadcasters, between domestic ethnic groups over certain foreign policy matters, and between importers and exporters over tariff laws and regulations. Similarly, interest group politics is evident in the tension among the military services over the allocation of the defense budget, between opposed interests in cases involving rights in conflict (such as the right to a fair trial versus the right to publish news), between parties competing before certain regulatory commissions (such as the Environmental Protection Agency or the Occupational Safety and Health Administration), and between blacks and whites in local communities with segregated schools.

Changing Cleavages in Society. The sources of interest group policy proposals are to be found in changing economic and social cleavages in society. The rise of new technologies, the altered shape of markets, the rise and decline of regions, and changes in the organizational skills and resources of previously unorganized (or weakly organized) groups provide opportunities for new interest group proposals. The debate over the Commerce Act of 1887 was set off by declining profits on the long-haul railroads, high monopolistic prices on many short-haul lines, rivalry among port cities for cheap access to the agricultural heartland of the country, and the rising importance of national and international markets for commercial farmers. Every interest had an incentive to organize for political action.

Though usually interest group policies by their very nature stimulate the organization of all relevant interests, sometimes one group is able to block the organizing efforts of its rival. Many industries were able to do this in the nineteenth and early twentieth centuries with respect to would-be labor unions; whites were able to do this in many communities with respect to blacks and other racial minorities. These restraints on equality of organizational opportunity were made possible by the privileged access one group already had to the coercive powers of the

66 The sources of interest group policy proposals are to be found in changing economic and social cleavages in society. **99**

Political activists tend to be young, and political movements tend to affect the young more than others. But there are important exceptions. Maggie Kuhn, shown here, is the founder of the Gray Panthers, a group of older activists.

government. Industries could for many years count on the police and the army as allies in breaking strikes just as southern whites could use laws and administrative regulations to keep large numbers of blacks from voting.

That privileged power position was sustained by widely shared attitudes. Many people disapproved of unions or objected to strikes that seemed intended to win exclusive control by the union over entry into a particular job market. Similarly, many citizens either were prejudiced against blacks or disapproved of black efforts to alter the distribution of political power. When these restraints to equal organizational opportunity existed, the disadvantaged group has had to employ a variety of tactics to change popular attitudes, attract legislative allies, and enlist the sympathy of the courts.

Political Parties.   When a policy is proposed by one interest group and opposed by another of comparable political power, the political parties will often be deeply divided and, as a consequence, play little or no role in the resolution of the matter. The issue cross-cuts partisan cleavages and, unlike parties in some European democracies, American parties are too weak to overcome such cross-cutting pressures. The passage of the Commerce Act, for example, was not a partisan matter; and both Democrats and Republicans were split for decades over the question of civil rights. A few interest group conflicts correspond to party lines—for example, labor-management issues have tended to parallel Democratic-Republican differences. But these are the exceptions.

Continuing Struggle.   Interest group politics does not end with the passage or defeat of the initial proposal. The struggle continues, but in other places—in the bureaucracy, before the courts, and in subsequent legislative sessions. The interest group struggle that resulted in the passage of the National Labor Relations Act and the Occupational Safety and Health Act was transferred from the lobbies of Congress to the offices and corridors of the National Labor Relations Board and the Occupational Safety and Health Administration. Such agencies are less likely to be "captured" by any single interest than are those created as a result of client politics. Nor will the affected interest groups accept gracefully the decisions of the bureaucracy; appeals will be taken to the federal courts and efforts will be made to get the law amended.

Public opinion and presidential leadership have some effect on the outcome of these struggles, but except in the formative stages that effect will ordinarily be weak. The public at large cannot possibly become so well informed or so concerned as to shape in important ways the conflict between well-organized, vitally involved opponents. The president can tilt the balance of power one way or another by whom he chooses to appoint to key bureaucratic agencies, but rarely does a president try to shape directly, deeply, or in detail the outcome of these conflicts. The public and the president are usually content to hope that the "right persons" are put in charge of refereeing interest group conflicts. And except to report on the more important outcomes and occasional scandals associated with interest group politics, the mass media rarely play an important role.

Client Politics

Sometimes the benefits of a policy are concentrated on one relatively small, easily organized group, and the costs are widely distributed over the public at large. In these cases client politics arises. We find this happening when the merchant marine or the dairy industry receives a government subsidy, when veterans obtain special benefits (in cash or in the form of preferential status in civil service competitions), and when various occupations are allowed by state licensing laws to govern themselves. Client politics is also at work when a community wishes to obtain a flood-control project or retain a military base, or when an economic or other interest obtains a "loophole" in the tax laws. Client politics need not involve obvious economic groups. We see client politics in action when teachers, organized as the National Education Association, seek the creation of a cabinet-level Department of Education, when organized Indians work to make certain the Bureau of Indian Affairs is sensitive to their demands, when professors insist that only other professors decide on what research projects the National Science Foundation will spend its money, and when civil rights groups dominate the work of the Civil Rights Commission.

Visibility.   Client politics is low-visibility politics—neither the public at large, nor (usually) the mass media have much interest in or knowledge about the policies involved. That can change, however. The regulations restricting the importation of foreign oil so that some oil companies are benefited became controversial. As a result of the steep rise in oil prices in the early 1970s, the costs that consumers had to bear suddenly became so visible and so high that no client group in the oil industry could any longer hope that its benefits would go unnoticed. Similarly with the cost of electricity: for decades technological advances steadily reduced the cost of electricity. The public was indifferent to the fact that state utility commissions charged with regulating the price of electricity usually did so in a perfunctory manner. When electricity prices began rising steeply in the 1970s, however, consumers complained and many state utility commissions began to take a tough line against utilities.

Noneconomic groups can also see their favored-client position deteriorate as a result of external forces. Extremist political groups may easily take advantage of the protection they enjoy from the First Amendment during tranquil times; when a national crisis, such as a war, occurs, the public may suddenly decide that the costs of free speech have become too great and demand restrictions.

Political Parties.   Political parties ordinarily play only a small role in client politics for an obvious reason: when a group makes an unopposed request, it would be foolhardy for most legislators to suppose that they had anything to gain by voting against it. Such measures typically pass with the support of lopsided majorities in both parties. Sometimes that outcome is facilitated by grouping a number of client proposals together in one package (a "pork barrel") so that there is something for everybody.

The political problem of a client group is ordinarily not that of winning a majority on the final vote, but of getting its proposal brought up for a vote at all. Thousands of groups want things from the government; the limits of time and of congressional committee interest reduce the number that will succeed. Finding a strategically placed congressional sponsor is essential. Because of the importance of having a sponsor and the ease of avoiding publicity, many of the cases of

> **"**The political problem of a client group is ordinarily not that of winning a majority on the final vote, but of getting its proposal brought up for a vote at all.**"**

Trying to get onto the political agenda: a right-to-life (antiabortion) activist in St. Louis.

political corruption occur in the arena of client politics. Some congressmen think they can charge for their services and get away with it. This is not to say that most or even many client-serving policies are the result of improper influence, but only that the conditions here are more conducive to such influence than they are in majoritarian politics.

Identifying the Clients.   Occasionally, a client-serving policy will be devised and proposed, not by the client group itself but by a self-appointed (or "vicarious") representative. The Economic Opportunity Act of 1964 was intended to benefit the urban poor, especially in minority neighborhoods, but it was not carried through Congress by an organization representing the urban poor.

This was done by professionals, bureaucrats, and political executives who thought it was time to act on behalf of the poor. Because they framed their proposals in harmony with the existing consensus on how needy people should be helped (chiefly with services rather than money), and because their proposals seemed then to impose no costs on any other distinct segment of society, the easy passage of the Economic Opportunity Act revealed a kind of client politics. Conflict later erupted, however, when mayors discovered that the Community Action Programs were a challenge to the institutional authority of city hall. From then on, the matter became one of interest group politics.

Serving the Clients.   Client-serving programs lead to the creation of client-serving government agencies. Some scholars have spoken of such agencies as the Civil Aeronautics Board or the Federal Communications Commission as having been "captured" by the groups they were supposed to regulate, but this is a misreading of history. These agencies and others like them were formed specifically to serve the interests of domestic aviation and radio broadcasting, just as the Veterans' Administration was created to serve the interests of veterans. At the time these laws were passed and for many years thereafter, people saw nothing wrong with such promotional ventures.

Important political changes have substantially reduced the freedom of action of client-serving agencies. The greater ease with which one can form and sustain groups purporting to represent mass or diffuse interests and the larger range of questions in which federal courts now intervene have made low-visibility client politics less common than in the past. Naderite groups, environmental protection groups, and organizations representing liberal and conservative causes use sophisticated fund-raising methods (including in some cases opportunities to get grants from the government itself) and take advantage of the easier access plaintiffs have to courts (owing to

changed rules on standing and provisions for fee-shifting). By these methods, such groups have reduced the extent to which diffuse interests go unrepresented in the arena of client politics but created new problems because that representation is often inaccurate.

Moreover, the proliferation of regulatory agencies in the government has resulted in the creation of offsetting pressure against some client interests. Client politics comes about because the majority of the people who must bear the costs (at a small per person amount) of a client group's benefits have no incentive to organize to contest those benefits. The government, because it can sustain organizations through taxation rather than voluntary contributions, can create agencies to contest client claims. Thus, the Antitrust Division of the Justice Department has challenged some of the practices of client-serving regulatory agencies, as when it criticized airline regulations for failing to promote competition.

Entrepreneurial Politics

Though opposition to client politics may eventually be institutionalized in the form of a new government agency, initially such opposition requires some form of entrepreneurial politics. An indifferent public can only be mobilized through skilled leadership that attracts substantial media attention. If real or imaginary threats to public well-being are pointed out, a congressional majority can be led to favor policies that impose substantial costs on even a well-organized minority. This happened when congressional— and ultimately popular—majorities were led to support policies that set tough standards on air and water pollution or tightened the regulations on patent medicines and prescription drugs. It also happened when the public was aroused against socialists, anarchists, Communists, and other radical political groups, and against high taxes.

Entrepreneurs can be found in the federal government, such as Dr. Harvey Wiley, the government chemist who dramatized the need for regulation of patent medicines, and Senator Estes Kefauver, who won headlines with his investigations of, first, organized crime and, later, the pharmaceutical industry. There were also Attorney General A. Mitchell Palmer and Senator Joseph McCarthy, who in different eras stimulated national passions directed at supposed subversives. Or the entrepreneurs can be found outside the federal government, as was Ralph Nader, who criticized various business practices; Upton Sinclair, who wrote about the conditions in meat-packing plants; and Howard Jarvis, who led a grass-roots attack on high property taxes in California.

Compelling Symbols. Policy entrepreneurs must achieve by emotional appeals what appeals to narrow self-interest cannot. Thus the rationale for a new policy must be presented in dramatic terms and evoke powerful symbols in the public's mind—"clean air," "pure water," "Americanism," "sinister plots," "confiscatory taxes," and so on. Legislative and administrative action based on such appeals is often cast in equally bold terms with strict standards, stern penalties, and short deadlines. Since the success of such proposals depends on arousing or taking advantage of a popular mood, the kinds of policies that can be adopted depend on the kinds of symbols to which people will respond. These symbols change from one generation to the next. At one time atheists and Communists seemed especially threatening forces; at another time people were largely indifferent to such groups. In an earlier era citizens might have accepted high levels of atmospheric pollution; in the modern era even low levels are a cause for popular concern. Some people may be indifferent to many deaths of coal miners caused by our dependence on coal as an energy source but deeply upset by even the chance of accidents caused by a shift to nuclear power.

Sometimes no compelling symbol can be found. Advocates of strict gun control, for example, have never been able to mobilize an intense

❝The mass media are of great importance in entrepreneurial politics, especially key reporters and editors who decide to give serious attention to the proponent of a policy.**❞**

A center of political influence: the newsroom of the *Washington Post.*

popular majority. This fact is sometimes explained by the "power" of the National Rifle Association. No doubt that group is influential, but so also have been the automobile industry, local pharmacists, and the American Medical Association. Nevertheless, each of these groups has lost decisively on important issues, because each was unable to cope with powerful symbolic appeals.

Promotion by the Media. The mass media are of great importance in entrepreneurial politics, especially key reporters and editors who decide to give serious attention to the proponent of a policy. Often a tacit alliance exists between a

Some "Rules" of Politics

Herewith some generalizations about American politics, distilled from what has been said in this book, offered in nervous awareness that our political system has a way of proving everybody wrong. (Before the 1960s it was a "rule" of politics that no Catholic could be elected president. John F. Kennedy took care of that.)

1. Policies once adopted tend to persist, whatever their value. (It is easier to start new programs than to end old ones.)

2. Almost all electoral politics is local politics. (Congressmen who forget "home base" tend not to remain congressmen for long.)

3. Whatever the size of their staff and budget, Congress and the White House will always be overworked. (More resources produce more work which produces more resources.)

4. Each branch of government tends to emulate the other. (Congress will become more bureaucratized to cope with an executive branch that is becoming more bureaucratized; judges will become more activist as Congress becomes more activist.)

5. Proposals that seem to confer widespread and immediate benefits will be enacted whatever their long-term costs.

6. Proposals that seem to confer delayed benefits will be enacted only if their costs are unknown, concealed, or deferred.*

7. Nobody—businessmen, bureaucrats, congressmen, judges, professors—likes competition, and everybody will do whatever he or she can to reduce or eliminate it.

8. "Planning" in government occurs after a crisis occurs.

9. The mass media never covers a story about things that are going well. Thus, the number of "problems" in society is a function of the number of reporters.

10. If you want something, you are claiming a right; if your opponent wants something, he is protecting a vested interest.

* This and similar rules are in William C. Mitchell, "The Anatomy of Public Failure: A Public Choice Perspective," Paper No. 13, International Institute for Economic Research, Los Angeles, 1978.

policy entrepreneur who supplies facts and arguments and a reporter who produces vivid "feature" stories. These stories often stimulate routine coverage of the issue by the press generally. Though political parties will play some role in this—one party is usually more sympathetic to the change than the other—that role is less significant than when majoritarian politics are involved. To the extent the symbols are powerful, members of both parties feel compelled to pay them lip service.

Capture of the Agencies. The government agencies created as a result of entrepreneurial politics are often vulnerable to "capture" by the interest group adversely affected by the policy. Since the policy adopted imposes significant costs on an organized group, that group has a strong incentive to weaken the administration of that policy. The pharmaceutical industry, for example, was from time to time able to weaken the enforcement of the food and drug laws by the Food and Drug Administration. In recognition of this possibility, advocates of such laws will sometimes create agencies that will encourage interest group competition (the regulations of the Environmental Protection Agency, for instance, impose costs on industries that must abide by them and create benefits to other industries that sell the equipment necessary to comply with the regulations).

The Courts. The courts play an important role in entrepreneurial politics. All affected parties, whether they be business firms or political movements, will seek court assistance in defending or resisting the new policy. Usually, the courts have deferred to the popular mood, at least initially, and thus upheld new environmental regulations or new restrictions on free speech. In time, however, and especially as popular passions abate, the courts tend to evolve balancing tests to assess the fairness of the regulations flowing from the new policy.

COMPETING THEORIES OF POLITICAL POWER

In Chapter 1 several competing theories of the distribution of political power in modern society were briefly sketched. Each of these theories—the Marxist, the pluralist, the bureaucratic, the elitist—is an attempt to characterize the political system *as a whole*. From the evidence summarized earlier in this chapter, the reader may already have surmised what in fact is the case—that no single description of the entire political system seems adequate, as different policies tend to arise out of somewhat different political processes. Of course, there is one description of the entire system that is roughly accurate: ours is a representative democracy with a high degree of personal freedom in the area of speech and opinion. But though that says a great deal, it does not say everything; in particular, it does not say much about the very different forms that "representative democracy" may take in particular policy areas. This point will become clearer if we review the more familiar theories of politics in light of what we have learned about policy-making. We should bear in mind that even a fairly extensive review of policies will of necessity omit much that is important and that policies, perceptions of policies, and the political system itself are constantly changing.

Marxist Theory

Orthodox Marxist theory argues that the economic structure, and in particular the pattern of ownership of the means of production, shapes politics and determines political outcomes. The aspects of American policy-making most frequently cited in support of this view are foreign policy, defense policy, and economic regulation. With regard to foreign and defense policies, we have seen that political considerations—public opinion, perceptions of international military and diplomatic necessities, and the world view of government elites—and not corporate ones are the decisive factors. Political considerations account for at least the major diplomatic and military initiatives of this country and explain the overall level of defense spending. Economic regulations can be of very different kinds depending on whether they are the product of interest group conflicts (as was the National Labor Relations Act), entrepreneurial skill (as was much environmental legislation), or client politics (as was an agency such as the Maritime Administration).

If a Marxist—or, more accurately, an economic determinist—theory of politics is appropriate, it is in the case where an economic client obtains a governmental advantage. An economic determinist can point to such client politics as maritime and dairy subsidies, price supports for large farmers, import quotas for oil, beef, steel, and other products, and favorable tax treatment for various economic groups. But even with respect to client politics, economic determinism gives an incomplete explanation, because a large and growing number of examples of client politics reflects the demands of non-economic organizations. The most notable example is that of ethnic, racial, and women's groups. The special status such groups enjoy with the Office for Civil Rights, the Equal Employment Opportunity Commission, the Civil Rights Commission, and the Civil Rights Division of the Justice Department is not the result of their economic power, nor are the benefits they seek exclusively economic.

Moreover, even client politics takes place within the boundaries of public and elite opinion. One can easily explain in economic terms how the Civil Aeronautics Board (CAB) was created since much of the work of that agency was directly beneficial to and protective of the major airline companies. It is harder to explain how the protected status of the airlines was drastically reduced over their intense opposition. A law passed in 1978 will produce much higher levels of competition in the domestic air travel business and will, in fact, lead to the abolition of the CAB by 1985.

A Marxist might rejoin that the principal influence of economic, and especially corporate, power is not in the details of legislation, but in the control of the agenda of politics, the shaping of the major thrust of policy (especially economic policy), and the distribution of political resources among potential participants in politics. Indeed, there have been periods in American history where such influences may well have been important. In an era of limited government, especially before the 1930s, many problems and practices never became political issues at all. Efforts to put them on the political agenda were met with the argument, often decisive, that it was wrong or illegitimate for the government to play any part in such matters as social welfare, income distribution, labor-management disputes, or the conditions of the workplace. Since the 1930s, and in particular since the 1960s, it is hard to think of any problem, real or imagined, that has not found its way onto the political agenda. The "legitimacy barrier" has long since collapsed; politics today is not just about a few obviously public things, but about nearly everything.

Similarly with the distribution of political resources: at one time access to such resources—money and votes—was sharply limited. The dollars were predominantly under the control of the wealthy; ballots, heavily under the influence of party bosses and machines. Newcomers to politics often experienced great difficulty in obtaining either. But in the modern era, a remarkable transformation occurred: there was a wholesale redistribution of political resources without a prior redistribution of income.

- Party machines decayed.
- Nominations for office were awarded by primary elections rather than by party organizations.
- The partisan and elite media were in part replaced by the mass media.

- Racial and sexual barriers to voting were torn down.
- Issue organizations became easier to form and to maintain as a result of the role of private foundations, direct-mail fund-raising techniques, government grants and contracts, and fee-shifting in court suits.

Moreover, the making of economic policy was profoundly altered when elite opinion accepted the propriety of budget deficits and of public responsibility for the maintenance of a high-employment economy. Once the earlier constraints had been removed—the belief that balanced budgets were essential and that economic growth should be maintained by governmental aids to investment but not to consumption—public officials were free to pursue economic policies with an eye chiefly to their impact on majority opinion.

In sum, though many examples of policy-making are dominated by economic advantage, no simple economic determinism offers an accurate and comprehensive view of American politics.

Elitist Theory

In one sense almost all politics is elitist in that almost all governmental decisions are made by the few rather than the many. But elitist theory says more than this: it asserts that it is always the same elite that makes policy, whatever the nature of the issue; that this elite acts in concert or at least has a common social, economic, or occupational background; and that the elite is only weakly influenced, if influenced at all, by popular opinion.

One could describe client politics as a partial confirmation of elite theory. Obviously, when a few persons—businessmen, union leaders, professors, state welfare directors—acquire substantial influence over a broad policy area from which they benefit, they are an elite. But these examples illustrate the inherent ambiguity in elite theory.

It makes all the difference whether a small group has power because it constitutes the direct *beneficiary* of some policy (as with dairy farmers, merchant seamen, or university research laboratories) or because it has certain general *characteristics* (wealth, prestige, social standing) that enable it to influence even policies that do not bear on the elite's material interests at all. Elite theory suggests that these personal attributes are the cause of its power.

Client politics should not be regarded as a confirmation of elite theory but as an illustration of how the distribution of the costs and benefits of a public policy differentially influences the abilities of the affected groups to shape that policy. The power of an activist federal judiciary is a better illustration of elite theory—not because judges are well paid or prestigious, but because they are drawn from a profession (the legal one) that provides them with cues and rewards that influence their decisions. Judges make decisions

George Meany, president of the AFL-CIO, is an outspoken advocate of many policies—in civil rights and foreign affairs—that are not directly related to the material interests of union members.

> **❝**The members of the foreign policy elite are distinctive more for their ideas than for their origins. These ideas are formed by experience, academic training, and personal ideology and tend to change from one generation to the next.**❞**

without being closely constrained by interest groups or voters but with considerable attention to the world of legal scholarship.

Foreign policy-making is a specially interesting case of elite influence because here, unlike in client politics, the power of the elite does not depend on its ability to win votes, mobilize interest groups, raise campaign funds, or represent the aspirations of ethnic or racial blocs. The influence of this elite depends on its members being part of a group that shares certain ideas and that has acquired experience in managing or writing about foreign affairs. At one time the foreign policy elite was also distinctive for its common social background—well-to-do white Anglo-Saxon Protestants who had attended Ivy League colleges. That is much less the case today. At present, the members of the foreign policy elite are distinctive more for their ideas than for their origins. These ideas are formed by experience, academic training, and personal ideology and tend to change from one generation to the next.

Bureaucratic Theory

The bureaucratization of almost all aspects of life, public and private, is one of the dominant facts of modern society. Some have argued that the number, size, and influence of governmental bureaucracies have become so great that elected officials and their key advisers are almost powerless to affect policy—whatever top officials propose, the bureaucracy can subvert. Criticisms of the bureaucratic state have evoked a rich verbal imagery: "Leading the bureaucracy is like pushing a wet string." Or, "Changing the bureaucracy is like moving a cemetery."

"Increasingly, the bureaucracy has become a source of the agenda of politics."

But it is as easy to overestimate as to underestimate bureaucratic power. Bureaucracy—that is, government by large organizations made up of appointed career officials—is most influential when the law confers on such officials wide discretion (i.e., freedom to choose among alternative courses of action). Such broad discretion exists in the area of weapons procurement by the military, the enforcement of civil rights laws, the making of foreign policy, and the regulation of business enterprise.

Some of this discretionary authority is inevitable. There is no way, for example, that Congress could write into law the precise specifications of the fighter planes the air force should buy or set the exact rates that railroads should charge for various classes of freight. But some discretion is the result of Congress being unwilling to make choices that could, in fact, be made. Congress could, for example, specify fairly precisely the penalties that ought to be imposed on convicted criminals rather than leave the matter almost entirely up to prosecutors, judges, and parole board members, and it could clarify the ambiguous laws now governing methods of school desegregation. Indeed, it has tried to do both of these things but found that congressional opinion on these matters is so divided that, willy nilly, the choice must be left to judicial and administrative officials.

Bureaucrats have the least power when their task is specified by statute in exact language. This is the case in the area of the social security laws that tell the administrator exactly how much money is to be sent to what classes of persons how often. Bureaucratic discretion is similarly narrow when it comes to providing benefits to veterans or to farmers. This is not to say that agencies working in these areas do not have bureaucratic problems, such as cumbersomeness, red tape, or delays. They do, as do all large organizations,

private or public. But those are very different problems from the kinds created by the existence of bureaucratic discretion.

Congress has of late taken note of this and tried in some areas to reduce bureaucratic discretion. The clean air and clean water laws specify rather exact standards for pollution control; the Endangered Species Act has given (at least until revised in 1978) nearly absolute protection to such exotic creatures as snail darters; the drug laws require the banning of certain foodstuffs and chemicals if they have *any* tendency to produce cancer. But if exact standards solve certain problems, they create others, such as the problem of keeping down the social cost of applying such strict standards.

There is at least one other way, besides exercising discretionary authority, in which bureaucracy has become more powerful. Increasingly, the bureaucracy has become a source of the agenda of politics. The Economic Opportunity Act of 1964, the Medicare Act of 1965, proposals for new weapons systems, and many other important measures come, not from private demands made on government, but from government generating demands on itself. Any president who tries to formulate a legislative program quickly discovers that he is heavily dependent on the bureaucracy for most of his ideas, just as any president who tries to reorganize the executive branch soon learns that his chief opponents are his nominal subordinates, the bureau chiefs.

In short, the power of bureaucracy may not depend so much on the kind of politics (interest group, client, or whatever) that led to its creation as on the substance of the policy it must apply and the clarity and consistency of the congressional laws governing it.

Pluralist Theory

The view that policies are made by conflict and bargaining among the organizations that represent affected groups is obviously an accurate description of what we have called interest group politics. Little more need be said on that score. But we have also seen the limits of the pluralist model: it overestimates the extent to which interest groups will form and be active. In client politics the large number of persons who must bear the widely distributed costs of a client-serving program have no incentive to organize and must rely instead on the vicarious (and perhaps inaccurate) representation supplied by "public interest" lobbies. In majoritarian politics important decisions can be made as the result of direct presidential leadership of, and congressional response to, majority views with interest groups playing only a marginal role.

With the rise of entrepreneurial politics and the collapse of some of the barriers to political participation, the pluralist theory has in a sense become more applicable to American government. Ironically, during the period (generally, the 1950s) in which the theory was most influential, it was least accurate. Broad categories of interest and opinion were not represented in politics at all, and some groups in society were experiencing great difficulty in organizing for political action. Today there is a greater variety of interests and of people represented, one way or another, in Washington than ever before. Indeed, some see in this an "atomization" of politics that has reduced sharply the power of government to do anything at all.[1]

But if the pluralist theory has become more descriptive of politics today, it still remains an inadequate one, not only because it does not take into account client or majoritarian politics, but because it offers no clear explanation of the special nature of entrepreneurial politics. The policy entrepreneur as folk hero is not a new phenomenon, but it has become a commonplace one. This could not have happened without the rise of a national mass media and of a shift in beliefs among the upper middle class (or at least that part of it that was called, in Chapter 5, the "New Class") in a direction that is supportive of certain kinds of entrepreneurship. Nor does pluralism take fully into account the extraordinary role that is played by the judiciary, an institution that can only with difficulty be described as a "group" with "interests." Rather, the courts are a constitutionally based source of authority, the exercise of which depends crucially on the ideas and beliefs of its individual members.

SUMMARY

There is no single answer to the question, "Who governs?" Everything depends on what policy is being proposed and on the opportunities different proponents and opponents have to mobilize on their behalf different parts of the fragmented institutions and processes of government. A crude classification can be made of some of the ways power is distributed by looking at the perceived costs and benefits of a policy. Four types of policies were identified: majoritarian, interest group, client, and entrepreneurial.

Using these four types, we can evaluate the claims made by advocates of a Marxist, an elitist, a bureaucratic, and a pluralist theory of politics. No single theory is generally true though some theories are correct in some cases. Any classification scheme and any evaluation of political theories must constantly be revised with changes in social reality, public perceptions of that reality, and ideas people have about the proper purposes of government.

23 To What Ends?

Growth of government • Competing interests •
Changes in the private sector • Disenchantment with government performance • The
influence of structure • The influence of ideas

The Liberty Bell in Philadelphia and the Statue of
Liberty on bicentennial day, July 4, 1976.

The most striking change in American government has been the dramatic expansion in the
scope of its activities. Until well into the twentieth century, who ruled in Washington, or to
what ends, made little difference in the lives of
most citizens except in wartime or when a dispute arose over the management of the currency. National politics was not a career for
many congressmen; governors and mayors were
more in the public eye than presidents; most
citizens never came into contact with a federal
official except when they received their mail.

When the federal establishment was relatively
small, one could supply a fairly simple answer to
the question of what ends the government
served. If the Republicans were in power, the
government sought high tariffs, tight money, and
for a while the punishment of the southern states
that had seceded from the Union. If the Democrats were in power, the government tended
to lower tariffs, enlarge the money supply, and

reach an accommodation with the South. From time to time, circumstances altered this tidy pattern—a brief flirtation with "Manifest Destiny" and the acquisition of an overseas empire, the recurrence of various social issues such as temperance and the enfranchisement of women, the bitter struggle between labor and management over union organization.

Today, if one wants to know the objectives of government, the answer is "practically everything." The expansion of the scope of government has meant the proliferation of the goals of government. No single philosophy animates public policy because public policy is not responsive to any single set of interests or influenced by any single set of political resources. Washington has policies (such as highway construction and mortgage insurance) that make it easier to move out of cities and policies (such as giving grants for neighborhood development) that are intended to encourage people to stay in cities. It has policies (such as pollution standards) designed to protect the environment even at the cost of economic growth and policies (such as tax deductions for investments) designed to stimulate economic growth. The government is formally committed to the goal of equal opportunity for all regardless of race and to programs that encourage employers to give special consideration to certain racial and ethnic groups in their hiring policies. In its foreign policy the government urges other nations to observe human rights and at the same time offers aid and alliances to nations that ignore fundamental rights.

COMPETING INTERESTS

It is not perversity or stupidity that leads the federal government to pursue so many apparently inconsistent goals. Because the interests and opinions of people conflict, the policies of any government seeking to serve those interests and opinions will of necessity be inconsistent.

People want different things. There is no "public opinion"; rather there are competing opinions of many different publics. As long as government is small, the competing desires of people are either reconciled by private arrangements (the market, voluntary agreements) or they are ignored. A large and active government might, of course, seek to be consistent, to follow a single philosophy, to serve some interests and not others. But if it is popularly elected, no such government will long survive.

A popular majority is a coalition of persons who want different things from government; to win and hold that majority, a government must do many different things. But since it cannot do everything a majority of the people want, it will lose the support of some who will then join with others formerly in the minority to form a new majority coalition wanting a slightly different set of policies. A new government is elected, and the process starts over again. In the long run, politicians win elections by promising to do things for persons who are either not represented by, or are disappointed by, the party in power. Promises tend to become programs.

Politicians are not being venal when they try to win votes by making promises. They are being democratic. Politicians who fail to make promises (usually) fail to win elections; politicians who fail to deliver on their promises may not win reelection.

RESTRAINTS ON GROWTH OF GOVERNMENT

For the better part of a century and a half, democratic politics in this country did not produce a rapid growth in the power and scope of the federal government. There were three reasons for this. First, the prevailing interpretation of the Constitution sharply limited what policies it could adopt. The Supreme Court restricted the authority of the government to regulate business and prevented it from levying an income tax. Most important, the Court

"There is no 'public opinion'; rather there are competing opinions of many different publics."

The "extended republic of the United States" embraces "a great variety of interests, parties and sects."

refused to allow, with some exceptions, the delegation of broad discretionary power to administrative agencies. This changed somewhat in the early decades of this century and changed fundamentally in the 1930s.

But, second, the Supreme Court could not have maintained this position for as long as it did if it had acted in the teeth of popular opposition. In fact, popular opinion, at least insofar as it was represented by interest groups and political parties, generally supported a restricted definition of federal authority. It was not thought legitimate for the federal government to intervene deeply in the economy (even the American Federation of Labor, led by Samuel Gompers, resisted federal involvement in labor-management issues). It was certainly not thought proper for Washington to upset racial segregation as it was practiced in

both the North and the South. It took constitutional amendments to persuade Congress that it had the authority to levy an income tax or to prohibit the sale of alcoholic beverages. Even in the 1930s public opinion polls showed that as many as half the voters were skeptical of a federal unemployment compensation program. Public opinion, of course, changed as a result of crises (such as the Great Depression), the spread of higher education, and other factors difficult to assess. Today people will quarrel about the *wisdom* of some government policy, but few persons any longer argue that the government has no *right* to enact the policy. Almost any policy—except for those that might restrict First Amendment freedoms—that can attract majority support can be enacted into law without a serious challenge to its legitimacy or constitutionality.

Third, the political system designed by the Framers was based on the assumption that the key problem was to prevent the government from doing too much. The separation of powers and other constitutional checks and balances were intended to make it difficult to enact a new policy unless that policy had broad support. No single faction would be able to dominate the government. For long, things worked pretty much as intended—it was difficult to introduce significant new programs except in emergency circumstances or when approval was both enduring and widespread. But the arrangements that make adopting new programs difficult make eliminating or revising old programs equally difficult. The very separation of powers that ensured that any new proposal would confront entrenched critics also ensured that any existing programs would have entrenched defenders. As a result, existing programs acquire a life of their own.

CONSEQUENCES OF ACTIVIST GOVERNMENT

It is tempting to make a sweeping judgment about a large and activist government, either praising it because it serves a variety of popular needs or condemning it because it is a bureaucratic affliction. Such generalizations are not entirely empty but neither are they very helpful. The worth of any given program, or of any collection of programs, can only be assessed by a careful consideration of its costs and benefits, of its effects and side effects. But there may be some general political consequences of the enlarged scope of governmental activity.

First, the expansion and bureaucratization of governmental programs stimulate the bureaucratization of private institutions. The more government seeks to accomplish, the more private organizations—business firms, labor unions, schools and colleges—must attempt to do. The

government will hire more persons when it is running eighty programs concerned with employment than when it is running one or two. By the same token, a private organization will hire (and give power to) more persons when it is the object of eighty government programs than when it is the object of only one or two. Of course, causality runs both ways—government may do more because private institutions, such as corporations, are becoming larger and more powerful; but private institutions may become larger and more bureaucratic because government is doing more.

Second, the more government does, the more it will appear to be acting in inconsistent, uncoordinated, and cumbersome ways. When people complain of "red tape," "bureaucracy," "stalemates," and "confusion," they often assume that these irritants are caused by incompetent or self-seeking public officials. There is incompetence and self-interest in government just as in every other part of life, but these character traits are not the chief cause of the problem. As citizens, we want different things.

An activist government tries to do as many different things as it can. The result is the rise of competing policies, the division of labor among separate administrative agencies, the diffusion of accountability and control, and the multiplication of paper work. And because Americans are especially energetic about asserting their rights, we must add to the above list of problems the regular use of the courts to challenge policies we do not like. That inconsistency and red tape are a result of activist government is not a decisive argument against such a government—the costs of making decisions in the public sector must be weighed against the benefits obtained from those decisions. That weighing process is beyond the scope of this book. For now, it is enough to remind the reader: whenever you encounter a policy or program that you think wasteful or indefensible, remember that someone else believes deeply in that policy or program.

Third, an activist government is less susceptible to control by electoral activity than a passive one. When the people in Washington did little, elections made a larger difference in policy than when they began to do a lot. We have pointed out in this book the extent to which political parties have declined in power and voters have reduced their voting turnout. There are many reasons for this, but an important one is often forgotten. If elections make less of a difference—because the few persons for whom one votes can do little to alter the ongoing programs of government—then it may make sense for people to spend less time in party or electoral activity and to spend more time in interest group activity aimed at specific agencies and programs.

The rapid increase in the number and variety of interest groups and their enlarged role in government is not pathological. It is a rational response to the fact that elected officials can only tend to a few things and therefore we must direct our energies at the appointed officials (and judges) who tend to everything else. Every president knows this and tries to do something about it, usually by trying to reorganize the executive branch. But no president and no reorganization plan can affect more than a tiny fraction of the millions of federal employees and thousands of government programs. "Coordination" from the top can, at best, occur selectively, for a few issues of exceptional importance.

Finally, the more government tries to do, the more things it will be held responsible for and the greater the risk of failure. From time to time in the nineteenth century, the business cycle made many people unhappy with the federal government—recall the rise of various protest parties—though then the government did very little. If federal officials were lucky, popular support would rise as soon as economic conditions improved. If they were unlucky, and a depression lasted into the election campaign, they would be thrown out of office. Today, however, the government—and the pres-

The expansion of government has brought it into contact with virtually every aspect of society. Senator Edmund Muskie of Maine has more than just voting to discuss with these factory workers.

ident in particular—is held responsible for crime, drug abuse, abortion, civil rights, the environment, the elderly, the status of women, the decay of central cities, the price of gasoline, and international tensions in half a dozen places on the globe. No government, and no president, can do well on all or even most of these matters most of the time. Indeed, some of these problems, such as crime, may be totally beyond the reach of the federal government no matter what its policy. It should not be surprising, therefore, that opinion surveys taken since the early 1960s have shown a steep decline in public confidence in government. There is no reason to believe this represents a loss of faith in our form of government or even in the design of its various institutions, but it clearly reflects a disappointment and even cynicism about the performance of government.

Disenchantment with government performance is not unique to the United States; it appears to be a feature of almost every political system in which public opinion is accurately measured. Indeed, the disenchantment is probably greater elsewhere. Americans who complain of high taxes might feel somewhat differently if they lived in Sweden where taxes are twice as high as here. Those who grouse about bureaucrats in this country probably have never dealt with the massive, centralized bureaucracies of Italy or France. Persons who are annoyed by congestion, pollution, and inflation ought to arrange a trip to Tokyo or Mexico City. However frustrating private life and public affairs may be in this country, every year thousands of persons living in other countries become immigrants to this country. Hardly any Americans want to emigrate to other places.

A question is asked from the audience at a "candidates' night" meeting. Such traditions help maintain the localistic nature of American politics and policies.

The enormous expansion of the scope and goals of the federal government has not been random or unguided. The government has tended to enlarge its powers more in some directions than in others; certain kinds of goals have been served more frequently than others. Though many factors shape this process of selection, two are of special importance. One is our constitutional structure, the other our political culture.

THE INFLUENCE OF STRUCTURE

To see the influence of structure, it is necessary to perform a mental experiment. Suppose the Founders had adopted a centralized, parliamentary regime instead of a decentralized, congressional one. The British model was right before their eyes. Every other European democracy adopted it. What difference would it have made had we followed the British example?

No one can be certain, of course, because the United States and Great Britain differ in many ways and not just in their political forms. At best, our mental experiment will be an educated guess. But the following possibilities seem plausible.

Because a parliamentary regime of the British sort centralizes power in the hands of an elected prime minister with a disciplined partisan majority in the legislature and frees him or her from most of the constraints and roadblocks created by independent congressional committees or independent and activist courts, we might have seen in the United States:

1. Quicker adoption of majoritarian policies, such as those in the area of social welfare. Broad popular desires would have been translated sooner into national policy when they were highly salient and conformed to the views of party leaders.

2. More centralization of bureaucratic authority—more national planning, less local au-

tonomy. More decisions would be made bureaucratically both because bureaucracies would be proportionately larger and because they would have wider discretionary authority delegated to them. (If the prime minister heads *both* the executive and the legislature, he or she sees no reason why decisions cannot be made as easily in one place as the other.)

3. Fewer opportunities for citizens to challenge or block government policies of which they disapproved. Without independent and activist courts, without local centers (state and city) of autonomous power, a citizen would have less of a chance to organize to stop a highway or an urban renewal project and hence fewer citizen organizations with these and similar purposes would exist.

4. Local authorities would not have been able to prevent groups of citizens from voting or otherwise participating in public life by maintaining at the local level segregated facilities that were illegal at the national level.

5. If "Watergate" occurred, we would never know about it. There would be no legislative investigating committees sufficiently independent of executive control to be able to investigate claims of executive wrongdoing.

6. We probably would have fought in about the same number of wars and under pretty much the same circumstances.

7. Taxes would be higher and a larger share of our tax money would be collected at the national level. Thus, we would find it harder to wage a "tax revolt" (since it is easier to block local spending decisions than national ones).

If this list of guesses is even approximately correct, it means that you would get more of some things you want and less of others. In general, it would have been easier for temporary majorities to govern and harder for individuals and groups to protect their interests.

The Founders would probably not be surprised at this list of differences. Though they could not have foreseen all the events and issues

66 By comparison, American politics remains far more sensitive to local concerns than does politics abroad. **99**

that would have led to these outcomes, they would have understood them, for many of them thought they were creating a system designed to keep central power weak and to enhance local and citizen power. They would have been amazed, of course, at the extent to which central power had been enhanced and local power weakened, but if they visited Europe they would learn that, by comparison, American politics remains far more sensitive to local concerns than does politics abroad.

THE INFLUENCE OF IDEAS

The broadly shared political culture of Americans—those attitudes toward governing that most of us have in common—would also have influenced the ends and means of government. Paramount among these attitudes is the preoccupation with rights. More than the citizens of perhaps any other nation, Americans define their relations with each other and with political authority in terms of rights. The civil liberties protected by the Bill of Rights have been assiduously defended and their interpretation significantly broadened even while the power of government has been growing.

For example: We expect that the groups affected by any governmental program will have a right to play a role in shaping and administering that program. In consequence, interest groups have proliferated. We think citizens should have the right to select the nominees of political parties as well as to choose between the parties; hence, primary elections have largely replaced party conventions. Individual members of Congress assert their rights and thus the power of congressional leaders and committee chair-

❝More than the citizens of perhaps any other nation, Americans define their relations with each other and with political authority in terms of rights.**❞**

Nuclear power is only the most dramatic of the many ways in which rights and wants are in conflict. People want more electric energy as well as assured safety; the government struggles, with uncertain knowledge, to provide both.

men is steadily diminished. We probably use the courts more frequently than the citizens of any other nation to make or change public policy; in doing so, we are asserting one set of rights against a competing set. The procedural rules that set forth how government is to act—the Freedom of Information Act, the Privacy Act, the Administrative Procedure Act—are more complex and demanding than the rules under which any other democratic government must operate. Each rule exists because it embodies what somebody has claimed to be a right: the right to know information, to maintain one's privacy, to participate in making decisions, and to bring suit against rival parties.

The more vigorously we assert our rights, the harder it is to make governmental decisions or to manage large institutions. We recognize this when we grumble about red tape and bureaucratic confusion, but we rarely give much support to proposals to centralize authority or simplify decision-making. We seem to accept whatever it costs in efficiency or effectiveness in order to maintain the capacity for asserting rights.

We do not always agree on which rights are most important, however. In addition to the influence of the widely shared commitment to rights generally, government is also shaped by the views some of us—certain political elites— have about which rights ought to be given the highest priority. Elite opinion tends to favor freedom of expression over freedom to manage or dispose of property. Mass opinion, though it has changed a good deal in the last few decades, is less committed to the preferred position of freedom of expression. Rank-and-file citizens often complain that what the elite calls essential liberty should instead be regarded as excessive permissiveness. Persons who own or manage property often lament the extent to which the rights governing its use have declined.

The changes in the relative security of personal and property freedom are linked to a fundamental and enduring tension in American thought. Tocqueville said it best. Americans, he wrote, "are far more ardently and tenaciously attached to equality than to freedom." Though democratic communities have a "natural taste for freedom," that freedom is hard to preserve because its excesses are immediate and obvious and its advantages are remote and uncertain. The advantages of equality, on the other hand, are readily apparent, and its costs are obscure and deferred.[1] Tocqueville may have underestimated the extent to which political liberties would endure because he did not foresee the determination of the courts to resist, in the long run if not the short, the passions of temporary majorities seeking to curtail such liberties. But he did not underestimate the extent to which in the economic and social realms Americans would decide that improving the conditions of life would justify restrictions on the right to dispose of property and manage private institutions. At first, the conflict was between liberty and equality of opportunity; more recently, it has become a conflict—among political elites if not within the citizenry itself—between equality of opportunity and equality of result.

Our concern for rights and the conflicts among us over which rights ought to be preferred affect politics profoundly. The fact that decisions can be influenced by opinions about rights indicates that decisions can be influenced by opinions generally. As the political system has become more fragmented, more individualized, and more atomized as a result of our collective assertion of rights, it has come more under the sway of ideas. When political parties were strong and congressional leadership was centralized (as they were in the latter part of the nineteenth and early part of the twentieth centuries), access to the decision-making process in Washington was difficult and the number of new ideas that stood a chance of adoption was small. However, those proposals that could command leadership support were more easily adopted—though there were powerful organizations that could say "no," these same organizations could also say "yes."

Today these and other institutions are fragmented and in disarray. Individual congressmen are far more important than congressional leadership. Political parties no longer control nominations for office. The media have given to candidates direct access to the voters; campaign finance laws have restricted, but not eliminated,

> **❝** At first, the conflict was between liberty and equality of opportunity; more recently, it has become a conflict . . . between equality of opportunity and equality of result. **❞**

the influence interest groups can wield by controlling money resources. Forming new, issue-oriented lobbying groups is much easier today than formerly, thanks to the capability of computers and direct-mail advertising.

These idea-based changes in institutions affect how policy is made. When there is widespread enthusiasm for an idea—especially among political elites but also in the public at large—new programs can be formulated and adopted with great speed. This happened when the "Great Society" legislation of Lyndon Johnson was proposed, when the environmental and consumer protection laws first arrived on the public agenda, when campaign finance reform was proposed in the wake of Watergate. So long as such symbols have a powerful appeal, so long as a consensus persists, change is possible. But when these ideas lose their appeal, or are challenged by new ideas, the competing pressures make change extremely difficult. Environmentalism today is challenged by concerns for creating jobs and economic growth; social legislation is challenged by skepticism about its effectiveness and concern over its cost; campaign finance reforms are, to some critics, merely devices for protecting incumbents.

This may all seem obvious to a reader raised in the world of contemporary politics. But it is different, in degree if not in kind, from the way politics was once carried out. In the 1920s, the 1930s, the 1940s—even in the 1950s—people described politics as a process of bargaining among organized interests or "blocs," representing business, farmers, labor, and ethnic and professional groups. With the expansion of the scope of government policy, there are no longer a few

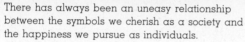

There has always been an uneasy relationship between the symbols we cherish as a society and the happiness we pursue as individuals.

major blocs that sit astride the policy process. There are instead hundreds, perhaps thousands, of highly specialized interests and constituencies that seek, above all, to protect what benefits, intangible as well as tangible, they get from government. This vast array of specialized interests can often be mobilized (or overcome) to produce broad changes. In the 1960s and early 1970s there was change aplenty. But when enthusiasm wanes, when symbols lose their appeal, when ideologies are in conflict, the political process becomes slow, cautious, and localistic. This, of course, was what the Founders intended, but they intended it for a government far smaller and less active than what we now have.

We have a large government—and large expectations about what it can achieve. But the government increasingly finds it difficult to satisfy those expectations. The public acceptance of an activist role for government has been accompanied by a decline in public confidence in those who manage that government. We expect more and more from government but are less and less certain we will get it, or get it in a form and at a cost we find acceptable. This constitutes, perhaps, the greatest challenge to statesmanship in the years ahead: to find a way to serve the true interests of the people while restoring and retaining their confidence in the legitimacy of government itself.

THE CONSTITUTION OF THE UNITED STATES

𝔚𝔢 𝔱𝔥𝔢 𝔓𝔢𝔬𝔭𝔩𝔢 *of the United States, in Order to form a more perfect Union, establish Justice, insure domestic Tranquility, provide for the common defence, promote the general Welfare, and secure the Blessings of Liberty to ourselves and our Posterity, do ordain and establish this Constitution for the United States of America.*

ARTICLE I.

Bicameral Congress

Section 1. All legislative Powers herein granted shall be vested in a Congress of the United States, which shall consist of a Senate and House of Representatives.

Membership of the House

Section 2. The House of Representatives shall be composed of Members chosen every second Year by the People of the several States, and the Electors in each State shall have the Qualifications requisite for Electors of the most numerous Branch of the State Legislature.

No Person shall be a Representative who shall not have attained to the age of twenty five Years, and been seven Years a Citizen of the United States, and who shall not, when elected, be an Inhabitant of that State in which he shall be chosen.

Representatives and direct Taxes shall be apportioned among the several States which may be included within this Union, according to their respective Numbers, which shall be determined by adding to the whole Number of free Persons, including those bound to Service for a Term of Years, and excluding Indians not taxed, three fifths of all other Persons.[1] The actual Enumeration shall be made within three Years after the first Meeting of the Congress of the United States, and within every subsequent Term of ten Years, in such Manner as they shall by Law direct. The Number of Representatives shall not exceed one for every thirty Thousand, but each State shall have at Least one Representative; and until such enumeration shall be made, the State of New Hampshire shall be entitled to chuse three, Massachusetts eight, Rhode-Island and Providence Plantations one, Connecticut five, New-York six, New Jersey four, Pennsylvania eight, Delaware one, Maryland six, Virginia ten, North Carolina five, South Carolina five, and Georgia three.

When vacancies happen in the Representation from any State, the Executive Authority thereof shall issue Writs of Election to fill such Vacancies.

[1] Changed by the Fourteenth Amendment, Section 2.

Note: The topical headings are not part of the original Constitution. Excluding the Preamble and Closing, those portions set in italic type have been superseded or changed by later amendments.

Power to impeach

The House of Representatives shall chuse their Speaker and other Officers; and shall have the sole Power of Impeachment.

Membership of the Senate

Section 3. The Senate of the United States shall be composed of two Senators from each State, *chosen by the Legislature thereof,*[2] for six Years; and each Senator shall have one Vote.

Immediately after they shall be assembled in Consequence of the first Election, they shall be divided as equally as may be into three Classes. The Seats of the Senators of the first Class shall be vacated at the Expiration of the second Year, of the second Class at the Expiration of the fourth Year, and of the third Class at the Expiration of the sixth Year, so that one third may be chosen every second Year; *and if Vacancies happen by Resignation, or otherwise, during the Recess of the Legislature of any State, the Executive thereof may make temporary Appointments until the next Meeting of the Legislature, which shall then fill such Vacancies.*[3]

No Person shall be a Senator who shall not have attained to the Age of thirty Years, and been nine Years a Citizen of the United States, and who shall not, when elected, be an Inhabitant of that State for which he shall be chosen.

The Vice President of the United States shall be President of the Senate, but shall have no Vote, unless they be equally divided.

The Senate shall chuse their other Officers, and also a President pro tempore, in the Absence of the Vice President, or when he shall exercise the Office of President of the United States.

Power to try impeachments

The Senate shall have the sole Power to try all Impeachments. When sitting for that Purpose, they shall be on Oath or Affirmation. When the President of the United States is tried the Chief Justice shall preside: And no Person shall be convicted without the Concurrence of two thirds of the Members present.

Judgment in Cases of Impeachment shall not extend further than to removal from Office, and disqualification to hold and enjoy any Office of honor, Trust or Profit under the United States: but the Party convicted shall nevertheless be liable and subject to Indictment, Trial, Judgment and Punishment, according to Law.

Laws governing elections

Section 4. The Times, Places and Manner of holding Elections for Senators and Representatives, shall be prescribed in each State by the Legislature thereof; but the Congress may at any time by Law make or alter such Regulations, except as to the Places of chusing Senators.

The Congress shall assemble at least once in every Year, and such Meeting shall be on the *first Monday in December, unless they shall by Law appoint a different Day.*[4]

Rules of Congress

Section 5. Each House shall be the Judge of the Elections, Returns and Qualifications of its own Members, and a Majority of each shall constitute a Quorum to do Business; but a smaller Number may adjourn from day to day, and may be authorized

[2] Changed by the Seventeenth Amendment.

[3] Changed by the Seventeenth Amendment.

[4] Changed by the Twentieth Amendment, Section 2.

to compel the Attendance of absent Members, in such Manner, and under such Penalties as each House may provide.

Each House may determine the Rules of its Proceedings, punish its Members for disorderly Behaviour, and, with the Concurrence of two thirds, expel a Member.

Each House shall keep a Journal of its Proceedings, and from time to time publish the same, excepting such Parts as may in their Judgment require Secrecy; and the Yeas and Nays of the Members of either House on any question shall, at the Desire of one fifth of those Present, be entered on the Journal.

Neither House, during the Session of Congress, shall, without the Consent of the other, adjourn for more than three days, nor to any other Place than that in which the two Houses shall be sitting.

Salaries and immunities of members

Section 6. The Senators and Representatives shall receive a Compensation for their Services, to be ascertained by Law, and paid out of the Treasury of the United States. They shall in all Cases, except Treason, Felony and Breach of the Peace, be privileged from Arrest during their Attendance at the Session of their respective Houses, and in going to and returning from the same; and for any Speech or Debate in either House, they shall not be questiond in any other Place.

Bar on members of Congress holding federal appointive office

No Senator or Representative shall, during the Time for which he was elected, be appointed to any civil Office under the Authority of the United States, which shall have been created, or the Emoluments whereof shall have been encreased during such time; and no Person holding any Office under the United States, shall be a Member of either House during his Continuance in Office.

Money bills originate in House
Procedure for enacting laws; veto power

Section 7. All Bills for raising Revenue shall originate in the House of Representatives; but the Senate may propose or concur with Amendments as on other Bills.

Every Bill which shall have passed the House of Representatives and the Senate, shall, before it become a Law, be presented to the President of the United States; If he approve he shall sign it, but if not he shall return it, with his Objections to that House in which it shall have originated, who shall enter the Objections at large on their Journal, and proceed to reconsider it. If after such Reconsideration two thirds of that House shall agree to pass the Bill, it shall be sent, together with the Objections, to the other House, by which it shall likewise be reconsidered, and if approved by two thirds of that House, it shall become a Law. But in all such Cases the Votes of both Houses shall be determined by yeas and Nays, and the Names of the Persons voting for and against the Bill shall be entered on the Journal of each House respectively. If any Bill shall not be returned by the President within ten Days (Sundays excepted) after it shall have been presented to him, the Same shall be a Law, in like Manner as if he had signed it, unless the Congress by their Adjournment prevent its Return, in which Case it shall not be a Law.

Every Order, Resolution, or Vote to which the Concurrence of the Senate and House of Representatives may be necessary (except on a question of Adjournment) shall be presented to the President of the United States; and before the Same shall take Effect, shall be approved by him, or being disapproved by him, shall be repassed by two thirds of the Senate and House of Representatives, according to the Rules and Limitations prescribed in the Case of a Bill.

Powers of Congress:
—taxes

Section 8.   The Congress shall have Power To lay and collect Taxes, Duties, Imposts and Excises, to pay the Debts and provide for the common Defence and general Welfare of the United States; but all Duties, Imposts and Excises shall be uniform throughout the United States;

—borrowing

To borrow Money on the credit of the United States;

—regulation of commerce

To regulate Commerce with foreign Nations, and among the several States, and with the Indian Tribes;

—naturalization and bankruptcy

To establish an uniform Rule of Naturalization, and uniform Laws on the subject of Bankruptcies throughout the United States;

—money

To coin Money, regulate the Value thereof, and of foreign Coin, and fix the Standard of Weights and Measures;

—counterfeiting

To provide for the Punishment of counterfeiting the Securities and current Coin of the United States;

—post office
—patents and copyrights

To establish Post Offices and post Roads;

To promote the Progress of Science and useful Arts, by securing for limited Times to Authors and Inventors the exclusive Right to their respective Writings and Discovcrics;

—create courts
—punish piracies

To constitute Tribunals inferior to the supreme Court;

To define and punish Piracies and Felonies committed on the high Seas, and Offences against the Law of Nations;

—declare war

To declare War, grant Letters of Marque and Reprisal, and make Rules concerning Captures on Land and Water;

—create army and navy

To raise and support Armies, but no Appropriation of Money to that Use shall be for a longer Term than two Years;

To provide and maintain a Navy;

To make Rules for the Government and Regulation of the land and naval Forces;

—call the militia

To provide for calling forth the Militia to execute the Laws of the Union, suppress Insurrections and repel Invasions;

To provide for organizing, arming, and disciplining, the Militia, and for governing such Part of them as may be employed in the Service of the United States, reserving to the States respectively, the Appointment of the Officers, and the Authority of training the Militia according to the discipline prescribed by Congress;

—govern District of Columbia

To exercise exclusive Legislation in all Cases whatsoever, over such District (not exceeding ten Miles square) as may, by Cession of Particular States, and the Acceptance of Congress, become the Seat of the Government of the United States, and to exercise like Authority over all Places purchased by the Consent of the Legislature of the State in which the Same shall be, for the Erection of Forts, Magazines, Arsenals, dock-Yards, and other needful Buildings;—And

—"necessary and proper" clause

To make all Laws which shall be necessary and proper for carrying into Execution the foregoing Powers, and all other Powers vested by this Constitution in the Government of the United States, or in any Department or Officer thereof.

Restrictions on powers of Congress

Section 9.   The Migration or Importation of such Persons as any of the States now existing shall think proper to admit, shall not be prohibited by the Congress prior to

—slave trade

the Year one thousand eight hundred and eight, but a Tax or duty may be imposed on such Importation, not exceeding ten dollars for each Person.

—habeas corpus

The Privilege of the Writ of Habeas Corpus shall not be suspended, unless when in Cases of Rebellion or Invasion the public Safety may require it.

—no bill of attainder or ex post facto law

No Bill of Attainder or ex post facto Law shall be passed.

No Capitation, or other direct, Tax shall be laid, *unless in Proportion to the Census or Enumeration herein before directed to be taken.*[5]

—no interstate tariffs
—no preferential treatment for some states

No Tax or Duty shall be laid on Articles exported from any State.

No Preference shall be given by any Regulation of Commerce or Revenue to the Ports of one State over those of another; nor shall Vessels bound to, or from, one State, be obliged to enter, clear or pay Duties in another.

—appropriations

No Money shall be drawn from the Treasury, but in Consequence of Appropriations made by Law; and a regular Statement and Account of the Receipts and Expenditures of all public Money shall be published from time to time.

—no titles of nobility

No Title of Nobility shall be granted by the United States: And no Person holding any Office of Profit or Trust under them, shall, without the Consent of the Congress, accept of any present, Emolument, Office, or Title, of any kind whatever, from any King, Prince, or foreign State.

Restrictions on powers of states

Section 10.   No State shall enter into any Treaty, Alliance, or Confederation; grant Letters of Marque and Reprisal; coin Money; emit Bills of Credit; make any Thing but gold and silver Coin a Tender in Payment of Debts; pass any Bill of Attainder, ex post facto Law, or Law impairing the Obligation of Contracts, or grant any Title of Nobility.

No State shall, without the Consent of the Congress, lay any Imposts or Duties on Imports or Exports, except what may be absolutely necessary for executing its inspection Laws: and the net Produce of all Duties and Imposts, laid by any State on Imports or Exports, shall be for the Use of the Treasury of the United States; and all such Laws shall be subject to the Revision and Controul of the Congress.

No State shall, without the Consent of Congress, lay any Duty of Tonnage, keep Troops, or Ships of War in time of Peace, enter into any Agreement or Compact with another State, or with a foreign Power, or engage in War, unless actually invaded, or in such imminent Danger as will not admit of delay.

ARTICLE II.

Office of president

Section 1.   The executive Power shall be vested in a President of the United States of America. He shall hold his Office during the Term of four Years, and, together with the Vice President, chosen for the same Term, be elected, as follows

Election of president

Each State shall appoint, in such Manner as the Legislature thereof may direct, a Number of Electors, equal to the whole Number of Senators and Representatives to which the State may be entitled in the Congress: but no Senator or Representative,

[5] Changed by the Sixteenth Amendment.

or Person holding an Office of Trust or Profit under the United States, shall be appointed an Elector.

The Electors shall meet in their respective States, and vote by Ballot for two Persons, of whom one at least shall not be an Inhabitant of the same State with themselves. And they shall make a List of all the Persons voted for, and of the Number of Votes for each; which List they shall sign and certify, and transmit sealed to the Seat of the Government of the United States, directed to the President of the Senate. The President of the Senate shall, in the Presence of the Senate and House of Representatives, open all the Certificates, and the Votes shall then be counted. The Person having the greatest Number of Votes shall be the President, if such Number be a Majority of the whole Number of Electors appointed; and if there be more than one who have such Majority, and have an equal Number of Votes, then the House of Representatives shall immediately chuse by Ballot one of them for President; and if no Person have a Majority, then from the five highest on the List the said House shall in like Manner chuse the President. But in chusing the President, the Votes shall be taken by States, the Representation from each State having one Vote; a quorum for this Purpose shall consist of a Member or Members from two thirds of the States, and a Majority of all the States shall be necessary to a Choice. In every Case, after the Choice of the President, the Person having the greatest Number of Votes of the Electors shall be the Vice President. But if there should remain two or more who have equal Votes, the Senate shall chuse from them by Ballot the Vice President.[6]

The Congress may determine the Time of chusing the Electors, and the Day on which they shall give their Votes; which Day shall be the same throughout the United States.

Requirements to be president

No Person except a natural born Citizen, or a Citizen of the United States, at the time of the Adoption of this Constitution, shall be eligible to the Office of President; neither shall any person be eligible to that Office who shall not have attained to the Age of thirty five Years, and been fourteen Years a Resident within the United States.

In Case of the Removal of the President from Office, or of his Death, Resignation, or Inability to discharge the Powers and Duties of the said Office, the Same shall devolve on the Vice President, and the Congress may by Law provide for the Case of Removal, Death, Resignation or Inability, both of the President and Vice President, declaring what Officer shall then act as President, and such Officer shall act accordingly, until the Disability be removed, or a President shall be elected.[7]

Pay of president

The President shall, at stated Times, receive for his Services, a Compensation, which shall neither be encreased nor diminished during the Period for which he shall have been elected, and he shall not receive within that Period any other Emolument from the United States, or any of them.

Before he enter on the Execution of his Office, he shall take the following Oath or Affirmation:—"I do solemnly swear (or affirm) that I will faithfully execute the Office of President of the United States, and will to the best of my Ability, preserve, protect and defend the Constitution of the United States."

[6] Superseded by the Twelfth Amendment.

[7] Modified by the Twenty-Fifth Amendment.

Powers of president
—*commander in chief*

Section 2.   The President shall be Commander in Chief of the Army and Navy of the United States, and of the Militia of the several States, when called into the actual Service of the United States; he may require the Opinion, in writing, of the principal Officer in each of the executive Departments, upon any Subject relating to the Duties

—*pardons*

of their respective Offices, and he shall have Power to grant Reprieves and Pardons for Offences against the United States, except in Cases of Impeachment.

—*treaties and appointments*

He shall have Power, by and with the Advice and Consent of the Senate, to make Treaties, provided two thirds of the Senators present concur; and he shall nominate, and by and with the Advice and Consent of the Senate, shall appoint Ambassadors, other public Ministers and Consuls, Judges of the supreme Court, and all other Officers of the United States, whose Appointments are not herein otherwise provided for, and which shall be established by Law: but the Congress may by Law vest the Appointment of such inferior Officers, as they think proper, in the President alone, in the Courts of Law, or in the Heads of Departments.

The President shall have Power to fill up all Vacancies that may happen during the Recess of the Senate, by granting Commissions which shall expire at the End of their next Session.

Relations of president
with Congress

Section 3.   He shall from time to time give to the Congress Information of the State of the Union, and recommend to their Consideration such Measures as he shall judge necessary and expedient; he may, on extraordinary Occasions, convene both Houses, or either of them, and in Case of Disagreement between them, with Respect to the Time of Adjournment, he may adjourn them to such Time as he shall think proper; he shall receive Ambassadors and other public Ministers; he shall take Care that the Laws be faithfully executed, and shall Commission all the Officers of the United States.

Impeachment

Section 4.   The President, Vice President and all civil Officers of the United States, shall be removed from Office on Impeachment for, and Conviction of, Treason, Bribery, or other high Crimes and Misdemeanors.

ARTICLE III.

Federal courts

Section 1.   The judicial Power of the United States, shall be vested in one supreme Court, and in such inferior Courts as the Congress may from time to time ordain and establish. The Judges, both of the supreme and inferior Courts, shall hold their Offices during good Behaviour, and shall, at stated Times, receive for their Services, a Compensation, which shall not be diminished during their Continuance in Office.

Jurisdiction of courts

Section 2.   The judicial Power shall extend to all Cases, in Law and Equity, arising under this Constitution, the Laws of the United States, and Treaties made, or which shall be made, under their Authority;—to all Cases affecting Ambassadors, other public Ministers and Consuls;—to all Cases of admiralty and maritime Jurisdiction;—

to Controversies to which the United States shall be a Party;—to Controversies between two or more States;—*between a State and Citizens of another State;*[8]—between Citizens of different States;—between Citizens of the same State claiming Lands under Grants of different States, and between a State, or the Citizens thereof, and foreign States, Citizens or Subjects.

—original

—appellate

In all Cases affecting Ambassadors, other public Ministers and Consuls, and those in which a State shall be Part, the supreme Court shall have original Jurisdiction. In all the other Cases before mentioned, the supreme Court shall have appellate Jurisdiction, both as to Law and Fact, with such Exceptions, and under such Regulations as the Congress shall make.

The Trial of all Crimes, except in Cases of Impeachment, shall be by Jury; and such Trial shall be held in the State where the said Crimes shall have been committed; but when not committed within any State, the Trial shall be at such Place or Places as the Congress may by Law have directed.

Treason

Section 3.   Treason against the United States, shall consist only in levying War against them, or in adhering to their Enemies, giving them Aid and Comfort. No Person shall be convicted of Treason unless on the Testimony of two Witnesses to the same overt Act, or on Confession in open Court.

The Congress shall have Power to declare the Punishment of Treason, but no Attainder of Treason shall work Corruption of Blood, or Forfeiture except during the Life of the Person attainted.

ARTICLE IV.

Full faith and credit

Section 1.   Full Faith and Credit shall be given in each State to the public Acts, Records, and judicial Proceedings of every other State. And the Congress may by general Laws prescribe the Manner in which such Acts, Records and Proceedings shall be proved, and the Effect thereof.

Privileges and immunities

Section 2.   The Citizens of each State shall be entitled to all Privileges and Immunities of Citizens in the several States.

Extradition

A person charged in any State with Treason, Felony, or other Crime, who shall flee from Justice, and be found in another State, shall on Demand of the executive Authority of the State from which he fled, be delivered up, to be removed to the State having Jurisdiction of the Crime.

No Person held to Service or Labour in one State, under the Laws thereof, escaping into another, shall, in Consequence of any Law or Regulation therein, be discharged from such Service or Labour, but shall be delivered up on Claim of the Party to whom such Service or Labour may be due.[9]

Creation of new states

Section 3.   New States may be admitted by the Congress into this Union; but no new State shall be formed or erected within the Jurisdiction of any other State; nor any

[8] Modified by the Eleventh Amendment.

[9] Changed by the Thirteenth Amendment.

State be formed by the Junction of two or more States, or Parts of States, without the Consent of the Legislatures of the States concerned as well as of the Congress.

Governing territories

The Congress shall have Power to dispose of and make all needful Rules and Regulations respecting the Territory or other Property belonging to the United States; and nothing in this Constitution shall be so construed as to Prejudice any Claims of the United States, or of any particular State.

Protection of states

Section 4.   The United States shall guarantee to every State in this Union a Republican Form of Government, and shall protect each of them against Invasion; and on Application of the Legislature, or of the Executive (when the Legislature cannot be convened) against domestic Violence.

ARTICLE V.

Amending the Constitution

The Congress, whenever two thirds of both Houses shall deem it necessary, shall propose Amendments to this Constitution, or, on the Application of the Legislatures of two thirds of the several States, shall call a Convention for proposing Amendments, which, in either Case, shall be valid to all Intents and Purposes, as Part of this Constitution, when ratified by the Legislatures of three fourths of the several States, or by Conventions in three fourths thereof, as the one or the other Mode of Ratification may be proposed by the Congress; Provided that no Amendment which may be made prior to the Year One thousand eight hundred and eight shall in any Manner affect the first and fourth Clauses in the Ninth Section of the first Article; and that no State, without its Consent, shall be deprived of its equal Suffrage in the Senate.

ARTICLE VI.

Assumption of debts
of Confederation

All Debts contracted and Engagements entered into, before the Adoption of this Constitution, shall be as valid against the United States under this Constitution, as under the Confederation.

Supremacy of federal
laws and treaties

This Constitution, and the Laws of the United States which shall be made in Pursuance thereof; and all Treaties made, or which shall be made, under the Authority of the United States, shall be the supreme Law of the Land; and the Judges in every State shall be bound thereby, any Thing in the Constitution or Laws of any State to the Contrary notwithstanding.

The Senators and Representatives before mentioned, and the Members of the several State Legislatures, and all executive and judicial Officers, both of the United States and of the several States, shall be bound by Oath or Affirmation, to support this Constitution; but no religious Test shall ever be required as a Qualification to any Office or public Trust under the United States.

No religious test

ARTICLE VII.

Ratification procedure

The Ratification of the Conventions of nine States, shall be sufficient for the Establishment of this Constitution between the States so ratifying the Same.

Done in Convention by the Unanimous Consent of the States present the Seventeenth Day of September in the Year of our Lord one thousand seven hundred and Eighty seven and of the Independence of the United States of America the Twelfth In witness whereof We have hereunto subscribed our Names,

G⁰ WASHINGTON—*Presidᵗ*
and deputy from Virginia

New Hampshire	JOHN LANGDON NICHOLAS GILMAN		GEO: READ GUNNING BEDFORD jun
Massachusetts	NATHANIEL GORHAM RUFUS KING	Delaware	JOHN DICKINSON RICHARD BASSETT JACO: BROOM
Connecticut	Wᴹ SAMᴸ JOHNSON ROGER SHERMAN		JAMES MᶜHENRY
New York	ALEXANDER HAMILTON	Maryland	DAN of Sᵀ THOˢ JENIFER DANᴸ CARROLL
New Jersey	WIL: LIVINGSTON DAVID BREARLEY. Wᴹ PATERSON. JONA: DAYTON	Virginia	JOHN BLAIR— JAMES MADISON Jr.
	B FRANKLIN	North Carolina	Wᴹ BLOUNT RICHᴰ DOBBS SPAIGHT. HU WILLIAMSON
	THOMAS MIFFLIN		
	ROBᵀ MORRIS		
Pensylvania	GEO. CLYMER THOˢ FITZSIMONS	South Carolina	J. RUTLEDGE CHARLES COTESWORTH PINCKNEY CHARLES PINCKNEY PIERCE BUTLER
	JARED INGERSOLL		
	JAMES WILSON	Georgia	WILLIAM FEW ABR BALDWIN
	GOUV MORRIS		

[*The first ten amendments, known as the "Bill of Rights," were ratified in 1791.*]

AMENDMENT I

Freedom of religion, speech, press, assembly

Congress shall make no law respecting an establishment of religion, or prohibiting the free exercise thereof; or abridging the freedom of speech, or of the press; or the right of the people peaceably to assemble, and to petition the Government for a redress of grievances.

AMENDMENT II

Right to bear arms

A well regulated Militia, being necessary to the security of a free State, the right of the people to keep and bear Arms, shall not be infringed.

AMENDMENT III

Quartering troops in private homes

No Soldier shall, in time of peace be quartered in any house, without the consent of the Owner, nor in time of war, but in a manner to be prescribed by law.

AMENDMENT IV

Prohibition on unreasonable searches and seizures

The right of the people to be secure in their persons, houses, papers, and effects, against unreasonable searches and seizures, shall not be violated, and no Warrants shall issue, but upon probable cause, supported by Oath or affirmation, and particularly describing the place to be searched, and the persons or things to be seized.

AMENDMENT V

Rights when accused; "due process" clause

No person shall be held to answer for a capital, or otherwise infamous crime, unless on a presentment or indictment of a Grand Jury, except in cases arising in the land or naval forces, or in the Militia, when in actual service in time of War or public danger; nor shall any person be subject for the same offence to be twice put in jeopardy of life or limb; nor shall be compelled in any criminal case to be a witness against himself, nor be deprived of life, liberty, or property, without due process of law; nor shall private property be taken for public use, without just compensation.

AMENDMENT VI

Rights when on trial

In all criminal prosecutions, the accused shall enjoy the right to a speedy and public trial, by an impartial jury of the State and district wherein the crime shall have been committed, which district shall have been previously ascertained by law, and to be informed of the nature and cause of the accusation; to be confronted with the witnesses against him; to have compulsory process for obtaining witnesses in his favor, and to have Assistance of Counsel for his defence.

AMENDMENT VII

Common-law suits

In Suits at common law, where the value in controversy shall exceed twenty dollars, the right of trial by jury shall be preserved, and no fact tried by a jury, shall be otherwise reexamined in any Court of the United States, than according to the rules of the common law.

AMENDMENT VIII

Bail; no "cruel and unusual" punishments

Excessive bail shall not be required, nor excessive fines imposed, nor cruel and unusual punishments inflicted.

AMENDMENT IX

Unenumerated rights protected

The enumeration in the Constitution, of certain rights, shall not be construed to deny or disparage others retained by the people.

AMENDMENT X

Powers reserved for states

The powers not delegated to the United States by the Constitution, nor prohibited by it to the States, are reserved to the States respectively, or to the people.

AMENDMENT XI
[Ratified in 1795.]

Limits on suits
against states

The Judicial power of the United States shall not be construed to extend to any suit in law or equity, commenced or prosecuted against one of the United States by Citizens of another State, or by Citizens or Subjects of any Foreign State.

AMENDMENT XII
[Ratified in 1804.]

Revision of Electoral
College procedure

The Electors shall meet in their respective states and vote by ballot for President and Vice President, one of whom, at least, shall not be an inhabitant of the same state with themselves; they shall name in their ballots the person voted for as President, and in distinct ballots the person voted for as Vice President, and they shall make distinct lists of all persons voted for as President, and of all persons voted for as Vice President, and of the number of votes for each, which lists they shall sign and certify, and trasmit sealed to the seat of the government of the United States, directed to the President of the Senate;—The President of the Senate shall, in the presence of the Senate and House of Representatives, open all the certificates and the votes shall then be counted;—The person having the greatest number of votes for President, shall be the President, if such number be a majority of the whole number of Electors appointed; and if no person have such majority, then from the persons having the highest numbers not exceeding three on the list of those voted for as President, the House of Representatives shall choose immediately, by ballot, the President. But in choosing the President, the votes shall be taken by states, the representation from each state having one vote; a quorum for this purpose shall consist of a member or members from two-thirds of the states, and a majority of all the states shall be necessary to a choice. *And if the House of Representatives shall not choose a President whenever the right of choice shall devolve upon them, before the fourth day of March next following, then the Vice President shall act as President, as in the case of the death or other constitutional disability of the President.*—[10] The person having the greatest number of votes as Vice President, shall be the Vice President, if such number be a majority of the whole number of Electors appointed, and if no person have a majority, then from the two highest numbers on the list, the Senate shall choose the Vice President; a quorum for the purpose shall consist of two-thirds of the whole number of Senators, and a majority of the whole number shall be necessary to a choice. But no person constitutionally ineligible to the office of President shall be eligible to that of Vice President of the United States.

[10] Changed by the Twentieth Amendment, Section 3.

AMENDMENT XIII
[*Ratified in 1865.*]

Slavery prohibited

Section 1. Neither slavery nor involuntary servitude, except as a punishment for crime whereof the party shall have been duly convicted, shall exist within the United States, or any place subject to their jurisdiction.

Section 2. Congress shall have power to enforce this article by appropriate legislation.

AMENDMENT XIV
[*Ratified in 1868.*]

Ex-slaves made citizens

"Due process" clause applied to states

"Equal protection" clause

Section 1. All persons born or naturalized in the United States and subject to the jurisdiction thereof, are citizens of the United States and of the State wherein they reside. No State shall make or enforce any law which shall abridge the privileges or immunities of citizens of the United States; nor shall any State deprive any person of life, liberty, or property, without due process of law; nor deny to any person within its jurisdiction the equal protection of the laws.

Reduction in congressional representation for states denying adult males the right to vote

Section 2. Representatives shall be apportioned among the several States according to their respective numbers, counting the whole number of persons in each State, excluding Indians not taxed. But when the right to vote at any election for the choice of electors for President and Vice President of the United States, Representatives in Congress, the Executive and Judicial officers of a State, or the members of the Legislature thereof, is denied to any of the male inhabitants of such State, being *twenty-one*[11] years of age, and citizens of the United States, or in any way abridged, except for participation in rebellion, or other crime, the basis of representation therein shall be reduced in the proportion which the number of such male citizens shall bear to the whole number of male citizens twenty-one years of age in such State.

Southern rebels denied federal office

Section 3. No person shall be a Senator or Representative in Congress, or elector of President and Vice President, or hold any office, civil or military, under the United States, or under any State, who, having previously taken an oath, as a member of Congress, or as an officer of the United States, or as a member of any State legislature, or as an executive or judicial officer of any State, to support the Constitution of the United States, shall have engaged in insurrection or rebellion against the same, or given aid or comfort to the enemies thereof. But Congress may by a vote of two-thirds of each House, remove such disability.

Rebel debts repudiated

Section 4. The validity of the public debt of the United States, authorized by law, including debts incurred for payment of pensions and bounties for services in suppressing insurrection or rebellion, shall not be questioned. But neither the United States nor any State shall assume or pay any debt or obligation incurred in aid of insurrection or rebellion against the United States, or any claim for the loss or eman-

[11] Changed by the Twenty-Sixth Amendment.

cipation of any slave; but all such debts, obligations and claims shall be held illegal and void.

Section 5.   The Congress shall have power to enforce, by appropriate legislation, the provisions of this article.

AMENDMENT XV
[*Ratified in 1870.*]

Blacks given right
to vote

Section 1.   The right of citizens of the United States to vote shall not be denied or abridged by the United States or by any State on account of race, color, or previous condition of servitude.

Section 2.   The Congress shall have power to enforce this article by appropriate legislation.

AMENDMENT XVI
[*Ratified in 1913.*]

Authorizes federal
income tax

The Congress shall have power to lay and collect taxes on incomes, from whatever source derived, without apportionment among the several States, and without regard to any census or enumeration.

AMENDMENT XVII
[*Ratified in 1913.*]

Requires popular election
of senators

The Senate of the United States shall be composed of two Senators from each State, elected by the people thereof, for six years; and each Senator shall have one vote. The electors in each State shall have the qualifications requisite for electors of the most numerous branch of the State legislatures.

   When vacancies happen in the representation of any State in the Senate, the executive authority of such State shall issue writs of election to fill such vacancies: *Provided,* That the legislature of any State may empower the executive thereof to make temporary appointments until the people fill the vacancies by election as the legislature may direct.

   This amendment shall not be so construed as to affect the election or term of any Senator chosen before it becomes valid as part of the Constitution.

AMENDMENT XVIII
[*Ratified in 1919.*]

Prohibits manufacture
and sale of liquor

Section 1.   *After one year from the ratification of this article the manufacture, sale, or transportation of intoxicating liquors within, the importation thereof into, or the exportation thereof from the United States and all territory subject to the jurisdiction thereof for beverage purposes is hereby prohibited.*

Section 2. *The Congress and the several States shall have concurrent power to enforce this article by appropriate legislation.*

Section 3. *This article shall be inoperative unless it shall have been ratified as an amendment to the Constitution by the legislatures of the several States, as provided in the Constitution, within seven years from the date of the submission hereof to the States by the Congress.*[12]

AMENDMENT XIX
[*Ratified in 1920.*]

Right to vote
for women

The right of citizens of the United States to vote shall not be denied or abridged by the United States or by any State on account of sex.

Congress shall have power to enforce this article by appropriate legislation.

AMENDMENT XX
[*Ratified in 1933.*]

Federal terms of
office to begin
in January

Section 1. The terms of the President and Vice President shall end at noon on the 20th day of January, and the terms of Senators and Representatives at noon on the 3d day of January, of the years in which such terms would have ended if this article had not been ratified; and the terms of their successors shall then begin.

Section 2. The Congress shall assemble at least once in every year, and such meeting shall begin at noon on the 3d day of January, unless they shall by law appoint a different day.

Emergency presidential
succession

Section 3. If, at the time fixed for the beginning of the term of the President, the President elect shall have died, the Vice President elect shall become President. If a President shall not have been chosen before the time fixed for the beginning of his term, or if the President elect shall have failed to qualify, then the Vice President elect shall act as President until a President shall have qualified; and the Congress may by law provide for the case wherein neither a President elect nor a Vice President elect shall have qualified, declaring who shall then act as President, or the manner in which one who is to act shall be selected, and such person shall act accordingly until a President or Vice President shall have qualified.

Section 4. The Congress may by law provide for the case of the death of any of the persons from whom the House of Representatives may choose a President whenever the right of choice shall have devolved upon them, and for the case of the death of any of the persons from whom the Senate may choose a Vice President whenever the right of choice shall have devolved upon them.

[12]Repealed by the Twenty-First Amendment.

Section 5.   Sections 1 and 2 shall take effect on the 15th day of October following the ratification of this article.

Section 6.   This article shall be inoperative unless it shall have been ratified as an amendment to the Constitution by the legislatures of three-fourths of the several States within seven years from the date of its submission.

AMENDMENT XXI
[Ratified in 1933.]

Repeals Prohibition

Section 1.   The eighteenth article of amendment to the Constitution of the United States is hereby repealed.

Section 2.   The transportation or importation into any State, Territory, or possession of the United States for delivery or use therein of intoxicating liquors, in violation of the laws thereof, is hereby prohibited.

Section 3.   This article shall be inoperative unless it shall have been ratified as an amendment to the Constitution by conventions in the several States, as provided in the Constitution, within seven years from the date of the submission hereof to the States by the Congress.

AMENDMENT XXII
[Ratified in 1951.]

Two-term limit for president

Section 1.   No person shall be elected to the office of the President more than twice, and no person who has held the office of President, or acted as President, for more than two years of a term to which some other person was elected President shall be elected to the office of the President more than once. But this Article shall not apply to any person holding the office of President when this Article was proposed by the Congress, and shall not prevent any person who may be holding the office of President, or acting as President, during the term within which this Article becomes operative from holding the office of President or acting as President during the remainder of such term.

Section 2.   This Article shall be inoperative unless it shall have been ratified as an amendment to the Constitution by the legislatures of three-fourths of the several States within seven years from the date of its submission to the States by the Congress.

AMENDMENT XXIII
[Ratified in 1961.]

Right to vote for president in District of Columbia

Section 1.   The District constituting the seat of Government of the United States shall appoint in such manner as the Congress may direct:
A number of electors of President and Vice President equal to the whole number of Senators and Representatives in Congress to which the District would be entitled

if it were a State, but in no event more than the least populous State; they shall be in addition to those appointed by the States, but they shall be considered, for the purposes of the election of President and Vice President, to be electors appointed by a State; and they shall meet in the District and perform such duties as provided by the twelfth article of amendment.

Section 2.　The Congress shall have power to enforce this article by appropriate legislation.

AMENDMENT XXIV
[Ratified in 1964.]

Prohibits poll taxes in federal elections

Section 1.　The right of citizens of the United States to vote in any primary or other election for President or Vice President, for electors for President or Vice President, or for Senator or Representative in Congress, shall not be denied or abridged by the United States or any State by reason of failure to pay any poll tax or other tax.

Section 2.　The Congress shall have power to enforce this article by appropriate legislation.

AMENDMENT XXV
[Ratified in 1967.]

Presidential disability and succession

Section 1.　In case of the removal of the President from office or of his death or resignation, the Vice President shall become President.

Section 2.　Whenever there is a vacancy in the office of the Vice President, the President shall nominate a Vice President who shall take office upon confirmation by a majority vote of both Houses of Congress.

Section 3.　Whenever the President transmits to the President pro tempore of the Senate and the Speaker of the House of Representatives his written declaration that he is unable to discharge the powers and duties of his office, and until he transmits to them a written declaration to the contrary, such powers and duties shall be discharged by the Vice President as Acting President.

Section 4.　Whenever the Vice President and a majority of either the principal officers of the executive departments or of such other body as Congress may by law provide, transmit to the President pro tempore of the Senate and the Speaker of the House of Representatives their written declaration that the President is unable to discharge the powers and duties of his office, the Vice President shall immediately assume the powers and duties of the office as Acting President.

Thereafter, when the President transmits to the President pro tempore of the Senate and the Speaker of the House of Representatives his written declaration that no inability exists, he shall resume the powers and duties of his office unless the Vice President and a majority of either the principal officers of the executive department or of such other body as Congress may by law provide, transmit within four days to the President pro tempore of the Senate and the Speaker of the House of Representatives their written declaration that the President is unable to discharge the powers and duties of his office. Thereupon Congress shall decide the issue, assembling within forty-eight hours for that purpose if not in session. If the Congress, within twenty-one days after receipt of the latter written declaration, or, if Congress is not in session, within twenty-one days after Congress is required to assemble, determines by two-thirds vote of both Houses that the President is unable to discharge the powers and duties of his office, the Vice President shall continue to discharge the same as Acting President; otherwise, the President shall resume the powers and duties of his office.

AMENDMENT XXVI
[*Ratified in 1971.*]

Voting age lowered to eighteen

Section 1.   The right of citizens of the United States, who are eighteen years of age or older, to vote shall not be denied or abridged by the United States or by any State on account of age.

Section 2.   The Congress shall have power to enforce this article by appropriate legislation.

AMENDMENT XXVII
[*Proposed in 1972; not ratified as of 1979.*]

Proposed Equal Rights Amendment

Section 1.   Equality of rights under the law shall not be denied or abridged by the United States or by any State on account of sex.

Section 2.   The Congress shall have power to enforce, by appropriate legislation, the provisions of this article.

Section 3.   This amendment shall take effect two years after date of ratification.

PRESIDENTS AND CONGRESSES, 1789–1980

				House		Senate	
Year	President and Vice-President	Party of President	Congress	Majority Party	Minority Party	Majority Party	Minority Party
1789–1797	**George Washington** John Adams	None	1st 2nd 3rd 4th	38 Admin 37 Fed 57 Dem-Rep 54 Fed	26 Opp 33 Dem-Rep 48 Fed 52 Dem-Rep	17 Admin 16 Fed 17 Fed 19 Fed	9 Opp 13 Dem-Rep 13 Dem-Rep 13 Dem-Rep
1797–1801	**John Adams** Thomas Jefferson	Federalist	5th 6th	58 Fed 64 Fed	48 Dem-Rep 42 Dem-Rep	20 Fed 19 Fed	12 Dem-Rep 13 Dem-Rep
1801–1809	**Thomas Jefferson** Aaron Burr (to 1805) George Clinton (to 1809)	Democratic-Republican	7th 8th 9th 10th	69 Dem-Rep 102 Dem-Rep 116 Dem-Rep 118 Dem-Rep	36 Fed 39 Fed 25 Fed 24 Fed	18 Dem-Rep 25 Dem-Rep 27 Dem-Rep 28 Dem-Rep	13 Fed 9 Fed 7 Fed 6 Fed
1809–1817	**James Madison** George Clinton (to 1813) Elbridge Gerry (to 1817)	Democratic-Republican	11th 12th 13th 14th	94 Dem-Rep 108 Dem-Rep 112 Dem-Rep 117 Dem-Rep	48 Fed 36 Fed 68 Fed 65 Fed	28 Dem-Rep 30 Dem-Rep 27 Dem-Rep 25 Dem-Rep	6 Fed 6 Fed 9 Fed 11 Fed
1817–1825	**James Monroe** Daniel D. Tompkins	Democratic-Republican	15th 16th 17th 18th	141 Dem-Rep 156 Dem-Rep 158 Dem-Rep 187 Dem-Rep	42 Fed 27 Fed 25 Fed 26 Fed	34 Dem-Rep 35 Dem-Rep 44 Dem-Rep 44 Dem-Rep	10 Fed 7 Fed 4 Fed 4 Fed
1825–1829	**John Quincy Adams** John C. Calhoun	National-Republican	19th 20th	105 Admin 119 Jack	97 Jack 94 Admin	26 Admin 28 Jack	20 Jack 20 Admin
1829–1837	**Andrew Jackson** John C. Calhoun (to 1833) Martin Van Buren (to 1837)	Democrat	21st 22nd 23rd 24th	139 Dem 141 Dem 147 Dem 145 Dem	74 Nat Rep 58 Nat Rep 53 AntiMas 98 Whig	26 Dem 25 Dem 20 Dem 27 Dem	22 Nat Rep 21 Nat Rep 20 Nat Rep 25 Whig
1837–1841	**Martin Van Buren** Richard M. Johnson	Democrat	25th 26th	108 Dem 124 Dem	107 Whig 118 Whig	30 Dem 28 Dem	18 Whig 22 Whig
1841	**William H. Harrison*** John Tyler	Whig					

*Died in office.   †Resigned from the presidency.

Notes

Only members of two major parties in Congress are shown; omitted are independents, members of minor parties, and vacancies.

Party balance as of beginning of Congress.

Congresses in which one or both houses are controlled by party other than that of the president are shown in color.

During administrations of George Washington and (in part) John Quincy Adams, Congress was not organized by formal parties; the split shown is between supporters and opponents of the administration.

Abbreviations

Admin = Administration supporters; **AntiMas** = Anti-Masonic; **Dem** = Democratic; **Dem-Rep** = Democratic-Republican; **Fed** = Federalist; **Jack** = Jacksonian Democrats; **Nat Rep** = National Republican; **Opp** = Opponents of administration; **Rep** = Republican; **Union** = Unionist; **Whig** = Whig.

Year	President and Vice-President	Party of President	Congress	House Majority Party	House Minority Party	Senate Majority Party	Senate Minority Party
1841–1845	**John Tyler** (VP vacant)	Whig	27th 28th	133 Whig 142 Dem	102 Dem 79 Whig	28 Whig 28 Whig	22 Dem 25 Dem
1845–1849	**James K. Polk** George M. Dallas	Democrat	29th 30th	143 Dem 115 Whig	77 Whig 108 Dem	31 Dem 36 Dem	25 Whig 21 Whig
1849–1850	**Zachary Taylor*** Millard Fillmore	Whig	31st	112 Dem	109 Whig	35 Dem	25 Whig
1850–1853	**Millard Fillmore** (VP vacant)	Whig	32nd	140 Dem	88 Whig	35 Dem	24 Whig
1853–1857	**Franklin Pierce** William R. King	Democrat	33rd 34th	159 Dem 108 Rep	71 Whig 83 Dem	38 Dem 40 Dem	22 Whig 15 Rep
1857–1861	**James Buchanan** John C. Breckinridge	Democrat	35th 36th	118 Dem 114 Rep	92 Rep 92 Dem	36 Dem 36 Dem	20 Rep 26 Rep
1861–1865	**Abraham Lincoln*** Hannibal Hamlin (to 1865) Andrew Johnson (1865)	Republican	37th 38th	105 Rep 102 Rep	43 Dem 75 Dem	31 Rep 36 Rep	10 Dem 9 Dem
1865–1869	**Andrew Johnson** (VP vacant)	Republican	39th 40th	149 Union 143 Rep	42 Dem 49 Dem	42 Union 42 Rep	10 Dem 11 Dem
1869–1877	**Ulysses S. Grant** Schuyler Colfax (to 1873) Henry Wilson (to 1877)	Republican	41st 42nd 43rd 44th	149 Rep 134 Rep 194 Rep 169 Rep	63 Dem 104 Dem 92 Dem 109 Dem	56 Rep 52 Rep 49 Rep 45 Rep	11 Dem 17 Dem 19 Dem 29 Dem
1877–1881	**Rutherford B. Hayes** William A. Wheeler	Republican	45th 46th	153 Dem 149 Dem	140 Rep 130 Rep	39 Rep 42 Dem	36 Dem 33 Rep
1881	**James A. Garfield*** Chester A. Arthur	Republican	47th	147 Rep	135 Dem	37 Rep	37 Dem
1881–1885	**Chester A. Arthur** (VP vacant)	Republican	48th	197 Dem	118 Rep	38 Rep	36 Dem
1885–1889	**Grover Cleveland** Thomas A. Hendricks	Democrat	49th 50th	183 Dem 169 Dem	140 Rep 152 Rep	43 Rep 39 Rep	34 Dem 37 Dem
1889–1893	**Benjamin Harrison** Levi P. Morton	Republican	51st 52nd	166 Rep 235 Dem	159 Dem 88 Rep	39 Rep 47 Rep	37 Dem 39 Dem
1893–1897	**Grover Cleveland** Adlai E. Stevenson	Democrat	53rd 54th	218 Dem 244 Rep	127 Rep 105 Dem	44 Dem 43 Rep	38 Rep 39 Dem
1897–1901	**William McKinley*** Garret A. Hobart (to 1901) Theodore Roosevelt (1901)	Republican	55th 56th	204 Rep 185 Rep	113 Dem 163 Dem	47 Rep 53 Rep	34 Dem 26 Dem
1901–1909	**Theodore Roosevelt** (VP vacant, 1901–1905) Charles W. Fairbanks (1905–1909)	Republican	57th 58th 59th 60th	197 Rep 208 Rep 250 Rep 222 Rep	151 Dem 178 Dem 136 Dem 164 Dem	55 Rep 57 Rep 57 Rep 61 Rep	31 Dem 33 Dem 33 Dem 31 Dem

Year	President and Vice-President	Party of President	Congress	House Majority Party	House Minority Party	Senate Majority Party	Senate Minority Party
1909–1913	**William Howard Taft** James S. Sherman	Republican	61st 62nd	219 Rep 228 Dem	172 Dem 161 Rep	61 Rep 51 Rep	32 Dem 41 Dem
1913–1921	**Woodrow Wilson** Thomas R. Marshall	Democrat	63rd 64th 65th 66th	291 Dem 230 Dem 216 Dem 240 Rep	127 Rep 196 Rep 210 Rep 190 Dem	51 Dem 56 Dem 53 Dem 49 Rep	44 Rep 40 Rep 42 Rep 47 Dem
1921–1923	**Warren G. Harding*** Calvin Coolidge	Republican	67th	301 Rep	131 Dem	59 Rep	37 Dem
1923–1929	**Calvin Coolidge** (VP vacant, 1923–1925) Charles G. Dawes (1925–1929)	Republican	68th 69th 70th	225 Rep 247 Rep 237 Rep	205 Dem 183 Dem 195 Dem	51 Rep 56 Rep 49 Rep	43 Dem 39 Dem 46 Dem
1929–1933	**Herbert Hoover** Charles Curtis	Republican	71st 72nd	267 Rep 220 Dem	167 Dem 214 Rep	56 Rep 48 Rep	39 Dem 47 Dem
1933–1945	**Franklin D. Roosevelt*** John N. Garner (1933–1941) Henry A. Wallace (1941–1945) Harry S. Truman (1945)	Democrat	73rd 74th 75th 76th 77th 78th	310 Dem 319 Dem 331 Dem 261 Dem 268 Dem 218 Dem	117 Rep 103 Rep 89 Rep 164 Rep 162 Rep 208 Rep	60 Dem 69 Dem 76 Dem 69 Dem 66 Dem 58 Dem	35 Rep 25 Rep 16 Rep 23 Rep 28 Rep 37 Rep
1945–1953	**Harry S. Truman** (VP vacant, 1945–1949) Alben W. Barkley	Democrat	79th 80th 81st 82nd	242 Dem 245 Rep 263 Dem 234 Dem	190 Rep 188 Dem 171 Rep 199 Rep	56 Dem 51 Rep 54 Dem 49 Dem	38 Rep 45 Dem 42 Rep 47 Rep
1953–1961	**Dwight D. Eisenhower** Richard M. Nixon	Republican	83rd 84th 85th 86th	221 Rep 232 Dem 233 Dem 283 Dem	211 Dem 203 Rep 200 Rep 153 Rep	48 Rep 48 Dem 49 Dem 64 Dem	47 Dem 47 Rep 47 Rep 34 Rep
1961–1963	**John F. Kennedy*** Lyndon B. Johnson	Democrat	87th	263 Dem	174 Rep	65 Dem	35 Rep
1963–1969	**Lyndon B. Johnson** (VP vacant, 1963–1965) Hubert H. Humphrey (1965–1969)	Democrat	88th 89th 90th	258 Dem 295 Dem 247 Dem	177 Rep 140 Rep 187 Rep	67 Dem 68 Dem 64 Dem	33 Rep 32 Rep 36 Rep
1969–1974	**Richard M. Nixon†** Spiro T. Agnew	Republican	91st 92nd	243 Dem 254 Dem	192 Rep 180 Rep	57 Dem 54 Dem	43 Rep 44 Rep
1974–1977	**Gerald R. Ford** Nelson A. Rockefeller	Republican	93rd 94th	239 Dem 291 Dem	192 Rep 144 Rep	56 Dem 60 Dem	42 Rep 37 Rep
1977–	**Jimmy Carter** Walter Mondale	Democrat	95th 96th	292 Dem 280 Dem	143 Rep 155 Rep	61 Dem 58 Dem	38 Rep 41 Rep

GLOSSARY

Acquittal   The formal determination by a court that the accused is not guilty of the offense as charged.

Activist   An individual who is extensively and vigorously involved in political activity, either within or outside the party system.

Administrative oversight   The attempt by Congress to ensure that the executive branch bureaucracy is doing what Congress told it to do and is doing it efficiently.

Affirmative action   The requirement, imposed by law or administrative regulation, that an organization (business firm, government agency, labor union, school, or college) take positive steps to increase the number or proportion of women, blacks, or other minorities in its membership.

Agenda   A list of specific items of business to be considered at a legislative session, conference, or meeting. *See also* Calendar

Amendment (constitutional)   Changes in, or additions to, a constitution. Proposed by a two-thirds vote of both houses of Congress or by a convention called by Congress at the request of two-thirds of the state legislatures. Ratified by approval of three-fourths of the state legislatures.

Amicus curiae   A legal term meaning "friend of the court." As amicus curiae, individuals or groups not parties to a lawsuit may file a brief (or written argument) with a court.

Appellate jurisdiction   Authority of a court to review decisions of a lower court. *See also* Jurisdiction

Apportionment   The determination of the number of congressional representatives each state shall elect. The Constitution requires that the apportionment be adjusted every ten years based upon the national census.

Appropriation   A legislative grant of money to finance a government program. *See also* Authorization

Australian ballot   A secret ballot, first used in the United States in 1888, which is prepared, distributed, and tabulated by government officials. Oral voting or voting on party-supplied ballots, often of different colors, was employed before the Australian ballot, thus allowing errors or fraud.

Authorization   Legislative permission to begin or continue a government program. An authorization bill may grant permission to spend a certain sum of money, but that money does not ordinarily become available unless it is also appropriated. *See also* Appropriation

Bicameral legislature   A law-making body made up of two chambers or parts. The United States Congress, composed of a House of Representatives and Senate, is a bicameral legislature.

Bill of attainder   A law that declares a person, without a trial, to be guilty of a crime. The state legislatures and Congress are forbidden to pass such acts by Article I, Sections 9 and 10, of the Constitution.

Bill of Rights   The first ten amendments to the United States Constitution. Contains a list of individual rights and liberties, such as freedom of speech, religion, and the press.

Block grants   Grants of money from the federal government to states for programs in certain general areas rather than for specific kinds of programs. *See also* Grant-in-aid

Boycott   An organized refusal to deal with a person, organization, or nation. Designed to bring about policy changes by exerting economic or social pressures. The term originated from the ostracizing of a land agent, Captain Boycott, by his neighbors during the Land League troubles in Ireland in 1880.

Bureaucracy   A large, complex organization composed of appointed officials. The departments and agencies of the United States government make up its bureaucracy.

Cabinet An advisory group selected by the president to aid him in making decisions. Traditionally, members include the vice-president and the heads of the major departments.

Calendar A legislative schedule that contains the names of all bills to be considered before committees or in either legislative chamber. When a House committee reports out a bill, it is placed on one of five calendars: *Consent* (noncontroversial bills), *Discharge* (discharge petitions), *House* (nonfiscal public bills), *Private* (private bills), or *Union* (revenue and appropriations bills). In the Senate all bills go on a single calendar; nonlegislative matters, however, are placed on the *Executive* calendar.

Calendar Wednesday A procedure of the House of Representatives whereby Wednesdays may be used to call the roll of the standing committees for the purpose of bringing up any of their bills for consideration from the House or Union Calendars.

Capitalism An economic system based on private ownership of the means of production and on a market economy. *See also* Laissez-faire

Caucus (legislative) A meeting of all the members of one party in a particular house of Congress for the purpose of selecting party leaders and deciding on legislative business. The Democrats use the term "caucus"; the Republicans use the term "conference." *See also* Caucus (nominating)

Caucus (nominating) A closed meeting of party leaders to select party candidates. The term "to caucus" is also used to describe any private meeting of politicians seeking to reach agreement on a course of political action. The term was originally an Indian word meaning "Counsellor." *See also* Caucus (legislative)

Censorship Broadly, any government restrictions on speech or writing. More precisely, government restrictions on expression before they are disseminated. Except in time of war or national emergency, prior restraint upon freedom of speech or of the press is ordinarily forbidden.

Certiorari, writ of An order issued by a higher court to a lower court to send up the record of a case for review. Most cases reach the Supreme Court through the writ of certiorari, issued when at least four of the nine justices feel that the case should be reviewed. *Certiorari* is a Latin term that means "made more certain."

Civil case A court case involving a dispute between private persons or between the government and individuals over noncriminal matters. *See also* Criminal case

Civil liberties The freedoms of speech, press, religion, and petition together with freedom from arbitrary arrest or prosecution.

Civil rights The rights of citizens to vote, to receive equal treatment before the law, and to share equally with other citizens the benefits of public facilities (such as schools).

Civil service Those persons employed by government (excluding the military) who are appointed or promoted under the merit system as distinguished from those appointed for political reasons.

Class-action suits A case brought into court by a person on behalf, not only of himself, but of all other persons in the country under similar circumstances. For example, in *Brown* v. *Board of Education of Topeka, Kansas,* the Court decided that not only Linda Brown but all others similarly situated had the right to attend an unsegregated school.

Clear and present danger rule (*Schenck* v. *United States*) A test formulated by Justice Oliver Wendell Holmes in *Schenck* v. *United States* to measure the permissible bounds of free speech: "The question in every case is whether the words are used in circumstances and are of such a nature as to create a clear and present danger that they will bring about substantive evils that Congress has a right to prevent."

Clientele agency A federal agency having a clearly defined constituency that maintains a close relationship with the agency. Example: Veterans' Administration.

Client politics The politics of policy-making in which some small group receives the benefits of the policy and the public at large bears the costs. Because those who benefit find it easier to organize, they will strongly influence the making of policy.

Closed primary The selection of a party's candidates

in an election limited to registered party members. Prevents members of other parties from "crossing over" to influence the nomination of an opposing party's candidate. *See also* Open primary; Primary election

Closed rule   An order, from the House Rules Committee, that sets a time limit on debate and forbids a particular bill from being amended on the legislative floor. *See also* Open rule; Rule

Closed shop   A workplace that hires only union members. Outlawed by the Taft-Hartley Act of 1947. *See also* Union shop

Cloture   A parliamentary technique (Rule 22 in the Senate) used by a legislative body to end or limit debate. Designed to prevent "talking a bill to death" by filibuster. *See also* Filibuster

Coalition   A combination of two or more factions or parties for the purpose of achieving some political goal. An example is the coalition sometimes formed in Congress between southern Democrats and conservative Republicans.

Coattail effect   The tendency of lesser-known or weaker candidates to profit in an election by the presence on the ticket of a more popular candidate. Derives from a speech by President Lincoln in which he accused certain unpopular candidates of hiding under the coattails of a popular politician in their party.

Commerce clause   A clause in Article I of the Constitution that grants to Congress the authority to regulate commerce with foreign nations and among the states.

Committee of the Whole   The members of the House of Representatives organized into a committee for the consideration of bills and other matters. Most House business is transacted in the Committee of the Whole so that the formal requirements of its regular sessions, such as having a quorum of one-half the membership, can be avoided.

Committee on Committees   Party committees in Congress that determine assignments to standing committees.

Common law   Judge-made law that originated in England from decisions shaped by prevailing custom and precedents.

Concurrent powers   Authority shared by both the state and national governments. Examples include the power to tax, to maintain courts, and to charter banks.

See also Delegated powers; Implied powers

Concurrent resolution   An expression of congressional opinion without the force of law that requires the approval of both the House and Senate but not of the president. Often used to set the time of final adjournment. *See also* Joint resolution; Resolution

Concurring opinion   A written opinion of one or more judges that supports the conclusions of a majority of the court but offers different reasons for reaching those conclusions. *See also* Dissenting opinion

Confederation   A political system in which states or regional governments retain ultimate authority except for those powers they expressly delegate to a central government. The United States was a confederation from 1776 to 1787 under the Articles of Confederation. *See also* Unitary state; Federalism

Conference committee   A special joint committee of the House and Senate that reconciles differences when a bill passes the two houses of Congress in different forms.

Conflict of interest   A situation in which an official's public actions are or may be affected by his or her private interests.

Congressional Record   The daily printed account of proceedings, debates, and statements in both the House and Senate. Members may edit and revise remarks made on the floor and have additional remarks printed in an appendix.

Consent Calendar   The legislative schedule for the consideration of noncontroversial items in the House of Representatives.

Constituent   A resident of a legislator's district. The district itself is referred to as the legislator's constituency.

Constitution   The set of fundamental laws and principles that prescribe the nature, functions, offices, and limits of a government. A constitution may be written (as in the United States) or unwritten (as in Great Britain).

Constitutional court   A federal court established under the provisions of Article III of the Constitution, as distinguished from a "legislative court" created by Congress. The major constitutional courts are the district courts, courts of appeal, and the Supreme Court. *See also* Legislative court

Containment policy   A policy adopted in 1947 by

the Truman administration to build "situations of strength" around the globe in order to contain Soviet power.

Cooperative federalism Arrangements permitting local, state, and national governments to share the responsibility for providing services to the citizens. Examples: grant-in-aid programs and interstate highway systems. *See also* Grant-in-aid

Criminal case A court case involving an alleged violation of criminal laws; that is, an offense against the state. There are three categories of criminal cases: felonies, misdemeanors, and petty offenses. *See also* Civil case

Critical election *See* Realigning election

De facto segregation Racial segregation in schools that occurs, not because of laws or administrative decisions, but as a result of patterns of residential settlement. To the extent blacks and whites live in separate neighborhoods, neighborhood schools will often be segregated "de facto." *See also* De jure segregation

De jure segregation Racial segregation that occurs because of laws or administrative decisions by public agencies. When state laws, for example, required blacks and whites to attend separate schools or sit in separate sections of a bus, "de jure" segregation resulted. It may also occur because of administrative decisions about the site of a new school building or the residential boundaries for neighborhood schools that make it impossible for blacks and whites to attend the same school. *See also* De facto segregation

Delegated powers Powers expressly granted to the national government by the Constitution. These powers, found in Article I, Section 8, include the authority to provide for the common defense, to coin money, and to regulate commerce.

Depression A serious economic slump characterized by very high unemployment.

Direct primary *See* Primary election

Discharge Calendar The legislative schedule for bills brought out of committee by discharge petitions.

Discharge petition A device by which any member of the House, after a committee has had a bill for thirty days, may petition to have it brought to the floor. If a majority of the members agree, the bill is discharged from the Committee. Designed to prevent a committee from killing a bill by holding it for too long. *See also* Discharge Calendar

Dissenting opinion A written opinion of one or more judges that disagrees with the decision reached by a majority of the Court. *See also* Concurring opinion

District court The federal court of "original jurisdiction," where most federal cases begin. It is the only federal court where trials are held, juries are used, and witnesses are called; there are 94 district courts in the United States and its territories.

Division vote A method of voting used in a legislative body in which members voting for or against the motion alternately rise and are counted by the presiding officer. Under this procedure a total vote count is secured, but it is difficult to know who voted for or against a measure. Often referred to as a "standing vote."

Double jeopardy The guarantee in the Fifth Amendment to the Constitution that one may not be tried twice for the same crime. For example, an individual declared "not guilty" of murdering a neighbor cannot be tried again for that murder. The person is not, however, exempt from being tried for the murder of another individual.

Due process of law Protection against arbitrary deprivation of life, liberty, or property as guaranteed in the Fifth and Fourteenth Amendments.

Elastic clause *See* Necessary and proper clause

Electoral College A group of persons called "electors," selected by the voters in each state, that officially elects the president and vice-president. The number of electors in each state is equal to its number of representatives in both houses of Congress.

Elite Persons who possess a disproportionate share of some valued resource (money, power, beauty, intelligence, strength), *or* who exercise disproportionate influence on the making of public policy, or both.

Eminent domain The constitutional power to take private property, provided that it is taken for a public purpose and that just compensation is awarded.

Entrepreneurial politics The politics of policy-making in which some small group bears the costs of a policy that allegedly will benefit everyone. For the policy to be adopted, a "policy entrepreneur" must arise who will find ways of pulling together a legislative majority on behalf of unorganized interests over the objections of organized ones.

Enumerated powers *See* Delegated powers

Equal time provision A regulation that requires that all candidates for a public office be given equal access to the use of television and radio. Thus, if a radio or television station provides time for one candidate or party, it must offer equal time to the opposition candidates or parties.

Establishment clause First Amendment clause that forbids the passage of any law "respecting an establishment of religion."

Executive agreement An international agreement made between the president and foreign nations that, unlike a treaty, does not require Senate consent (though it is usually made pursuant to some congressional authorization).

Executive Calendar The Senate schedule for all non-legislative matters, such as treaties and appointments.

Executive privilege The claimed right of executive officials to refuse to appear before, or to withhold information from, the legislature or courts on the grounds that the information is confidential and would damage the national interest. For example, President Nixon refused, unsuccessfully, to surrender his subpoenaed White House tapes by claiming executive privilege.

Ex post facto law A law that makes criminal an act that was legal when it was committed, or that increases the penalty for a crime after it has been committed, or that changes the rules of evidence to make conviction easier; a retroactive criminal law. A Latin term meaning "after the fact."

Extradition Provision of Article IV of the Constitution that an individual charged in any state with treason, felony, or other crimes, who has fled from justice and is found in another state, shall be returned to the state having jurisdiction over the crime.

Fairness doctrine A rule that requires broadcasters to present both sides of a controversial public issue and to give a person who is attacked free time in which to reply.

Favorite son A presidential nominee whose support is exclusively or largely from his home state's delegation. Usually a favorite son is not a serious candidate and his nomination is merely a means of honoring him or of delaying commitment of the state delegation's vote.

Federalism (or federation) A political system in which ultimate authority is shared between a central government and state or regional governments. *See also* Confederation; Unitary state

Federalist Papers A series of eighty-five essays written by Alexander Hamilton, James Madison, and John Jay (all using the name "Publius"), which was published in New York newspapers in 1787 to convince New Yorkers to adopt the newly proposed Constitution.

Fee-shifting When the losing party pays the legal costs of the winning party in a court case.

Filibuster Attempting to defeat a bill in the Senate by talking indefinitely, thus preventing the Senate from doing any other work. From the Spanish *filibustero,* which means a "freebooter," a military adventurer.

Fiscal policy Efforts to manage the economy by altering the level of government spending and taxation. Ordinarily, the government will endeavor to run a surplus (take in more by taxation than it spends) when there is inflation and to run a deficit (spend more than it takes in by taxes) during a recession. *See also* Monetary policy

Franking privilege A policy that enables members of Congress to send material through the mail free of charge by substituting their facsimile signature (frank) for postage. From the Latin *francus,* meaning "free."

Free rider An individual who benefits from the success of an organization or project without having helped to bring about that success. For example, a free rider benefits from, but does not participate in, an ecology group's clear-air efforts.

Full faith and credit Provision of Article IV, Section 1, of the Constitution, that requires states to honor the civil rulings of other states: "Full faith and credit shall be given in each state to the public acts, records, and judicial proceedings of every other state."

Gag rule A legislative rule that limits the time available for debate or consideration of a measure.

General election   An election to fill public offices. *See also* Primary election

Gerrymander   The drawing of legislative district boundaries in such a way as to give special advantage to one party or special-interest group. The term arose when a political artist in 1812 drew a picture of a sprawling Massachusetts district that resembled a salamander. An editor changed the title to "Gerrymander" because the governor at that time was Elbridge Gerry.

Grandfather clause   Originally, a legal provision granting the franchise to persons otherwise ineligible to vote whose ancestors ("grandfathers") had voted prior to the passage of the Fifteenth Amendment. The clause was intended to keep blacks from voting. Refers today to any legal provision protecting persons having some right or benefit from changes in that right or benefit.

Grant-in-aid   Funds made available by Congress to state and local governments for expenditure in accordance with prescribed standards and conditions. Major functions financed through grants-in-aid include highways, airports, education, welfare, and health. *See also* Block grants

Gross national product (GNP)   The total value of all the goods and services produced by a nation during a specified period. The GNP is the most common measure of economic activity and growth.

Habeas corpus   A court order directing a police officer, sheriff, or warden who has a person in custody to bring the prisoner before a judge and show sufficient cause for his detention. Designed to prevent illegal arrests and unlawful imprisonment. A Latin term meaning "you shall have the body."

Hearing   A public or private session of a legislative body in which witnesses present testimony on matters under consideration by the committee. The objective is to gather information that will help determine whether new legislation should be passed or to build political support for a policy already preferred by the committee.

House Calendar   The legislative schedule in the House for the consideration of nonfiscal public bills.

Ideology   A comprehensive set of political, economic, and social views or ideas, particularly concerned with the form and role of government. Thus, we speak of a "liberal," "conservative," or "Marxist" ideology.

Impeach   A formal accusation against a public official by the lower house of a legislative body. Impeachment is merely an accusation and not a conviction. Only one president, Andrew Johnson in 1868, was ever impeached. He was not, however, convicted, for the Senate failed by one vote to obtain the necessary two-thirds vote required for conviction.

Implied powers   Authority possessed by the national government by inference from those powers expressly delegated to it in the Constitution. For example, the national government's power to draft persons into the armed forces is deduced from its delegated power to raise armies and navies. Based on the national government's constitutional authority to do all things "necessary and proper" to carry out its delegated powers. *See also* Concurrent, Delegated, and Reserved powers

Impoundment   A refusal by the president to spend money appropriated by Congress, usually because he opposes the program being financed.

Incumbent   The person currently in office.

Independent regulatory commission   An agency, partially independent of the executive branch, designed to regulate some important aspect of the economy. Examples include the Federal Communications Commission, the Interstate Commerce Commission, and the Federal Reserve Board.

Indiana ballot   *See* Party-column ballot

Inflation   A time of generally rising prices for goods and services.

In forma pauperis   A procedure whereby an indigent can file and be heard in court as a pauper, free of charge.

Initiative   An electoral procedure whereby citizens can propose legislation or constitutional amendments and refer the decision to popular vote by obtaining the required number of signatures on a petition.

Injunction   A court order requiring some specified action or preventing some anticipated action.

Interest group   An organization of persons that seeks to influence the making of public policy.

Interest group politics   The politics of policy-making in which one small group bears the costs of the policy and another small group receives the benefits. Each group has an incentive to organize and press its interests.

Interstate compact   An agreement between two or more states for the solution of common problems. According to Article I, Section 10, of the Constitution, such compacts are forbidden without the consent of Congress. Compacts cover such things as flood control and the management of ports.

Interstate rendition   *See* Extradition

Item veto   The power (exercised by governors in all but a few states) to veto sections or items of an appropriation bill while signing the remainder of the bill into law. The president does not have an item veto. *See also* Veto; Pocket veto

Jawboning   Efforts by the president to persuade businesses and labor unions to avoid or minimize increases in prices and wages.

Jim Crow laws   Laws or governmental practices designed to segregate blacks or otherwise keep them in a subordinate or politically powerless position.

Joint committee   A legislative committee composed of members of both houses.

Joint resolution   A formal expression of congressional opinion, in the form of a bill, that must be approved by both houses of Congress and by the president. Joint resolutions proposing a constitutional amendment need not be signed by the president. *See also* Concurrent resolution; Resolution

Judicial activism   The tendency of courts, or of individual judges, to enlarge the scope of their authority or to decide cases on the basis of their beliefs as to what public policy ought to be. *See also* Judicial self-restraint

Judicial review   The power of the courts to declare acts of the legislature and of the executive to be unconstitutional and hence null and void.

Judicial self-restraint   The tendency of judges to decide cases in such a way as to defer to the enactments of the legislature except where that enactment plainly contradicts the Constitution or is otherwise patently unreasonable. *See also* Judicial activism

Jurisdiction   Authority vested in a court to hear and decide certain types of cases. The term literally means "to say the law."

Laissez-faire   An economic doctrine emphasizing little or no government intervention in the economy; a "hands off" policy, based on the assumption that if everyone competes in pursuit of his or her own self-interest, all will benefit. From a French phrase meaning "let do" or "let alone."

Lame duck   A person, legislature, or administration that has been defeated in an election but still holds office for a period of time. For example, after Jimmy Carter defeated Gerald Ford, Ford was a lame duck president from November until January when Carter was inaugurated.

Legislative court   A court, not mentioned in the Constitution, set up by Congress for some specialized purpose. Legislative courts include the Court of Military Appeals and the Tax Court. *See also* Constitutional court

Legitimacy   The acceptance by citizens of a political system or governmental order as proper, lawful, and entitled to obedience.

Libel   To defame or injure a person's reputation by a published writing; often punishable under criminal law.

Libertarianism   The political doctrine or ideology holding that personal liberty is the supreme value society ought to protect and that the powers of government should be kept to a minimum.

Lobbyist   A person, usually acting as an agent for a group, who seeks to bring about the passage or defeat of legislative bills, to influence their contents, or to influence administrative actions. The term originates from the practice of persons meeting legislators in the lobbies of the Capitol to express their views or to influence officeholders.

Logrolling   Trading votes on different bills; for example, a rural congressman supports a mass-transit bill and in return gets a vote for a farm bill from an urban representative. The term originates from the practice of backwoodsmen who would join together to roll large timber logs to an area for burning. "You help me roll my logs, and I'll help you roll yours."

Machine   A hierarchically organized, centrally led state or local party organization that rewards members with material benefits (patronage).

Majoritarian politics The politics of policy-making in which all or most citizens receive some benefits and pay the costs.

Majority leader (floor leader) The chief spokesman and strategist of the majority party in a legislative body. *See also* Minority leader

Mandamus, writ of A court order issued to an individual, corporation, or public official to compel performance of a specified act of public, official, or ministerial duty. Thus, a contract must be fulfilled as agreed upon or a writ of mandamus will be issued to order its enforcement. Mandamus is a Latin term meaning "we command."

Markup Revising a legislative proposal in a committee.

Marxism Economic, political, and philosophical theories, developed by Karl Marx, which maintain that economic factors determine the structure of society and its politics and that society is controlled by those who own the means of production.

Massachusetts ballot *See* Office-bloc ballot

Merit system The selection or promotion of government employees on the basis of demonstrated merit rather than on the basis of political patronage. *See also* Civil service

Military-industrial complex An alleged alliance among key military, governmental, and corporate decision-makers involved in weapons procurement and military-support systems. The phrase was coined by Dwight D. Eisenhower.

Minority leader (floor leader) The chief spokesman and strategist of the minority party in a legislative body. *See also* Majority leader

Monetary policy Government policy that alters the money supply and the availability of credit in order to manage the economy. For example, the Federal Reserve Board uses "tight money" policies to fight inflation and "loose money" policies to fight recession.

Multimember district An area represented in the legislature by two or more persons. *See also* Single-member district

National supremacy *See* Supremacy clause

Necessary and proper clause (elastic clause) The final paragraph of Article I, Section 8, of the Constitution, which authorizes Congress to pass all laws "necessary and proper" to carry out the enumerated powers. Sometimes called the "elastic clause" because of the flexibility it provides to Congress.

North Atlantic Treaty Organization (NATO) The alliance of certain North American and European nations, established under the North Atlantic Treaty of 1949, to create a single unified defense force to safeguard the security of the North Atlantic area.

Office-bloc ballot A ballot listing all candidates for a given office under the name of that office; also called a "Massachusetts" ballot. *See also* Party-column ballot

Oligarchy A system of government in which political power is exercised by a small group of people, usually self-selected.

Open primary An election that permits voters to choose on election day the party primary in which they wish to vote. They may vote for candidates of only one party. *See also* Closed primary; Primary election

Open rule An order, from the House Rules Committee, that permits a bill to be amended on the legislative floor. *See also* Closed rule; Rule

Opinion (of the Court) A written statement giving the reasons for the decision in a particular case. When agreed to by a majority of the judges, it becomes the opinion of the Court. *See also* Concurring opinion; Dissenting opinion

Original jurisdiction The authority of a court to hear a case at its inception. Generally courts of original jurisdiction are trial courts. Courts of appellate jurisdiction hear cases on appeal from courts of original jurisdiction. *See also* Appellate jurisdiction

Pardon The granting of a release from the punishment or legal consequences of a crime by the proper executive authority before or after conviction. An "absolute pardon" restores the individual to the position enjoyed prior to conviction; a "conditional pardon" requires that certain obligations be met before the pardon becomes effective.

Parliamentary government A political system in which the legislature selects the executive head of the government (usually called the prime minister).

Participatory democracy A system of governance in which all or most citizens participate directly by either holding office or helping to make policy. The town meeting, in which citizens vote on major issues, is an example of participatory democracy.

Party boss A political leader who controls a strong party organization or machine. Richard Daley of Chicago was a well-known party boss.

Party-column ballot A ballot listing all candidates of a given party together under the name of that party; also called an "Indiana" ballot. *See also* Office-bloc ballot.

Party identification The feeling of individuals that a particular party is their party and deserves their support because it represents their point of view.

Party-line vote A vote in a legislature in which a majority of one party votes together against a majority of the other party or parties.

Party platform The principles, policies, and promises adopted by a party.

Patronage Material rewards—jobs, contracts, favors—given by political leaders and organizations to supporters and friends. *See also* Spoils system

Pentagon The headquarters of the Department of Defense, which includes the departments of the navy, army, and air force. The name comes from the shape of the five-sided building.

Plaintiff In civil law, the person who initiates the lawsuit or brings an action to court.

Pluralism A concept describing a society in which many interests vie through the political process to achieve their objective, as opposed to one in which one interest or group dominates the process to the exclusion of the interests of others.

Plurality A number of votes received by a candidate that is greater than that received by any other candidate, but less than a majority of the total vote.

Pocket veto A special veto power exercised when the legislative body adjourns, whereby bills not signed by the chief executive die after a specified time. The president puts the bill "in his pocket" and therefore kills it. *See also* Item veto; Veto

Political action committee (PAC) A committee set up by and representing a corporation, labor union, or special-interest group that raises and gives campaign contributions on behalf of the organization or group it represents.

Political culture A broadly shared set of ways of thinking about how politics and governing ought to be carried out.

Political efficacy The belief of citizens that they can affect the workings of government or that government takes citizen opinions into account in making its decisions.

Political power The ability to affect in accordance with one's intentions the selection of persons who will hold governmental office or the decisions made by them.

Political question A doctrine enunciated by the Supreme Court holding that certain constitutional issues cannot be decided by the courts, but are to be decided by the executive or legislative branches. Examples: presidential power to recognize foreign governments and congressional power to determine whether constitutional amendments have been ratified within a reasonable time.

Poll tax A tax that must be paid before one can vote; it is now unconstitutional.

Pork barrel Legislation that gives tangible benefits (such as highways, dams, and post offices) to a congressman's constituents. Origin: Congressmen, in their eagerness to get appropriations for local projects, behaved like hungry slaves in the South who rushed to the pork barrel to get their meager rations.

Preferred-position doctrine The judicial doctrine, not fully accepted, that the rights guaranteed by the First Amendment to the Constitution are more important than other parts of the Bill of Rights and thus occupy a "preferred position." *See also* Civil liberties

President pro tempore The temporary presiding officer of the Senate in the absence of the vice-president; usually the most senior senator. *Pro tempore* is a Latin term that means "for the time being," "temporarily."

Primary election (direct primary) An election prior to the general election in which voters select the candidates who will run on each party's ticket. Primaries are also used to choose convention delegates and party leaders, and may be open or closed. *See also* Closed primary; Open primary

Private bill A bill that deals only with specific private, personal, or local matters rather than with general legislative affairs. The main kinds include immigration and naturalization bills referring to particular individuals and personal claim bills. *See also* Public bill

Private Calendar   The legislative schedule for private bills to be considered by the House.

"Privileged" bills   Bills that go directly to the floor of the House after being in committee, rather than to the Rules Committee.

Progressive tax   Any tax in which the tax *rate* increases as the amount to be taxed increases. For example, those in high-income brackets might pay income taxes of 50 percent while those in lower brackets might pay only 15 percent. *See also* Regressive tax

Proletariat   The working class as distinguished from the propertied class, the bourgeoisie, or the nobility.

Proportional representation   A system of allocating seats in a legislature so that each political party is given a percentage of seats roughly equivalent to its percentage of the popular vote. For example, a minority party that receives 5 percent of the total vote will win 5 percent of the legislative seats. Not used in American elections for national offices.

Public bill   A legislative bill that deals with matters of general concern. A bill involving defense expenditures is a public bill; a bill pertaining to an individual becoming a naturalized citizen is not. *See also* Private bill

Quorum   The minimum number of members of a legislative chamber who must be present in order to transact business. Fewer than a quorum may be present if no votes on legislation are to be taken. The Constitution specifies that "a majority of each house shall constitute a quorum to do business." (Article I, Sec. 5). This means 218 congressmen and 51 senators.

Ranking member   The member of a legislative committee with the greatest seniority on that committee of any member of the same political party. The ranking member of the majority party ordinarily becomes chairman of the committee; the most senior member of the minority party is often called the "ranking member."

Realigning election   An election in which a new and lasting coalition of voters is formed under the names of one or both of the major parties; also called a "critical election."

Referendum   An electoral device available in half the

states by which voters can approve or disapprove a state constitutional amendment or legislative act. The legislature "refers" its proposal to the electorate.

Regressive tax   Any tax in which the burden falls relatively more heavily upon low-income persons than upon more affluent ones. Opposite of progressive tax in which tax rates increase as ability to pay increases. Sales taxes on food or other necessities are usually regressive, since it is harder for the poor to pay the tax than the wealthy. *See also* Progressive tax

Representative democracy   A principle of governance in which leaders and representatives acquire political power by means of a competitive struggle for the people's vote.

Reserved powers   Powers not delegated to the national government nor prohibited to the states by the Constitution are reserved for the states under the Tenth Amendment to the Constitution. *See also* Delegated powers

Resolution   A formal expression of the opinion or will of one house of Congress, adopted by vote and in the form of a bill, but unlike a bill having no enforcement clause. *See also* Concurrent resolution; Joint resolution

Revenue sharing   A law providing that the federal government will automatically return to the states and localities some fixed amount or share of federal tax revenues.

Rider   A provision, unlikely to pass on its own merits, added to an important bill so that it will "ride" through the legislative process. A farm-price provision added to a defense bill is an example of a rider.

Roll-call vote (or record vote)   A vote taken in a legislative body in which each member votes yes or no, either by answering an oral roll call or by electronic voting.

Rule   The procedure, determined by the Rules Committee, by which a bill is considered on the house floor. For example, a rule might set a time limit on debate or forbid the introduction of amendments. *See also* Closed rule; Open rule

Sampling   A method by which the characteristics or responses of a population are estimated by choosing at random individuals from that population. A public opinion poll is based upon a sample of a local or national population.

Sampling error The difference between the results of two surveys or samples. For example, if one random sample showed that 60 percent of all Americans like cats and another random sample taken at the same time showed that 65 percent do, the sampling error is 5 percent. *See also* Sampling

Sedition Actions that incite rebellion or discontent against a duly established government. Espionage, sabotage, or attempts to overthrow the government constitute sedition.

Select committee A legislative committee established for a limited time period and for a special purpose. Examples include the House Assassinations Committee and the Select Committee on Aging.

Senatorial courtesy The tradition of referring the names of candidates for appointive office to the senators of the states in which they reside and withdrawing any nominee deemed objectionable by a senator of the president's party.

Seniority A tradition widely observed in Congress of assigning positions of authority, especially committee chairmanships, on the basis of length of service in a legislative chamber or on the committee.

Separate but equal doctrine The doctrine, established in *Plessy* v. *Ferguson* (1896), in which the Supreme Court ruled that a state could provide separate but equal facilities for blacks.

Separation of powers A principle of American government whereby constitutional authority is distributed among three branches of government—the legislative, the executive, and the judicial.

Single-member district An electoral district from which a single legislator is chosen, usually by a plurality vote. This system of representation is used in the United States Congress and in most (but not all) state legislatures. *See also* Multimember district

Split-ticket voting Voting for candidates of different parties for various offices in the same election. For example, voting for a Republican for senator and a Democrat for president. *See also* Straight-ticket voting

Spoils system The award of government jobs to political supporters and friends. The term derives from Senator William Marcy's 1832 statement, "To the victors belong the spoils." *See also* Patronage

Standing A legal concept referring to who is entitled to bring a lawsuit to court. For example, an individual must ordinarily show personal harm in order to acquire standing and be heard in court.

Standing committee A permanently established legislative committee that considers and is responsible for legislation within a certain subject area. Examples: the House Ways and Means Committee, the Appropriations Committee, the Judiciary Committee.

Stare decisis The practice of basing judicial decisions on similar cases decided in the past. A Latin phrase meaning "let the decision stand."

States' rights Technically, those rights which, under the Tenth Amendment to the Constitution, are reserved to the states. More broadly, the term is used to connote opposition to increasing the national government's power at the expense of state power or authority.

Steering committee (or policy committee) A committee, composed of leaders of the same party in a legislative body, which coordinates the party's legislative program and attempts to secure its adoption.

Straight-ticket voting Voting for candidates who are all of the same party. For example, voting for a Republican senator, a Republican representative, and a Republican president. *See also* Split-ticket voting

Subpoena An order of a court, grand jury, or any authorized administrative agency or congressional committee that commands a witness to appear and give testimony. A Latin term meaning "under penalty."

Supremacy clause A clause in Article VI of the Constitution providing that the Constitution, laws passed by the national government under its constitutional powers, and all treaties are the supreme law of the land.

Symbolic speech The claim that an otherwise illegal act, such as burning a draft card, is constitutionally protected if the act is meant to convey a political message.

Teller vote A vote taken in a legislative body in which members are counted as they file past designated "tellers" who count first those who are in favor of an action and then those who are opposed.

Third party Any political party other than the two major parties; a minor party. Examples: Socialist party, Bull Moose party, Libertarian party.

Ticket-splitting   *See* Split-ticket voting

Unicameral legislature   A legislature with only one legislative body, as contrasted with a two-house legislature, such as that of the United States Congress. Nebraska has the only unicameral state legislature. *See also* Bicameral legislature

Union Calendar   (Calendar of the Whole House on the State of the Union) The legislative schedule in the House for all revenue and appropriations bills.

Union shop   An establishment that hires nonunion employees on the condition that they join the union within a given number of days. *See also* Closed shop

Unitary state   A centralized government in which local or state governments exercise only those powers given to them by the central government. It differs from a federal system (such as that of the United States) in which power is constitutionally divided between the central government and subdivisional governments.

Unit rule   A rule once applicable in Democratic national conventions providing that a state delegation may cast its total vote in a block for the presidential candidate preferred by a majority of that state's delegation.

Veto   The power of a president, governor, or mayor to kill a piece of legislation by refusing to sign the act. *Veto* is a Latin term meaning "I forbid."

Whip   An assistant to the majority or minority party leader whose duties include organizing the party members and inducing them to vote with the leadership. The term originates from the English fox-hunting term "whipper": the one who keeps the hounds from wandering by whipping them into their line of chase.

White primary   A primary election in which blacks and other nonwhites are systematically excluded from voting. In *Smith* v. *Allwright* (1944), the Supreme Court ruled that the white primary violated the Fifteenth Amendment.

REFERENCES

Chapter 1 The Study of American Government

1. Aristotle, *Politics*, iv, 4, 1290^b. More precisely, Aristotle's definition was this: Democracy is a "constitution in which the free-born and poor control the government—being at the same time a majority." He distinguished this from an oligarchy "in which the rich and well-born control the government—being at the same time a minority." Aristotle listed several varieties of democracy, depending on whether, for example, there was a property qualification for citizenship.
2. Joseph A. Schumpeter, *Capitalism, Socialism, and Democracy,* 3rd ed. (New York: Harper Torchbooks, 1950), p. 269. (This book was first published in 1942.)
3. Karl Marx and Friedrich Engels, "The Manifesto of the Communist Party," in Robert C. Tucker, ed., *The Marx-Engels Reader,* 2nd ed. (New York: W. W. Norton, 1978), pp. 469–500.
4. C. Wright Mills, *The Power Elite* (New York: Oxford University Press, 1956).
5. Richard Rovere, *The American Establishment* (New York: Harcourt, Brace, 1962).
6. H. H. Gerth and C. Wright Mills, trans. and ed., *From Max Weber: Essays in Sociology* (London: Routledge & Kegan Paul, 1948), pp. 232–235.
7. Among the authors whose interpretations of American politics are essentially pluralist is David B. Truman, *The Governmental Process,* 2nd ed. (New York: Alfred A. Knopf, 1971).
8. Alexis de Tocqueville, *Democracy in America,* ed. by Phillips Bradley (New York: Alfred A. Knopf, 1951), Vol. II, Book 2, Ch. 8, p. 122.
9. Derek C. Bok and John T. Dunlop, *Labor and the American Community* (New York: Simon & Schuster, 1970), p. 134.

Chapter 2 The Constitution

1. Quoted in Bernard Bailyn, *The Ideological Origins of the American Revolution* (Cambridge, Mass.: Harvard University Press, 1967), p. 61, fn. 6.
2. Quoted in Bailyn, *op. cit.,* pp. 135–137.
3. Quoted in Bailyn, *op. cit.,* p. 77.
4. Quoted in Bailyn, *op. cit.,* p. 160. Italics in the original.
5. *Federalist* No. 37.
6. Gordon S. Wood, *The Creation of the American Republic* (Chapel Hill: University of North Carolina Press, 1969). See also *Federalist* No. 49.
7. Letter of George Washington to Henry Lee, October 31, 1787. In John C. Fitzpatrick, ed., *Writings of George Washington* (Washington, D.C.: Government Printing Office, 1939), Vol. 29, p. 34.
8. Letters of Thomas Jefferson to James Madison (January 30, 1787) and to Colonel William S. Smith (November 13, 1787). In Bernard Mayo, ed., *Jefferson Himself* (Boston: Houghton Mifflin, 1942), p. 145.
9. *Federalist* No. 51.
10. *Federalist* No. 48.
11. *Federalist* No. 51.
12. *Ibid.*
13. *Ibid.*
14. Max Farrand, *The Framing of the Constitution of the United States* (New Haven: Yale University Press, 1913), p. 185.
15. See, for example, John Hope Franklin, *Racial Equality in America* (Chicago: University of Chicago Press, 1976), Ch. 1, esp. pp. 12–20.
16. Bailyn, *op. cit.,* pp. 235–246.
17. Max Farrand, *The Records of the Federal Convention of 1787,* 4 vols. (New Haven: Yale University Press, 1911–1937).
18. Theodore J. Lowi, *American Government:*
Incomplete Conquest (Hinsdale, Ill.: The Dryden Press, 1976), p. 97.
19. Article I, Section 2, para. 3.
20. Article I, Section 9, para. 1.
21. Article IV, Section 2, para. 3.
22. Charles A. Beard, *An Economic Interpretation of the Constitution* (New York: Macmillan, 1913).
23. Beard, *op. cit.,* pp. 26–51, 149–151, 324–325.
24. Forrest McDonald, *We the People* (Chicago: University of Chicago Press, 1958), Ch. 8.
25. Robert E. Brown, *Charles Beard and the Constitution* (Princeton, N.J.: Princeton University Press, 1956), pp. 20, 54, 102, 108, 200.
26. Quoted in Robert H. Horwitz, "Locke and the Preservation of Liberty: A Perennial Problem of Civic Education," in Horwitz, ed., *The Moral Foundations of the American Republic* (Charlottesville: University of Virginia Press, 1977), p. 129.
27. Quoted in Wood, *op. cit.,* p. 429.
28. *Ibid.,* p. 52.
29. *Federalist* No. 51.
30. J. R. Pole, *The Pursuit of Equality in American History* (Berkeley: University of California Press, 1978), p. 55.

Chapter 3 Federalism and the States

1. William H. Riker, "Federalism," in Fred I. Greenstein and Nelson W. Polsby, eds., *Handbook of Political Science* (Reading, Mass.: Addison-Wesley, 1975), Vol. V, p. 101.
2. David B. Truman, "Federalism and the Party System," in Arthur MacMahon, ed., *Federalism: Mature and Emergent* (Garden City, N.Y.: Doubleday, 1955), p. 123.

3. Harold J. Laski, "The Obsolescence of Federalism," *New Republic* (May 3, 1939), pp. 367–369.
4. Riker, *op. cit.,* p. 154.
5. Daniel J. Elazar, *American Federalism: A View from the States* (New York: Thomas Y. Crowell, 1966), p. 216.
6. Martin Diamond, "The Federalists' View of Federalism," in George C. S. Benson, ed., *Essays in Federalism* (Claremont, Calif.: Institute for Studies in Federalism, 1961), pp. 21–64, and Samuel H. Beer, "Federalism, National-ism, and Democracy in America," *American Political Science Review,* Vol. 72 (March 1978), pp. 9–21.
7. United States v. Sprague, 282 U.S. 716 (1931).
8. Article I, Section 8, paragraph 18.
9. McCulloch v. Maryland, 4 Wheat. 316 (1819).
10. Collector v. Day, 11 Wall. 113 (1870). This was in part overruled in Graves v. New York, 306 U.S. 466 (1939).
11. Laurence H. Tribe, "Intergovernmental Immunities in Litigation, Taxation, and Regulation," *Harvard Law Review,* Vol. 89 (1976), pp. 682–713.
12. Champion v. Ames, 188 U.S. 321 (1903).
13. Hoke v. United States, 227 U.S. 308 (1913).
14. Clark Distilling Co. v. W. Md. Ry., 242 U.S. 311 (1917).
15. Hipolite Egg Co. v. United States, 220 U.S. 45 (1911).
16. United States v. E. C. Knight Co., 156 U.S. 1 (1895).
17. Paul v. Virginia, 8 Wall. 168 (1869).
18. Veazie Bank v. Fenno, 8 Wall. 533 (1869).
19. Brown v. Maryland, 12 Wheat. 419 (1827).
20. Wickard v. Filburn, 317 U.S. 111 (1942); NLRB v. Jones & Laughlin Steel Corp., 301 U.S. 58 (1937).
21. Kirschbaum Co. v. Walling, 316 U.S. 517 (1942).
22. Goldfarb v. Virginia State Bar, 421 U.S. 773 (1975); Flood v. Kuhn, 407 U.S. 258 (1972).
23. United States v. California, 332 U.S. 19 (1947).
24. Morton Grodzins, *The American System* (Chicago: Rand McNally, 1966), pp. 49–50.
25. Morton Keller, *Affairs of State* (Cambridge, Mass.: Harvard University Press, 1977), pp. 310, 381–382.

26. Neal R. Pierce, "Partnership for City Aid," *Boston Globe,* March 30, 1978.
27. Samuel H. Beer, "The Modernization of American Federalism," *Publius,* Vol. 3 (Fall 1973), esp. pp. 74–79, and Beer, "Federalism, . . . ," *op. cit.,* pp. 18–19.
28. Paul R. Dommel, *The Politics of Revenue Sharing* (Bloomington: Indiana University Press, 1974).
29. Calculated from *Special Analyses: Budget of the U.S. Government, Fiscal Year 1979* (Washington, D.C.: Government Printing Office, 1978), p. 187.
30. Quoted in *National Journal,* September 18, 1976, p. 1321.
31. Congressional Budget Office, *Troubled Local Economies and the Distribution of Federal Dollars* (Washington, D.C.: Government Printing Office, 1977), pp. 5–10.
32. Quoted in *U.S. News and World Report,* December 5, 1977, p. 40.
33. Edward C. Banfield, "Making a New Federal Program: Model Cities, 1964–1968," in Allan P. Sindler, ed., *Policy and Politics in America* (Boston: Little, Brown, 1973), pp. 124–158.
34. Jerome T. Murphy, "The Education Bureaucracies Implement a Novel Policy: The Politics of Title I of ESEA, 1965–1972," in Sindler, *op. cit.,* pp. 160–198.
35. Judy Feder, "The Social Security Administration and Medicare: The Politics of Federal Hospital Insurance," unpublished Ph.D. dissertation, Harvard University, 1977.
36. Martha Derthick, *The Influence of Federal Grants: Public Assistance in Massachusetts* (Cambridge, Mass.: Harvard University Press, 1970), Ch. 8.
37. Helen Ingram, "Policy Implementation Through Bargaining: The Case of Federal Grants-in-Aid," *Public Policy,* Vol. 25 (Fall 1977), pp. 499–526.
38. Jeffrey L. Pressman and Aaron B. Wildavsky, *Implementation* (Berkeley: University of California Press, 1973).
39. Edward C. Banfield and James Q. Wilson, *City Politics* (Cambridge, Mass.: Harvard University Press, 1963), pp. 38–44, 56–58, 138–150, 187–203; James Q. Wilson and Edward C. Banfield, "Public-Regardingness as a Value Premise in Voting Behavior," *American Political Science Review,* Vol. 58 (December 1964), pp. 876–887; James Q. Wilson and Edward C. Banfield,

"Political Ethos Revisited," *American Political Science Review,* Vol. 65 (December 1971), pp. 1048–1062.
40. Sarah McCally Morehouse, "The Governor as Political Leader," in Herbert Jacob and Kenneth N. Vines, *Politics in the American States,* 3rd ed. (Boston: Little, Brown, 1976), p. 198, and recent news accounts.
41. Thomas R. Dye, *Politics in States and Communities,* 2nd ed. (Englewood Cliffs, N.J.: Prentice-Hall, 1973), p. 188.
42. *Ibid.,* p. 178.
43. *Ibid.,* pp. 180–181.
44. Joseph A. Schlesinger, "The Politics of the Executive," in Herbert Jacob and Kenneth N. Vines, *Politics in the American States,* 2nd ed., (Boston: Little, Brown, 1971), p. 232.
45. Samuel C. Patterson, "State Legis-latures," In Jacob and Vines, *Politics in the American States,* 3rd ed., p. 179.
46. Banfield and Wilson, *op. cit.,* pp. 63–68.
47. *Ibid.,* p. 80.
48. *Ibid.,* pp. 286–288; J. David Greenstone, *Labor in American Politics* (New York: Alfred A. Knopf, 1969), Ch. 4.
49. Morehouse, *op. cit.,* p. 202.
50. J. David Greenstone and Paul E. Peterson, "Reformers, Machines, and the War on Poverty," In James Q. Wilson, ed., *City Politics and Public Policy* (New York: John Wiley, 1968), pp. 267–292.
51. David R. Cameron and Richard I. Hofferbert, "The Impact of Federalism on Education Finance: A Comparative Analysis," *European Journal of Political Research,* Vol. 2 (1974), pp. 240, 245.
52. Robert Albritton, "Welfare Policy," in Jacob and Vines, *op. cit.,* 3rd ed., pp. 363–373.

Chapter 4 American Political Culture

1. Alexis de Tocqueville, *Democracy in America,* ed. by Phillips Bradley (New York: Alfred A. Knopf, 1951), Vol. I p. 288. (First published in 1835.)
2. *Ibid.,* Vol. I, pp. 319–320.
3. *Ibid.,* Vol. I, p. 319.
4. Donald J. Devine, *The Political Culture of the United States* (Boston: Little, Brown, 1972), p. 185.
5. Gunnar Myrdal, *An American Dilemma: The Negro Problem in Modern Democracy* (New York: Harper, 1944), Intro. and Ch. 1.

6. Frank R. Westie, "The American Dilemma: An Empirical Test," *American Sociological Review,* Vol. 30 (August 1965), pp. 536–537.

7. Eric L. McKitrick, "Party Politics and the Union and Confederate War Efforts," in William Nisbet Chambers and Walter Dean Burnham, eds., *The American Party Systems,* 2nd ed. (New York: Oxford University Press, 1975), pp. 117–121.

8. Gabriel Almond and Sidney Verba, *The Civic Culture* (Princeton, N.J.: Princeton University Press, 1963).

9. Thomas J. Anton, "Policy-Making and Political Culture in Sweden," *Scandinavian Political Studies,* Vol. 4 (1969), pp. 88–100; M. Donald Hancock, *Sweden: The Politics of Post-Industrial Change* (Hinsdale, Ill.: The Dryden Press, 1972); Sten Johansson, "Liberal-Democratic Theory and Political Processes," in Richard Scarse, ed., *Readings in the Swedish Class Structure* (New York: Pergamon Press, 1976); Steven J. Kelman, "Regulating Job Safety and Health: A Comparison of the U.S. Occupational Safety and Health Administration and the Swedish Worker Protection Board" (unpublished Ph.D. dissertation, Harvard University, 1978).

10. Lewis Austin, *Saints and Samurai: The Political Culture of American and Japanese Elites* (New Haven, Conn.: Yale University Press, 1975).

11. Richard Simeon and David J. Elkins, "Regional Political Cultures in Canada," *Canadian Journal of Political Science,* Vol. 7 (September 1974), pp. 397–437.

12. Seymour Martin Lipset, *The First New Nation* (New York: Basic Books, 1963), pp. 36–45.

13. Max Weber, *The Protestant Ethic and the Spirit of Capitalism,* trans. by Talcott Parsons (New York: Scribner's, 1930). (First published in 1904.)

14. Erik H. Erikson, *Childhood and Society* (New York: W. W. Norton, 1950), Ch. 8.

15. "Inner-directed" and "other-directed" are terms introduced in David Riesman, Nathan Glazer, and Reuell Denney, *The Lonely Crowd* (Garden City, N.Y.: Doubleday, 1953).

16. Arthur H. Miller, "Political Issues and Trust in Government: 1964–1970," *American Political Science Review,* Vol. 68 (September 1974), pp. 951–972. These data were updated through 1976 by John McAdams using surveys from the Survey Research Center of the University of Michigan.

17. Jack Citrin, "Comment: The Political Relevance of Trust in Government," *American Political Science Review,* Vol. 68 (September 1974), pp. 973–988.

18. Miller, *op. cit.;* James S. House and William M. Mason, "Political Alienation in America, 1958–1968," *American Sociological Review,* Vol. 40 (April 1975), pp. 123–147; James Q. Wilson, "The Riddle of the Middle Class," *The Public Interest* (Spring 1975), pp. 125–129.

19. Citrin, *op. cit.,* p. 975.

20. F. Christopher Arterton, "Watergate and Children's Attitudes Toward Political Authority Revisited," *Political Science Quarterly,* Vol. 90 (Fall 1975), pp. 477–496.

21. Philip E. Converse, "Change in the American Electorate," in Angus Campbell and Philip E. Converse, eds., *The Human Meaning of Social Change* (New York: Russell Sage Foundation, 1972), p. 328, and Richard W. Boyd, "Electoral Trends in Postwar Politics," in James D. Barber, ed., *Choosing the President* (Englewood Cliffs, N.J.: Prentice-Hall, 1974). The figures were updated through 1976 by John McAdams.

22. Survey Research Center, University of Michigan; Norman H. Nie, Sidney Verba, and John R. Petrocik, *The Changing American Voter* (Cambridge, Mass.: Harvard University Press, 1976), pp. 125–128.

23. James W. Prothro and Charles M. Grigg, "Fundamental Principles of Democracy: Bases of Agreement and Disagreement," *Journal of Politics,* Vol. 22 (Spring 1960), pp. 275–294.

24. Prothro and Grigg, *op. cit.;* Samuel A. Stouffer, *Communism, Conformity, and Civil Liberties* (Garden City, N. Y.: Doubleday, 1954); Herbert McClosky, "Consensus and Ideology in American Politics," *American Political Science Review,* Vol. 58 (June 1964), pp. 361–382.

25. David G. Lawrence, "Procedural Norms and Tolerance: A Reassessment," *American Political Science Review,* Vol. 70 (March 1976), p. 88; James D. Wright, *The Dissent of the Governed* (New York: Academic Press, 1976), p. 295.

26. Lawrence, *op. cit.,* p. 91. See also Robert W. Jackman, "Political Elites, Mass Publics, and Support for Democratic Principles," *Journal of Politics,* Vol. 34 (August 1972), p. 765. A contrasting view is Mary R. Jackman, "General and Applied Tolerance: Does Education Increase Commitment to Racial Integration?" *American Journal of Political Science,* Vol. 22 (May 1978), pp. 302–324.

Chapter 5 Public Opinion and Political Participation

1. M. Kent Jennings and Richard G. Niemi, "The Transmission of Political Values from Parent to Child," *American Political Science Review,* Vol. 62 (March 1968), p. 173.

2. Robert D. Hess and Judith V. Torney, *The Development of Political Attitudes in Children* (Chicago: Aldine, 1967), p. 90.

3. Several studies of child-parent agreement on party preference are summarized in David O. Sears, "Political Behavior," in Gardner Lindzey and Elliot Aronson, eds., *The Handbook of Social Psychology,* 2nd ed. (Reading, Mass.: Addison-Wesley, 1969), Vol. V, p. 376.

4. Norman H. Nie, Sidney Verba, and John R. Petrocik, *The Changing American Voter* (Cambridge, Mass.: Harvard University Press, 1976), Ch. 4.

5. Jennings and Niemi, *op. cit.*

6. Robert S. Erikson and Norman R. Luttbeg, *American Public Opinion: Its Origins, Content, and Impact* (New York: John Wiley, 1973), p. 197; and Seymour Martin Lipset, *Revolution and Counterrevolution,* rev. ed. (Garden City, N.Y.: Doubleday Anchor Books, 1970), pp. 338–342.

7. Erikson and Luttbeg, *op. cit.,* p. 194.

8. *Ibid.,* pp. 133–134.

9. *Ibid.,* pp. 135–136.

10. *Ibid.,* pp. 139–140; and Alexander M. Astin, *Four Critical Years: Effects of College on Beliefs, Attitudes, and Knowledge* (San Francisco: Jossey-Bass, 1978), pp. 36–38.

11. Astin, *op. cit.,* p. 38.

12. Erikson and Luttbeg, *op. cit.,* p. 138.

13. J. L. Spaeth and Andrew M. Greeley, *Recent Alumni and Higher Education* (New York: McGraw-Hill, 1970), pp. 100–110; and Erland Nelson, "Persistence of Attitudes of College Students Fourteen Years Later," *Psychological Monographs,* Vol. 68 (1954), pp. 1–13.

14. Kenneth A. Feldman and Theodore M. Newcomb, *The Impact of College on Students* (San Francisco: Jossey-Bass, 1969), Vol. 1, pp. 99–100, 312–320.

15. Everett Carll Ladd, Jr., and Seymour Martin Lipset, *The Divided Academy:*

Professors and Politics (New York: McGraw-Hill, 1975), pp. 26–27, 55–67, 184–190.

16. *Statistical Abstract of the United States, 1975,* p. 135.

17. David Butler and Donald Stokes, *Political Change in Great Britain* (New York: St. Martin's Press, 1969), pp. 70, 77.

18. Erikson and Luttbeg, *op. cit.,* p. 184.

19. V. O. Key, Jr., *Public Opinion and American Democracy* (New York: Alfred A. Knopf, 1961), pp. 122–138.

20. *Ibid.,* pp. 124, 126, 131.

21. Richard E. Dawson, *Public Opinion and Contemporary Disarray* (New York: Harper & Row, 1973), Ch. 4.

22. Erikson and Luttbeg, *op. cit.,* pp. 186–187; Dawson, *op. cit.,* pp. 116–124.

23. Norman H. Nie, Sidney Verba, and John R. Petrocik, *The Changing American Voter* (Cambridge, Mass.: Harvard University Press, 1976), pp. 253–256.

24. Michael J. Hindelang, *Public Opinion Regarding Crime, Criminal Justice, and Related Topics,* Analytic Report No. 1 of the National Criminal Justice Information and Statistics Service of the Law Enforcement Assistance Administration, U.S. Department of Justice (Washington, D.C., 1975), pp. 11, 13.

25. Everett Carll Ladd, Jr., *Transformations of the American Party System,* 2nd ed. (New York: W. W. Norton, 1978), pp. 147–150.

26. Nie, Verba, and Petrocik, *op. cit.,* pp. 247–250.

27. *Ibid.,* p. 218.

28. Ladd, *op. cit.,* p. 280.

29. Philip E. Converse, "The Nature of Belief Systems in Mass Publics," in David Apter, ed., *Ideology and Discontent* (New York: The Free Press of Glencoe, 1964), pp. 206–261.

30. Christopher H. Achen, "Mass Political Attitudes and the Survey Proposal," *American Political Science Review,* Vol. 69 (December 1975), pp. 1218–1231.

31. Nie, Verba, and Petrocik, *op. cit.,* pp. 115, 129, 142.

32. John L. Sullivan *et al.,* "Ideological Constraint in the Mass Public: A Methodological Critique and Some New Findings," *American Journal of Political Science,* Vol. 22 (May 1978), pp. 233–249, and George F. Bishop *et al.,* "Change in the Structure of American Political Attitudes: The Nagging

Question of Question Wording," *American Journal of Political Science,* Vol. 22 (May 1978), pp. 250–269.

33. Converse, *op. cit.*

34. Seymour Martin Lipset and Earl Rabb, *The Politics of Unreason* (New York: Harper & Row, 1970), Ch. 11; and James A. Stimson, "Belief Systems: Constraint, Complexity, and the 1972 Election," *American Journal of Political Science,* Vol. 19 (1975), pp. 393–417.

35. Stimson, *op. cit.* See also Allen H. Barton and R. Wayne Parsons, "Measuring Belief System Structure," *Public Opinion Quarterly,* Vol. 41 (Summer 1977), pp. 159–180.

36. Seymour Martin Lipset and David Riesman, *Education and Politics at Harvard* (New York: McGraw-Hill, 1975), Ch. 8; Ladd, *op. cit.,* p. 253.

37. Ladd, *op. cit.,* p. 284.

38. *Ibid.,* pp. 287, 289.

39. Nie, Verba, and Petrocik, *op. cit.,* pp. 262–263.

40. Tabulated from data in Barry Bruce-Briggs, *The New Class?* (New Brunswick, N.J.: Trans-Action Books, 1979), p. 221.

41. See the differing views of Irving Kristol and Daniel Bell in Bruce-Briggs, *ibid.*

42. Gabriel A. Almond and Sidney Verba, *The Civic Culture* (Princeton, N.J.: Princeton University Press, 1963), p. 171.

43. Lester W. Milbrath and M. L. Goel, *Political Participation,* 2nd ed. (Chicago: Rand McNally, 1977), pp. 98–102; and Raymond E. Wolfinger and Steven J. Rosenstone, "Who Votes?" paper delivered at the 1977 Annual Meeting of the American Political Science Association, Washington, D.C.

44. Milbrath and Goel, *op. cit.,* pp. 114, 116.

45. Sidney Verba and Norman H. Nie, *Participation in America* (New York: Harper & Row, 1972), pp. 151–157; and Milbrath and Goel, *op. cit.,* p. 120.

46. Verba and Nie, *op. cit.,* pp. 160–164.

47. Richard A. Brody, "The Puzzle of Political Participation in America," in Anthony King, ed., *The New American Political System* (Washington, D.C.: American Enterprise Institute, 1978), pp. 315–323; and Charles Lewis Taylor and Michael C. Hudson, *World Handbook of Political and Social Indicators,* 2nd ed. (New Haven, Conn.: Yale University Press, 1972), Table 3.1.

48. Verba and Nie, *op. cit.,* Ch. 18.

49. Angus Campbell, Philip E. Converse,

Warren E. Miller, and Donald E. Stokes, *The American Voter* (New York: John Wiley, 1960), Ch. 8.

50. V. O. Key, Jr., *The Responsible Electorate* (Cambridge, Mass.: Harvard University Press, 1966).

51. David RePass, "Issue Salience and Party Choice," *American Political Science Review,* Vol. 65 (June 1971), pp. 389–400.

52. Gerald M. Pomper, "From Confusion to Clarity: Issues and American Voters, 1956–1968," *American Political Science Review,* Vol. 66 (June 1972), pp. 415–428; and Arthur H. Miller *et al.,* "A Majority Party in Disarray: Policy Polarization in the 1972 Election," *American Political Science Review,* Vol. 70 (September 1976).

53. Erikson and Luttbeg, *op. cit.,* pp. 41–42.

54. Lloyd A. Free and Hadley Cantril, *The Political Beliefs of Americans* (New Brunswick, N.J.: Rutgers University Press, 1967), p. 72; Erikson and Luttbeg, *op. cit.,* p. 51; George H. Gallup, *The Gallup Poll: Public Opinion, 1935–1971* (New York: Random House, 1972), Vol. III, p. 2161; Seymour Martin Lipset and William Schneider, "The Bakke Case: How Would It Be Decided at the Bar of Public Opinion?" *Public Opinion,* Vol. I (March–April 1978), pp. 38–44; and Peter Skerry, "The Class Conflict Over Abortion," *The Public Interest* (Summer 1978), pp. 69–84.

Chapter 6   Political Parties

1. Leon D. Epstein, "Political Parties," in Fred I. Greenstein and Nelson W. Polsby, eds., *Handbook of Political Science* (Reading, Mass.: Addison-Wesley, 1975), Vol. IV, p. 230.

2. This account draws heavily on William Nisbet Chambers and Walter Dean Burnham, eds., *The American Party Systems: Stages of Political Development,* 2nd ed. (New York: Oxford University Press, 1975).

3. Quoted in Henry Adams, *History of the United States of America During the Administrations of Jefferson and Madison,* abridged edition ed. by Ernest Samuels (Chicago: University of Chicago Press, 1967), p. 147.

4. Morton Keller, *Affairs of State* (Cambridge, Mass.: Harvard University Press, 1977), p. 239.

5. Quoted in Keller, *op. cit.,* p. 256.

6. Martin Shefter, "Parties, Bureaucracy, and Political Change in the United States," in Louis Maisel and Joseph Cooper, eds., *The Development of Political Parties*, Sage Electoral Studies Yearbook, Vol. 4 (Beverly Hills, Calif.: Sage Publications, 1978).

7. James Q. Wilson, *The Amateur Democrat: Club Politics in Three Cities* (Chicago: University of Chicago Press, 1962).

8. Dwain Marvick and Charles R. Nixon, "Recruitment Contrasts in Rival Campaign Groups," in Dwaine Marvick, ed., *Political Decision-Makers* (New York: The Free Press, 1961), pp. 212–213; and David Nexon, "Asymmetry in the Political System," *American Political Science Review*, Vol. 65 (September 1971), 716–730.

9. Samuel J. Eldersveld, *Political Parties: A Behavioral Analysis* (Chicago: Rand McNally, 1964), pp. 278, 287.

10. Robert H. Salisbury, "The Urban Party Organization Member," *Public Opinion Quarterly*, Vol. 29 (Winter 1965–1966), pp. 550–564.

11. *Ibid.*, pp. 557, 559.

12. Eldersveld, *op. cit.;* and J. David Greenstone, *Labor in American Politics* (New York: Alfred A. Knopf, 1969), p. 187.

13. V. O. Key, Jr., *Southern Politics in State and Nation* (New York: Alfred A. Knopf, 1950), Ch. 14.

14. Chambers and Burnham, *op. cit.*, p. 6.

15. Williams v. Rhodes, 393 U.S. 23 (1968).

16. James Q. Wilson, *Political Organizations* (New York: Basic Books, 1973), Ch. 12; and Samuel Stouffer, *Communism, Conformity, and Civil Liberties* (Garden City, N.Y.: Doubleday, 1955).

17. Jeane Kirkpatrick, *The New Presidential Elite* (New York: Russell Sage Foundation and Twentieth Century Fund, 1976), pp. 297–315. Another study of the 1972 convention reaches somewhat different conclusions, but on the basis of a more primitive methodology and less detailed questions: Denis G. Sullivan *et al.*, *The Politics of Representation* (New York: St. Martin's Press, 1974).

18. Austin Ranney, *Participation in American Presidential Nominations, 1976* (Washington, D.C.: American Enterprise Institute, 1977), p. 20.

19. Austin Ranney, *Curing the Mischiefs of Faction: Party Reform in America* (Berkeley: University of California Press, 1975), pp. 128–130; and Ranney, "Turnout

and Representation in Presidential Primary Elections," *American Political Science Review*, Vol. 66 (March 1972), pp. 21–37.

20. Kirkpatrick, *op. cit.*, pp. 66–67; Ch. 4; and Sullivan, *op. cit.*, Ch. 5.

21. Kirkpatrick, *op. cit.*, Ch. 4.

22. Norman H. Nie, Sidney Verba, and John R. Petrocik, *The Changing American Voter* (Cambridge, Mass.: Harvard University Press, 1976), p. 203.

23. Barry Sussman, "Elites in America," *Washington Post*, September 26–30, 1976.

24. Nie *et al.*, *op. cit.*, p. 203.

Chapter 7 Elections and Campaigns

1. Richard Smolka, quoted in William J. Crotty, *Political Reform and the American Experiment* (New York: Thomas Y. Crowell, 1977), pp. 86–87.

2. Morton Keller, *Affairs of State* (Cambridge, Mass.: Harvard University Press, 1977), p. 523.

3. United States v. Reese, 92 U.S. 214 (1876); United States v. Cruikshank, 92 U.S. 556 (1876); and Ex parte Yarbrough, 110 U.S. 651 (1884).

4. Guinn and Beall v. United States, 238 U.S. 347 (1915).

5. Smith v. Allwright, 321 U.S. 649 (1944).

6. Schnell v. Davis, 336 U.S. 933 (1949).

7. Congressional Quarterly, *Congress and the Nation*, Vol. III: 1969–1972 (Washington, D.C.: Congressional Quarterly, Inc., 1973), p. 1006; and *Statistical Abstract of the United States, 1975*, p. 450.

8. *Historical Statistics of the United States: Colonial Times to 1970*, Part 2, pp. 1071–1072.

9. Walter Dean Burnham, "The Changing Shape of the American Political Universe," *American Political Science Review*, Vol. 59 (March 1965), p. 11; and William H. Flanigan and Nancy H. Zingale, *Political Behavior of the American Electorate*, 3rd ed. (Boston: Allyn and Bacon, 1975), p. 15.

10. Burnham, *op. cit.;* E. E. Schattschneider, *The Semisovereign People* (New York: Holt, Rinehart and Winston, 1960), Chs. 5, 6.

11. Keller, *op. cit.*, p. 523.

12. *Ibid.*, p. 524.

13. Philip E. Converse, "Change in the American Electorate," in Angus Campbell and Philip E. Converse, eds., *The Human Meaning of Social Change*

(New York: Russell Sage Foundation, 1972), pp. 263–338.

14. Gary Hart, in Ernest R. May and Janet Fraser, eds., *Campaign '72: The Managers Speak* (Cambridge, Mass.: Harvard University Press, 1973), p. 73.

15. Xandra Kayden, "The Political Campaign as an Organization," *Public Policy*, Vol. 21 (Spring 1973), pp. 263–290.

16. Thomas E. Patterson and Robert D. McClure, *The Unseeing Eye: The Myth of Television in National Politics* (New York: G. P. Putnam's Sons, 1976); and Xandra Kayden, *Campaign Organization* (Lexington, Mass.: D. C. Heath, 1978), Ch. 6.

17. *Wall Street Journal*, March 15, 1978.

18. Flanigan and Zingale, *op. cit.*, pp. 158–162.

19. John F. Becker and Eugene E. Heaton, Jr., "The Election of Senator Edward M. Brooke," *Public Opinion Quarterly*, Vol. 31 (Fall 1967), pp. 346–358.

20. Seymour Martin Lipset and Earl Rabb, "The Election and the National Mood," *Commentary* (January 1973), pp. 43–44.

21. Arthur H. Miller *et al.*, "A Majority Party in Disarray: Policy Polarization in the 1972 Election," *American Political Science Review*, Vol. 70 (September 1976), p. 757.

22. Daniel Katz and Samuel J. Eldersveld, "The Impact of Local Party Activity on the Electorate," *Public Opinion Quarterly* (Spring 1961), pp. 1–24; Phillips Cutright and Peter H. Rossi, "Grass Roots Politicians and the Vote," *American Sociological Review* (April 1958), pp. 171–179; and Edward C. Banfield and James Q. Wilson, *City Politics* (Cambridge, Mass.: Harvard University Press, 1963), pp. 227–229.

23. Flanigan and Zingale, *op. cit.*, p. 162.

24. Norman H. Nie, Sidney Verba, and John R. Petrocik, *The Changing American Voter* (Cambridge, Mass.: Harvard University Press, 1976).

25. Walter Dean Burnham, *Critical Elections and the Mainsprings of American Politics* (New York: W. W. Norton, 1970), p. 10.

26. James L. Sundquist, *Dynamics of the Party System* (Washington, D.C.: Brookings Institution, 1973), Ch. 7.

27. Kevin Phillips, *The Emerging Republican Majority* (New Rochelle, N. Y.: Arlington House, 1969).

28. Jerrold D. Rusk, "The Effect of the Australian Ballot Reform on Split-

Ticket Voting: 1876–1908," *American Political Science Review,* Vol. 64 (December 1970), pp. 1220–1238.

29. Robert Axelrod, "Where the Votes Come From: An Analysis of Electoral Coalitions, 1952–1968," *American Political Science Review,* Vol. 66 (March 1972), pp. 11–20; and Axelrod, "Communication," *American Political Science Review,* Vol. 68 (June 1974), 718–719.

30. Gerald M. Pomper, *Elections in America* (New York: Dodd, Mead, 1971), p. 178.

31. Benjamin Ginsberg, "Elections and Public Policy," *American Political Science Review,* Vol. 70 (March 1976), pp. 41–49.

32. Stanley Kelley, Jr., Richard E. Ayres, and William G. Bowen, "Registration and Voting: Putting First Things First," *American Political Science Review,* Vol. 61 (June 1967), pp. 359–379.

33. Dunn v. Blumstein, 405 U.S. 330 (1972).

34. Richard G. Smolka, *Election Day Registration: The Minnesota and Wisconsin Experience in 1976* (Washington, D.C.: American Enterprise Institute, 1977), p. 5.

35. *Ibid.,* p. 68.

36. Herbert Asher, *Presidential Elections and American Politics* (Homewood, Ill.: The Dorsey Press, 1976), p. 211.

37. Roland J. Cole, *Campaign Spending in Senate Elections* (A Report to the Campaign Study Group, School of Government, Harvard University, January 1975), p. 46.

38. Buckley v. Valeo, 424 U.S. 1 (1976).

39. Congressional Quarterly, *Dollar Politics* (Washington, D.C.: Congressional Quarterly, Inc., 1974), pp. 66–69.

40. Buckley v. Valeo, 424 U.S. 1 (1976).

41. Congressional Quarterly, *Dollar Politics, op. cit.,* pp. 49–54.

42. Crotty, *op. cit.,* p. 121.

43. Buckley v. Valeo, 424 U.S. 1 (1976).

44. Crotty, *op. cit.,* p. 114, reporting data from Common Cause.

Chapter 8   Interest Groups

1. L. Harmon Zeigler and Hendrik van Dalen, "Interest Groups in the States," in Herbert Jacob and Kenneth N. Vines, eds., *Politics in the American States,* 2nd ed. (Boston: Little, Brown, 1974), pp. 122–160; and Edward C. Banfield and James Q. Wilson, *City Politics* (Cambridge, Mass.: Harvard University Press, 1963), Chs. 18, 19.

2. *New York Times,* March 26, 1978.

3. Joseph LaPalombara, *Interest Groups in Italian Politics* (Princeton, N.J.: Princeton University Press, 1964).

4. David B. Truman, *The Governmental Process,* 2nd ed. (New York: Alfred A. Knopf, 1971), p. 59.

5. The use of injuctions in labor disputes was restricted by the Norris-La Guardia Act of 1932; the rights to collective bargaining and to the union shop were guaranteed by the Wagner Act of 1935.

6. *Historical Statistics of the United States, Colonial Times to 1970,* Vol. I, p. 386.

7. Gabriel A. Almond and Sidney Verba, *The Civic Culture* (Princeton, N.J.: Princeton University Press, 1963), p. 302.

8. Derek C. Bok and John T. Dunlop, *Labor and the American Community* (New York: Simon & Schuster, 1970), p. 49; and *Statistical Abstract of the United States, 1975,* p. 373.

9. Almond and Verba, *op. cit.,* p. 194.

10. *Ibid.,* p. 203.

11. *Ibid,* p. 207.

12. Morris Axelrod, "Urban Structure and Social Participation," *American Sociological Review,* Vol. 21 (February 1956), pp. 13–18; and Herbert H. Hyman and Charles R. Wright, "Trends in Voluntary Association Memberships of American Adults," *American Sociological Review,* Vol. 36 (April 1971), pp. 191–206.

13. E. E. Schattschneider, *The Semisovereign People* (New York: Holt, Rinehart and Winston, 1960), p. 32.

14. James Q. Wilson, *Political Organizations* (New York: Basic Books, 1973), p. 61.

15. Bok and Dunlop, *op. cit.,* p. 134.

16. Gerhard Lenski, *The Religious Factor* (Garden City, N.Y.: Doubleday, 1961), Ch. 4.

17. Henry J. Pratt, *The Liberalization of American Protestantism* (Detroit: Wayne State University Press, 1972), Ch. 12.

18. Raymond A. Bauer, Ithiel de Sola Pool, and Lewis Anthony Dexter, *American Business and Public Policy* (New York: Atherton Press, 1963), pp. 363–372.

19. Mancur Olson, Jr., *The Logic of Collective Action* (Cambridge, Mass.: Harvard University Press, 1965), pp. 33–36; but compare Wilson, *op. cit.,* Ch. 2.

20. Olson, *op. cit.,* pp. 153–157.

21. *National Journal,* October 10, 1976, pp. 1386–1387. See also Henry J. Pratt, *The Gray Lobby* (Chicago: University of Chicago Press, 1976), Chs. 7, 14.

22. Jeffrey M. Berry, *Lobbying for the People* (Princeton, N.J.: Princeton University Press, 1977), pp. 71–76, 93–96, 186–202.

23. *New York Times,* January 29, 1978, p. E-3.

24. Bauer, Pool, and Dexter, *op. cit.,* Ch. 30.

25. Berry, *op cit.,* pp. 136–140.

26. *National Journal,* January 23, 1976, p. 1520.

27. *New York Times,* March 7, 1977.

28. *New York Times,* January 16, 1977.

29. *Ibid.*

30. *Congressional Quarterly Weekly Report,* March 24, 1979, pp. 512–513.

31. *National Journal,* November 19, 1977, p. 1800.

32. Suzanne Weaver, *Decision to Prosecute* (Cambridge, Mass.: MIT Press, 1977), pp. 154–163.

33. *National Journal,* November 19, 1977, p. 1800, quoting a study by the staff of Senator William Proxmire.

34. United States v. Harriss, 347 U.S. 612 (1954).

35. Hope Eastman, *Lobbying: A Constitutionally-Protected Right* (Washington, D.C.: American Enterprise Institute, 1977), p. 30.

36. One such bill was S. 1785, 95th Congress. See Eastman, *op. cit.,* p. 10.

37. Eastman, *op. cit.,* pp. 20–21.

38. *United States Code,* Title 26, Sec. 501 (c) (3).

39. Wilson, *op. cit.,* p. 321.

Chapter 9   The Media

1. R. L. Lowenstein, *World Press Freedom, 1966* (Columbia, Mo.: Freedom of Information Center, 1967), Publication No. 11.

2. D. E. Butler, "Why American Political Reporting Is Better than England's," *Harper's* (May 1963), pp. 15–25.

3. *New York Times,* March 15, 1975.

4. *New York Times,* January 28, 1974.

5. Douglass Cater, *The Fourth Branch of Government* (Boston: Houghton Mifflin, 1959), p. 76; and William L. Rivers, "The Press as a Communication System," In Ithiel de Sola Pool, Wilbur Schramm, *et al., Handbook of Communication* (Chicago: Rand McNally, 1973), pp. 522–526.

6. Quoted in F. L. Mott, *American Journalism, 1690–1960,* 3rd ed. (New York: Macmillan, 1962), p. 529, as cited in Rivers, *op. cit.,* p. 526.

7. Edward Jay Epstein, *News from Nowhere: Television and the News* (New York: Random House, 1973), p. 37.

8. Allen H. Barton, "Consensus and Conflict Among American Leaders,"

Public Opinion Quarterly, Vol. 38 (Winter 1974–1975), pp. 507–530.

9. Paul H. Weaver, "The New Journalism and the Old—Thoughts After Watergate," *The Public Interest* (Spring 1974), pp. 67–88.

10. Michael J. Robinson, "TV's Newest Program: The 'Presidential Nominations Game,'" *Public Opinion* (May/June 1978), pp. 41–46.

11. Near v. Minnesota, 283 U.S. 697 (1931).

12. New York Times v. United States, 403 U.S. 713 (1971).

13. New York Times v. Sullivan, 376 U.S. 254 (1964).

14. Yates v. United States, 354 U.S. 298 (1957).

15. Peter M. Sandman *et al., Media* (Englewood Cliffs, N.J.: Prentice-Hall, 1972), p. 182.

16. Branzburg v. Hayes, 408 U.S. 665 (1972).

17. Epstein, *op. cit.,* pp. 64, 285.

18. George Howard White, "Political Television in Congressional and Senatorial Campaigns," senior honors thesis, Department of Government, Harvard University (March 1977), pp. 8–9, 42–43.

19. Thomas E. Patterson and Robert D. McClure, *The Unseeing Eye: The Myth of Television Power in National Elections* (New York: G. P. Putnam, 1976); and Herbert Asher, *Presidential Elections and American Politics* (Homewood, Ill.: The Dorsey Press, 1976), pp. 239–240 (and studies cited therein).

20. David O. Sears and Richard E. Whitney, "Political Persuasion," in Pool and Schramm, *op. cit.,* pp. 253–289.

21. Robert S. Erikson, "The Influence of Newspaper Endorsements in Presidential Elections: The Case of 1964," *American Journal of Political Science,* Vol. 20 (May 1976), pp. 207–233.

22. Maxwell E. McCombs and Donald R. Shaw, "The Agenda Setting Function of the Mass Media," *Public Opinion Quarterly,* Vol. 36 (Summer 1972), pp. 176–187.

23. G. Ray Funkhouser, "The Issues of the Sixties," *Public Opinion Quarterly,* Vol. 37 (Spring 1973), pp. 62–75.

24. Henry Fairlie, "The Rise of the Press Secretary," *The New Republic* (March 18, 1978), pp. 20–23.

25. Michael J. Robinson, "A Twentieth-Century Medium in a Nineteenth-Century Legislature: The Effects of Television on the American Congress," in Norman J. Ornstein, ed., *Congress*

in Change (New York: Praeger, 1975), pp. 240–261.

26. Barton, *op. cit.*

27. Barry Sussman, "Media Leaders Want Less Influence" (a report of a survey of media leaders), *Washington Post,* September 29, 1976.

28. Peter Braestrup, *Big Story: How the American Press and Television Reported and Interpreted the Crises of Tet 1968 in Vietnam and Washington* (Boulder, Col.: Westview Press, 1977), 2 vols.

Chapter 10 Congress

1. H. Douglas Price, "Careers and Committees in the American Congress," in William O. Aydelotte, ed., *The History of Parliamentary Behavior* (Princeton, N.J.: Princeton University Press, 1977), pp. 28–62.

2. David R. Mayhew, *Congress: The Electoral Connection* (New Haven, Conn.: Yale University Press, 1974).

3. David R. Mayhew, "Congressional Elections: The Case of the Vanishing Marginals," *Polity,* Vol. 6 (Fall 1974), pp. 295–317, reprinted in Robert L. Peabody and Nelson W. Polsby, eds., *New Perspectives on the House of Representatives,* 3rd ed. (Chicago: Rand McNally, 1977), pp. 26–43.

4. Mayhew, *Congress: The Electoral Connection, op. cit.;* Morris P. Fiorina, *Congress: Keystone of the Washington Establishment* (New Haven, Conn.: Yale University Press, 1977); Walter Dean Burnham, "Communication," *American Political Science Review,* Vol. 68 (March 1974), p. 210; and John Ferejohn, "On the Decline of Competition in Congressional Elections," *American Political Science Review,* Vol. 71 (March 1977), pp. 166–175.

5. Wesberry v. Sanders, 376 U.S. 1 (1964).

6. Richard F. Fenno, Jr., "U.S. House Members and Their Constituencies: An Exploration," *American Political Science Review,* Vol. 71 (September 1977), pp. 883–917, esp. p. 914.

7. Lawrence C. Dodd and Bruce I. Oppenheimer, "The House in Transition," in Dodd and Oppenheimer, eds., *Congress Reconsidered* (New York: Praeger, 1977), p. 40.

8. Richard F. Fenno, Jr., *Congressmen in Committees* (Boston: Little, Brown, 1973).

9. John S. Saloma III, *Congress and the New Politics* (Boston: Little, Brown, 1969), pp. 184–185.

10. Fiorina, *op. cit.*

11. Data on congressional staffs and related matters can be found in Commission on Administrative Review, *Report on Administrative Units and Report on Work Management* (95th Congress, 1st Session, 1977), House Document 93–232, Vols. 1 and 2; and Commission on the Operation of the Senate, *Senators: Offices, Ethics, and Pressures* (94th Congress, 2nd Session, 1977).

12. Lawrence H. Chamberlain, "The President, Congress, and Legislation," in Aaron Wildavsky, ed., *The Presidency* (Boston: Little, Brown, 1969), pp. 444–445.

13. Ronald C. Moe and Steven C. Teel, "Congress as a Policy-Maker: A Necessary Reappraisal," *Political Science Quarterly,* Vol. 85 (September 1970), pp. 443–470.

14. Malcolm E. Jewell and Samuel C. Patterson, *The Legislative Process in the United States,* 3rd ed. (New York: Random House, 1977), p. 439.

15. Warren E. Miller and Donald E. Stokes, "Constituency Influence in Congress," in Angus Campbell *et al.,* eds., *Elections and the Political Order* (New York: John Wiley, 1966), p. 359.

16. John E. Jackson, *Constituencies and Leaders in Congress* (Cambridge, Mass.: Harvard University Press, 1974); and Otto Davis and John E. Jackson, "The Political Economy of Income Distribution," cited in Daniel P. Moynihan, *The Politics of a Guaranteed Income* (New York: Random House, 1973), p. 389.

17. Robert S. Erikson and Norman R. Luttbeg, *American Public Opinion* (New York: John Wiley, 1973), p. 257.

18. Lewis A. Froman, *Congressmen and Their Constituencies* (Chicago: Rand McNally, 1963), Ch. 6.

19. *Congressional Quarterly Weekly Report,* December 17 and December 23, 1978.

20. *National Journal,* September 9, 1978.

21. Quoted in *Congressional Quarterly Weekly Report,* September 2, 1978, p. 2315.

Chapter 11 The Presidency

1. Jean Blondel, *An Introduction to Comparative Government* (New York: Praeger, 1969), as cited in Nelson W. Polsby, "Legislatures," in Fred I. Greenstein and Nelson W. Polsby, eds., *Handbook of Political Science* (Reading, Mass.: Addison-Wesley, 1975), Vol. 5, p. 275.

2. Woodrow Wilson, *Congressional Government* (New York: Meridian

Books, 1956), pp. 167–168, 170. (First published in 1885.)

3. Stephen Hess, *Organizing the Presidency* (Washington, D.C.: Brookings Institution, 1976), p. 3.

4. Committee on Post Office and Civil Service, U.S. House of Representatives, *Policy and Supporting Positions* (94th Congress, 2nd Session, November 1976).

5. David T. Stanley *et al., Men Who Govern* (Washington, D.C.: Brookings Institution, 1967), pp. 41–42, 50.

6. Daniel J. Elazar, "Which Road to the Presidency?" in Aaron Wildavsky, ed., *The Presidency* (Boston: Little, Brown, 1969), p. 340.

7. Richard E. Neustadt, *Presidential Power*, rev. ed. (New York: John Wiley, 1976), Ch. 4.

8. Marbury v. Madison, 1 Cranch 137 (1803).

9. United States v. Nixon, 418 U.S. 683 (1974).

10. Joseph A. Califano, Jr., *A Presidential Nation* (New York: W. W. Norton, 1975), p. 51.

11. Marcus Cunliffe, *American Presidents and the Presidency* (New York: American Heritage Press/McGraw Hill, 1972), pp. 63, 65.

12. *Ibid.*, p. 214.

Chapter 12   The Bureaucracy

1. Charles E. Lindblom, *Politics and Markets* (New York: Basic Books, 1977), p. 114.

2. Article II, Section 2, paragraph 2.

3. Article II, Section 3.

4. Calculated from data in *Historical Statistics of the United States: Colonial Times to 1970* (Washington, D.C.: Government Printing Office, 1975), Vol. II, pp. 1102–1103.

5. Panama Refining Co. v. Ryan, 293 U.S. 388 (1935).

6. Hampton Jr. & Co. v. United States, 276 U.S. 394 (1928).

7. Edward S. Corwin, *The Constitution and What It Means Today*, 13th ed. (Princeton: Princeton University Press, 1973), p. 151.

8. I am indebted to Bruce Porter for this research on the growth of federal employment in wartime.

9. See the cases cited in Corwin, *op. cit.*, p. 8.

10. *U.S. Statutes*, Vol. 84, Sec. 799 (1970).

11. *Historical Statistics of the United States*, Vol. II, p. 1107.

12. *Statistical Abstract of the United States, 1975* (Washington, D.C.: Government Printing Office, 1975), p. 242.

13. Hugh Heclo, "Issue Networks and the Executive Establishment," in Anthony King, ed., *The New American Political System* (Washington, D.C.: American Enterprise Institute, 1978), pp. 87–124.

14. *Ibid.*, p. 118.

15. Quoted in Hugh Heclo, *A Government of Strangers* (Washington, D.C.: Brookings Institution, 1977), p. 225.

16. J. Donald Kingsley, *Representative Bureaucracy* (Yellow Springs, Ohio: Antioch Press, 1944).

17. See Richard P. Nathan, *The Plot That Failed: Nixon and the Administrative Presidency* (New York: John Wiley, 1975).

18. Kenneth Meier and Lloyd Nigro, "Representative Bureaucracy and Policy Preferences: A Study of the Attitudes of Federal Executives," *Public Administration Review*, Vol. 36 (July–August 1976), pp. 458–467.

19. Bernard Mennis, *American Foreign Policy Officials* (Columbus, Ohio: Ohio State University Press, 1971).

20. Joel D. Aberbach and Bert A. Rockman, "Clashing Beliefs Within the Executive Branch: The Nixon Administration Bureaucracy," *American Political Science Review*, Vol. 70 (June 1976), pp. 456–468.

21. Herbert Kaufman, *The Forest Ranger* (Baltimore, Md.: Johns Hopkins University Press, 1960); and Ashley Schiff, *Fire and Water* (Cambridge, Mass.: Harvard University Press, 1962).

22. James Q. Wilson, *The Investigators* (New York: Basic Books, 1978).

23. Graham K. Wilson, "Are Department Secretaries Really a President's Natural Enemies?" *British Journal of Political Science*, Vol. 7 (1977), pp. 273–299.

24. Richard F. Fenno, Jr., *The Power of the Purse* (Boston: Little, Brown, 1966), pp. 450, 597.

25. John E. Schwartz and L. Earl Shaw, *The United States Congress in Comparative Perspective* (Hinsdale, Ill.: The Dryden Press, 1976), pp. 262–263; and Herbert Stephens, "The Role of Legislative Committees in the Appropriations Process," *Western Political Quarterly*, Vol. 24 (March 1971), pp. 147, 152.

26. *National Journal*, August 6, 1977, pp. 1228–1232.

27. See cases cited in Corwin, *op. cit.*, p. 22.

28. Daniel Katz *et al., Bureaucratic Encounters* (Ann Arbor: Survey Research Center of the University of Michigan, 1975), pp. 63–69, 118–120, 184–188.

Chapter 13   The Judiciary

1. Henry J. Abraham, *The Judicial Process*, 3rd ed. (New York: Oxford University Press, 1975), pp. 279–280.

2. Robert G. McCloskey, *The American Supreme Court* (Chicago: University of Chicago Press, 1960), p. 27.

3. Marbury v. Madison, 1 Cranch 137 (1803); and McCulloch v. Maryland, 4 Wheaton 316 (1819).

4. Martin v. Hunter's Lessee, 1 Wheaton 304 (1816); and Cohens v. Virginia, 6 Wheaton 264 (1821).

5. Gibbons v. Ogden, 9 Wheaton 1 (1824).

6. Quoted in Albert J. Beveridge, *The Life of John Marshall* (Boston: Houghton Mifflin, 1919), Vol. IV, p. 551.

7. Dred Scott v. Sanford, 19 Howard 393 (1857).

8. Abraham, *op. cit.*, p. 286.

9. *In re* Debs, 158 U.S. 564 (1895).

10. Pollock v. Farmers' Loan & Trust Co., 157 U.S. 429 (1895).

11. United States v. Knight, 156 U.S. 1 (1895).

12. Cincinnati, N.O. & T.P. Railway Co. v. Interstate Commerce Commission, 162 U.S. 184 (1896).

13. Hammer v. Dagenhart, 247 U.S. 251 (1918).

14. Lochner v. New York, 198 U.S. 45 (1905).

15. McCloskey, *op. cit.*, p. 151.

16. Munn v. Illinois, 94 U.S. 113 (1877).

17. Dayton-Goose Creek Railway Co. v. United States, 263 U.S. 456 (1924).

18. Atchison, Topeka, and Santa Fe Railroad Co. v. Matthews, 174 U.S. 96 (1899).

19. Mugler v. Kansas, 123 U.S. 623 (1887).

20. St. Louis Consolidated Coal Co. v. Illinois, 185 U.S. 203 (1902).

21. New York Central Railroad Co. v. White, 243 U.S. 188 (1917).

22. Wabash Railway Co. v. Illinois, 118 U.S. 557 (1886).

23. Morton Keller, *Affairs of State* (Cambridge, Mass.: Harvard University

Press, 1977), p. 369. See also Mary Cornelia Porter, "That Commerce Shall be Free: A New Look at the Old Laissez-Faire Court," in Philip B. Kurland, ed., *The Supreme Court Review* (Chicago: University of Chicago Press, 1976), pp. 135–159.

24. Chief of Capital Police v. Jeannette Rankin Brigade, 409 U.S. 972 (1972).

25. Aptheker v. Secretary of State, 378 U.S. 500 (1964).

26. Trop v. Dulles, 356 U.S. 86 (1958); Afroyim v. Rusk, 387 U.S. 253 (1967); and Schneider v. Rusk, 377 U.S. 163 (1964).

27. Lamont v. Postmaster General, 381 U.S. 301 (1965); and Blount v. Rizzi, 400 U.S. 410 (1971).

28. Richardson v. Davis, 409 U.S. 1069 (1972); U.S. Department of Agriculture v. Murry, 413 U.S. 508 (1973); Jimenez v. Weinberger, 417 U.S. 628 (1974); and Washington v. Legrant, 394 U.S. 618 (1969).

29. Quoted in Henry J. Abraham, *Justices and Presidents* (New York: Oxford University Press, 1974), p. 74.

30. *Ibid.*, p. 75.

31. Gideon v. Wainwright, 372 U.S. 335 (1963). The story is told in Anthony Lewis, *Gideon's Trumpet* (New York: Random House, 1964).

32. Erwin Griswold, "Rationing Justice: The Supreme Court's Case Load and What the Court Does Not Do," *Cornell Law Review*, Vol. 60 (1975), pp. 335–354.

33. Paul A. Freund, *Report of the Study Group on the Caseload of the Supreme Court* (Washington, D.C.: Federal Judicial Center, 1972).

34. The Supreme Court decided in 1975 that it would not allow fee-shifting except in cases authorized by Congress. Alyeska Pipeline Service Co. v. Wilderness Society, 421 U.S. 240.

35. Flast v. Cohen, 392 U.S. 83 (1968), which modified the earlier Frothingham v. Mellon, 262 U.S. 447 (1923); United States v. Richardson, 418 U.S. 166 (1947).

36. Brown v. Board of Education of Topeka, 347 U.S. 483 (1954).

37. Baker v. Carr, 369 U.S. 186 (1962).

38. See Louise Weinberg, "A New Judicial Federalism?" *Daedalus* (Winter 1978), pp. 129–141.

39. Glendon Schubert, *The Judicial Mind Revisited* (New York: Oxford University Press, 1974); and Sheldon Goldman and Thomas P. Jahnige,

The Federal Courts as a Political System, 2nd ed. (New York: Harper & Row, 1976), pp. 167–170.

40. Bruce E. Fein, *Significant Decisions of the Supreme Court, 1975–1976 Term* (Washington, D.C.: American Enterprise Institute, 1977), p. 19.

41. Quoted in Abraham, *The Judicial Process*, p. 330.

42. A. P. Blaustein and A. H. Field, "Overruling Opinions in the Supreme Court," *Michigan Law Review*, Vol. 57 (1957), p. 2.

43. Colegrove v. Green, 328 U.S. 549 (1946).

44. Baker v. Carr, 369 U.S. 186 (1962).

45. Donald L. Horowitz, *The Courts and Social Policy* (Washington, D.C.: Brookings Institution, 1977), p. 6.

46. Gates v. Collier, 349 F. Supp. 881 (1972).

47. Lau v. Nichols, 414 U.S. 563 (1974).

48. *International Directory of Bar Associations,* 3nd ed. (Chicago: American Bar Foundation, 1973).

49. Joel B. Grossman and Austin Sarat, "Litigation in the Federal Courts: A Comparative Perspective," *Law and Society Review*, Vol. 9 (Winter 1975), pp. 321–346.

50. Warner W. Gardner, "Federal Courts and Agencies: An Audit of the Partnership Books," *Columbia Law Review*, Vol. 75 (1975), pp. 800–822.

51. Jack W. Peltason, *Fifty-Eight Lonely Men: Southern Federal Judges and School Desegregation* (New York: Harcourt, Brace, 1961).

52. Anthony Patridge and William B. Eldridge, *The Second Circuit Sentencing Study* (Washington, D.C.: Federal Judicial Center, 1974).

53. Abington School District v. Schempp, 374 U.S. 203 (1963).

54. Abraham, *The Judicial Process*, p. 337.

55. *Ibid.*, pp. 41–42.

56. *Ibid.*, p. 332.

57. *Ex Parte* McCardle, 7 Wallace 506 (1869).

58. Walter F. Murphy, *Congress and the Court* (Chicago: University of Chicago Press, 1962); and C. Herman Pritchett, *Congress versus the Supreme Court* (Minneapolis: University of Minnesota Press, 1961).

Chapter 14   The Policy-Making Process

1. E. E. Schattschneider, *The Semi-sovereign People* (New York: Holt,

Rinehart and Winston, 1960), p. 68.

2. Jack L. Walker, "Setting the Agenda in the U.S. Senate: A Theory of Problem Selection," *British Journal of Political Science*, Vol. 7 (1977), pp. 343, 441.

3. *Statistical Abstract of the United States, 1975* (Washington, D.C.: Government Printing Office, 1975), pp. 342–343, 349.

4. Alexis de Tocqueville, *The Old Regime and the French Revolution,* trans. by Gilbert Stuart (Garden City, N.Y.: Doubleday Anchor Books, 1955), pp. 176–177 (first published in 1856).

5. David O. Sears and J. B. McConahay, *The Politics of Violence* (Boston: Houghton Mifflin, 1973). Compare Abraham H. Miller *et al.*, "The New Urban Blacks," *Ethnicity*, Vol. 3 (1976), pp. 338–367.

6. Daniel Patrick Moynihan, *Maximum Feasible Misunderstanding* (New York: The Free Press, 1969), Ch. 2.

7. Nelson W. Polsby, "Goodbye to the Senate's Inner Club," in Norman J. Ornstein, ed., *Congress in Change: Evolution and Reform* (New York: Praeger, 1975), pp. 208–215.

8. Walker, *op. cit.*, pp. 427–430.

9. *Ibid.*, pp. 434, 439, 441.

10. This is a revised version of a theory originally presented in James Q. Wilson, *Political Organizations* (New York: Basic Books, 1973), Ch. 16. There are other ways of classifying public policies, notably that of Theodore J. Lowi, "American Business, Public Policy, Case Studies, and Political Theory," *World Politics*, Vol. 16 (July 1964).

11. *Congressional Quarterly Almanac, 1970* (Washington, D.C.: Congressional Quarterly Service, 1971), p. 376.

12. The flag salute requirement was upheld in Minersville School District v. Gobitis, 310 U.S. 586 (1940), and overturned in West Virginia Board of Education v. Barnette, 319 U.S. 624 (1943).

Chapter 15   Business Regulation

1. Arguments that business dominates American politics can be found in Edward S. Greenberg, *Serving the Few: Corporate Capitalism and the Bias of Government Policy* (New York: John Wiley, 1974) and Charles E. Lindblom, *Politics and Markets* (New York: Basic Books, 1977).

2. The inability of capitalism to survive democratic politics is argued in Joseph Schumpeter, *Capitalism, Socialism, and Democracy* (New York: Harper & Row, 1950).

3. Paul W. MacAvoy, ed., *Federal Milk Marketing Orders and Price Supports* (Washington, D.C.: American Enterprise Institute, 1977).

4. *Ibid.*, p. 111.

5. Gerald R. Jantscher, *Bread Upon the Waters: Federal Aids to the Maritime Industries* (Washington, D.C.: Brookings Institution, 1975).

6. Richard E. Caves, *Air Transport and Its Regulators* (Cambridge, Mass.: Harvard University Press, 1962); and William A. Jordan, *Airline Regulation in America* (Baltimore, Md.: Johns Hopkins University Press, 1970).

7. Charles R. Plott, "Occupational Self-Regulation: A Case Study of the Oklahoma Dry Cleaners," *Journal of Law and Economics,* Vol. 8 (October 1965), pp. 195–222.

8. Herbert E. Alexander, *Financing Politics* (Washington, D.C.: Congressional Quarterly Press, 1976), p. 229.

9. *Ibid.,* pp. 114–155, 118–120; and William J. Crotty, *Political Reform and the American Experiment* (New York: Thomas Y. Crowell, 1977), pp. 140–144.

10. Steven J. Kelman, "Regulating Job Safety and Health: A Comparison of the U.S. Occupational Safety and Health Administration and the Swedish Worker Protection Board" (unpublished Ph.D. dissertation, Harvard University, 1978).

11. Robert E. Cushman, *The Independent Regulatory Commissions* (New York: Oxford University Press, 1941), pp. 37–54.

12. Gabriel Kolko, *Railroads and Regulation, 1877–1916* (Princeton, N.J.: Princeton University Press, 1965); and George J. Stigler, *The Citizen and the State: Essays on Regulation* (Chicago: University of Chicago Press, 1975), Ch. 8.

13. John A. Garraty, *The New Commonwealth, 1877–1890* (New York: Harper & Row, 1968); Edward A. Purcell, Jr., "Ideas and Interests: Businessmen and the Interstate Commerce Act," *Journal of American History,* Vol. 54 (December 1967), pp. 561–578; Robert W. Harbeson, "Railroads and Regulation, 1877–1916: Conspiracy or Public Interest?"

Journal of Economic History, Vol. 27 (June 1967), pp. 230–242; and Albro Martin, *Enterprise Denied: Origins of the Decline of American Railroads, 1897–1917* (New York: Columbia University Press, 1971).

14. Paul W. MacAvoy, *The Economic Effects of Regulation* (Cambridge, Mass.: MIT Press, 1965); and John R. Meyer *et al., The Economics of Competition in the Transportation Industries* (Cambridge, Mass.: Harvard University Press, 1964).

15. Louis Galambos, *The Public Image of Big Business in America, 1880–1940* (Baltimore, Md.: Johns Hopkins University Press, 1975).

16. Richard A. Posner, *Antitrust Law: An Economic Perspective* (Chicago: University of Chicago Press, 1976), p. 25.

17. *Ibid.*

18. Standard Oil Company of New Jersey v. United States, 221 U.S. 1 (1911); United States v. American Tobacco Company, 221 U.S. 106 (1911). The scope of the Sherman Act was also narrowed by a ruling that manufacturing (in this case, of refined sugar) was not interstate commerce and thus monopolizing that manufacture, as in fact had occurred, was not a violation of the Sherman Act. United States v. E. C. Knight Co., 156 U.S. 1 (1895).

19. Alan Stone, *Economic Regulation and the Public Interest: The Federal Trade Commission in Theory and Practice* (Ithaca, N.Y.: Cornell University Press, 1977), Ch. 2.

20. On the role of Wilson, see Alan L. Seltzer, "Woodrow Wilson as 'Corporate-Liberal': Toward a Reconsideration of Left Revisionist Historiography," *Western Political Quarterly,* Vol. 30 (June 1977), pp. 183–212.

21. Suzanne Weaver, *Decision to Prosecute: Organization and Public Policy in the Antitrust Division* (Cambridge, Mass.: MIT Press, 1977), Ch. 7; and Robert A. Katzmann, "Antitrust Decision-Making in the Federal Trade Commission: A Study in Bureaucracy and Public Policy" (unpublished Ph.D. dissertation, Harvard University, 1978).

22. Mark J. Green *et al., The Closed Enterprise System* (New York: Grossman, 1972), Ch. 2.

23. Weaver, *op. cit.,* pp. 154–163.

24. Paul J. Halpern, "Consumer Politics and Corporate Behavior: The Case of Automobile Safety" (unpublished Ph.D. dissertation, Harvard University, 1972).

25. Upton Sinclair, *The Jungle* (New York: Doubleday, Page and Co., 1906).

26. Mark V. Nadel, *The Politics of Consumer Protection* (Indianapolis, Ind.: Bobbs-Merrill, 1971), pp. 143–144.

27. Jack L. Walker, "Setting the Agenda in the U.S. Senate: A Theory of Problem Selection," *British Journal of Political Science,* Vol. 7 (1977), pp. 423–445.

28. Alfred Marcus, "What Does Reorganization Accomplish? The Case of the EPA" (unpublished Ph.D. dissertation, Harvard University, 1977).

29. Charles McGarry, *Citizen Nader* (New York: Saturday Review Press, 1972), pp. 94–106.

30. Nadel, *op. cit.,* pp. 66–80.

31. Walter J. Mead, "Energy and the Environment: Conflict in Public Policy," paper published by the American Enterprise Institute (1978), pp. 17–20.

32. *New York Times,* October 31, 1977, and private correspondence from Mark V. Nadel.

Chapter 16 Economic Policy

1. Edward R. Tufte, *Political Control of the Economy* (Princeton, N.J.: Princeton University Press, 1978), pp. 71–88.

2. Douglas A. Hibbs, Jr., "The Mass Public and Macroeconomic Policy: The Dynamics of Public Opinion Toward Unemployment and Inflation," paper delivered at 1978 annual meeting of the American Political Science Association, Figure 4.

3. *Ibid.,* Figure 2.

4. Tufte, *op. cit.,* pp. 71–83.

5. Herbert Stein, *The Fiscal Revolution in America* (Chicago: University of Chicago Press, 1969), pp. 67, 118, 219.

6. David J. Ott and Attiat F. Ott, *Federal Budget Policy,* 3rd ed. (Washington, D.C.: Brookings Institution, 1977), p. 159.

7. Gallup Polls, 1978, reported in *Public Opinion,* Vol. 1 (May-June 1978), p. 24.

8. Joseph A. Pechman, *Federal Tax Policy,* 3rd ed. (Washington, D.C.: Brookings Institution, 1977), p. 35.

9. Peter B. Natchez and Irwin T. Bupp,

"Policy and Priority in the Budgetary Process," *American Political Science Review,* Vol. 67 (September 1973), pp. 947–963.

10. Pechman, *op. cit.,* pp. 49–50.
11. Tufte, *op. cit.,* pp. 11–12.
12. *Ibid.,* pp. 19–21; and William D. Nordhaus, "The Political Business Cycle," *Review of Economic Studies,* Vol. 42 (April 1975), pp. 169–190.
13. William C. Mitchell, *The Popularity of Social Security: A Paradox in Public Choice* (Washington, D.C.: American Enterprise Institute, 1977), p. 11.
14. Tufte, *op. cit.,* pp. 36–39.
15. *Ibid.,* p. 53.
16. *Ibid.,* pp. 52–54.
17. *Ibid.,* p. 136.
18. *Ibid.,* Ch. 5; Gerald H. Kramer, "Short-Term Fluctuations in U.S. Voting Behavior, 1896–1964," *American Political Science Review,* Vol. 65 (March 1971), pp. 131–143; Saul Goodman and Gerald H. Kramer, "Comment on Arcelus and Meltzer," *American Political Science Review,* Vol. 69 (December 1975), pp. 1255–1265; and Howard S. Bloom and H. Douglas Price, "Voter Response to Short-Run Economic Conditions: The Asymmetric Effect of Prosperity and Recession," *American Political Science Review,* Vol. 69 (December 1975), pp. 1240–1254. But compare Francisco Arcelus and Allan H. Meltzer, "The Effect of Aggregate Economic Variables on Congressional Elections," *American Political Science Review,* Vol. 69 (December 1975), pp. 1232–1239.

Chapter 17 Social Welfare

1. For a general discussion, see Charles E. Gilbert, "Welfare Policy," in Fred I. Greenstein and Nelson W. Polsby, eds., *Handbook of Political Science* (Reading, Mass.: Addison-Wesley, 1975), Vol. VI, Ch. 4.
2. Congressional Quarterly, *Congress and the Nation, 1945–1964* (Washington, D.C.: Congressional Quarterly Service, 1965), p. 1225.
3. Harold E. Raynes, *Social Security in Britain: A History* (London: Pitman, 1960), Ch. 18. See also Hugh Heclo, *Modern Social Politics in Britain and Sweden* (New Haven, Conn.: Yale University Press, 1974).
4. Histories of the 1935 act include Edwin E. Witte, *The Development of the Social Security Act* (Madison:

University of Wisconsin Press, 1962). A different view, offering a neo-Marxist interpretation of the act, can be found in Frances Fox Piven and Richard A. Cloward, *Regulating the Poor* (New York: Pantheon, 1971).
5. The development of the War on Poverty is told in Daniel Patrick Moynihan, *Maximum Feasible Misunderstanding* (New York: The Free Press, 1969) and James Sundquist, *Politics and Policy* (Washington, D.C.: Brookings Institution, 1968).
6. Michael Harrington, *The Other America* (Baltimore, Md.: Penguin Books, 1962).
7. The Lampman work was given wide circulation in the government by the Joint Economic Committee of the U.S. Congress in the late 1950s.
8. The development of Medicare is described in Sundquist, *op. cit.,* and Theodore Marmor, "Doctors, Politics, and Health Insurance for the Aged: The Enactment of Medicare," in Allan Sindler, ed., *Cases in Contemporary American Government* (Boston: Little, Brown, 1969).
9. The development of FAP is the subject of several studies: Daniel Patrick Moynihan, *The Politics of a Guaranteed Income* (New York: Random House, 1973); Kenneth M. Bowler, *The Nixon Guaranteed Income Proposal* (Cambridge, Mass.: Ballinger, 1974); and Vincent J. and Vee Burke, *Nixon's Good Deed—Welfare Reform* (New York: Columbia University Press, 1974).
10. Quoted in Bowler, *op. cit.,* p. 47.
11. Michael E. Schiltz, *Public Attitudes Toward Social Security, 1935–1965,* Research Report No. 3, Social Security Administration, U.S. Department of Health, Education, and Welfare (Washington, D.C.: Government Printing Office, 1970), pp. 36, 98.
12. *Ibid.,* pp. 128, 140.
13. *Ibid.,* Ch. 4.
14. *Ibid.,* pp. 154–165.
15. See the studies cited in Moynihan, *The Politics of a Guaranteed Income,* pp. 268–269, and Otto A. Davis and John E. Jackson, "The Political Economy of Income Distribution" (Washington, D.C.: Urban Institute, March 1972).
16. Alicia H. Munnell, *The Future of Social Security* (Washington, D.C.: Brookings Institution, 1977), Appendix.
17. Martha Derthick, "How Easy Votes on Social Security Came to an End," *Public Interest* (Winter 1979), p. 96; and

William C. Mitchell, *The Popularity of Social Security: A Paradox in Public Choice* (Washington, D.C.: American Enterprise Institute, 1977).
18. Quoted in William E. Leuchtenburg, *Franklin D. Roosevelt and the New Deal* (New York: Harper & Row, 1963), p. 133.

Chapter 18 Civil Liberties

1. Sheppard v. Maxwell, 384 U.S. 333 (1966); New York Times Co. v. United States, 403 U.S. 713 (1971); and Kunz v. New York, 340 U.S. 290 (1951).
2. Gordon S. Wood, "The Democratization of Mind in the American Revolution," in Robert H. Horowitz, ed., *The Moral Foundations of the American Republic* (Charlottesville: University of Virginia Press, 1977), pp. 120–121.
3. Jefferson's remarks are from a letter to Abigail Adams, quoted in Walter Berns, *The First Amendment and the Future of American Democracy* (New York: Basic Books, 1976), p. 82.
4. Thomas Jefferson to Thomas McKean, Governor of Pennsylvania, February 19, 1803. From Paul L. Ford, ed., *The Writings of Thomas Jefferson: 1801–1806* (New York: G. P. Putnam's Sons, 1897), Vol. 8, p. 218. See also Leonard W. Levy, *Legacy of Suppression: Freedom of Speech and Press in Early American History* (Cambridge, Mass.: Harvard University Press, 1960).
5. Harry N. Scheiber, *The Wilson Administration and Civil Liberties, 1917–1921* (Ithaca, N.Y.: Cornell University Press, 1960), Ch. 2.
6. Robert K. Murray, *Red Scare: A Study in National Hysteria, 1919–1920* (Minneapolis: University of Minnesota Press, 1955), p. 239.
7. Schenck v. United States, 249 U.S. 47 (1919), at p. 52.
8. Frohwerk v. United States, 249 U.S. 204 (1919); and Debs v. United States, 249 U.S. 211 (1919).
9. Abrams v. United States, 250 U.S. 616 (1919).
10. In addition to the Abrams case, *supra,* see Gitlow v. New York, 268 U.S. 652 (1925), and Whitney v. California 274 U.S. 357 (1927).
11. Edward S. Corwin, *Total War and the Constitution* (Plainview, N.Y.: Books for Libraries, 1947).
12. Dennis v. United States, 341 U.S. 494 (1951), at pp. 510 ff. The Supreme Court here adopted a formula first proposed by Judge Learned Hand of

the Court of Appeals: see Dennis v. United States, 183 F. 2d 201 (1950), at p. 212.

13. Henry J. Abraham, *Freedom and the Court: Civil Rights and Liberties in the United States,* 3rd ed. (New York: Oxford University Press, 1977), p. 202.

14. Yates v. United States, 354 U.S. 298 (1957); and Abraham, *op. cit.,* p. 203.

15. Scales v. United States, 367 U.S. 203 (1961).

16. Communist Party v. Subversive Activities Control Board, 367 U.S. 1 (1961); United States v. Communist Party, 377 U.S. 968 (1964), declining to review Communist Party v. United States, 331 F. 2d 807 (1963).

17. Aptheker v. Secretary of State, 378 U.S. 500 (1964).

18. Albertson v. Subversive Activities Control Board, 382 U.S. 70 (1965).

19. Dellinger v. United States, 410 U.S. 970 (1973), denying certiorari in Dellinger v. United States, 472 F. 2d 340 (1972).

20. Brandenburg v. Ohio, 395 U.S. 444 (1969).

21. Abraham, *op. cit.,* p. 228; and Edward S. Corwin, *The Constitution and What It Means Today,* revised by Harold W. Chase and Craig R. Ducat, 13th ed. (Princeton: Princeton University Press, 1973), p. 286.

22. Raymond D. Gastil, "The Comparative Survey of Freedom—VIII," *Freedom at Issue,* No. 44 (January-February 1978), p. 5, lists twenty-one nations as "most free" in terms of civil liberties.

23. From Holmes's dissenting opinion in Northern Securities Co. v. United States, 193 U.S. 197 (1904). This dissent is what provoked the attack (quoted in Chapter 13) on Holmes by the man who had apppointed him to the Court, President Theodore Roosevelt.

24. Barron v. Baltimore, 7 Peters 243 (1833).

25. Gitlow v. New York, 268 U.S. 652 (1925), at p. 666.

26. Fiske v. Kansas, 274 U.S. 380 (1927); and Stromberg v. California, 283 U.S. 359 (1931).

27. Near v. Minnesota, 283 U.S. 697 (1931).

28. De Jonge v. Oregon, 299 U.S. 353 (1937).

29. Palko v. Connecticut, 302 U.S. 319 (1937); and Abraham, *op. cit.,* p. 70.

30. Wolf v. Colorado, 338 U.S. 25 (1949).

31. Mapp v. Ohio, 367 U.S. 643 (1961).

32. Gideon v. Wainwright, 372 U.S. 335 (1963).

33. Malloy v. Hogan, 378 U.S. 1 (1964).

34. Pointer v. Texas, 380 U.S. 400 (1965).

35. Klopfer v. North Carolina, 386 U.S. 213 (1967); and Duncan v. Louisiana, 391 U.S. 145 (1968).

36. Robinson v. California, 370 U.S. 660 (1962).

37. Benton v. Maryland, 395 U.S. 784 (1969).

38. Escobedo v. Illinois, 378 U.S. 478 (1964); and Miranda v. Arizona, 384 U.S. 436 (1966).

39. Gyuro v. Connecticut, 393 U.S. 937 (1968); and McBeth v. Texas & Pacific Railway, 390 U.S. 987 (1968). The Second Amendment ("the right to bear arms") and the Third Amendment (quartering soldiers in private homes) also do not apply to the states.

40. Griswold v. Connecticut, 381 U.S. 479 (1965); and Abraham, *op. cit.,* pp. 83–88.

41. Roe v. Wade, 410 U.S. 113 (1973).

42. See the dissenting opinion of Justice Black in Griswold v. Connecticut, 381 U.S. 479 (1965), at pp. 509, 511, and his book, *A Constitutional Faith* (New York: Alfred A. Knopf, 1968).

43. Abraham, *op. cit.,* pp. 209–210.

44. New York Times v. Sullivan, 376 U.S. 254 (1964); but compare Time, Inc. v. Firestone, 424 U.S. 448 (1976).

45. United States v. O'Brien, 391 U.S. 367 (1968).

46. Tinker v. Des Moines Community School District, 393 U.S. 503 (1969).

47. Chaplinsky v. New Hampshire, 315 U.S. 568 (1942); but compare Gooding v. Wilson, 405 U.S. 518 (1972) and Rosenfeld v. New Jersey, 408 U.S. 901 (1972).

48. Village of Skokie v. National Socialist Party, 97 S. Ct. 2205 (1977); 366 N.E. 2d 349 (1977); and 373 N.E. 2d 21 (1978). The U.S. Supreme Court ordered the Illinois state courts to consider the First Amendment issues, which they did.

49. Abraham, *op. cit.,* pp. 214–215, fn. 178.

50. Justice Stewart's famous remark was made in his concurring opinion in Jacobellis v. Ohio, 378 U.S. 184 (1964), at p. 197.

51. Miller v. California, 413 U.S. 15 (1973).

52. Jenkins v. Georgia, 418 U.S. 153 (1974).

53. Miranda v. Arizona, 384 U.S. 436 (1966).

54. Malloy v. Hogan, 378 U.S. 1 (1964).

55. Abraham, *op. cit.,* p. 146.

56. Mapp v. Ohio, 367 U.S. 643 (1961).

57. Edward S. Corwin, *The Constitution and What It Means Today,* revised by Harold W. Chase and Craig R. Ducat, 14th ed. (Princeton, N.J.: Princeton University

Press, 1978), pp. 346–360, provides the relevant cases.

58. Harris v. New York, 401 U.S. 222 (1971); Younger v. Harris, 401 U.S. 37 (1971); Hicks v. Miranda, 422 U.S. 332 (1975); and Juidice v. Vail, 97 S. Ct. 1211 (1977).

59. Stone v. Powell, 428 U.S. 465 (1976); United States v. Janis, 428 U.S. 433 (1976); and the dissent by Chief Justice Burger in Bivens v. Six Unknown Agents, 403 U.S. 388 (1971), at p. 415.

Chapter 19   Civil Rights

1. United States v. Carolene Products Co., 304 U.S. 144 (1938); and San Antonio Independent School District v. Rodriguez, 411 U.S. 1 (1973).

2. Gunnar Myrdal, *An American Dilemma* (New York: Harper, 1944), Ch. 27.

3. Richard Kluger, *Simple Justice* (New York: Random House/Vintage Books, 1977), pp. 89–90.

4. Paul B. Sheatsley, "White Attitudes Toward the Negro," in Talcott Parsons and Kenneth B. Clark, eds., *The Negro American* (Boston: Houghton Mifflin, 1966), pp. 305, 308, 317.

5. Kluger, *op. cit.,* pp. 626–634.

6. Slaughterhouse Cases, 16 Wall. 36 (1873).

7. Civil Rights Cases, 109 U.S. 3 (1883).

8. Plessy v. Ferguson, 163 U.S. 537 (1896).

9. Cumming v. Richmond County Board of Education, 175 U.S. 528 (1899).

10. Missouri ex rel. Gaines v. Canada, 305 U.S. 337 (1938).

11. Sipuel v. Board of Regents of the University of Oklahoma, 332 U.S. 631 (1948).

12. Fisher v. Hurst, 333 U.S. 147 (1948).

13. Sweatt v. Painter, 339 U.S. 629 (1950); and McLaurin v. Oklahoma State Regents for Higher Education, 339 U.S. 637 (1950).

14. Kluger, *op. cit.,* pp. 291–294.

15. Brown v. Board of Education of Topeka, 347 U.S. 483 (1954).

16. Brown v. Board of Education of Topeka, 349 U.S. 294 (1955). This case is often referred to as "Brown II."

17. Francis M. Wilhoit, *The Politics of Massive Resistance* (New York: George Braziller, 1973), p. 289.

18. Frederick S. Mosteller and Daniel P. Moynihan, eds., *On Equality of Educational Opportunity* (New York: Random House, 1972), pp. 60–62.

19. United States v. Jefferson County Board of Education, 372 F. 2d 836 (1966).

20. Green *et al.* v. County School Board of New Kent County, 391 U.S. 430 (1968).
21. Swann v. Charlotte-Mecklenburg Board of Education, 402 U.S. 1 (1971).
22. Keyes v. School District No. 1 of Denver, 413 U.S. 189 (1973).
23. Milliken v. Bradley, 418 U.S. 717 (1974).
24. Evans v. Buchanan, 423 U.S. 963 (1975); Board of Education v. Newburg Area Council, 421 U.S. 931 (1975); and Board of School Commissioners of Indianapolis v. Buckley, 97 S. Ct. 802 (1977).
25. Pasadena City Board of Education v. Spangler, 423 U.S. 1335 (1975).
26. Robert S. Erikson and Norman R. Luttbeg, *American Public Opinion* (New York: John Wiley, 1973), p. 49; and Hazel Erskine, "The Polls: Demonstrations and Race Riots," *Public Opinion Quarterly*, Vol. 31 (Winter 1967–1968), pp. 654–677.
27. Martin Luther King, Jr., *Why We Can't Wait* (New York: Signet Books, 1963), p. 69.
28. Howard Hubbard, "Five Long Hot Summers and How They Grew," *The Public Interest* (Summer 1968), pp. 8–9; and Martin Luther King, Jr., "Behind the Selma March," *Saturday Review*, April 3, 1965, pp. 16–17.
29. Harper v. Virginia State Board of Elections, 383 U.S. 663 (1966).
30. *Statistical Abstract of the United States, 1975* (Washington, D.C.: Government Printing Office, 1975), p. 449.
31. Gary Orfield, *Congressional Power: Congress and Social Change* (New York: Harcourt Brace Jovanovich, 1975), p. 69.
32. Congressional Quarterly, *Congress and the Nation, 1973–1976* (Washington, D.C.: Congressional Quarterly, 1977), Vol. 4, p. 666.
33. *Ibid.*, pp. 664–665.
34. Regents of the University of California v. Bakke, 98 S. Ct. 2733 (1978); and Allan P. Sindler, *Bakke, DeFunis, and Minority Admissions* (New York: Longman, 1978).

Chapter 20 Foreign Policy

1. Alexis de Tocqueville, *Democracy in America*, ed. by Phillips Bradley (New York: Alfred A. Knopf, 1951), Vol. I, p. 235.
2. Edward S. Corwin, *The President: Office and Powers* (New York: New York University Press, 1940), p. 200.
3. The exact number varies with who is doing the counting. See Louis Henkin, *Foreign Affairs and the Constitution* (New York: W. W. Norton, 1972), pp. 53, 306 fn 43.
4. Louis W. Koenig, *The Chief Executive*, 3rd ed. (New York: Harcourt Brace Jovanovich, 1975), p. 217.
5. Louis Fisher, *President and Congress* (New York: The Free Press, 1972), p. 45; and United States v. Belmont, 301 U.S. 324 (1937).
6. Aaron Wildavsky, "The Two Presidencies," in Wildavsky, ed., *The Presidency* (Boston: Little, Brown, 1969), p. 231.
7. *Ibid.*
8. Peter G. Richards, *Parliament and Foreign Affairs* (London: George Allen & Unwin, 1967), pp. 37–38; and John E. Schwarz and L. Earl Shaw, *The United States Congress in Comparative Perspective* (Hinsdale, Ill.: The Dryden Press, 1976), p. 235.
9. Bernard E. Brown, "The Decision to End the Algerian War," in James B. Christoph, ed., *Cases in Comparative Politics* (Boston: Little, Brown, 1965), pp. 154–180; Roy C. Macridis, "De Gaulle and NATO," in Macridis, ed., *Modern European Governments* (Englewood Cliffs, N.J.: Prentice-Hall, 1968), pp. 92–115; and Schwarz and Shaw, *op. cit.*, pp. 235–236.
10. Loch Johnson and James M. McCormick, "The Making of International Agreements: A Reappraisal of Congressional Involvement," *Journal of Politics*, Vol. 40 (1978), pp. 468–478.
11. Arthur M. Schlesinger, Jr., *A Thousand Days: John F. Kennedy in the White House* (Boston: Houghton Mifflin, 1965), Ch. 30, 31. Schlesinger, at p. 841, described Kennedy's actions as a "brilliantly controlled," "matchlessly calibrated" combination of "nerve and wisdom." His view of Nixon's action was a good deal less charitable in *The Imperial Presidency* (Boston: Houghton Mifflin, 1974), Ch. 7.
12. United States v. Curtiss-Wright Export Co., 299 U.S. 304 (1936).
13. Mitchell v. Laird, 488 F. 2d 611 (1973).
14. Prize Cases, 67 U.S. 635 (1863).
15. Mora v. McNamara, 389 U.S. 934 (1967); and Massachusetts v. Laird, 400 U.S. 886 (1970).
16. Korematsu v. United States, 323 U.S. 214 (1944).
17. Youngstown Sheet & Tube Co. v. Sawyer, 343 U.S. 579 (1952).
18. Richard M. Pious, *The American Presidency* (New York: Basic Books, 1979), p. 400.
19. Robert S. Erikson and Norman R. Luttbeg, *American Public Opinion* (New York: John Wiley, 1973), pp. 50–51.
20. William R. Caspary, "The 'Mood Theory': A Study of Public Opinion and Foreign Policy," *American Political Science Review*, Vol. 64 (June 1970), pp. 536–547.
21. Erikson and Luttbeg, *op. cit.*, p. 52.
22. John E. Mueller, *War, Presidents, and Public Opinion* (New York: John Wiley, 1973), p. 110.
23. *Ibid.*, p. 112.
24. Milton J. Rosenberg, Sidney Verba, and Philip E. Converse, *Vietnam and the Silent Majority* (New York: Harper & Row, 1970), pp. 26–27.
25. Erikson and Luttbeg, *op. cit.*, p. 155.
26. Mueller, *op. cit.*, Ch. 9.
27. *Ibid.*, p. 169.
28. *Ibid.*, pp. 45–47.
29. *Ibid.*, pp. 54–56.
30. *Ibid.*, Ch. 6.
31. Philip E. Converse, Warren E. Miller, Jerrold G. Rusk, and Arthur C. Wolfe, "Continuity and Change in American Politics: Parties and Issues in the 1968 Elections," *American Political Science Review*, Vol. 63 (December 1969), pp. 1083–1105; and John P. Robinson, "Public Reaction to Political Protest: Chicago, 1968," *Public Opinion Quarterly*, Vol. 34 (Spring 1970), pp. 1–9.
32. Mueller, *op. cit.*, pp. 125, 139.
33. *Ibid.*, p. 127.
34. *Ibid.*, p. 126.
35. X, "The Sources of Soviet Conduct," *Foreign Affairs*, Vol. 25 (July 1947), p. 566.
36. Walter Lippmann, *The Cold War* (New York: Harper and Brothers, 1947).
37. Erikson and Luttbeg, *op. cit.*, p. 52.
38. Mueller, *op. cit.*, p. 40.
39. Wayne S. Cole, *America First: The Battle Against Intervention, 1940–1941* (Madison: University of Wisconsin Free Press, 1953), Ch. 1, 2.
40. Quoted in Michael Roskin, "From Pearl Harbor to Vietnam: Shifting Generational Paradigms and Foreign Policy," *Political Science Quarterly*, Vol. 89 (Fall 1974), p. 567.
41. *Ibid.*
42. Frank L. Klingberg, "The Historical Alternation of Moods in American Foreign Policy," *World Politics*, Vol. 4 (1952), pp. 239–273.
43. Ernest R. May, *American Imperialism*

(New York: Atheneum, 1968), Ch. 1.

44. Walter LaFeber, *The New Empire: An Interpretation of American Expansion, 1860–1898* (Ithaca, N.Y.: Cornell University Press, 1963).

45. Alfred T. Mahan, *The Influence of Sea Power Upon History: 1660–1783* (New York: Hill & Wang, 1963). First published in 1890.

46. Gar Alperovitz, *Atomic Diplomacy: Hiroshima and Potsdam* (New York: Simon & Schuster, 1965); and D. F. Fleming, *The Cold War and Its Origins* (Garden City, N.Y.: Doubleday, 1961).

47. Richard J. Barnet, *Roots of War* (New York: Atheneum, 1972).

48. Gabriel Kolko, *The Politics of War* (New York: Random House, 1968). See also William Appleman Williams, *The Tragedy of American Diplomacy*, rev. ed. (New York: Dell Books, 1962); and Lloyd Gardner, *Economic Aspects of New Deal Diplomacy* (Madison: University of Wisconsin Press, 1964).

49. Jagdish Bhagwati, *Economics and World Order* (New York: Macmillan, 1972); Paul A. Baran and Paul M. Sweezy, *Monopoly Capital* (New York: Monthly Review Press, 1966); and Harry Magdoff; *The Age of Imperialism* (New York: Monthly Review Press, 1969).

50. Robert James Maddox, *The New Left and the Origins of the Cold War* (Princeton, N.J.: Princeton University Press, 1973).

51. Benjamin J. Cohen, *The Question of Imperialism* (New York: Basic Books, 1973); Charles S. Maier, "Revisionism and the Interpretation of Cold War Origins," in Donald Fleming and Bernard Bailyn, eds., *Perspectives in American History*, Vol. 4 (1970), pp. 313–345; and Robert W. Tucker, *The Radical Left and American Foreign Policy* (Baltimore, Md.: Johns Hopkins University Press, 1971).

52. *Public Papers of Harry S. Truman, 1952–1953*, p. 708.

53. Leslie H. Gelb, "Vietnam: The System Worked," *Foreign Policy*, Vol. 3 (November 1971), pp. 140–167; James C. Thomson, Jr., "How Could Vietnam Happen? An Autopsy," *Atlantic* (April 1968), pp. 47–53; and Doris Kearns, *Lyndon Johnson and the American Dream* (New York: Harper & Row, 1976), Ch. 9.

54. Marvin Feuerwerger, "Congress, Foreign Aid, and American Policy Toward Israel, 1969–1976," unpublished Ph.D. dissertation, Harvard University, 1977.

55. Roberta Wohlstetter, *Pearl Harbor: Warning and Decision* (Stanford, Calif.: Stanford University Press, 1962).

56. Graham Allison and Peter Szanton, *Remaking Foreign Policy: The Organizational Connection* (New York: Basic Books, 1976), pp. 36–37.

57. *Ibid.,* pp. 37, 196–197.

Chapter 21 Military Spending

1. See Michael Reich, "Military Spending and the U.S. Economy," in Steven Rosen, ed., *Testing the Theory of the Military-Industrial Complex* (Lexington, Mass.: D.C. Heath/Lexington Books, 1973), pp. 85–102; and Paul Baran and Paul Sweezy, *Monopoly Capital* (New York: Monthly Review Press, 1965).

2. John Kenneth Galbraith, *How to Control the Military* (New York: Signet, 1969), pp. 10, 33.

3. Marc Pilisuk and Tom Hayden, "Is There a Miliatry-Industrial Complex that Prevents Peace?" in Robert Perruci and Marc Pilisuk, eds., *The Triple Revolution* (Boston: Little, Brown, 1971).

4. Stanley Lieberson, "An Empirical Study of the Military-Industrial Linkages," in Rosen, *op. cit.,* p. 74.

5. Lawrence J. Korb, "The Secretary of Defense and the Joint Chiefs of Staff: The Budgetary Process," in Sam C. Sarkesian, ed., *The Military-Industrial Complex: A Reassessment* (Beverly Hills, Calif.: Sage Publications, 1972), pp. 301–340.

6. An important study relating perceived Soviet threats, total federal budget needs, and congressional interest in economizing to the level of defense spending can be found in Charles W. Ostrom, Jr., "A Reactive Linkage Model of the U.S. Defense Expenditure Policymaking Process," *American Political Science Review*, Vol. 72 (September 1978), pp. 941–957.

7. *Wall Street Journal,* March 14, 1978.

8. Arnold Kanter, "Congress and the Defense Budget: 1960–1970," *American Political Science Review,* Vol. 66 (March 1972), pp. 129–143.

9. Robert A. Bernstein and William W. Anthony, "The ABM Issue in the Senate, 1968–1970," *American Political Science Review,* Vol. 68 (September 1974), pp. 1198–1206.

10. Stephen Cobb, "Defense Spending and Defense Voting in the House: An Empirical Study of an Aspect of the Military-Industrial Complex Thesis," *American Journal of Sociology,* Vol. 82 (July 1976), pp. 163–182.

11. Charles Gray and Glen Gregory, "Military Spending and Senate Voting," *Journal of Peace Research,* Vol. 1 (1968), pp. 44–54; Bruce Russett, *What Price Vigilance?* (New Haven, Conn.: Yale University Press, 1970); and Stephen Cobb, "The United States Senate and the Impact of Defense Spending Concentrations," in Rosen, *op. cit.,* pp. 197–223.

12. Lieberson, *op. cit.,* p. 66.

13. Murray L. Weidenbaum, *The Military-Space Market* (St. Louis, Mo.: Washington University Department of Economics, 1967).

14. Comptroller General of the United States, *Defense Industry Profit Study,* Report B-159896 (March 1971); and J. Ronald Fox, *Arming America* (Boston: Harvard University School of Business Administration, 1974), Ch. 15.

15. James R. Kurth, "Aerospace Production Lines and American Defense Spending," in Rosen, *op. cit.,* pp. 135–156.

16. Robert J. Art, "Why We Overspend and Underaccomplish: Weapons Procurement and the Military-Industrial Complex," in Rosen, *op. cit.,* p. 249.

17. Congressman Henry B. Gonzalez (D., Texas), quoted in Fox, *op. cit.,* p. 5.

18. Victor A. Thompson, *Bureaucracy and the Modern World* (Morristown, N.J.: General Learning Press, 1976), p. 89.

19. Quoted in Robert J. Art, *The TFX Decision: McNamara and the Military* (Boston: Little, Brown, 1968), p. 126.

20. See Art, *op. cit.,* and Fox, *op. cit.,* for similar descriptions of this process.

Chapter 22 Who Governs?

1. Anthony King, "The American Polity in the Late 1970s: Building Coalitions in the Sand," in King, ed., *The New American Political System* (Washington, D.C.: American Enterprise Institute, 1978), p. 391; and James Q. Wilson, "American Politics, Then and Now," *Commentary* (February 1979), pp. 39–46.

Chapter 23 To What Ends?

1. Alexis de Tocqueville, *Democracy in America,* ed. by Phillips Bradley (New York: Alfred A. Knopf, 1951), Vol. II, Book II, Ch. 1.

INDEX TO REFERENCES

INDEX

Italic page numbers indicate illustrations.

and Vietnam War, 550
workload of, 282
Congressional agencies, 367
Congressional Black Caucus, 276
Congressional Budget Office (CBO), 283
Congressional committees, organization of,
    277-281. *See also* Committees
Congressional Directory, 297
Congressional District Data Book, 297
Congressional districts, 267
    marginal, 264
    Supreme Court on, 399
Congressional Quarterly, 297
Congressional Record, 297
Congressional Research Service (CRS), 282
Congressmen. *See also* Representatives;
    Senators
    and constituents, 73
    local offices of, 281
    opinion of, 294
    policy views of, 275
    staffs of, 281-282
    vote of, 292
Congress of Racial Equality (CORE), 523,
    530, 535
Congress Watch, 217, 366
Conkling, Roscoe, 260
Connally, Tom, 547
Connecticut, and slavery issue, 36
Connor, Eugene "Bull," 525
Consensus, in political culture, 96
Conservative coalition, 294
Conservatives, 111, 112, 113-116, 130
    in Congress, 275
    economic, 453, 455
    and interest groups, 220
    and military spending, 580
    and protest movements, 91
    regional basis for, 110
    in Supreme Court, 397
Constitution, U.S. *See also* Amendments;
    Articles
    commerce clause, 51
    and democracy, 30-33
    early reactions to, 33
    elastic language of, 49-50
    on election procedures, 167
    and *The Federalist* papers, 32
    and foreign policy, 544
    legitimacy of, 345
    liberties guaranteed in, 33-35
    and New Jersey Plan, 26-27
    process for amending, 30-31
    ratification of, 34
    on segregation, 514
    and slavery, 35-37
    and states, 49
    and Virginia Plan, 26
Constitution, U.S., Framers of, 7, 8, 23-25,
    30
    and Bill of Rights, 34

and civil liberties, 484
and Congress, 257
motives of, 37-39
and purpose of government, 100
on slavery, 36-37, 41
on union, 40
Constitutional Convention of 1787, 6,
    21-25, 27
Constitutional Union party, 187
Constitutions
    English, 18
    of states, 20, 22
Consumer Federation of America, 220
Consumer interests, and government
    interests, 435. *See also* Interest groups
Consumer preferences, nationalization of,
    65
Consumer protection laws, 13
Consumers Union, 215
Containment policy, 558, 562
Conventions, national nominating,
    143-146, 244
    origin of, 138
    outcomes, 160
Cook County Democratic "machine," 134,
    207-208, 276
Coolidge, Calvin, 316, 334, 343
Corporations. *See also* Business
    and defense contracts, 581-584
    government regulation of, 412
    Marxist view of, 10
Cosmopolitan, 236
Costa Rica, political culture of, 88
Cost of Living Council, 354
Council of Economic Advisers, 321, 453
    and presidency, 455, 465
    tax cuts proposed by, 459
Council on Environmental Quality, 321
Council on Foreign Relations, 562
Court of Military Appeals, 385
Court-packing plan, 384, 405
Courts. *See also* Supreme Court
    activism of, 400
    checks on, 402-406
    civil rights campaign in, 512-521
    and Congress, 407
    district, 323, 388, 407
    and entrepreneurial politics, 598
    political influence of, 407
    and public opinion, 406
    and quotas, 533-534
Courts, federal
    development of, 378-385
    and funding, 63-64
    jurisdiction of, 387-395
    power of, 398-400
    structure of, 385-387
Courts of Appeals, 323, 407
    on desegregation of schools, 518
    jurisdiction of, 388
    and regulatory agencies, 402

Cranston, Alan, 271
Crawford, William H., 311
Crime, and due process, 502-506
Crisis, The, 514
Critical Mass, 217
Cronkite, Walter, *231*
Cuban missile crisis, 548, 553
Culture, political, 80-89, 136, 351, 401,
    611-614. *See also* Attitudes; Beliefs;
    Values
Curley, James Michael, 71
Customs Service, 373

Dairy industry, regulation of, 427
Dairy interests, client politics of, 429
Daley, Richard, 72, 276
Data processing, 353
Davis, John W., 146
Debates, presidential, 182, 243
Debs, Eugene, 155, *164*
Decision-making, 417-419, 571-573. *See
    also* Policy-making
Declaration of Independence, 16, 19, 40
Defense Department, 571
    and cost overruns, 582
    decision-making in, 571-573
    employees of, 362
    organization of, 572
Defense, national
    and corporations, 581-584
    money spent on, *574 (see also* Military
        spending)
De Gaulle, Charles, 547
Delaware, and slavery issue, 36
Delegates, to national conventions, 144-145,
    159-160
Democracy
    Constitution and, 30-33
    direct, 7, 8
    elitist theory of, 7
    nature of, 6-8, 14
    participatory, 7, 8
    power distribution in, 8-11
    representative, 7
    role of elections in, 164
Democratic centralism, 6
Democratic party. *See also* Political parties
    attitudes in, 161, 162
    black support for, 109
    in Congress, 265
    delegate selection, 145
    dominance of, 185
    earlier position of, 604, 606
    effect of education on ideology of, 121
    electoral objectives of, 157
    identification with, 161
    industrial unions in, 156
    national committee of, 143
    national convention of, *143*
    during 1972 election, 177
    and party vote, 274

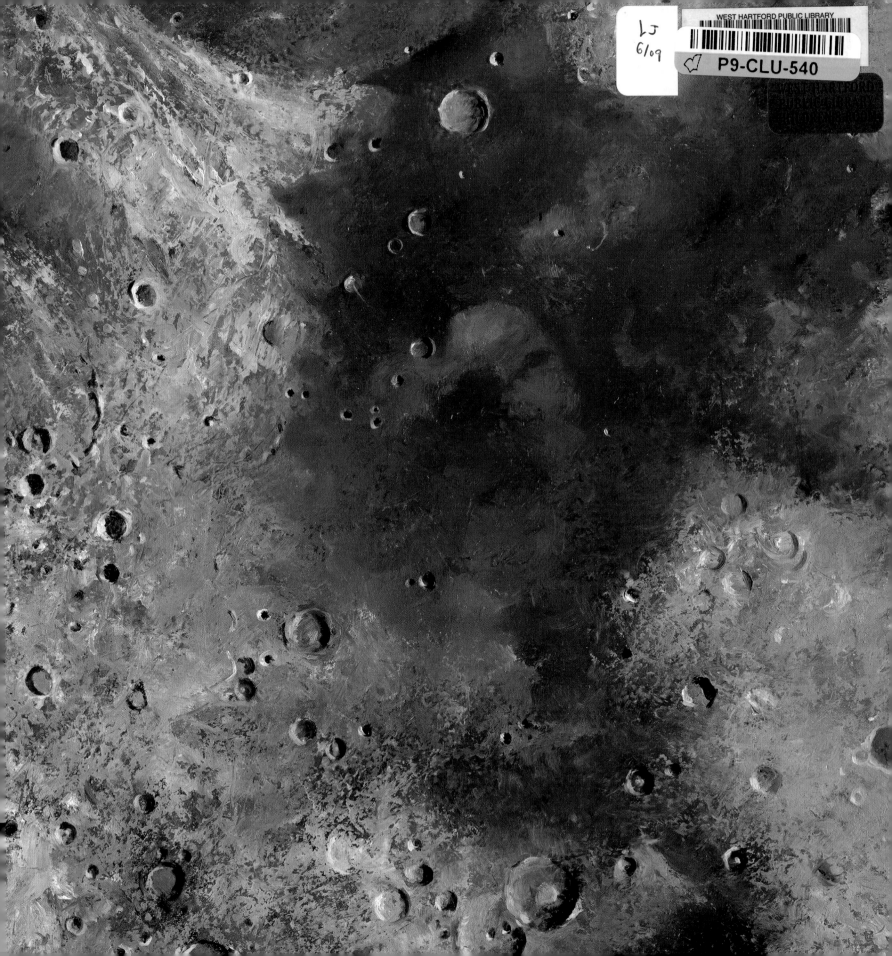

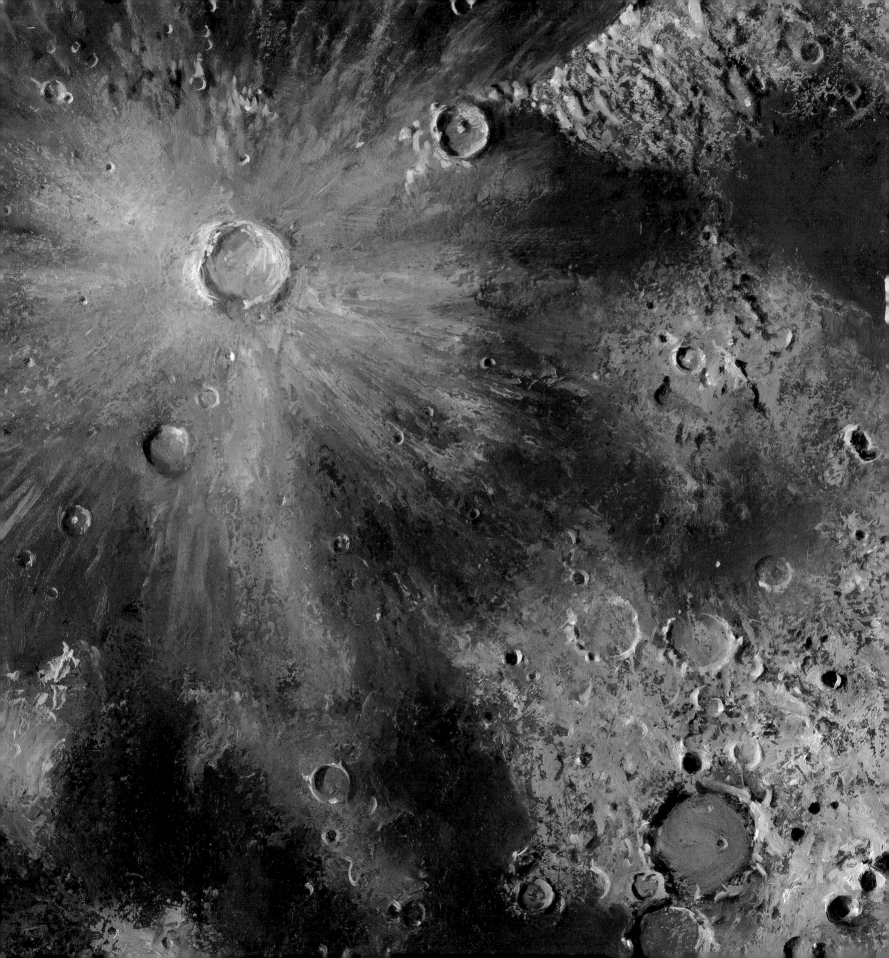

ONE GIANT LEAP

ONE GIANT LEAP

Robert Burleigh PAINTINGS BY Mike Wimmer

PHILOMEL BOOKS

For Aiden and Austin Scott

(along with Robin, Ryan, Sue and Ralph)

R. B.

This book is dedicated to the men and women who look to the heavens, not just for inspiration but for a destination. I would like to recognize the following people for their invaluable help with research and getting the facts straight, which helped bring this historic event to life: Max Ary; J. Milt Heflin, Associate Director (Technical), Office of the Director, NASA—Johnson Space Center; Mike Gentry, Media Resource, Centers NASA—Johnson Space Center; Suzette Ellison, Oklahoma Science Museum.

M. W.

July 20, 1969. Seventy miles up,

The two spaceships, *Eagle* and *Columbia*, separate.

They orbit in sight of each other one last time.

Then the *Eagle* begins to descend—

To where no human has ever been.

To the moon.

The *Eagle* is like a gold-speckled bug falling out of the sky—

Its odd-shaped body plastered with many boxes,

Its outer walls thinner than human skin.

The spacecraft's spindly legs poke out as it rides on its back.

At 8,000 feet, it tilts and straightens.

Brakes its descent. Slows.

Drifts down through space.

The astronauts look out at last.

Neil Armstrong. Buzz Aldrin.

They stand upright before two small windows.

Their eyes widen.

Look—rushing up toward them—

The moon!

It is gray, it is brown, it is blue-edged.

Its billion-year-old landscape is cracked and scarred,

Its surface gouged and cratered and pitted with tiny holes,

Like a battlefield from some ancient war.

The radio voice crackles from Earth, 240,000 miles away:

"*EAGLE*, HOUSTON: YOU ARE *GO* FOR LANDING."

Armstrong tenses forward, feeling the seconds tick,

Aware that the fuel is sinking toward zero.

Timing is everything.

His gaze darts between nearby rows of switches

And the strange world below.

Dark ridges rise like forbidding walls,

Spidery shadows creep in the rising sunlight,

Boulders loom up as big as cars.

He glances again at the flashing dial: *fuel running short*.

Where can he land?

"*EAGLE*: 90 SECONDS OF DESCENT FUEL LEFT."

Armstrong hears the warning.

Now. All he has ever learned is focused on this.

Nothing matters but this exact moment.

Aldrin's nonstop voice calls out altitude numbers:

"Forty feet, thirty-five, thirty . . ."

Down they move, down and down.

Fast enough to conserve precious fuel.

Slow enough to land somewhere safely.

He hopes.

The *Eagle* dips. Hovers. Zigs. Zags.

Dances over its own dark shadow.

The seconds tick toward eternity. Time stops.

Clouds of moondust swirl like blackening fog.

An almost terrifying blindness.

And then—with only the very slightest bump—

The small craft touches down.

Whew!

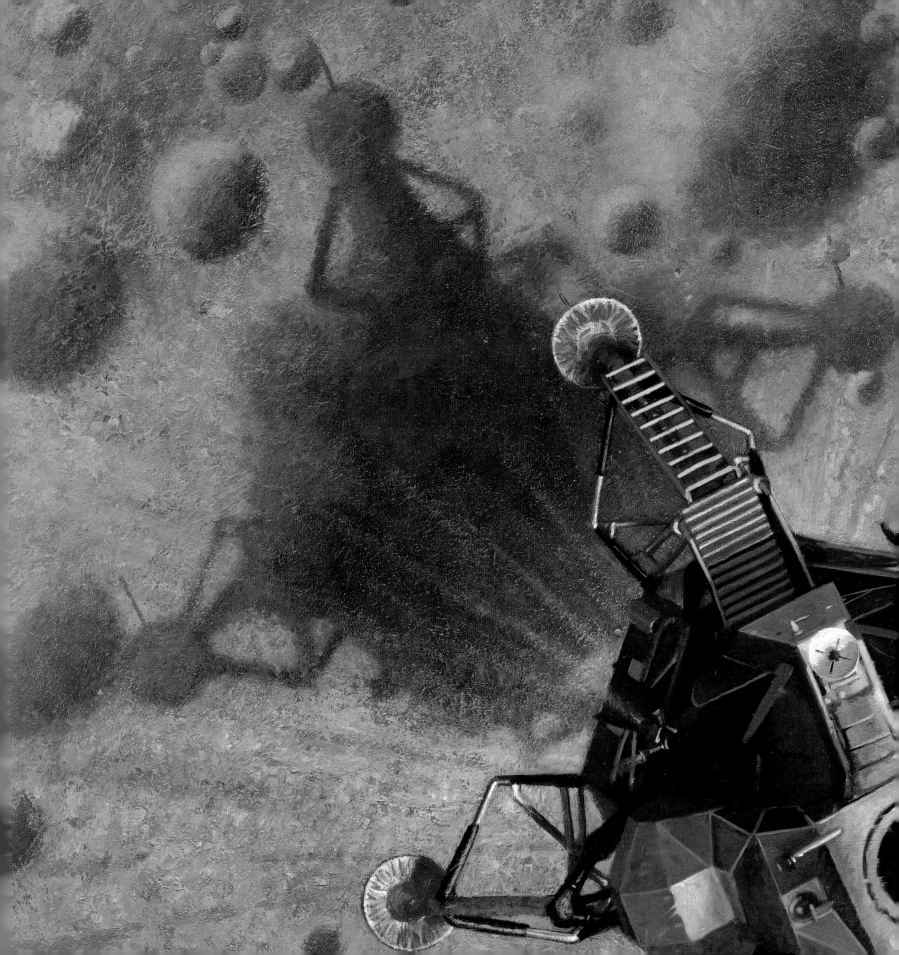

"The *Eagle* has landed."

High overhead, Michael Collins listens, but cannot see.

They made it. They made it!

The *Columbia* orbits—and waits.

Collins has waited a lifetime for this.

Yet for him, the waiting is not over.

In Houston, on Earth, hundreds in the control room break into wild cheers.

The first humans on the moon!

But in this other place it is very quiet.

It is lunar morning on the Sea of Tranquility.

Armstrong lets out another deep breath and turns.

He raises his gloved hand and meets Aldrin's gloved hand halfway.

We did it. We're here.

Exploration time!

Armstrong and Aldrin add still more to their spacesuits.

There are new overshoes and heavier gloves,

A visored helmet to protect against sunlight,

And an oxygen-filled backpack thick as a sofa pillow.

They pause to gaze out:

An endless, mysterious wasteland,

Whose distant hills are as sharply outlined as nearby stones.

No water. No wind. No sound.

No life at all.

Unbelievable.

A hatch opens.

Armstrong, on all fours, crawls through its small space.

He moves awkwardly in his "moon cocoon."

Outside, on the narrow porch,

Where a ladder is attached to one landing leg,

He climbs to the bottom rung and stops.

A TV camera, placed in the *Eagle*'s hatchway, is pointed down.

Armstrong knows that back on Earth,

Hundreds of millions of people are watching.

He jumps to the landing leg's round footpad.

He holds on. He pauses. He points his foot and steps off.

The surface is as fine as powdered charcoal.

The treads of his boot leave a perfectly crisp print in the dust.

On the weatherless moon, it will last for millions of years.

His voice sounds staticky and far away:

"That's one small step for man—one giant leap for mankind."

In orbit, Michael Collins listens. And waits.

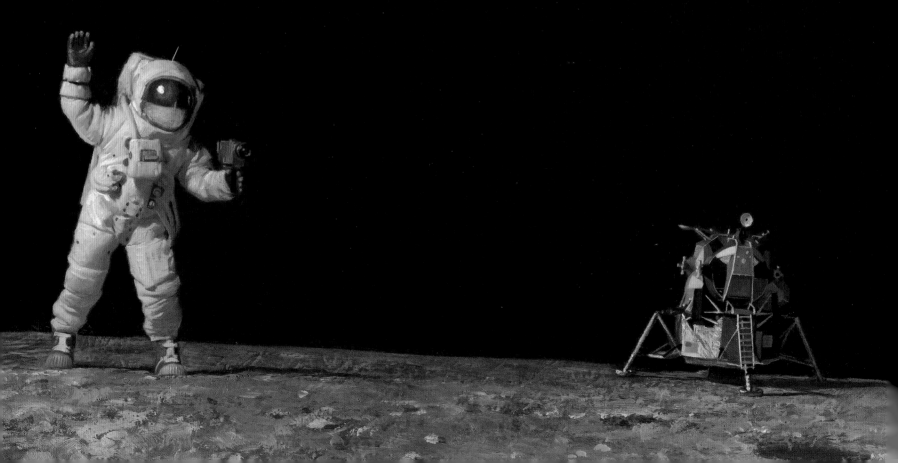

Now it is Buzz Aldrin's turn.

He climbs down, feeling full of goose pimples.

Together the astronauts go moon-walking.

Flexing their toes and ankles, they walk stiffly,

As if navigating inside a rigid balloon.

But moving about is easier than they expect.

They twirl like slow-motion tiptoe dancers.

They jog. They kangaroo-hop,

Like two boys bouncing on a trampoline.

Because of the moon's lesser gravity, they feel light as air.

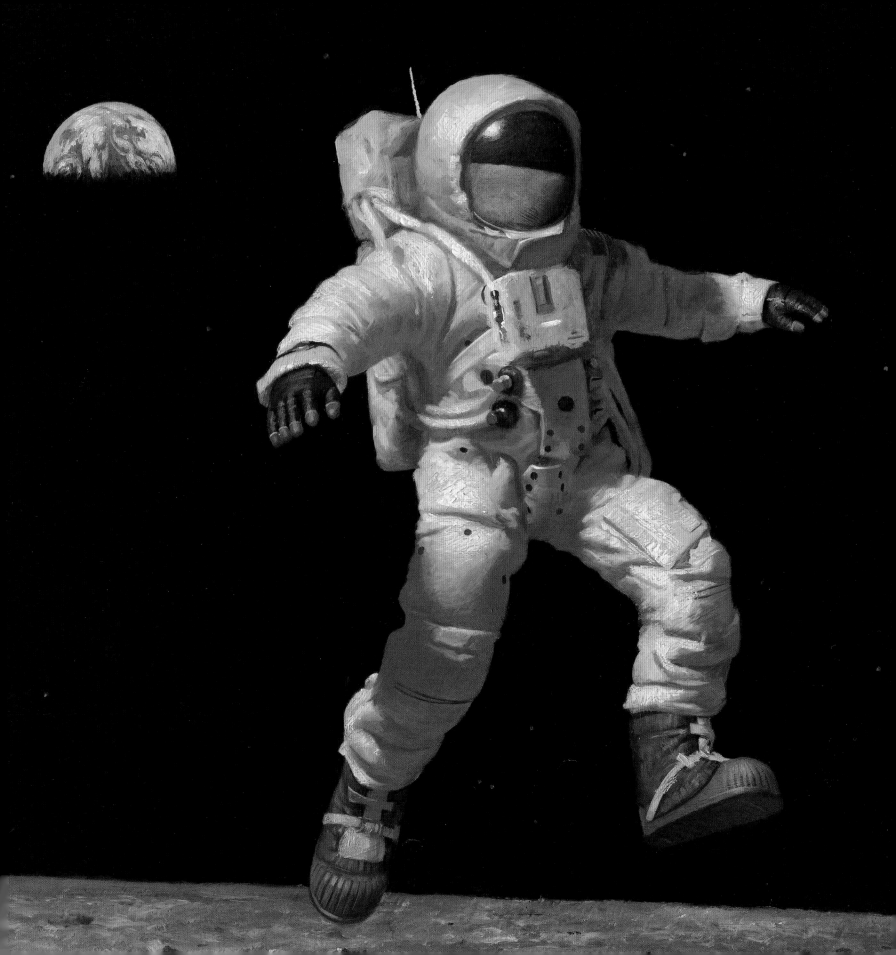

Armstrong checks the time. They must hurry.

They have just two hours on this strange and beautiful world.

They use long metal tongs to collect rocks.

Some are slippery with dust.

Some sparkle. Some look tan or even purple.

The rocks go into two large boxes that scientists will open back on Earth.

They try to plant the American flag.

But underneath its surface dust, the moon is like steel.

They jab the pole into the hard crust.

They twist and turn, leaning with all their might.

At last they are able to balance the staff—just barely.

A rod across the top keeps the flag unfurled.

Then *click*. Armstrong takes a picture of Aldrin saluting the flag.

A surprise call comes from the President:

"For a priceless moment, all the people on this earth are truly one."

A tightness rises in the throats of the astronauts.

They feel part of something so much larger than themselves.

Yet soon it is over. They are inside again.

This world is not theirs. Not their own.

Streaks of dirt cover their spacesuits.

The smell of the moondust hits them as they remove their helmets.

"Like spent cap pistols," they tell each other.

They have been awake for eighteen hours straight, but it feels like much more.

Can they sleep now? Maybe.

It is shivery cold in the cramped *Eagle*.

Aldrin curls up on the floor.

Armstrong lies in a hammock stretched across the room.

Exhausted.

He looks up. Above him, there is an unshuttered porthole.

The earth stares down. "A big blue eyeball," he thinks.

He blinks back at the bright blue eye.

Then turns. And tries to sleep.

July 21. Unease. Uncertainty.

This is the part they are most afraid of.

This is the place where things can go terribly wrong.

Armstrong and Aldrin stand quietly in the tiny cockpit.

Liftoff in one minute. Away from here—*maybe*.

The *Eagle* will split into two parts.

The upper half must fly up.

The lower will stay on the moon—a permanent monument.

Will the engine light? Will it keep on burning?

They try to ease their worries—but there is no escape from this.

No backing up. No doing it again. No second try.

They know one thing only: failure means death.

The second hand winds down. Now or never.

Aldrin's voice cuts into the awful stillness.

"Three, two, one . . . ascent . . ."

At first—a frightening pause. What is happening?

Then bang! Whoosh! Zoom!

It feels as if the floor is coming up at them.

The *Eagle*'s top half rises like a fast-moving elevator.

Its engine leaves a trail of wide, white light.

The *Eagle* soars skyward, silently, faster and faster:

Fifty miles up. Almost a mile a second!

Aldrin glances sideways. Nods and grins.

Into moon orbit. On our way.

Higher still, Michael Collins peers through his sextant.

Still waiting. *Where are they?*

He scans the sky and sees—only blackness.

The *Columbia* has been circling now for over twenty hours.

From the far side of the moon,

Collins cannot even radio back to people on Earth.

He squints through the sextant's eyepiece again.

There! A tiny blinking light in the darkness!

He locks his computer on the distant speck, tracking its approach.

The *Eagle* keeps climbing and climbing. Up and up.

It is like an intricate dance: *Columbia* leads; *Eagle* follows.

All at speeds of over 3,000 miles an hour!

Now they fly in perfect formation. Closer. Closer.

Collins punches hundreds of keystrokes to make the docking work.

They touch. They connect. The capture latches snap shut.

A small door opens into a tunnel.

Look who's here! Welcome!

Armstrong and Aldrin come floating through . . .

It is the final orbit around the moon . . .

Can a photo capture the wonder of what they've seen? Not likely.

Still, the astronauts hover beside the *Columbia*'s windows taking pictures.

The spacecraft accelerates.

It curls around the moon's far edge.

It is flung free like the tail-end skater in a game of crack-the-whip.

It soars into the emptiness of space.

The astronauts look back with a sad-happy feeling.

Hours go by. They can rest at last.

They sleep. Read. Talk. Play music.

Sometimes they glimpse the slowly receding moon.

Was it all a dream? No, we were there. We were there!

But mostly their eyes are fixed on another place:

Blue, white, light brown and shining below them.

They want that now. More than anything.

A planet of oceans and rivers. Of grass and green hills.

A world of trees and family and friends.

A place called Earth: fragile, beautiful, home.

A man on the moon! On the moon! The moon!

It was July 20, 1969. For one miraculous moment, the playfulness of nursery rhymes, the fantasy of science fiction, and the reality of true science were joined. We—a billion, more or less, of Earth's inhabitants— watched on snow-flecked, black-and-white television screens as a stiff figure climbed down a ladder and planted a boot in the soft dust of another world.

How did it come about? When President John F. Kennedy proclaimed in the early 1960s that America would land an astronaut on the moon within the decade, it sounded to many like an unreachable dream or, at most, simple politics. And in one sense, it was. Kennedy's promise came during the Cold War between the United States and the Soviet Union. The Russians had earlier sent a cosmonaut around the earth. America responded with its own space program. The big prize was the moon. And the race was on!

The amount of money, the people-hours, the planning, the trials and errors, and the dogged belief of thousands of men and women—all that went into that first step in the soft dust—is beyond the scope of this book. But the result of that dedicated effort— America's moon landing—may well be the single most concentrated and successful effort to achieve one great goal in human history.

Where the United States space program is going today is unclear. Our technological power has increased to an amazing degree in the past half-century. Today one tiny chip can hold far more information and facilitate far more activities than even the hugest, bulkiest computer a half-century ago.

What we do with this new power, in regard to space travel, is still to be decided. What is our next destination? There are millions of galaxies in the universe besides ours (the Milky Way). Traveling to one of them—perhaps at the speed of light!— may seem impossible now. But remember: Space exploration of any kind once seemed impossible. So don't be too sure.

One thing, though, is certain. Regardless of what occurs in the future, nothing can diminish the heroic achievement and sublime beauty of the moment when humans first landed on Earth's one and only moon.

PHILOMEL BOOKS

A division of Penguin Young Readers Group.

Published by The Penguin Group. Penguin Group (USA) Inc., 375 Hudson Street, New York, NY 10014, U.S.A. Penguin Group (Canada), 90 Eglinton Avenue East, Suite 700, Toronto, Ontario M4P 2Y3, Canada (a division of Pearson Penguin Canada Inc.). Penguin Books Ltd, 80 Strand, London WC2R 0RL, England. Penguin Ireland, 25 St. Stephen's Green, Dublin 2, Ireland (a division of Penguin Books Ltd). Penguin Group (Australia), 250 Camberwell Road, Camberwell, Victoria 3124, Australia (a division of Pearson Australia Group Pty Ltd). Penguin Books India Pvt Ltd, 11 Community Centre, Panchsheel Park, New Delhi - 110 017, India. Penguin Group (NZ), 67 Apollo Drive, Rosedale, North Shore 0632, New Zealand (a division of Pearson New Zealand Ltd). Penguin Books (South Africa) (Pty) Ltd, 24 Sturdee Avenue, Rosebank, Johannesburg 2196, South Africa. Penguin Books Ltd, Registered Offices: 80 Strand, London WC2R 0RL, England.

Published simultaneously in Canada.

Manufactured in China by South China Printing Co. Ltd.

Design by Richard Amari.

Text set in Boton Medium.

The illustrations were created in oils on paper mounted onto board.

Library of Congress Cataloging-in-Publication Data

Burleigh, Robert. One giant leap / Robert Burleigh ; illustrated by Mike Wimmer. p. cm. 1. Project Apollo (U.S.)—History—Juvenile literature. 2. Space flight to the moon—History—Juvenile literature. I. Wimmer, Mike, ill. II. Title. TL789.8.U6A52423 2008 629.45'4—dc22   2008015695

ISBN 978-0-399-23883-3

1 3 5 7 9 10 8 6 4 2

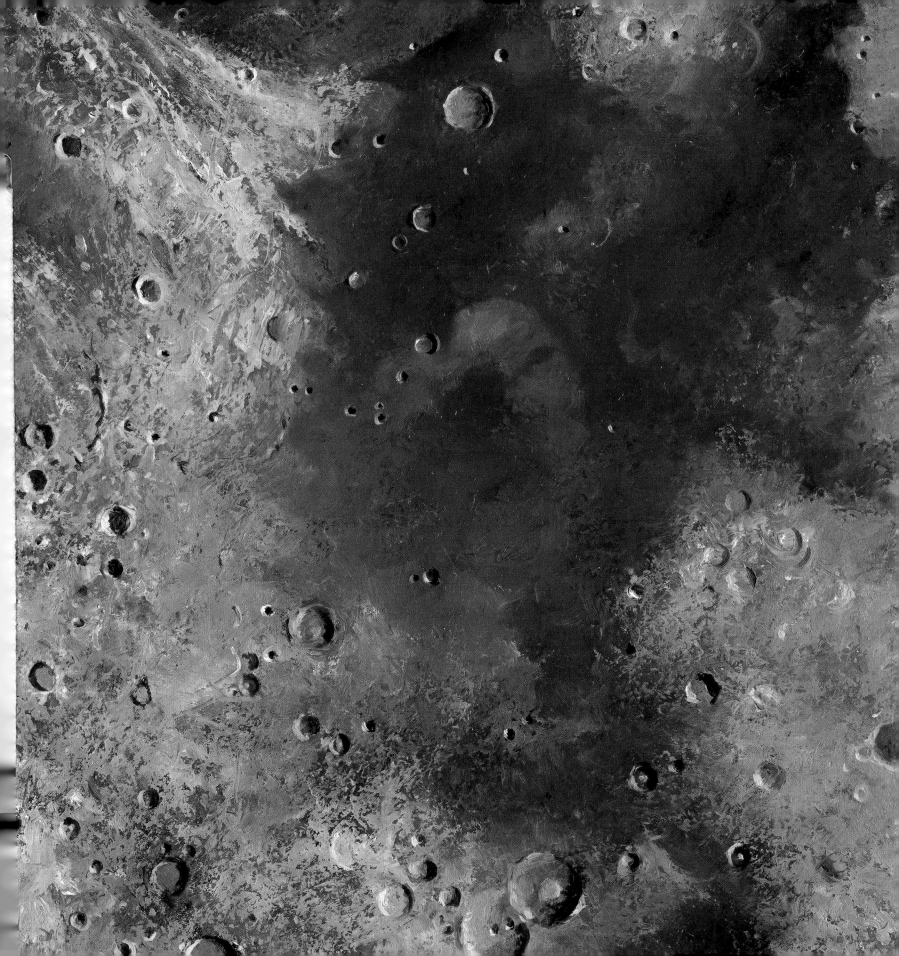

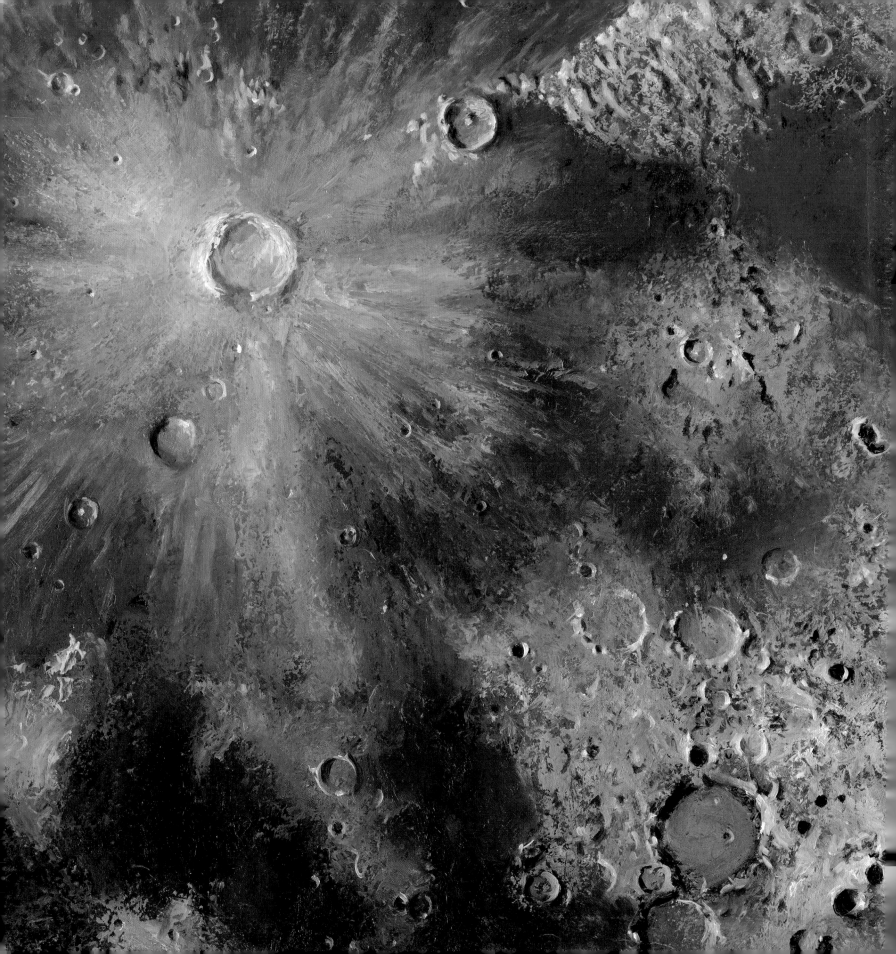